CASTLES, CUSTOMS, AND KINGS

TRUE TALES BY ENGLISH HISTORICAL FICTION AUTHORS

VOLUME 2

Castles, Customs, and Kings

True Tales by English Historical Fiction Authors

VOLUME 2

Edited by

Debra Brown and Sue Millard

MADISON STREET
PUBLISHING

Paperback ISBN: 978-0-9962648-1-5
Hardback ISBN: 978-0-9962648-2-2
Publisher: Madison Street Publishing
3 5 7 9 10 8 6 4

Dedicated to the memory of

M.M. BENNETTS

book critic, author, pianist, equestrienne
mother, friend, member of English Historical Fiction Authors

CONTENTS

INTRODUCTION

By DEBRA BROWN

PERHAPS YOU KNOW THE SIGNIFICANCE OF THE YEAR 1066, OR THE GIST OF THE English Civil War, or that Mary, Queen of Scots, lost her throne. Perhaps these events stuck in your memory but never unlocked your interest.

Dry dates and details—is this all that British history is? Not hardly! These are but the backbone of the past, the mere skeleton on which life stories hang.

Castles, Customs, and Kings: True Tales by English Historical Fiction Authors is designed to flesh out the history, capturing the soul of the past with personal stories and strange happenings. How did people eat, sleep, and play? What rules, dangers, and beliefs controlled their existence?

As a child I marveled at the things I read in *My Bookhouse Books*. I put myself into that faraway land of castles, maidens, and knights. It formed my love for history, something that resurfaced when adult life slowed down enough for me to dream again. I realized that the places I had looked for in my travels, the things I had drawn or painted, and the movies I had sought out all took me back to that childhood place.

L. P. Hartley wrote that *"the past is a foreign country: they do things differently there."* Grab your passport, pack a bag: these essays from English Historical Fiction Authors will carry you away for an extended visit.

The English Historical Fiction Authors have rejoiced in the good reception of Volume I of this series. Author Tom Williams called it *"an amusing trot through British history and excellent bedtime reading...literary comfort food—a recollection of childhood, warm and satisfying."*

We look forward to sharing more stories from our fascinating research, and we hope you enjoy this second volume of selected posts from the English Historical Fiction Authors blog just as much as the first.

CONTRIBUTING AUTHORS

ARNOPP, JUDITH

After a lifetime of reading and studying history, Judith Arnopp is now the author of seven historical fiction novels. Her earliest works are set in the Anglo-Saxon/early medieval era while her more recent books take place during the Tudor period. She is currently working on the life of Margaret Beaufort, mother of Henry VII. All Judith's books are available in paperback and on Kindle.

ASHE, KATHERINE

Katherine Ashe Is the author of the *Montfort* series of books on the life of Simon de Montfort, the founder of Parliament. Historical research into original period documents is her forte. She lives in rural Pennsylvania with her husband, dogs, and farm animals. Her most recent book is *An Evening with Edgar Allan Poe* originally commissioned by the New York City Historic House Trust for performance at the Poe Cottage.

BEARD, J.A.

J.A. Beard is a restless soul married to an equally restless soul. They have mildly restless children. When he hasn't been writing, studying history, or making excuses for not writing, he's tried his hand at several careers including intelligence analysis, programming, and research science. Though he likes to declare himself the Pie Master, he's yet to prove his worth in the brutal baking show-downs of Celebration, Florida.

BYRD, SANDRA

Sandra Byrd's historically sound Gothic romance series launched in 2015 with Book One: *Mist of Midnight*. That book earned a coveted Editor's Choice from the Historical Novel Society. *To Die For: A Novel of Anne Boleyn* was named a Library Journal Best Books for 2011 and *The Secret Keeper: A Novel of Kateryn Parr* earned that same award for 2012. *Roses Have Thorns: A Novel of Elizabeth I* published in 2013.

BELFRAGE, ANNA

Had Anna been allowed to choose, she'd have become a professional time-traveller. As this was impossible, she became a financial professional with two absorbing interests: history and writing. Anna has authored the acclaimed The Graham Saga, winner of multiple awards including the HNS Indie Award 2015. Her new series set in the 1320s will feature Adam de Guirande, his wife Kit, and their adventures during Roger Mortimer's rise to power.

BENNETTS, M.M.

A former book critic for the Pulitzer Prize-winning *Christian Science Monitor*, M.M. Bennetts was an historian specialising in early nineteenth century Europe and the author of two novels set amidst the turbulence of the Napoleonic wars: *May 1812* and *Of Honest Fame*. A keen cross-country rider, Bennetts was also an accomplished pianist and a dedicated researcher. M.M. died in 2014 before being able to complete her third novel, *Or Fear of Peace*.

BILYEAU, NANCY

Nancy Bilyeau is the author of the suspense trilogy *The Crown*, *The Chalice* and *The Tapestry*, set in Tudor England. *The Chalice* won the award for Best Historical Mystery of the Year from RT Reviewers. A magazine editor, Nancy has worked on the staffs of *Good Housekeeping*, *InStyle* and *Entertainment Weekly*. She lives in New York City with her husband and two children.

BRACEWELL, PATRICIA

Patricia Bracewell taught high school English before turning to a writing career and producing essays, short stories, and novels. She has traveled extensively for historical research, and in the fall of 2014 she served as Writer-in-Residence at Gladstone's Library, Wales. She is currently at work on the final novel of her *Emma of Normandy Trilogy*. She has two grown sons and lives with her husband in Oakland, California.

BROWN, DEBRA

Debra has topped off a lifetime of creative pursuits with writing. The promotion of her first novel, *The Companion of Lady Holmeshire*, led her to establish the English Historical Fiction Authors blog and the Goodreads group Historical Info for Historical Fiction Readers. Many friends later, she continues to try to find time to write. Debra is the President of the M.M. Bennetts Award for Historical Fiction.

BURNS, MARY F.

Mary F. Burns is the author of several historical novels, including *Portraits of an Artist: A Novel about John Singer Sargent*, *J-The Woman Who Wrote the Bible*, *Isaac and Ishmael*, and the first of a brand new historical mystery series, *The Spoils of Avalon*, featuring amateur sleuths Violet Paget and John Singer Sargent. She is a member of and book reviewer for the Historical Novel Society.

CALKINS, SUSANNA

Susanna Calkins holds a PhD in early modern British history from Purdue University, and writes the Lucy Campion historical mysteries set in seventeenth century England. Her series, featuring a chambermaid-turned-printer's apprentice, have been shortlisted for several historical mystery awards, including the Sue Feder Historical Mystery award and the Bruce Alexander Historical Mystery award. She works at Northwestern University and lives outside Chicago with her husband and two sons.

COWELL, STEPHANIE

Stephanie Cowell is the author of *Nicholas Cooke, The Physician of London, The Players: a novel of the young Shakespeare, Marrying Mozart* and *Claude & Camille: a novel of Monet*. She is the recipient of an American Book Award. Her next novel is on the love story of the Brownings in Victorian London to be followed by the conclusion of the Nicholas trilogy. Her work has been translated into nine languages.

DENNING, RICHARD

Richard Denning was born in Ilkeston in Derbyshire and lives in Sutton Coldfield in the West Midlands, where he works as a General Practitioner. He is married and has two children. He has always been fascinated by historical settings as well as horror and fantasy. Other than writing, his main interests are games of all types. He is the designer of a board game based on the Great Fire of London.

EAKES, LAURIE ALICE

With more than twenty books in print, Laurie Alice Eakes lives her dream job of full-time author from her home in Texas, where her cat sleeps on her desk to "help" and her husband shows great patience with her absent-mindedness. She loves to read, go for long walks, and watch old movies. The only reason why her house is clean is because vacuuming is when she plots her next novel.

ELLIOT, GRACE

Grace Elliot has a pet passion for history—indeed, she is a veterinarian with a special interest in history and attitudes to pets over the ages. Her current works include historical romance and a non-fiction book of feline historical trivia. For more details visit Grace's blog: Fall in Love with History.

ENGLISH, CHRISTY

Ever since Christy English picked up a fake sword in stage combat class at the age of fourteen, she has lived vicariously through the strong women of her imagination. Sometimes an actor, always a storyteller, a banker by day and a writer by night, Christy loves eating chocolate, drinking too many soft drinks, and walking the mountain trails of her home in western North Carolina.

FARRAR, P.L.

P.L. Farrar is a young writer, currently studying history and Italian at university in the UK. An enthusiastic horseback rider, cook, and violinist, Farrar is also working on her first historical novel, set in early nineteenth century England.

GILBERT, LAUREN

An avid reader, Lauren Gilbert was introduced to English authors early in life, reading classic literature by Jane Austen, period romances by Victoria Holt/Jean Plaidy/Philippa Carr, the mysteries of Dorothy Sayers, and others. Lauren is fascinated by England and its history, and multiple visits to England have only heightened her interest. A member of JASNA, Lauren released her first book, *Heyerwood,* in 2011, and her second book, *A Rational Attachment*, will be released in 2015.

GRACE, MARIA

Though Maria Grace has been writing fiction since she was ten years old, those early efforts happily reside in a file drawer and are unlikely to see the light of day again, for which many are grateful. After penning five file-drawer novels in high school, she took a break from writing to pursue college and earn her doctorate in Educational Psychology. After sixteen years of university teaching, she returned to her first love, fiction writing.

HILL, DAVID WESLEY

David Wesley Hill is the award-winning author of two novels and more than thirty short stories. In 1997 he was presented with the Golden Bridge award at an international conference in Beijing, and in 1999 he placed second in the Writers of the Future contest. He studied under Joseph Heller and Jack Cady and received a Masters in creative writing from the City University of New York.

HOPKINS, JONATHAN

Jonathan Hopkins works as a kitchen designer and equine saddle fitter. A lifelong horse-keeper and long term chair of an affiliated riding club close to his home in South Wales, his interest in the cavalrymen who served under the Duke of Wellington and Napoleon originally grew out of research into saddlery worn by English troop horses, for which there are no surviving patterns.

HOWARD, SCOTT

Scott Howard holds a B.S. in Marketing and an MBA from Northwest Missouri State University; he has just finished an MA at Luther Rice University. In the U.S. Navy, he trained in nuclear propulsion and spent nine years as a Reactor Operator. He is now employed as an engineer in Georgia. His pursuits include reading, writing, and collecting battle-ready swords; he is currently working on a fourth novel set during the Crusades.

JACKSON, DIANA

Following a teaching career, Diana Jackson now writes and runs a small writer's publishing cooperative in Bedfordshire. Love of social history and historical research drives much of Diana's writing, including compiling a memoir going back over 100 years and also her recent murder mystery, inspired by an unsolved murder in 1919. Diana's interest in aviation, especially flying boats and sea planes, stems from her second novel *Ancasta*.

JOHNSON, ANNE E.

Anne E. Johnson lives in Brooklyn, New York. With degrees in Classical Languages and Medieval Musicology, she has had four of her essays on early music published in the *New York Times* and is currently an editor at *Early Music America Magazine*. Besides historical fiction, Johnson also loves to write science fiction and fantasy and has had dozens of short stories and two novels published in speculative genres.

KROENUNG, TERRY

Terry Kroenung began as a playwright but has moved on to historical fantasy novels, taking care that the fantasy serves the history and not the other way around. M.M. Bennetts drilled that into him with her steely glare. He teaches Bartitsu (Sherlock Holmes' martial art, an actual Victorian discipline). *Paragon of the Eccentric*, his prequel to Wells' *War of the Worlds*, won the 2013 Colorado Gold writing contest.

KYLE, BARBARA

Barbara Kyle is the author of the acclaimed *Thornleigh Saga* novels, a 7-book series with over 450,000 copies sold in seven countries. Before becoming an author Barbara enjoyed a twenty-year acting career in television, film, and stage. Barbara has taught writers at the University of Toronto and is a regular presenter at writers' conferences. Through her master classes and manuscript evaluations, she has helped launch many writers to published success.

LAKE, MARTIN

Martin Lake wrote for many years before combining his love of writing and history and finding that this really worked for him. He self-published his first e-book in 2011 and has since published a further six novels and three collections of short stories. One of his novels has been republished by Lake Union Publishing and a sequel will be published in January 2016. He lives in the French Riviera.

LAMB, VICTORIA

Victoria Lamb writes historicals for Penguin Random House. As Elizabeth Moss, she also writes indie Regency romance and Tudor romance for Hodder & Stoughton, and as Beth Good, writes rom coms for Thimblerig Books. Daughter of prolific romance queen, Charlotte Lamb, Victoria has been a professional writer since 1994, winning various awards for fiction and poetry. She has five children, three of whom are home-schooled, and lives in the rainy South-West of England.

LOFTING, PAULA

Paula Lofting was born in the UK, migrated with her family at the age of two to Australia, returned to England at the age of sixteen, and now lives in Sussex. After having her family and training to be a psychiatric nurse, she decided to fulfill her childhood dream to write. She published *Sons of the Wolf* in 2012 and is now working on the sequel, *The Wolf Banner*.

LORTZ, ROSANNE E.

When she's not writing medieval adventures or Regency romances, Rosanne E. Lortz teaches Latin grammar and English composition and reads picture books to her four boys four and under. She and husband David co-own Madison Street Publishing.

MCGRATH, CAROL

Carol McGrath lives in Oxfordshire with her husband and family. She taught History until she took an MA in Creative Writing at The Seamus Heaney Centre, Queens University Belfast, followed by an MPhil in Creative Writing at Royal Holloway, University of London. Her debut novel, *The Handfasted Wife*, first in the best-selling trilogy *The Daughters of Hastings*, was shortlisted for the RoNAS, 2014. Carol reviews for the HNS and is coordinating the 2016 Conference.

MILLARD, SUE

Sue Millard lives in Cumbria, England. Her website showcases her published output of novels and non-fiction which tend to feature horses, carriage-driving, romance, rural life, history, and artistic but inept dragons. Her poems have been published by The Interpreter's House, Pennine Platform, Pirene's Fountain, Butcher's Dog, Lighten Up Online, and Snakeskin. Her recent collection, *Ash Tree,* is published by Prole.

MOSS, TOM

Tom Moss lives in north-east Cumbria, England in the delightful village of Walton, just a few miles south of the English-Scottish Border, with Tina, his partner of many years. He has always loved British history and, since his move to Cumbria, the life and times of the Border Reivers. Their history is unique, replete with bitter feuds between the clans and families that often lasted for generations.

O'BRIEN, ANNE

Anne O'Brien lives in the UK. After gaining a B.A. Honours degree in History at Manchester University and a Master's in Education at Hull, she became a teacher of history. Leaving teaching, Anne turned to writing historical fiction to give voice to the medieval women who fascinated her. Today Anne lives in an eighteenth century cottage in Herefordshire, an area full of inspiration for her work.

PATTON, MARK

Mark Patton was born on the island of Jersey and studied Archaeology and Anthropology at Clare College, Cambridge, and University College, London. He is the author of several academic works on history and archaeology, as well as three historical novels.

PYM, KATHERINE

Katherine Pym and her husband divide their time between Seattle, WA and Austin, TX. Katherine writes rumpus good tales in 1660s London before the great fire that burned the city to the ground. The decade is so exciting, filled with human interest stories as people adjust from one government to another, and all their changing rules and regulations.

RANDOLPH, OCTAVIA

Octavia Randolph is the author of *The Circle of Ceridwen Saga* set in ninth century England and Scandinavia; *Light, Descending*, a biographical novel of the great nineteenth century art and social critic John Ruskin; *Ride*, a retelling of the story of Lady Godiva; and *The Tale of Melkorka*, taken from the Icelandic Sagas. She is the recipient of fellowships at the MacDowell Colony, Ledig House International, and Byrdcliffe.

RENDELL, MIKE

Mike Rendell is the custodian of a treasure-trove of diaries and ephemera left by his 4x-great-grandfather Richard Hall. When he retired after spending thirty years as a lawyer in Bristol, Mike wrote up Richard's life story as a social history of the eighteenth century—the world seen through Richard's eyes—published under the title of the *Journal of a Georgian Gentleman*.

ROOT, LINDA

Linda Root is a former major crimes prosecutor whose cases were widely featured in the media. Since 2010, she has written seven novels set in sixteenth and seventeenth century Scotland. Root is a member of the English Historical Fiction Authors blog, the board of the M.M. Bennetts Award, and both the State Bar of California and the United States Supreme Court. She lives in Yucca Valley, California.

RUSSELL, ARTHUR

Arthur Russell lives in Navan, Co Meath, Ireland with his wife Mary. He is a professional Agriculturalist who has worked in Ireland, Eastern Europe, Central Asia, and Mongolia. He has a keen interest in history, especially the history of his native place, which features in his first book *Morgallion*, published in 2012, which is set in the early fourteenth century during the Bruce invasion of Ireland.

SCHRADER, HELENA P.

Award–winning novelist Helena P. Schrader has a PhD in History. She has published non-fiction books on WWII and novels set in Ancient Sparta, the crusades, and WWII. The first book in her three-part biography of Balian d'Ibelin, Knight of Jerusalem, was a finalist for the Chaucer Award, and the second book in the series will be released in September 2015. Helena is a U.S. diplomat currently serving in Africa.

SKEA, MARGARET

Margaret Skea lives in Scotland but grew up in Ulster during the "Troubles". An award-winning short story writer, she won both the Historical Fiction section in the Harper Collins/ Alan Titchmarsh People's Novelist Competition 2011 and the Beryl Bainbridge Best 1st Time Novelist 2014 for her debut novel, *Turn of the Tide*. Both it and the sequel, *A House Divided*, focus on a notorious vendetta in sixteenth century Scotland.

STUART, ALISON

Alison Stuart is an award winning Australian writer of cross-genre historical romances. Alison is a lapsed lawyer who has worked in the military and fire service, which may explain a predisposition to soldier heroes and men in uniform. She is a digital first author, published by Harlequin Australia and independently. If your taste is for duelling cavaliers, wayward ghosts, time travel, and murder mysteries—sometimes all in the same book—Alison's stories are for you.

SWIFT, DEBORAH

Deborah Swift is an ex-costume designer with a love of old buildings and antiques, and a passion for the seventeenth century. Her novels are *The Lady's Slipper*, *The Gilded Lily*, *A Divided Inheritance*, *Pleasing Mr Pepys*, and *The Highway Trilogy* (for young adults). Deborah also writes WWII novels under the pen-name Davina Blake. She lives in a picturesque stone village in the North of England close to the mountains and the sea.

THOMAS, SAM

Sam Thomas writes historical fiction in his basement and teaches historical fact at University School, an independent K-12 school outside Cleveland. He is the author of the Midwife Mysteries, featuring Bridget Hodgson.

VANNER, ANTOINE

Antoine Vanner has lived long-term in eight countries and has travelled extensively in every continent except Antarctica. He has particularly relished his exposure to developing countries where there are few certainties as regards security or social stability. This gave him a particular interest in situations of moral ambiguity, as is reflected in his adventure novels set in the Late-Victorian Era.

VON STAATS, BETH

Beth von Staats is an American history writer of both fiction and non-fiction short works. A life-long history enthusiast, Beth is the owner of the Queen Anne Boleyn Historical Writers website. Beth's most pronounced interest lies with the men and women who drove the course of events and/or were most poignantly impacted by the English and Protestant Reformations, as well as the Tudor Dynasty of English and Welsh History in general.

WILLIAMS, LANA

Lana Williams is an Amazon bestselling author who writes historical romance filled with mystery and adventure. Her medieval trilogy is set in England and follows heroes seeking vengeance only to find love when they least expect it. Her Victorian London trilogy shares the stories of three lords injured in an electromagnetic experiment that went terribly wrong and the women who help heal them through the power of love.

YARDE, LISA J.

Lisa J. Yarde writes fiction inspired by the Middle Ages in Europe.

LIST OF NOVELS BY
CONTRIBUTING AUTHORS

PRE-ROMAN TO EARLY MEDIEVAL BRITAIN (PRE-55 B.C.-A.D. 1000)

The Song of Heledd, by Judith Arnopp

The Amber Treasure (Northern Crown Series), by Richard Denning

Child of Loki (Northern Crown Series), by Richard Denning

Princes in Exile (Northern Crown Series), by Richard Denning

Shield Maiden (Nine Worlds Series), by Richard Denning

The Catacombs of Vanaheim (Nine Worlds Series), by Richard Denning

A Kiss at Vespers, by Anne E. Johnson

Land of Blood and Water, by Martin Lake

Undreamed Shores, by Mark Patton

An Accidental King, by Mark Patton

The Circle of Ceridwen, by Octavia Randolph

Ceridwen of Kilton (Circle of Ceridwen Saga), by Octavia Randolph

The Claiming (Circle of Ceridwen Saga), by Octavia Randolph

The Hall of Tyr (Circle of Ceridwen Saga), by Octavia Randolph

Ride: The Story of Lady Godiva, by Octavia Randolph

The Tale of Melkorka, by Octavia Randolph

Leonidas of Sparta: A Boy of the Agoge, by Helena P. Schrader

Leonidas of Sparta: A Peerless Peer, by Helena P. Schrader

Leonidas of Sparta: A Heroic King, by Helena P. Schrader

LATE MEDIEVAL PERIOD (1001-1485)

Peaceweaver, by Judith Arnopp

The Forest Dwellers, by Judith Arnopp

Montfort the Early Years 1229 to 1243, by Katherine Ashe

Montfort the Viceroy 1243 to 1253, by Katherine Ashe

Montfort the Revolutionary 1253 to 1260, by Katherine Ashe

Montfort the Angel with the Sword 1260 to 1265, by Katherine Ashe

Shadow on the Crown, by Patricia Bracewell

The Price of Blood, by Patricia Bracewell

The Queen's Pawn, by Christy English

To Be Queen: A Novel of the Early Life of Eleanor of Aquitaine, by Christy English

A Soul's Ransom, by Scott Howard

For a Thousand Generations, by Scott Howard

A Matter of Honor, by Scott Howard

Trouble at the Scriptorium, by Anne E. Johnson

Resistance (The Lost King 1), by Martin Lake

Wasteland (The Lost King 2), by Martin Lake

Blood of Ironside (The Lost King 3), by Martin Lake

Outcasts, by Martin Lake

Sons of the Wolf, by Paula Lofting

I Serve: A Novel of the Black Prince, by Rosanne E. Lortz

The Handfasted Wife, by Carol McGrath

The Swan-Daughter, by Carol McGrath

The Betrothed Sister, by Carol McGrath

Virgin Widow: A Novel of Anne Neville, by Anne O'Brien

Devil's Consort: A Novel of Eleanor of Aquitaine, by Anne O'Brien

The King's Concubine: A Novel of Alice Perrers, Mistress of Edward III, by Anne O'Brien

The Forbidden Queen: A Novel of Katherine de Valois, by Anne O'Brien

The Scandalous Duchess: A Novel of Katherine Swynford, by Anne O'Brien

The King's Sister: A Novel of Elizabeth of Lancaster, by Anne O'Brien

The Queen's Choice: A Novel of Joanna of Navarre (to be pub. 2016), by Anne O'Brien

Morgallion, by Arthur Russell

Knight of Jerusalem: A Biographical Novel of Balian d'Ibelin, by Helena P. Schrader

Defender of Jerusalem: A Biographical Novel of Balian d'Ibelin, by Helena P. Schrader

St. Louis Knight, by Helena P. Schrader

The Disinherited, by Helena P. Schrader

A Widow's Crusade, by Helena P. Schrader

A Vow to Keep, by Lana Williams

A Knight's Kiss: A Medieval Novella, by Lana Williams

Trust in Me, by Lana Williams

Believe in Me, by Lana Williams

A Knight's Christmas Wish: A Medieval Novella, by Lana Williams

A Knight's Quest, by Lana Williams

On Falcon's Wings, by Lisa J. Yarde

The Burning Candle, by Lisa J. Yarde

TUDOR PERIOD (1485-1603)

The Winchester Goose: At the Court of Henry VIII, by Judith Arnopp

The Kiss of the Concubine: A Story of Anne Boleyn, by Judith Arnopp

Intractable Heart: The Story of Katheryn Parr, by Judith Arnopp

A Song of Sixpence: The Story of Elizabeth of York and Perkin Warbeck, by Judith Arnopp

The Beaufort Chronicles (to be released), by Judith Arnopp

The Crown, by Nancy Bilyeau

The Chalice, by Nancy Bilyeau

The Tapestry, by Nancy Bilyeau

To Die For: A Novel of Anne Boleyn, by Sandra Byrd

The Secret Keeper: A Novel of Kateryn Parr, by Sandra Byrd

Roses Have Thorns: A Novel of Elizabeth I, by Sandra Byrd

Nicholas Cooke, by Stephanie Cowell

The Players: A Novel of the Young Shakespeare, by Stephanie Cowell

At Drake's Command: The Adventures of Peregrine James during the Second Circumnavigation of the World, by David Wesley Hill

The Queen's Lady (Thornleigh Saga), by Barbara Kyle

The King's Daughter (Thornleigh Saga), by Barbara Kyle

The Queen's Captive (Thornleigh Saga), by Barbara Kyle

The Queen's Gamble (Thornleigh Saga), by Barbara Kyle

Blood between Queens (Thornleigh Saga), by Barbara Kyle

The Queen's Exiles (Thornleigh Saga), by Barbara Kyle

The Traitor's Daughter (Thornleigh Saga), by Barbara Kyle

A Love Most Dangerous, by Martin Lake

Wolf Bride (Lust in the Tudor Court 1), by Elizabeth Moss

Rebel Bride (Lust in the Tudor Court 2), by Elizabeth Moss

Rose Bride (Lust in the Tudor Court 3), by Elizabeth Moss

Deadlock and Deliverance: The Capture and Rescue of Kinmont Willie Armstrong, by Tom Moss

Ballads of the Anglo/Scottish Border Reivers (nonfiction), by Tom Moss

Bandits of the English Scottish Border Lands (nonfiction), by Tom Moss

The First Marie and the Queen of Scots, by Linda Root

The Last Knight and the Queen of Scots, by Linda Root

The Midwife's Secret: The Mystery of the Hidden Princess, by Linda Root

The Other Daughter, Midwife's Secret II, by Linda Root

1603: The Queen's Revenge, by Linda Root

Turn of the Tide, by Margaret Skea

A House Divided (to be released), *by Margaret Skea*

STUART PERIOD (1603-1714)

A Rip in the Veil (Graham Saga 1), by Anna Belfrage

Like Chaff in the Wind (Graham Saga 2), by Anna Belfrage

The Prodigal Son (Graham Saga 3), by Anna Belfrage

A Newfound Land (Graham Saga 4), by Anna Belfrage

Serpents in the Garden (Graham Saga 5), by Anna Belfrage

Revenge and Retribution (Graham Saga 6), by Anna Belfrage

Whither Thou Goest (Graham Saga 7), by Anna Belfrage

To Catch a Falling Star (Graham Saga 8), by Anna Belfrage

A Murder at Rosamund's Gate, by Susanna Calkins

From the Charred Remains, by Susanna Calkins

The Masque of a Murderer, by Susanna Calkins

A Death Along the River Fleet (to be released 2016), by Susanna Calkins

The Physician of London, by Stephanie Cowell

The Last Seal, by Richard Denning

Viola, a Woeful Tale of Marriage, by Katherine Pym

Twins, by Katherine Pym

Of Carrion Feathers, by Katherine Pym

In the Shadow of the Gallows, by Linda Root

The Green Woman: A Scottish Fantasy, by Linda Root

Secrets in Time, by Alison Stuart

Her Rebel Heart, by Alison Stuart

By the Sword (Guardians of the Crown 1), by Alison Stuart

The King's Man (Guardians of the Crown 2), by Alison Stuart

The Lady's Slipper, by Deborah Swift

The Gilded Lily, by Deborah Swift

A Divided Inheritance, by Deborah Swift

Pleasing Mr Pepys, by Deborah Swift

Shadow on the Highway (The Highway Trilogy), by Deborah Swift

Spirit of the Highway (The Highway Trilogy), by Deborah Swift

Lady of the Highway (The Highway Trilogy - to be released), by Deborah Swift

The Midwife's Tale, by Sam Thomas

The Harlot's Tale, by Sam Thomas

The Witch Hunter's Tale, by Sam Thomas

The Midwife and the Assassin, by Sam Thomas

EARLY GEORGIAN ERA (1715-1800)

Marrying Mozart, by Stephanie Cowell

The Ringmaster's Daughter, by Grace Elliot

The Cook's Apprentice, by Grace Elliot

The First Apostle, by Katherine Pym

The Journal of a Georgian Gentleman (nonfiction), by Mike Rendell

English Paper-Cutting in the 18th Century (nonfiction), by Mike Rendell

Astley's Circus: The Story of an English Hussar (nonfiction), by Mike Rendell

Bristol Blue Glass (nonfiction), by Mike Rendell

An Illustrated Introduction to the Georgians (nonfiction), by Mike Rendell

100 Facts about the Georgians (nonfiction), by Mike Rendell

LATE GEORGIAN AND REGENCY ERA (1800-1837)

May 1812, by M.M. Bennetts

Of Honest Fame, by M.M. Bennetts

Family Guardian, by Laurie Alice Eakes

A Necessary Deception, by Laurie Alice Eakes

A Flight of Fancy, by Laurie Alice Eakes

A Reluctant Courtship, by Laurie Alice Eakes

A Lady's Honor, by Laurie Alice Eakes

A Stranger's Secret, by Laurie Alice Eakes

A Dead Man's Debt, by Grace Elliot

Eulogy's Secret, by Grace Elliot

Hope's Betrayal, by Grace Elliot

Verity's Lie, by Grace Elliot

Heyerwood: A Novel, by Lauren Gilbert

A Rational Attachment (to be released), by Lauren Gilbert

Darcy's Decision, by Maria Grace

The Future Mrs. Darcy, by Maria Grace

All the Appearance of Goodness, by Maria Grace

Twelfth Night at Longbourn, by Maria Grace

Remember the Past, by Maria Grace

The Darcy Brothers, by Maria Grace

Mistaking Her Character, by Maria Grace

A Jane Austen Christmas: Regency Christmas Traditions (nonfiction), by Maria Grace

Walls of Jericho, by Jonathan Hopkins

Leopardkill, by Jonathan Hopkins

To Wed an Heiress, by Rosanne E. Lortz

The Earl and His Tiger, by Elizabeth Moss

The Uncatchable Miss Faversham, by Elizabeth Moss

Lavinia in Love, by Elizabeth Moss

A Dangerous Lady, by Elizabeth Moss

The Petticoat Club, by Elizabeth Moss

Poppeia and the Petticoat Club, by Elizabeth Moss

An Illustrated Introduction to the Regency (nonfiction), by Mike Rendell and Philippa Sutcliffe

Lord Somerton's Heir, by Alison Stuart

VICTORIAN ERA (1837-1901)

An Evening with Edgar Allan Poe (biographical), by Katherine Ashe

The Companion of Lady Holmeshire, by Debra Brown

Portraits of an Artist, by Mary F. Burns

The Spoils of Avalon, by Mary F. Burns

Mist of Midnight: A Novel, by Sandra Byrd

Bride of a Distant Isle: A Novel, by Sandra Byrd

Claude & Camille: A Novel of Monet, by Stephanie Cowell

Elizabeth's Sonnets (to be released 2017), by Stephanie Cowell

Gentle Rebels: An Edwardian Love Story (to be released 2017), by Stephanie Cowell

Cat Pies: Feline Historical Trivia (nonfiction), by Grace Elliot

Riduna (Riduna Series 1), by Diana Jackson

Brimstone and Lily, by Terry Kroenung

Jasper's Foul Tongue, by Terry Kroenung

Jasper's Magick Corset, by Terry Kroenung

The Artful Dodger, by Martin Lake

Light, Descending: A Novel of John Ruskin, by Octavia Randolph

Britannia's Wolf, by Antoine Vanner

Britannia's Reach, by Antoine Vanner

Britannia's Shark, by Antoine Vanner

Unraveling Secrets, by Lana Williams

Passionate Secrets, by Lana Williams

Shattered Secrets, by Lana Williams

TWENTIETH CENTURY

Past Encounters, by Davina Blake

Ancasta: Guide Me Swiftly Home (Riduna Series 2), by Diana Jackson

The Life and Demise of Norman Campbell (memoir), by Diana Jackson

Murder, Now and Then, by Diana Jackson

Omphalos, by Mark Patton

Chasing the Wind (Kindle title: *Where Eagles Never Flew: A Battle of Britain Novel*), by Helena P. Schrader

An Obsolete Honor: A Novel of the German Resistance to Hitler (Kindle title: *Hitler's Demons*), by Helena P. Schrader

The Blockade Breakers: The Berlin Airlift (nonfiction), by Helena P. Schrader

Sisters in Arms: The Women Who Flew in WWII (nonfiction), by Helena P. Schrader

Codename Valkyrie: General Friedrich Olbricht and the Plot Against Hitler (nonfiction), by Helena P. Schrader

Gather the Bones, by Alison Stuart

CASTLES, CUSTOMS, AND KINGS

TRUE TALES BY ENGLISH HISTORICAL FICTION AUTHORS

VOLUME 2

ACROSS THE ATLANTIC

By NANCY BILYEAU

O N A JULY DAY, I TOOK A TRAIN 40 MINUTES SOUTH OF LONDON CHARING CROSS TO THE town of Dartford. Armed with a well-studied map, I walked through the center of town, past shops and pubs on the High Street, past blocks of small houses, to a building called the Manor Gatehouse on Priory Road. Just inside is a registration office to record the births, marriages, and deaths that occur in Kent. The property is also a popular place for nuptials: two rooms provide a place to hold the ceremony, and the sweeping walled garden yields some exquisite photos afterward. *"Make your dreams come true,"* boast the advertisements.

My dream was indeed coming true as I stood in the garden, staring at the red-brick building, that high arch over the door, but it had nothing to do with a wedding. My husband of twenty years and my two children were thousands of miles away in New York City. I'd come alone to England, at considerable expense, to see, among other things, this gatehouse, part of a royal manor raised by orders of King Henry VIII in 1538. It was built on the rubble of a demolished priory for Dominican sisters. And it is one of the places that appears in my novels.

My desire to write fiction set in England long ago comes from my love of that genre, a deep and lasting love that began when I was a child, watching *Elizabeth R* on *Masterpiece Theatre* with my parents in suburban Detroit. Today my daughter reads the adventures of Percy Jackson, by Rick Riordan. When I was her age, I devoured Mary Stewart's tales of Merlin. I was a teenage bookworm; I went to bed with novels by Norah Lofts, Jean Plaidy, and Anya Seton, reading until my eyes failed. My sister still jokes about how she'd be woken by a thundering noise. It was my library books falling off the bed as I turned over in my sleep.

I kept reading historical novels—and mysteries, too—as I grew older. I found the work of E.L. Doctorow, Mary Renault, Bernard Cornwell, Ellis Peters, Robert Graves, Caleb Carr, Ken Follett, Sarah Waters. I also devoured nonfiction about history, from the lives of Henry II and Eleanor of Aquitaine all the way to the reign of Queen Victoria. But it was the sixteenth century that pulled at me the hardest. I cherished my books by Jasper Ridley, Garrett Mattingly, and, most of all, Antonia Fraser. My pregnancy with my first child became difficult in the final two months, when I had to stop working as a magazine editor and go to bed, lying on my side to keep my son from being born prematurely. I was both frightened and bored, trapped in the tiny bedroom of our Upper West Side apartment, its window facing a narrow passageway. It was an unusually hot June. If I turned on the air conditioning, I froze; if I switched it off, I soon boiled again. Desperate to take my mind off this, I opened my paperback of Fraser's *Mary Queen of Scots* and read that opening chapter for the umpteenth time:

The winter of 1542 was marked by tempestuous weather throughout the British Isles: in the north, on the borders of Scotland and England, there were heavy snow-falls in December and frosts so savage that by January the ships were frozen into the harbor at Newcastle....

I'll be forever grateful to Fraser's elegant, evocative prose for getting me through those weeks.

Ten years ago, in a fiction workshop I joined on impulse, I decided to try to write a novel that built on my devotion to English history and my knowledge of the time. I chose the tumultuous reign of Henry VIII and created a main character of a Dominican novice caught in the crosswinds of time.

I loved plotting my story, creating characters, and ratcheting up the suspense. But months turned into years; the research became my obsession. I wanted to get it all right. In a strange way I felt I owed it to my beloved sixteenth century. I felt that a working knowledge of the Tudor time was not enough to write these novels. I needed to know what material a habit or a doublet was made of; how fast the horses drew the wagons; how large a bedroom would be; what a nun ate for breakfast. I turned to my journalist side and ended up "reporting" my book. Through email I chased down experts. For example, I found a curatorial intern at the Tower of London who sent me details of prisoners' confinement, such as a PDF of the diet sheet of the king's doomed uncle, Edward Seymour, duke of Somerset. (He actually ate quite well.)

The details of the lives of the Dominican sisters were the most elusive of all. Henry VIII's Dissolution of the Monasteries destroyed their centuries' old priory. For all of the Tudor nuns, not much remains, except for a few letters and wills. I read all the books I could find about medieval English monastics, and also the traditions of the abbeys in France and the Netherlands in the sixteenth century. A breakthrough came when I found at the New York Public Library, main branch, a book that helped me understand the lives of those who took vows in the sixteenth century: F.A. Gasquet's *English Monastic Life*, published in 1904.

I knew that I wouldn't uncover hidden treasures if I were to go in person to Dartford. I'd learned pretty much all I could thanks to my years of reading and the two helpful men who worked at the town's small museum. But I wanted to walk the same ground that my Sister Joanna Stafford walked, in Dartford and in London. I zeroed in on a discount fare on Expedia and booked it, my hands trembling.

Why was I so overcome with emotion over arranging this trip? I was far from a sheltered person. I lived in New York City! As a journalist I'd been flown places. One magazine sent me to Austin, Texas, to interview Laura Bush. I'd had to be pretty tough from the beginning of my career. At my first job, a newspaper in Florida, I saw corpses, interviewed the police. I was once chased off someone's property by two Dobermans.

Yet the nervous excitement over traveling to England to research my novels didn't let up. It just kept building. I was set to take a red-eye flight from JFK to London. Expecting the food at the airport to be dire, I ate a cheese sandwich that evening, kissed my husband and children, and made my way to the front of our apartment, to take a cab to the airport. There was no line at the Virgin Atlantic counter; I was quite early for the flight. In the international terminal I spotted the glittering Caviar House and Prunier and, on impulse, ordered champagne. Next to me a couple dined on Chardonnay, crab legs, and salad. I sipped my drink and scribbled in a brown-leather Italian journal I'd bought just for this trip (it was too heavy to be easily toted around but I was determined to do this old school).

Some of the giddiness wore off after I found my seat in the back of the enormous plane: 63K. My neighbor was a man jabbering into his cell phone, calling his friend "Dude" every five seconds, and complaining that the weather made his face break out and that while in New York he'd fought with his girlfriend. But finally he had no choice but to turn off his phone and once that happened, he settled down.

The plane groaned to life. I wrote in my journal at 10:46 p.m.: *"I am in this giant dark beast gliding down the runway. All the lights had to be turned off. There are tiny spotlights for reading. We are turning...we are in the air. Millions of sparkling lights below. The plane banks. I see a star. The Atlantic."*

I slept no more than 90 minutes on that flight. I kept lifting the window shade to peer at the black ocean. Once dawn peeked over the horizon, there was no question of rest. At 3:30 a.m. East Coast Time, I had lemon cake and coffee. I was ready to go. Not even a grueling line at Heathrow's customs could defeat me. I'd been advised to take a nap at the hotel, to orient myself to the new time zone. But I changed clothes and ran back onto the Strand. London awaited me.

It was late in the day when I found myself at the bank of the Thames and a statue of Boudicca, ferocious female warrior. It was also where the tour boats pick up customers. I had grown to loathe the tour buses and boats of New York City. But I eagerly paid for one here, for this was my way to the Tower of London. My main character, Sister Joanna, spent months in the Tower in *The Crown*. I couldn't wait to walk across the grounds, peer into the cells.

After finishing our tour, the last one of the day, I could feel the exhaustion creeping over me. I went to one of the fish-and-chips stalls facing the Tower of London and sat at a folding table, outside, nibbling the food, and gazed on the walls raised by William the Conqueror, the green where Anne Boleyn and Catherine Howard lost their lives, the river that Princess Elizabeth's boat took to convey her to her imprisonment.

And I was completely happy.

Pre-Roman to Early Medieval Britain (pre-55 B.C.–A.D. 1000)

STONE CIRCLES: SEEKING THE PEOPLE BEHIND THE STONES

By MARK PATTON

FOR MORE THAN THIRTY YEARS I HAVE BEEN ACTIVELY INVOLVED IN THE STUDY OF Europe's megalithic monuments. From passage graves such as Maes Howe in Orkney and Newgrange in Ireland to the long barrows and stone circles of the Cotswolds, the standing stones of Brittany, and the stone temples of Malta, guide books and museum displays tell us that these structures were built between seven thousand and four thousand years ago by Neolithic farmers who grew wheat and barley, kept cattle, sheep, and pigs, and used pottery, but who had no knowledge of either metals or writing.

Generally, the monuments themselves are assumed to have played some role in the religion of these people. Some were collective tombs, others clearly were not. Some of them are aligned towards particular rising or setting points of the sun. Those built six thousand years ago did not necessarily have the same function or significance as those built four thousand years ago.

I grew up in Jersey surrounded by these monuments. At the age of seventeen I hitch-hiked through France to the great stone alignments of Carnac in Brittany. Since then I have visited hundreds of these monuments all over Europe, spent many days in museum stores examining, measuring, and drawing the artefacts found within them and many months directing excavations of my own. In the course of this research I published several works of non-fiction.

The cold stones of a monument, however, and the stone tools, pottery fragments, and bones found within them can tell us only so much about the people who built the monuments and the societies in which they lived. The great archaeologist Christopher Hawkes used to talk about a "ladder of inference"; it was relatively easy, he argued, to talk about prehistoric technology, rather more difficult to talk about the economics of prehistoric communities, and almost impossible to draw inferences from the archaeological evidence about the belief systems or emotional lives of prehistoric people. For my part, however, I could never stand in a stone circle or hold a stone axe in my hand without wanting to understand these people in fully human terms. As an archaeologist, this frequently left me perching, somewhat precariously, at the very top of Hawkes' ladder. Ultimately it is what inspired me to write fiction about the distant past.

Recent archaeological discoveries have shed new light on these monuments. Some megaliths in Brittany, which had been thought to have been among the earliest (carbon dated to around 4500 B.C.), have been shown to have been made up of the broken fragments of monuments that were earlier still. At Gobeckli Tepe in Turkey, a stone "temple" has been found to be more than eleven thousand years old, built not by Neolithic farmers but by Mesolithic hunters and gatherers. In England, in the area around Stonehenge (one of the most iconic, but also one of the later monuments, built around four and a half thousand years ago), archaeologists have excavated the houses and the graves of some of the people who may have built the monument. Scientific analysis of the bones shows that some of these people (the first in Britain to use metals) came from far afield: from West Wales, the origin, also, of some of the stones at Stonehenge, and in at least one case, from Austria or Switzerland (where copper, bronze, and gold were worked long before their first appearance in Britain). A grave found near Stonehenge has some of the earliest copper and gold objects ever found in Britain. Chemical analysis of the man's teeth shows that he grew up in Central Europe (probably in Austria or Switzerland).

Each individual discovery is like a piece in a jigsaw puzzle, and together they allow us to build up a picture of a dynamic society in which some people must have travelled great distances, in which new technologies were developed in some regions and carried to others, and in which new ideas about life and death were circulating and being debated.

THE COLIGNY CALENDAR AND THE RHYTHMS OF THE IRON AGE YEAR

By MARK PATTON

THE COLIGNY CALENDAR IS AN ENGRAVED COPPER ALLOY TABLET WHICH WAS ORIGI-nally 1.48 metres wide and 0.9 metres high. It is broken and incomplete, but the 73 fragments preserved in the Gallo-Roman Museum in Lyon give us a great deal of information about how the calendar was structured. It dates to the late second century A.D., by which time Lyon and its surrounding district was, in most respects, thoroughly Roman-ised, yet the months it lists are not the familiar ones of the Julian calendar.

Presumably it mattered, at least to some people, to keep in mind the calendar of their pre-Roman ancestors. Since Julius Caesar and other writers emphasise the unity of Gaulish and British culture, with druids moving freely across tribal boundaries, the like-lihood is that this calendar, or some variant of it, applied in Britain just as it did in Gaul.

The list below shows the names of the months (in the Gaulish language), the equiva-lents in our calendar, and suggested translations (academics do not always agree on these).

> Samonios: October/November: Seed-Fall.
> Dumannios: November/December: Darkest Depths.
> Riuros: December/January: Cold-Time.
> Anagantios: January/February: Stay-Home Time.
> Ogronios: February/March: Time of Ice.
> Cutios: March/April: Time of Winds.
> Giamonios: April/May: Shoot-Show.
> Simivisionios: May/June: Time of Brightness.
> Equos: June/July: Horse Time.
> Elembivos: July/August: Claim Time.
> Edrinios: August/September: Arbitration Time.
> Cantios: September/October: Song Time.

The years are grouped into five year cycles, and these five year cycles are in turn grouped into "ages" of thirty years which corresponds to what Pliny the Elder has to say about the druidic understanding of the passage of time. Intercalary months were added in some years to synchronise the solar and lunar cycles (as with modern "leap years").

The major festivals within the year were Samhain (31 October, when all household fires were extinguished and re-lit from a ceremonial bonfire), Imbolc (1 February, marking the return of light to the world), Bealtaine (1 May, the feast of Belenos, God of Fire), and Lughnasa (1 August, a harvest festival at which marriages were also celebrated).

It is impossible to know how far back in time this calendar extends.

THE FLAVIAN PALACE AT FISHBOURNE: LUXURY UNPARALLELED IN EUROPE NORTH OF THE ALPS

BY MARK PATTON

CLOSE TO THE MODERN CITY OF CHICHESTER IS A ROMAN PALACE THAT BEARS COMparison with Nero's "Golden House" and the Palace of Domitian in Rome itself. Much of it is now hidden beneath modern housing but in its heyday it had a larger footprint than Buckingham Palace. Not only is it, by far, the most lavish Roman dwelling ever built in Britain, it is also one of the earliest, having been built within a few decades of the Roman invasion of 43 A.D.

There are two main theories regarding the construction and ownership of the palace. The first, suggested by the original excavator, Professor Sir Barry Cunliffe, is that it was built between 73 and 79 A.D. for Tiberius Claudius Cogidubnus, a native British king known for his loyalty to Rome. The second, suggested by Dr. Miles Russell of Bournemouth University, is that it was built in the A.D. 90s, possibly for the Roman Governor, Sallustius Lucullus. I have always found the first hypothesis to be the more compelling, but there is no conclusive proof either way.

What is clear is that it must have been erected by Roman builders and craftsmen brought to Britain especially for the purpose. Nothing remotely like this had ever been seen in Britain before. The palace has an entrance-hall, a formal audience chamber, residential suites with mosaics and under-floor heating, a bath complex, accommodation for guests and for servants or slaves. It also has an "aisled hall" (an unusual feature with a door onto the street, which may have been used in religious ceremonies, public addresses, and/or entertainments), and an elaborate formal garden.

The earliest mosaics of the Flavian Palace are predominantly black and white, featuring geometric motifs.

It was not the first building on the site. Beneath the garden of the Flavian palace (the Flavian period encompassed the reigns of Vespasian and his sons, Titus and Domitian, and lasted from 69 to 96 A.D.) were found the remains of an earlier palace, built in the 60s A.D., two substantial timber buildings of the 50s A.D., and military granaries built soon after the Roman invasion.

If Cogidubnus provided the Emperor Claudius with a safe harbour and a supply base for his legions, this might go some way towards explaining why Claudius' eventual successor, Vespasian, rewarded him so generously. Vespasian and Cogidubnus may have become friends in the months following the invasion. We know that the Second Legion, which Vespasian then commanded, campaigned in Hampshire and Dorset. Vespasian may have cultivated Cogidubnus as he would later cultivate the Jewish leader, Josephus.

We do not know the name of the architect who designed the palace, but there are close parallels between Fishbourne and the Palace of Domitian in Rome, close enough to suggest that it may have been designed by the same man and built with the assistance of some of the same craftsmen or by their former apprentices.

> Awesome and vast is the edifice, distinguished not by a hundred columns but by as many as could shoulder the gods and the sky, if Atlas were let off. The Thunderer's palace next door gapes at it, and the gods rejoice that you are lodged in a like abode.... So great extends the structure and the sweep of the far-flung hall, more expansive than that of an open plain, embracing much enclosed sky and lesser only than its master....
>
> —Statius, *Silvae*, 4, describing the Palace of Domitian.

The Fishbourne palace remained in use until it was destroyed by fire in around 270 A.D. and may have passed through several hands. Some of the more elaborately coloured mosaics date to the second and third centuries A.D.

A GLIMPSE INSIDE THE ROMAN HOME

BY MARK PATTON

WHEN ARCHAEOLOGISTS EXCAVATE A ROMAN HOUSE IN BRITAIN, THEY TYPICALLY find only the foundations. The walls, ceilings, and roof-timbers have always disappeared and, even if the concrete or mosaic floors remain intact, the buildings had, in most cases, been abandoned by their owners before they were buried, leaving only rubbish behind. It can make it quite difficult to imagine what the domestic world of Roman times was really like, the more so since Roman literature has almost nothing to say about the home lives of ordinary people. (The *Satyricon* is a notable exception, but it provides only a few tantalising hints.)

The 2012 Pompeii and Herculaneum exhibition at the British Museum put some welcome flesh on the normally bare archaeological bones. The focus of the exhibition was very specifically on domestic life and, although it included objects from across the two towns destroyed by the eruption of 79 A.D., the starting point around which everything else was structured was the floor-plan of one specific home, the "House of the Tragic Poet" in Pompeii.

Because of the way in which Pompeii and Herculaneum were destroyed, objects were preserved that have rarely survived elsewhere and certainly not in Roman Britain. From kitchen utensils to chamber-pots, food-warmers, portable stoves, wooden stools, tables, and a baby's cradle, these objects are like the missing pieces in an ancient and very incomplete jigsaw puzzle.

There are some significant surprises, too. It has long been known that religion played a major part in most Roman homes with domestic altars and shrines to the Lares or household gods. What is less well known is that the slaves of the household often had their own shrine, typically located in or adjacent to the kitchen.

We might not expect to see graffiti in our own homes, but it is present in many Pompeian ones. Was it a subtle means by which slaves could communicate their concerns with one another or even with their masters without having to take the risk of speaking up publicly and being identified individually?

Pompeians of the first century A.D. seem to have been unembarrassed by nudity or by depictions of sex. Early scholars of Pompeii often assumed that a building adorned with sexually explicit images must be a brothel. There certainly were brothels in Pompeii and Herculaneum (and presumably in all the major towns of Roman Britain), but there are also plenty of sexually explicit wall-paintings in what appear to have been regular family homes. In some of the imagery and in the graffiti, one starts to pick up an echo of the sense of humour prevalent, perhaps especially among the slaves, and providing us with a glimpse, not only into the Roman home, but also into the Roman mind. Was the mosaic of a skeleton bearing wine to the table an Epicurean exhortation to enjoy life whilst one may or a statement about householders who work their slaves to death?

Of course, Pompeii and Herculaneum were not Silchester or Caerwent, and we cannot take the analogies too far or make too many assumptions. I doubt, however, that I will ever look at a family home of the first century A.D. (whether in Britain or in Italy) in quite the same way again. More than anything, it is the garish colours and the raucous noise of the Pompeian houses that will stay with me and influence my writing.

THE MISSION OF ST. AUGUSTINE

BY RICHARD DENNING

CHRISTIANITY HAD COME TO BRITAIN IN ROMAN TIMES BUT, FOLLOWING THE ROMAN withdrawal in about 416 A.D. and the steady conquest of what would one day be England by the Anglo-Saxon immigrants, it was confined mostly to the lands under the control of the Romano-British Welsh (increasingly confined to the west), the Irish, and the Scots. The vast bulk of the land under the rule of the Saxons was pagan.

The church in Rome was certainly aware of the reversal of its fortunes in the former province of Britannia. According to legend, Pope Gregory I (590-604) once saw fair haired Anglo-Saxon boy slaves in the forum in Rome. He enquired who these were and was told they were Angles, to which he poetically replied *"Non Angli, sed Angeli"* ("Not Angles, but Angels") and determined that this race should be converted to Christianity. When he became Pope, he set about just this task. But he needed a man for the job.

In the 580s Gregory had founded and been the Abbot of the Monastery of St. Andrews on the Caelian Hill in Rome. One of his former monks had now risen to become Prior of St. Andrews and it was to this man, Augustine, and forty of his monks that Gregory now turned. In the year 595 Gregory asked Augustine to go to Britain and convert the English.

We know little about Augustine prior to his appointment. He was probably the son of a wealthy Roman, but beyond that there is a scarcity of information. This is *not* St. Augustine of Hippo who wrote many of the religious essays that shaped medieval Christianity but a totally different man.

THE MISSION

There is uncertainty over where the idea for this mission originated. The official version, as we have seen, is that it was the idea of the Pope. There has also been a suggestion that Gregory was approached by Bertha, the Queen of Kent. Bertha was the daughter of a king of the Franks and a Christian. Her husband, Aethelberht of Kent, was pagan but tolerated his wife's religion. Possibly Aethelberht saw political advantage in requesting ties with Rome.

In any event, Kent was the logical choice for the mission to take place. Its ruler would not oppose their presence, and moreover, Kent's alliance with Burgundy and the Franks would allow safe passage for Augustine, especially after Gregory wrote to their rulers requesting assistance. Augustine's route was laid out, but after departing from Rome he and his party almost turned back in France. It needed another push from Gregory to finally get them to England in 597 A.D.

Kent and its ruler were receptive to the message. Baptisms and the establishment of a monastery soon followed, and Aethelberht himself converted after some months. In Canterbury at the same spot where an old Roman church stood (St. Martin's) the foundations were laid for what would one day be the cathedral that today is the senior cathedral of the Church of England.

In 601 A.D., Gregory confirmed Augustine as Archbishop of Canterbury and sent more missionaries with instructions to appoint bishops, a plan to have an Archbishop at York (this would not occur for 25 more years), and also encouragement to spread out and incorporate other kingdoms under his authority.

WHAT TO DO ABOUT PAGAN TEMPLES AND TRADITIONS?

As the Augustine mission expanded, it was faced with the issue of the pre-existing pagan culture of the English and their temples and traditions. Should the Roman Christians ban the festivals and destroy the temples? The Pope sent instructions to Augustine on this matter via one of the new Abbots.

> *Tell Augustine that he should be no means destroy the temples of the gods but rather the idols within those temples. Let him, after he has purified them with holy water, place altars and relics of the saints in them. For, if those temples are well built, they should be converted from the worship of demons to the service of the true God. Thus, seeing that their places of worship are not destroyed, the people will banish error from their hearts and come to places familiar and dear to them in acknowledgement and worship of the true God. Further, since it has been their custom to slaughter oxen in sacrifice, they should receive some solemnity in exchange. Let them therefore, on the day of the dedication of their churches, or on the feast of the martyrs whose relics are preserved in them, build themselves huts around their one-time temples and celebrate the occasion with religious feasting. They will sacrifice and eat the animals not any more as an offering to the devil, but for the glory of God to whom, as the giver of all things, they will give thanks for having been satiated. Thus, if they are not deprived of all exterior joys, they will more easily taste the interior ones. For surely it is impossible to efface all at once everything from their strong minds, just as, when one wishes to reach the top of a mountain, he must climb by stages and step by step, not by leaps and bounds.... Mention this to our brother the bishop, that he may dispose of the matter as he sees fit according to the conditions of time and place.*

So the church was to be pragmatic. It would re-use pagan temples as the people were already used to worshipping in them. It would not ban pagan festivals but adapt them. Saints' days and holy days would often fit in with pre-existing pagan dates and so, rather than expect the people to lay aside their parties and festivals, the Church would take them over as times of joy and celebration.

THE MISSION GETS HARDER

Britain was not one nation. It was divided into Anglo-Saxon eastern kingdoms and Romano-British Welsh western kingdoms as well as the kingdoms of the Irish, Picts, and Scots. There were dozens of kingdoms, and each of the Saxon lands were pagan. Some were receptive, some very resistant. Some kingdoms would convert only to revert to paganism when a new king came along. Mercia would not become totally Christian until as late as the eighth century. Nevertheless, gradually Augustine was able to penetrate other lands, and the Augustine mission was deemed a success.

That was until he came across the Welsh....

MEETING THE WELSH

In around 603, Augustine requested a meeting with the Welsh bishops at a place known as Augustine's Oak—somewhere around the border of Mercia, Hwicee, and the Welsh lands. From the start there was trouble. The Welsh bishops had maintained a Christian church in the land for 300 years. Effectively separated from Rome by the English lands, the church had evolved independently after Rome abandoned Britannia. This led to several differences: the method of appointing bishops, the timing of Easter, the approach to converting the pagan English, and even the tonsure (the style of a monk's hair cut).

Augustine insisted that the Welsh abandon their traditions and conform to Rome's teachings. His attitude was so arrogant that the meeting broke up.

Another meeting was arranged some months later. The Welsh bishops were uncertain how to approach it and sought advice from a wise man who suggested that they allow Augustine to arrive first and then go in. If he rose when they entered (as if he were greeting equals) then they should try and reach accommodation. If he did not rise, they would know that he looked down on them and treated them as inferior. To Augustine's mind *he* was the Archbishop, and these *were* inferior. The Welsh did not see it that way and left. It would take many years to reach accommodation after this failure.

THE END OF HIS MISSION

It is believed that Augustine died between 604 and 609 A.D. In his brief years as Archbishop he had re-established the Christian church in the land ruled by the English and set the foundation of a structure that would last until Henry VIII separated from Rome. Canterbury is still the seat of the Archbishop, so in that regard he was a success. Certainly his mission had a powerful effect on the evolving land that would one day become England. His failing was arrogance, as witnessed by his dealings with the Welsh. He is venerated as a saint in the Roman Catholic Church and accepted as the father of the Church in England.

DARK AGES GWYNEDD

By RICHARD DENNING

THE KINGDOM OF GWYNEDD ALONG THE NORTH WALES COAST IS OFTEN ASSOCIATED with the mighty Llewelyn ap Gruffydd who unified Wales in the thirteenth century and opposed England's expansion. Today, though, I am looking at the origins of this great Welsh kingdom. For that we go back in time to the years after the Romans abandoned Britannia and the centuries thereafter.

Gwynedd covers most of North Wales and the Isle of Anglesey. The name might mean "Desirable Land" or "Warrior Land" or might relate to the names of Irish tribes who settled it before the Romans.

It seems that before the Romans came to Britain an Irish presence existed in North Wales. Tribes from Leinster travelled across the Irish Sea in the first century B.C. and settled in Ynys Mon (Anglesey) and along the north coast as far as the Llyn (or Lleyn) peninsula. Ancestors of the Welsh known as the Ordovices may also have lived in the area. The Romans who arrived in the vicinity in the 70s A.D. called the region Venedotia.

Venedotia remained under Roman control until around 380 when the Roman legions withdrew from the region. Nennius, a ninth century monk, recorded that after this time the region was defenceless and became victim to increasing raids from Ireland.

So, soon after the Romans left, the northwest area of Wales was in effect an Irish province. The expanding Irish domains in South and North Wales, along with the Picts raiding down the east coast and the Saxons along the east and south, created a crisis that required action.

In the mid-fifth century a certain Cunedda led his sons and their followers in a migration from Manau Goddodin (around Edinburgh) to the North Welsh coast. It is possible that this was at the instigation or suggestion of Vortigern who also (according to tradition) invited the Saxons Hengest and Horsa to settle in Kent. The suggestion is that Vortigern was high king of the British and was responding to Irish raids in the Gwynedd area as well as Pictish raids down the east coast.

Cunedda was married to the daughter of Coel Hen, the powerful King of the whole of the north and the man immortalized by the children's rhyme "Old King Cole". Cunedda's sons would rule not just Gwynedd but also huge chunks of the north and west of Britain.

The same monk, Nennius, records how Cunedda fought the Irish in North Wales and drove them out. He then established the kingdom of Gwynedd. His was a dynasty that would last 800 years until the English finally occupied the region in the thirteenth century.

The period I am most interested in at present is the early seventh century. Gwynedd played a pivotal role in the history of the English of the Anglo-Saxon Kingdom of Northumbria. Around 604 A.D. the King of Bernicia (the northern half of Northumbria) had taken over Deira (the southern half) probably in battle or possibly by political means. The heirs to the throne of Deira were young princes in their teens—Edwin and Hereric. These boys were forced to flee into exile. One of the places where Edwin, at least, spent a good deal of time was Gwynedd. We do not know exactly how and when he got there or exactly in what circumstances.

What is laid down in traditions is that Edwin became the adopted son of King Cadfan of Gwynedd and became baptized at some stage (although he later was baptized again when king in Northumbria, so this may well have been a political step).

It is probable that as a result of its sponsorship of Edwin, Gwynedd became one of the targets of Aethelfrith who attacked the City of Chester which was possibly in the hands of Gwynedd (or Powys—another allied Welsh Kingdom) around 612 to 614 A.D.

This battle was a disaster for the Welsh and probably forced Edwin to go on the road again looking for shelter and protection. He eventually ended up in East Anglia where he was able to persuade King Redwald to support him in battle. This battle in 616 at the River Idle led to the death of Aethelfrith and to Edwin regaining his throne.

Meanwhile, back in Gwynedd, Cadfan was soon afterwards succeeded by Cadwallon. Cadwallon and Edwin would have been step-brothers, but any affection they had turned sour, for Edwin invaded and attacked Gwynedd and managed to occupy almost all of it.

Cadwallon was a friend of the Saxon king, Penda of Mercia. He was able to forge an alliance with Penda and then counter-attack. So in 632 they killed King Edwin of Northumbria and conquered his kingdom.

With Northumbria at his feet it is possible that Cadwallon could have re-established a powerful Welsh kingdom in the North—an echo of the kingdoms of Coel Hen himself, Cadwallon's illustrious grand sire. But it was not to be. In 633, Oswald, a son of Aethelfrith—who had spent sixteen years in exile himself like Edwin—returned to Northumbria and with Pictish help defeated and killed Cadwallon at the Battle of Heavenfield near Hadrian's Wall.

The Kings of Gwynedd retreated to their own boundaries where their power and strength would wax and wane over the years. This mountain fastness would provide a stubborn opponent to the English for centuries to come.

AN ANGLO-SAXON CHRISTMAS

By RICHARD DENNING

CHRISTMAS, ALONG WITH THE NEW YEAR CELEBRATIONS THAT FOLLOW IT, IS IN Britain the most important festival and holiday of the year. Families get together, give and receive presents, eat and drink, and have a good time. Many businesses close down for almost two weeks, and very little work gets done even in those places that are actually open—unless of course they are pubs and restaurants!

In celebrating this time of year we recreate festivals that predate even the coming of Christianity to Anglo-Saxon England. Here it is deep winter. It is a time of long nights and short days. It is cold and dark and not a time to be out. This is a time to feast and create our own light and warmth and to look forward with hope to the return of the sun.

That at least is how our ancestors saw things. Christmas coincides with Yuletide—the ancient celebration that occupied midwinter. Here in England it was celebrated for a number of days running on from the twenty-fifth of December. At that time, under the old Julian calendar, December 25 was also the winter solstice. (Today it is December 20 or 21, of course.)

How do we know that the early Saxons celebrated Yuletide at this time? Well, the eighth century scholar Bede tells us this in an essay he wrote on the Saxon calendar:

> They began the year with December 25, the day we now celebrate as Christmas; and the very night to which we attach special sanctity they designated by the heathen mothers' night—a name bestowed, I suspect, on account of the ceremonies they performed while watching this night through.

The very name for the months that straddled Yuletide—December and January—were considered "Giuli" or Yule by the Anglo-Saxons. As Bede said, the Anglo-Saxons celebrated the beginning of the year on December 25, which they called "Modranect"—that is, Mothers' Night. This celebration was linked to the rebirth of "Mother" Earth, and the whole idea of ceremonies conducted at the time was to ensure fertility in the coming spring season. The Saxon gods of fertility were Freyja, who governed love and fertility, and her twin brother Freyr, and they may well have been linked to the celebrations.

FORGET THE TURKEY—BRING OUT THE BOAR

It is probable that the feasts involved boars. Freyja and Freyr were associated with the boar. This was the primary animal represented in Yuletide customs and, indeed, in Anglo-Saxon culture in general. It is mentioned in epic warrior poetry like *Beowulf*. A boar's head may well have been sacrificed to appease the gods, and the boar continued to ornament brooches, bowls, and jewellery as well as more military objects for centuries.

It was not only boars that were eaten but cows and other animals. We can get some idea of Yuletide ceremonies from Icelandic writings. (We have to rely on Scandinavian writing often as not many writings exist from the early Anglo-Saxon period.)

This is an excerpt from *The Saga of Hakon the Good*.

> *It was ancient custom that when sacrifice was to be made, all farmers were to come to the heathen temple and bring along with them the food they needed while the feast lasted. At this feast all were to take part of the drinking of ale. Also all kinds of livestock were killed in connection with it, horses also; and all the blood from them was...smeared all over...the pedestals of the idols and also the walls of the temple within and without; and likewise the men present were to be sprinkled with blood. But the meat of the animals was to be boiled and served as food at the banquet. Fires were to be lighted in the middle of the temple floor, and kettles hung over them. The sacrificial beaker was to be borne around the fire, and he who made the feast and was chieftain, was to bless the beaker as well as all the sacrificial meat.*

The narrative continues that toasts were to be drunk. The first toast was to be drunk to Odin *"for victory and power to the king"*, the second to the gods Njörðr and Freyr *"for good harvests and for peace"*, and third, a beaker was to be drunk to the king himself. In addition, toasts were drunk to the memory of departed kinsfolk.

So sacrifices were made to the gods, the fertility gods as well as Odin (Woden in England), and then much drinking of ale and eating of meat ensued. The main celebration lasted three days and it seems that fighting and duels were put off for this period. The *Svarfdæla* saga records a story in which a berserker put off a duel until three days after Yule to honour the sanctity of the holiday. Grettis Saga refers to Yule as a time of *"greatest mirth and joy among men."*

THE MISSIONARIES ARRIVE

In the year 597, the Pope sent Augustine to England to try and convert it to Christianity. The process would take centuries, but quite early on it appears that a decision was made to amalgamate the pagan festival of Yuletide with Christianity.

The Roman church had already decided to use December 25 as the date of Christ's birth some centuries before. Christmas as a festivity celebrating the birth of Jesus originated in Egypt sometime in the second century; here it took over a previous festival, most likely the birth of Osiris. In Europe, Christianity encountered the Roman cult of Mithras. Mithras was an Iranic deity associated with Sun-worship whose cult became so widespread in the Roman Empire as to become a serious threat to Christianity. The twenty-fifth of December is accepted as Mithras' birthday. When the Emperor Constantine declared that Christianity was the official religion of the Empire, from 336 A.D. onwards, the Western Church used the twenty-fifth as the date of Christmas. The church often took this pragmatic view; rather than attempt to do away with pagan celebrations and traditions and temples, they took them over and eventually replaced them—although often older traditions still show themselves in little things we do.

A significant step in this process occurred in 567 A.D. In order to encourage the people to abandon pagan holidays, the Council of Tours declared the twelve days of Christmas to be a festival. Historically, the twelve days of Christmas followed December 25. These dozen days ended the day before Epiphany (the coming of the Magi), which was celebrated on January 6.

When Augustine arrived in Britain in 597, he was encouraged by the Pope to bring the Saxons' Yuletide into line with Christmas.

> Because they are accustomed to slay many oxen in sacrifices to demons, some solemnity should be put in place of this.... [T]hey may make bowers of branches of trees around those churches which have been changed from heathen temples, and may celebrate the solemnity with religious feasting. Nor let them now sacrifice animals to the Devil, but for the praise of God kill animals for their own eating....

Christian influence, however, remained superficial until the time of the Norman Conquest. Many older pagan rites persisted and to some extent do today. Rites included Yule logs, which may have been a Celtic tradition adopted by the Anglo-Saxons. The idea was that since the sun was far away it could be persuaded to return if the log could be kept burning throughout Yuletide. The use of evergreens and mistletoe originated in ancient fertility customs—an echo of Mothers' Night.

Gradually, old Germanic Yule celebrations combined with nativity feasts, and the English Christmas began to take shape. Alfred the Great insisted that no business be done during the Twelve Days. By 1066 the Christianisation of England was complete, and the Twelve Days were the main annual holiday. When we sit down to our Christmas lunch, we recreate traditions that stretch back through fifteen centuries and more and celebrate both a Merry Christmas and a Happy Yuletide!

MEDIEVAL GAMES AND PASTIMES

BY OCTAVIA RANDOLPH

ALL CULTURES, REGARDLESS OF HOW ARDUOUS THE TIMES THEY LIVE IN, HAVE SOME kinds of sport, games, and pastimes to engage in during leisure hours, and thankfully children have always played. In Anglo-Saxon times (roughly 450-1100) life was largely lived outdoors for most people, for the continuance of life was predicated on agricultural labour. The interiors of most buildings were dark, smoky, and often cramped, and many tasks whether for livelihood or leisure required the clear, strong light of daylight.

Children played with many more natural objects than they do today; a later medieval sermon, which still holds true for the Anglo-Saxon era, mentions children playing:

> with flowers...with sticks, and with small bits of wood, to build a chamber, buttery, and hall, to make a white horse of a wand, a sailing ship of broken bread, a burly spear from a ragwort stalk, and of a sedge a sword of war, a comely lady from cloth, and be right busy to deck it elegantly with flowers.

Grave finds from early heathen burials contain carved wooden toys such as horses and small wooden boats, tenderly laid to rest with their little owner. But childhood was short for the Anglo-Saxon girl or boy, and girls of five or six were already spending part of their day learning to spin wool, card fleece, or help with the younger children in the family. Boys tended animals or helped in the fields. Boys also played with small spears and knives carved of wood, learning the arts of hunting and defense at a young age.

Miniature tools sized for a child's hand have been found, much like children's sized gardening implements today, but since a child would be more useful at an activity such as egg gathering or sheep tending perhaps such tools were meant as playthings rather than actual implements of labour for young hands (although no one pulls weeds better than an industrious six year old!).

Sometimes, for adults, work and play were mingled. In some villages plough races were held by the men on Plough Monday, the first Monday after Twelfth Night (Epiphany), the end of the Yuletide season.

Physical fitness was obviously of paramount importance to people of all classes: life was hard and demanding, and being physically able to cope with the realities of farming, tree-felling, and of course, battle, could mean the literal difference between life and death. Young men in particular held foot-races, participated in wrestling matches, and practiced the martial arts such as spear throwing, archery, and mock sword play. Those who were rich enough to own horses would have raced them to see whose was the fastest; the Old English epic *Beowulf* mentions young men doing just that:

The warriors let their bay horses go
a contest for the best horse
galloping through whatever path looked fair.

Hunting was not purely sport, as it was relied upon to bring food to the table, but it could be very exciting and therefore enjoyable. Huge numbers of deer roamed the vast forests and marshes of Britain and provided a good supply of game to those able to stalk and bring them down. Wolves too were hunted as a protection to the flocks of sheep on which so much depended. These intelligent predators later suffered the same fate as the bear, which was hunted to extinction on the island in the tenth century. Boar hunting was hunting of the most challenging kind, and many dogs, horses, and men were killed while trying to hunt this speedy, ferocious, and clever beast.

Good hounds were cherished both as working animals and as companions, and the rich oftentimes made gifts of such dogs. King Ælfred, greatest king of the Anglo-Saxon era and perhaps indeed of any other, sent a brace of fine hounds to the archbishop of Reims.

Only the very richest lords kept falcons specially trained to bring down pigeons and starlings and the like. Riding out on horseback and releasing the falcon and watching it swoop down on its prey was a very aristocratic sport indeed. Many of these falcons were from Viking traders who captured and trained them in Scandinavia, and then sold them to the rich in Britain, Northern Europe, and as far east as Arabia.

Although most fish were captured in weirs set up in rivers, streams, and narrow ocean channels, line fishing was practiced and was undoubtedly found to be as enjoyably frustrating as it is today.

The Anglo-Saxons had a great love of ornament on even everyday objects, and men and women spent long hours decorating the spines of wood, bone, and horn hair combs with drawings of animals, embellishing gowns and tunics with gaily coloured embroidery, and decorating leather goods by stamping them with metal dies and burning designs into the surface with heated pokers. The most utilitarian of items such as wooden buckets and dippers generally carried some decoration, even if only simple incised lines or dots around the perimeter. Many of these handcrafts would have been practiced out of doors to take advantage of the good light.

Indoor pastimes included games using dice and a variety of board games that used little clay and carved markers. Just as today almost everybody enjoyed such pastimes, and our modern word "game" comes from the Old English "gamen". Dice games were very popular (so popular that even clergy played them) and many dice have been found. Betting played a large role in dice games, just as it does today.

The game of *tæfl* was played on a board using game pieces in opposition. The rules of early games probably varied quite a bit, but many of these games featured a piece which represented the "king" which needed to be protected by the other pieces.

The stunning contents of a grave of an Anglo-Saxon prince or king (possibly of King Sabert who died in 616) discovered near Southend in Essex in 2003 and known as the

Prittlewell Find contained 57 gaming pieces carved of bone and two very large dice carved from antler. This shows us that games were important enough in the lives of the Anglo-Saxons that they accompanied their owners into the afterlife.

In the latter Anglo-Saxon period, from the twelfth century onward, chess (a particular favourite of my own), originally created in India, was brought to Britain. With its war lords, warriors, and horsemen it echoed the battle-driven lives of the noblemen and women who played it. Two forms of chess were played, one quite similar to the challenging intellectual game we know today, and one simplified version which employed dice, and thus introduced an element of luck.

Storytelling, singing, and dancing were also part of the long indoor winter evenings.

Harps such as the beautiful one buried with the Sutton Hoo treasure (the burial goods of a great king from about 625 C.E., now on display at the British Museum) were played by professional story tellers called *scops*, but small hide drums, wood pipes, and whistles are easily made from everyday materials and were probably played by a wide variety of children and adults. Listening was an active art, and when the professional storyteller or scop began his tale, all turned attentively to him and listened raptly, picturing in their mind's eye the great heroes, battles, hunts, and religious episodes he sang of.

There was also pleasure to be taken in the simple contemplation of unspoilt nature. A fourteenth century treatise on the duties and pleasures of a nobleman lists "Watching the snow fall" as an act worthy of his rank, and indeed during winter when many agricultural duties were suspended and war rarely waged one can also imagine his earlier forbears doing the same.

The love of word-play extended to riddles, and close to one hundred riddles of the Anglo-Saxon period have been recorded in *The Exeter Book*, a manuscript written about 975, and still kept at Exeter Cathedral Library. Here is one:

> *A creature came slinking where men were sitting, many of them in council, men shrewd in mind. It had one eye and two ears and two feet, twelve hundred heads, a back and a belly and two hands, arms and shoulders, one neck and two sides. Say what I am called.*
>
> (S.A.J. Bradley translation)

Can you guess it? The answer is: A one eyed garlic seller.

SOURCES

Bradley, S. A. J. *Anglo-Saxon Poetry*. Everyman Paperback, 1995.

Breeden, David, trans. *The Adventures of Beowulf*. CreateSpace, 2011.

Owst, G. R. *Literature and Pulpit in Medieval England*. Oxford, 1961.

SAXON HEALING HERBS

By RICHARD DENNING

Wʜᴀᴛ ᴅɪᴅ ᴛʜᴇ Aɴɢʟᴏ-Sᴀxᴏɴs ᴋɴᴏw ᴏғ ᴛʜᴇ ʜᴇᴀʟɪɴɢ ᴀʀᴛs, ᴀɴᴅ ᴡʜᴀᴛ ᴛᴇxᴛ-books did they refer to, if any? Today I take a look at the oldest surviving documents from the Anglo-Saxon period relating to healing. These are *Bald's Leechbook,* the *Lacnunga* manuscript, and the *Old English Herbarium.*

BALD'S LEECHBOOK

Bald's Leechbook is the only document whose content appears to reflect a fairly pure English tradition and is free of much influence from the Mediterranean world. The plant names are given in English, for example. The surviving manuscript which is held at the British Museum was probably compiled in the ninth century, possibly around 850 A.D. The book's title is from an inscription which reads *"Bald habet hunc librum Cild quem conscribere iussit,"* meaning *"Bald owns this book which he ordered Cild to compile."* Who Bald and Cild are we have no idea.

SAXON TRADITIONS AND THE CHRISTIAN FAITH

What is interesting is that although this book was written during the mid-Anglo-Saxon period when Christianity was well established, it is clear that many beliefs from the earlier pagan religions were still held as well as the new faith. This is shown by these examples of illness caused by dark-elves (whom the Saxons believed attacked people during the night) or by relations with the devil.

> *For elf sickness, a leechdom…one must sing over the plants before one takes them and one must place them under an altar.*

> *Make a salve for the elvish race and nightgoers and the people with whom the devil has intercourse.*

SOME INTERESTING METHODS OF TREATMENT

> *For palsy, if the mouth be crooked or deficient, take coriander, crush it into a woman's milk and put it in the healthy ear.*

Here they seem to be talking about what we today call Bell's Palsy which causes paralysis and dropping of the side of the face. Not sure what putting milk in the other ear would do.

> *For Lice, give him boiled cabbage to eat often having fasted overnight, he will be protected from lice.*

Not sure how that was meant to work—unless the smell of boiled cabbage drove the lice away!

> For that one be moon mad, take a dolphin's hide, make it into a scourge, beat him with it, he will soon be better.

Maybe I won't suggest this one to my patients.

> For if a man's skull be wrenched, lay the man out flat, drive in two pegs at the shoulders then lay a board crosswise over the feet, then strike on it thrice with a hammer and it will go aright shortly.

Or else I guess the patient would have broken legs and be unable to run after you!

NOT ENTIRELY WITHOUT BASIS

Despite these more outlandish treatments, areas where the Saxons had remedies that often do make sense is either in the creation of salves and ointments for external wounds—using herbs with known antiseptic effects—or in the recipes for drinks for internal consumption for gripes, abdominal pains, and vomiting.

> For gripes and ache of the lower abdomen take bethony and wormwood, marche, radish, fennel, pound them and put into ale. Drink a cupful.

Here wormwood does have known effects on suppressing harmful abdominal bacteria whilst fennel has antispasmodic effects and can relieve a fever; both are used in herbal remedies today.

NINTH CENTURY LEAGUE TABLES?

> If a man be hacked and you may have to cure him, if you see that he be facing towards you when you go in, then he may live; if he be facing away, do not attend him. (Bald's Leechbook)

The ninth century way of avoiding treating patients likely to die! In today's world such a man would affect your ranking on surgeon's league tables, so don't be touching him! I wonder if a similar thing is going on here. A healer's reputation was as important then as now, after all.

THE *LACNUNGA* MANUSCRIPT

The *Lacnunga* is a collection of medical texts and prayers, written in a mix of Old English and Latin. It is found in a larger codex of manuscripts in the possession of the British Library. This manuscript was probably compiled in England in the late tenth or early eleventh century. It appears to be the work of at least two writers. One wrote mainly in

English and the other in Latin. The word *Lacnunga* is old English for "remedies" and was the name given to this collection by a nineteenth century collector.

The *Lacnunga* has no particular order or organisation. It is almost a scrapbook of ideas, remedies, cures, and prayers—rather like a cookbook passed down through generations with each cook adding their own notes.

It does however contain one entry of great significance. It contains the text of *The Nine Herbs Charm*. The charm is intended to be an antidote to poison and to heal infection. It contains both Pagan and Christian elements and details the Nine Sacred Herbs of Woden/Odin. It may have been written during the Pagan era and edited by Christian monks. Therefore it probably predates the Christian era and give us a glimpse of healing beliefs from the early Saxon period.

For Woden took nine glory-twigs,
he smote the adder that it flew apart into nine parts.
Now there nine herbs have power against nine evil spirits,
against nine poisons and against nine infections:
against the red poison, against the foul poison,
against the yellow poison, against the green poison,
against the black poison, against the blue poison,
against the brown poison, against the crimson poison.
Against worm-blister, against water-blister,
against thorn-blister, against thistle-blister,
against ice-blister, against poison-blister.
Against harmfulness of the air,
against harmfulness of the ground,
against harmfulness of the sea.
If any poison comes flying from the east,
or any from the north, or any from the south,
or any from the west among the people.
Woden [later Christ] stood over diseases of every kind.

THE *OLD ENGLISH HERBARIUM*

This is an English translation of an original Latin text from around the ninth century. Four Old English manuscripts still survive. This book takes a different approach from the other two. Rather than listing medical ailments and then specifying cures, this is more like a Pharmacopoeia or a formulary in that it lists the plants and then says what they can be used for:

LXX The Herb Crision that is clover
1. For pain of the gum

LXXVI Herb Solate that is nightshade
1. For a swelling 2. For pain in the ears 3. For toothache 4. For blood coming from the nostrils.

IN CONCLUSION

Although many of the remedies listed in these early textbooks are of extremely doubtful value, what we see here is an early attempt in the Anglo-Saxon world to put together a formal approach to medicine. It also gives us a fascinating glimpse of the mindset where many ills are blamed on the works of the Christian devil, or the pagan elves, dwarves, or other denizens—a mindset that would last for well over a thousand years in some places.

Women's Rights in Anglo-Saxon England: Why They Were Much Greater Than You Think

By OCTAVIA RANDOLPH

HERE IN THE TWENTY-FIRST CENTURY IT IS EASY, AND EVEN NATURAL, TO BELIEVE IN an ever-improving continuum of human rights. We look back to the banning of slavery in Britain in 1834, the signing of the 13th Amendment to the Constitution of the United States in 1865, the granting of the vote to women in the U.S. in 1920 and in Britain in 1928, the passing of Civil Rights laws in the 1960s, recent legal recognition of same-sex marriage in many nations, and feel: "This is the natural progression of things. People gain more rights as time goes on."

But you might be surprised to learn that if you are of English descent, your maternal ancestors of 1000 years ago enjoyed more legal rights than did your great-grandmother. Shocking, but true. Women's legal rights under, say, King Ælfred the Great (King of Wessex, 844-899 A.D.) were far greater than under Queen Victoria (r. 1837-1901).

(Indeed, the Victorian era was the nadir of women's rights in Britain, as women were reduced to the state of near-complete legal dependence on fathers and husbands, and divorce required an act of Parliament until 1857. The most powerful woman in the world repeatedly claimed her own sex unfit to win suffrage. But that is another essay....)

The fact is that women enjoyed legal rights under Anglo-Saxon law that they were to lose after the Battle of Hastings (1066) and for many hundreds of years afterwards. So let us return to the more congenial ninth century and learn more.

Ælfred's ninth century law code has survived and provides us with valuable insight into women's legal status. His laws were predicated upon those of earlier kings, particularly Ine, King of the West Saxons (688-726). In his preface, Ælfred explains that he examined many existing law codes from the Old Testament to those of previous Anglo-Saxon kings in neighbouring kingdoms:

> Then I, King Ælfred, gathered them together and ordered to be written many
> of the ones that our forefathers observed—those that pleased me; and many
> of the ones that did not please me I rejected with the advice of my council-
> lors, and commanded them to be observed in a different way. For I dared not
> presume to set down in writing at all many of my own, since it was unknown
> to me what would please those who should come after us. But those which I

found either in the days of Ine, my kinsman, or of Offa, king of the Mercians, or of Ælthelberht (who first among the English people received baptism), and which seemed to me most just, I collected herein, and omitted the others.

Crimes are categorised along class lines. Here are penalties owed by men for adultery:

If anyone lies with the wife of a twelve-hundred man, he is to pay 120 shillings compensation to the husband; to a six-hundred man, he is to pay 100 shillings compensation; to a ceorl, he is to pay forty shillings compensation.

A "twelve-hundred man" refers to the individual's wergild (man-gold), or valuation. Twelve hundred shillings would signify a nobleman, or at least a thegn (the forerunner of the later knight). The ceorl ("churl") was a common free man, usually an agricultural worker, but possibly a skilled craftsman as well. The ceorl's wergild was set at 200 shillings. We do not know the exact figure of Ælfred's own wergild, but it is thought to have been 6,000 shillings.

Wergild was an important legal concept, for without it all feuds were settled "eye for an eye": If you kill my kinsman, I kill your kinsman. If you rape my daughter, I rape yours. Wergild, the notion of a cash valuation for each person's life, allowed the ruling noble to command that grievances be redressed not by violence but by silver or gold payments, thus limiting the escalation of vendetta.

All persons (except slaves) had a wergild, and Ælfred's laws spell out reparations for the loss of bodily parts as well, even unto the loss of the little fingernail (one shilling fine).

Ælfred's laws cover penalties owed for kidnapping (or luring) a woman from a nunnery; for assault, sexual and otherwise, of a woman; rape of a slave woman; rape of underage girls; and for the death of a pregnant woman. While it is true that the financial penalties exacted from the wrongdoer typically went to the woman's father or husband, it is also true that crimes against women were treated with as much seriousness as crimes against men. And no woman of any age could be forced into marriage: "*No woman or maiden shall ever be forced to marry one whom she dislikes, nor be sold for money.*"

Other rights that an Anglo-Saxon woman enjoyed were the right to own land in her own name and to sell such land or give it away without her father's or husband's consent, the right to defend herself in court, and the right to act as *compurgator* in law suits, that is, to testify to another's truthfulness. She could also freely manumit her slaves. Her morgen-gifu, or morning-gift, that gift of land, jewellery, livestock or such that a bride received from her new husband the morning after their wedding, was hers to keep for life. (Compare these rights to those of your great-grandmother in London, the chattel of her father until marriage and then the legal "property" of her husband afterward.)

One of the greatest indicators of women's rights is women's ability to end an abusive or otherwise unsatisfactory marriage. Divorce was extremely common amongst upper-class Anglo-Saxons; indeed (and to the chagrin of the Church), both men and women practised serial "marrying up" as a form of social climbing. (More humble folk simply separated without ado, to take up with another or remain single as they wished.)

Early divorce laws granted the wife half the household goods, including any goods she had brought into the union, and full custody of the children. As only women's wills from the era mention the disposition of things such as linens, furniture, plate, and so on, there is reason to assume that the majority of household furnishings by default followed the woman in case of divorce. Instead of impoverishing women, divorce laws ensured an equitable sharing of goods and property.

In the ninth century daughters inherited goods or land from either parent, or both, and these bequests were theirs without challenge or question. One exception was that of heathens: in the opening of *The Circle of Ceridwen* the eponymous character is denied her inheritance from her uncle because as a heathen she has no standing in the eyes of the law. Her rightful lands are given to a nearby priory for its maintenance, and she becomes their ward.

All of these advantages were to come to a crushing end after the catastrophe of October 1066. The Normans ("northmen") carried across the Channel with them the vestiges of their earlier Viking mores towards property and women. A legal "golden age" for English women had come to an end.

SOURCES

For more about Anglo-Saxon law and society, I highly recommend *The Beginnings of English Society* by Dorothy Whitelock (Penguin Books, 1974); and *Alfred the Great: Asser's Life of King Alfred and Other Contemporary Sources,* translated by Simon Keynes and Michael Lapidge (Penguin Books, 1983), from which I excerpted portions of Ælfred's law code.

HOW MUCH FOR AN EAR?
SAXON LEGAL CODES

BY RICHARD DENNING

IN THE FIRST DECADE OF THE SEVENTH CENTURY, KING AETHELBERHT OF KENT LAID down the first set of Legal Codes that survive from the Anglo-Saxon period. The codes still exist although in a copied volume of law codes and genealogical records called the *Textus Roffensius*—the Rochester Book—which was made (and is still held) at Rochester Cathedral around 1120. This document gives us our first glimpse of laws and legal traditions from the Saxon Period.

One fundamental principle of these law codes that date back to Germanic and Anglo-Saxon traditions is that of *weregild* and compensation. In essence these laws laid down the means whereby a man guilty of a crime would be expected to pay a fine to the victim. In our modern world we look to punish crime by imprisonment or (until the 1960s in the U.K.) death in the case of murder, but the Saxons took an approach that tried to avoid a blood feud.

To understand this, one has to think back on years where these law codes evolved. In the chaotic and bloody years of the Anglo-Saxon settlement (probably drawing from earlier traditions in the Germanic homelands when there was no real legal structure), it would be very easy for harm to a man to be avenged by the victim's family. This could easily lead to tit-for-tat retaliation. So in those years the principle of a *weregild* evolved meaning literally "man's worth". Every man had his weregild. If he died at another man's hand, the value of this would be paid to avoid retribution.

For centuries the exact values of weregild were recorded and passed on orally—or if written down, we have no record of them in the U.K. There are however earlier legal codes compiled by the Franks, the earliest of which was written by Clovis, the first king of the Franks, as early as the late fifth century, which contain these principles.

In England, this first legal code of Aethelberht gives us a snapshot of these fines as they existed during his time. *"If someone slays another man he shall pay-over a proper compensation of 100 shillings."* The code even goes on to specify that 20 shillings must be paid over the grave as the man was being buried and the rest within 40 days.

Not all men are born equal in these codes. A slave killed would lead to compensation of between 40 and 80 shillings dependent on the value of the slave.

The law codes are incredibly elaborate and do not just talk of fines for murder. In fact they go on to specify just about every conceivable injury:

> *If the ear is pierced the compensation shall be 3 shillings.*
> *If the eye is put out the aggressor shall pay in compensation 50 shillings.*
> *For each finger nail, a shilling.*

There is even an attempt to establish rules for separations:

If she (a wife) wishes to leave with the children let her have half the money.

And rules for adultery:

If one freeman lies with another's wife he shall render the weregild [code is not clear how much] and procure with his own money a second wife for the man.

The codes also cover property damage, trespass and other areas of non-violent crime:

If someone is first to force his way into someone else's premises he shall pay in compensation 6 shillings, the next 3 and each subsequent man 1 shilling. If someone seizes goods whilst inside he shall pay back three fold.

These codes do something else which is vital in the development of the land that will one day be called England. They establish the authority of the king, place the king at the heart of the law, and also provide revenue for the crown. Many of the codes deal with much larger and heavier fines due to the king in the event of harm to him or his property or household: "*If a freeman steals from the king he shall pay back ninefold.*"

Any crime committed near the king, in his presence or even in the same locality whilst he was resident would lead to fines being paid to the king in addition to the weregild going to the family of the victim. A king was entitled to compensation for every freeman killed. "*50 shillings shall go to the king as compensation for loss of a subject.*"

This approach did not just extend to the king. Aethelberht was the first Anglo-Saxon King to convert to Christianity and, mindful of potential threat to the incoming missionaries from reluctant Saxons, he enshrined within his codes protection for the church and its property: "*God's property will be compensated twelvefold.*" This meant he was placing in a very clear way a higher value on the church than that which he placed on himself.

What we see here are the beginnings of the legal system being formalized and drawn under state control. Later codes such as those of Alfred the Great would establish legal courts and elaborate on these basic codes, but this set of laws written fourteen centuries ago is the earliest record we have of people in England striving towards an orderly state.

There is a superb book on this subject called *Early English Law* by Bill Griffiths.

Alfred the Great and the Importance of the Oath

By ROSANNE E. LORTZ

On the list of English kings, only one has the honor to be called "the Great." What was it that made Alfred of Wessex such an unforgettable monarch? How did he achieve the title that no subsequent English king has ever received?

Alfred's military exploits are one possible reason for the title. During his reign of twenty-eight years, he brought back the realm of Wessex from near extinction, fighting off several Danish invasions and establishing himself as the high king of the Anglo-Saxons. His most memorable victory was at the Battle of Edington in 878, where he defeated a Danish host led by Guthrum, forcing the Danes to sign a treaty where they would withdraw from Alfred's domains and convert to the Christian religion.

Alfred's educational reform and literary achievements are another possible reason for the title. The previous century had seen a great decline in the literacy of the British Isles, with Latin being completely forgotten and only a few still remembering how to read in the Anglo-Saxon language. Alfred imported scholars from the continent and set up schools to teach his people their letters. Always one to lead by example, he mastered the difficult Latin language himself and then set about translating important works himself into the popular tongue.

But out of all the reasons why Alfred might be considered "the Great," the one that I want to focus on today is the law code that he created for the Anglo-Saxons, a seminal work that would influence the laws of England and the nations she colonized for centuries to come.

William of Malmesbury, writing several centuries later, tells us that Alfred, *"amid the din of war, enacted statutes...."* In the midst of battle, rape, and pillage, Alfred strove to establish a society where those things would not occur, and he did this by means of law.

The importance of Alfred's law code does not lie in its originality. The introduction contains a translation of the Ten Commandments, a recital of many of the case laws in the book of Exodus, an excerpt of Christ's Sermon on the Mount, and a history of the Apostles with quotes from the book of Acts. Some historians have seen in this Alfred's attempts to show how the Old Testament laws should be contextualized in an Anglo-Saxon society.

The historian F.N. Lee notes that:

> Alfred had already: *first re-enjoined the Decalogue or the Ten Commandments (Exodus 20:1-17); then illustrated their concrete application by way of case law (Exodus 21:1 to 23:9); and next assured his readers that Christ had*

not come to break the Ten Commandments, but to approve them well (Mat-
thew 5:5-19). Indeed, Alfred had then gone on, together with all of Christ's
Twelve Apostles, to enjoin...God's Law for man. This is seen quite clearly in
the apostolic prohibitions enjoining abstinence from idolatry, bloodshed and
fornication (Acts 15:23-29).

Clearly, then, Alfred believed that the Apostles here (at the Synod of Jeru-
salem or the first General Assembly of the Christian Church) enjoined God's
Commandments upon all of the Gentile [non-Jewish] Christians who had
heard it—and who indeed should keep it.

Alfred, by quoting extensively from certain Scripture passages, was making an argument that Biblical law should be kept by the Anglo-Saxons. Following his introduction,
Alfred continues his non-originality by quoting laws given by earlier kings.

Now I, King Alfred, have collected these laws, and have given orders for copies
to be made of many of those which our predecessors observed, and which I
myself approved.... I have not dared to presume to set down in writing much
of my own; for I cannot tell what [innovations of mine] will meet with the
approval of our successors. But those which were the most just of the laws I
found—whether they dated from the time of Ina my kinsman, or of Offa King
of the Mercians, or of Aethelberht who was the first [Anglo-Saxon or Anglo-
Jutish king] to be baptized in England—these I have collected....

One can only assume that Alfred used the criteria of Biblical law (as outlined at length
in his introduction) to determine which of his predecessors' laws were "most just" and
should be included. The laws of these previous monarchs include all sorts of subjects—
murder, maiming, perjury, theft—but when Alfred does finally launch into promulgating
new laws of his own, the first law he gives is most instructive.

Of oaths and of weds [pledges].

1. At the first we teach, that it is most needful that every man warily keep
his oath and his wed [pledge]. If anyone be constrained to either of these
wrongfully, either to treason against his lord, or to any unlawful aid; then
it is juster to belie than to fulfill. But if he pledge himself to that which it is
lawful to fulfill, and in that belie himself, let him submissively deliver up his
weapon and his goods to the keeping of his friends, and be in prison forty
days.... Let him there suffer whatever the bishop may prescribe to him; and let
his kinsmen feed him, if he himself have no food.... But if he escape, let him be
held a fugitive, and be excommunicate of all Christ's churches....

In Alfred's mind, the "most needful" thing in the kingdom was for men to keep their word. It was good faith and trust between men that built the fabric of a stable society. Peace, commerce, and learning were only possible in a world where a man's word was his bond.

The Anglo-Saxon society was one plagued by failure to keep oaths. The epic poem *Beowulf* records a story of a truce made and broken between the Danes and the Frisians.

> *So, a truce was offered....*
> *Both sides then sealed their agreement.*
> *With oaths to Hengest, Finn swore*
> *Openly, solemnly, that the battle survivors*
> *Would be guaranteed honor and status.*
> *No infringement by word or deed,*
> *No provocation would be permitted.*

It is only a few lines later that the "unpermitted provocations" occur, and the truce is broken in violent bloodshed.

> *...longing woke*
> *In the cooped up exile for a voyage home—*
> *But more for vengeance, some way of bringing*
> *Things to a head: his sword arm hankered*
> *To greet the Jutes...*
> *Thus blood was spilled....*

This sort of oath-breaking was commonplace in the Anglo-Saxon world—and not just betrayal between two people groups, but also betrayal of a lord by his men. At the end of the epic, when Beowulf's sword fails to cut through the dragon's scales, his servant Wiglaf exhorts the other men to go help their lord!

> *I remember that time when mead was flowing,*
> *How we pledged loyalty to our lord in the hall,*
> *Promised our ring-giver we would be worth our price,*
> *Make good the gift of the war-gear,*
> *Those swords and helmets, as and when*
> *His need required...*
> *...now the day has come*
> *When this lord we serve needs sound men*
> *To give him their support. Let us go to him,*
> *Help our leader through the hot flame*
> *And dread of the fire....*

Unfortunately, rather than keep their oaths to Beowulf, the men ignore Wiglaf's entreaties and leave their ring-giver to his fate.

Alfred's world was beset with the same rampant oath-breaking that we see in *Beowulf*. Benjamin Merkle, in his biography *The White Horse King*, writes:

> To understand the significance of oath-keeping to the king of Wessex, one need only think back on the many times when the integrity and strength of Alfred's shieldwall during the crushing combat depended on the faithfulness of the oaths that his thegns had pledged during those less-dangerous moments of feasting and boasting in the mead hall. Similarly, one can remember the habitual treachery of the pagan Vikings, whose unctuous pledges of peace were disregarded by the Danes within hours of making the pledge.

These "unctuous pledges of peace" were the bane of Alfred's existence when dealing with the Danes. Two years prior to the Battle of Edington, Bishop Asser's *Life of King Alfred* records that this same warband led by Guthrum had made a treaty with Alfred at Wareham,

> to the effect that they should depart out of the kingdom, and for this they made no hesitation to give as many hostages as he named; also they swore an oath over the Christian relics...that they would depart speedily from the kingdom. But they again practiced their usual treachery, and caring nothing for the hostages or their oaths, they broke the treaty, and sallying forth by night, slew all the horsemen that the king had round him....

This earlier betrayal would undoubtedly have been in the back of Alfred's mind when he parleyed with Guthrum after the Battle of Edington, but nevertheless, Alfred—determined to show the importance of an oath—still swore the treaty. And Guthrum, surprisingly, kept it. Over the course of the next few years, some of Guthrum's nobles again resumed their depredations, but Guthrum refrained from attacking Alfred's borders or breaking his baptismal vows.

Alfred, through legislation and through personal example, was resolved to make his country a place where false witness would not be borne. Merkle sums it up well when he says:

> By giving so much weight to truthfulness in oath-making...Alfred helped to ensure that no man could break his oath without dire consequences. If a man was found to have sworn falsely, he would be ostracized from society, losing his right to weapons, to property, and even to testify to his own innocence in court. Thus, the men of Alfred's day took great care to ensure that they did not make careless oaths or pledges.

There is, perhaps, little of originality in Alfred's law code, but the pre-eminence he gives to a man's oath had a powerful impact on his culture, and it is this law—the foundation for law in England and the countries she colonized—that can be considered the main reason why Alfred of Wessex is called "the Great."

SOURCES

Asser. *The Life of King Alfred.* Trans. J.A. Giles. http://omacl.org/KingAlfred/ (accessed May 6, 2013).

Heaney, Seamus, trans. *Beowulf.* New York: W.W. Norton & Company, 2000.

Lee, F.N. "King Alfred the Great and Our Common Law." http://www.dr-fnlee.org/docs6/alfred/alfred.pdf (accessed May 6, 2013).

Merkle, Benjamin. *The White Horse King: The Life of Alfred the Great.* Nashville, TN: Thomas Nelson, 2009.

William of Malmesbury. *The Kings before the Norman Conquest.* Trans. Joseph Stephenson. Wales: Llancerch, 1989.

AETHELFLAED, LADY
OF THE MERCIANS

By LISA YARDE

DURING THE LATE NINTH CENTURY IN ENGLAND, THE ANGLO-SAXON KING ALFRED OF Wessex and his wife Ealhswith, a descendant of the royal family of Mercia, welcomed their first child.

Their newborn daughter Aethelflaed entered a dangerous world, made so by frequent incursions from the Danes who had harried the English coasts and countryside for decades. Aethelflaed would have two brothers and two sisters; she shared pivotal roles with them or else eclipsed them entirely.

During the children's early years, their father Alfred brokered a treaty with the Dane, Guthrum. This chieftain had carved out a portion of northwestern England called the Danelaw, which included a ravaged portion of Mercia. The ensuing period of peace allowed for a marriage between Aethelflaed and the warrior Athelred, alternatively called an ealdorman or Lord of the Mercians.

Alfred supported his regime and gave him control of London and part of the Oxford area. The bride might have been in her late teens when the marriage took place, but Athelred's age remains uncertain. They would have one child, a daughter named Aelfwynn. During the marriage, the couple issued joint charters. They also transferred the relics of Saint Oswald of Northumbria to the Gloucester priory they founded in his name.

In 899, Aethelflaed lost her father, whose son Edward eventually succeeded after fending off a rival claim for the throne from Alfred's cousin. Aethelflaed and her husband continued to govern Mercia, though all of the country's coinage bore King Edward's name.

After the year 900, Athelred's health steadily declined. His wife's responsibilities increased until she became the *de facto* ruler. It is possible her power exceeded that of most women of her time as she fortified the defenses against Mercia's Welsh and Danish enemies.

On the west, Mercia abutted northern Wales, and Athelred had endured several conflicts with its people which continued under Aethelflaed's reign. In 905 when the Danes attacked Chester, she safeguarded the town. Aethelflaed also established new defenses at the boroughs of Bridgnorth and Bromsgrove.

For four years after Athelred's death and his burial at Saint Oswald's priory in 911, Aethelflaed also allegedly began strengthening several areas around Tamworth, Stafford, Warwick, Runcorn, and Eddisbury; there is some dispute as to whether Edward ordered the work instead. He reclaimed the London and Oxford lands his father had granted Athelred rather than allowing the widowed Aethelflaed to rule them.

It remains certain that she also struck out against Mercia's foes. In 916, she led an incursion into Wales to avenge the death of a Mercian abbot. She allied with her brother Edward for a fight against Northumberland's Danes in 917. She gained Derby and Leicester in the struggle. Aethelflaed also pledged to intervene in the fight against Norse raiders determined to take York, but she died at Tamworth before this could occur. Interred at Saint Oswald's priory after death, her tireless efforts against the Danes and Welsh gained her the title Lady of the Mercians.

SYMBOLISM IN ANGLO-SAXON ART

By CAROL MCGRATH

URING THE ANGLO-SAXON ERA THE INTERIORS OF CHURCHES WOULD HAVE GLOWED with colour. The walls of the halls were painted with decorative scenes from the imagination, telling stories of monsters and heroes like those in the poem *Beowulf.* Although nothing much is left of the wall paintings, we can discover evidence of pictorial art in Bibles and Psalters. Monasteries gave religious artists the stability they needed to advance a native style in illuminated manuscripts which were to become the envy of Europe. Much beautiful work was produced by monks in their scriptoriums.

This early beautiful illumination work is apparent in the Lindisfarne Gospels of the seventh century. They show a mixture of Byzantine influence and a very lively distinctive English style. The colours and the lines used are fabulous.

The golden age of early Anglo-Saxon art came with the period of King Alfred (871-970). There was a resurgence of learning in Wessex, and King Alfred himself translated tracts from the Bible into English. These illuminated texts contained beautiful, sophisticated illustrations alive with much symbolism. What follows is just an outline of a few of the symbols to be found in religious manuscripts.

Man, angel, lion, bull, or calf feature in gospel books either alone or accompanying representations of the evangelists in human form. They emerge from the description of God's throne in the Apocalypse. Each gospel is associated with its related symbol.

The Trinity cannot be depicted, as it is without form, so only through metaphors and symbols and analogies can the notion be represented. The symbols are often inclusive of the lamb and the dove. Since there are many references to God's right hand in the Old Testament we have *Dextera Dei* to represent God. The lamb is a reference to Christ with origins in the notion of the Passover lamb in John the Baptist's words, *"Look, there is the lamb of God that takes away the sin of the world."* The dove appeared at Christ's baptism in Matt iii.16. The dove and lamb appear in symbolic images of the Trinity and in scenes such as the Crucifixion are placed above the head of Christ to symbolise God's approval of Christ's sacrifice.

Evangelists are portrayed holding books just as St. Peter holds keys. Martyred saints hold palm branches, and Mary is shown holding the Christ child to indicate her role as mother of the saviour.

Angels are very significant in Anglo-Saxon paintings and sculpture. They are placed above canon tables in gospel books often with sceptres as a sign of Christ's royal status. They blow trumpets and hold scales in reference to the coming of judgement. Other motifs vary. For example in a crucifixion scene, Christ may be depicted wearing a diadem, and the symbols of the sun and moon are occasionally placed above the arms of the cross to remind the viewer of the darkness that covered the earth at Christ's death and to remind us of the belief that the world mourned the death of its creator.

As a writer of fiction set in this period, I find that looking closely at the art and embroidery helps me to come closer to grasping the mindset of the characters in my novels. Equally, it is interesting to recognise how brilliant and talented our early medieval ancestors were when they produced such painstakingly beautiful works of art.

Manufacturing a Mythology: Brutus, the Legendary Founder of Britain

By Rosanne E. Lortz

I F YOU'RE AN ANCIENT GREEK, YOUR MYTHOLOGICAL HERO IS WRATHFUL ACHILLES, THE "swift-footed son of Peleus" who defeats Priam's mighty son Hector and paves the way for the eventual destruction of Troy. Or if guile is more your style, you have Odysseus, the resourceful hero who wanders the world for ten years on his homeward voyage, braving Cyclops, Sirens, Scylla and Charybdis before slaying the scores of suitors ensconced in his own halls.

If you're an imperial Roman, you have Aeneas, striding proudly out of the flames of Troy, escaping the wiles of Dido of Carthage and carving out a new home in Italy.

But if you're British and living in the ninth century A.D., you have...nothing. And frankly, it's kind of embarrassing. Or, at least, it was to the historian Nennius.

How could a country have a proper pedigree if it could not trace its ancestors back to the siege of Troy?

The answer? It couldn't. And so Nennius began his *Historia Brittonum* with this story of the legendary "founder" of Britain, a story that seems, almost certainly, concocted from his own fertile imagination since no other versions of the tale precede it.

> *Aeneas, after the Trojan War, arrived with his son* [Ascanius] *in Italy; and having vanquished Turnus, married Lavinia, the daughter of king Latinus....*
>
> *But Ascanius married a wife, who conceived and became pregnant. And Aeneas, having been informed that his daughter-in-law was pregnant, ordered his son to send his magician to examine his wife, whether the child conceived were male or female. The magician came and examined the wife and pronounced it to be a son, who should become the most valiant among the Italians, and the most beloved of all men.*
>
> *In consequence of this prediction, the magician was put to death by Ascanius* [who presumably thought that he should be the most valiant and most beloved?]; *but it happened that the mother of the child dying at its birth, he was named Brutus; and after a certain interval agreeably to what the magician had foretold, whilst he was playing with some others he shot his father with an arrow, not intentionally but by accident.*
>
> *He was, for this cause, expelled from Italy, and came to the islands of the Tyrrhene sea, when he was exiled on account of the death of Turnus, slain by*

Aeneas. He then went among the Gauls, and built the city of Turones, called Turnis. At length he came to this island, named from him Britannia, dwelt there, and filled it with his own descendants, and it has been inhabited from that time to the present period.

This story, spun by Nennius, was taken by Geoffrey of Monmouth in his twelfth century *Historia Regum Britanniae* and embellished even further. He expanded the simple tale into a chapter that numbers twenty-one pages in my edition of the work.

Brutus, now the great-grandson (not the grandson) of Aeneas, shows his cunning and prowess as he assembles an army of exiled Trojans, wins victories in Gaul, and crosses the channel into Britain where he must defeat a fierce band of giants. He even builds a capital city on the banks of the Thames, calling it *Troia Nova*—"New Troy."

After Geoffrey of Monmouth, the legend of Brutus became widely known and promulgated. The anonymous author of *Sir Gawain and the Green Knight* commences his story thus:

When the last assault had been delivered, and the siege of Troy was over, and the city was destroyed by fire and lay in ashes, Prince Aeneas sailed away with his noble kindred, and they conquered new realms.... And far over the French flood [i.e. the English Channel] Felix Brutus, with joy in his heart, founded a broad realm on the hills of Britain....

And in a charming *inclusio*, once the story of Sir Gawain has been fully told, the author brings us back to Brutus to conclude his tale:

This adventure happened in the days of King Arthur, and the books about Britain, that Brutus founded, record it. And many other adventures like it have befallen since the siege and assault ceased at Troy and the bold knight Brutus first made his way to this land.

Sir Gawain and the Green Knight is just one example among many of how the story of the legendary Brutus became commonplace over the next several centuries. Holinshed's *Chronicles of England, Scotland, and Ireland*, which were published in the sixteenth century during the life of Shakespeare, give more than a nod to the story and treat it as proper history:

After...came Brutus the son of Sylvius with a great train of the posterity of the dispersed Trojans in 324 ships.... [He] brought them also wholly under his rule and governance, and dispossessing the peers & inferior owners of their lands and possessions, he divided the country among such princes and captains as he in his arrival here had led out of Greece with him.

Although Shakespeare, to my knowledge, did not mention Brutus (or, at least, *this* Brutus), he did use Holinshed's *Chronicles* as a source for some of the works in his corpus.

His plays *King Lear* and *Cymbeline*, both about semi-mythical kings of Britain, show that he was fascinated by the early, legendary days of England. His play *Troilus and Cressida* (which is set during the fall of Troy) shows that he was also fascinated by the "matter of Rome"—as they called classical mythology.

Geoffrey of Monmouth took Nennius' few short paragraphs and penned an adventure-filled saga of twenty-one pages. What literary brilliance could Shakespeare have achieved if he had taken Geoffrey of Monmouth's history and plotted a play about Brutus, the legendary founder of Britain? That is a play I would have enjoyed reading....

SOURCES

Geoffrey of Monmouth. *The History of the Kings of Britain*. Trans. Lewis Thorpe. London: Penguin Books, 1966.

Holinshed's *Chronicles of England, Scotland, and Ireland*. 1587 Edition. Found at The Holinshed Project. http://www.english.ox.ac.uk/holinshed/toc.php?edition=1587

Ridley, M.R., trans. *Sir Gawain and the Green Knight*. Found in *Medieval Romances,* edited by Roger Sherman Loomis and Laura Hibbard Loomis. U.S.A.: Random House, 1957.

THE SCIENCE OF HISTORY

BY PATRICIA BRACEWELL

MUCH OF WHAT WE KNOW OF EARLY ENGLAND HAS BEEN GLEANED FROM THE ANNALS known today as the *Anglo-Saxon Chronicle*. This compilation of the history of the English people, written down in Old English over three centuries, is concerned not only with events such as battles, the passing of kings, or matters relating to church hierarchy but also recounts natural events which must have been significant at the time. The chroniclers were fascinated especially by celestial events—eclipses, shooting stars, and comets. Often, what they recorded in their annals can be compared to observations made elsewhere, and so verified.

Consider this entry from 1066:

> *There was over all England such a token seen as no man ever saw before. Some men said that it was the comet-star, which others denominate the long-hair'd star. It appeared first...on the eighth before the Calends of May; and so shone all the week.*

The Irish annals for that year corroborate the sighting:

> *A star appeared on the seventh of the Calends of May, on Tuesday after Little Easter, than whose light the brilliance or light of the moon was not greater; and it was visible to all in this manner till the end of four nights afterwards.*

Seven hundred years later Edmund Halley would verify that sighting as the comet that bears his name.

In 1098 the chronicler described another celestial event in this way: *"The heaven was of such a hue, as if it were burning, nearly all the night."*

And again in 1131: *"After Christmas was the heaven on the northern hemisphere all as if it were burning fire; so that all who saw it were so dismayed as they never were before."*

Here is the aurora borealis, described by men who could not have imagined that high above the earth, gaseous particles were colliding to form terrifying lights in the sky.

But it was not only celestial events that drew the attention of the chroniclers. Part of the entry for 1014 reads:

> *This year, on the eve of St. Michael's day, came the great sea-flood, which spread wide over this land, and ran so far up as it never did before, overwhelming many towns, and an innumerable multitude of people.*

Anyone reading this today would recognize it as a description of a tsunami. We've already experienced two such massive sea floods in this young century, and we know what devastation such events can cause. The word itself would not be incorporated into the English language until the nineteenth century, thanks to the Japanese who, like the English, live surrounded by water. But although the word we use today did not exist in 1014, the great sea-flood of that year was corroborated all over southern Britain by annalists writing in Wales, Cornwall, Kent, Sussex and Hampshire. In addition, a chronicle written at the Convent of Quedlinburg Abbey in Saxony states that in that year a great flood struck Juteland, Holstein, Friesland, the Netherlands, and Belgium.

There is no question that the great sea-flood of 1014 was a tsunami. But what caused it? To answer that question, scientists have looked to the earth, gathered data, and then, like the writers of the *Anglo-Saxon Chronicle*, they have looked to the skies.

The first bit of data comes from North Carolina. Geologists tell us that in the eleventh century a Class 5 hurricane or a tsunami destroyed a chain of barrier islands off the coast of that state, and that the Outer Banks are a remnant of those islands.

The next bit of evidence was found in bog core samples from the Black Rock Forest Area of New York, and dated to the eleventh century. They contained exotic components from an area of the ocean floor some 3700 km away, and their presence can only be explained by some kind of impact event in the mid-Atlantic.

What was that impact event? Forensic geologist Dallas Abbott suggests that it was a meteor strike, creating a tsunami that swept westward to North America and eastward through the English Channel.

The meteor, landing in the middle of the Atlantic Ocean, would have been seen by no one. The innumerable multitude of people who were inundated by the wave that followed could not have imagined what was heading toward them. The men who wrote the chronicles, though, took note of that wave. They used the words and the experiences that they had at their disposal to describe it. It was a great sea-flood, overwhelming and deadly. A thousand years later we are able to combine their observations with scientific research to determine that the terrible devastation wrought by the sea in October of 1014 probably had its origins in the sky.

SOURCES

Abbott, Dallas. "Exotic Grains in a core from Cornwall, NY—Do They Have an Impact Source?" *Journal of Siberian Federal University*. http://elib.sfu-kras.ru/bitstream/2311/1632/1/01.pdf (accessed August 16, 2013).

"Anglo Saxon Chronicle." *Britannia History*. http://www.britannia.com/history/docs/asintro2.html

Haslett, Simon K. "The Hell of High Water: Tsunami and the Cornish Coast." Slideshow presentation. http://www.slideshare.net/ProfSimonHaslett/the-hell-of-high-water-tsunami-and-the-cornish-coast

Uncovering Lady Godiva

By OCTAVIA RANDOLPH

No other early Englishwoman has been remembered as long, or as provoca- tively, as Lady Godiva. The name instantly conjures up an image of a woman on horseback, clad only in her hair. Whether depicted in a fifteenth century print or gracing a modern chocolate box, Godiva lives—and rides—on in our imaginations.

Godiva is the Latinised form of the Old English name Godgyfu or Godgifu (liter- ally, "God's gift" or "good gift"). Godgyfu was an eleventh century Anglo-Saxon aristocrat whose life spanned one of the most tumultuous periods in early English history. Despite her illustrious husband, renowned piety, and religious benefactions, without the tan- talising legend of her ride through the Midlands town of Coventry she would likely be completely forgotten.

What is known of Godgyfu is found in the chronicles of various religious founda- tions, mentions of her or her husband in charters, and the post-Conquest compilation known as the Domesday Book. The first positive record of her is in 1035, when she was already married to Leofric, Earl of Mercia. Her birth date is unknown. Similarly, the date of her ride through Coventry cannot be known; possibly it was linked to the dedication of the Priory she and Leofric built there in 1043.

Here I must also acknowledge that despite records dating to the late twelfth century concerning her ride, there are some modern scholars who doubt that it ever took place. I am persuaded that it did.

To return to fact: like other Anglo-Saxon women of her class, Godgyfu owned property in her own right, both given to her by her parents and acquired through other means—gifts from her husband, inheritance from relatives, and purchases and exchanges from individ- uals and religious foundations. The modest farming village of Coventry was one of them. The Domesday Book lists it, twenty years after her death, as having sixty-nine families.

It is not known why Godgyfu and Leofric turned their attention to Coventry, which, after all, was a small and seemingly unremarkable farming community. As early as 1024 Bishop Æthelnoth (later to be Archbishop of Canterbury) gave to Leofric a priceless relic, the arm of St. Augustine of Hippo, which had been purchased by the bishop in Rome and which he apparently indicated was intended—we do not know why—for Coventry.

The response of Leofric and Godgyfu was to create a suitable sanctuary to house this exceptional relic. The lavishly decorated Benedictine Priory of St. Mary, St. Osburgh, and All Saints was dedicated by Archbishop of Canterbury Eadsige in 1043, on property owned by Godgyfu. Within was a shrine to St. Osburgh (a local holy woman who had ear- lier founded a nunnery in Coventry) which held her head encased in copper and gold. St. Augustine's arm took its place in a special shrine, and Godgyfu and Leofric also presented to the new Priory many ornaments of gold, silver, and precious stones, so that it was famed for its richness. Leofric further endowed the Priory with estates in Warwickshire, Gloucestershire, Leicestershire, Northamptonshire, and Worcestershire.

Their religious endowments were many, restoring, enriching, or founding houses in Much Wenlock, Worcester, Evesham, Chester, Leominster, and Stow in Lincolnshire. This last, the Priory Church of St. Mary's Stow-in-Lindsey, is of particular interest as a significant portion of the beautiful and impressive extant church there issued from their hands. The earliest stonework in the church dates from 955; Godgyfu and Leofric greatly endowed and enriched it from 1053 to 1055. The lofty crossing features four soaring rounded Saxon arches (which now enclose later pointed Norman arches built within the original Saxon arches). A tenth or eleventh century graffito of an oared ship is scratched into the base of one of the Saxon arches, possibly a memento from a Danish raider who sailed up the nearby Trent.

The north transept houses a narrow, deep Saxon doorway of honey-coloured stone, which would originally have been lime-washed and over-painted with decorative designs. It likely led to a chapel in Godgyfu's day, and surely she passed through this very arch. To experience St. Mary's Stow, built just ten years after the dedication of the Coventry church, is to begin to imagine what the Priory Church of St. Mary, St. Osburgh, and All Saints may have been like.

Leofric was a man of considerable talent and statesmanship; no man could survive forty years as Earl without these qualities. Elevated to Earl (a title and position new to the English, replacing and expanding the Anglo-Saxon ealdorman) in 1017 by the Dane Cnut, he survived and thrived through Cnut's reign. Then followed that of Harold Harefoot (1035-1040), in whose selection as successor to Cnut Leofric was instrumental. Hardacnut, Cnut's other son, reigned next (1040-1042), and then began Edward the Confessor's rule (1042-1066).

Unsurprisingly for his age, Leofric could alternate between great rapacity and great piety, his depredations and subsequent generous benefactions upon the town of Worcester being a case in point. In 1041, when Hardacnut was king, two of his tax collectors were murdered by an angry and over-taxed group of Worcester citizens.

An act of this nature, upon the direct representatives of the king, was seen as almost an assault upon the king's body itself. In reprisal Hardacnut ordered Leofric to lay waste to Worcester, which Leofric did with complete and horrifying efficiency, made perhaps even more reprehensible as Worcester was the cathedral city of his own people. Afterwards (and seemingly as personal reparation) Leofric bestowed many gifts of treasure and lands upon the religious foundation there, enough to ensure that his memory would be revered and not reviled.

He seems to have been successful in this. Near the end of his life Leofric experienced four religious visions which were carefully recorded by the monks at Worcester and published after his death in 1057. The *Anglo-Saxon Chronicle* entry for 1057 noted:

...In this same year, on 30 October, Earl Leofric passed away. He was very wise in all matters, both religious and secular, that benefited all this nation. He was buried at Coventry, and his son Ælfgar succeeded to his authority....
(G.N. Garmonsway translation)

Following his death, Godgyfu made additional gifts to the religious foundation at Worcester to aid in the repose of Leofric's soul and for the benefit of her own. These gifts included altar frontals, wall hangings, bench covers, candlesticks, and a Bible, and joined a long list of items and estates the two had granted to Worcester in the years prior to Leofric's death.

Leofric and Godgyfu had one known child, the above-mentioned Ælfgar, who died in 1062. His daughter Ealdgyth was wed briefly first to a Welsh king and, following his death, to Harold Godwineson, who was killed by William of Normandy's men on the field at Hastings. Thus for nine months Godgyfu was grandmother to the queen of England.

Godgyfu died in 1067, the year following Hastings. At her death she was one of the four or five richest women in England with estates valued at £160 of silver. Her lands were then forfeit to the new king William.

Godgyfu was buried next to her husband in the Priory church in Coventry they had created. According to chronicler William of Malmesbury, her dying act was characteristically pious: as a final gift to the Priory, she ordered hung about the neck of a statue of the Virgin Mary her personal rosary of precious stones. (The church was, alas, destroyed like so many others during the Reformation, the treasures looted and dispersed.)

Late Medieval Period (1001-1485)

A King, an Earl, and the Terrible Death of a Prince

By PAULA LOFTING

EDWARD THE CONFESSOR CAME TO THE THRONE AFTER HIS HALF-BROTHER HARthacnut died in June 1042. Harthacnut had designated Edward as his heir; however, it was not a foregone conclusion, and Edward needed to rally the support of the English nobility. One of the most powerful nobles with whom it was necessary for him to ingratiate himself was Godwin of Wessex.

Godwin was a dominant figure in the politics of the time and had control of a large part of what was once Alfred the Great's kingdom of Wessex. Godwin must have played a large part in rallying the other nobles and thegns to Edward's cause and, for this, Edward may have felt obliged to agree to wed Godwin's daughter Edith, despite the fact he despised him.

The origin of Edward's animosity toward Godwin lay in the part that Godwin had played in Edward's brother Alfred's death. Alfred's unpleasant demise occurred in 1036 when the brothers, living as exiles in Normandy for more than twenty years, received a letter, allegedly written by their mother Queen Emma. She invited them to England on the premise that she needed their aid. The brothers, for some reason, decided to travel separately to England.

The expedition appears to have been a failure for both of them, but at least Edward escaped with his life. Alfred, unfortunately, did not.

Some sources lay the blame for his death totally at Godwin's door, although others are less inclined to show Godwin in a bad light. What appears to have happened is that Alfred and his party were met by Godwin who was to escort them to meet with Harold Harefoot, then the monarch. At Guildford, however, they were intercepted by Harold's men and taken from Godwin's custody. What happened next ended with poor Alfred being blinded and dying of his wounds at Ely.

This is what the Abingdon Manuscript (C) tells us:

> But then Godwine stopped him, and set him in captivity,
> And drove off his companions, and some variously killed;
> Some of them were sold for money, some cruelly destroyed,
> Some of them were fettered and some of them were blinded,
> Some maimed, some scalped,
> No more horrible deed was done in this country
> Since the Danes came and made peace here....

...The atheling still lived; he was threatened with every evil;

Until it was decided that he would be led to Ely town, fettered thus

As soon as he came on ship he was blinded, and blind thus brought to the monks,

And there he dwelt as long as he lived,

Afterwards he was buried as well as befitted him,

Full honourably, as he was entitled...

...His soul is with Christ.

It seemed that Edward would forever hold it against Godwin for what happened to Alfred even though Godwin was to be cleared before the court on oath more than once. To Edward, Godwin was like a boil on his backside that would never go away, and when one day the opportunity came for Edward to be rid of the whole Godwin family, he grasped it firmly in his hands.

Robert Champart of Jumièges was the newly appointed Archbishop of Canterbury and a longstanding enemy of Godwin's. According to the sources, he began whispering in the king's ear that Godwin had murdered his brother Alfred and was now plotting to murder him. A visit from Edward's brother-in-law, Eustace of Boulogne, seemed to fuel the fire that was, thanks to Champart, burning in Edward's heart. When on his way home to Boulogne, Eustace and his men stopped at the town of Dover and caused a fight with the townspeople. Some of Eustace's men were killed in the fight as well as an equal number of townsfolk. Godwin was ordered by the king to punish the town by razing it to the ground. He refused. Dover was in Godwin's jurisdiction and he may have heard the Doverian townsfolk's side of the sad, sorry tale and believed the fracas to be the fault of Eustace and his men. In any case, his refusal to punish them resulted in a stand-off between the Godwins and the king and his supporters, ominously including the northern earls and all of their thegns. The Godwins were, consequently, all exiled, and although Edward later accepted Godwin and his family back, restoring his lands and his office as earl after a year in exile, their relationship would always be strained.

Edward's unforgiving attitude towards Godwin later shows in his behaviour at the earl's death in 1053 at a court reunion with his family and the king. During the feast, Edward is allegedly said to have made acrimonious remarks toward Godwin regarding his involvement in Alfred's death. It is said that Godwin was so enraged that it caused him to have a stroke, and he died later in Edward's private apartment. Perhaps Edward at last, after all those years of haranguing the earl about Alfred, felt a pang of guilt and offered him the comfort of his own chamber and doctor to ease his way into the next life. Finally, Edward was now rid of the thorn in his side.

After Godwin's death, his oldest surviving son Harold became the next earl of Wessex. Harold went on to become the most powerful man at court, second only to the king. He took the throne in January 1066 and died later that year at the Battle of Hastings after only ten months of rule.

SOURCES

Barlow, Frank. *Edward the Confessor*. London: Yale University Press, 1970.

Barlow, Frank. *The Godwins*. Edinburgh: Pearson Education Ltd, 2002.

Stanton, M., trans. *Anglo Saxon Chronicle*.

THE LAST ENGLISH KING

By MARTIN LAKE

IF YOU WERE TO ASK SOMEONE THE NAME OF THE LAST ANGLO-SAXON KING OF ENGLAND you would probably be told it was King Harold, the man who lost his eye, the Battle of Hastings, and his throne.

But if you were to ask someone the question in the autumn of 1066 they would have given a different answer. They would tell you that the last English King was Edgar Ætheling.

Since that time, Edgar has been almost forgotten. At best he has become a footnote of history and is often referred to in dismissive terms. It is as if his story has been deliberately erased from history. As George Orwell said, *"History is written by the winners."*

Yet Edgar was proclaimed King of England and was a key figure in the resistance to the Norman Conquest. After his eventual submission to William the Conqueror, he continued to shape the events of his day.

When Edward the Confessor died early in 1066, the Witan deemed the times too perilous for a man of Edgar's youth to take the throne. Two of the greatest warriors in Europe were preparing to invade, and Edgar was an untried youth of thirteen or fourteen. The Witan gave the throne instead to the experienced Harold Godwinson. Ten months later, Harold was dead and the Witan needed to choose a new king to replace him. This time they chose Edgar.

There were a number of requirements to become King of the English in the eleventh century. One was to be a member of the ruling dynasty of England, the dynasty which had once ruled the Kingdom of Wessex. The second was to be crowned. The third, and arguably most important, was to be proclaimed King by the Witan, the council of the great men of the kingdom.

There were other people who could have been proclaimed King: Edwin, Earl of Mercia, the most obvious. So why did the Witan ignore him and other experienced leaders and put their faith in a young boy?

Edgar Ætheling was the grandson of Edmund Ironside and the direct heir of Edward the Confessor. The Witan decided that only a man with the blood of Alfred the Great in his veins could unite the Kingdom against the invader. He was proclaimed King. There was no time for a coronation, and soon after the defeat at Hastings Edgar and the English leaders led a second English army to fight the Normans. But his advisers were overawed by the power and destructiveness of the Norman army and advised him to surrender.

Edgar was now firmly in William's power, and that may well have seemed like the end of the story. In fact, there are very few details regarding the rest of Edgar's life. It seems as if the conquerors were determined to erase all memory of him. Some details persist across the centuries, however.

Edgar spent a few years in William's hands. In 1068 he fled, probably with his family, to the court of Malcolm, King of the Scots. Malcolm fell in love with Edgar's sister, Margaret. At first, sister and brother rebuffed his advances, but eventually they gave in to the inevitable. Margaret set out to humanise Malcolm, and Edgar set out to win his support to invade England. Malcolm agreed, and Edgar led a small force over the border to join with an army already being gathered by Earl Gospatric of Northumbria.

The English army defeated the Normans in Durham, inflicting a greater Norman death toll upon them than they had suffered at Hastings. Buoyed by their success, they marched south, but William moved more swiftly. William's generalship proved too much for the poorly equipped English army, and Edgar was forced to flee back to Scotland.

Later that year he crossed Hadrian's Wall a second time and raised another army.

The Danish King, Swein Estrifthson, felt he had a good claim to the throne of England and sent a huge fleet under his brother and sons to contest the Kingdom with the Normans. Edgar and his supporters now faced two potential threats. They solved it by doing something remarkable. They allied themselves to their ancient enemies, the Danes, and prepared to do battle with the Normans. Nobody knows what deal they negotiated. Detractors of Edgar say that he fought on the side of the Danes, but this seems to me to be highly unlikely. Some division of the kingdom seems a much more likely scenario.

The joint English and Danish force captured the city of York, the most important city in the north, destroying two castles and slaying all but a handful of the Norman defenders. Then they moved south in order to bring William to battle. But the Danes seemed reluctant to engage, and Edgar decided to lead a small force on his own to capture Lincoln. This attempt was over-ambitious and ended in defeat.

Later that winter Esbjorn, the Danish leader, was bought off by the Normans. The joint strategy was in tatters. The English army drifted away, and the earls who had fought alongside Edgar submitted to William.

Edgar refused to submit, however, and was pursued across northern England by the Normans, who wreaked mass destruction and near-genocide upon the north. Edgar and his men escaped and made their way back to Scotland once again. He had been successful against the Norman armies but not when they were led by William.

Two years later, in 1072, William attacked the Scots in a devastating campaign, and Malcolm was forced to sue for peace. The peace treaty required him to expel his young brother-in-law from his kingdom.

Edgar sailed to the court of one of William's most determined enemies, Count Robert of Flanders. He returned to Scotland two years later, but he did not stay with Malcolm for long. Philip, the young King of the Franks, was determined to break the power of the Normans and offered Edgar lands close to Normandy so that he could attack William in his own homeland. Edgar was quick to accept the offer and sailed for the south. Fate was against him yet again, and his ships were shipwrecked with great loss of life. Edgar and a handful of followers were hunted by the Normans but finally made their way once more to Malcolm's court.

Edgar had been fighting against the Normans for six years and was still a young man of only twenty-one years or so. This time the pressure from Malcolm and his sister persuaded him to offer William his submission.

He was treated with great pomp by William and given lands and a pension of one pound of silver a day. This was an immense amount and made him one of the wealthiest men in the Kingdom. He did not take part in the botched revolt of the Earls the following year. He was wise not to have done so.

We hear little of Edgar during the next ten years. The few Norman accounts describe him as childish and lazy although a good horseman and a fluent talker. An example of his stupidity is illustrated by the fact that he is supposed to have given William his pension in exchange for a horse. The horse must have been exceptionally fine to be worth such a stupendous amount. Presumably it was Pegasus complete with wings and the gift of speech. Easily worth a pound of silver. Either that or this story is indicative of the Norman campaign to discredit Edgar in the eyes of Normans, the English, and posterity.

In 1085, complaining that he received little honour and respect, he secured William's agreement to leave England with two hundred followers. He went to Apulia, which was part of the Norman territories in Italy. We do not know what he did there, although he may have taken part in the dispute between Roger Borsa and Bohemond for the Dukedom of Apulia and Calabria.

A few years later 5,000 Englishmen left England for Constantinople under the leadership of one of Edgar's oldest friends. Given later events in Edgar's life it is plausible that Edgar joined them.

Within a few years, however, he had returned to Normandy where he became one of the principal advisers to William's successor as Duke of Normandy, Robert Curthose. He appears to have given up any hope of regaining his lost throne. But ahead of him were years of warfare in England, Normandy, and Scotland, the making and unmaking of kings, and an important role in the First Crusade.

What I found most remarkable is that although Edgar spent much of his life leading the resistance to William the Conqueror and his successors he was never punished in the way that others were. Many were imprisoned for life, a few lost their lives. Not so, Edgar. He seems to have been the great survivor of these dangerous years.

Nobody knows the reason for this. Was it that the Norman kings feared to do him any harm, that they felt guilty because they knew he was the legitimate king of England? Was it that he was just incredibly lucky? Or was it that he was a highly intelligent man who learnt how to survive in a world which had turned upside down?

The Alternate Histories of the Norman Conquest, Part One

By ROSANNE E. LORTZ

ONE DISSERVICE THAT MANY HISTORIANS DO TO READERS IS TO WEIGH TWO SIDES OF a disputed issue, form a judgment on what they think happened, and then present their judgment as if it is incontrovertible fact. The events leading up to the Norman Conquest are one such issue. School children everywhere learn that prior to Edward the Confessor's death, Harold Godwinson, the most powerful earl in England, made a trip to Normandy and swore to support Duke William's claim to the crown. After Edward's death, Harold reneged on his oath, precipitating the Norman Conquest and his own death at the Battle of Hastings.

It is interesting to note, however, that most of the primary sources of the period have fairly different versions of this tale. Things are not as cut and dried as the historians would have us imagine. Did Harold actually make a journey to Normandy? And if so, did King Edward send him? Was his purpose in going to swear an oath of support to William? Or was the oath exacted under compulsion? Did Edward the Confessor, upon his deathbed, name Harold as his successor? If so, was this a change from having previously named William?

A brief look at the primary sources of this period will show us that there are no easy answers to these questions. To tell only one version of the story is glib, at best, or deceptive, at worst.

SOURCE 1: *THE ANGLO-SAXON CHRONICLE*

The first sources that we will examine are from the English side of the Channel. The *Anglo-Saxon Chronicle* (a source written at a monastery and regularly updated by the record-keepers) makes no mention of Harold's visit to Normandy. At King Edward's death, it includes an epitaph that commends Harold as Edward's choice for successor:

> *Yet did the wise king entrust his kingdom*
> *To a man of high rank, to Harold himself,*
> *The noble earl, who ever*
> *Faithfully obeyed his noble lord*
> *In words and deeds, neglecting nothing*
> *Whereof the national king stood in need.*

An argument from silence is not a strong one. It is possible that Harold's visit to Normandy was a secret one and not common knowledge to the people of England. This source does indicate, however, that King Edward gave the crown to Harold upon his deathbed.

SOURCE 2: *CHRONICON EX CHRONICIS*

Another chronicle, the eleventh century *Chronicon ex Chronicis* from Worcester Abbey also makes no mention of Harold's journey to Normandy. As in the *Anglo-Saxon Chronicle*, we see the claim that Edward chose Harold to succeed.

> When [Edward] *was entombed, the underking* [subregulus], *Harold, son of Earl Godwine, whom the king had chosen before his demise as successor to the kingdom, was elected by the primates of all England to the dignity of kingship, and was consecrated king with due ceremony by Ealdred, archbishop of York, on the same day.*

This source also gives us another important detail, that Harold *"was elected by the primates of all England to the dignity of kingship."* During the later Anglo-Saxon period, the king's heir was usually elected by a group of nobles called the Witan, adding a bit of oligarchic democracy into the monarchical succession.

SOURCE 3: *VITA AEDWARDI REGIS*

A third English source worth looking at is the *Vita Aedwardi Regis* (The Life of King Edward), a hagiographic work that King Edward's wife commissioned immediately following his death. Edward's wife Edith was the sister of Harold Godwinson—meaning she was probably very much in favor of her brother being the chosen heir to the kingdom.

The *Vita Aedwardi* says that there were three people present at the deathbed of the king: Edith, Harold, and the Archbishop of Canterbury. According to this source, the dying Edward looked at Harold and said: *"I entrust this woman and all the kingdom to your protection."*

Some historians have wondered about the veracity of this account. If Edward really had chosen William earlier (as we will find the Norman accounts attest), why did he change his mind at the last minute? Wouldn't it have been very easy for Edith and Harold to fabricate a story about Edward's last words? The only person they would have to suborn would be Archbishop Stigand, who from other sources, seems to have been quite friendly with the house of Godwin.

But although this theory is an interesting one, it is both impossible to prove and a conspiracy theory that none of Edward's contemporaries ever considered. The two preceding sources confirm that the entire country of England believed Edward to have bestowed the crown on Harold.

SOURCE 4: *GESTA NORMANNORUM DUCUM*

Although Harold's trip to Normandy is ignored in these early English sources, the Norman chroniclers are extremely eager to highlight it. William of Jumièges, a Norman monk in a monastery near Rouen, lived through the Norman Conquest and wrote an account of it in the *Gesta Normannorum Ducum* (Deeds of the Norman Dukes). He writes that King Edward sent Harold to Normandy in order to *"swear fealty to the duke concerning his crown and, according to the Christian custom, pledge it with oaths."* After crossing the channel and landing in Ponthieu, Harold fell into the hands of Guy, Count of Abbeville, who threw Harold into prison. William sent envoys to Guy to secure Harold's freedom. Then, *"after Harold had stayed with* [William] *for some time and had sworn fealty to him about the kingdom with many oaths he sent him back to the king with many gifts."*

Notice the details in the above work. Harold was sent by King Edward to pledge his support to William for the crown. If this is true, and if Edward did indeed bequeath the crown to Harold on his deathbed, then something must have happened in between to change the old king's mind. The account goes on to say that William rescued Harold from a local baron named Guy. There is no suggestion that William held Harold captive himself, only that he treated him as a guest, loading him down with presents after he swore the requisite fealty.

SOURCE 5: WILLIAM OF POITIERS

William of Poitiers, another Norman writing during the Conquest years, confirms the story as told by William of Jumièges. King Edward sent Harold to Normandy for the express purpose of strengthening Duke William's right to inherit the English throne. Harold was captured by Guy in Ponthieu, rescued by William, and then...

> Harold swore fealty to him according to the holy rite of Christians. And, as the most truthful and distinguished men who were there as witnesses have told, at the crucial point in the oath he clearly and of his own free will pronounced these words that as long as he lived he would be the vicar of Duke William in the court of his lord King Edward; that he would strive to the utmost with his counsel and his wealth to ensure that the English monarchy should be pledged to him after Edward's death.... For there was no hope that Edward, already sick, could live much longer.

Notice, the emphasis that Harold swore *"clearly"* and *"of his own free will,"* indicating that there may have been claims circulating that the oath was under compulsion. While the Anglo-Saxon sources are clear that Edward promised the crown to Harold on his deathbed, the Norman sources are equally clear that Edward sent Harold to promise the crown to William just a short while earlier.

SOURCE: 6: *CARMEN DE HASTINGAE PROELIO*

The *Carmen de Hastingae Proelio* (Song of the Battle of Hastings), an epic poem that was probably composed for William's coronation, confirms the official Norman view of how events transpired. In the poem, after William lands in England, he responds to a threatening delegation sent by Harold, making clear reference to the earlier oath:

> *Although he threatens, unjustly, to make war, my men, trusting in the Lord, will not retreat. Is he not aware of the oath made to me and covertly forsworn? Does he not in his heart remember that he was my vassal? If his perjured hand does not yet recoil condemned, it has already been found guilty by the judgement of God. If he seeks peace and wants to confess his crimes, I will be indulgent and promptly overlook his faults. I will grant him the lands which formerly his father held if he is willing to be, as before, my vassal.*

SOURCE 7: THE BAYEUX TAPESTRY

The Bayeux Tapestry, a long embroidery documenting the history of the Norman Conquest, is enigmatic in the way that pictures often are. The pictures tell us that Harold went to Normandy, was captured by Guy, and swore an oath to William, but the captions do not tell us why Harold went and what were the terms of the oath he swore. The pictures do indicate that the oath was of a serious nature, for Harold's hands are placed on two reliquaries.

When Harold returns to England, the picture where Edward the Confessor receives him almost looks as if the king is rebuking him—but then pictures like these are hard to use as conclusive evidence. Perhaps Edward did not want Harold to make that oath (whatever the oath was), or perhaps there is some other explanation for Harold's obsequious posture and King Edward's admonishing finger.

CONCLUSION

The seven sources we have examined thus far can all be somewhat harmonized. Perhaps the English sources simply omitted Harold's voyage to Normandy. Perhaps the Norman version of Edward sending Harold to Normandy is correct. They do leave us with one serious gap in knowledge, however. What caused Edward the Confessor to change his mind? Why would he acknowledge William as his heir and then change the plan of succession on his deathbed to Harold?

In Part Two we will look at more sources, histories written several decades after the event, that throw even more elements of mystery into the mix, showing that there is more than one way to tell the story of how the Norman Conquest came about....

The Alternate Histories of the Norman Conquest, Part Two

By ROSANNE E. LORTZ

In Part One we considered seven different primary sources relating to the Norman Conquest, trying to discover the true story of what happened with the English succession. Three Anglo-Saxon sources told us that Edward the Confessor, on his deathbed, gave the crown to Harold, but they made no mention of Harold taking an earlier trip to Normandy to pledge the crown to William. Four Norman sources placed great emphasis on this trip and on Harold's oath, although some of them, like the Bayeux Tapestry, were not clear on what the actual terms of the oath were.

Here we will consider some sources written a little bit after the fact—fifty to a hundred years after the Norman Conquest.

SOURCE 8: ORDERIC VITALIS

William of Jumièges' work, one of the Norman sources that we looked at in the previous essay, was revised in the early twelfth century by Orderic Vitalis. In the passage discussing Harold's trip to Normandy, Orderic Vitalis adds these interesting details: (1) After Harold swore fealty to William, William *"promised he would give him his daughter Adeliza with half the kingdom of England,"* and (2) after these transactions, William sent Harold *"back to the king with many gifts but kept as hostage his handsome brother Wulfnoth."*

These additions by Orderic Vitalis indicate that the oath Harold swore was more of a treaty, an agreement between two men, each who had something to gain. In exchange for Harold's support, William would make Harold his Number Two Man, and he would seal the deal with his daughter's hand. William keeping Harold's brother Wulfnoth as a hostage was a standard way for lords of this time to guarantee a treaty.

These additions also make us question: where did Orderic Vitalis get his information? The detail of the daughter is not mentioned in any of the earliest sources. How did Orderic come by this evidence? And how much weight should be given to these sources that were written a generation or two after the fact? Are they less reliable? More?

SOURCES 9 AND 10: EADMER AND WACE

Like Orderic Vitalis' additions, the rest of the sources telling us about the Norman Conquest come late to the game. In the *Historia Novorum in Anglia*, penned sometime between 1095 and 1123, Eadmer wrote that Harold intended to see William on his journey, but for the purpose of retrieving hostages not to swear an oath. Significantly, Eadmer says that Harold did swear an oath to William, but he did so under compulsion.

Another writer, Wace, wrote his *Roman de Rou* in the first half of Henry II's reign (1155-1170). He includes a fantastic story of Harold swearing an oath to Duke William, then being surprised to discover that William had hidden relics below his hands, which made the oath sacred and inviolable. This story is often repeated in history books, although the earliest sources have no mention of such a dramatic surprise.

SOURCE 11: WILLIAM OF MALMESBURY

The last source for this discussion is, in my opinion, the most interesting of them all. William of Malmesbury wrote the *Gesta Regum Anglorum* (Deeds of the English Kings) around 1120. He had a Norman father and an English mother and spent his whole life in England. To the degree that it is possible for a historian to be without national bias, William of Malmesbury seems to be.

His explanation of why Harold took that fateful voyage to Normandy is a unique one.

> *Some say that Harold himself was sent to Normandy for this purpose by the king; others, more familiar with his secret intentions, maintain that he was driven there against his will by the violence of the wind, and to protect himself invented a story which, since it looks very close to the truth, I will now tell. Harold had gone to an estate of his at Bosham, and there, by way of pastime, he boarded a fishing-boat and for a time, pressing his entertainment rather far, proceeded out to sea; but a storm blew up suddenly from the wrong quarter, and he and his companions were driven to the country of Ponthieu. The men of that country, as is their national habit, flocked together suddenly from all directions, and the party, being few and unarmed, were easily overwhelmed by a larger force of armed men; their hands were bound and feet shackled. Harold, pondering with all his ingenuity how to mend the situation, suborned a man with large promises and sent him to William. He had been sent to Normandy by the king, he said, as the best man to confirm by his presence the message haltingly conveyed to lesser envoys; he was being held in chains by Guy count of Ponthieu, to prevent him carrying out his mission. So Harold was freed on William's orders, and taken personally to Normandy by Guy.*

According to William of Malmesbury, Edward the Confessor did not send Harold to promise the crown to William. But when Harold ended up in a tight pinch, captured by Guy of Ponthieu, he invented that story to save himself from duress. If this version of events is true, it would make sense why the English sources record no such embassy and why the Norman sources are adamant that Edward sent Harold.

William of Malmesbury's version of Edward's deathbed bequest conflicts slightly with the early English sources:

> When king Edward died, England, fluctuating with doubtful favour, was
> uncertain to which ruler she should commit herself; to Harold, William, or
> Edgar [the young grandson of Edward's half-brother]; *for the king had rec-*
> *ommended him also to the nobility, as nearest to the sovereignty in point of*
> *birth; concealing his better judgment from the tenderness of his disposition.*

Here it seems as if the dying Edward offered no clear choice of successor, and perhaps even leaned toward preferring Edgar who was closest to him in blood.

William of Malmesbury goes on to relate what happened after Edward's death:

> *...Harold, once crowned, did not spare a thought for the agreement between*
> *himself and William, declaring himself released from his oath because Wil-*
> *liam's daughter, to whom he had been betrothed, had died before she was*
> *old enough to marry.... [Harold] added with regard to the kingdom that it*
> *had been presumptuous to promise on oath a succession that was not his,*
> *without the general assembly and decision of his council and his folk; and*
> *so a foolish oath deserved to be broken. If an oath or vow disposing of her*
> *hand taken voluntarily by a maiden in her father's house without her par-*
> *ents' knowledge is held to be null and void, how much less weight should*
> *be given to the oath by which he had disposed the kingdom, while under*
> *the king's authority, without the knowledge of all England and compelled*
> *by circumstances! It was moreover unfair to demand that he should resign*
> *the authority conferred upon him with such popular support; this would be*
> *unwelcome to his countrymen and perilous for his knights.*

Once again, we see the promised marriage alliance that showed up in Orderic Vitalis' interpolations. Here, however, Harold claims that William's daughter has died before the marriage could take place, thus terminating the treaty and freeing him from any obligation to William. He also argues that the oath was under compulsion, and that he had promised something that did not actually belong to him. If Edward did not actually send Harold, then how could an earl pledge away the crown of England? And if the Witan was responsible for electing the next king, then how could Harold force them to give the crown to William?

CONCLUSION

So, what really happened? There are a couple things that we can say with a fair amount of certainty. Harold probably did go on a voyage to Normandy and probably did swear some kind of oath to William. Conspiracy theories aside, Edward probably did bequeath the crown to Harold upon his deathbed. Other matters are very much open for debate. Did Edward send Harold to Normandy? What were the terms of the oath? Was it under compulsion? Was a marriage alliance mentioned? Did William's daughter die, thus ter-minating the agreement?

All of these questions are questions still. But of two things I am more than certain—with an issue this complex, a historical novelist may take whatever version of the story she chooses and craft a brilliant novel; and conversely, with so many tangled strands of evidence, no modern historian should give just one version of events and then leave his readers believing that his story is the Gospel truth.

Aesop's Fables and the Bayeux Tapestry

By ROSANNE E. LORTZ

A Crow having stolen a bit of cheese, perched in a tree and held it in her beak. A Fox, seeing this, longed to possess the cheese himself, and by a wily stratagem succeeded. "How handsome is the Crow," he exclaimed, "in the beauty of her shape and in the fairness of her complexion! Oh, if her voice were only equal to her beauty, she would deservedly be considered the Queen of Birds!" This he said deceitfully; but the Crow, anxious to refute the reflection cast upon her voice, set up a loud caw and dropped the cheese. The Fox quickly picked it up, and thus addressed the Crow: "My good Crow, your voice is right enough, but your wit is wanting."

THIS FABLE, ATTRIBUTED TO THE ANCIENT GREEK SLAVE AESOP, APPEARS PICTORIALLY three different times in the margins of the Bayeux Tapestry. Other fables, also from Aesop, show up as well, leading historians to pose an interesting question: Why were they included? Are they merely decoration? Or are they commentary on the larger narrative of the Tapestry itself?

The Bayeux Tapestry is an embroidered cloth over 70 meters long that tells the story of the Norman Conquest of England. The Tapestry begins with the depiction of Harold Godwinson, Earl of Wessex, journeying to Normandy. There he is taken captive by the Normans and brought to Duke William, to whom he swears some kind of oath, most probably an oath pledging his support to William in the matter of the English succession. The Tapestry goes on to show Harold sailing back to England and becoming king himself after Edward the Confessor's death. Duke William then launches an invasion, defeats and kills Harold, and takes the crown.

The origins of the Bayeux Tapestry are debated by historians. Most agree that it was commissioned by a Norman in the decades following the Conquest (since it seems to tell the version of events given by Norman historians like William of Poitiers and William of Jumieges). But the jury is out on whether it was commissioned by the Conqueror's wife Matilda, the Conqueror's brother Odo, or someone else entirely. There is also healthy discussion on whether it was created in the French town of Bayeux or embroidered somewhere in England.

One segment of thought believes that the Tapestry, although commissioned by a Norman, was embroidered by the conquered Anglo-Saxons, and thus has a subversive subtext stitched into its borders. The fables and their interpretation play a key part in this fascinating theory. While I do not have time to look at each fable in depth, I want to show you how the embroiderers' use of "The Fox and the Crow" bears out this idea of an Anglo-Saxon subtext rebelliously commenting on the larger narrative.

In the story of "The Fox and the Crow", we see a strong animal taking advantage of a weak one. The fox uses guile to trick the foolish crow into giving up the coveted piece of cheese. The moral of the fable, "Flatterers are not to be trusted," leads the reader to identify with the unfortunate crow as the hero of the story. The Fox, although clever, is still the villain of the piece. The cheese was never rightfully his—it was something that he stole through deceit.

There are several pictorial clues in the Tapestry linking the Crow to Harold and the Fox to William. The first time the fable appears, it is beneath the scene where Harold is setting sail for Normandy. The Crow is on the left, and the Fox on the right. If the Crow is symbolizing Harold, then this is exactly what we would expect since in the historical narrative Harold is leaving England on the left, journeying toward Normandy and William on the right.

The cheese has already dropped from the Crow's mouth and is halfway between the Crow and the Fox. What does this indicate? Perhaps that Harold, just by setting sail has as good as lost the prize. Or perhaps it is a foreshadowing of what is to come.

The second instance of this fable occurs after Harold has been captured by Guy of Ponthieu and brought to William. It is shown beneath the scene where Harold is accompanying William to the Breton war. In this picture of the fable, the cheese is already in the Fox's mouth. Harold, now in William's clutches, has already lost the prize.

The third instance of the fable comes in the upper margin just as Harold has left Normandy to return to England. The arrangement of the Fox and the Crow in this third version of the fable is interesting. The Fox (which we have already established as William) is on the left, in the direction of the Normandy that Harold has just left. The Crow is on the right, in the direction of Harold's voyage. The historian David Bernstein notes that the Fox and the Crow are *"no longer in the same compartment."* They are *"separated by a panel, a spatial composition similar to that of William and Harold below,"* for Harold has just put the sea between William and himself.

In a strange twist, the Crow now has the cheese in her mouth. You will recall that in the two previous showings of this fable, the cheese was either in mid-air, or firmly in the clutches of the Fox. Escaping from Normandy unscathed, Harold has regained his prize for a time by putting a watery barrier between William and himself.

Throughout this story, the cheese in question is a symbol of the throne of England. Harold has it. William wants it. And somehow, through trickery, William will contrive to get it. Harold may have been as foolish as the flattered bird to travel to Normandy in the first place, but it is only because William is as rapacious and guileful as a Fox that Harold's cheese is in any danger.

The clever use of Aesop's Fables in the Bayeux Tapestry—of which "The Fox and the Crow" is just one example—provides us with an even greater appreciation for the makers of the Tapestry. Were they members of the oppressed Anglo-Saxon race, trying to hint at their own perception of events, even while they stitched out the story their conquerors demanded? The use of the Fables hints that such a subtext could be possible, and though the evidence might not be enough to make an unqualified historical claim, it could be enough to inspire the story for another historical novel.

SOURCES

Bernstein, David J. T*he Mystery of the Bayeux Tapestry*. Chicago: University of Chicago Press, 1986.

Bridgeford, Andrew. *1066: The Hidden History of the Bayeux Tapestry*. London: Harper Perennial, 2004.

Townsend, Rev. George Fyler, Trans. *Aesop's Fables*. [on-line collection]. Available from http://www.pacificnet.net/~johnr/aesop/

Wilson, David M. *The Bayeux Tapestry*. New York: Thames & Hudson, Inc. 1985.

THE LONDON TORNADO OF 1091

By RICHARD DENNING

As A WEATHER PHENOMENON TORNADOS ARE NOT PARTICULARLY ASSOCIATED WITH the U.K. However a recent report by the Met office that said that actually the U.K. gets more per square kilometre than the U.S.A. Yet our tornados are babies for the most part and of very little power. Occasionally though we do get a whopper!

Such a huge tornado occurred on October 17, 1091 during the reign of King William II (called Rufus). This was the first recorded tornado in the British Isles, and it hit London hard. It is estimated to have been about T8 strength.

The London Tornado of 1091 is reckoned to have only killed two people, but dramatically the then-wooden London Bridge was completely demolished. This bridge had been built by William I after the Norman Conquest. After the tornado William II rebuilt the bridge, but this too was short lived as a fire destroyed it only 40 years later.

The nearby church of St. Mary-le-Bow was badly damaged. There are reports that such was the elemental power unleashed that four rafters recorded as 26 feet long were driven so deeply into the ground that only four feet protruded. Around 600 houses were also destroyed.

William had recently been raiding church treasuries for funds, and so there is speculation that the English would have seen this storm as a judgement by God on the wickedness of the king in the same way that some people saw the Great Fire of London as also allowed "by permission of heaven".

THE FORGOTTEN MILITANT ORDER: THE KNIGHTS OF ST. LAZARUS

By HELENA P. SCHRADER

THE SO-CALLED MILITANT ORDERS—MONASTIC ORDERS OPEN TO FIGHTING MEN— were children of the Crusades. Scollins and Wise (in *The Knights of Christ*) list no less than seventeen military orders, eight of which were founded in the Iberian Peninsula, two of which were Italian, and two German. The most famous and most powerful militant orders, however, were the Templars and the Hospitallers, both founded in the Holy Land and international in their structures and membership.

Initially, true to the Word of Christ, the Church of Rome condemned violence of any kind. By the fifth century, however, the Church conceded that there were circumstances under which the use of force—even homicide—was necessary, excusable, and potentially pious. The concept of the "just war" emerged and was recognized theologically by St. Augustine.

Furthermore, the more Islam threatened the Christian world, the more the Church recognized the need for armed men to defend it against armies determined to spread Islam with the sword. Meanwhile, wherever secular power was weak, the need for men willing to protect clerics, women, and peasants against everything from Viking raids to common robbers was equally evident and urgent.

The fact that the Church drew its leadership from the ruling class—the secular lords with strong military traditions—meant that most clerics in the Middle Ages were themselves imbued with a warrior ethos. This is demonstrated by the number of bishops who donned armor and took an active part in warfare, from the Battle of Hastings to the Battle of Crécy. Thus it is not surprising that by the end of the first Christian millennium, Christianity recognized the need for armed force and men who wielded it, but that did not mean the Church had completely abandoned its principles.

On the contrary, the Church sought repeatedly to restrict, reduce, control, and direct warfare and violence. Violence against churches and clergy was punished with excommunication, for example, and there were frequent clerical diatribes against the vanity, arrogance, and violence of the warrior class.

When the Byzantine Emperor appealed to Pope Urban II for aid in fighting the Seljuk Turks and freeing the Holy Land, there is little doubt that Urban II had dual motives for calling for a crusade: on the one hand, he wanted to free the Holy Land, but on the other he wanted to free France and Western Europe from excess numbers of violent young men, trained in the profession of arms, who were too quick to fight each other and prey upon the defenseless.

Balderic, one chronicler of Urban II's speech calling for the First Crusade, quotes the Pope as saying:

> *Christian warriors, who continually and vainly seek pretexts for war, rejoice, for you have today found a true pretext. You, who have so often been the terror of your fellow men, go and fight for the deliverance of the holy places. You, who sell for vile pay the strength of your arms to the fury of others, armed with the sword of the Maccabees, go and merit eternal reward.... If you must have blood, bathe in the blood of the infidels.... Soldiers of Hell, become soldiers of the living God!*

What is remarkable in retrospect is the extent to which Pope Urban II struck a chord with his audience. Not only did men take the cross in great numbers (and proceed to bathe in the blood of infidels when they reached Jerusalem), but for the next 200 years fighting men flocked to serve Christ, not just in crusades, but as fighting monks bound by monastic vows of chastity, poverty, and obedience. This was made possible by the creation of new monastic orders that enabled men to be both monks and knights.

While members of these orders were expected to abjure all wealth and property, to attend Mass multiple times a day, to fast, pray, and eat in silence, and to live in controlled communities cut off from the outside world, especially women, members were not required to give up the profession of arms. Rather, these orders were designed to capture the religious zeal of the time and funnel the fervor and energy of fighting men into religious channels.

The most famous of the "fighting orders" or militant orders were of course the Knights Templar and the Knights Hospitaller (Knights of St. John), two orders founded in the Holy Land and, for their age, truly international in character. Although not powerful and now largely forgotten, there was a third military order also founded in the Holy Land, the Order of St. Lazarus.

The Order of St. Lazarus evolved from a leper hospital that had existed in Jerusalem prior to the First Crusade. After the Christian Kingdom of Jerusalem was established, it became part of the Hospitaller network of hospitals, but by 1142 the Order of St. Lazarus broke away, and by 1147 it was known as the Leper Brothers of Jerusalem.

About this time the Order also started to expand, eventually having houses in Tiberias, Ascalon, Acre, Caesarea, Beirut, and possibly other cities as well. Furthermore, it began to have military brethren, whose role was primarily the defense of the leper hospitals. These military men were most likely former Templars and Hospitallers who had contracted leprosy, because we know that both the Templar and Hospitaller Rules required members with leprosy to join the Order of St. Lazarus.

Possibly some knights and sergeants joined St. Lazarus without being lepers, however, because there are recorded incidents of the Order of St. Lazarus taking part in military operations—possibly at the Battle of Hattin; certainly at the Battle of Gaza in 1244, at Ramla in 1253, and during the defense of Acre in 1291.

After the fall of Acre, the Order of St. Lazarus moved its headquarters to Cyprus, abandoned all military activities, and thereafter concentrated on its mission of providing comfort and care for the victims of leprosy until the mid-fourteenth century.

SOURCES

Hopkins, Andrea. *Knights*. London: Grange, 1990. Pp. 82-83.

Wise, Terrence. *The Knights of Christ. London:* Osprey Publishing, 1984.

THE ARCHBISHOP WHO DEFIED TWO KINGS: ANSELM OF CANTERBURY

BY ROSANNE E. LORTZ

WE HAVE ALL HEARD THE STORY OF THOMAS BECKET, THE ARCHBISHOP WHO refused to surrender to the will of King Henry II and ended up lying murdered on the floor of the church at Canterbury. What many people do not know, however, is that Thomas Becket was not the first Archbishop of Canterbury to defy a king in order to protect the power of the Church against the encroachments of the monarchy. He was simply following in the grand tradition of his illustrious predecessor, Anselm of Canterbury.

When William the Conqueror died in 1087, his son William Rufus inherited the throne of England. The office of Archbishop of Canterbury fell vacant. For four years, the king refused to allow the office to be filled, declaring that he would be his own archbishop. The flock of England was thus left with no shepherd to tend her while a wolf wore the crown.

Eventually, King William Rufus was prevailed upon to fill the office in Canterbury. He selected Anselm of Bec for this privilege, an aging abbot famous for his ontological proof of the existence of God. William knew that he had chosen one of the most scholarly men of the age, but he was perhaps unaware that he had also chosen one of the most tenacious.

Anselm was no sooner selected to fill the see of Canterbury than he denied the king's right to make that selection. William Rufus, so Anselm said, had no right or power to appoint clergy. The dispute over lay investiture that was surfacing in courts and cathedrals all across Europe had come at last to England. This issue would dominate the struggle between Anselm and William Rufus and prove a proper prelude to the clash between Thomas Becket and Henry II.

William Rufus believed that it was his God-given prerogative to fill any vacant church office in his realm. In his mind, bishops, as well as barons, were his vassals. When an eleventh century bishop received his see, he also received a large portion of English land and thus acquired feudal obligations to the English king. Like William Rufus' more secular vassals, the bishops owed him fealty and knight service. Therefore, the king wanted to have a say on who his servants would be.

Anselm contended that a bishop, by the very nature of his office, could not be a vassal to the king without compromising his position as vassal to Christ. The material possessions that went along with the office changed nothing. Scripture prescribed that the Church should choose her ministers, and no prescription of William Rufus could annul this mandate from God.

In this stance Anselm was supported by the Church throughout Europe. Twenty-five years earlier, Gregory VII, the Bishop of Rome, had stated the Church's official position on this issue: *"We decree that no one of the clergy shall receive the investiture of a bishopric or abbey or church from the hand of an emperor or king or of any lay person, male or female."* Any clergyman or lay lord who presumed to violate this mandate was subject to excommunication for his presumption.

When soon-to-be-Emperor Henry IV ignored the Church's decision and appointed a bishop for Milan, Gregory VII censured him for this action. The Emperor responded by declaring Gregory a false pope. With lighter measures having failed, Gregory threatened the German Emperor with excommunication. This was no idle threat. Excommunication could result in a de facto deposition since God-fearing subjects would be reticent to serve an apostate emperor. Henry IV would not be warned. Haughtily, he announced these words to the representative of the Church: *"I am to be judged by God alone and am not to be deposed for any crime unless—may it never happen—I should deviate from the faith."* Gregory met scorn with scorn. He excommunicated the Emperor from the pale of the Church and absolved all of his subjects from their allegiance to him.

With his country in revolt, the Emperor was forced to back down and abase himself before the pope. In that famous scene outside the castle of Canossa in northern Italy, the Holy Roman Emperor Henry IV prostrated himself before Gregory and besought forgiveness for his rash actions. When forgiveness had been received and his country once again set in order, the Emperor showed his gratitude to Gregory by sending an army against Rome. He forcibly removed Gregory his seat in St. Peter's and installed a new pope. Gregory died a few months later, weary in soul and sad in heart. Thus had the controversy over lay investiture begun in Germany and Italy.

In England, Anselm was more fortunate than Gregory had been. His resistance to William Rufus' policies led to a voluntary exile, but through it all he managed to keep his position as archbishop and continue his theological writings. He developed a theory of Christ's substitutionary atonement to be published in the book *Cur Deus Homo* (Why God Became Man).

When Henry I (the grandfather of Thomas Becket's Henry) succeeded his brother William Rufus to the throne, he invited Anselm back to England, needing the archbishop's support against his older brother Robert Curthose. But if Henry I had known what was best for his interests, the invitation would never have been issued. Robert Bartlett writes:

> *During his exile Anselm absorbed the more radical demands of the reformers, including their objection to the practice of ecclesiastics doing homage to lay people, even kings. Hence it was that when Rufus's successor, Henry I, invited the archbishop to return to England in 1100, there was, instead of the anticipated settlement and reconciliation, a dispute in which much deeper issues of principle were raised.*

Anselm no longer simply objected to the king appointing bishops; he also objected to the king receiving homage from any member of the Church.

After several years of harsh conflict and a second exile for Anselm, a compromise was finally reached. The king was not allowed to choose ecclesiastics or invest them with their spiritual authority. He could, however, receive homage from them for the lands that were attached to their benefice. Neither archbishop nor king was entirely pleased with the arrangement. It was a makeshift settlement that would last only half a century.

Anselm had peace for two years after his settlement with Henry I, tending to his duties as archbishop and continuing the written outpourings of one of the best minds in Europe. He died in 1109, and interestingly enough, it was Archbishop Thomas Becket who, fifty-four years later, requested that Anselm be canonized as a saint. Perhaps he knew how much he owed to the man who had come before him.

Anselm, in many ways, showed just as much courage and stubbornness as Thomas Becket would, defying the sons of William the Conqueror and standing up for the rights of the Church against two kings of England. But because his last breath was not spilled out in blood on the flagstones of Canterbury, his stand is less memorable. History loves a martyr. A seventy-six-year-old bishop who died in his bed is a little more prosaic.

SOURCE

Bartlett, Robert. *England under the Norman and Angevin Kings 1075-1225*. New York: Oxford University Press, 2000.

THE HISTORY THAT NEVER HAPPENED: GEOFFREY OF MONMOUTH

BY ROSANNE E. LORTZ

WHAT'S THE PROPER RATIO OF FACT TO FICTION? IT'S A COMMON DISCUSSION among writers of historical fiction. Some authors feel bound to honor every known fact and only invent material where the historical record is silent. Others use history as a rough guideline and let their imaginations run wild. Some sit solidly on the historical side of the spectrum while others fly their flag more freely in the opposing field of fiction.

But in both cases, historical novelists' books meet the requirements of their genre. They are, to a greater or lesser degree, inspired by and based on the actual events of history, but no one mistakes them for history itself. No one looks for historical novels in the nonfiction section of the bookstore.

Geoffrey of Monmouth lived in the twelfth century, an age where distinctions like history and historical fiction had yet to be drawn. His book, *The History of the Kings of Britain*, traced the history of Britain from its alleged establishment by Brutus to the arrival of the Saxons some two thousand years later. It drew from previous historical records like Gildas' *On The Destruction and Conquest of Britain* and Bede's *The Ecclesiastical History of the English People*, but it also incorporated a great deal of material from the fertile ground of Geoffrey's own imagination.

In one chapter Geoffrey would recount well-researched events like Julius Caesar's foray into Britain. In another he would discuss King Arthur's plans to attack *"Leo, the Emperor of the Romans."* Geoffrey's *History* is one of the most colorful accounts of the early Middle Ages; it is also one of the most unhistorical accounts to ever be written.

William of Newburgh, a fellow chronicler writing less than half a century after Geoffrey's death, had this critique to offer:

> It is quite clear that everything this man wrote about Arthur and his successors, or indeed about his predecessors from Vortigern onwards, was made up, partly by himself and partly by others, either from an inordinate love of lying, or for the sake of pleasing the Britons.

Not all the chroniclers were as discerning as William of Newburgh, however. Some of them, like William, panned Geoffrey's work vociferously, but others saw it as a valuable source, borrowing from it and embedding his legends in the fabric of popular English history.

Today's historians put little stock in anything *The History of the Kings of Britain* has to say. Historian and translator Lewis Thorpe notes that:

> *the* History of the Kings of Britain *rests primarily upon the life-history of three great men: Brutus, grandson of Aeneas; Belinus, who sacked Rome; and Arthur, King of Britain. This particular Brutus never existed; Rome was never sacked by a Briton called Belinus; and Geoffrey's Arthur is far nearer to the fictional hero of the later Arthurian romances...than to the historical Arthur....*

And yet, despite its historical inaccuracies, Geoffrey of Monmouth's book went on to influence hundreds of writers and provide enjoyment for readers across the ages. The courtly love poets of the next century drew from his work when they wrote on "the matter of Britain." William Shakespeare took the stories of Lear and Cymbeline, two British kings described by Geoffrey, and penned some of the world's greatest plays. Tennyson crafted his epic *Idylls of the King* in part from the flesh that Geoffrey had added to the few facts earlier historians had recorded about Arthur.

Geoffrey of Monmouth is mostly remembered for being a very bad historian, but perhaps what he should be remembered for is being a very good storyteller. If only poor Geoffrey of Monmouth had lived in a later century. If only poor Geoffrey of Monmouth had known enough to market his book as historical fiction instead of history.

SOURCE

Geoffrey of Monmouth. *The History of the Kings of Britain.* Trans. Lewis Thorpe. London: Penguin Books, 1966.

ROMANISING THE CELTIC CHRISTIAN CHURCH

By ARTHUR RUSSELL

T HE TWIN TWELFTH CENTURY ABBEYS OF MELLIFONT AND BECTIVE IN IRELAND WERE founded by the Cistercian Order as a major part of a process to bring the Celtic Church into line with Roman practices. The need for this arose from the fact that the Celtic Church had evolved significantly differently in several respects over the centuries since Ireland, which had never been subjected to Imperial Roman conquest, was Christianised during the fifth century.

The Roman Briton Bishop Patrick, who started his mission to Christianise Ireland in 432 A.D., is popularly credited with Ireland becoming *"the island of Saints and Scholars"* over the next two centuries. Those centuries coincided with the barbarian invasions of Continental Europe which ushered in the so-called Dark Ages that almost destroyed European learning and culture which had developed over the previous millennium in Greece and in Imperial and early Christian Rome.

CHAOS IN EUROPE—AN IRISH SOLUTION

The chaos of fifth and sixth century Europe contrasted sharply with the peace of Ireland. This meant that the island became a repository for Christian learning and scholarship. This period of history is considered a "Golden Age" which positioned Ireland to become the wellspring of renewal and regeneration for Britain and Europe in the aftermath of the barbarian invasions. Located so far west in the Atlantic Ocean, Ireland escaped the attention of Goths, Visigoths, Vandals, Huns, Franks, Jutes, Saxons, Angles and other pagan tribes who swept through what was left of the failing Roman Empire which had dominated Europe for so long and under whose shadow the Christian Church had grown and developed since the reign of the Emperor Constantine.

This happy circumstance allowed Ireland to "give back" to Europe what it had received from Patrick. The process of European re-Christianising began in Scotland where Colmcille established a monastic settlement on the island of Iona that went on to establish further daughter houses in Britain, the most notable of which was Lindisfarne on the north-eastern coast of England.

Further afield in Continental Europe, Irish missionaries such as Columbanus (in France and Italy), Killian (in Southern Germany), and Gallen (in Switzerland) were prime movers in proselytizing the new peoples who had settled across Europe. As they traversed from one district to the next, the missionaries established monasteries and centres of learning and religion, some of which still survive: Luxueil (in France), Bobbio (in Italy), St. Gallen (in Switzerland). The record of their visitations is recalled in place-names, churches, and shrines scattered throughout western Europe. Most institutions of learning of the day, all over Europe were likely to have one or more Irish scholars on their academic staffs.

Irish monasteries became a focus for students and scholars from Britain and the Continent who came to them to be educated in relative peace and stability.

One noted Irish academic, Johannes Scotus Eriugena (which means "John born in Ireland), lived from 817 to 877 A.D and was considered the foremost scholar of the Carolingian era. His writings and theories made significant contribution to the development of late medieval and modern philosophy and theology. (Johannes Scotus propounded the seemingly contradictory but thought-provoking theory that: Authority is the source of knowledge, but reason of mankind is the norm by which all authority is justified. Such an idea was never likely to sit well with an authoritarian Church that was then beginning to recover its position of power and influence across the Continent!)

THE ROMAN CHURCH'S "IRISH PROBLEM"

Problems arose when the Roman Church began to reassert itself as Europe finally emerged from the Dark Ages, finding itself at odds with what it saw to be different and peculiarly Celtic practices. While there were no fundamental conflicts in the area of teaching and doctrines, there were differences in the way religious practice had diverged between the Celtic Church and the re-emerging Roman Church. The most striking differences were in monastic discipline, where Celtic rule was seen as being noticeably harsher than the Roman system as developed by the likes of the Cistercian Order. Other differences, such as the timing of Easter, took quite a long time to resolve and were not without their share of dispute and controversy.

The following quotation from a letter sent by one of the earliest Irish missionaries, Columbanus, to the Pope, discussing these differences, is revealing:

> We Irish, though dwelling at the far ends of the earth, are all disciples of St.
> Peter and St. Paul.... We are bound to the Chair of Peter, and although Rome
> is great and renowned, through that Chair alone is she looked on as great
> and illustrious among us.... On account of the two Apostles of Christ, you are
> almost celestial, and Rome is the head of the whole world, and of the Churches.

The letter describes the Pope as "Lord and Father in Christ", the "Chosen Watchman", and the "First Pastor, set higher than all mortals."

What this shows is that Columbanus, never the most patient of men when it came to his own missionary work, was prepared, to some extent at least, to bow to what he saw as the ultimate authority of Rome. But many of his activities and letters also show that Columbanus was always ready to argue the Celtic point of view in matters ecclesiastic, with local bishops and even with the Pope himself.

At that early stage, with so much to be done to re-establish the Church in Europe, pragmatism prevailed on both sides of various disputes. Both Celtic and Roman systems managed to coexist and even to accommodate each other. However, Rome was never going to allow such diversity in Christendom to continue indefinitely—that, coupled with the fact that the influence of the Celtic Church in Britain and on the Continent was suffering decline due to the Viking invasions of Britain and Ireland which were increasing during the early eighth century. It meant that the Celtic Church was by then under considerable stress which resulted in a much reduced flow of scholars and teachers from Ireland and Scotland to man their English and European religious foundations.

The disruption caused by Viking attacks also meant that the Celtic Church was effectively isolated from and beyond the reach of the now resurgent Roman Church which was a dominant influence on the establishment of the feudal system in Europe. Under these circumstances, the Celtic Church demonstrated an increasing level of independence in adopting existing and new directives from Rome, which was the cause of great concern there. As the end of the first millennium approached, Rome's desire to standardise practice across Christendom increased.

During the ninth and tenth centuries, Britain had become a front line of sorts in the "war" between the two competing Church traditions, with the added element that Canterbury desired to increase its influence over territories (including Ireland), which it saw as part of its domain.

The normalising of religious practice in Ireland was always going to take much longer to resolve than in Britain. It was not until a Synod held during the iconic year of 1111 A.D. in Rath Breasail in the Irish midlands that the Celtic Church made the significant move of establishing the Roman diocesan system. Here the country was divided into the twenty dioceses that have substantially survived until the present.

Three further Synods during the twelfth century removed most of the remaining differences in practice, so that by the time of the issue of the Papal Bull "Laudabiliter" by Pope Adrian IV in 1152, during the reign of King Henry II, the Roman Church's "Celtic problem" was well on the way to be resolved.

Note: After the Norman invasion of 1169, "Laudabiliter" was used to confer dubious Church and Papal sanction and legitimacy on the claim to Ireland by the Angevin King. (It was always Politics, stupid!)

THE CISTERCIANS IN IRELAND—AGENTS OF CHANGE

These Synods, along with the influence of the Cistercian Order, who had established themselves in Mellifont, and later in Bective in the Kingdom of Meath can be credited with making a significant contribution to bring the two church traditions together. In 1139, Bishop Malachy Ó'Morgair from Armagh visited St. Bernard in Clairvaux, France, on his way to visit Pope Innocent II, and was so impressed by the life of the Cistercians that he asked the Pope's permission to join that community.

The Pope regarded Malachy's reforming work of the Irish Church to be of much higher importance and would not allow him to do this. On his way back from Rome,

Malachy left some of his travelling companion clerics to be trained as Cistercians and sent more clerics from Ireland to join them after he arrived home. After a period of training, Bernard sent a mixed group of French and Irish Cistercians from Clairvaux to Ireland in 1142 under the leadership of a monk called Gillacríst O'Conarchy, who was duly appointed the first Irish Cistercian abbot.

Years later, Malachy died in Clairvaux while travelling from Rome and was buried with his friend Bernard in the French mother-house where their bones are still venerated, after both men were canonised as saints by the Pope.

Back in Ireland, many Gaelic chieftains were happy to invite the Cistercians to establish houses in their territories and generously endowed them with lands and houses. So by the time of the Norman invasion of Ireland in 1169, there were ten Cistercian houses scattered all over the island. After the invasion, more Cistercian houses would continue to be established in both Gaelic and Norman controlled territories during the second half of the twelfth and thirteenth century, with the support of whoever ruled in each area.

BECTIVE ABBEY

The first Cistercian foundation in Ireland had been built at Mellifont in 1142. The first daughter house was established in 1147 with the support of the King of Meath, Murchad MacLochlainn. This impressive foundation was located on the banks of the River Boyne, close to the ancient Hill of Tara, the ancient seat of the High Kings of Ireland.

After Meath was conquered and occupied by the Norman invaders, both Mellifont and Bective were firmly in Norman territory and in the Norman sphere of influence. This meant that they were recipients of support and funds from the new power who was now the Lord of Meath, the Norman baron, Sir Hugh deLacy. After deLacy was killed by an Irish workman at Durrow in 1186, there was an unseemly dispute between the Cistercian monasteries of Durrow and Bective about where his mortal remains should be buried.

After nine years of disputation, Bective temporarily won the privilege to have Hugh's body buried in its grounds in 1195, while his head was buried in the Abbey of St. Thomas in Dublin, another Cistercian abbey that was also a recipient of deLacy patronage during his life. Subsequently and finally, the body was taken from Bective to be reunited with the head in St. Thomas'.

In subsequent centuries, the Abbot of Bective came to have considerable status at both political and ecclesiastical level and was an *ex officio* spiritual lord of Parliament.

Bective continued as a Cistercian house until King Henry VIII suppressed all monasteries in the early sixteenth century. After this, the monastery building was turned into a fortified mansion by Thomas Agard, the civil servant who took over its lease. The possessions of the abbey at the time of its dissolution included 1600 acres of land, a water mill, and a fishing weir on the nearby River Boyne.

It was the end of an era.

KNIGHTS TEMPLAR:
BANKING AND SECRECY

By SCOTT HOWARD

THE KNIGHTS TEMPLAR MERGED THE IDEAL OF A KNIGHT WITH THE MONASTIC LIFE. They observed the hours of service in the same fashion as monks but relaxed those duties during times of war. However, these warrior monks had their hands in more than just warfare and ecclesiastical duties—they were merchants, landowners, and bankers. And running hard on the heels of their banking innovations, a system of secure communication and codes developed, demonstrating a sophisticated military intelligence network.

Pilgrimage to the Holy Land was fraught with danger. Bandits preyed on the faithful as an easy source of income as most pilgrims would not have the funds to hire a personal army. Modern travelers use a combination of cash, debit, and credit cards (not all in one purse or wallet) when they travel to spread the risk in case of theft—the wisest course. There were no banks, ATMs, or credit cards during the Crusades or along the pilgrimage routes. Of course not. Or does history prove our ill-conceived notions wrong?

Historical fact is indeed stranger than fiction. The Knights Templar were pioneers in more than just their unique role as that of warrior monks; they developed a system of banking, complete with a shadow of the system of checking accounts and credit cards that we enjoy today. As mentioned before, the Templars were landowners and merchants; moreover, they received donations in the form of land and coin from wealthy nobles and monarchs but were exempt from paying taxes and homage to any earthly person, save the Pope. Their wealth grew from their humble beginning as their star rose. As a consequence, banking became another revenue stream and a safer means of travel for pilgrims.

The revenues from their estates funded their operations in Outremer, and they had become savvy in business and even owned a fleet of ships to transfer goods, people, soldiers, and gold to the Holy Land. *Temple of Mysteries* tell us that as a direct result of this:

> *The Order also had to develop a sophisticated financial and banking operation. Money raised by its estates had to be transmitted to the "sharp end"—the Holy Land. As the Templars developed a reputation for the secure transfer of funds, the demand grew for them to do the same on behalf of pilgrims and other travellers. From this developed a system of credit, so that a pilgrim could deposit funds at a Templar preceptory in his home country, and then draw goods and services from other Templar houses along his route. And so, in effect, the Templars invented the principles of the modern chequebook and credit card.*

The banking service was not free, but most pilgrims found this method a better alternative than traveling with one's life savings. But what about fraud? Where there is innovation, thieves search for ways around the system, however, these red-crossed monks and savvy bankers knew a little about secrecy:

> The other consequence of the banking operations came from a demand for secure communications. As can be seen from today's credit card crimes, a move away from hard cash is open to fraud and forgery—how, for example, could one Templar house be sure that a document presented to them really did come from another Templar house on the other side of Europe? The knights therefore developed a system of codes, both for identification and for the safe passing of information. This system of banking required deposit and withdrawal information, which was secured by coded ciphers—its ancillary effects led to a sophisticated network of information exchange from one preceptory to another, chiefly military intelligence.

The Knights Templar were more than just knights following a strict monastic rule. They were also bankers who developed codes, networks, contacts, and an almost unhealthy obsession with privacy—some would call it conspiracy. It is this devotion to secrecy that allows the facts and their legend to endure.

SOURCE

Temple of Mysteries (2010-12-01). *The Knights Templar* (Kindle Locations 534-538; 541-544). Temple of Mysteries. Kindle Edition.

KNIGHTS TEMPLAR: CULTURE AND MINDSET

By SCOTT HOWARD

THE KNIGHTS TEMPLAR HELD FAST TO THE VOWS OF POVERTY, CHASTITY, AND OBEDI-ence. Austerity was the hallmark of their lives, and they even went as far as disavowing their families and loved ones when they joined the order. Fellow knights in this fraternity were referred to as brethren, effectively creating a strict, yet rather large extended family that followed The Rule. Charles G. Addison writes that:

> The rule enjoins severe devotional exercises, self-mortification, fasting, and prayer, and a constant attendance at matins, vespers, and on all the services of the church, "that being refreshed and satisfied with heavenly food, instructed and stablished with heavenly precepts, after the consummation of the divine mysteries," none might be afraid of the fight, but be prepared for the crown.

Among the many restrictions of the 72-chapter Rule, feminine contact was strictly forbidden!

However, there was a reasoning to what modern people would call this madness. In addition to receiving constant training, a newly-inducted Knight Templar was stripped of all vestiges of his former life. One would be "broken down", then remade into the Templar mold. Looking back to the preceding quote, the harshness of their lives and how they lived as brothers served to create a culture that resulted in fearlessness in battle, unity of mind, order, and obedience, even unto death where they would receive their heavenly crown.

These well-disciplined soldiers could be likened to the present day U.S. Navy SEALS or the British SAS based on their military bearing and quiet confidence—soldiers who have been remade for a specific purpose.

> An eye-witness of the conduct of the Templars in the field tells us that they were always foremost in the fight and the last in the retreat; that they proceeded to battle with the greatest order, silence, and circumspection, and carefully attended to the commands of their Master.

Moreover, concerning a Templar who had been captured by Saladin around 1180 A.D., Charles G. Addison provides some illumination of the brotherhood's proud culture:

> Saladin offered Odo de St. Amand his liberty in exchange for the freedom of his own nephew, who was a prisoner in the hands of the Templars; but the

Master of the Temple haughtily replied, that he would never, by his example, encourage any of his knights to be mean enough to surrender, that a Templar ought either to vanquish or die, and that he had nothing to give for his ransom but his girdle and his knife. The proud spirit of Odo de St. Amand could but ill brook confinement; he languished and died in the dungeons of Damascus, and was succeeded by Brother Arnold de Torroge, who had filled some of the chief situations of the order in Europe.

But these formidable knights were still constrained by human limitations. There were harsh consequences for cowardice or even having its appearance. Breaking faith on the field of battle brought disunity and disorder, potentially poisoning the ranks. Offenders were shunned and penance was meted:

If any one of them should by chance turn back, or bear himself less manfully than he ought, the white mantle, the emblem of their order, is ignominiously stripped off his shoulders, the cross worn by the fraternity is taken away from him, and he is cast out from the fellowship of the brethren; he is compelled to eat on the ground without a napkin or a table-cloth for the space of one year; and the dogs who gather around him and torment him he is not permitted to drive away. At the expiration of the year, if he be truly penitent, the Master and the brethren restore to him the military girdle and his pristine habit and cross, and receive him again into the fellowship and community of the brethren.

It took a special breed to become a Knight Templar; you were stripped of all earthly trappings, yet your induction into the order gave you entrance into a unique brotherhood. There was strict adherence to one's religious duties, The Rule, and you had to be fearless unto death. Capture meant that you would likely die imprisoned as surrender was not an option. Additionally, feminine contact, whether romantic or filial was anathema. However, for those that embraced this band of brothers and their ideals, history is not lacking in tales of their sacrifices; modern special operations groups have too many similarities to say that the legacy and military culture of the Knights Templar has ever died.

SOURCE

Addison, Charles G. (2012-01-17). *The History of the Knights Templars, the Temple Church, and the Temple.* Kindle Locations 339-342; 1094-1096; 1099-1103; 1160-1165. Kindle Edition.

KNIGHTS TEMPLAR: ORGANIZATIONAL STRUCTURE

By SCOTT HOWARD

LIKE ANY WELL-OILED MODERN MILITARY MACHINE, THE KNIGHTS TEMPLAR HAD A hierarchy comprised of members that served various functions. For every soldier that entered the field of battle there were support personnel that managed finances, coordinated shipments of material and troops, and performed clerical duties.

Alas, not every member could wear the white mantle with the red cross and spur his destrier to glory or wield a sword and lance in the thick of battle. Some had to manage the organization, cook, or tend to the horses and their diverse needs. The lowliest grooms had to muck out stalls for certain!

At the top rung of this hierarchy was the Grand Master—a title which evokes those comical images of older men wearing strange hats with tassels. However, the Grand Master was a lofty position that came with great responsibility. One had to have risen through the ranks and proven himself in battle to be elected into this position. Temple of Mysteries says that, *"The Grand Master in Jerusalem was in overall, autocratic charge. He was elected by a 'college' made up of 13 senior knights, representing (it is said) Jesus and his disciples."* The preceding quote underscores how important they believed this position was, owing to the mystical references to Jesus and the twelve disciples.

The knights who wore the white mantle emblazoned with the red cross comprised about 10% of the fighting force while the rest of the members had non-military functions or duties that were less than glorious. The ranks of this order were as follows:

Knights: free men of noble birth who wore the white mantle and red Templar cross.

Sergeants (a rank invented by the Templars): free men of lower class who acted as men-at-arms and sentries. The sergeants wore a black or brown mantle emblazoned with the red cross.

Clerics and chaplains: the priests of the Order, who also acted as scribes and record-keepers.

Of these general ranks there were certain titles and positions of authority that were held. Temples and preceptories scattered across Europe and the Holy Land had their own unique organizational structures that fulfilled the localized needs. There were marshals, regional commanders, provincial masters, and seneschals.

Imagine a medieval estate with its army of people ensuring smooth management and then you get an idea of the variety of faces and functions that populate the organization. An army requires cooks, blacksmiths, grooms, armorers, priests, surgeons, and so on—the list quickly becomes endless. Additionally, the order built fortresses and preceptories around Europe which required craftsmen to build and maintain.

Moreover, how could these men of European extraction survive and prosper the way they did without knowledge of the land, language, and customs? For this reason they employed Turcopoles who were savvy in language and were highly aggressive warriors. Temple of Mysteries says:

> *Perhaps surprisingly, the majority of the Templar army was actually made up of warriors of Arab extraction, often of mixed Arab and European blood—Turcopoles, who were familiar with the Saracens' ways of warfare. For this reason the Order employed many Arab interpreters.*

Owing to their far-reaching military and organizational structure and the fact that the Knights Templar rendered allegiance solely to the Pope, they effectively were a country operating within and without borders. The idea of this group operating as a "fifth column" does not seem so far-fetched, thus making them ripe for all manner of speculation concerning their true mission. So are the conspiracies and the games and books they spawned true?

SOURCE
Temple of Mysteries (2010-12-01). *The Knights Templar*. Kindle Locations 599-609. Temple of Mysteries. Kindle Edition.

HENRY II AND THE RULE OF LAW

By CHRISTY ENGLISH

HENRY II FOUGHT THROUGHOUT HIS REIGN TO CONSOLIDATE CONTROL INTO THE monarchy's hands and to extend the king's peace.

When he took the throne in 1154, England had been at war for almost two decades as Stephen the Usurper and Mathilda of Normandy fought for the English throne. It was Henry II who at the age of nineteen finally settled this question, defeating Stephen in a decisive battle during the same summer when Stephen's son and heir died of a fever.

Needless to say, during the twenty years of civil war, the king's peace was more than broken. It was crushed, along with many villages, people, and crops. By the time Henry II took the throne in December of 1154, England was desperately in need of the king's peace. At first, this peace only extended to the room the king was in: if you drew your sword in anger in the king's presence, your life was forfeit.

During Henry II's reign, for the first time since the Norman invasion, the king's peace began to extend beyond his presence. Henry worked to make sure that if the king's peace was broken anywhere in England, secular law would deal with the culprit. This was seen as power-mongering among his barons, but for the peasants of England, the king's peace meant that if someone was raped or killed or brutalized, they or their loved ones had legal recourse.

Henry II's famous conflict with Thomas Becket stemmed from this concern over the rule of law. When Thomas was Henry's chancellor, he worked along with him to strengthen law in England. But once he was made Archbishop of Canterbury, his loyalties were with the Church and Rome.

When a priest, even a layman, committed a crime, he was not charged in the secular courts but in an ecclesiastical one. This meant that any priest could rape or kill with complete impunity, because often ecclesiastical courts chose to look the other way when dealing with errant priests.

Henry II fought long and hard over this issue, but his work hit a setback with the death of Thomas Becket in December of 1170. As difficult as the unruly archbishop had been, once Becket was martyred, Henry lost the moral high ground. Forced to do penance for Thomas' murder in 1174, Henry spent the rest of his reign fighting his sons for control the empire he had built.

In spite of the end of his reign, Henry II did the most of any other Norman king to further the rule of law in England. We remember him most for his family conflicts, but perhaps we should remember him for his love of the law instead.

Understanding the Archbishop: Thomas Becket and the Case of the Criminous Clerks

By Rosanne E. Lortz

Thomas Becket is known far and wide as the archbishop who wrangled with England's Henry II and ended up being slain in the church at Canterbury. Although most consider Becket's murder a deplorable event, historical opinion is divided over whether Becket was in the right in the first place. Did he really have any justification for standing in Henry's way? Was he not simply quibbling over minutiae and defending an indefensible position?

The place that I will pick up in the story is just after Henry finagled matters so that Becket could become the Archbishop of Canterbury. Previously, Becket had been Henry's royal chancellor and had proved his usefulness and loyalty to the king time and again. But within the month of his election as archbishop, he resigned his position as royal chancellor. It was a move he did not have to make. In the king's mind, Becket could have retained both positions without any conflict of interest. Becket thought otherwise. This resignation of the chancellorship was the first manifestation that he was not the king's man any longer.

Those inside of Becket's household began to see a change in their master. John of Salisbury wrote that, *"Upon his consecration he immediately put off the old man, and put on the hairshirt of the monk, crucifying the flesh with its passions and desires."* No longer was his house a scene of Epicurean delights. The gold was gone from the tables. The fare was frugal and spare. Becket also took seriously his liturgical duties. He performed the office of the sacraments with all the reverence that was required but that had never been expected of him. He withdrew as often as he could into prayer and study in order that he might be better equipped for his office of teacher and pastor.

Right away the pulpit of Canterbury resounded with a new voice, a voice powerful and persuasive, the like of which had not been heard since the days of Archbishop Anselm. The chronicler Roger of Pontigny gives us a taste of Becket's preaching:

> It happened at that time in certain crowded gathering that Thomas delivered
> a sermon to the clergy and people in the presence of the king. His sermon con-
> cerned the kingdom of Christ the Lord, which is the Church, and the worldly
> kingdom, and the powers of each realm, priestly and royal, and also the two
> swords, the spiritual and the material. And as on this occasion he discussed
> much about ecclesiastical and secular power in a wonderful way—for he was

very eloquent—the king took note of each of his words, and recognizing that he rated ecclesiastical dignity far above any secular title, he did not receive his sermon with a placid spirit. For he sensed from his words how distant the archbishop was from his own position.

Becket had changed, and not—in Henry's mind—for the better.

The first open dispute between archbishop and king was over money. Traditionally, all of the manors and churches in an English county would pay small sums to support the local sheriffs in their own area. These sheriffs were the king's men, but they also provided the people with security and protection from regional bandits and extortionists. In July of 1163, Henry decided to divert this tax money away from the local government and into the moneybags of the royal exchequer.

Although this plan affected lay folk as well as clergy, Becket was the only one out of all the barons and bishops to protest. Roger of Pontigny records that he rose to his feet and spoke to Henry before all the council of the realm:

> *Lord, it does not become your excellence to deflect something that belongs to another to your use, especially when these two shillings are conferred on your ministers not out of necessity or duty, but rather as a favour. For if your sheriffs conduct themselves peacefully and respectfully towards our men, we will indeed give freely. But if they do not we will not, nor can we be forced by law.*

The archbishop's tone was calm, but there was nothing calm about the king's reply. *"By the eyes of God, they will be enrolled immediately!"* Henry roared, meaning that the tax money would be recorded on the parchment rolls that keep an account of royal revenues. Then he berated the archbishop for taking a stand against him: *"You yourself well ought to assent to my wish in this regard."*

With formidable frankness, the archbishop shot back a reply: *"By the eyes by which you swear, never while I am living will they be given from my land."*

Near the time of this tax dispute, another conflict arose between Henry and Becket. The archbishop had excommunicated William of Eynsford, an influential landholder. The reason? Becket had appointed a clerk to preside over a vacant church on one of William's holdings. William had objected to the appointment and had expelled the clerk from his land. Frank Barlow summarizes the ensuing fray:

> *Thomas, without consulting or even notifying Henry, excommunicated William, who complained to the king. Henry, by means of a writ, ordered Thomas to absolve William. The archbishop replied that absolution, like excommunication, was a matter for him not for the king. Henry answered that it was a royal prerogative that tenants-in-chief should not be excommunicated without his consent. There was a blazing quarrel over this, and in the end Thomas gave way.*

One round to Becket, one round to Henry, and the third round still to come. These first two disputes reveal fairly clearly what lay at the heart of the quarrel between Church and king. The arguments over who would hold the Church's purse strings and who would wield her sword of excommunication were smaller pieces of the larger question: was the Church subservient to the crown? Could Henry ride roughshod over the ecclesiastical authorities simply because they dwelt in the land of which he was king? It is well to keep the heart of this quarrel in mind, for the next dispute, a dispute far more violent and publicized than the previous two, stirred up a whirlwind of accusations and obscurities that clouded the issue.

The next dispute was actually a series of cases that all involved a common thread. Men of the cloth were committing crimes. One clerk stole a silver cup from the church of his bishop; another clerk lay with a woman and then slew her father. The most famous of these cases was that of the canon Philip de Broi who was accused of killing a knight. In each of these cases, Henry wished to take the offending clergyman and try him for his offenses in the royal court.

Becket refused to allow this. It is not right, he contended, for a man of the Church to be judged in the court of the world. The Church will discipline her own. And moreover, if the king should punish a man for a crime that the Church had already disciplined, then he would wrong the man by punishing him twice for the same sin.

Henry took exception to this. The bishops were notoriously lenient in their correction of the criminous clerks, and the clerks seemed to become more notoriously lawless every year. Stricter measures must be had, and where better to enforce them than in his own courts? In the two previous disputes, Henry was acting on nothing stronger than his royal greed for gold and power, but in this dispute over the criminous clerks, Henry claimed to have tradition on his side.

Both William Rufus and Henry I had exercised considerable power over the affairs of the Church, and since his immediate predecessors had all been as power-hungry as he was, Henry could claim that English custom was on his side. The dictates of tradition are hard to deny, but Thomas refused to be swayed by them. Richard Mortimer writes that:

> The only legitimacy Henry II could allege for his demands in his conflict with archbishop Thomas Becket was that conferred by the custom of the realm, and to this Thomas's answer came readily: 'Christ did not say "I am custom", but "I am truth".'

Many in retrospect have derided Thomas for his stand on this issue. What could he have been thinking? Church historian Philip Schaff thanks God that the Reformation has given us *"a more just appreciation of the virtues and faults of Thomas Becket than was possible in the age in which he lived and died."* He goes on to say, *"To most of his countrymen, as to the English-speaking people at large, his name has remained the synonym for priestly pride and pretension, for an arrogant invasion of the rights of the civil estate."*

But such blanket condemnation of Becket's stance ignores the historical context surrounding the dispute. For decades, the kings of England, the Holy Roman Emperors, and other European potentates had been trying to insert their tentacles into the hierarchy of the church. Because bishops were landholders in their demesnes, they were insisting that they had the right to interfere with the Church's elections and appointments. As we saw in the second conflict between Henry and Becket, kings were going so far as to say that the Church must ask permission of the crown before wielding the sword of excommunication.

The relationship between Church and State had already rubbed raw in England and was chafing the backs of ecclesiastics and seculars all over Europe. When kings claimed the right to ordain and defrock the clergy as it pleased them, is it any wonder that the Church's response—that kings had no power whatsoever over the persons of the clergy—savored of the reactionary? By denying that Henry had the right to try clerks for their crimes, Becket believed that he was holding ground in a larger struggle. Instead of picking his battles, he was manning the walls against all attacks.

The events that follow the case of the criminous clerks are well known. Becket, for a time, stood *contra* Henry and, without the support of his fellow bishops, seemingly *contra mundum*. Eventually, he recanted his position and agreed to support the king's demands at Clarendon—until on second thought, he recanted his recantation, leading to his exile from England and his eventual return and martyrdom.

Becket's stance on the criminous clerks, taken out of context, seems a prime piece of folly. Did he really want men of the cloth to be able to get away with murder? But looked at in the light of the Church/State controversies throughout the previous century, it becomes a more understandable—though perhaps still misguided—step to take. Becket saw this as one more area where the king was trying to erode the power of the Church. His response was an over-reaction, but an over-reaction that occurred in the heat of battle. And when arrows and missiles are flying all around, it's not always easy for a man to rein his horse in the wisest direction.

SOURCES

Barlow, Frank. *Thomas Becket*. Berkeley: University of California Press, 1986.

Bartlett, Robert. *England under the Norman and Angevin Kings 1075-1225*. New York: Oxford University Press, 2000.

Schaff, Philip. *History of the Christian Church*, Vol. 5, The Middle Ages, A. D. 1049-1294. Grand Rapids, MI: William B. Eerdmans Publishing Co., 1907.

Staunton, Michael, trans. and ed., *The Lives of Thomas Becket*. NY: Manchester University Press, 2001.

A Different "Type" of History: Medieval Historiography and Thomas Becket

By ROSANNE E. LORTZ

ONE OF THE MOST STARTLING DIFFERENCES BETWEEN THE WAY MEDIEVAL HISTO-rians "did" history and the way modern historians do it is the medieval use of typology. Defined briefly, typology is the use of a real (historical) person, thing, or event as a metaphor for another real person, thing, or event.

Typology is the language of the Bible. Abraham's near-sacrifice of Isaac typifies—or prefigures, if you'd prefer a different word—God the Father's sacrifice of his son Jesus Christ. Jonah's three days in the belly of the whale typify the three days that Christ spent in the tomb.

Medieval historians, many of them monks and steeped in Scripture, were used to expressing themselves with the same language and ideas that they saw in the Biblical text. They evaluated historical personages, saw them in a Biblical framework, and drew typological connections for their readers' benefit. There was no strangeness to them in considering their historical king Alfred to have the same role as the Biblical king David—a ruler who typified Christ.

One of the beauties to be appreciated in the medieval historians is their subtlety in using this literary device. Most of their typological connections are hidden in the text, wrapped in allusion, and veiled with implicit metaphor.

They did not treat the reader like an obtuse child. They did not say: "Now, when Germanus came over to give the gospel to the pagan Britons, he was acting like a type of Christ, and we know this because...." No, rather they simply told the story, and told it in such a way that the reader (or at least the Scripture-literate reader) would make the connection himself.

Consider this example from Bede's *Ecclesiastical History of England*. In this passage, the bishop Germanus is coming across the English Channel to evangelize the Britons. A storm has arisen, threatening the safety of the ship:

> As it happened, their leader, the bishop, was worn out and fell asleep. Their champion having thus deserted his post (or so it seemed), the storm increased in fury and the ship, overwhelmed by the waves, was about to sink. Then St. Lupus and all the rest in their dismay awakened their leader so that

he might oppose the fury of the elements. More resolute than they in the face of frightful danger, Germanus called on Christ and in the name of the Holy Trinity took a little water and sprinkled it on the raging billows. At the same time he admonished his colleague and encouraged them all, whereupon with one consent and one voice they offered up their prayers. Divine help was forthcoming, the adversaries were put to flight, peace and calm followed, and the contrary winds veered round and helped them on their way.

Those conversant with the Scriptures will see the obvious allusion. Germanus, awakened from sleep by his "disciples", calms the wind and the waves just like Christ did in the Gospels. This parallel action (and not the voice of the narrator) tells us how we should think of Germanus—as a type of Christ.

In this subtlety, the medieval historians were mimicking the subtlety that the Bible itself often displays. In the Book of Acts, Luke does not tell us outright that Stephen in his martyrdom is a type of Christ.

Rather, he signals it to us by recording and emphasizing the last words of Stephen: *"Lord Jesus, receive my spirit,"* and *"Lord, do not charge them with this sin"* (Acts 7:59-60). These words closely echo the words of Christ on the cross, and thereby evoke (rather than simply tell) the typological connection.

This typological tradition of historiography continues on from Bede into the following centuries. One of the chroniclers of Archbishop Thomas Becket's life wrote this about the dispute between Becket and King Henry:

And when he [Henry II] continued to press, asking again and again if the archbishop of Canterbury would promise to observe his customs entirely, absolutely and without adding the exception of his order, he was unable to obtain what he wanted from the vicar of Christ [Becket]. Therefore the king was greatly troubled, and all Jerusalem with him, and in this heated mood he left London without notice, with all his business unfinished, and lawsuits left hanging.

Did you catch it? The line at the end that says, *"the king was greatly troubled, and all Jerusalem with him"*?

This allusion is a zinger of an accusation. By quoting Matthew 2:3 (*"When Herod the king had heard these things, he was troubled, and all Jerusalem with him."*), the historian lets us know more about Henry and his ambitions than he could have explained in ten pages of plain language. Henry is Herod, the enemy of the Messiah. All of the negative baggage that the name Herod carries is hereby transferred to Henry.

In the above passage, we see that Henry's enemy is in fact Thomas. This leads us to another typological connection: Herod's enemy was Christ, Henry's enemy is Thomas, and so Thomas represents Christ in this story. He is Christ's "vicar" in a very real sense.

The events surrounding the quotation in its original context also affect the text of the chronicle. What is the context of Herod being "troubled" in Matthew 2:3? It is when he sees the Magi—when they inform him that there is another King besides him. This is the same thing that troubles Henry. There is another King besides him in England, a King whom Becket is choosing to honor instead.

In the book of Matthew, Herod follows his agitation with action. He slaughters the innocents. This gives us an indication of how far Henry will go. He will not stop at murder to keep this other King from capturing the obedience of his kingdom.

I strongly doubt that medieval historians, when using these typological connections, considered them to be a mere literary device that they themselves had imposed on the story. To the writer of the above excerpt, Henry *was* Herod. Becket *was* Christ. The typological connections were not something that historians had to invent—they were already there, written into the real-life story and waiting to be discovered.

With the story seen through this typological framework, it would have made perfect sense to the chroniclers that when Becket returned from exile, there was a crowd waiting to greet him in England, throwing down their coats before him and shouting, *"Blessed is he who comes in the name of the Lord!"* His time of martyrdom must be preceded by a Triumphal Entry, even as Christ's was.

For modern historians, however, the similarities between Biblical and medieval accounts can create doubt as to the veracity of the medieval historians. Was Germanus really asleep in the boat during the storm, or was that just a convenient way for Bede to make the allusion to Christ? Did the English really shout, *"Blessed is he who comes in the name of the Lord!"* or did Becket's chroniclers ad lib some dialogue that fit the scene they wanted to depict?

That subject could be debated to good purpose and with interesting points from either side. But instead of questioning the accuracy of medieval historians, I find it far more interesting to ponder this question: did historical personages of this era see themselves as types of Biblical figures in the grand scheme of a divinely-ordained history?

Let me explain.... In one instance, when Becket is rebuking his fellow clergy members, he says, *"Who put a spell on you, foolish bishops?"* This is more than reminiscent of Paul's rebuke to the Galatians (cf. Galatians 3:1). He goes on to disparage them for serving man to the detriment of serving God: *"If an angel came down from the sky and gave me such advice I would curse it"* (cf. Galatians 1:8).

If the chronicler's quotation of Becket's words is accurate, it causes one to wonder—were these just convenient quotations to use, or did Becket see himself as a type of Paul, one who had formerly persecuted the Church as Henry's chancellor and was now her champion after a Road to Damascus experience?

Perhaps it was not just the medieval historians who were determined to draw typological connections. Perhaps the subjects they wrote about were determined to bring those connections about.

Perhaps Becket, who prophesied his own death before he returned to England, was determined to be a type of Christ. And perhaps the chroniclers, with all their typological language, were merely giving his actions their stamp of approval and acknowledging how successful his efforts had been.

SOURCES

Bede. *The Ecclesiastical History of the English People.* Edited and translated by Judith McClure and Roger Collins. New York: Oxford University Press, 1969.

Staunton, Michael, trans. and ed. *The Lives of Thomas Becket.* NY: Manchester University Press, 2001.

THE DUTIES OF A DEAD SAINT, OR THOMAS BECKET'S BUSY SCHEDULE AS A MARTYR

BY ROSANNE E. LORTZ

DECEMBER 29, 1170—THE DAY THAT ARCHBISHOP THOMAS BECKET MET HIS DEATH AT the hands of King Henry II's knights in the cathedral at Canterbury.

Within three years of his death he had been canonized (i.e. made a "saint") by the church. The speed with which he was canonized is telling—in a century where the church was careful only to canonize "legitimate" saints, it often took decades before a saint's holy life and post mortem miracles were documented and accepted as legitimate.

The new saint was also exceptional in gaining a multi-national following. Historian Thomas Head writes that Becket was such a "prominent" member of the saintly set that *"the date of his martyrdom...was annually commemorated all over Europe with special prayers and lessons, and often with special music as well."*

Head goes on to say that:

> *The standard office for Thomas's December feast day was evidently written soon after the canonization in 1173 by Benedict of Peterborough, a monk who belonged to the community of Christ Church, Canterbury, until 1177 and served as the first recorder of miracles at the saint's tomb.*

The readings in the Mass, interspersed between the complex antiphons, are as much a history lesson as a sermon, telling the story of Becket's disagreement with Henry, his exile, and his martyrdom.

The text of the Mass is interesting, not just because of what it tells us about Thomas Becket, but because of what it tells us about twelfth century Europe's veneration of the saints. Here is one of the responsorial readings:

> *O kind Jesus, through Thomas's merits, release us from our debts; watch over our home, city gate, and tomb; and arouse us from threefold death. Restore, by your wonted mercy, what we have lost by act, thought, or habit....*
>
> *Through Thomas's blood, O Christ, which he shed for thee, make us too to rise where he ascended.*

Note that the words, though they reference "Thomas's merits," are directed to Jesus. The medievals were entreating Christ to look upon Becket's supererogatory merit (deeds done over and above what is required for salvation) and apply it to their own accounts. Becket had gone above and beyond the call of duty, as it were, and his good conduct was something that the pious but not-quite-so-holy could take advantage of as they sought to measure up to the mark.

The popularity of Becket's feast day throughout Europe shows that there was a high regard for his "merits"...and for their effectiveness in being transferred to others. But besides celebrating the twenty-ninth of December, there was another even more effective way of seeking the help of the dead saint....

Every year, thousands of pilgrims congregated at Becket's tomb at Canterbury. There they sought a physical connection with the bones and long dried up blood of the martyr, and, while touching the relics of the saint on earth, beseeched him to intercede for them in heaven.

The medieval veneration for relics—a finger bone, a vial of dried up blood, a skull—is often confusing and faintly disturbing to moderns. But rather than being based on macabre superstition, it was actually rooted in the Christian doctrine of the bodily resurrection.

Becket's soul was in heaven with God. His body was here on earth. There was still a link between the two, for, at the end of time, Becket's body would be resurrected and reunited with his soul.

Because of this link, the pilgrims who came into contact with Becket's body had a connection with Becket's soul. Since the soul was in the presence of God, it could make intercession for them with the Almighty, for whom nothing is impossible. This is why the medievals believed that relics could produce miracles. (For a fuller discussion of this idea, see Peter Brown's *The Cult of the Saints: Its Rise and Function in Latin Christianity*.)

Thomas Becket spent eight long, weary years combating Henry II's program to erode the liberty of the church. In the end, he certainly did nothing to avoid the grisly death that awaited him, refusing to let the monks bar the door against the murderers and refusing to recant any of his past pronouncements in the face of four drawn swords. Perhaps he was tired of fighting. Perhaps he was ready for death.

But rather than entering a well-deserved rest in the afterlife, it seems that Becket's duties were only increased. Now, instead of having the cares of the see of Canterbury on his shoulders, he was inundated with the cares of Christians across Europe. When he put off this mortal flesh he put on the role of mediator between the ordinary Christian and the Christ enthroned in heaven. And if he truly was making intercession for each and every pilgrim who murmured a prayer beside his tomb, he would hardly have time for harp-strumming or taking it easy on a floating cloud.

In the twelfth century conception of things, Thomas Becket, the martyr, would find himself with a busier schedule than Thomas Becket, the Archbishop of Canterbury, ever had. For a medieval saint, death was only the beginning....

SOURCES

Brown, Peter. *The Cult of the Saints: Its Rise and Function in Latin Christianity.* Chicago: University of Chicago Press, 1981.

Head, Thomas, ed. and trans. *Medieval Hagiography: An Anthology.* New York: Routledge, 2001.

THE SONG OF DERMOT AND THE EARL

BY ARTHUR RUSSELL

THE STORY OF THE INVASION OF ENGLAND IN 1066 BY WILLIAM THE CONQUEROR IS graphically told in the Bayeux Tapestry. By any standard it was a total success from the perspective of the invader as England was brought under the sway of William and his Plantagenet successors. Just over a century later (1169), the descendants of the soldiers from Normandy who marched with William made their first landfall on the neighbouring island of Ireland. They also had conquest on their minds. Their story is told in a long narrative called *The Song of Dermot and the Earl* written in French by an unknown author. (It complements another version written by a cleric called Giraldus Cambrensis [Gerald of Wales] who accompanied King Henry II in 1171 during the first ever visit of a foreign monarch to Ireland.) The *Song* was translated into English and published by Goddard Henry Orpen in 1899 and is considered to be the definitive record of the Norman invasion and conquest of almost half of Ireland in the second half of the twelfth century.

As with the Bayeux Tapestry, the narrative is rather biased and written from the invaders' perspective, many of whom hailed from the Welsh marchlands and who could trace their ancestry to the Welsh Princess Nesta (1085-1136). Nesta was a notable beauty of her day and was sister of Gruffyd, the unconquered Prince of Wales, on whose head King Henry I had set "a mountain of gold". She was mother to numerous sons and daughters by various fathers (husbands as well as lovers, one of whom was King Henry himself). Nesta's sons and grandsons went on to feature prominently in the initial invasion force that landed at Bannow Strand in Wexford, Ireland in May 1169. Among the surnames represented in that group were Fitzgerald, FitzMaurice, FitzWilliam, FitzStephen, deBarry, names that went on to figure in a future Irish aristocracy. No wonder Nesta became known as *"the mother of the Invasion of Ireland"*. The invasion actually served as a useful outlet for an energetic and restive group of knights and barons from the Welsh marchlands who had a history of being hard to control and were not overly loyal to the Plantagenet monarchy.

The two heroes commemorated in *The Song of Dermot* are Dermot MacMurrough (the "rich king" of Leinster) and Richard deClare (Earl of Pembroke), now best remembered by his nickname "Strongbow".

Dermot MacMurrough is the man blamed for inviting the first Norman invaders to Ireland to help him win back the kingdom of Leinster, from which he had recently been expelled by the Irish Ard-Rí (High King) Rory O'Connor and his ally Tiernan O'Rourke. The *Song* is sympathetic to Dermot as indicated by this reference to him:

About King Dermot I will tell you;
In Ireland, at this day,
There was no more worthy king:
Very rich and powerful he was;
He loved the generous, he hated the mean.

THE NATIVE IRISH PERSPECTIVE OF DERMOT

By contrast, the Gaelic Irish view of Dermot is not at all flattering as described in the *Annals of the Four Masters,* written during the sixteenth century.

> *Diarmaid MacMurchadha, King of Leinster, by whom a trembly sod was made of all Ireland. After having brought over the Saxons, after having done extensive injuries to the Irish. After plundering and burning many churches, as Ceanannus* [Kells], *Cluain Irair* [Clonard], *died of an insufferable and unknown disease; for he became putrid while living, through the miracle of God, Columcille and Finian, and the other saints of Ireland, whose churches he had profaned and burned some time before;*
>
> *And he died at Fearnamor* [Ferns], *without making a will, without penance, without the body of Christ, without unction, as his evil deeds deserved.*

These surely are not the most Christian sentiments as articulated by the monk scribes.

The *Annals of Tigernach* further describes Dermot as *"the disturber and the destroyer of Banba"* (Banba is an old name for Ireland).

In truth, the altercation between Dermot and Ard-Rí Rory O'Connor in the late 1160s was just another of the endless wars, raids, and skirmishes of tribal kings and chieftains that were endemic in Ireland and its clan-based society since earliest history. What marked this particular altercation from all others was the fact that Dermot fled overseas to the court of King Henry II in Aquitaine to seek outside help and was given the King's blessing to look for whatever manpower he required from among his subjects. Dermot McMurrough would henceforth be remembered as the man who brought foreign invaders to Ireland, and things would never be the same again.

THE SONG OF DERMOT AND THE EARL—AN OBJECTIVE CHRONICLE?

The Song's view of the native Irish chiefs, kings, and people, especially those who resisted the invaders, is largely negative, to say the least, and certainly far from objective. It seemed the invaders fully expected the Irish to simply roll over and acquiesce to foreign interlopers who were aggressively intruding into their territories and way of life. Interestingly, those few Gaelic chieftains who formed alliances with and helped the invaders were deemed "wise", "loyal" and "brave"; while those who resisted were considered "treacherous" and "traitors".

In the area of propaganda, the native kings and chieftains were at serious disadvantage.

The Song of Dermot's author as well as Giraldus were better positioned to get their message across, in contrast to the perceived Gaelic "enemies" who were portrayed as being "uncivilized" and much less worthy. Even the Church of the day had a jaundiced view of certain aspects of the Celtic Church, something which Henry II had been commissioned by Pope Adrian IV (who coincidentally was also an Englishman) to resolve—once he had conquered the island.

It has to be remembered that like most European countries in the Middle Ages, Ireland did not have a national sense of itself. Irish nationalism would take centuries of occupation and outside exploitation to evolve. Lack of cohesion among the Irish therefore allowed the relatively better focused and single-minded invaders to exploit tribal and regional disputes as they went through the countryside. They had nothing to lose (except their lives, which they were determined and eminently able to preserve) and everything to gain (land and titles), all with the blessing of their King.

In this and subsequent incursions into Irish territories, the Normans were helped in no small measure by their superior arms and armour. The Norman way of fighting was something completely new in Ireland. Every armoured soldier was almost impregnable to lightly armed and armoured soldiers. This was especially true when fighting on open ground, which forced the Irish to increasingly resort to guerrilla tactics—something the Normans considered "unchivalrous".

AN INTERESTING INSIGHT INTO THE FIGHTING

The invading soldiers brought with them a number of camp followers including one called Alice of Abergavenny who accompanied her beau to Bannow. This man was killed in one of the earlier skirmishes, leaving Alice bereft and quite angry with those responsible for killing him. Part of her "revenge therapy" was to be allowed to behead 70 unfortunate enemy soldiers who had been captured in the same battle. (Tough ladies, those ladies from the Welsh marchlands! The Geneva Convention for prisoners did not apply as far as the "noble knights" or their ladies [wenches] were concerned!)

> *Of the Irish there were taken, quite as many as seventy.*
> *But the noble knights had them beheaded.*
> *To a wench they gave an axe of tempered steel,*
> *And she beheaded them all and threw their bodies over the cliff,*
> *Because she had that day lost her lover in the combat.*
> *Alice of Abergavenny was her name, who served the Irish thus.*

THE ARRIVAL OF "STRONGBOW"—HIS CAPTURE OF WATERFORD; HIS MARRIAGE TO AOIFE

The narrative describes the arrival of Earl Richard (Strongbow) and his role in the taking of the town of Waterford which had been established by Danish seafarers as a trading outpost on the south coast of Ireland two centuries before. After this important victory,

Dermot was happy to give his daughter Aoife to the Earl as a bride. The marriage took place in Waterford amid scenes of death and destruction following the attack, capture, and subsequent slaughter of Waterford citizens after Strongbow's forces broke into the city. The marriage of the Earl and Aoife was part of the bargain made to persuade Strongbow to help Dermot win back his kingdom—that and the promise of making his son-in-law heir to his title after his death. Of course Dermot had no right to do this according to existing Irish law, under which the succession should be decided by an election confined to designated members of the MacMurrough clan.

> When the earl by his power had taken the city,
> The earl immediately sent word to King Dermot by messenger
> That he had come to Waterford and had won the city;
> That the rich king should come to him and should bring his English.
> King Dermot speedily came there, be sure, right royally.
> The king in his company brought there many of his barons,
> And his daughter he brought there; to the noble earl he gave her.
> The earl honourably wedded her in the presence of the people.
> King Dermot then gave to the earl, who was so renowned,
> Leinster he gave to him with his daughter, whom he so much loved;
> Provided only that he should have the lordship of Leinster during his life.

KING HENRY II VISITS HIS NEW LORDSHIP

Later, the narrative describes the visit of King Henry to Ireland during the winter of 1171-72, when he effectively gave the invasion a permanence that was to last for over seven centuries. It unashamedly targeted the complete conquest of what he clearly considered his new kingdom, totally setting at nought the ancient rights of indigenous kings and chieftains, even the Ard-Rí himself. In doing this he was following a precedent set by his ancestor, William the Conqueror, after the battle of Hastings, a century earlier in England. His actions also helped establish the model for creating future colonies all over the world which, while it purported to "civilize" benighted and wayward peoples, was really more interested in rewarding and enriching the invading colonists as well as the mother country.

> Before the feast of St. Martin King Henry at length came to Ireland.
> With the king there crossed over vassals of good kindred.
> William the son of Audeline came with him on this occasion,
> Also Humphrey de Bohun, and the baron Hugh de Lacy.
> With the king himself there came the son of Bernard,
> Robert, I trow; a renowned baron came, Bertram de Verdun he was called;
> Earls and barons of great worth came in numbers with Henry.

FIXING CONQUESTS ALREADY MADE

During those winter months while he held court in Dublin, Henry confirmed his ownership of all the lands and cities that had already been conquered by the invading knight
adventurers. He had brought with him Sir Hugh deLacy and made him Constable of the
city of Dublin, to be henceforth considered the capital city of Ireland.

> Then the king summoned Hugh de Lacy, first of all,
> And his earls and his vassals and his free-born barons.
> The rich king then gave the custody of the city of Dublin
> And of the castle and the keep to the baron Hugh de Lacy,
> And Waterford, on the other hand, to the baron Robert the son of Bernard.
> The son of Stephen at this juncture was left at Dublin,
> And Meiler the son of Henry and Miles the son of David;
> With Hugh these were left by the command of King Henry.

DIRECTING THE NEXT PHASE—THE CONQUEST OF MEATH AND ULSTER

Having already fixed the conquered territories and cities of his new kingdom, Henry
immediately turned his attention to the territories that had yet to be conquered.

> To Hugh de Lacy he granted all Meath in fee.
> Meath the warrior granted for fifty knights
> Whose service the baron should let him have whenever he should have need of it.
> To one John he granted Ulster, if he could conquer it by force;
> John de Courcy was his name, who afterwards suffered many a trouble there.

The King obviously had high regard for Hugh deLacy and deCourcy as people who
could push the boundaries of the conquest further. Armed with Royal authority both of
these worthies spent the next few years making good on Henry's grants.

> Of Hugh de Lacy I shall tell you,
> How he enfeoffed his barons, Knights, serjeants, and retainers.
> Castle Knock, in the first place, he gave to Hugh Tyrrell, whom he loved so
> much;
> And Castle Brack, according to the writing, to baron William le Petit,
> Magheradernon likewise and the land of Rathkenny;
> The cantred of Ardnorcher then to Meiler, who was of great worth,
> Gave Hugh de Lacy to the good Meiler Fitz Henry;
> To Gilbert de Nangle, moreover, he gave the whole of Morgallion;
> To Jocelin he gave the Navan, and the land of Ardbraccan,
> (The one was son, the other father, according to the statement of the mother);
> To Richard Tuite likewise he gave a rich fief;
> Rathwire he gave moreover to the baron Robert de Lacy;

To Richard de la Chapelle he gave good and fine land;
To Geoffrey de Constantine Kilbixi near to Rathconarty;
And Skreen he then gave by charter to Adam de Phepoe he gave it;
To Gilbert de Nugent, and likewise to William de Musset,
He gave lands and honours, in the presence of barons and vavassours;
And to the baron Hugh de Hussey he then gave fair lands;
To Adam Dullard likewise the land of 'Rathenuarthi'.
To one Thomas de Craville he gave in heritage Emlagh Beccon
In quiet enjoyment, at the north east of Kells,
Laraghcalyn likewise, and Shanonagh, according to the people,
Gave Hugh de Lacy, know in sooth, to this Thomas.
Crandone then to a baron, Richard the Fleming was his name.
Twenty fiefs he gave him of a truth, if the geste does not deceive you.
A fortress this man erected in order to harass his enemies,
Knights and a goodly force he kept there, Archers, serjeants,
Likewise, in order to destroy his enemies.

THE SIEGE OF DUBLIN

Despite making his own submission to Henry and concluding the Treaty of Windsor in 1172 which should have guaranteed his position in the new scheme of things, the Ard-Rí was enraged to learn that his territories in Meath had been almost casually granted to deLacy. This determined him to resist. Rory managed, with great difficulty, to cobble a temporary alliance of chieftains to initiate a siege of Dublin which, while it did come close to dislodging the invaders, failed due to lack of cohesion on the Irish side coupled with remarkable determination and daring from the desperate defenders who succeeded in breaking out and scattering their protagonists.

IRISH RESISTANCE

The narrative tells that deLacy (in Meath) and deCourcy (in Ulster) did not have everything their own way as the native Irish resisted their planned systematic takeover of their lands. Their growing resistance meant that the conquest of Ireland was not completed as it ground to a halt during the fourteenth century.

Often he brought them from bad to worse.
But afterwards there came against him O'Carroll, who was king of Oriel,
And the rebel MacDunlevy of the region of Ulster;
O'Rourke was there, also, and the king Melaghlin.
Full twenty thousand at this time of the Irish came upon them.
Very fiercely they attacked them,
And the barons defended themselves so long as they could have.
Defence in the fortress;

But the Irish from all sides hurled their javelins and their darts.
The fortress indeed they destroyed and slew the garrison within;
But many were previously slain of the Irish of the northern districts.
In such manner, know ye all, was the country planted with castles and with cities,
With keeps and with strongholds.
Thus well rooted were the noble renowned vassals.

In reality, the Norman conquest was not completed and petered out into a kind of stalemate that resulted in Norman lords and Gaelic chieftains coexisting in dynamic tension with each other for the next four centuries. It can be speculated that this gave late medieval Ireland the worst of both worlds which prevented it from developing into a post-feudal nation as happened elsewhere in Europe. To a large extent, it influenced the direction of Irish history right down to the present.

ENGLAND AND THE CRUSADES

By HELENA P. SCHRADER

WHEN WE LOOK BACK ON THE CRUSADES, WE ARE MORE LIKELY TO THINK OF THE French, who dominated the Christian crusader kingdoms in "Outremer," than the English. Alternatively, we might think of the Germans, who contributed huge contingents of troops to the First, Second, Third, and Children's Crusades, not to mention that the Holy Roman Emperor Friedrich II was supposed to lead the Fourth Crusade and, having failed to show up for that, finally launched his own crusade, the Sixth Crusade. Meanwhile, the Spaniards were perpetually "on crusade" at home on the Iberian Peninsula, pushing back the "Moors."

By comparison, the English appear to have been conspicuously absent from crusading. Yet such an assessment is superficial and misleading. In fact, Plantagenet kings and vassals and English knights and nobles played key roles in the history of the crusades, while England, no less than the rest of the Western Europe, was significantly altered by the impact of the crusades.

HENRY II, HATTIN, AND THE SALADIN TITHE

The most famous of all English crusaders was, of course, Richard I, the "Lionheart," but we should not forget that his father too had taken a strong interest in the fate of the crusader kingdoms. His grandfather, Fulk d'Anjou had turned over his French inheritance to his son, Henry's father Geoffrey, in order to go to the Holy Land to marry the heiress of Jerusalem, Melisende. He was crowned King in Jerusalem in 1131 and ruled until his death in 1143. His sons by Melisende, Baldwin III and Aimery (or Amalric) I of Jerusalem, were thus Henry's uncles and Amalric's children, Baldwin IV and Sibylla were Henry's cousins. Two years before the fateful Battle of Hattin in 1187, Henry instituted a tax known as the "Saladin Tax" which was deposited in equal amounts with the Templars and Hospitallers to finance a future crusade. During Saladin's invasion of 1187, the Templars used the treasure Henry II had deposited with them to hire mercenaries, including some 200 knights. In consequence, 200 "English" knights fought at Hattin, although sources are unclear as to whether these knights were Englishmen, subjects of Henry Plantagenet, or simply knights financed by Henry II. Regardless of their exact nationality, two hundred knights out of a total of 1200 to 1500 is significant.

The portion of his treasure deposited with the Hospitallers, on the other hand, was used to buy the freedom of thousands Christians after the fall of Jerusalem. The terms of the surrender gave Christians 40 days to raise a ransom of ten dinars per man, five per woman, or two per child or otherwise face slavery. Balian d'Ibelin, who negotiated the surrender (after the walls had been breached!), knew that the city was flooded with refugees who could not possibly pay this ransom, so he also negotiated a "lump sum" payment of 30,000 dinars for (depending on source) eight to eighteen thousand paupers, and the Hospitallers provided the money from King Henry's deposits with them.

Thus, while Henry II did not personally take part in a crusade, he provided something arguably more important at this juncture in time—the means to outfit, transport, and sustain many other fighting men—and freedom for thousands of poor Christians, predominantly women and children, who would otherwise have been enslaved.

THE THIRD CRUSADE: 1189-1192

Significant as Henry II's contributions were, they pale beside those of his son. Although the Third Crusade was jointly led by the Holy Roman Emperor, Philip II of France, and Richard of England, its achievements can be attributed to Richard alone.

The Holy Roman Emperor, Friedrich Barbarossa, drowned before reaching Jerusalem, and most of his army turned back. Philip II, conscious (and jealous) of being in Richard's shadow, returned to France after the first victory of the campaign, the re-capture of Acre. But Richard stayed on, and it was his subsequent accomplishments that are so significant. The fact that the Third Crusade failed in the stated objective of re-capturing Jerusalem has misled many to see the crusade as a failure. Nothing could be further from the truth.

In 1191, when Richard I arrived in Outremer, the Kingdom of Jerusalem had virtually ceased to exist. The Kingdom, which had once reached beyond the Jordan and stretched along the Mediterranean coast from Beirut to Ascalon, had been reduced to the city of Tyre—and Tyre was beleaguered.

Not only had Jerusalem been lost, the important pilgrimage sites of Bethlehem and Nazareth were also in Saracen hands. Tiberius, Nablus, and Toron had fallen within days of the victory at Hattin, after which Saladin had taken the important coastal cities of Ascalon, Jaffa, Caesarea, Haifa, Acre, Sidon, and Beirut, while his subordinate commanders subdued all resistance further inland both on the West Bank and beyond the Jordan.

The great crusader castles had surrendered one after another until only a handful, notably the Templar stronghold of Tortosa and the Hospitallers' great fortress Krak de Chevaliers, still held out. An estimated 100,000 Latin Christians had been taken captive during this campaign, and the captives included the King of Jerusalem and the Grand Master of the Knights Templar. Although there was still a Christian County of Tripoli and a Christian Principality of Antioch, the Kingdom of Jerusalem had effectively been wiped off the map.

When Richard I left the Holy Land roughly a year after his arrival, the entire coastline of Palestine had been restored to Christian control, and a viable Kingdom had been re-established that was to endure another 100 years. Although the new borders were drawn just short of Jerusalem and Bethlehem, they did include sufficient hinterland to create a continuous if narrow territory that stretched along the coast. Furthermore, that narrow kingdom had been made sustainable by another of Richard's deeds: the capture of the Island of Cyprus.

The creation of a Latin Kingdom on Cyprus ensured that the Kingdom of Jerusalem had a secure source of food, particularly grain. Furthermore, the Latin Kingdom of Cyprus also kept the sea lanes open, since no Arab fleet could blockade the cities of Palestine as long as Cyprus was controlled by Christians.

In short, Richard I of England ensured that the Kingdom of Jerusalem existed 100 years longer than would have been the case without his Third Crusade. In so doing, he ensured that there would be another six crusades to Outremer, not counting the "Children's Crusade." Not exactly an insignificant accomplishment in the history of the crusades!

THE LAST CRUSADE: EDWARD OF ENGLAND'S CRUSADE OF 1271-1272

Richard I's deeds in Outremer were clearly a hard act to follow; nevertheless, it was not the end of English involvement in the crusades. Richard's nephew and namesake, Richard of Cornwall, the able younger brother of Henry III, took the cross, and Richard's great nephew, a man who would prove his military capabilities against the Welsh and the Scots, also led a crusade.

Because the latter was not yet king at the time and had too few resources to affect much, the crusade of Edward I of England tends to get overlooked in crusader history. Nevertheless, it demonstrates that the Plantagenet kings had not lost interest in the Holy Land. Furthermore, despite the overwhelming strength of his opponent, Baibars—a highly successful, ruthless and treacherous Mamluke sultan—Edward obtained a ten year truce. He also reinforced the walls of Acre with an additional tower (and Edward was to prove a master castle builder as his castles in Wales demonstrate), the "King Edward Tower."

PLANTAGENET VASSALS AND ENGLISH NOBLEMEN AND KNIGHTS

But kings alone do not make a crusade, and therefore, when considering the English contribution to the crusades, it is important to look at the contribution of noblemen and knights as well as kings. For example, the most famous of all English knights in the twelfth century, William Marshal, is known to have gone to the Holy Land and fought with the Knights Templar.

His fame was such that his example doubtless inspired countless others to follow in his footsteps and take the cross as well. We know too that William, Earl of Salisbury led a contingent of English knights on the Seventh Crusade and died at the Battle of Mansourah. Likewise, a contingent of English knights under Otto de Grandson took part in the final, futile defense of Acre in 1291. In between, hundreds if not thousands of Englishmen took part in the defense of the crusader kingdoms as Knights Templar and Knights Hospitaller. At least one Templar Grand Master was English, Thomas Berard (1256-1273).

By far the most important Plantagenet vassals to play a role in Outremer, however, were the Lusignans. Although not English, the Lusignans were Poitevin nobility that owed fealty to the Plantagenet kings in the twelfth and thirteenth centuries. The Lusignans were involved in rebellions against Henry II (which of his vassals wasn't at one time or another?), but the family was restored to royal favor at the latest when King John married a Lusignan.

In the meantime, however, the cadet branch of the family had established itself in Outremer. Aimery and Guy de Lusignan, the younger sons of Hugh de Lusignan, were both to be Kings of Jerusalem, in both cases by right of their respective wife. Guy married the elder daughter of King Amalric I and ruled as King of Jerusalem from 1187 until his wife's death in 1190. Aimery de Lusignan, although older than Guy, ruled after him, when he married the younger daughter of King Amalric I, Isabella of Jerusalem. Aimery was King of Jerusalem from 1198 to 1205. Both brothers also ruled Cyprus, establishing a dynasty there that lasted until 1398.

Guy, furthermore, has the distinction of being widely blamed for the catastrophic Christian defeat at the Battle of Hattin. He was vain, arrogant, militarily incompetent, and completely immune to good advice. Saladin was not invincible; before and after Hattin, Christian kings (Baldwin IV of Jerusalem, a leper, in 1177, and Richard I of England in 1191) defeated Saladin in battle.

Had the crusaders followed the advice and plan put forward by the High Court of Jerusalem, notably by Raymond III of Tripoli and Balian d'Ibelin, the exhausted Christian army would not have been trapped on the Horns of Hattin. However, Guy de Lusignan ignored the advice of the local barons and preferred to listen to another interloper, Gerard de Rideford, who happened to be the Grand Master of the Knights Templar—but that is a story for another day (and the subject of my current project, a biographical novel in three parts about Balian d'Ibelin.)

IMPACT OF THE CRUSADES ON ENGLAND

Having discussed the English role in the crusades and the crusader kingdoms, I'd like to close this essay with a brief summary of the reverse side of the coin: the impact the crusades and crusader kingdoms had on England. The first obvious effects of the crusades were almost all negative. From Henry II's "Saladin Tithe" to Richard I's ransom payments, it is clear that England paid dearly for her kings' interest in the crusader kingdoms.

Arguably, Richard did more good for the Kingdom of Jerusalem than he did for the Kingdom of England! But such an assessment has the benefit of hindsight and is further colored by modern distaste for the very concept of crusades. In fact, support for the crusades was widespread and intense in Western Europe in the twelfth century, at least, and Richard's contemporaries were more critical of him for not doing enough (failing to take Jerusalem) than for going on crusade in the first place.

As with all sustained military operations, the crusades furthered a number of technological developments. European armor, saddles, siege equipment, and weapons developed rapidly in the period of the crusades as the Western Europeans adapted and improved on the weapons employed by the Byzantines and their enemies. Castle and palace-building advanced dramatically in this period, as did ship-building. The latter particularly was an area in which the West had a clear superiority over Constantinople and their Arab and Turkish enemies.

Certainly, the entire Western world benefited significantly from the trade that developed throughout the Mediterranean after the establishment of the crusader kingdoms in the Levant. From the capture of Jerusalem by the crusaders in 1099 until the rise of the Ottoman Empire, Christian fleets dominated the Mediterranean, turning it back into the center of trade it had been at the height of the Roman Empire.

That meant that all the products of the East, from as far away as China and India, could be imported into Western Europe, and Western goods and products could be sold to much more extensive markets. Furthermore, Western Europeans now came into regular contact with the Byzantine Empire, a highly advanced civilization, and to a lesser extent with the Armenians, the Seljuk Turks, and the Arabs themselves. All parties benefited from the exchange of goods, technology, and ideas.

SOURCES

Barber, Richard. *The Knight and Chivalry*. Woodbridge: Boydell & Brewer Inc., 1995.

Edbury, Peter W. *The Kingdom of Cyprus and the Crusades, 1191-1374*. Cambridge: Cambridge University Press, 1991.

Harl, Kenneth. *The Era of the Crusades*. The Great Courses. Chantilly: The Teaching Company, 2003.

Hopkins, Andrea. *Knights*. London: Grange, 1990.

Nicolle, David. *Hattin 1187: Saladin's Greatest Victory*. London: Osprey Publishing, 1993.

Robinson, John J. *Dungeon, Fire and Sword: The Knights Templar in the Crusades*. London: M. Evans and Co., 1991.

The Strange Death of Richard the Lionheart

By NANCY BILYEAU

I N APRIL 1199, THE FRENCH KING, PHILIP II, THANKED GOD FOR THE PROVIDENTIAL death of his great rival: Richard I. Ever since the English king had been freed from his prison in Austria in 1194, he had turned his war machine on the French, reclaiming the lands and castles that were taken while he was captive. Had he continued his relentless campaign, Richard might well have conquered the whole of France, and medieval history would have turned out quite differently.

But at the age of 42, Richard died of an infection caused by an arrow wound. He was slain during a siege of a small and seemingly unimportant French castle, and certain aspects of his death struck the chroniclers of his time—and later historians—as strange, almost sordid. It was an anticlimactic end to the life of the Lionheart.

Richard was taken captive on his way back from the Third Crusade. Leopold of Austria held grudges against Richard, and he put him in a secret prison. Once Queen Eleanor, Richard's mother, discovered where her beloved son was, she appealed to the Pope. The Holy Roman Emperor set a ransom of 150,000 marks—65,000 pounds of silver. It was an astronomical sum, estimated to be three times the annual income of the English crown. But Eleanor raised it.

In the legends of Robin Hood, Richard is a benevolent ruler, who after being freed forgives his brother John and returns to the task of governing England. But Richard had little interest in England his whole life—he is rumored to have said, *"If I could have found a buyer, I would have sold London itself"*—and was passionate about going on Crusades or fighting for more French territory than he already possessed as the ruler of the Aquitaine.

Richard decided what he needed was an impregnable castle from which to defend Normandy and then retake critical French land. The vast one that he built required two years of punishing around-the-clock labor and cost an estimated £20,000, more than had been spent on any English castle in the last decade. Legend has it that while building the Chateau-Gaillard, Richard and his men were drenched with "rain of blood," but he refused to take it as an evil omen.

In March 1199, Richard was in the Limousin, suppressing a revolt by the Viscount of Limoges. He *"devastated the Viscount's land with fire and sword."* Then he besieged the nearby small chateau of Chalus-Chabrol. Accounts differ on why; some say it was because a peasant found treasure underground—either Roman gold or valuable objects—and Richard was so desperate for money, he laid siege to the castle. But some historians say that this entire area was of strategic importance to Richard's hold on France, and he was only there to suppress rebellion.

What most historians agree on is that Richard was walking the chateau's perimeter without wearing his chain mail and he was shot by a castle defender using a crossbow. The wound in his left shoulder turned gangrenous. It steadily grew worse over the next ten days. Some wrote that while dying Richard asked that the bowman be brought to him. He then forgave the man, who was named Peter Basil, and instructed that he should not be harmed. Richard died in the arms of his mother on April 6. Later, in defiance of Richard's orders, Peter Basil was flayed alive and hanged.

Why did Richard I, a seasoned and expert warrior, expose himself to a bowman's shot? Did the king and crusader put his life at risk to claim some grubby treasure dug up from the ground—why?

Following the custom of the time, Richard's body was buried in different places. His heart was buried at Rouen in Normandy, his entrails in Chalus, and the rest of his body near his father's remains in Anjou. A French forensics expert received permission in May 2011 to analyze a small sample of Richard I's heart to determine if the cause of the king's death was indeed septicemia, an infection of the blood. Tests results have not yet been released (2012). When completed, they may confirm what disease killed Richard. What's harder to understand is what put him at that particular castle at that particular time so that he was killed while in his prime. There is no test for that.

Eustache the Monk: Medieval Outlaw or Hero?

By Lana Williams

As with many tales of old, whether the protagonist is an outlaw or hero depends on the view of the one telling the story. Such is the case with *Eustache the Monk,* a manuscript written in Old French between 1223 and 1284. While the author's identity remains in question, the story is known to be based on an actual person, Eustache Busquet, who was born in Northern France in 1170 and died in 1217.

Eustache lived an extraordinary life. He trained as a knight, then as a seaman, and traveled to Spain to study black magic, though no historical evidence supports this. The story embellishes his deeds, telling readers how Eustache and his companions got into a fight in a tavern and cast a magic spell and made the tavern keeper and her customers strip naked, straddle wine casks, and get a bit crazy. Or maybe that should be a lot crazy. Eustache continues his journey and casts another spell on a man driving a cart, making the cart and horse appear to go backwards.

Soon after, he joins a Benedictine abbey at the age of twenty and wreaks havoc there by casting more spells. The monks eat when they should be fasting, go barefoot when they should wear shoes, and swear when they're supposed to be silent. He also casts a spell on a side of bacon, changing it into an old ugly woman, which frightens the cook.

Eustache remained at the monastery until his father was murdered by a man named Hainfrois de Heresinghen. As would any good son, Eustache left the monastery to demand justice from his father's overlord, the Count of Boulogne, for his father's murder. A judicial duel was arranged, but alas, Eustache's champion lost. Apparently the count was impressed with Eustache, for he appointed him seneschal for an expedition with King Philip of France to win back territories in Normandy held by King John of England. Unfortunately, Eustache's enemy, de Heresinghen, returned to the picture and accused Eustache of mismanaging the finances of the expedition, convincing the count of Eustache's guilt as well.

Eustache suspected treachery and fled into the forests near Boulogne. The count, displeased with Eustache, seized his properties and burned his fields. That is when the story grows even more interesting. Eustache began to methodically harass the count, his allies, and his soldiers. The story tells of Eustache leading a band of up to 30 men, as well as operating alone, often in disguise. As the story progresses, Eustache moves from casting spells to using trickery and deception instead. While this period of outlawry was brief as it lasted only a year, it takes up the majority of the story. Not so different from the action movies at the theaters these days!

Leaving his homeland, Eustache wandered the English Channel where he acted as a pirate, eventually offering his services as a mariner to King John. As a reward, Eustache was given lands in Swaffam, Norfolk. Soon after, while he still served King John, he acted as English ambassador to the Count of Boulogne. That did not go well though, for as soon as King Philip learned of his return to France, he outlawed Eustache.

In London in 1212, the Count of Boulogne was able to negotiate a charter of allegiance with King John. Again fearing treachery, Eustache fled, this time back to France where he joined King Philip. Nothing like changing allegiances as circumstances dictate. In 1214, King John was faced with a rebellion of his English barons, and Eustache was said to have supplied them with arms. Needless to say, King John was less than pleased and seized the lands he'd previously given Eustache in Norfolk.

Over the next few years, Eustache continued to control the English Channel and to support the English barons. He provided transport to Prince Louis of France to the Isle of Thanet during the Barons' War. Alas, Louis' ship was later attacked by four English ships. They captured him and beheaded him immediately in August of 1217.

Despite his time as an outlaw, Eustache was supported by his family and friends, suggesting he was worthy of loyalty, a heroic quality for certain. The story written about him tells of the code by which he lived. Following such rules is also a quality we can admire and suggests chivalric behavior. He rewarded those who were truthful and loyal to him. If someone betrayed him, they were killed, but he did release some adversaries unharmed. If someone lied to him about the amount of money they had on their person, they were robbed. However, if a person told the truth about the amount of money they had, they were allowed to keep it.

There are similarities in Eustache the Monk's story to Robin Hood and other "good outlaw" legends. Eustache was of noble birth, he set out to avenge his father's murder, and he lived by his own version of chivalry. However, the story also contains rather shocking cruelties, which put the term "hero" in question. He forces a young man to twist his own rope from which to hang. When several of his men have their eyes gouged out, he retaliates by chopping off the feet of four of the culprit's men. He tortures another person in a mud pit. There's also a passage in the story of Eustache disguising himself as a prostitute, then humiliating the count's man, and taunting him for trying to sodomize a monk. None of those acts seem heroic.

As with all great heroes and villains/outlaws, there are shades of gray in both characters and real people, some darker than others. Often how we authors tell the story determines what the reader decides.

SOURCE

Kelly, Thomas E. "Eustache the Monk." *Medieval Outlaws: Ten Tales in Modern English*. Ed. Thomas H. Ohlgren. Thrupp, Stroud, Gloucestershire: Sutton Pub., 1998. 61-98.

THE BOOK OF HOURS

By CAROL MCGRATH

AMONGST MY FAVOURITE TREASURES OF THE MIDDLE AGES ARE THE BOOKS OF Hours. They really belong to the High Middle Ages but have an earlier history also. The very first Book of Hours has been attributed to one William de Brailles of Oxford between 1230 and 1260. Throughout the rest of the period we know as the Middle Ages this little decorated book of prayers, *A Book of Hours,* was a favourite with everyone in Western Europe. In other words it was "the" medieval bestseller. Now, Books of Hours are invaluable resources for researchers of the period 1230 until the end of the fifteenth century because they give a fabulous insight into the daily life of the Middle Ages. They are also very valuable.

They began as an addition to the end of the Psalter in the early Middle Ages. The name Book of Hours is associated with the Benedictine hours of the day. The medieval hour was actually an inexact space of time that was allocated to religious or to business duties. It derives from the notion that the monastic orders specified particular prayers and rituals which were to be observed eight times a day.

Therefore, the objective of the Book of Hours is to encourage the secular world to emulate the monastic programme of daily devotion. The Book of Hours was a book of private prayer and meditation owned by ordinary people. They were, for instance, often read in bed each morning, a notion that I find enchanting because they must have been beautiful to look upon just as you wake up—and I am not a religious person!

The manuscript for a Book of Hours is divided into sections. The core of the Book of Hours is known as "Hours of the Virgin". This set of psalms and prayers is designed to be used in honour of the Virgin Mary at each of the canonical hours of the day: Matins (2 a.m.), Lauds (5 a.m.), Prime (before daybreak), Terce (9 a.m.), Sext (noon), Nones (2 p.m.), Vespers (sunset), and Compline (7 p.m.).

There will always be a calendar showing saints' days and four short readings from the Gospel at the front of the book. Preceding the hours of the Virgin there usually are two prayers to the Virgin.

After the Hours of the Virgin there would be the Hours of the Cross and the Holy Spirit, usually short, with a hymn, an antiphon, and a prayer. Then there are Seven Penitential Psalms with the Litany and the Offices of the Dead. Coming to the end of the book there might be the Fifteen Joys of the Virgin and finally the important Invocations of the Saints.

If the patron commissioning the book was wealthy, the book's pages could be emblazoned with initials in gold and colours and often with miniatures and decorative borders. Miniature originally came from the Latin word *minium,* the red pigment used to emphasise initial letters.

The term "Red Letter Day" derives from the practice of writing important saints' days in red ink within the calendar section of the Book of Hours. Borders became more elaborate through time. By the end of the fifteenth century they contained fabulous naturalistic animals and flowers.

Miniatures, too, developed to contain successive episodes from Biblical stories. And of course, occasionally, the owner of the book would be painted within a miniature. The notion of a Primer as a first reading book comes from the hour of Prime and the Book of Hours. It indicates just how important and widely used these small lovely little books became!

The Calendar lists the saints' days for each month and festivals such as Christmas and the feast day of the Virgin Mary. Local saints were written in gold, red, or blue, and local events such as consecration of churches or deaths of important people in the diocese were recorded. Each month may occupy two pages with illustrations showing the occupations of the month and the zodiac signs.

The Sequences of the Gospels show the Hours of the Virgin and the Office of the Dead. The Office of the Dead has two parts, Vespers and Matins, and often miniatures show the last judgement. Later the illustrations varied and often included skeletons prancing with spears. The prayers were said over coffins! It contains readings from the Gospels—extracts from Matthew, Mark, Luke, and John usually accompanied with a pictorial attribute (eagle for John, lion for Mark, angel for Matthew, and ox for Luke). In the readings from the Penitential Psalms, King David usually is depicted in illustrations as he had an adventurous life; thus the illustrations are varied.

The most highly illustrated section after Hours of the Virgin would be the Memorials of the Saints. The section opens with prayers to the Trinity followed by prayers to the Virgin Mary, St. Michael, St. John the Baptist, and finally a collection of local and popular saints. Like the Gospel saints, they too have their own particular emblems. There are too many to list here, but who can ever forget St. Catherine and her wheel!

KING JOHN'S CASTLE: MEDIEVAL STRONGHOLD

By ANTOINE VANNER

THE TERM "MEDIEVAL CASTLE" BRINGS IMMEDIATELY TO MIND IMAGES OF HIGH CAS-tellated walls, massive gatehouses, and vast keeps, and many such fortresses did indeed exist. The vast majority of castles were, however, much smaller structures, "strong-holds" built for local defence, even if on occasion they did serve as royal residences. One such is King John's Castle, near Odiham, Hampshire. Though it is little more than a ruined shell today, it has a most spectacular history and provides insights into what many more like it looked like.

The castle consisted of a single massive octagonal keep of three stories and was sur-rounded by one or possibly more deep moats, which survive today only as dry, overgrown ditches. The walls, with cores of flint boulders held together by mortar, were externally clad with stone. This has however been stripped away over the centuries since here, as elsewhere in Britain, neighbouring communities exploited it as a quarry after it had been abandoned.

Now only the cores remain and indeed two sides of the octagon are gone completely. The site is preserved by Hampshire County Council as well as is possible given the cas-tle's ruined condition. A number of very informative notices are provided, each featuring delightful illustrations in the medieval style by the artist Andy Bardell.

The structure was built in the 1207-1214 period on the orders of King John, a monarch who has had a deservedly bad reputation, as compared with his older brother Richard, who had an undeservedly good one. John's entire reign consisted of conflicts with the Church, with the French, and with his own barons. The castle at Odiham is associated with the single most important event of John's reign as it was from here in 1215 that he rode to Runnymede, under pressure from his rebellious barons, to sign the Magna Carta and thereby to lay the foundation for the liberties of the English-speaking world in cen-turies to come.

A year later, invading French troops besieged the castle for two weeks. The defenders were allowed to surrender with honour and were found, to the amazement of the French, to consist of fourteen men only. This is a commentary on just how invulnerable such structures were in the days before gunpowder and when hunger and thirst were the most effective weapons against determined defenders.

King John's young son, Henry III, ordered repairs to the castle in 1225, the refur-bished roof being of lead and weighing some twenty-two tons. It was supported by the outer walls and by a central column that no longer exists. On each of the two floors above ground level beams extended from this central beam, like spokes of a wheel, to joist holes in the outer walls.

Eleven years later Henry III gave the castle to his younger sister, Eleanor, who was married to the powerful French nobleman, Simon de Montfort. He in due course became Earl of Leicester and was a key figure in the "Barons' War" against his royal brother-in-law. While a residence in this period, the castle's interior was likely to have been richly furnished. It can only however have been very cramped by modern standards and one assumes that most of the retainers and servants were lodged in smaller dwellings, of which no trace now remains, in the area between the castle walls and the moat.

This period ended when Simon de Montfort was killed in 1265 at the Battle of Evesham, in which he was fighting the future King Edward I, son of Henry III. Family ties notwithstanding, Eleanor was exiled to France, where she spent the rest of her days, taking with her the household rolls which give an insight to life at the castle.

Edward succeeded his father in due course and spent Christmas 1302 there. His own son, Edward II, proved to be one of the most disastrous kings in English history and his reign was not only marred by civil war but by his ultimate overthrow by his wife, Isabella, abetted by her lover. Odiham Castle was once more besieged in 1322, but again survived.

Edward III, unlike his father, proved to be perhaps the most powerful English king of the medieval period, and he not only initiated the Hundred Years' War against France but scored notable victories over the Scots—Scotland at that time still being an independent kingdom and almost invariably an ally of France. Edward granted Odiham Castle to his queen, Philippa of Hainault, and it appears that she may have had a garden planted around it, an indication that its role was no longer primarily military.

The castle was to play its last significant role in history in this period. In 1346 Edward's army smashed an invading Scots force at Neville's Cross (today a suburb of Durham) and in the process captured the Scottish king, David II. Held captive until an enormous ransom of 100,000 marks was paid, David was held for part of the time at the Tower of London and for three years at Odiham. Here, in the agreeable rural surroundings of East Hampshire, he was provided with a well-furnished room and with good food, wine, and other luxuries. The nature of his detention was unlikely to have been rigorous since honour would forbid escape prior to payment of ransom, and one can well imagine David hunting in the surrounding area.

With David's release, Odiham Castle, now relegated to the status of a hunting lodge, started to fade from history. By 1600 it seems to have been in ruins, and the process of quarrying it for stone seems to have started. Its day, however, had been a long one and despite its small size it was witness to some of the most dramatic events of England's Middle Ages.

A particularly attractive way to reach the castle today is by barge from the nearby modern village of Odiham.

In preparing this article I am indebted to the splendid notices posted by Hampshire County Council at the site and which are so beautifully enhanced by Andy Bardell's illustrations.

KENILWORTH CASTLE

By KATHERINE ASHE

KENILWORTH: THE NAME RINGS WITH THE ROMANCE OF TUDOR ENGLAND, WITH images of the great feast and water festival staged by Robert Dudley, Earl of Leicester, for Queen Elizabeth I.

But of course the castle's history begins long before that, perhaps in those pre-history times when a castle was a hill or mound, for just such a mound is enclosed within the masonry of the great tower. A favorite retreat of John of Gaunt and Richard III, its court-yard was filled in late medieval and renaissance times with elaborate buildings whose stone filigree now reaches roofless to the sky.

And before that, it was the most secure castle in England, withstanding siege, in 1265-6, for eighteen months until the defenders surrendered to what seemed at the time generous terms.

The castle was never taken. So formidable was it that, lest it be used by the royalists, Cromwell had its walls destroyed and its massive tower packed with dynamite. Three walls of the tower still stand, mighty looking even in their dissolution.

It was Simon de Montfort who turned the neglected royal holding into an impregnable fortress. In his autobiography (Montfort Archive, *Bibliotheque Nationale*) he complains that the property, as given to him in 1238, was in severe disrepair and cost him much to make it habitable. By the following summer, having offended King Henry III, Montfort had fled to France and Palestine.

King Henry found he rather fancied the place and continued the repairs. His accounts record his cutting a large window to give view of the Mere, repainting the chapel and furnishing it with two seats decorated with the royal arms. A pretty boat was added to the Mere, the lake formed by the dammed stream surrounding the castle on three sides. (The fourth side has a channel, completing the waterworks and the defences.)

Returned to royal favor, in 1244 Montfort again received Kenilworth. He was married to the king's sister and was Earl of Leicester, so the gift was no more out of the ordinary than Henry's bestowing numerous other royal properties upon his relatives.

By 1258 Montfort was one of six baronial leaders demanding a revolutionary reorganization of the government to offset King Henry's disastrous incompetence. Henry had pledged the Crown of England to Pope Alexander IV if he failed to pay the costs of a papal army to seize Sicily for his son Edmund. Henry failed to pay and the Pope was about to claim England as a papal fief, much as he had claimed Sicily and offered its Crown to Henry.

A meeting of England's barons and high clergy gathered at Oxford, supposedly to raise the needed funds. Instead, the lord and clerics produced the Provisions of Oxford, the template for Parliament and modern elective government. And they refused to raise the tax for Sicily, instead demanding that all properties given from the royal holdings be returned to the Crown. Montfort was first to respond and volunteered Kenilworth. The castle became again a royal holding—which is not to say the Montfort family vacated. They did not.

Simon de Montfort was the foremost military strategist in England. When the royalist faction managed to organize themselves and bring an army against the reformers, it was Montfort who was the leader of the baronial side. To provide a refuge, preparing for the worst should the royalists prevail, Montfort used tax monies and the incomes of royalists he vanquished in battle to develop Kenilworth along the lines of the crusader castles he had seen in Palestine: castles impregnable and defendable by just a few knights.

Kenilworth's bailey wall—fronting the Mere and separating the tower, its chapel, cook and laundry buildings, and immediate gardens from the barns, stables, orchards, and paddocks that occupied the rest of the island—was strengthened. The causeway that crossed the Mere was walled, with barbicans at either end, the farthest one reinforced to protect the sluice that kept the Mere from draining to a little stream trickling through a meadow (as it is today). And the entire island, bounded by the Mere and channel, was walled and studded with towers.

The decorative banquet halls and ranges made in later times have been destroyed by pilferers, weathering, and time. The fortress walls that the Earl Montfort created merited total demolition by Cromwell. But three walls of the tower stand to this day, grand with their soaring arches and massive red masonry.

THE MEDIEVAL GARDEN

BY CAROL MCGRATH

IN THE MEDIEVAL PERIOD THE WORLD WAS A QUIET PLACE.
Robert Lacey writes in his book, *The Year 1000*, "*Yet in the year 1000 hedgerows actually had a sound.*" He points out that you were able to hear baby birds chirping in their nests, and that the only mechanical noise you would ever hear in a medieval village would come from the blacksmith's bellows, the church bell, or the cogs clanking around the water mill.

Lacey reminds us that in the countryside bees buzzed and wood pigeons cooed. Towns were so small in the early eleventh century that these would be sounds one might hear there also.

Of course, another peaceful place was the medieval garden. Medieval gardens begin with Charlemagne circa 800 and the period of the medieval garden ends in England circa 1500.

Orchards were valued for the joy of the blossom and for scent and shade and, indeed, their produce. Orchards, however, are difficult to find evidence for, never mind their planting plans. There is evidently detailed evidence for three or four orchards. One was at Llanthony Priory, Gwent in 1199. It contained twelve acres with 400 and more trees. A second was the cemetery orchard on the Swiss, ninth century, St. Gall monastery plan. This orchard was home to around thirteen trees, planted between the tombs of dead monks. Another orchard is Rosamund's Bower, Everswell where a hundred pear trees were planted by Henry III in 1268. And finally we have plans for the orchard in the Curia at Cuxham which contained 139 apple trees.

The Herber or small enclosed garden was generally square, and it might have four borders placed around a small lawn. Sometimes they were half bed and half lawn, and the beds could be filled with aromatic herbs. The culinary herbs would have belonged to the utilitarian garden.

This type of garden came into its own during the twelfth century and could be found in enclosed castle sites. Small herbers romantically might be placed beneath the bed chambers of royalty and nobility as has been evidenced at Windsor, Arundel, Marlborough, Gloucester, and Nottingham castles.

The pleasure garden was a park-like garden, generally walled. One might find there diverse trees and wild creatures such as hares, stags, rabbits, and various little creatures. It might have a timber-framed summer palace where a king and queen might relax. Rows of trees ran down from a palace so that the animals could be observed. These gardens also contained rivers and pools for fish and fowl. I imagine they must have been beautiful gardens.

Somersham Palace, Cambridgeshire, a residence of the bishops of Ely, contained a pleasure garden during the fifteenth century. But on a smaller scale many English manors had such gardens during the thirteenth and fourteenth centuries.

In addition to farm buildings, Cuxham had an eleven acre garden containing spinneys, coppices, river, fishpond, a nut garden, and vegetable areas as well as two dovecots.

Finally, the kitchen garden contained food and medicinal plants as well as plants for strewing on floors, making hand waters, chasing away insects, and general household purposes.

The kitchen garden was filled with brassicas such as kale, leeks, parsley, leaf beet, and root crops such as parsnips. Beans and peas were grown to be eaten as a green vegetable although they were grown generally as a field crop and dried. Garlic, chives, bulb onions, hemp, and flax were grown in the kitchen garden as well as in vast quantities. Popular herbs were hyssop, parsley, and sage. Salad plants included borage, marigold, heartsease, langdebeef, and poppy.

So with the month of March heralding the arrival of spring and the medieval winter finally loosening its grip a cycle of cultivation could indeed get under way.

SOURCES

Lacey, Robert and Danny Danziger. *The Year 1000: What Life Was Like at the Turn of the First Millennium, An Englishman's World*. Black Bay Books, 2000.

Landsberg, Sylvia. *The Medieval Garden*. Thames and Hudson, 1996.

THE RISE, RISE, AND FALL OF SIR ROGER MORTIMER

BY ARTHUR RUSSELL

AFTER THE DEFEAT OF EDWARD BRUCE AT FAUGHART IN IRELAND IN OCTOBER 1318, Sir Roger Mortimer's reputation as an effective soldier and administrator made him a vital ally of King Edward II of England. The King was facing a resurgence of rebellion from his barons mostly arising from the activities of his latest favourite at court, Sir Hugh Despenser, his closest adviser. Established laws and agreements were being set aside to endow Despenser's family with lands and titles as Despenser took over roles the King was too lazy or unwilling to perform himself. The pattern for this been set a decade earlier with a former Royal favourite, Piers Gaveston.

The difference from Mortimer's point of view was that while Gaveston had been his mentor and friend, Despenser was a mortal enemy arising from an old marchland dispute in which Despenser's grandfather was killed by Mortimer's grandfather. This meant that Mortimer had to be careful. The King might appreciate his talents but showed that he had no qualms ignoring everything when it came to pleasing Despenser. Mortimer was somewhat relieved to be sent back to Ireland as Justiciar, thereby taking him away from court intrigues until he saw how things developed. For the moment he was "out of sight, out of mind".

Over the next two years he restored the post-Bruce Irish colony to a healthy state so that by the time he left, the country had not known such peace and prosperity for generations. By contrast, the England he returned to in late 1320, was on the brink of civil war due to the continuing actions of Despenser.

MORTIMER JOINS THE REBELLION

Mortimer's English interests had suffered considerably in his absence. He felt constrained to join an alliance of barons who resisted what Despenser and through him the King were doing. As a Marcher Lord with rights and privileges that were guaranteed under Magna Carta, Mortimer simply had no other choice.

The King was alarmed by this latest challenge to his authority and summoned the barons to court to declare their loyalty. The rebel barons ignored the summons and attacked Despenser territory in South Wales. Despenser pressured the King to declare them traitors, which meant their lands and titles were forfeit. At this point, the rebels were at pains to say their opposition was not against the King, but against the Despensers (father and son). Edward offered concessions, but refused the barons' demand to banish the Despensers. Mortimer was stripped of his Irish Justicarship in favour of a Despenser relative who proceeded to return Ireland to the anarchy from which it had been rescued a short time before by Mortimer.

During the next months, the King was forced by the rebels to banish the Despensers. The elder Despenser fled to Bordeaux, blaming his son's greed for his family's downfall. Sir Hugh became a pirate exacting revenge on ships conducting trade and commerce between England and the Continent. This caused economic damage as well as severe embarrassment to Edward, who seemed less disturbed by this than by the anger and insult he held against the rebel barons, now clearly led by Mortimer.

What followed was one of the most rapid changes of fortunes in history.

ROYAL REVENGE

Having won their campaign against the Despensers, the rebel alliance immediately fell apart. The event that sparked King Edward's revenge was the refusal of one of them to allow Queen Isabella to shelter in Leeds Castle as she went on pilgrimage to Canterbury. The King ordered the castle to be besieged, but none of the baron alliance came to help. The offending lord and some followers were executed by the King who now, with the help of barons who had not previously taken sides, felt strong enough to move against the remaining rebels. Mortimer quickly realized that his best course lay in making his own peace with the King, who accepted his submission and imprisoned him in the Tower of London. All Mortimer's titles and properties were seized by the crown.

In the following months, the King exacted terrible revenge on the barons with a series of horrific executions, while Sir Hugh Despenser was recalled from exile and restored to his former position at the King's court. Despenser wanted Mortimer executed but bowed to the King's wish to commute this to perpetual incarceration in the Tower.

The King now had absolute power, which meant that no castle or estate was safe from Despenser who continued to enrich himself and his family at the expense of those he considered the King's (and his) enemies. This drew the enmity of the bishops and Queen Isabella, the sister of the French King Charles IV, who increasingly saw Mortimer as the best focus for growing opposition to what had become Royal tyranny.

In 1322, Isabella accompanied the King and Despenser on a disastrous Scottish campaign and was treated to the sight of her husband and his chief minister ungallantly fleeing from Scottish King Robert's army, leaving her to fend for herself. With the help of her ladies, two of whom died, she eventually managed to find her way back to court.

MORTIMER THE EXILE

Both Despenser and the King now saw the threat that Mortimer posed while he lived, even as a prisoner. Despenser determined to kill him, confident that the King would have to allow it. Before this could happen, Mortimer, with the connivance of the Queen and the sub-lieutenant of the Tower, escaped and fled to France. It was months before the enraged King learned where Mortimer was. He suspected the Queen's role in the escape and punished her by stopping her income. The four royal children were taken from Isabella and put in the care of Lady Despenser.

France and England were by now edging towards war with one another, due mainly to Despenser's aggressive policies towards France, which he was forcing on the King. This meant that the fugitive Mortimer was welcomed by King Charles as an ally. All England now feared imminent invasion by Mortimer, who was cast in the role of bogeyman supreme and the focus for everyone who resented Royal tyranny.

In March 1325 Edward II allowed his Queen to travel to France to use her influence to defuse the political situation with her brother. He sent handpicked servants with her with instructions to spy and report "disloyal" actions and words. In truth the Queen was delighted to leave England and her ruined marriage behind her. She managed to forge a peace between Edward and Charles, which while distasteful to Edward, was as good as he could have hoped. One significant condition was that the fourteen-year-old heir, Prince Edward, had to present himself in France to pay homage to Charles. This brought the Prince to his mother's side and under her influence to fulfil what Edward considered a most distasteful but necessary condition. Once this was done, Edward demanded that his Queen and their son return immediately to England. With the encouragement of her brother, Isabella refused to accede to her husband's request, blaming the obnoxious (to her) presence of Despenser at the English court as her reason.

On Christmas Day 1325, Mortimer finally met Isabella at the French court and thus began the most notable romance (and Royal scandal) of the Middle Ages between the exiled baron and the fugitive Queen. Isabella's marital desertion was an extreme humiliation for Edward when he publicly acknowledged it in February 1326 and had to ask his subjects to prepare for an invasion led by Isabella and her lover. Meantime, Mortimer's wife, the unfortunate Joan, along with their three sons, was being held prisoner by Edward. Mortimer's mother managed to keep herself out of the King's hands.

ISABELLA AND MORTIMER INVADE ENGLAND

On 20 September 1326, Roger and Isabella joined the fleet and small army of 1500 mercenaries they had assembled across the English Channel at Rotterdam to invade England. They landed in Suffolk on September 24. Surprised that the invaders came with such a small military force, the King assembled one of the largest armies ever seen in medieval England to destroy them. He did not reckon on the love the common people had for their Queen who, with the young Prince at her side, won them over to her cause. What should have been Edward's overwhelming victory turned into a demoralizing retreat as the Queen succeeded in winning the hearts and minds of her subjects as she progressed through the English countryside.

With all the resources of his kingdom at his disposal, the King was effectively paralysed and isolated. He could not even count on the loyalty of the citizens of London and felt obliged to abandon the city in early October. Anarchy reigned on the streets as high ranking Royal supporters were lynched by a mob and brutally executed. Edward fled to Despenser's territories in Wales in the vain hope that the Welsh might support him. Despenser senior was captured and executed by Mortimer after a siege in Bristol. The King, having lost all hope of resisting the wrath to come, attempted to take a ship to Ireland but his attempt to escape failed due to adverse weather. At the end of October the King and his remaining supporters, including Hugh Despenser, were captured. Mortimer immediately exacted full and final revenge on Hugh Despenser, who was tried, condemned, and publicly hanged, drawn, and quartered in Hereford.

ROYAL ABDICATION

Mortimer and Queen Isabella were now *de facto* master and mistress of England, but needed legitimacy in the eyes of the people and the world. King Edward II had to be made to abdicate in favour of his fourteen-year-old son, who was firmly under their control. A Parliament was duly convened at which the King was given no other option but to abdicate and pledge support to his son, who was immediately crowned to replace him. It was the first but not the last time that the power of Parliament (representing People Power), was pitted against "the Divine right of Kings". The ousted King was charged and found guilty of a long list of crimes against his people and realm and was imprisoned in Kenilworth Castle.

The new regime found that a live ex-King is not an easy thing to manage as the Royal prisoner became the focus of plots and conspiracies. Life was further complicated by the need to embark on another inevitable campaign against Scotland's King Robert Bruce who was pillaging the North of England. This took Mortimer away from court, earning him blame from the newly crowned King when Roger refused to let him lead his army against a superior Scottish army who in his experienced military opinion, were too numerous and much too well positioned to risk putting the young king in harm's way. After weeks of pointless skirmishing and chasing across Northern England, the Scots tired of their adventure south of the border and simply returned home.

CONSPIRACY AND REGICIDE

What happened after this has been the cause of much argument and debate, theory, and counter-theory. The narrative goes that the deposed King Edward died or was murdered while under the care of Mortimer's subordinates in Berkeley castle on 21 September 1327. Speculation (then and since) suggests that Mortimer was the prime mover in Edward's death as he had much to gain from the King's demise. (Ian Mortimer proposes in his book *The Greatest Traitor* that the deposed King's death and funeral were faked, with both the Queen and the young King "buying into" the ensuing deception for their own good reasons.)

Mortimer and Isabella now proceeded to act as virtual rulers of England. Inevitably, the young King Edward III was growing older and becoming impatient with his overbearing mentor who was losing the support of many former allies who were envious of his power and influence. Mortimer was blamed for concluding a peace treaty with the Scots which effectively stripped many Northern Lords of their Scottish estates. Opposition finally came to a head when Mortimer insisted on having the King's uncle, the Earl of Kent, executed for conspiring to rescue the ex-King from Corfe Castle, where rumour had it he was being secretly kept. By that time, Mortimer had become used to using Royal power against his own enemies, many of whom fled England.

(The death of heirless Charles IV of France, in February 1328, had far-reaching effects as it opened the possibility that his nephew, King Edward III of England, should inherit the French throne. This would lead to the outbreak of the Hundred Years' War in 1337.)

THE FALL OF MORTIMER

It now seemed to many that Mortimer's tyranny was no better that that of Despenser. This became more obvious when Mortimer began to take over huge territories and titles for himself and his supporters. After five years reigning in Mortimer's shadow, it was time for King Edward III to exert control over his most powerful subject if he was going to hold onto his crown—a crown many feared Mortimer was about to seize for himself unless something was swiftly done about him.

With the King's approval and connivance, Roger Mortimer was arrested in his castle at Nottingham in October 1330. A month later he was tried and executed in Tyburn, being spared the drawing and quartering that had been meted out to Hugh Despenser years before. The main charge against him (one of fourteen) was the regicide of King Edward II. Queen Isabella, who had pleaded for her lover Mortimer's life to be spared, was retired with a comfortable pension and lived privately until her death in 1358.

Sir Roger Mortimer is arguably one of the most colourful figures of medieval England. Many of his political activities were cloaked in secrecy, which means that his true importance in the age is often overlooked and understated. His relatively short life provides a rich source of material to inspire many books of more than one genre, be it romance, political drama, or even a detective novel for any writer feeling inclined to delve into the machinations surrounding King Edward II's murder (or not?). He was a true Machiavellian operator in a pre-Machiavellian age who eventually lost out to an equally unscrupulous King whom he had done so much to place on England's throne. Mortimer inevitably became the final victim of his own insatiable ambition.

THE LUTTRELL PSALTER

BY JUDITH ARNOPP

THE LUTTRELL PSALTER, WRITTEN AND ILLUMINATED IN THE SECOND QUARTER OF the fourteenth century, contains the Psalms and Canticles, a calendar of church festivals and saints' days, and a Litany with Collects and the Office of the dead. A single scribe was responsible for the Latin text which covers three hundred and nine leaves of vellum, but a variety of hands assisted with the marginal decoration.

The text is of a distinctive square script possibly designed to be read at a distance, and the work is illuminated in a manner undetected in other contemporary work. The resulting manuscript is testament to the grandeur of the man who commissioned it, and the work remains as strikingly symbolic of his status today as it was during his lifetime.

The portrait of Sir Geoffrey Luttrell together with its inscription *"Dns Galfridus louterell me fieri fecit"* (*The Lord Geoffrey Luttrell caused me to be made*) ensures that his name and the splendid Psalter will be forever connected, each gracing the other. The purpose of the book was to glorify both the life of Christ and that of Sir Geoffrey Luttrell.

It is not, however, the liturgical content that has made the manuscript so uniquely famous but the scenes of domesticity and rural idyll that decorate the borders.

Modern history books, ranging from primary school histories to treatises on medieval farming, are often illustrated with scenes from the psalter. It is generally accepted that the work provides an honest account of fourteenth century life.

Janet Backhouse, an authority on medieval manuscripts, comments that the Luttrell Psalter is permeated with *"a general atmosphere of satisfaction and rejoicing"*, but close examination shows that this is not necessarily so. The illustrations of the labourers seem to me to be notable for their marked lack of satisfaction and joy. For all the colourful clothing and depictions of leisure they still come across as repressed and resentful. In fact, there is not the slightest suggestion of a smile in the entire manuscript.

The inhabitants of the margins seem to be acting out an idyll, perhaps more for the sake of the intended reader than for any attempt to represent reality. Their clothes are inappropriate both to their station and lifestyle which would have been one of toil, their role being to provide luxury for the Knight and his family. It is as if the artist has been instructed to show scenes of idyll (possibly at the behest of his employer) but has been unable or unwilling to disguise an underlying dissent.

William Langland depicts similar scenes in his prelude to his poem *The Vision of Piers Plowman.* He sees the idyll of the scene before him but is aware of the discord beneath. His poem, however, is of a vision or a dream, and the idealisation of rural life is more obvious than in Geoffrey Luttrell's vision of his country estate:

of alle manere men, the mene and the pore,

worschyng and wandryng as this world ascuth.

Somme otte hem to the plogh, playde ful selde,

In settynge and in sowynge swonken ful harde

And wone pat pis wastors with glotony destrueth.

And summe putte hem to pruyde and parayled hem per-aftir

In continence of clothing in many kyne gyse.

In preiers and penaunces potten hem mony,

Al for love of oure Lord lyuenden swythe harde

In hope to haue a good ende and heuenriche blisse.

The Luttrell Psalter was produced at the end of one of the most tumultuous periods in history; rebellion, civil conflict, failed harvests, and famine resulted in a social chaos that threatened the stability of every social strata, not least that of the landed classes.

The resulting insecurity meant that the maintenance of social position was paramount, and the nobility needed to be perceived as secure in an uncertain world.

The comfort of the lord of the manor took precedence over that of his tenants; the freeholder tenants paid a monetary rent to the lord, but the servile tenants were required to pay their dues with labour. The Lord owned the mill (or maybe more than one) and required every villager to use it and pay the customary fee which usually took the form of a portion of the milled flour.

This monopoly caused rancour and gave birth to the stereotypical untrustworthy miller of contemporary literature. Other capitalist enterprises controlled by the landowner were fishing, bird snaring, sheep, and arable farming; all of these activities can be seen in the Luttrell Psalter.

Images of farming dominate the margins—ploughing, sowing (f.170), weeding, and harvesting (f.172), but how far should we trust these images as being representational of rural reality? The illustrations may provide evidence of types of tools that were currently in use, but it remains unlikely that the workers were provided with such costly attire as their warm hoods and protective gloves, which are more probably a part of Sir Geoffrey's idyll. In medieval England, dress was an indication of social status. Sumptuary laws prohibited anyone below the rank of knight from wearing satin, and some limitation was placed upon the fur and colours he was allowed to wear.

As Michael Camille confirms, *"the peasants are being dressed up to Sir Geoffrey's level of taste and cosmeticized, much as they are in Bruegel's later paintings."* Other aspects also suggest that we should be wary of taking the images too literally, for example the reaping scene (f.172).

This illustration depicts two women cutting the standing corn while a third eases her aching back (f.172) and a man binds the cut corn into sheaves. Studies of almost one hundred medieval images of reaping reveal only one other illustration of women performing farming work. This strongly suggests that it was a task largely carried out by men. So, these images are likely a projection of Sir Geoffrey Luttrell's ideal world where he is the centre of an ordered, prosperous society. However, the Psalter's illustrations suggest that, actually, the opposite was true. The reality is glorified in order to convince those around Geofrey Luttrell of his unassailable power and virtue.

The idyllic representation magnifies his status to that of a Christ figure. Nowhere is this more apparent than in the comparison of the illustration of the Luttrell family at table (Fol. 208v) with the representation of the Last Supper (Fol. 90v).

The design and symmetry of the two illustrations are almost exact. Sir Geoffrey sits at the centre of his family just as Christ sits at the centre of his disciples. He is the focus of attention, and there is even a servant standing to one side waiting to serve him, just as Judas kneels before Christ.

One notable difference is that at the table of the Last Supper Jesus is giving Judas "the sop" whereas Sir Geoffrey is preparing to drink himself from the cup which he holds in his right hand.

Michael Camille notes that the cup Sir Geoffrey is holding illustrates the verse from the accompanying psalm: *"Calicem salutaris accipiam et nomen domini invocabo"* (*I will take the chalice of salvation, and I will call upon the name of the Lord. Psalm 115.13*).

Emmerson and Goldberg state in their paper "Lordship and Labour in the Luttrell Psalter" that in their view,

> the visual allusion to the chalice of salvation and the possible invocation of the Lord's name further underscore the eucharistic allusions and the entire scene's association with the Last Supper. Such deliberate, and to our minds, perhaps slightly shocking, juxtaposition of the secular lord with the Lord is also found elsewhere in the psalter.

In fact, the most lavish illustration in the manuscript is the portrait of Geoffrey being armed by his wife and daughter-in-law. The prominent use of heraldry, which can be observed on his surcoat, shoulders, helmet, pennon, and horse trappings, together with the inscription *"Dominus Galfridus Louterell me fieri fecit"* all serve to promote his importance. God created the world, David wrote the psalms, and Sir Geoffrey commissioned the Luttrell Psalter.

The importance of Sir Geoffrey's lordship is crucial to the understanding of the Psalter itself. It is intended as a glorification of his status as the Lord of his estates, so he is depicted as a great knight (although he would have been long past fighting age when the work was commissioned) and worthy of homage. The peasants who inhabit his estate spend their lives working for his continued prosperity and eminence in much the same way that Christians are expected to live their lives for the greater glory of God. This self-canonisation does not necessarily denote confidence or stability but rather suggests the opposite, the impulse to self-aggrandise often springing from insecurity or anxiety.

Many of the illustrations seem to involve representations of theft or the fear of loss—for instance the crows that attempt to steal the grain (f.170 and f.171) or the hawks preying upon the poultry (f.169). The image of the small boy stealing cherries from the tree described by Janet Backhouse as "a lively scene" is undoubtedly finely drawn and informative, but while Backhouse notes the detail of the tree bark and clothing she understates the threat of punishment that the older man's "club" represents. The child is stealing cherries that are intended for the Luttrell table, and his punishment may well be severe, another dark undertone to the colourful peasant lifestyle presented by the artist.

Even the miller, whose stereotypical untrustworthy nature has been recorded by Chaucer, *"a theef he was for sothe of corn mele / and that a sly, and usuant for to stele"* (3939) seems afraid of becoming the victim of theft and has armed himself with a fierce dog to protect his Lord's property. These images of plunder suggest insecurity and fear of loss. One explanation of the proliferation of these images is that the deprivations of the great famine of 1315-16 and the civil war of 1321-22 would have still been fresh in the medieval mind.

The scenes of farming and food preparation culminate in the feast at the Luttrell table, the grain provides the flour for the bread, the poultry provide the meat, the sheep provide the milk, and the hens provide the eggs. The labourers strive to put food, not into the mouths of their families but into the mouths of the Luttrell family.

The entire ritual of tilling the soil, sowing the grain, harvesting the crop, milling the flour, and cooking the meal is for the benefit of the Lord while those who labour receive little or no benefit at all. The back-breaking labour of the lower classes is consumed by the upper and, just as the seeds of their labour are consumed by the crows, so are the end results of their toil consumed by the Luttrells.

The mouths of the labourers in the margins are largely painted as downturned grimaces which lend discontent to their expressions. The rowers of the boat are among those illustrations that depict the open mouth; whether this is meant to depict horror, surprise, or singing is unclear, but what is clear is that they are not representative of joy or contentment. The men in the boat retain their impassive expressions and subjugated body language, which paired with their peculiarly open mouths lends a mask-like appearance to their faces. The open mouth is extended to include biting and consuming activities elsewhere in the margins, and there is scarcely a page that fails to depict a human or beast biting another life form or even in some cases biting itself.

Fol. 59v shows an image of swine feeding on acorns thrown down to them by the swineherd; Camille interprets this in conjunction with St. Bernard's Sermon which describes the oak as barren: *"And if they bear fruit it is not fit for human consumption but for pigs. Such are the children of this world, living in carousing and drunkenness, in overdrinking and overeating, in beds and shameless acts."*

St. Apollonia (who stands nearby) wears her teeth on a rosary to illustrate how they were extracted as part of her torture and martyrdom, and her mouth is a crimson gash across her face. The porcine illustration of gluttony and sexual excess contrasts sharply with the toothless saint. Teeth, often associated with hell and vice, are used by the pigs to indulge in that from which St. Apollonia abstains.

The gaping mouth of hell is represented on fol. 157v and serves as a vivid reminder of the consequence which waits to consume the ungodly sinner. The unfortunate man who walks in naked trepidation to his fate looks suitably repentant and illustrates the futility of earthly sin.

Interestingly, at the foot of this page is a mysterious illustration that has baffled historians for some time. Backhouse sees it as *"an unidentified game of skill"* while the less idealistic Camille views it as *"water torture."*

The illustration could represent an early drinking game wherein the victim is required to measure the quantity of ale he can consume. This would fit nicely alongside other representations of vice and gluttony and also complement the accompanying representations of death and descent into hell.

The combined images urge the reader to repent of the sin of gluttony before it is too late, and we must remember that peasants were not usually in the position to commit that particular sin.

There are clearly more questions raised by this manuscript than can be answered, but what is quite clear is that it is not representative of the social idyll that Geoffrey Luttrell desired.

Of course, images of hybrids and grotesques are found elsewhere in medieval art and architecture, usually in the margins of a civilised space like church or monastic portals, and it is apparent that they represent some long lost meaning. Their presence however does emphasise that there is more occurring in this manuscript than we can as yet understand and, if we accept that the grotesques have cryptic connotations, then it seems naïve to accept that any part of the manuscript is truly representative of the fourteenth century.

There are many images in the margins that are distinctly separate from the Luttrell family yet necessary to their continued prosperity. Labourers, foreigners, grotesques, and women are depicted in terms of excess and sin, the clothes of the lower class women that fly about them denote their sinful state and can be directly contrasted to the discreet dress of Agnes and Beatrice Luttrell. Images of greed, lust, and sin dominate the margins, juxtaposed with the devotional doctrine of the Psalms. Monsters and sinners mingle with saints and martyrs.

There are many aspects of the Psalter that adhere to Sir Geoffrey's (apparent) desire for an idealised representation of life, but his perfect world is undermined by labourers with surly faces, women carrying out inappropriate tasks, monks wielding weapons of war, the ever-present consuming mouth, the scenes of theft. All of these turn Geoffrey Luttrell's world into one of insecurity and even dread.

In the words of Michael Camille,

> *Rather than being a reflection of fourteenth century reality the Luttrell Psalter, like most important works of art, restructures reality and shores up the conflicts and discontinuities of late medieval England. It presents its*

noble owner as an active knight at a time when not only were his chivalric values outdated but he could no longer ride a horse. It presents him as the paterfamilias in his hall and a supporter of his church during the very period when he was faced with charges of incest and when the nobility was withdrawing into an ever-more private world at home and in private oratories. It displays his peasants as idealised labourers during the decades of agricultural crisis. The artists who made this monument for their patron in the third decade of the fourteenth century were creating an account of the contradictions of their age.

The Psalter provides a cameo of a period when rural England was on the brink of major agricultural reform, when discontent was present but the means of reform not yet available, resulting in insecurity and hunger jostling for dominance over subjugation.

Geoffrey Luttrell desired to be commemorated and aggrandised in this manuscript, but it is obvious that the scribe had other ideas. The status of a scribe would have been no higher than that of a ploughman, so the artists may have been from the very peasant class they were requested to depict. Perhaps it was impossible to resist representing Geoffrey Luttrell's "perfect world" from the perspective of the labouring class from which the illustrator sprung.

SOURCES

Backhouse, Janet. *The Luttrell Psalter.* Warwick: The Roundwood Press, 1989, pp. 56; 61.

Camille, Michael. *Mirror in Parchment.* Guildford: Reaktion Books Ltd., 1998, pp. 175; 184; 196; 336; 348.

The Problem of Labour in Fourteenth Century England, ed., by J. Bothwell, P.J.P. Goldberg, W.M. Ormrod. Bury St. Edmunds: York Medieval Press, 2000, p. 53.

The Riverside Chaucer. ed. by Larry D. Benson. Bath: Oxford University Press, 1988, p. 79.

John Wycliffe and the Necessity of Taking Sides in History

By Rosanne E. Lortz

Ascribing motivations—I've heard it said before that this is one of the main differences between historical novelists and historians. The historian aims to tell what historical characters did. The historical novelist aims to tell why they did it. The historian gives us the facts. The historical novelist embroiders the facts with what was going on in the actors' heads and hearts. The historian gives us an impartial account of what happened. The historical novelist biases the account by giving us a hero and a villain and manipulating events to create a story arc.

While it is certainly true that good historical novelists try to get inside the heads of their characters, it's also true that historians do the very same thing. Historians are telling a story, just as historical novelists are, so instead of assuming that everything we read in a history book is plain, unadulterated fact, we should instead learn to look at it as a piece of literature that must be evaluated. Who is the historian casting as the hero? Who is the historian casting as the villain? What events is the historian including in order to shape the story into the arc he wants? What events is he leaving out?

The story of John Wycliffe is a prime example of a man who has been dealt with in many different ways by historians. John Wycliffe was a fourteenth century intellectual who tried to reform the corruption in the church. He was an opponent of papal authority in England, which had gradually increased over the centuries until the Roman Pope claimed complete authority over all matters spiritual and secular. He believed that the Bible should be the sole authority for Christians and urged it to be made available in the vernacular so that every man could read it. He condemned pilgrimages, veneration of the saints, and transubstantiation.

Wycliffe's followers became known as the Lollards. They agitated against the established church with their anti-clerical views and were eventually suppressed by the civil rulers. Wycliffe's teachings were condemned posthumously at the Council of Constance in 1415, and since he was no longer alive to face the punishment for his heresy, the church exhumed his bones and burned them. Historians would later refer to Wycliffe as "The Morning Star of the Reformation" since so many of his ideas were seminal to the ideas of men like Martin Luther and John Calvin.

Thomas Walsingham, a fourteenth century monk of St. Albans, was quite clear what role Wycliffe played in the storybook of history:

There arose in the university of Oxford a northerner called John Wycliffe, a doctor in theology, who maintained publicly in the schools and elsewhere, erroneous, absurd and heretical conclusions against the teachings of the whole Church, resounding poisonously against monks and other religious possessioners.... The lords and magnates of the realm and many of the people favoured John Wycliffe and his followers in their preachings of such errors, especially since by their assertions they gave great power to the laity to take away the temporal possessions of the clergy and the religious.

To Thomas Walsingham, Wycliffe was a villain with "poisonous" teachings. His followers flocked to him only because it was to their own material advantage. They hoped to take the wealth belonging to the clergy.

Foxe's *Book of Martyrs*, a work written two centuries later during the English Reformation, has a much different part assigned to Wycliffe. Foxe wrote:

This Wickliff, perceiving the true doctrine of Christ's Gospel to be adulterated and defiled with so many filthy inventions and dark errors of bishops and monks...determined with himself to help and to remedy such things.... This holy man took great pains, protesting, as they said, openly in the schools, that it was his principal purpose to call back the Church from her idolatry, especially in the matter of the sacrament of the body and blood of Christ. But this boil or sore could not be touched without the great grief and pain of the whole world: for, first of all, the whole glut of monks and begging friars was set in a rage and madness, who, even as hornets with their sharp stings, did assail this good man on every side; fighting, as is said, for their altars, paunches, and bellies.... Notwithstanding, the said Wickliff, being somewhat friended and supported by the king, bore out the malice of the friars and of the archbishop; John of Gaunt, Duke of Lancaster, the king's son, and Lord Henry Percy, being his special maintainers.

To Foxe, Wycliffe's words are not poisonous; rather, it is the *"filthy inventions and dark errors"* of the established clergy which come under censure. The accusation of greed, which Walsingham said motivated Wycliffe's followers, is now leveled against Wycliffe's opponents who rejected Wycliffe's teachings for the sake of *"their altars, paunches, and bellies."*

In a later passage, Foxe goes out of his way to show that John of Gaunt, the Duke of Lancaster, was a true believer in Wycliffe's teaching, not just an opportunist. He quotes a sermon given by Philip Reppyngdon, a colleague of Wycliffe's, in which he said *"that the Duke of Lancaster was very earnestly affected and minded in this manner, and would that all such* [those who held Wycliffe's views] *should be received under his protection."*

The bias shown by each of these medieval historians is easy to spot. Their work is weighed down with adjectives containing moral judgments: holy, filthy, poisonous, dark, erroneous, absurd, heretical, good. Modern historians take more pains to hide their judgments, but the judgments are there all the same.

Jackson Spielvogel, in his monumental tome *Western Civilization*, tells the story in a way of which Foxe would probably approve:

> *Wyclif has sometimes been viewed as a forerunner of the Reformation of the sixteenth century because his arguments attacked the foundations of the medieval Catholic church's organization and practices. His attacks on church property were especially popular, and he attracted a number of followers who came to be known as Lollards. Persecution by royal and church authorities who feared the socioeconomic consequences of Wyclif's ideas forced the Lollards to go underground after 1400.*

Spielvogel steers clear of the word "greedy", but notice that it is Wycliffe's opponents who *"fear the socioeconomic consequences of Wyclif's ideas."*

Brian Tierney, in *Western Europe in the Middle Ages: 300-1475*, describes things with a bit more skeptical tone:

> *John Wyclif (ca. 1330-1384), a theologian of Oxford University, first became prominent around 1375 for attacking the wealth and luxury of the church and for maintaining that all church property was held only at the discretion of the secular authorities. At this time, a group of English nobles headed by John of Ghent, duke of Lancaster, were looking with greedy eyes on the possessions of the church and were delighted to find an ecclesiastical supporter. Wyclif was lucky in having the protection of the powerful duke of Lancaster for the rest of his life.*

Tierney does not go so far as to impugn Wycliffe's motives, but John of Gaunt is certainly only in it for the money—just like the monk from St. Albans asserted.

Elizabeth Hallam, in one of the essays included in *Chronicles of the Age of Chivalry*, shows even more skepticism than Tierney:

> *Desperate for money to prosecute the faltering war with France, Gaunt looked to the English clergy, already hard-pressed by papal taxation. He needed to stem papal demands and also to coerce the clergy into paying even higher taxes to the state. To do this he harnessed prevailing anti-clerical and anti-papal prejudices and used Wycliffe as his propagandist. The don relished the task, developing the doctrine that it was laity's right and duty to reform the erring Church.*

With the loaded words "prejudices" and "propagandist", Hallam manages to imply that Wycliffe was a tool in the hands of the money-grubbing John of Gaunt and that he might not even have truly believed in the doctrines he was drawing up.

In all of the examples I have given, the historians—both medieval and modern—ascribed motivations to John Wycliffe's followers, John Wycliffe's opponents, or John Wycliffe himself. The differing treatment from the pens of different historians is an eye-opening example of how moral judgments permeate history books. Like it or not, we must admit that historians take sides in the same way that historical novelists do.

But at the same time, we must also realize that bias, *per se*, is not a failing for a historian. Bias is an inevitability. The historian puts John Wycliffe in the role of hero or villain because stories—even real stories—have good guys and bad guys. The historian makes a moral judgment about John Wycliffe's teachings because there really are some right views and some wrong views in the world. And the historian—the modern historian—makes a concerted effort to hide his bias as best he can, because everyone knows that history books don't take sides. That's what historical novelists do.

SOURCES

Foxe, John. *Foxe's Book of Martyrs*. U.S.A.: Whitaker House, 1981.

Hallam, Elizabeth, ed. *Chronicles of the Age of Chivalry*. London: Greenwich Editions, 2002.

Spielvogel, Jackson J. *Western Civilization*. Third Edition. Minneapolis: West Publishing Company, 1997.

Tierney, Brian. *Western Europe in the Middle Ages: 300-1475*. Sixth Edition. U.S.A.: McGraw-Hill College, 1999.

THE POWER OF A RED DRESS

By ANNE O'BRIEN

RED, THE COLOUR OF FESTIVITY AND ENJOYMENT, THE COLOUR OF YOUTH AND BEAUTY. Of seduction. The colour of sin....

Red is not a colour I ever wear, but I can see its attraction, and it was highly popular with women in the Middle Ages.

Geoffrey Chaucer in his *Canterbury Tales* tells of the Wife of Bath, an energetic and dominant woman said to be based on Alice Perrers, although she had five husbands, unlike Alice.

The Wife tells the tale in her Prologue of her life with her fifth husband. And most notably the impact of her Red Dress.

Here she goes, on her way to Canterbury: the Wife of Bath, with her hat as big as a buckler and her gap-toothed smile—denoting passion of course—and wearing red:

> *My fifth and last—God keep his soul in health!*
> *The one I took for love and not for wealth,*
> *Had been at Oxford not so long before*
> *But had left school and gone to lodge next door.*
> *Yes, it was to my godmother's he'd gone,*
> *God bless her soul! Her name was Alison.*
> *She knew my heart and more of what I thought*
> *Than did the parish priest, and so she ought!*

Does this suggest that her fifth husband was a much younger man, recently out of his training? Perhaps it does. This is what happened:

> *And so one time it happened that in Lent,*
> *As I so often did, I rose and went*
> *To see her (Alison), ever wanting to be gay*
> *And go a-strolling, March, April and May,*
> *From house to house for chat and village malice.*
> *Jenkin the clerk (from Oxford) and dame Alis*
> *And I myself into the fields we went.*
> *My husband was in London all that Lent;*
> *All the more fun for me....*

So our Wife of Bath, it would seem, was still wed to husband number four while dallying with number five. But where did the Red Dress figure?

And so I made a round of visitations,
Went to processions, festivals, orations,
Preachments and pilgrimages, watched the carriages
They used for plays and pageants, went to marriages,
And always wore my gayest scarlet dress.

Which sounds innocent enough, until our lively lady adds this cautionary note about her favourite item of clothing:

These worms, these moths, these mites, I must confess
Got little chance to eat it, by the way,
Why not? Because I wore it every day.

Ah, but did scarlet denote our colour red? The name scarlet derives from the Latin *scarlata* for "fine cloth" and that again from the Persian *saqirlat*. Scarlet cloth was produced in red, white, green, blue, and brown colours among others, although the most common colour was carmine red.

I would wager that our Wife of Bath had a carmine red dress rather than one of green or brown for her lengthy festivities.

And then as an after-thought to her marital situation:

When my fourth husband lay upon his bier,
I wept enough and made but sorry cheer,
As wives must always, for it's custom's grace,
And with my kerchief covered up my face,
But since I was provided with a mate (Jenkin)
I really wept but little, I may state.

And our Wife married the fortunate Jenkin. I expect she wore her red frock for the occasion. But it was not a happy marriage, with some violence between the pair, until she took her new husband in hand so that Jenkin finally says to her:

My own true wedded wife,
Do as you please the term of all your life.

A lady after my own heart.

So beware, ladies, if you decide to wear red. Who knows what might be the end result? Or perhaps this tale might just encourage you to buy that scarlet dress....

WHAT PRICE A CROWN?

BY ANNA BELFRAGE

O N JULY 4, 1399, A MAN LANDED AT RAVENSPUR, YORKSHIRE, RETURNING FROM HIS exile in France. With him came a handful of companions, and I suppose the man must have been nervous, no matter how determined. He was, after all, risking his life and his future. Henry Bolingbroke had come to claim the English crown.

It reads like an improbable adventure. The red-headed Henry, son of John of Gaunt, speedily took control over most of England, further helped along by the fact that Richard II was in Ireland, having taken his loyal lords with him.

By the time Richard made it back in late July, it was too late. Inexplicably, Richard left his main host in Pembrokeshire and, disguised as a friar, rode north, there to meet with the Earl of Salisbury, whom he had charged with raising a royal army. No such army materialised. At Conwy Castle, Richard was forced to receive Henry's messengers. On August 19, Richard II surrendered to his cousin at Flint Castle and rode in his retinue all the way back to London, no doubt most indignant at having to ride behind Henry rather than in front of him.

Richard presented his abdication to Parliament on September 29, and on October 13, Henry Bolingbroke was crowned as Henry IV, the first of the Lancastrian kings. A quick and neat usurpation, taking no more than twelve weeks.

Three Plantagenet kings have been named Richard. Apart from their name, they also have in common the fact that none of them had a son to which to bequeath their throne. The first died—rather ingloriously for this embodiment of chivalric virtues—from a crossbow quarrel in his armpit. The other two share the distinction of being ousted from their thrones by a man called Henry. While Richard III's death at Bosworth and the subsequent enthronement of Henry Tudor still inspires a lot of controversy and opinionated discussions, in general Henry IV's usurpation back in 1399 is met with little more than a shrug. Why is that? Well, I believe it is due to Henry Bolingbroke, a man far less controversial to his future subjects than Henry Tudor.

Henry Bolingbroke was a respected man—admired for his prowess at tournaments and loved because of his largesse. A renowned warrior and leader of men, a crusader, the father of a bevy of sons where Richard II had none, Henry epitomised the male ideals of the time. Add to this a thorough education, an excellent role model in his father, a reputation for fairness, and it is easy to understand why so many considered Henry a far more palatable choice for king than Richard II.

Poor Richard never succeeded in living up to his subjects' expectations of becoming like his father, the beloved Black Prince. Besides, Richard had a tendency to expend huge amounts of money on his court, himself, and his beloved arts. Just like his great-grandfather

Edward II, Richard II also liked handing out gifts and lands to his favourites, often at the expense of the public purse.

In addition to this, Henry Bolingbroke could claim he had been most unfairly treated by his royal cousin. Despite loyal and steadfast service to the crown, Richard had rewarded him by forcing him into exile, and even worse, when John of Gaunt died, Richard had refused to honour the laws of inheritance, effectively disinheriting Henry. Not a popular thing to do, not in a country where more and more of his people were beginning to consider the King petty and unreliable, prone to consider himself well above the laws and customs of the realm. Richard's barons were even more worried; if the king chose to act so unjustly towards his first cousin, what was to stop him from acting in a similar way towards other rich and powerful noblemen?

When Henry Bolingbroke initiated his armed rebellion, he officially stated that he was in England only to claim his paternal inheritance, wrongfully denied him by the King. Smart move, as everyone could sympathise with that. He made a big show of proclaiming his desire to help reform government in England, to bring order and stability, reinstate the rule of law rather than that of royal prerogative. Not once did he say, "I want the crown", as had he voiced his intent to claim the throne he might have had a problem rallying support. Richard's subjects were sick of their king's high-handed rule, but to depose a king was a grievous sin.

This presented something of a conundrum to Henry. Having once before experienced just how capable Richard was of holding a grudge (it took him more than a decade to plan his cunning revenge on the Lords Appellant, a group of men, including Henry, who had protested against the mismanagement of the government—rumours had it he had even ordered the murder of one of the Lords Appellant, his own uncle, Thomas of Woodstock), Henry was disinclined to allow Richard to remain on the throne. Somehow, the king had to be convinced to abdicate in favour of Henry, preferably in such a way as to allow Henry to emerge untarnished from this whole sordid matter.

In hindsight, that didn't work. To ensure Richard's cooperation, Henry's supporters lied to him. At Conwy Castle, the Earl of Northumberland and the Earl of Westmoreland perjured themselves by swearing on holy relics that the intention was not to relieve Richard of his crown, rather to "help" him govern. Richard was an intelligent man and wasn't convinced, but he played for time, hoping that by pretending to accept these lies, he'd get the opportunity to flee and gather support. Not to be, as next morning Richard was forcibly taken into custody by the Earl of Northumberland and transported to Flint Castle, there to wait for Henry.

Henry went out of his way to be as courteous as possible towards his unhappy cousin. A steel hand in a velvet glove, one could say, as there was no doubt in either man's mind as to who was presently in charge, but all the same, Henry attempted to make things as comfortable as possible for Richard, treating him always with respect. I suspect Henry was uncomfortably aware of just how displeased his father, John of Gaunt, would have been with this whole mess. John would never have countenanced deposing the Lord's anointed—but then John had died (obviously) before Richard committed the unforgive-able act of denying Henry his inheritance.

What forces were brought to bear on Richard for him to sign his abdication remain unclear. Undoubtedly, threats to his life would have been made—never by Henry per-sonally, of course. And maybe Richard believed that signing the abdication was the only thing he could do at present, hoping to turn the tables on his cousin at a future date.

Once on his throne, it seems Henry IV was quite willing to let Richard live. This was his first cousin, and while they were too different to have much of a natural liking for each other, they were both aware of their blood-ties. Maybe Henry's intention was to keep Richard in comfortable captivity—although choosing Pontefract as the future home of the retired king indicates Henry didn't want him too comfortable (or too close to London).

All that changed when several of Richard's former favourites became involved in a plot against the new king, with the intention of murdering not only Henry but also his four sons, all of them children. The Epiphany Rising in 1400 might not have implicated Richard per se, but it underlined the risk of keeping the former king alive, a potential rallying point to all future discontent.

Conveniently, sometime in February 1400, Richard II died. It was said he starved to death—whether voluntarily or not is still up for debate. Personally, I believe he was mur-dered. To have kept him alive would have been too much of a risk.

To take a crown comes at a price. Henry was never entirely comfortable on his throne, and to make matters worse, his relationship with his eldest son was permanently dam-aged by his usurpation. Young Henry was very fond of Richard and never forgave his father for having deposed him. Besides, there was the matter of guilt. By all accounts, Henry Bolingbroke was a man of tender conscience, a devout man who worked hard at being good and just. Mostly he succeeded.

But the false promises made to Richard back in August of 1399, promises that Richard would remain king, no matter that Henry would rule, gnawed at Henry for the rest of his life. Then there's the matter of Richard's death, a millstone of guilt for a man as upright as Henry to carry. It broke him, and over the coming years of his life, the once so powerful, so vibrant Henry Bolingbroke transformed into a sick and melancholy man. Upon his death, he left no instructions as to how he was to be buried, and his will breathes of humility and guilt, in glaring contrast to most other wills of the period.

I guess the lesson is easy: never do anything that makes it difficult to meet your eyes in the mirror. Fate, however, now and then obliges us to act against our conscience. Henry Bolingbroke felt he had no choice—he had to safeguard his inheritance, for himself and for his sons. I dare say he never forgave himself; I dare say he found the price too steep.

Rebellion in Wales: Owain Glyn Dŵr and Cydweli Castle, Carmarthenshire

By JUDITH ARNOPP

STANDING PROUD ABOVE A SMALL VILLAGE, OVERLOOKING THE RIVER GWENDRAETH near Carmarthen in West Wales, is Cydweli Castle. Of Norman origin, the fortress is testament to the years of Anglo/Welsh conflict, its dominant position in the landscape making it quite clear who was in control of whom.

The earliest castle was a Norman earth and timber construction built shortly after the conquest, the village growing up around it. During the twelfth century the castle fell several times into Welsh hands and by the thirteenth century it had been rebuilt in stone with the latest in defensive design.

Today, we see most phases of building: a square inner bailey defended by four round towers, a semi-circular outer curtain wall to protect the landward side, and the massive gatehouse and jutting tower defending the riverside walls.

Cydweli (or the anglicised Kidwelly) is of concentric design with defensive walls set one within the other providing the best defence possible at the time of building. The gate house was still under construction when Owain Glyn Dŵr held it under siege during his campaign against the English.

Owain Glyn Dŵr was born around 1359 and through his parents, Gruffydd Fychan II and Elen ferch Tomas ap Llywelyn, descended from the Welsh princes of Powys and Deheubarth. His early life is quite unremarkable and law-abiding. He was educated in London and served as a squire and a soldier, fighting for the English king in campaigns in Scotland. By the year 1400 he had become a well-respected Welsh gentleman, but events over the next few years pushed Glyn Dŵr further into rebellion.

Baron Grey de Ruthyn, a neighbour of Glyn Dŵr's, had seized control of some land, forcing him to appeal to the English Parliament. In 1400, Lord Grey failed to inform Glyn Dŵr in time of a royal command to levy feudal troops for service on the Scottish border. This apparent dereliction of duty enabled the Welshman to be named a traitor in London court circles.

Possibly due to Lord Grey's personal friendship with King Henry IV, Glyn Dŵr lost the case and when, in January 1400, civil disorder broke out in Chester in support of the deposed king, Richard II, Glyn Dŵr's relationship with Henry IV broke down completely.

In September 1400, Owain Glyn Dŵr was created Prince of Wales by the dissenting Welsh.

By 1401, after a series of confrontations between Owain's followers and Henry IV, the revolt began to spread. Welshmen studying at Oxford abandoned their studies, labourers laid down their tools and returned to Wales and flocked to Owain's banner; Welsh troops who had fought for the king in France and Scotland also joined the cause; Welsh archers and men-at-arms abandoned the English king to join the Welsh rebellion.

Early in the campaign the Welsh skill at guerrilla warfare gained them some notable success. They were victorious at the battle of Bryn Glas in Powys in 1402, inflicted much damage on many towns (including Cardiff), and took control of several of the strongest castles in Wales, notably Aberystwyth and Harlech.

During the fourth year of the revolt, Owain Glyn Dŵr and his armies turned up in the Tywi Valley and captured a number of castles, including Dyslwyn and Carmarthen and persuaded Henry Don, a former steward of the Duchy of Lancaster and a fellow of considerable standing and power, to throw in his lot with the rebels. It was Henry Don who led the attack on Cydweli Town and castle.

However, around 1405 the rebels began to lose ground. They were defeated at Usk, and sometime between 1408-9 the castles at Aberystwyth and Harlech were retaken by the crown. Owain himself was never captured but faded from history, believed to be dead by 1416. Many tales are told about the circumstances of his death.

A supporter of Glyn Dŵr, Adam of Usk, wrote in his *Chronicle* in the year 1415 that:

> *After four years in hiding, from the king and the realm, Owain Glyndŵr died, and was buried by his followers in the darkness of night. His grave was discovered by his enemies, however, so he had to be re-buried, though it is impossible to discover where he was laid.*

Adrien Jones, the president of the Owain Glyn Dŵr Society, as late as 2006 visited Sir John Scudamore who is a direct descendant of Glyndŵr and lives near Abergavenny. He told him that Glyn Dŵr spent his last years with his daughter Alys at Monnington Straddel in Herefordshire and eventually died there. The family kept the secret for six hundred years, but Sir John claimed that Glyn Dŵr is buried beneath a mound nearby at Monnington Straddel.

Whatever the truth of the matter may be, Owain Glyn Dŵr is gone but never forgotten, and remains a hero in Wales, a household name, and an icon of Welsh nationalism.

LLEWELLYN AP GRUFFYDD FYCHAN: WELSH HERO

By JUDITH ARNOPP

EDWARD I'S DEFEAT OF LLEWELLYN THE LAST IN 1282 AND HIS SUBSEQUENT SUBJUGA-tion of the Welsh people caused seething discontent among the Welsh. After a hundred years of continuing discontent, things finally reached a boiling point when the English crown refused to settle a land dispute between Baron Grey de Ruthyn and the forty-something, grey-haired, and law abiding Owain Glyn Dŵr. It is difficult to access the details of this matter, but we do know that events quickly spiralled out of control and ultimately, Glyn Dŵr took up arms against King Henry IV.

Glyn Dŵr himself, on calling for Welsh assistance, is likely to have been surprised at the alacrity of response. In September 1400 when he raised his banner at Ruthin, supporters came from far and wide and, due to his descent from the Welsh Princes, they dubbed him the Prince of Wales.

In response, the English king marched his army through North Wales burning and looting without mercy. The population were easily quelled and sought peace with Henry, leaving Glyn Dŵr and a few remaining supporters to take to the hills.

But things weren't over yet, and the rebellion took off again when Conway Castle was taken by the Welsh, allowing Glyn Dŵr access to mid and south Wales. Consequently, the rebellion picked up momentum, and Welshmen living and working in England laid down their tools and returned home to join his ranks.

It was around this time that Henry IV, following Glyn Dŵr into the wilds of Wales, called at the home of Llewellyn ap Gruffydd Fychan who lived in Caeo in Carmarthenshire.

According to the chronicle of Adam of Usk, Llewellyn was a "bountiful" member of the Carmarthenshire gentry, a country squire whose household used "fifteen pipes of wine" annually. This is not to imply that the man was a drunk but shows him to be a wealthy and generous host.

At the time in question, Llewellyn was around sixty years of age, too old to fight perhaps, but it is believed two of his sons were at Glyn Dŵr's side. Henry IV forced Llewellyn to lead him to Glyn Dŵr's base camp, and for several weeks the old man led the King on a goose chase through the wild uplands of Deheubarth, allowing Glyn Dŵr time to escape into Gwynedd and gain a position of greater strength.

King Henry, cold, tired, and frustrated, realising somewhat belatedly what was afoot, forced Llewellyn to admit his stratagem. Knowing full well what punishment lay in store, the Welshman spoke out bravely as a loyal follower of Glyn Dŵr and supporter of Wales.

On October 9, 1401 Llewellyn was dragged to the gallows at Llandovery Castle where he was publicly disembowelled and dismembered in front of his eldest son. (Documentation does not make clear whether this refers to Llewellyn's eldest son or Henry's.) As a deterrent to future rebels, Llewellyn's remains were displayed in towns across Wales and his lands were granted to Henry's supporter Gruffydd ap Rhys. But the rebels weren't done with Henry yet, and unrest continued for more than a decade.

It seems that Llewellyn ap Gruffydd was not alone in his loyalty to the last Welsh Prince of Wales for, although Henry IV led one of the largest, most feared armies in Europe (remember Agincourt a few years later in 1415), Owain Glyn Dŵr, who had re-united the Welsh nation, was never captured, mostly because his countrymen refused to betray him. His final end remains a mystery today.

Six hundred years later, in 1998, a campaign was started by residents of Llandovery to construct some sort of a monument to their local hero, Llewelyn, and after an exhibition of proposed designs in the year 2000, a statue by Toby and Gideon Peterson of St. Clears was chosen.

The effigy stands sixteen feet tall and is fashioned of stainless steel, standing on a base of stone brought from near Llewellyn's home in Caeo. The figure of Llewellyn, clothed in cloak, armour, and wearing an empty helmet, stands proudly on the skyline, looking out across the town of Llandovery as a mark of Welsh solidarity.

HENRY V: KING, CONQUEROR, AND...MUSICIAN?

BY ROSANNE E. LORTZ

WESTMORELAND:

> O that we now had here
> But one ten thousand of those men in England
> That do no work to-day!

KING HENRY V:

> What's he that wishes so?
> My cousin Westmoreland? No, my fair cousin;
> If we are mark'd to die, we are enow
> To do our country loss; and if to live,
> The fewer men, the greater share of honour....

Henry V is best remembered as the Lancastrian king of England who fought the French at the Battle of Agincourt, and, against overwhelming odds, carried the field and claimed the crown of France. He is not remembered for being a musical composer during the glorious era of fifteenth century English choral music.

Yet although the story of longbows has won out over the story of the lute, it is certain that music was an important aspect of Henry's life. Thomas Elmham, a contemporary chronicler who would become one of Henry's chaplains, described Henry's early life thus:

> He was in the days of his youth a diligent follower of idle practices, much given to instruments of music, and one who, loosing the reins of modesty, though zealously serving Mars, was yet fired with the torches of Venus herself, and, in the intervals of his brave deeds as a soldier, wont to occupy himself with the other extravagances that attend the days of undisciplined youth.

Here we see that along with fighting and wenching, the young Henry numbered playing musical instruments among his other "extravagances." This idea is confirmed by Tito Livio Frulovisi, an Italian biographer later employed by Henry's brother, who wrote that the young Henry *"delighted in song and musical instruments."*

The prince's predilection for playing musical instruments lent itself to the penning of musical compositions as well. In the Old Hall Manuscript, the best extant source for late Medieval English music (now located at the British Library), there are two compositions attributed to "Roy Henry"—which is translated "King Henry." Most musicologists accept that the king referred to is in fact Henry V, although some wish to attribute the pieces to his father, Henry IV.

Richard Taruskin, in the *Oxford History of Western Music*, offers a suggestion that could harmonize the two camps of thought about the Old Hall Manuscript:

> *Henry IV and Henry V...both reigned during the period of its compiling. Opinions still differ as to which of them may have composed the two pieces attributed to Roy Henry...but as the two pieces differ radically in style it is not impossible that each of the two kings may have written one.*

Even with the remote possibility that Henry IV may have written one of the pieces, it is almost certain that the other was composed by Henry V.

The first piece is a Sanctus, a standard piece from the medieval mass with the words:

> *Sanctus, Sanctus, Sanctus*
> *Dominus Deus Sabaoth.*
> *Pleni sunt caeli et terra gloria tua.*
> *Hosanna in excelsis.*
> *Benedictus qui venit in nomine Domini.*
> *Hosanna in excelsis.*

> *Holy, Holy, Holy*
> *Lord God of Hosts.*
> *Heaven and earth are full of your glory.*
> *Hosanna in the highest.*
> *Blessed is he who comes in the name of the Lord*
> *Hosanna in the highest.*

Taruskin describes Roy Henry's Sanctus as *"smoothly and skillfully written"* with full, rich chords. *"It can be taken as representative of 'normal' English style...just before that style became widely known and momentously influential on the continent."*

The second Roy Henry piece is a Gloria, another standard piece from the medieval mass, which begins with the words spoken by the angels, *"Glory to God in the highest, and on earth peace to men of goodwill."* The parts for this one are written out separately, *"choirbook fashion,"* with the predominant top voice being supported by the others *"in an advanced* ars nova *cantilena style."*

Putting musical terminology aside, suffice it to say that both Roy Henry pieces are up to par with the rest of the works in the collection. Henry was no slouch on the battlefield, and he was, apparently, no slouch at writing music either.

Interestingly enough, the early fifteenth century during which Henry lived marked a golden age for English music. Historian Elizabeth Hallam writes:

The English had a reputation as musicians. On its way to the Council of Con-stance (1414-1418), the delegation led by the bishops of Norwich and Lichfield delighted the congregation in Cologne Cathedral with singing, 'better than any had heard these thirty years'.

The magnificent sounds of English choirs taking their show on the road soon began to impact musicians and composers on the continent. French and Italian composers started using the full, harmonious chords of English music, giving up the stark paral-lelism of an earlier musical tradition.

Elizabeth Hallam writes:

The early 15th century was the only time in history that English musicians helped shape the direction of European music. Henry V's victory at Agin-court, celebrated in the 'Agincourt Carol', meant that a generation of English nobles and churchmen were regular visitors to northern France—and with them came their music.

Although Henry V will probably always be most remembered as the warlike Harry of Shakespeare's immortal play, with *"famine, sword and fire...leash'd in like hounds"* at his heels, it rounds out our picture of the man to remember the musical Harry as well. And ironically enough, it was his success with the sword that transported the voices of English choirs and the scribblings of English composers across the Channel—with such great success that *"not until the 20th century did English music again win such prestige."*

SOURCES

Church, Alfred John. *Henry V.* London: MacMillan and Co., 1891.

Hallam, Elizabeth, ed. *The Wars of the Roses: From Richard II to the Fall of Richard III at Bosworth Field—Seen through the Eyes of Their Contemporaries.* New York: Weiden-feld & Nicolson, 1988.

Taruskin, Richard. *Oxford History of Western Music: Music from the Earliest Notations to the Sixteenth Century.* New York: Oxford University Press, 2010.

The "English Sound" in the Late Medieval Catholic Church

By ANNE E. JOHNSON

O NE OF CHARLEMAGNE'S MANY INFLUENCES ON EUROPEAN CULTURE DEALT WITH how liturgical chant was used by the Catholic Church. Before the ninth century and the formation of the Holy Roman Empire, each region of Europe had its own tradition of singing for Catholic worship. When he came to power, Charlemagne realized that standardizing the rituals of the Church would help his Empire stabilize its many component peoples. He looked to the monasteries of England, where some of the world's best scholars dwelled, and hired a monk named Alcuin to devise a collection of chants to become the official music of Catholics everywhere and replace the regional styles.

To create these universal chants, Alcuin needed to pick one of the regional types of chant to use as a starting point. Interestingly, he did not choose the very distinctive Sarum rite popular in England. Instead, he chose Charlemagne's favorite, a style of chant now known as Old Roman, which was widely used in Charlemagne's native Frankish lands (i.e., Germany).

In order to convince Catholics that altering their worship at Charlemagne's command was a mandate from God, Alcuin's people started a very persuasive rumour: It was claimed that, over 200 years before, God had sent a dove to Pope Gregory I to sing God's chosen chants into the Pope's ear. Those songs, according to the story, were the only official chant of the Catholic Church. With this story to justify them, Alcuin's new melodies became known as Gregorian chant, and European monasteries did accept these songs over the coming century.

England, however, being physically separate from Europe, was a last holdout, defending its regional Sarum rite despite Charlemagne's directive. In fact, this British stubbornness resulted in important developments in music history. In particular, the way monks decorated or harmonized against their chant was unique in the Catholic world. The lush quality of English polyphony was caused by the English monks' use of "chords" (in modern terms) in ways that nobody in Europe had thought of yet, in an English Catholic singing tradition called "fa-burden."

By the fifteenth century, long after Charlemagne, it became clear to French and Flemish composers that the English church music had a very special sound that did not exist on the Continent. They referred to the sweetness and richness of English harmonies, for example "Quam pulchra es," by the fifteenth century English composer John Dunstable, as the *contenance angloise.*

After the Middle Ages, British composers continued to experiment with using that patented English richness in more and more sophisticated ways, such as the early seventeenth century "Tu es Pastor Ovium" by William Byrd.

Continental composers came up with a way to approximate that special English sound, and music would never be the same. All the great European Renaissance musicians, and even famous Baroque composers like Vivaldi and Bach, can trace the richness of their counterpoint back to the European co-opting of the *contenance angloise.* Thank goodness the English held onto their individuality, or the classical music tradition would have turned out very differently!

THE MAKING OF A MEDIEVAL QUEEN, OR HOW TO THROW A PARTY IN LENT...

By ANNE O'BRIEN

O N THE DAY THAT KATHERINE DE VALOIS WAS CROWNED QUEEN OF ENGLAND IN Westminster Abbey on 23 February 1421, her husband of nine months, Henry V, was not present at the ceremony or the resulting festivities. It is suggested that he absented himself in order not to detract from the new Queen's glory, that his time was too valuable to waste on such "junketings", or that it was not tradition for the King to attend the coronation of the Queen. Or even that his initial affection for her had cooled. Whatever the truth of it, I imagine that Katherine might have valued his company at such heavy ceremonial. She was neglected as a child, raised for much of her young life in the convent at Poissy, and her command of English or any language other than French was not very good.

We know that Katherine rode through the streets of London which were hung with cloth of gold, silks and velvets. The crowning by Archbishop Chichele was *"performed with such magnificence that the like had never been seen at any coronation since the time of the noble knight Arthur, King of the English."*

It was a very popular marriage and a splendid occasion.

After the ceremony there came the coronation feast, which was so notable that we have the complete menu for three vast courses. Since it was Lent, fish was definitely the order of the day:

- *pike in herbiage*
- *eeles in burneax*
- *lamprie fresh baked*
- *smelts fried*
- *fresh sturgeon with welks*
- *cervisse de eau doure*
- *eeles roasted with lamprie*
- *pearch with goion*
- *carp de ore*

...and so on, with a vast array of trout, plaice, whiting, crabs, sole, halibut, salmon and lobster.

There were two interesting exceptions to the fish:

Roasted porpoise was served, which since it lived in water was frequently considered to be "fish" as were beaver and water birds (which were not on the menu on this occasion).

Also brawn, which is a traditional, classic, English dish cooked from the meat of a pig's head, trotters and other parts of porcine offal.

I think I would stick with the fish!

At the end of each course there was a superb subtlety produced for the admiration of all, full of political symbolism for the marriage and heraldic meaning, made of pastry and sugar and marzipan:

- *a pelican sitting on her nest with St. Catherine (Katherine's own saint) holding a book in her hand;*
- *a panther and St. Catherine with her terrible wheel and holding a scroll of poetry;*
- *St. Catherine with angels;*
- *a tiger with a mirror, and an armed man on horseback holding the tiger's cub.*

They must have been wonderful to see.

What did Katherine think of all this? What did she wear for the occasion? Sadly we do not know either her thoughts or her appearance. We have no indication of Katherine's sentiments on any aspects of her life until the final months when on entering Bermondsey Abbey she comments on her state of health, and *The Pageant of the Birth, Life and Death of Richard Beauchamp, Earl of Warwick K.G. 1389-1439* which is always a valuable source does not include an illustration of Katherine's coronation. But if it was anything like her marriage, she wore an ermine trimmed gown and mantle and an eye-catching collar.

I doubt that Katherine's experience as Queen of England was a stimulating one, but the fishy coronation feast was obviously a memorable occasion.

An Unfortunate End for a Remarkable Queen of England

By ANNE O'BRIEN

KATHERINE DE VALOIS DIED 3 JANUARY 1437 AT BERMONDSEY ABBEY. THE ABBEY NO longer exists except for its foundations under the streets of London.

She was clearly ill as she herself had commented: *"in grievous malady, in which I have been long, and yet am troubled and vexed."* She had already made her will on January 1, appointing her son Henry VI as executor, and the execution of it to be supervised by Cardinal Beaufort and the Duke of Gloucester (Henry V's uncle and brother) and Bishop Alnwick of Lincoln.

She was 36 years old. Were her problems mental or physical? It seems that some of her servants secured favourable bequests from her—far too favourable—which were annulled afterwards, so perhaps she was too open to suggestion in those final weeks. Perhaps it was the fragility of mind that had struck down her father and was to affect her son. It has been suggested that she suffered from cancer, or she may have been pregnant with a baby that was born and died at Bermondsey. We have no clear evidence.

Katherine was buried in Westminster Abbey but she was not allowed to lie in peace, and it is a tale of neglect and terrible insensitivity. When Henry Tudor became king as Henry VII, he replaced the original inscription on his grandmother's grave, which made no mention of her second marriage to Owen Tudor, with one that did.

In 1503 or thereabouts, during some rebuilding at the abbey, Katherine's body, loosely wrapped in lead, was taken from the original tomb and placed in Henry V's tomb, but it appears to have been openly on view there in its embalmed form. Shockingly to our eyes, until the eighteenth century, it was often on display as a curiosity. On 23 February 1669 the diarist Samuel Pepys was allowed *"by particular favour"* to take Katherine's body into his hands and he *"planted a kiss on her mouth reflecting upon it that I did kiss a queen and that it was my birthday."* It is a macabre thought.

In 1776 the dean of Westminster at last ordered Katherine's reburial but the corpse was still visible in 1793. It was not until 1878 that she finally arrived at her present resting place in Henry V's chantry. We have Queen Victoria to thank for this compassionate decision.

The inscription for her on the altar can be translated:

> *Under this slab (once the altar of this chapel) for long cast down and broken up by fire, rest at last, after various vicissitudes, finally deposited here by command of Queen Victoria, the bones of Catherine de Valois, daughter of*

Charles VI of France, wife of Henry V, mother of Henry VI, grandmother of Henry VII, born 1400, crowned 1421, died 1438.

The date of her death is wrong, but at least Katherine has been allowed peace at last. It is what she deserved, to rest with dignity and seemliness.

Richard III and the Lost World of Greyfriars

By NANCY BILYEAU

THE DISCOVERY IN A LEICESTER CARPARK OF THE REMAINS OF AN ADULT MALE WITH A cleaved skull and spinal abnormalities prompted all sorts of impassioned debate. Was this indeed the body of Richard III, the last Yorkist monarch, slain in the Battle of Bosworth on August 22, 1485, his corpse exposed to the public for all to see by orders of the victor, an obscure, exiled Lancastrian earl named Henry Tudor?

As argument rages anew over Richard III's role in the disappearance of the princes, or whether Sir Thomas More and William Shakespeare defamed Richard with their descriptions of deformity of body and spirit, the location of his burial—the church of a Franciscan friary—and the actions of those who bravely took custody of a battered and naked royal corpse have gone largely unremarked.

Why has Richard rested there? Clearly the last Plantagenet ruler did not designate Greyfriars of Leicester for this honor. His dead queen, Anne, was buried at Westminster; his older brother, Edward IV, was entombed at Windsor. But then, Richard did not expect to die on the field of battle. With greater numbers and far more experience in combat, he was confident of victory. After the crown tumbled off his head—literally—in the immediate shock and chaos of Bosworth, no Yorkist ally or family member claimed the body.

It was a group of Franciscan friars that came forward. The court historian of Henry VII, Polydor Vergil, wrote that Richard was *"buried two days after without any pomp or solemn funeral in the abbey of monks Franciscan at Leicester."* Ten years later, Henry VII assigned 50 pounds to the creation of a tomb. An inscription asked for prayers for Richard's soul *"to atone my crimes and ease my pains below."*

In the late 1530s, the victor's son, Henry VIII, brought about the destruction of the Catholic monasteries as he pushed through the laws creating himself supreme head of the Church of England. The friary in Leicester, like many other structures housing friars, monks, or nuns, was stripped of its value and knocked down. The monument for Richard III was lost. At some point, the ground swallowed up the church where the friars prayed, sang, and chanted.

Over the centuries there were rumors that Richard's body was moved, either soon after death or during the Dissolution, but the leading theory was that he never left Greyfriars. And in 2012, excavation workers funded by the Richard III Society, using historical maps, pinpointed where the friary was once located. Digging began. To the amazement of the world, a body fitting Richard's description was located in the choir of the church, where someone of importance would have been buried.

In exposing the centuries-old church—as well as the chapter house and other rooms of the cloister—the archaeologists have revealed a lost world. To some, the Greyfriars themselves are no more than shadowy figures, extinct specters like the Knights Templar. But what a vital force the Franciscans were for the three centuries preceding the Dissolution, in not only the daily lives of the people but also the intimate lives of kings and queens. By the sixteenth century a branch of Franciscans had become so intertwined with the royal family that when Henry VIII crushed the monasteries, his behavior when dealing with these particular friars veered between inexplicable mercy and shocking savagery.

It all began in Italy, as so many things do, when a wealthy cloth merchant's son gone soldiering saw a series of visions that led to a life of poverty and repentance. Francis of Assisi gained the approval of Pope Innocent III to form a new order. The brotherhood spread incredibly fast; in 1224, nine friars landed at Dover, eager to open shop.

The Franciscans were called "Greyfriars" because of the color of their habits: gray, loose garments of coarse material reaching their ankles, girded with cords. All of their friaries were dubbed Greyfriars as well. Along with the Dominicans, the Franciscans were an important mendicant order in England. These were not monks, shut away to pray in seclusion. Their purpose was to go out and about. According to the 1887 book written by Walter Stanhope, *Monastic London*:

> They were, as it may be termed, the spiritual democrats; they were to mingle with the people, yet without being of the people; they were to take cognizance of all private and public affairs, of all those domestic concerns and sympathies, duties and pleasures, from which their vows put them off. They were to possess nothing they could call their own, either as a body or individually. They were to beg from their fellow Christians food and raiment—such at least was their original rule, a rule soon modified.... Their creative vocation was to look after the stray sheep of the fold of Christ; to pray with those who wept, to preach glad tidings, to exhort to repentance, to rebuke sin and Satan; to advise the doubtful and comfort the weak without distinction of place or person.

Greyfriars' churches sprang up across England, Scotland, and Ireland: in Canterbury, London, Oxford, Northampton, Norwich, York, Salisbury, and, of course, Leicester. At the time of the Dissolution, there were 1,700 Franciscan friars in England.

The largest friary church was in London, on Ludgate Street. Queen Marguerite, the pious second wife of Edward I, sponsored a "spacious and handsome church" for the friars. It became a respected burial place for the nobility as well as for royalty, setting a precedent perhaps for the later interment of Richard III in Leicester. In fact, four queens rested in London's Greyfriars: Queen Marguerite herself; Queen Isabella, the wife of Edward II; Queen Joan, wife of Edward Bruce, king of Scotland; and Queen Isabella, titular queen of the Isle of Man. (After the Dissolution, the friary church was transformed into one for the parish. but all was destroyed in the Great Fire of 1666.)

The benefits bestowed by the Franciscans are beyond question. They espoused the importance of fresh water and built conduits to their friaries, shared by citizens in half a dozen cities. In 1256, they intervened along with the Dominicans to protect a group of Jews who were accused of crucifying a Christian child. As a result, a chronicler said, Londoners gave the Franciscans less alms.

What is interesting is how often the Franciscans interjected themselves into politics. Simon de Montfort, the founder of Parliament and thorn in the side of Henry III, was advised by Franciscans. In a later reign, the friars based in Leicester got into even more serious trouble. They openly supported the deposed Richard II instead of the new king, Henry IV. When word got out, a group of nine were brought to London, tried, and executed. It would not be the last time the Franciscans paid a terrible price for being on the losing side.

But these episodes were nothing compared to what happened after the creation of the Observant Friars of Greenwich. A movement had sprung up in Europe calling for greater asceticism in the Franciscan Order. King Edward IV, despite his devotion to wine, women, and the latest fashions, approved, and in 1480 Pope Sixtus IV sanctioned the foundation of a friary specifically for the Observants in Greenwich. *"The proximity of the Observant Franciscans to what was a much-used royal palace gave them an influence and a prominence far beyond what might have been expected,"* wrote G.W. Bernard in *The King's Reformation.*

There is no record of what Richard III thought of the Franciscans, Observant or otherwise, but considering that they braved a ferocious political climate to give him Christian burial, the relationship could only have been good. His successor, Henry VII, rather surprisingly, held the friars of Greenwich in high esteem as well. He confirmed their grant, arranged for the installment of stained glass in their church, and left them 200 pounds in his will as he *"knew that they had been many times in peril of ruin for lack of food."*

But perhaps the greatest sign of Henry VII's regard for the Observant Franciscans is that he chose to have his second son, the future Henry VIII, baptized in their chapel at Greenwich.

For a time, all was well in the new reign. Henry VIII arranged for the Observants to say two Masses daily for his father's soul. In 1513, he wrote to Pope Leo X saying he could not commend enough the Franciscans' strict adherence to poverty and sincerity, charity, and devotion. His wife, the Spanish Catherine of Aragon, went even further. She was often accompanied by her Franciscan confessors and, in middle age, wore a habit under her royal robes.

All the players were in place, then, for one of the greatest clashes of the King's Divorce. When Henry VIII sought to have his marriage to Catherine annulled so that he could father a son with the young Anne Boleyn, the Observant friars opposed him, showing tremendous—if not suicidal—amounts of courage.

After Catherine of Aragon had been banished from court, Franciscan Friar William Peto, in his Easter Sunday sermon in 1532, preached to a full church, with both Henry and Anne Boleyn in attendance, that if the king pursued his divorce, he would incur the same fate as Ahab and the dogs would lick his blood. After the sermon, Peto told the king to his face that divorce put his throne in jeopardy and that there were mutterings that Henry had slept with both Anne's sister and mother. There is no known record of greater defiance in the presence of the king. Yet Henry VIII did not strike back. Astonishingly, Friar Peto was not arrested; he was later allowed to leave England and go into exile. The following year, Henry VIII had his daughter with Anne Boleyn, Elizabeth, baptized in the same Greenwich friary church as he had been.

But the controversial executions of Sir Thomas More and Cardinal John Fisher for treason followed by the Pilgrimage of Grace, a religion-fueled rebellion against the king, made mercy harder to come by. Another Observant Franciscan, Friar John Forest, a former confessor to Catherine of Aragon, bore the full brunt of Henry VIII's rage. He refused to swear to the authority of Henry VIII as supreme head of the Church of England. After several years of imprisonment, Forest, 67 years old, was taken to Smithfield on May 22, 1538, and burned to death. About 200 Franciscans are believed to have been imprisoned for refusing to swear loyalty to king over pope; perhaps 50 died in captivity.

Such violence over choice of faith leaves one shaken. But there is a quieter sorrow, too, that of the loss of the medieval friaries themselves. The identity of Richard III has been confirmed thanks to DNA advances, but the beauty of the Greyfriars church where he was bravely laid to rest cannot be re-created.

Most of the friars' homes and churches were destroyed utterly; in a few cases, as in Norwich, stone skeletons teeter, hinting at past glory. As Stanhope says in *Monastic London*:

> But even though it was necessary in Protestant England to confiscate and suppress the monasteries, why should the exquisitely wrought buildings have been overthrown? The ruins might at least have been preserved, and future generations been permitted to behold their funereal beauty.

Tudor Period
(1485–1603)

Prophecy: The Curse of the Tudors

By NANCY BILYEAU

The Yorkists were a hard-headed lot, basing their right to rule on blood-line. When their last king, Richard Plantagenet, was slain at the Battle of Bosworth on August 22, 1485, his devastated Yorkist supporters—as well as the rest of the country—waited to hear what claim to the throne the victor, Henry Tudor, Earl of Richmond, would put forth.

It was a delicate question.

Tudor was the leader of the Lancastrian house, but strictly by default. Stronger claim-ants had been mown down a while ago. Yes, he'd won the crown in battle, but there were laws in England. To hold the crown, he'd have to convince everyone he was the legiti-mate king. Tudor's father, Edmund, had no English royal blood; he was the son of French Queen Dowager Katherine of Valois and her Welsh servant, Owen Tudor. (And so half-brother to the last Lancaster king, Henry VI.) Through his mother, Margaret Beaufort, Henry Tudor had a stronger claim, as she was in direct descent from Edward III, but the Beauforts were barred from the succession.

We can imagine there was a certain level of suspense as the country waited. Most assumed that the newly declared Henry VII would swiftly marry Elizabeth of York, oldest living child of the dead Edward IV, and attach his weak claim to her greater one. But he did not marry her right away.

When he invaded England with French-financed troops, Tudor had marched through his family stronghold of Wales gaining support and men under the banner of the red dragon, the battle standard of King Arthur and other Celtic leaders. Now it was announced that Henry Tudor was descended from Arthur himself through Cadwaladr and the Welsh chieftains who were ancestors of Owen Tudor. Genealogists had confirmed this, the skeptical court was informed. Henry's ascension was the fulfillment of prophecy.

Despite such grandiose claims, Henry married Elizabeth of York. But he did not drop the Arthur business. Far from it: He insisted that his first child be born in Winchester, sometimes identified as Camelot in legend. And when that baby boy was born, he was named...Arthur.

What could not be accidental is that in 1485 something else happened in England besides Bosworth. The first printing of *Le Morte d'Arthur* appeared, a compilation of tales by Sir Thomas Malory of Arthur and Guinevere, Launcelot, Mordred, and the magician Merlin. The tales were so popular they were reprinted.

Henry VII would not be the first ruler to seize on the romance of Camelot to bol-ster his regime. But the direct connection of his legal claim to rule to a work of mythic entertainment is bold indeed—if not bizarre. It was as if, in 1977, the year *Star Wars* hit theaters, a president appeared who announced himself descended from Luke Skywalker.

But there were darker elements to this claim to Camelot. In legitimizing a mystical prophecy, Henry VII was unleashing a certain kind of power that would reach across the entire sixteenth century. Rebels against various Tudor regimes would repeatedly use their own prophecies to rally support. They effectively co-opted Henry VII's *modus operandi*, down to the symbolic banners. A frustrated Henry VIII sought to ban prophecy from his kingdom after he was nearly engulfed by seers, witches, and necromancers spouting predictions, many of them derived, allegedly, from Merlin and yet coded and obscure, open to many interpretations.

"The craving to gaze into the future arises naturally in times of great danger and distress," said Madeleine Hope Dodds in the paper "Political Prophecies in the Reign of Henry VIII." It would be hard to imagine more distress caused than the Reformation and Dissolution of the Monasteries. Some of the rebels who rose up in the Pilgrimage of Grace spouted the "wisdom" of Merlin to lead them.

Again and again, strange prophecies emerged in times of political distress. After a young nobleman named Anthony Babington was arrested for a treasonous conspiracy to murder Elizabeth I and replace her with Mary, Queen of Scots, a book of Merlin prophecies was found in Babington's London home.

More than any other Tudor ruler since Henry VII, Elizabeth tried to harness prophecy, to understand it through her consultations with Dr. John Dee and his colleague, the bizarre necromancer Edward Kelley.

But as her grandfather learned so many years before, prophecy was difficult to control.

MOTHER SHIPTON AND THE END OF THE WORLD

By NANCY BILYEAU

IN THE SPRING OF 1881, FAMILIES ACROSS ENGLAND DESERTED THEIR HOMES, TOO DIS-traught to sleep in their beds. They slept in fields or prayed in churches and chapels for God to spare their lives in the apocalypse that was foretold: *"The world to an end shall come / in eighteen hundred and eighty one."*

The author of their terror was Mother Shipton, also known as Ursula Shipton, a woman whose prophecies had been circulating through England and beyond for centuries. The first famous man whose life she prophesied was Cardinal Thomas Wolsey, the minister to Henry VIII until 1530. In often cryptic verse, the crone-like seer predicted wars, rebellions, and all matter of natural disasters. After London burned in 1666, Samuel Pepys wrote in his diary: *"Mother Shipton's word is out."* Her prophecies were published in one form or another over twenty times between 1641 and 1700. In the 1800s, her predictions grew even more terrifying: The end-of-the-world was foretold in a book published in 1862. Its other prophetic verse included: *"A carriage without a horse shall go / Disaster fill the world with woe / In water iron then shall float / As easy as a wooden boat."*

The world did not end in 1881. People began sleeping in their beds once more. It was not the first time that fear of a Mother Shipton prediction convulsed a nation, and it would not be the last.

Today there is considerable skepticism that a voluble prophetess named Mother Shipton ever existed. Many of her written predictions are, after all, confirmed forgeries, created to sell greater numbers of chapbooks and almanacs. Her 1684 "biographer" spun spooky details of her birth and existence; the 1881 end-of-the-world prophecy was debunked when the Victorian editor Charles Hindley publicly confessed to concocting the verses himself.

Nonetheless, belief in Mother Shipton persisted. Today a thriving tourist attraction called Mother Shipton's Cave, at Knaresborough, North Yorkshire, features the cave where she was born and the petrifying well where objects can turn to stone. There's also a shop selling mugs, tea towels, thimbles, and wishing-well water in dark pink, ruby red, and kelly green.

But just because Mother Shipton has become the label on kelly-green wishing-well water does not mean that she has no basis in fact. Like Robin Hood or King Arthur, it's believed that if we were able to trace the myth-making back to the very beginning, a living, breathing person could be identified.

There are no written references to Mother Shipton in the 1500s. That name does not appear in print until 1641. But a mention of a "witch of York" in a chilling letter written by King Henry VIII himself could be the elusive source of the legend.

The context of the letter is critical. It was written to Thomas Howard, Duke of Norfolk, while the Duke was in the middle of a clean-up operation following the Northern rebellion against the King known as the Pilgrimage of Grace. Thousands of commoners and a fair number of nobles rose up against the reforms in religion forced on the country by Henry VIII. The rebels were particularly aggrieved by the fresh taxes and the closing of the monasteries, which in the poorer regions of the North were needed sources of food, shelter, and medical care. The Duke of Norfolk had easily defeated this 1537 outbreak, which followed the main rebellion of 1536, and he was now imprisoning and then executing people without trial, imposing martial law. He wrote his King that he hanged more than 70.

Henry VIII dictated the following letter to Norfolk in response:

> We shall not forget your services, and are glad to hear also from sundry of our servants how you advance the truth, declaring the usurpation of the bishop of Rome.... We approve of your proceedings in the displaying of our banner, which being now spread, till it is closed again the course of our laws must give place to martial law; and before you close it up again, you must cause such dreadful execution upon a good number of inhabitants, hanging them on trees, quartering them, and setting their heads and quarters in every town, as shall be a fearful warning, whereby shall ensue the preservation of a great multitude.... You shall send up to us the traitors Bigod, the friar of Knareborough, Leche, if he may be taken, the vicar of Penrith and Towneley, late chancellor to the bishop of Carlise, who has been a great promoter of these rebellions, the witch of York and one Dr. Pykering, a canon. You are to see to the lands and goods of such as shall now be attainted, that we may have them in safety, to be given, if we be so disposed, to those who have truly served us....

"The witch of York"—could this be a contemporary reference to a woman who not only caused enough trouble to incite the wrath of Henry VIII but also transformed into Mother Shipton? Her legend grew and grew in the 1600s, in published almanacs: Ursula was born in a cave in 1488, the child of an orphan servant girl and an unknown father—perhaps Lucifer himself. She was singularly ugly, called "Devil's Bastard" and "Hag-face." Nonetheless, Ursula married a builder named Toby Shipton and lived quietly with him, never prosecuted for witchcraft though regularly uttering prophecy. "Her stature," wrote her biographer, "was larger than common, her body crooked, her face frightful; but her understanding extraordinary." How much of this describes the same "witch of York" cited by Henry VIII is unknown.

The fact that Mother Shipton's first known prediction concerned the fate of Cardinal Wolsey is significant. According to Wolsey's gentleman usher and later biographer, George Cavendish, Wolsey, near the end of his life, was disturbed by a prophecy heard. Cavendish wrote: "'There is a saying,' quoth he, 'that *When this cow rideth the bull, then priest beware thy skull.*'" According to Tudor-court interpretation, the cow was Anne Boleyn who, holding sway over Henry VIII and convincing him to divorce his Queen to marry her, triggered the break with the Catholic Church. This prophecy was not attributed to Mother Shipton by Cavendish. But in the future, her soothsaying would intertwine with Wolsey's fate.

Belief in prophecy ran through every level of Tudor society. It reached a fever pitch during the dangerous 1530s when queens and courtiers were beheaded, monasteries fell, and rebels were hanged from trees across the North of England.

Many prophecies were used for political purposes. Uprisers against Henry VII said they were following the ancient sages. The rebels of the Pilgrimage of Grace cried that Henry VIII was the ancient "Mouldwarp," a monster ruler foretold by Merlin who would be "cast down." Anthony Babington, who conspired to assassinate Elizabeth I, carried a prediction of Merlin's sayings. One popular prophecy during Elizabeth's time was *"When HEMPE is soon, England's done."* HEMPE was thought to stand for Henry-Edward-Mary-Philip-Elizabeth. Madeleine Dodds in "Political Prophecies in the Reign of Henry VIII" wrote: *"Political prophecies tended to be invoked at a time of crisis, usually to demonstrate that some drastic change, either desired or already accomplished, had been foreseen by the sages of the past."*

In the 1700s and 1800s, Mother Shipton's prophecies broadened to cataclysmic disasters, amazing inventions, and, of course, the end of the world. Stripped of politics, they were more potent than ever. Perhaps they filled a deep craving within to feel that everything happens by some design, even if it is drawn by an ancient mystic, sage, or witch. We are all of us fulfilling an obscure and coded destiny.

It's a craving that we still see around us today. It just might be part of being human.

LISTENING TO BLACKFRIARS

BY NANCY BILYEAU

"*CATHERINE, QUEEN OF ENGLAND, COME INTO THE COURT!*"

It was the third call made by the crier, commanded by Henry VIII to stop the Queen from leaving the tribunal court convened to inquire into the legality of their twenty-year marriage. On that day, June 21, 1529, before a vast room occupied by two scarlet-clad cardinals, nobles of the realm, and a throng of spectators, Catherine threw herself at the feet of the man who was desperate to divorce her in order to marry another woman.

Immortalized by Shakespeare, Queen Catherine said:

> *Sir, I desire you do me right and justice; and to bestow your pity on me; for I am a most poor woman, and a stranger; born out of your dominions; having here no judge indifferent, nor no more assurance of equal friendship and proceedings. Alas, Sir, in what way have I offended you? What cause hath my behavior given to your displeasure, that thus you should proceed to put me off, and take your good grace from me?*

After finishing her entreaty to an embarrassed and unmoved husband, Catherine rose, ignored the crier, saying, "*It matters not, this is no indifferent court for me. I will not tarry.*" And she left. When the Queen reached the sight of the crowd of commoners gathered outside, they cheered for her, the sound of it wafting into the chamber she'd left behind.

It is an unforgettable scene, one that has shaken and moved me each time I read Catherine of Aragon's plea to be spared such a humiliating rejection. Perhaps it was the draw of such high drama—the cheers and cries and arguments of The Great Matter—that led me to search that section of London for the place where the royal confrontation took place: Blackfriars. But there is another reason too.

In my novels *The Crown* and *The Chalice*, I write the stories through the eyes of a Dominican novice who lives at the priory of Dartford in Kent. It was the sole house of Dominican sisters in the kingdom. But the largest male Dominican establishment in England—and one of the most prestigious in all of Europe—was the monastery of friars dubbed Blackfriars. In its vast complex, the upper frater building, 110 feet long and 52 feet wide with two-foot-thick stone walls, had a second-story room called the Parliamentary Chamber. Many important sessions of government were held there.

It's natural to be surprised that a friary would possess such a chamber; the medieval monarchs' respect for the large monastic orders—Dominicans, Benedictines, and Franciscans—is not much written about. The first followers of St. Dominic arrived in England in 1221. Over the next 50 years, their influence and their numbers grew as, pledged to humility and poverty, they stayed in various churches. They were nicknamed "Black-friars" because of the color of their robes.

Edward I was the principal patron of the new Blackfriars friary in London. He made a gift of 200 marks in 1280 to raise the church; construction of all the buildings—cloister, frater, infirmary, chapel, dormitory, vestry, buttery, brewery—lasted at least 20 years. King Edward took its creation so seriously that he extended the western perimeter wall of the city of London so the friars could have more room. Their property extended from the Thames River to Ludgate; the friars, moreover, were not answerable to the mayor or any governmental officials of the city. They were a city within the city.

After the work was finished, King Edward I conducted state business in Blackfriars and even slept there on occasion. Did nights spent on a friar's pallet afford more peace for Edward Longshanks, the Hammer of the Scots? Perhaps.

The Dominicans were grateful to their patron, so much so that they staunchly defended his son, Edward II, when no one else did. After Edward II was deposed by his French wife and her allies, the Blackfriars were distrusted and blamed for a time and had to go into hiding.

There are no more instances of Dominicans' dangerous interference with political affairs. On the property, houses were built and lent to those not affiliated with the friars. It became a fashionable place to live, known for its gardens. Sir William Kingston retired to Blackfriars precinct after his years of service managing the Tower of London, dealing with such prisoners as King Henry's second wife, Anne Boleyn. The Parr family also had a house in Blackfriars, and Henry VIII's sixth wife, also named Catherine, was born there in 1512.

When the end came in the 1530s and Henry VIII, denied his divorce by Rome, declared himself head of the Church of England, the Dominicans did not martyr themselves, like the Carthusian monks. The prior, John Hilsey, surrendered Blackfriars without any known objection in November 1538. The fifteen friars living there were ejected and the friary officially closed. For his cooperation, Prior Hilsey received a pension of 60 pounds for the rest of his life and could stay in prior's lodgings, which included larders, buttery, kitchen, storeroom, cellar, gallery, and other parcels.

Throughout the rest of the sixteenth century, the buildings and gardens of Black-friars were sold to various courtiers. Large structures were broken up; later, some of the halls were put back together to become a playhouse for Shakespeare and other Elizabeth playwrights. In the Great Fire of London, that building was destroyed.

I knew very well that nothing of Blackfriars remained when I visited London in the summer of 2011 to research *The Chalice*. But it was hard to believe. It had functioned as more than a friary and parliamentary-session house—it was a palace. When Charles V, the Holy Roman Emperor, visited his aunt, Catherine of Aragon, he stayed not in any of Henry VIII's castles but in the guesthouse of Blackfriars.

I bought some historical maps and guidebooks at the fantastic bookstore at the Museum of London. Armed with my research suggesting some bits and pieces of the medieval complex remained, I headed for the neighborhood early in the evening. I took the underground to—what else?—Blackfriars station.

I walked the neighborhood, my backpack stuffed with books growing heavier by the minute. It's not really a tourist area, and the financial workers, ties loosened, drinking beer outside a shiny pub, glanced at me, bemused, as I rounded their corner yet again, a map of the city in my hand.

Tired and hungry, I was about to give up when I heard something very strange on a deserted side street. It was singing, a beautiful hymn of some sort. I followed the sound of the voices to a set of stairs leading up. At the top was a small, leafy courtyard park, and a group of twenty middle-aged men and women gathered, singing. A priest stood by.

I learned that this day, July 26, was St. Anne's Day, and they sang to honor her, the mother of the Virgin Mary. I sat on a bench and listened to their program. At twilight, I got up to leave and saw a scrap of low stone wall and near it a line of centuries-old tombstones on the edge of the park pavement.

They were the graves of friars of the Dominican Order. The Church of St. Anne was built in 1550, twelve years after the surrender, to serve as the house of worship for those still living in the precinct. One thing they did was gather and protect some of the graves.

I had found Blackfriars.

OLD LONDON BRIDGE

By KATHERINE PYM

O LD LONDON BRIDGE WAS A WORLD UNTO ITSELF. NOT CONSIDERED LONDON, IT WAS a Liberty, or suburb. People were born, lived, married, and died there, some without stepping off the Bridge the whole of their lives.

Built in the years between 1176 and 1209, it was begun by King Henry II, the first Plantagenet king of England, and finished during the reign of King John (who was forced to sign the Magna Carta). A massive structure that acted like a dam, it stood stalwart against heavy tides and ice during cold winters, and prevented invading ships from passing upriver.

So strongly built, the Old London Bridge lasted 622 years before being pulled down in the 1830s. (The location of the current London Bridge is some 180 feet upriver from the old.) It was a stone structure of nineteen arches and a wooden drawbridge. Houses, shops, churches, and other assorted buildings stood on the bridge.

The anchors holding the bridge in place were called starlings. Massive and feet-like, they were comprised of broken stones and rubble. The starlings compressed the river flow into one-third of its width, causing the tides to rush through the arches like heavy waterfalls. The rush of water going out to sea could be as high as eight feet, depending on the phase of the moon.

It brought out the reckless, usually young men, to "shoot the bridge". Boats would gain speed, and (if the water wasn't too high, scraping the men's heads on the tops of the arches or drowning them) they'd fly through and shoot out the other side over London Pool. After a moment or two dangling over the Pool they'd drop like a rock to the water below. Many died upon a wager or from mishap by getting pulled into the fast current.

Generally, however, the wherryman pulled his boat to the river's edge, and his passenger got out to walk around the bridge. He'd catch another wherry in London Pool to finish his journey down river.

The bridge had a row of houses on either side of its length with shops at road level. This made the actual road from London to Southwark no more than twelve feet across. It was so narrow the bridge gridlocked with traffic. Coaches and dray wagons would meet and could not pass. Fist fights ensued, with blackened eyes and teeth knocked out.

Sources state that at one time there were about 138 shops on the bridge, the two story chapel of St. Thomas Becket, Nonesuch House, and the gatehouse. The bridge with its heavy flow used waterwheels to power corn mills, and on the London side sported the water works.

Then, there was the gateway at the Southwark side where heads of traitors were displayed. The Keeper of the Heads had full managerial control over this section of the bridge. He impaled newly removed heads on pikes and tossed the old ones into the river. When the original bridge was pulled down, workers found skulls in the mud.

Sometimes, when researching, one comes upon some strange things. I came across the following which I'd like to share with you (truth or fiction?):

When King Henry VIII demanded Catholicism no longer be the favorite religion of the land, Sir Thomas More refused to follow his liege lord. As a result he was beheaded. His body was placed in a coffin and his head put on a pike above London Bridge. After the allowable timeframe wherein the Keeper of the Heads knew gulls had feasted and nothing should remain but putrid flesh and hollow eye sockets, Sir Thomas' daughter beseeched the Keeper not to throw her father's head in the river. Instead, she requested he give her the head so she might join it with the body and they be interred together.

The Keeper agreed, but was amazed when he removed the head, for it remained pink and whole as if only sleeping and still alive....

SOURCE

Pierce, Patricia. *Old London Bridge, the Story of the Longest Inhabited Bridge in Europe.*
    Headline Book Publishing, 2001.

THE DEMISE OF THE
MEDIEVAL ROOD LOFT

BY JUDITH ARNOPP

BEFORE THE REFORMATION THE FOCAL POINT OF ALL CHURCHES, EVEN SMALL ONES, was the Holy Rood, a great crucifix that stood high above the congregation upon the Rood beam above the chancel. The cross was often accompanied by figures of Mary and John where candles were kept burning, paid for by the many bequests for *"the light to burn before the Rood."*

Access to the beam was by way of the Rood Loft, usually an ornately carved and painted structure set just above the Rood Screen beneath the chancel arch. On occasion the priest would preach from the loft, lit by the candles about the Rood, the added height and position providing extra impact to his sermons.

During the Reformation of the Church the changes did not at first affect the Roods, although it was ordered that the accompanying images be removed. There were those at this time who saw the Rood as a prime object of idolatry, and instances of vandalism are recorded, but the Rood was allowed to remain and there was no major demolition of the Roods until the reign of Edward VI.

Early in his reign his zealous reforms called for the removal of all shrines, images, candlesticks, and painted images on walls, screens, and even on the stained glass windows. This general destruction began in London in 1548 and spread throughout the realm.

Although many reformers regarded them as Popish idolatry, the figures about the Rood were highly valued in most parishes. When they were ordered to be destroyed, many parishes, unable to face their ruin, hid their prized images away and later, at the time of Queen Mary's reversal of the reforms, they were simply brought out of hiding and reinstated in the church.

It was during the Elizabethan Injunctions that irreversible damage occurred when anything connected with the old religion was ripped out and burnt on huge bonfires.

With the Roods and Rood figures gone, the loft itself had little use, and in the following years most of them slowly decayed until they were removed altogether. The stairs that led to them were largely blocked up and plastered over, but in a few churches the stairs still remain today, built into the solid walls, leading nowhere, a reminder of our medieval past.

There are no Rood Crosses left in Britain today, but some Screens remain, often ornately carved and painted. They stand as testament to the changes the church has endured and marking the medieval divisions between the earthly and divine. Very few

Rood Lofts are left although some have been reconstructed, as only a small amount survived the upheavals of reform.

I recently had the good luck to visit The Church of Merthyr Issui at Patricio in Mid-Wales which houses a splendid unspoiled example of an intact Rood Loft and Screen.

Patricio is a tiny church nestling on a hillside in a wooded valley, a valley infused with natural peace where the only sound is of grazing sheep and birdsong. The building has no ostentatious grandeur, no opulent riches on display, but for me, the simplicity adds to its charm. It is the sort of place that makes an atheist pause and begin to question his convictions.

Somehow, possibly due to its remote location, Patricio escaped the devastation of church reform and stands today pretty much as it did in the medieval period. On opening the door you are assailed by cold, the smell of damp, and the impact of a thousand years of prayer.

The floor is slate, the walls are stone, and here and there a wall painting peeps from beneath the layer of whitewash. There is the depiction of Time, a skeleton with scythe and hourglass reminding us of our mortality, the Royal Coat of Arms, a biblical text in thick, black, forbidding script...but it is the Rood Screen and Loft that draws your eye and pulls you toward the altar.

It lies beneath the chancel arch stretching the width of the church, a masterpiece of craftsmanship laden with carved leaves and flowers concealing a dragon, the emblem of evil, consuming a vine, the emblem of good.

The loft and screen are in an unpainted state; it has never been painted. The Irish oak has been left to flaunt its own natural beauty which makes it, as far as I know, quite unique. You are forced to stand and stare until, at length, you stretch out a finger to trace the path of the ancient chisel.

A short stone stairway is cut into the wall, the Tudor headed doorway suggesting it was added later than the two stone altars which have also somehow escaped the destruction ordered in the Elizabethan period.

I love this place. I do not want to leave. My camera clicks, recording what I see, but there are things the lens can never quite capture—the serenity of the graveyard, the cool tranquility of the interior, the brush strokes of long dead painters, the chisel marks of the carpenter on the Rood Loft and Screen, the antiquity of the incised consecration crosses on the altars. And, most of all, it can never capture the whispering echoes of the prayers of the long dead congregation.

You will have to make the journey there to experience that.

Rightful Head of England: Pope vs. King

By ROSANNE E. LORTZ

We thought that the clergy of our realm had been our subjects wholly, but now we have well perceived that they be but half our subjects, yea, and scarce our subjects: for all the prelates at their consecration make an oath to the Pope, clean contrary to the oath that they make to us, so that they seem to be his subjects, and not ours.

ON MAY 11, 1532, KING HENRY VIII UTTERED THIS COMPLAINT TO PARLIAMENT, THAT the clergy of the realm cared more for the Pope's commands than they did for his own. Any Tudor-phile can tell you what happened next. Two years later Henry issued the Act of Supremacy, severing the connection with Rome and making himself *"the only supreme head on earth of the Church in England."*

But how did the Church of England become so reliant on the Church of Rome in the first place? How did the Pope, the bishop of the far-away city of Rome, gain authority over what happened in the British Isles?

The story of the Pope's involvement with the island of England goes back to the sixth century, nearly a thousand years before Henry VIII's complaint. The island of Britain had been evangelized by Christian missionaries in the first several centuries A.D., but after the invasion of the Angles, Saxons, and Jutes, it became pagan once again. In the late sixth century, Pope Gregory the Great, the bishop of Rome, felt a great burden to Christianize these people. Bede records that Gregory, *"prompted by divine inspiration, sent a servant of God named Augustine and several more God-fearing monks with him to preach the word of God to the English race."*

With his mission accomplished, Augustine sent to Rome *"to inform the Pope St. Gregory that the English race had received the faith of Christ and that he himself had been made their bishop. At the same time he asked his advice about certain questions which seemed urgent."*

What follows is a list of questions about liturgy, governance, and conduct, but the important thing is the way it is phrased. Augustine seeks Pope Gregory's advice.

The Pope, as the successor of Saint Peter and the ruler of the "apostolic see", had always been seen as an important spiritual leader in the Church, but it is anachronistic to suppose that he wielded as much power in the early church as he did in days of the Tudors. Historian Gerd Tellenbach notes that after the collapse of the Western Roman Empire and the foundation of new kingdoms by the Germanic tribes, *"the national and regnal churches were to a greater or lesser extent autonomous and not easily influenced from outside."*

Tellenbach confirms what we observe in Bede, saying:

> *Only exceptionally did Popes play a significant role beyond their own region before the middle of the eleventh century. They were normally active only when called upon to be so, not on their own initiative; their advice or judgements were not compulsory; they could be accepted, ignored, or rejected at will.*

In the centuries subsequent to Augustine's missionary activities, we see the English kings looking up to the Pope with respect and rendering them obedience in spiritual matters. One example of this is Alfred the Great who, as a young child, accompanied his father on a pilgrimage to Rome to see Peter's Successor. The Pope later became a godfather of sorts to Alfred, but he made no attempt to interfere with his subjects' loyalties.

What happened then in the eleventh century to change things? Several successive "Reform" Popes, Gregory VII being the most famous, saw it as their divinely-appointed task to combat corruption in the church. One especial sin that needed to be purged was "lay investiture," the practice of political rulers appointing men for church office. In response to the Holy Roman Emperor arrogating to himself the power to appoint bishops, the Pope arrogated to himself the power to depose emperors (by excommunicating them, and thus freeing their subjects from the necessity of obeying them).

Henry IV, the Holy Roman Emperor whom Gregory would depose, saw no justification for the Pope throwing his weight around in such a manner:

> *You dared to threaten to take the kingship away from us—as though we had received the kingship from you, as though kingship and empire were in your hand and not in the hand of God.... As the tradition of the holy Fathers has taught, I am to be judged by God alone and am not to be deposed for any crime unless—may it never happen—I should deviate from the Faith. For the prudence of the holy bishops entrusted the judgment and the deposition even of Julian the Apostate not to themselves, but to God alone. The true Pope Saint Peter also exclaims, "Fear God, honor the king" (I Peter 2:17). You, however, since you do not fear God, dishonor me, ordained of Him.*

The battle between the Pope and the Holy Roman Emperor would soon have repercussions in England. In 1162, the English king Henry II installed his friend Thomas Becket as Archbishop of Canterbury. Unfortunately for the king, Becket soon came to see that his own ordination was just one example out of many of how Henry was encroaching upon the liberty of the church. He rebuked Henry for these incursions and took it upon himself to become the church's defender.

The story of the conflict between the two men is famous, and I will not take the time to tell it all here; however, it is interesting to note the role of the Pope during these events.

When Becket excommunicated lower clergymen who had dared to side with Henry, they appealed to the higher authority of the Pope in order to have their excommunications revoked. Several times throughout the conflict, both Henry and Becket appealed to the Pope to give a ruling, not in the sense of giving advice, but in the sense of giving a binding judgment. These instances show how a formal hierarchy had developed with the Pope at the apex, and how papal power was continuing to increase throughout the twelfth century.

The rule of Henry's son John in the thirteenth century would see an even greater increase in papal power. When John tried to follow in his father's footsteps and select the new Archbishop of Canterbury, Pope Innocent III rebuked him and put forward his own candidate for the position. John refused to comply. Pope Innocent put England under an interdict, prohibiting the clergy from conducting any religious services. John seized the lands of the clergy who followed the Pope's orders. More excommunications and seizures of money followed. When John still proved recalcitrant, the Pope incited the French king to prepare an invasion against him (not that Philip II needed much incitement...). Fearful of an attack from France, John finally submitted his will to the Pope's and did homage to Innocent for the country of England.

Innocent's letter to John following these events shows how outrageous the papal aggrandizement of power had become:

> The king of kings and lord of lords, Jesus Christ...has set over all one whom he appointed to be his vicar on earth so that, just as every knee on earth and in heaven and even under the earth is bowed to him, so all should obey his vicar and strive that there be one fold and one shepherd. The kings of the world so venerate this vicar for the sake of God that they do not regard themselves as reigning properly unless they take care to serve him devotedly. Prudently heeding this, beloved son...you have decreed that your person and your kingdom should be temporally subject to the one to whom you knew them to be spiritually subject, so that kingship and priesthood, like body and soul, should be united in the one person of the vicar of Christ to the great advantage and profit of both.

The Popes of the next three centuries tried, with varying degrees of success, to maintain the high position to which Innocent had elevated the papacy, but their rhetoric and resplendence never quite measured up. When the papacy removed to France for seventy years during the Avignon Papacy, the English lost a great deal of respect for Peter's Successor. After winning one of the early battles of the Hundred Years' War, the English bandied about a jest (which, yes, also appears in the Heath Ledger movie *A Knight's Tale*), saying, *"The Pope may be French, but Jesus Christ is English."*

The Papal Schism which followed the Avignon Papacy in 1378, saw two different Popes battling for the position over the course of forty years. This weakened the papacy even further as France, the Spanish kingdoms, and Scotland supported one Pope while England and the Holy Roman Empire supported the other.

By the time Henry VIII took the throne in England, the papacy was not as much of a force to be reckoned with. The Pope was still a political player in Europe, but no longer the eight-hundred-pound gorilla in the room.

So, all this goes to show that when Henry VIII was complaining to Parliament of the Pope's undue influence over English clergy, what he really should have been doing was counting his blessings. If he had had Innocent III to deal with instead of Clement VII, he might have met his match, he might have stayed married to Catherine of Aragon, and he might never have become the star of a Showtime television series. The title of "Supreme head of the Church in England" would have remained with the Pope, and the ill-fated Anne Boleyn might have contrived to keep her head.

SOURCES

Bede. *The Ecclesiastical History of the English People.* New York: Oxford University Press, 1969.

Tellenbach, Gerd. *The Church in Western Europe from the Tenth to the Early Twelfth Century.* Trans. Timothy Reuter. U.K.: Cambridge University Press, 1993.

Tierney, Brian. *The Crisis of Church and State 1050-1300.* Toronto: University of Toronto Press, 1988.

"Cruel and Abominable Tyrant": The Pope Who Took on Henry VIII

By NANCY BILYEAU

O<small>N</small> M<small>AY</small> 8, 1539, <small>MORE THAN</small> 20,000 L<small>ONDON MEN BETWEEN THE AGES OF SIXTEEN</small> and sixty put on white clothing and assembled before their King, Henry VIII, to prove their readiness to go to war. Before 6 a.m. they mustered in order of battle in the fields *"between White Chapel and Mile End"* and, to the sound of drums and fifes, marched with their weapons to Westminster, there to be surveyed by the King, his chief minister Thomas Cromwell and *"all the nobility."*

This was the great London muster, held to not only demonstrate to Henry VIII that his *"loving subjects"* were willing to fight to the death, but to make clear to hostile foreign powers how formidable were these *"goodly, tall and comely men"* toting *"rich jewels, chains and harness."*

Fifty years before King Philip II's famous Spanish Armada sailed for England to attempt to depose Elizabeth I, a less-well-known invasion was planned by Philip's father, Holy Roman Emperor Charles V, and his allies. In the end, no attack was launched on England. But the plan was real.

For Henry VIII, who in 1536 had (prematurely) declared on the death of his Spanish first wife Catherine of Aragon, *"God be praised we are freed from all suspicion of war,"* the threat of foreign invasion in the late 1530s was his worst nightmare coming true.

For it wasn't just Catherine's nephew, Charles V, who was poised to attack but King Francis I of France, along with King James V of Scotland, eager to swoop down for the kill. England was completely isolated.

The architect of war on Henry VIII was Pope Paul III, 71 years old, who on the day of the muster was called a *"cankered and venomous serpent."*

Those words wouldn't have scared His Holiness. Pope Paul was not afraid of Henry Tudor. He had pushed through a bull of excommunication on Henry in December 1538 that called him a *"most cruel and abominable tyrant"* and freed his subjects from obedience to the king who broke from Rome. The Pope was the one who worked feverishly to unite Charles V and Francis I, who distrusted each other, so that their combined armies could demolish Henry VIII's defenses.

Once Henry was gone, it was expected that his twenty-three-year-old daughter, Mary, the niece of Charles V, would rule, and not his tiny son by Jane Seymour.

In light of the seriousness of this foreign threat, Henry VIII's behavior during the late 1530s and early 1540s—his rash of horrific executions, his fourth marriage and rapid divorce, and his erratic religious policies—is better understood, if not excused.

Henry was a middle-aged man in poor health with an infant male heir and two daughters he'd deemed illegitimate, one of them half-Spanish. It was critical to Henry and Cromwell that there be absolutely no chance that anyone in England would rise to join in the foreign attack.

But the King was hardly in the strongest domestic position, since in 1536 and 1537 thousands of subjects in the North of England rebelled against him, saying they wanted a return to the Pope and the old ways of the Catholic Church. That rebellion was quashed, but for a while it looked as if it might triumph.

Henry VIII's enemy, Pope Paul III, was a man of determination but with his own dark side. He was born Alessandro Farnese, of an aristocratic family in Rome. He was the oldest brother of Julia Farnese, the beauty and acknowledged mistress of Roderigo Borgia, Pope Alexander VI. It was the Borgia Pope who made Farnese a cardinal-deacon at the age of 27.

While a cardinal, Farnese had four children by a mistress, Sylvia Ruffini. One of their sons would grow up to become the first Duke of Parma and live as a violent, amoral mercenary until he was stabbed to death in 1547, his assassins hanging his corpse from a palace window.

When Henry VIII tried to have his marriage with Catherine of Aragon annulled, the Pope in Rome was Clement VII, a vacillator who strung Henry along for years without an answer. He didn't want to upset either Henry VIII or Catherine's nephew, Charles V. That policy was a huge error. In frustration, Henry VIII had broken with Rome, made himself head of the Church of England, and annulled his own marriage.

When Farnese became Pope Paul III in 1534, his first act was to make two of his teenage grandsons cardinals. Another priority was to persuade Michelangelo to finish the fresco "The Last Judgment" in the Sistine Chapel.

But he was also determined to crush the defiant English King.

It was not just Henry VIII's break from Rome that brought about papal excommunication. Other monarchs were following the ideas of the Protestant reformation without being attacked by the Pope.

It was Henry's executions of Sir Thomas More and Cardinal Fisher, his destruction of the monasteries that were packed with friars, monks, and nuns loyal to Rome, and, most of all, his despoiling of the shrines of English saints that appalled the Catholic powers.

Pope Paul III labored to unite the two most powerful princes of Europe, Charles V and Francis I, both of whom had gone back and forth with Henry VIII, sometimes his friend and sometimes his enemy. Henry had been a sought-after ally because of his treasury and England's strategic location, and he enjoyed playing them off against each other.

After the death of his third wife, Jane Seymour, in 1537, Henry wanted a beautiful royal bride from the family of either Charles or Francis, but they played for time. One after another, the desirable Christina of Milan or Marie de Guise would be dangled before him, only to be yanked away after Henry made serious pursuit through diplomatic channels. (Marie de Guise married James V of Scotland, and they were the parents of Mary Queen of Scots who would one day cause endless headaches for Henry's daughter Elizabeth.)

After the Pope made clear his wish for war on England, the only ruling family that could conceivably make a marriage alliance with Henry VIII was a Protestant one, and Anne of Cleves, sister of the German Duke of Cleves, was chosen to be his fourth wife. But before she arrived, King Henry also turned his attention to his own nobility to weed out possible traitors.

Pope Paul had encouraged Reginald Pole, Henry VIII's cousin, in his public criticism of the English King from the safety of Rome, and he made Pole a cardinal in 1537. Reginald's mother, Countess Margaret, and brother, Baron Montague, both vulnerable, wrote to Reginald asking him not to provoke the King further, but, egged on by the Pope, he refused to tone down his blistering attacks. It was even thought that Pope Paul intended to replace Henry VIII with Reginald, or marry Reginald to Mary and have them rule together.

In retaliation, Henry lashed out at the Poles, executing sixty-nine-year-old Margaret Pole and Baron Montague with no proof of treachery. He also had arrested and executed his first cousin and childhood friend, Henry Courtenay, Marquess of Exeter, and imprisoned Courtenay's wife and teenage son.

The Poles and Courtenays had sympathized with Catherine of Aragon and were friends to Princess Mary. No evidence of conspiracy ever came to light. But they were wiped out because of their dangerous share of Plantagenet royal blood, their connection to Mary, and their Catholic beliefs.

In addition to issuing musters all over England to men ready to defend their kingdom, Henry VIII poured money into his navy and his land defenses near the shore. Detailed maps were commissioned, bulwarks and blockhouses raised. When France and Spain recalled their ambassadors in 1539, it looked as if war would come any day.

But the alliance between Charles V and Francis I did not hold. Their hatred of each other—which usually came to a boil over obsession with acquiring the same land and titles in Italy—led to a break in 1540. Also, despite all of the Pope's haranguing, neither of them possessed the same passion for war on England, not because of affection for Henry but because invading a well-defended island kingdom would be so expensive and promised to be full of casualties.

If only King Philip of Spain would, five decades later, have studied his father's example. He'd have saved himself an Armada.

The Fool and His King

By JUDITH ARNOPP

Q: When is a fool, not a fool?
A: When he is a fool.

IT DOESN'T MATTER HOW FAR BACK YOU RESEARCH INTO HISTORY, IF THERE IS A MONarch, then his fool will not be far away. In one form or another, be it tumbler, juggler, trickster, jester, or clown, every recorded culture had them, but, thanks to Shakespeare and other writers of the period, it is the motley fool of the English medieval kings that remains uppermost in our minds. But these fools were not simply to amuse the monarch; they had other, more subtle duties and their importance shouldn't be underestimated. As the sixteenth century author Erasmus pointed out:

> We have all seen how an appropriate and well-timed joke can sometimes influence even grim tyrants.... The most violent tyrants put up with their clowns and fools, though these often made them the butt of open insults. (Desiderius Erasmus, *In Praise of Folly*)

Throughout history there are fools. Dwarves, of course, and warrior fools, Norman buffoons, minstrel fools, and innocents; but it is the Tudor fool, Will Somer, whose influence and companionship to Henry VIII is so well documented, upon whom I wish to concentrate today.

Somer was not the only fool at court, but he seems to have been the favourite. His predecessor, Sexton (also known as Patch), was famous for his nonsensical wit, but the thing that set Somer apart from the others was the love of the King. He had the ability to turn Henry's mind when it needed turning the most.

The most famous quip afforded to Somer is by Thomas Wilson who quotes him in his *Art of Rhetoric* as follows.

> William Somer, seeing much ado for account-making, and that the King's Majesty of most worthy memory, Henry the eighth, wanted money such as was due unto him: As please your grace (quoth he) you have so many frauditers, so many conveyers, and so many deceivers to get up your money, that they get all to themselves....

The pun on "auditors, surveyors and receivers" is both a joke and a truth, and there are other similar witticisms recorded to Somer in other works of the period. For example:

Armin's *Foole upon Foole* (1600), Samuel Rowley's *When You See Me, You Know Me* (1605), or the anonymous, *A Pleasant History of the Life and Death of Will Summers* (1676).

John Southworth, author of *Fools and Jesters at the English Court* says that these documents do not offer much in the way of history but they all highlight Somer's use of his "merry prate" and spontaneous rhymes to improve his master's state of mind.

Other reports suggest he was less a wit than a "natural fool" (today we would refer to this as having learning difficulties), and I could go into a lengthy discussion about this, but I want to concentrate on Will's relationship with Henry VIII.

William Somer first emerges in 1535 when an order appears for new clothes for "William Somer, oure foole." Henry's "olde foole" Patch/Sexton had grown too old, and it was Will who was chosen to take his place.

His initial requirements included a fool's livery:

> a dubblette of wursteed, lined with canvas and coton...a coote and a cappe
> of grene clothe, fringed with red crule, and lined with fryse...a dublette of
> fustian, lyned with cotton and canvas...a coote of grene clothe, with a hood of
> the same, fringed with white crule lyned with fryse and bokerham.

It seems that throughout his service Somer was maintained by the Privy purse, for although there is a surviving record from Cromwell in January 1538 of a *"velvet purse for W. Somer"*, there is no mention of anything to fill it, his expenses being met by the court.

In this fine new apparel Will Somer's duty was to entertain and distract the King from his worldly care, and he seems to have done so admirably. His favour with Henry raised him so high that he appears in several portraits commissioned by the King himself, the most famous being the family portrait by an unknown artist which is now housed in the Royal Collection.

It depicts Henry at his most virile and vigorous best and Queen Jane who had already been dead for over a decade. On the King's right is their son Edward (whose birth caused his mother's death in 1537). Completing the Tudor idyll are the Princesses, Mary and Elizabeth, both girls bastardised and legitimised so many times they can have had no real idea as to their royal standing.

The entire royal family are assembled in a fantasy gathering, a made-up truth to please the King, and what makes this especially poignant is that, a little behind the royal sitters, the painting also shows Will Somer dressed in his "clothe coote", and his velvet purse is hanging from his belt. His pet monkey obligingly picks lice from the fool's hair.

Framed in the opposite archway is a likeness of a girl, believed to be of Jane, the innocent fool of Princess Mary, whom it is believed she took into her household after the death of Anne Boleyn. The presence of the royal fools in this very personal portrayal of Henry's family can only point to their importance.

Another glimpse we have of Will Somer is in a psalter commissioned by Henry (circa 1540). This time the King is drawn as an old man in the character of King David playing a Welsh harp, and Will is pictured with his back to the King. Again, he is dressed in the "grene cloth cote" recognisable from the descriptions in the Privy purse accounts.

Since most of Henry's old friends had, by this point, been executed, exiled, or (more rarely) died of natural causes, there must have been few left that he could safely trust or confide in. This makes the image of the lonely old King and his trusty fool a hauntingly unhappy one. I can almost be moved to pity him.

Records suggest that, as the reign progressed, only Will was able to take Henry's mind from the incessant pain of his ulcerated leg, the cares of state, and his growing ill-health and depression. Right until the end of the King's life, wherever Henry went Will went too, from palace to palace; his every need was catered and provided for. At Christmas 1545, just a year before the King's death, when a batch of sixteen horses were ferried across the Thames on a trip to Hampton Court, there were three mounts to carry the massively obese king and one for his fool, "Wyllyam Somer."

After Henry's death in 1547, Somer went on to serve at the court of Edward VI and Mary I, but he died early in the reign of Elizabeth. He is buried at St. Leonard's in Shoreditch, his name marked on a stone to commemorate players and musicians of the period who are buried in the church.

FURTHER READING

Southworth, John. *Fools and Jesters at the English Court.* The History Press, 2011.

ELIZABETH HOWARD: THE QUEEN'S MOTHER

By JUDITH ARNOPP

QUEEN ELIZABETH I, AS WE KNOW, WAS NAMED AFTER HER PATERNAL GRANDMOTHER, Elizabeth of York, the flower of the Plantagenets who, by marrying Henry Tudor, strengthened and secured his throne. Queen Elizabeth's other grandmother, the mother of Anne Boleyn, was also an Elizabeth but, unlike her daughter and granddaughter, is often bypassed in the history books.

She was Elizabeth Howard, the eldest daughter of Thomas Howard (2nd Duke of Norfolk) by his first wife, another Elizabeth—this time by the name of Tilney. Through her father's line Elizabeth Howard was directly descended from Edward II.

John Howard, the old Duke of Norfolk, fought in King Richard's vanguard and perished at the Battle of Bosworth. As a result his estates were forfeit and his heir, Thomas Howard, faced an uphill battle to gain favour with the new Tudor King. His estates were not restored until 1489. As a girl, Elizabeth served in the household of his Queen, Elizabeth of York, and later as lady-in-waiting to Catherine of Aragon. During this period rumours began to circulate that the young Henry VIII was romantically involved with Elizabeth Howard, but most historians now discount them.

Before Henry and Anne were married, because of his affair with Mary Boleyn (Anne's sister), he asked for a dispensation, ensuring there was no impediment to his marriage. He made no mention of a relationship with Elizabeth, and another story says that when it was suggested in his presence that Henry had slept with all three Boleyn women, the king scotched the rumour with the words, "Never with the Mother." It would make little sense to confess to one affair and lie about another when both would equally affect his marriage to Anne.

In her early years at court, Elizabeth was courted by a friend and ally of her father, the upwardly mobile Thomas Boleyn, a diplomat in the king's service. They were wed in the 1490s, and Elizabeth gained the titles of Countess of Ormond and Viscountess Rochford.

After many unsuccessful pregnancies Elizabeth presented Thomas with three surviving children, all of whom were to become notorious: Mary, later mistress to King Francis I and Henry VIII; Anne, to become Queen Consort to Henry VIII; and George who, had it not been for his proximity to his royal sister would have remained in relative obscurity, instead died with her on the scaffold accused of treason and incest.

While Thomas Boleyn was Ambassador in France, his daughters Mary and Anne served as ladies in waiting to Queen Claude. It is probable that Elizabeth was with them there. What she made of her eldest daughter's interlude with the French King is anybody's guess, but historian M. L. Bruce in his book *Anne Boleyn* claims that Thomas and Elizabeth developed "feelings of dislike" for Mary.

Later rumours that the French King referred to Mary as his *"English mare"* and a *"great whore, the most infamous of all"* may have made the situation worse. Possibly as a measure to protect her reputation a marriage was arranged between Mary and William Carey, a gentleman courtier and friend of Henry VIII. Unfortunately, this only served to put Mary in the way of the English king who was quickly smitten and began an affair with her.

When the ever-fickle Henry set his eyes on her sister Anne, his interest in Mary began to wane. The rumours that Mary's children, Henry and Catherine Carey, were in fact the King's persist to this day, and a study of the portraits do show some convincing resemblances to the monarch.

Mary's misdemeanors didn't end there, and after the death of her husband from the sweating sickness in 1528, she formed a liaison and secretly married a commoner, William Stafford. Mary could have made a brilliant second match, and the King and Queen saw her marriage to Stafford as a great insult. As a result Mary was banished from court, her relationship with her Boleyn family apparently severed. It is interesting to note that Mary was not shunned by her family while a royal mistress and valuable to the Boleyn cause but only after her unsuitable, unprofitable marriage.

Elizabeth's relationship with her younger daughter appears to be rather different. It may have been that Anne was more intellectual, less given to impulse than her sister, or it may have been that, unlike her sister, Anne did so much more to boost the standing of the Boleyn family, putting her head before her heart. Anne and her mother shared a love of music, theology, and reading, and when Anne arrived at court in the early years of her relationship with Henry, Elizabeth was at her side and remained part of her daughter's household until the Queen's execution in 1536.

As a mother myself I can scarcely contemplate even the idea of witnessing my own children reviled throughout the kingdom, accused of the most dreadful of crimes, treason, fornication, and incest, and finally executed as traitors to the King.

We can only speculate on Elizabeth's state of mind at this time, but I am quite certain that she would have known them to be innocent, she would have prayed for some sort of reprieve, and her feelings of powerlessness must have been immense. For Elizabeth, I am quite sure, the loss of her children in such circumstances, the bastardisation of her granddaughter and namesake, the Princess Elizabeth (now to be addressed only as Lady), would have outweighed the loss of her own status.

We do not know if she was present for the executions; I rather hope not. All we do know is that she retired from court life and died two years later in April 1538 at Baynard's Castle. She now lies, not with her husband in the Boleyn tomb at Hever, but in the Howard chapel at St. Mary's in Lambeth.

FURTHER READING

Bruce, M. L. *Anne Boleyn*. London, Collins. 1972.

Denny, Joanna *Anne Boleyn*. 2007.

Ives, Eric. *The Life and Death of Anne Boleyn*. 2004.

Ridgeway, Claire *The Anne Boleyn Collection*. 2012.

Weir, Alison. *The Lady in the Tower*. 2009.

Weir, Alison *Mary Boleyn: The Great and Infamous Whore*. 2001.

Thomas Wyatt: Courtier, Diplomat, Poet, Lover

By JUDITH ARNOPP

Thomas Wyatt's portrait by Holbein shows a discontented fellow. His eyes are troubled, mentally tortured even, his mouth down-turned, his cheeks sagging, as if he is tired of life and living. But maybe we are swayed by the stories we've all heard of his unhappy marriage, his unrequited love for Anne Boleyn, his lovelorn poetry, his enforced exile, and his false imprisonment. But what do we really know?

Was Tom Wyatt really the tortured poet and lover that we like to think he was? There are plenty of known facts about him, putting him in a certain place at a certain date, clues we can pick up and learn from. There is the aforementioned portrait by Holbein, various letters and papers, a biography of Anne Boleyn written by his grandson George Wyatt... and, closest to his heart of all, there is his poetry.

Born in 1503, Thomas Wyatt was destined for life in the royal court. His father remained in high favour since his support of Henry VII at Bosworth, and Wyatt's first recorded presence is in the entourage of the christening of Princess Mary (a future queen, incidentally, who would one day be responsible for the beheading of Wyatt's son after the Lady Jane Grey affair in 1554).

In a dynastic power match, Wyatt was married to Elizabeth Brooke in 1520, a union that, despite the birth of Thomas Wyatt the younger, proved both unhappy and unsuccessful. In later years Wyatt, after accusing her of adultery, parted company with his wife to live openly with his mistress, Elizabeth Darrell.

One of Henry VIII's esquires of the body, he became one of the King's intimates, entering into courtly pastimes—jousting, hunting, and dancing. Like Henry, Wyatt wrote verses, an important component of the courtly love games that were so popular among the royal household. These poems were often left where a girl could find them or offered as tokens; sometimes the poems were altered or embellished by another hand before being passed on. They were not published in his lifetime and in all probability never meant for close interpretation. Due to Wyatt's central role in the story of Anne Boleyn, however, history has decided otherwise.

It must have been during this carefree period of Henry VIII's reign that Wyatt's romantic interest in Anne Boleyn was first piqued. As part of Queen Katherine's household Anne would have been fair game for Wyatt's attention, but when it became clear that Henry had set his sights on the same target, Wyatt either withdrew or was sent by the King on a mission that took him away from court.

Most historians seem to agree that some sort of an attachment existed between

Thomas and Anne, but we can only guess at the extent of it. Some read a physical involvement into the poems, but it seems to me to have been one-sided. Although there seems little doubt in the depth of Wyatt's involvement, at the time he first began to make reference to Anne she was engaged in a liaison with Henry Percy, an affair that was quickly nipped in the bud by Cardinal Wolsey.

I am not skilled enough to judge the quality of Wyatt's poetry, but his particular choice of words and nuances of meaning can leave no doubt as to his state of mind. This is love if ever I saw it. A riddle, punning on the name "Anna", points to the possible identity of his secret lady.

> *What word is that that changeth not,*
> *Though it be turned and made in twain?*
> *It is mine answer, God it wot,*
> *And eke the causer of my pain.*
> *It love rewardeth with disdain:*
> *Yet is it loved. What would ye more?*
> *It is my health eke and my sore.*

It could, of course, be another Anna; it was a common enough name. It is not until you read all the poems as one unit that the argument for the object of his passion being Anne Boleyn becomes stronger.

The following poem is believed to have been written later, and the lines were altered at some point to make them less dangerous. The line *"Her that did set a country in a roar"* was changed to read *"Brunet, that set my wealth in such a roar"*. Obviously the initial reference to Anne was far too explicit; after all, what other "brunet" of his acquaintance had "set the country in a roar?"

> *If waker care, if sudden pale colour,*
> *If many sighs, with little speech to plain,*
> *Now Joy, now woe, if they my cheer disdain,*
> *For hope of small, if much to fear therefore;*
> *To haste to slack my pace less or more,*
> *Be sign of love, then do I love again.*
> *If thou ask whom; sure, since I did refrain*
> *Her that did set our country in a roar,*
> *Th'unfeigned cheer of Phyllis hath the place*
> *That Brunet had; she hath and ever shall.*
> *She from myself now hath me in her grace:*
> *She hath in hand my wit, my will, my all.*
> *My heart alone well worthy she doth stay,*
> *Without whose help, scant do I live a day.*

Taken individually, Wyatt's poetry could refer to anyone. It is not until you come to the most famous verse of all that arguments against it being Anne begin to collapse. It could, I suppose, have been poetic licence or wishful thinking but surely, the words are too personal for that. In my opinion these lines can only have been written by a man who has lived them, and it is this poem that endorses all the others. There is no need, I think, to explain the meaning; Wyatt speaks as clearly now as he did then, but he also illustrates, quite clearly, that the attachment was one-sided and, at least by the time that this verse was written, Anne belonged to Henry.

> Whoso list to hunt, I know where is an hind,
> But as for me, alas, I may no more,
> The vain travail hath wearied me so sore.
> I am of them that farthest cometh behind;
> Yet may I by no means my wearied mind
> Draw from the Deer: but as she fleeth afore,
> Fainting I follow. I leave off therefore,
> Since in a net I seek to hold the wind.
> Who list her hunt, I put him out of doubt,
> As well as I may spend his time in vain:
> And, graven with diamonds, in letters plain
> There is written her fair neck round about:
> Noli me tangere, for Caesar's I am,
> And wild for to hold, though I seem tame.

Another poem, possibly written after "Noli Me Tangere" shows Wyatt trying to reconcile himself to the fact that he has lost, trying to convince himself (and others perhaps) that his affection had been nothing but folly. But, all these years later, are we convinced? Or do the words smack of bravado? How many of us have shrugged our shoulders and said, "I never loved him anyway"?

> Some time I fled the fire that me brent
> By sea, by land, by water and by wind;
> And now I follow the coals that be quent,
> From Dover to Calais against my mind.
> Lo how desire is both sprung and spent!
> And he may see that whilom was so blind,
> And all his labour now he laugh to scorn,
> Meshed in the briars that erst was all to-torn.

Wyatt continued to serve the king. He was made High Marshal of Calais and Commissioner of the Peace of Essex. In 1532 he accompanied the King and Anne, who was by then the King's mistress, on their visit to Calais, and when the royal divorce was finally granted Anne Boleyn married the King in January 1533. Wyatt served in her coronation in June, and in 1535 he was knighted, but a year later when Anne's fortune turned, Wyatt's former attachment for the Queen almost dragged him down with her.

It is said that he witnessed Anne's execution from the window of his prison in the Bell Tower, writing a lengthy elegy to the men who died alongside her and making no secret of his broken heart. He also remembered her in another verse, although he still does not dare to mention her name.

> These bloody days have broken my heart.
> My lust, my youth did them depart,
> And blind desire of estate.
> Who hastes to climb seeks to revert.
> Of truth, circa Regna tonat. [around the throne it thunders]
> The bell tower showed me such sight
> That in my head sticks day and night.
> There did I learn out of a grate,
> For all favour, glory, or might,
> That yet circa Regna tonat.

Some say it was thanks to Cromwell that Thomas Wyatt escaped execution, but he may well have suffered the more for surviving. A diplomat as well as a politician, his subsequent career took him back to Europe where he became involved in intrigue and espionage, leading to his capture and ransom by Spain. His involvement in the attempted assassination of Reginald Pole led (somewhat ironically) to an accusation of treasonable contact with the King's enemies and a second spell in the Tower.

As a diplomat (some say spy) Wyatt was in constant danger, and wherever he travelled, he would have taken his memories with him. He doesn't seem to have achieved happiness, and some biographers have accused him of revelling in poetic misery. That may be a little harsh. It is easy to sit in our secure, warm environment and judge those who lived in tougher times. I think we can say Thomas Wyatt was a man who, although unfortunate in love, understood love. I think we can say he suffered for his love, and I think we can say he was a victim of the times he lived in—yet another victim of Henry VIII. He died of a fever in 1542, just six years after Anne, and in a letter written to his son in 1537, he described his life as *"a thousand dangers and hazards, enmities, hatreds, prisonments, despites and indignations".*

A Queen in Shadow: A Peek Back through Time at Anne Boleyn and Her Daughter, Elizabeth

By JUDITH ARNOPP

THE SUBJECT OF ANNE BOLEYN'S TRUE PHYSICAL APPEARANCE HAS BEEN DISCUSSED time and time again in books, blogs, and journals, yet it is a subject that remains endlessly fascinating, the varied opinions and theories almost as intriguing as the woman herself.

Almost instantly recognisable, Anne Boleyn's portrait graces thousands of book covers, mugs, tea towels, key rings...her face is everywhere. But is it really her face that we are seeing? Do the portraits show us what Anne was really like?

I don't intend to hold a full debate on the portraits here, but none we have are contemporary and the closest are copies made of likenesses painted in her lifetime.

After her execution it wasn't wise to have representations of a fallen queen gracing one's walls, so during the remainder of Henry's reign and the years of Edward and Mary's rule, her face and many artefacts belonging to her slipped away. It wasn't until her daughter Elizabeth ascended the throne that Anne became acceptable again, and the demand for her image increased. As a consequence most extant images were worked long after her death—some as late as the seventeenth century.

The likenesses attributed to be her range from softly pretty to plum ugly as do the textual descriptions. Opinions of Anne Boleyn depended enormously upon the political stance and agenda of the author, and as a consequence, the documentary evidence is as varied and unreliable as the pictorial.

Due to her efforts for religious reform and the displacement of Catherine of Aragon, Anne was never a favourite of Spain or the Catholic faction and this is clear from some of the descriptions of her. Roman Catholic Nicholas Sander saw her as:

> ...rather tall of stature, with black hair and an oval face of sallow complexion, as if troubled with jaundice. She had a projecting tooth under the upper lip, and on her right hand, six fingers. There was a large wen under her chin, and therefore to hide its ugliness, she wore a high dress covering her throat. In this she was followed by the ladies of the court, who also wore high dresses, having before been in the habit of leaving their necks and the upper portion of their persons uncovered. She was handsome to look at, with a pretty mouth.

Very nice of him to go to the trouble of saying so. And the Venetian ambassador was scarcely more flattering in his account.

> *Madame Anne is not one of the handsomest women in the world. She is of middling stature, swarthy complexion, long neck, wide mouth, bosom not much raised, and in fact has nothing but the King's great appetite, and her eyes, which are black and beautiful—and take great effect on those who served the Queen when she was on the throne. She lives like a queen, and the King accompanies her to Mass—and everywhere.*

It is quite clear that she was not a ravishing beauty although of course, what is considered beautiful today is vastly different to that favoured in the sixteenth century. If you look at the line-up of Henry's wives, the "Flanders Mare" of Henry's stable, Anne of Cleves, was by today's standards, rather pretty.

In a society that favoured delicately complexioned blondes, Anne's dark hair and olive skin were far from fashionable and neither did her slim, small breasted ("not much raised") figure fit the current vogue for voluptuous women.

But most descriptions, even the most unfavourable, agree that Anne possessed expressive eyes and a vivacious wit, and it must have been those attributes that captivated the king. Which, for once I think, speaks rather well of Henry in that he was able to see past contemporary ideals to what lay beneath. Shame it didn't last.

The only truly contemporary image we have of Anne is a badly damaged portrait medal that nevertheless bears some resemblance to the Anne we see depicted in later portraits. From this we can deduce that we can come quite close to discovering a likeness to the real woman.

The medal was struck in 1534 with Anne's motto, "The Most Happi" and the initials "A.R"—Anna Regina, so we can be quite sure that it is her. These medals were usually struck to commemorate a great event, often a coronation, but since the date does not tie in with this, Eric Ives believes that it was more likely to have been intended to mark the birth of Anne's second child in the autumn of 1534 that she miscarried. This theory also explains why few copies survive.

Other portraits include the familiar Hever portrait and the one at the National Portrait Gallery as well as some sketches by Holbein which receive varying degrees of certainty from the experts. The Nidd Hall portrait shows an aging Anne which is closer to some of the less favourable documented descriptions discussed previously. Another rather touching artefact is the Chequers Ring, a jewel removed from the finger of Elizabeth I on her death bed and found to contain the image of herself and her mother, Anne.

Of course we can never know the extent of Elizabeth's attachment to her mother but some documented incidents point to a curiosity about her. Although Elizabeth was just two years old when Anne was executed and is not likely to have had strong memories of her, there were those around her who had known Anne and would have been able to keep her memory alive. If Elizabeth was satisfied that the image bore a likeness to her mother, then I think we can be fairly confident too.

The recent (and not so recent) discussions of Anne's appearance have led to the assumption that she and her daughter bore a close resemblance. Apart from Elizabeth's colouring which was auburn and Tudor in origin, there are likenesses to Anne, especially in the earlier portraits before Royal iconography began to overshadow Elizabeth's personality. The dark eyes are particularly similar.

I spend a lot of time looking at paintings of historical figures, and recently with the matter of Anne and Elizabeth at the forefront of my mind I came across a painting of Margaret Beaufort. Of course, I had seen it many times before, but for the first time it struck me that Elizabeth did in fact come to closely resemble her great-grandmother in her later years. I suppose it should come as no surprise that there is also a look of Henry VII, Elizabeth's grandfather. Perhaps there is more Tudor in Elizabeth than we thought, after all.

THE SOFTER SIDE OF THOMAS CROMWELL, 1ST EARL OF ESSEX

BY BETH VON STAATS

His speech is low and rapid, his manner assured; he is at home in courtroom or waterfront, bishop's palace or inn yard. He can draft a contract, train a falcon, draw a map, stop a street fight, furnish a house and fix a jury. He will quote you a nice point in the old authors, from Plato to Plautus and back again. He knows new poetry, and can say it in Italian. He works all hours, first up and last to bed. He makes money and he spends it. He will take a bet on anything.

—Hilary Mantel, *Wolf Hall*

THOMAS CROMWELL, 1ST EARL OF ESSEX, VICE-GERENT AND CHIEF MINISTER OF KING Henry VIII, suddenly is a very popular man in contemporary British culture. With the huge literary award winning acclaim for Hilary Mantel's brilliant novels, *Wolf Hall* and *Bring Up the Bodies*, the Lord Privy Seal made an amazing resurgence, not only in recognition as an important historical figure, but also in a greatly enhanced respect of Cromwell's legacy.

The sinister antagonist in Robert Bolt's *A Man for All Seasons* is now a lead heroic figure himself in two positively reviewed plays based on Mantel's novels performed by none other than the Royal Shakespeare Company.

Was Thomas Cromwell really as heroic as Hilary Mantel's prose would suggest or as conniving as Robert Bolt highlights in his screenplay? The answers are both "yes" and "yes", for this brilliant and highly complex statesman had far more layers to his personality than most men, alive or dead.

A man of the sixteenth century, his decisions and actions often conflict with our modern sensibilities, and frankly sometimes to many living in his own era. Historians and history lovers will debate Thomas Cromwell endlessly, and justifiably so.

Some Tudor enthusiasts will argue that Thomas Cromwell was an evil historical villain of the highest order—a man capable of dissolving an entire nation's monasteries, displacing thousands, while also orchestrating the deaths of any and all subjects with dissenting opinions, popular courtiers, Roman Catholic religious figures, and even a reigning queen consort.

In stark contrast, others will profess that instead Cromwell was a genius statesman worthy of admiration, a man who revolutionized Parliamentary Law, united the kingdom through nationalized government, successfully counseled King Henry VIII to refrain from fruitless wars abroad, patronized the arts and brought the English language Bible to all English and Welsh subjects (an accomplishment often unfairly attributed to Thomas Cranmer).

One can argue both mindsets convincingly, because this was a man with a mission, a man who wanted to make a difference, a man who sought to change how government works, a man who sought to bring scripture to all people, and a man who was 100% devoted to his God, his faith as justified solely by his faith, and the King he served with steadfast loyalty—all the way to the scaffold.

In short, Thomas Cromwell was a man who viewed that the means always justified the end, so long as that end was either his perception of God's will or, more importantly to his tainted legacy, the King's will.

Most people who are familiar with Tudor era history are very knowledgeable of the "evil side" of Thomas Cromwell. After all, whether by active manipulation for his own agenda or far more likely at the command of King Henry VIII, he was at the epicenter of the course of events that changed the face of England forever, many of the realm's subjects becoming displaced, destitute, or dead in the process.

But, did Thomas Cromwell have a softer side? Was the King's Chief Minister capable of compassion? Kindness? Fun? Love? Of course he was, but with no memoirs and only a precious few private correspondences to guide us to this conclusion, how do we know? Let's explore the ways in this admittedly incomplete accounting.

THOMAS CROMWELL, FAMILY MAN

Admittedly, very little is known of Thomas Cromwell's private life. Still, most people assume that beyond his commitment to his son Gregory, the Earl of Essex was distant, aloof and egocentric. In fact, Thomas Cromwell was actually a devoted "family man". Married to Elizabeth Wykys in 1515, Thomas raised three children with her: Gregory, Anne, and Grace.

Tragically, Cromwell's wife died most likely of the sweating sickness in 1528. His two daughters perished together shortly thereafter. Poignantly, the will Cromwell wrote soon after Elizabeth's death refers to his late wife and details careful provisions made for Gregory, Anne and *"myne little daughter Grace"*. These deaths obviously had a profound impact on Thomas Cromwell, as in an age where remarriage was not only common but expected, this wealthy and highly eligible widower remained single for the remainder of his lifetime.

Beyond Cromwell's commitment to his immediate family, the King's Chief Minister was gracious and loving to his extended family. Cromwell continued to share his home with his wife's mother throughout her lifetime, laid provisions in his will for his sister who sadly predeceased him, and funded rich educations for not only all of his nephews and children of close family friends, but also his niece.

Thomas Cromwell had a special affinity for his nephew Richard Williams, son of his sister Katherine. Cromwell's influence was obvious, as his nephew requested to take Cromwell's name after his own father's death. Richard Cromwell, great-grandfather of Lord Protector Oliver Cromwell, entered his uncle's service and became a highly successful courtier, ultimately serving in Parliament and as High Sheriff of Cambridgeshire and Huntingdonshire.

Likely most telling of Cromwell's commitment and love for family was his wardship of Sir Ralph Sadleir. In the sixteenth century, many people of means were wards of orphaned children of the rich, usually arranged as a sign of favor from the King. Such wardships were highly lucrative, as while the child remained a minor, the income from the deceased parent's properties was diverted to the guardian.

Courtiers as esteemed as Saint Thomas More and Charles Brandon, Duke of Suffolk gained substantial incomes from their wards. Brandon even married one of his wards, none other than Catherine Willoughby, Duchess of Suffolk. The fourteen-year-old Willoughby was initially contracted to his son.

Thomas Cromwell, in contrast, became guardian of the seven-year-old Ralph Sadleir while his parents still lived at their behest in their desire for the child's best interest. Instead of generating income from the arrangement, Cromwell raised Sadleir as his own, alongside his children at Austin Friars. Their freely given relationship was exceptionally close.

Due to Cromwell's influence and patronage, Sadleir became King Henry VIII's Principal Secretary and later was knighted by King Edward VI. Ultimately, Sir Ralph Sadleir, an esteemed diplomat essential to England's foreign policy with Scotland, became England's most influential and wealthy commoner, far eclipsing both Cromwell's own son and nephew.

THOMAS CROMWELL, RELIGIOUS SCHOLAR AND REFORMER

Many Tudor history lovers view that Thomas Cromwell's belief system was devoid of true religious conviction, and point to his actions as Vice-gerent and Chief Minister as self-serving, in short, a way to gain properties and riches for himself at the expense of others. One historian goes so far as to list pages of Cromwell's obsessive financial accounting to detail alleged exorbitant bribes and kick-backs garnished during the Dissolution of the Monasteries, as well as alleged bribes received to secure favor from the King through Cromwell's influence.

Although Thomas Cromwell certainly became an extremely wealthy man and owner of extensive property, his wealth gained through the King's pleasure, through his own good fortune, and, most tellingly, through his exceptionally hard work in no way discredits his obvious religious convictions.

Prior to 1531, Thomas Cromwell was a Roman Catholic. There is strong evidence of his convictions, including his success in gaining bulls for the Boston Guild's Chapel of the Virgin Mary, St. Botolph's Church. Yes, Cromwell did resourcefully entice His Holy Father with music and sweetmeats to gain advantage, but the fact remained, with his help, the Boston Guild received papal authority to sell indulgences in "perpetuity"—well, at least until the Henrician Reformation Cromwell authored criminalized the practice.

Though the example above more humorously illustrates Cromwell's resourcefulness than truly reflecting his religious devotion, what he accomplished while on route to visit His Holy Father to secure these bulls most certainly does. Thomas Cromwell memorized in full Desiderius Erasmus' 1516 translation of the New Testament, book by book, psalm by psalm, scripture by scripture, word by word.

Other small hints speak to Cromwell's religious mindedness before his evangelical conversion. For example, George Cavendish teaches us in his biography of Thomas Cardinal Wolsey that he came upon Thomas Cromwell during a weak moment on the day Cromwell left Wolsey's service. With English modernized for the reader, Cavendish records....

> It chanced upon me on the morning of Hallow's Eve to come there into the great chamber to give my attendance where I found Master Cromwell leaning in the great window with a primer in his hand saying "Our Lady Maddens" (which had been a very strange sight). He prayed not more earnestly than the tears from his eyes.

Not long after leaving Thomas Cardinal Wolsey's service, evidence begins to show plainly that Thomas Cromwell's love of scripture was gradually drawing him toward more evangelical leanings. Gaining a seat in Parliament representing Taunton and securing employment in the King's service as a low ranking councilor, Cromwell worked in partnership with his friend Stephen Vaughan through Dr. Augustine de Augustinis to secure the *Apology of the Augsburg Confession*, by German theologian Philipp Melanchthon, along with other Lutheran writings.

There is also ample circumstantial evidence to suggest Vaughan and Cromwell were smuggling evangelical works into England through Antwerp cloth merchants. Beyond this, Christopher Mont, another evangelical ally, was translating German religious works *in Thomas Cromwell's home*.

Thomas Cromwell, Stephen Vaughan, and Christopher Mont were playing with fire—quite literally. Concurrently, Lord Chancellor Thomas More and John Stokesley, Bishop of London, were chasing, arresting, and burning at the stake people guilty of Lutheran heresies. Thus, it can hardly be argued that Thomas Cromwell feigned religious piety to gain wealth and riches. The fact is clear that he risked his career and life repeatedly to practice his faith and bring it to others.

Even Thomas Cromwell's decisions to send clergy to Europe for teaching from evangelical theologians and introduction of a Bible in English while at the height of his power held inherent risks. In fact, Cromwell's staunch evangelical position contributed significantly to his ultimate downfall, since he was viewed as a huge impediment towards the goals of the conservative faction, most notably Thomas Howard, Duke of Norfolk and Stephen Gardiner, Bishop of Winchester.

THOMAS CROMWELL, PHILANTHROPIST AND ADVOCATE FOR THE POOR

Obviously, Thomas Cromwell was the architect of the Henrician Reformation and driving force of the Dissolution of the Monasteries. During the course of four short years, every abbey, monastery, and priory—literally every religious house in England and Wales, without exception—was dismantled; all nuns, monks, friars, and priests displaced with small pensions; and all poor reliant on the religious houses for charity scrambling for food and emergency housing.

If we are to believe Queen Anne Boleyn who chastised Thomas Cromwell in 1535, the Vice-gerent's motivations were far from religious and lacked all charity. To her way of thinking, Cromwell's goals were to fill the King's treasuries, reward and buy off allies and courtiers through the sale of property at bargain prices, and line his own pockets. Enraged, she famously threatened to have his head smitten off. Was Her Majesty's thinking fair and accurate? In short, no.

In the same year Anne Boleyn and Thomas Cromwell "spiritedly debated" how monastery proceeds should be dispersed, Cromwell began drafting legislation that ultimately resulted in the "Relief of the Poor Bill of 1536". Prepared after a yearlong investigation of the causes of poverty, Cromwell set about, albeit unsuccessfully, to seek a revolutionary solution to the challenges faced by the poor and downtrodden.

Cromwell's ideas included a highly elaborate plan of public works, erecting new buildings, repairing poorly maintained harbors, and dredging waterways throughout the kingdom in exchange for fair pay for work completed. The legislation also proposed free medical care for abandoned or orphaned children, the disabled, the elderly or the chronically ill. Of course, this all would be policed by officials to ensure no abuse. Although the ultimate law that was submitted to Parliament was less far reaching that the original drafts, the ideas were revolutionary just the same.

Now is this all sounding a bit familiar? Was Thomas Cromwell world history's first socialist? Did he influence the thinking of American President Franklin D. Roosevelt? Perhaps so, but indirectly of course.

Unfortunately, Cromwell's originally proposed Bill to benefit the realm's most vulnerable failed to pass Parliament. Had Cromwell's efforts succeeded, his legacy of charity and compassion for others would have been indisputable.

Even before Thomas Cromwell held power second only to King Henry VIII, he showed strong support for the common man. He had obvious reason. Cromwell was born and raised "base born" himself, the son of the Putney town drunk.

George Cavendish teaches us in his biography of Thomas Cardinal Wolsey that Thomas Cromwell was greatly concerned for the plight of Wolsey's servants who were to abruptly lose their wages and board due to the Cardinal's startling fall. On the last day Cromwell spent in Wolsey's service, he indignantly shamed the clergy to pony up some of their lavish wealth to provide each servant a month's wages.

Cromwell dug into his purse and tossed five pounds in gold of his own money on the table, and chided, *"Now let us see what you chaplains will do."* The men, embarrassed by Cromwell's assessment of their lack of charity, contributed substantial funds dispersed to those displaced by Wolsey's misfortune.

Thomas Cromwell throughout his lifetime contributed to a variety of worthy causes and was a strong patron of the arts, but most likely, the people most tragically impacted by his execution beyond his blood family and the six men, three evangelical and three Roman Catholic, executed in his wake, were the over 200 men, women and children that were fed each day through "doles" at his London home. They were abruptly left hungry and scrambling to find a meager meal.

THOMAS CROMWELL, MEDIATOR

As first a lawyer and then the King's Secretary, Thomas Cromwell was often drawn in to mediate an endless variety of grievances, such as property ownership, fair compensation for purchases and services rendered, and marriage disputes. Even Elizabeth Howard, Duchess of Norfolk sought Cromwell's help in mediating issues between herself and her estranged husband, the powerful and ornery Thomas Howard. I can't imagine that he enjoyed the task.

The most critical and historically relevant mediation Thomas Cromwell successfully brokered, however, was the submission of the Lady Mary to her father's ultimate Supremacy and recognition that King Henry VIII's marriage to Catherine of Aragon was never valid. Though Mary Tudor was not of like mind given her staunch loyalty to her mother and the bullying she endured by those councilors and clergy sent by the King to force the issue, Cromwell's actions, in partnership with his ally in the cause, Imperial Ambassador Eustace Chapuys, saved her life and eventually restored her to the succession that led to her ultimate Queenship.

THOMAS CROMWELL, LIFE OF THE PARTY

When I look at the famous portrait of Thomas Cromwell painted by Hans Holbein the Younger, I am struck by the seriousness and aloof nature Cromwell projects. It is a common perception, and with good reason given many historical accounts and popular historical fiction, that Cromwell was all-business, stern, aggressive, a henchman, a "work-a-holic"—in short, a man "lurking in the shadows" and cruel to the extreme.

Even the contemporary and admittedly hostile source Cardinal and later Archbishop of Canterbury Reginald Pole described Thomas Cromwell to be the *"Emissary of Satan"*. Was he?

I will leave that to the historians and history lovers to debate, but I will say this. Thomas Cromwell was affable, surprisingly fun-loving, exceptionally witty, and a man who enjoyed a great party. There was not a courtier, minister, foreign diplomat, queen, or maid in King Henry's Court that didn't add Thomas Cromwell's lavish parties to their social calendars. In one perhaps apocryphal accounting, he is said to have paid 4000 pounds for an elaborate costume to entertain the King. Yes, Thomas Cromwell reportedly paraded around for His Majesty in costume—imagine that.

Thomas Cromwell's quick wit was legendary. It seems the man had an answer for everything. To prove the point, I will highlight his thoughts as a young Parliamentarian, words that not only illustrate his wit, but also prove that *the more things change, the more they stay the same*". In a 1523 letter to his friend John Creke, Cromwell writes:

I among others have endured a parliament which continued by the space of seventeen whole weeks, where we commoned of war, peace, strife, contention, debate, murmur, grudge, riches, poverty, perjury, truth, falsehood, justice, equity, deceit, oppression, magnanimity, activity, force, attemprance, treason, murder, felony, conciliation, and also how a commonwealth might be edified and also contained within our realm. Howbeit, in conclusion we have done as our predecessors have been wont to do, that is to say as well as we might, and left where we began.

Touché! Britain's ultimate Parliamentarian, politician and lawyer has the last word. Case closed. Let the deliberations begin.

SOURCES

Cavendish, George. *The Life and Death of Cardinal Wolsey.* http://www.library.utoronto.ca/utel/ret/cavendish/cavendish.html

Hutchinson, Robert. *Thomas Cromwell: The Rise and Fall of Henry VIII's Most Notorious Minister.* Weidenfeld & Nicolson, 2007.

Loades, David. *Thomas Cromwell: Servant to Henry VIII.* Amberley Publishing, 2013.

Schofield, John. *Thomas Cromwell: Henry VIII's Most Faithful Servant.* The History Press, 2011.

SEVEN SURPRISING FACTS
ABOUT ANNE OF CLEVES

BY NANCY BILYEAU

EVERYONE THINKS THEY KNOW THE STORY OF THE FOURTH WIFE OF HENRY VIII. SHE was the German princess whom he married for diplomatic reasons, but when the forty-eight-year-old widower first set eyes on his twenty-four-year-old bride-to-be, he was repulsed.

With great reluctance, Henry went through with the wedding—saying darkly, *"I am not well handled"*—but after six months he'd managed to get an annulment, and the unconsummated marriage was no more. Although Anne had behaved impeccably as Queen, she accepted her new status as "sister" and lived a quiet, comfortable existence in England until 1557, when she became the last of the wives of King Henry VIII to die.

And so Anne of Cleves has either been treated as a punchline in the serio-comic saga of Henry VIII's wives or someone who was smart enough to agree to a divorce, trading in an obese tyrant for a rich settlement. But the life of Anne of Cleves is more complex than the stereotypes would have you believe.

1. Anne's father was a Renaissance thinker. The assumption is that Anne grew up in a backward German duchy, too awkward and ignorant to impress a monarch who'd once moved a kingdom for the sophisticated charms of Anne Boleyn. But her father, Duke John, was a patron of Erasmus, the Dutch Renaissance scholar.

The Cleves court was liberal and fair with low taxes for its citizens. And the Duke made great efforts to steer a calm course through the religious uproar engulfing Germany in the 1520s and 1530s, earning the name John the Peaceful. He died in 1538, so his must have been the greatest influence on Anne, rather than her more bellicose brother, William. In Germany, highborn ladies were not expected to sing or play musical instruments, but Anne would have been exposed to the moderate, thoughtful political ideals espoused by John the Peaceful.

2. Anne was born a Catholic and died a Catholic. Her mother, Princess Maria of Julich-Berg, had traditional religious values and brought up her daughters as Catholics, no matter what Martin Luther said. Their brother, Duke William, was an avowed Protestant, and the family seems to have moved in that direction when he succeeded to his father's title.

Anne was accommodating when it came to religion. She did not hesitate to follow the lead of her husband Henry VIII, who was head of the Church of England. But in 1553, when her step-daughter Mary took the throne, she asked that Anne become a Catholic.

Anne agreed. When she was dying, she requested that she have *"the suffrages of the holy church according to the Catholic faith."*

3. Anne's brother had a marriage that wasn't consummated either. Duke William was not as interested in peace as his father. What he wanted more than anything else was to add Guelders to Cleves—but the Holy Roman Emperor Charles V had other ideas. William took the bold step of a French marriage so that France would support him should it come to war.

His bride was Jeanne D'Albret, the daughter of Marguerite of Angouleme and niece of King Francis. The "high-spirited" Jeanne was only twelve and did not want to marry William. She was whipped by her family and physically carried to the altar by the Constable of France. But when Charles V took hold of Guelders, France did nothing to help William of Cleves. The four-year-old marriage was annulled—it had never been consummated. Jeanne's next husband was Antoine de Bourbon, whom she loved. Their son would one day become Henry IV, King of France.

4. Hans Holbein painted Anne accurately. The question of Anne's appearance continues to baffle modern minds. In portraits she looks attractive, certainly prettier than Jane Seymour. A French ambassador who saw her in Cleves said she was *"of middling beauty and of very assured and resolute countenance."*

It is still unclear how hard Thomas Cromwell pushed for this marriage, but certainly he was not stupid enough to trick his volatile King into wedding someone hideous. The famous Hans Holbein was told to paint truthful portraits of Anne and her sister Amelia. After looking at them, Henry VIII chose Anne. Later, the King blamed people for over-praising her beauty, but he did not blame or punish Holbein. The portrait captures her true appearance. While we don't find her repulsive, Henry did.

5. Henry VIII never called her a "Flanders Mare." The English King's attitude toward his fourth wife was very unusual for a sixteenth century monarch. Royal marriages sealed diplomatic alliances, and queens were expected to be pious and gracious, not sexy.

Henry wanted more than anything to send Anne home and not marry her, which would have devastated the young woman. He was only prevented from such cruelty by the (temporary) need for this foreign alliance. But while he fumed to his councilors and friends, he did not publicly ridicule her appearance. The report that Henry VIII cried loudly that she was a "Flanders mare" is not based on contemporary documents.

6. Anne of Cleves wanted to remarry Henry VIII. After the king's fifth wife, young Catherine Howard, was divorced and then executed for adultery, Anne wanted to be Queen again. Her brother, William of Cleves, asked his ambassador to pursue her reinstatement. But Henry said no. When he took a sixth wife, the widow Catherine Parr, Anne felt humiliated and received medical treatment for melancholy. Her name came up as a possible wife for various men, including Thomas Seymour, but nothing came of it. She never remarried or left England.

7. Anne of Cleves is the only one of Henry's wives to be buried in Westminster Abbey. Henry himself is buried at Windsor with favorite wife Jane Seymour, but Anne is interred in the same structure as Edward the Confessor and most of the Plantagenet, Tudor, and Stuart rulers. In her will she remembered all of her servants and bequeathed her best jewels to the stepdaughters she loved, Mary and Elizabeth.

KATHERINE HOWARD: SCHEMER OR VICTIM?

By JUDITH ARNOPP

ON FEBRUARY 12, 1542 (SOME SOURCES SAY FEBRUARY 13) A YOUNG QUEEN WENT TO the scaffold accused of adultery and treason, leaving history to make of her what it would. Katherine Howard has been dismissed as a bit of a trollop, a superficial girl interested only in jewellery, gowns, and dancing. Since she clearly lacked her cousin Anne Boleyn's poise, intelligent wit, and sparkling personality, it is not easy to pinpoint exactly what it was about Katherine that so entranced Henry VIII.

Perhaps it was just her seeming simplicity and her youth.

Although of good pedigree Katherine was born to impoverished parents and placed in the care of her grandmother, Agnes Howard (née Tilney), the Dowager Duchess of Norfolk who ran a very lax household. The other ladies that served the Dowager were left to run wild and did nothing to protect Katherine from their sexual indiscretions and gave no credence to her position in life. Indeed, Katherine while still at an impressionable age seems to have been embraced as "one of the gang" and subjected to what would now be seen as sexual abuse.

The first man to know Katherine intimately was her music master, Henry Mannox. Although the relationship was not fully consummated, Katherine later confessed that Mannox had completely crossed the bounds of gentlemanly behaviour. *"At the flattering and fair persuasions of Mannox, being but a young girl, I suffered him at sundry times to handle and touch the secret parts of my body...."*

She was just a little older when Francis Dereham took Mannox's place. This time there seems to have been a deeper commitment, and the couple formed a sort of pseudo-marriage, naming each other "husband" and "wife." Such arrangements were commonplace but not lightly undertaken and considered to be binding betrothals. The relationship did not stop at an exchange of vows, and after her arrest Katherine confessed that Dereham *"lay with me naked and used me in such sort as a man doth his wife many and sundry times but how often I know not."*

A girl in Katherine's position was an invaluable bartering tool in the marriage market, and any stain upon her character could completely devalue her. When the Dowager Duchess got wind of the affair (one report says she was tipped off and burst into the chamber, catching the couple in a compromising position) there is little doubt that Norfolk was informed. Katherine was reprimanded and Dereham sent away, but Norfolk was left in the position of having a disgraced female relative to marry off respectably, and he knew just how hard that would be. It is not a surprise that Norfolk kept quiet about the affair; the surprising thing is that he had the nerve to go ahead and dangle soiled goods before the king himself.

After a string of unsuccessful marriages, the thing that Henry desired most was a soft pliant wife in his bed—one who could be relied upon not to meddle in politics. Although Henry now had his heir, Prince Edward, Katherine's primary role was to provide the ageing, sick King with another son, a Duke of York to secure the Tudor dynasty once and for all. The fact that she was young, pretty, and affectionate could only be a bonus for Henry. It was Katherine who was faced with the problem of conceiving, and if she failed to do so the fault would be laid at her door.

Since the break from Rome, the royal court had split into two factions: those who favoured Rome, notably Stephen Gardiner (Bishop of Winchester) and Thomas Howard (Duke of Norfolk), and those who were on the side of religious reform, Thomas Cranmer and the King's Secretary, Thomas Cromwell.

It was Cromwell who had introduced to Henry the idea of marriage to Anne of Cleves, and when she failed to please, he fell into disfavour and was executed as a result. The way was cleared for a new bride, and Norfolk lost no time in trying to regain Henry's favour; filling the gap left by Cromwell, he placed his pretty niece, Katherine Howard, in the King's way.

Katherine was first brought to Henry's notice at the home of Norfolk's friend, Bishop Gardiner in Southwark, and it is often said that the marriage was engineered by the two men to weaken the cause for reform. Although there were many party to the knowledge of Katherine's earlier indiscretions, Norfolk still went to the risk of bringing her to the King's notice. Of course, whether Henry took the bait or not was out of Norfolk's hands, and his relief must have been great when Henry took to her straight away. They were married in July 1540.

In the beginning the marriage seemed to go very well. Henry was openly content with his bride, describing her as his "rose without a thorn." The royal party embarked upon a progress to the north of England, and it is believed that during this time Katherine and Thomas Culpepper, a gentleman of the King's privy chamber, became lovers. There have been many romantic stories built around this relationship; they were childhood sweet-hearts and distant cousins reunited at court. Often Thomas is depicted as a romantic swain whom Katherine couldn't resist. In actual fact the Culpeppers seem to have been a dysfunctional family, and Thomas (although we must acknowledge it could have been his elder brother who was also called Thomas) was involved in rape and murder. What-ever the truth of his character, it is quite clear that he and Katherine risked everything and formed an illicit and deeply dangerous relationship. This may be seen as romantic or foolhardy depending on one's perspective.

Once Queen, Katherine failed to see the importance of leaving her dissolute past behind and seems instead to have embraced it. Not content with embarking on a madcap liaison with a member of the King's household, she also took into her own household those who should never have been allowed anywhere near.

Slowly, women she had known whilst in the care of the Dowager Duchess came to be placed in her household. Most puzzling of all was the engagement of Francis Dereham into her household as her private secretary. Since the relationship between them was not resumed, it could be deduced that Katherine was "buying his silence" or felt she owed him something but, either way, it was a bad move and undeniably stupid. Young and inexperienced as she was, even Katherine must have known that she would never sit easy on the throne while surrounded by those in possession of such volatile information.

Unsurprisingly, it wasn't long before word of her former indiscretions began to leak out and arrests and torture followed. Dereham, eager to salvage himself, wasted no time in mentioning Culpepper's name. Katherine was sent upriver to Syon Abbey while investigations were carried out. While Norfolk made himself scarce, the Tower began to fill with Katherine's relatives and friends. Culpepper was beheaded, Dereham hung, drawn, and quartered, and their heads were placed on London Bridge. Katherine herself was condemned to death without trial and beheaded at the Tower on February 12 or 13, 1542, the same place her cousin, Anne Boleyn, had met her own death six years previously.

Opinion of Katherine Howard varies. She has been seen as a brazen adulteress, a reckless, greedy doxy, an innocent victim of her scheming uncle. As always, we will never know the real truth of the matter, and it is for each to make up their own mind. To me, she will always be a mixture of all of the above.

Today it is difficult not to see her as a victim of child abuse, and her story illustrates that she was sexually liberal as an adult. Her main downfall was that her physical attraction provided a tool for Norfolk's political schemes which, in turn, put her in the way of the king.

Unable to reject an offer of marriage from her monarch, the idea of jewels and parties and pretty dresses galore may have been some compensation, but, once married and finding herself expected to provide an heir for an ageing (and possibly impotent) husband, Katherine was now in an impossible position. It may have been her reason for falling so foolishly into Culpepper's bed (perhaps she didn't need much persuasion), but either way, she didn't deserve to die for it.

If her pre-contract to Dereham is to be believed, then Henry's marriage to Katherine was never valid. This in turn raises the question of the legality of her execution. If she was not married to the King, then she was not guilty of adultery.

The king had been fending off old age for some time, and, whether he managed it in private or not, Katherine helped to restore the illusion of his vitality. With her on his arm he could pretend to still be in his prime. In cuckolding him she destroyed the remaining vestiges of his youth and caused the whole world to snigger behind their hands. It was something Henry could not allow.

On her death, to mark the end of his fifth marriage and restore his self-esteem, Henry returned to Whitehall and embarked upon three successive days of feasting and celebration and, as Chapuys reported, *"received* [women] *with much gaiety without however showing particular affection for any of them."* This is classic behaviour of a cuckolded man. Henry, to hide his hurt and anger, buried himself in gaiety and sought the company of women who would soothe his damaged ego.

Katherine died because she had injured Henry's self-esteem. She had ruined his carefully constructed image.

A RESPLENDENT MONUMENT TO HENRY VIII OF ENGLAND

By JUDITH ARNOPP

MOST PEOPLE WOULD AGREE THAT ENGLAND'S MOST MEMORABLE MONARCH IS Henry VIII. The bloody years of his reign, the executions, the break with Rome, his complex sex life have all left their mark on our imagination. He is so synonymous with England that you might even assume that a magnificent memorial stands prominently in Westminster such as the one his parents share, or the superb edifice that enshrines the resting place of his daughter Elizabeth. But you'd be quite wrong to think so.

Indeed, although buried at Windsor alongside his third wife, Jane Seymour, Henry has no glorious shrine, no gilded angels, just a slab set in the floor. Where once people trembled before King Henry, now many of us do not even notice when we walk over him. Death is a great leveller.

In the sixteenth century, monuments were intended to mark wealth, status, and power, and the building of them was usually undertaken during the lifetime of the person for whom the tomb was intended. Always conscious of the need to emphasise his own supremacy, Henry laid down elaborate plans for a suitable edifice. You have only to consider the most famous portrait of Henry to imagine the impact he intended his memorial to have. Henry was dominant, self-obsessed, and power hungry. His burial tomb was intended to reflect that.

As early as 1518, while still married to his first queen, Katherine of Aragon, a contract was signed by a Florentine sculptor, Pietro Torrigiano, the same man who created the fabulous tomb of Henry VII and Elizabeth of York. It was to be similar in design, of black and white marble, yet twenty-five per cent bigger and *"finished in beauty, fairness, costs and adornments."*

Unfortunately, an issue arose over payment between the sculptor and Wolsey (who was in charge of the project), and the Florentine left without completing, or perhaps not even beginning the work.

Henry and Wolsey quickly sought other craftsmen and made further plans for even more splendid designs. Robert Hutchinson in his book, *The Last Days of Henry VIII*, notes that the design was based on one originally intended for Pope Leo X.

> It was to be 28ft high, 15ft long and topped by an effigy of the king on horse-back in grand Italian Renaissance style. Beneath this the high canopy were to lie the effigies of the king and queen. In its sheer megalomaniac scale, it

was deliberately intended to be a monument to outshine that of any Pope or monarch found within the churches and abbeys of Europe.

Wow, splendid indeed...and expensive.

At around this time Cardinal Wolsey had also begun plans for his own shrine. As equally status-conscious as his King, Wolsey's tomb was to outdo that of Henry VII's both in ostentation and in cost. Unfortunately, his downfall preceded the completion of his monument and having fallen foul of his King, he was instead buried ignominiously at Abbey Park in Leicestershire.

Henry, never one to let a good thing go to waste, lost no time in acquiring elements of Wolsey's tomb for his own use, and Cromwell, who was now the project manager, made several payments to Italian and English metal founders. A giant effigy of the King was produced in gilt bronze, and work continued until the last decade of Henry's reign when war with France and Scotland put pressure on the royal coffers. By this time the project was well underway. In his will Henry stated that his tomb was *"well onward and almost made therefore already with a fair grate about it, in which we will also the bones of our true and loving wife Queen Jane be put also."*

But with the King out of the picture the project for his grand burial was no longer of primary importance, even to his children.

Under his successor, Edward VI, work continued half-heartedly and under the new Protestant regime even the chantry priests who had been asked to pray for Henry and Jane's souls were forbidden to continue. The King's tomb was shelved, and after Edward's early demise in 1553 work on his own tomb took precedence over Henry's.

When Mary Tudor assumed the throne she declined to continue with the work for fear she should be seen as supporting one who broke with Rome, and when Elizabeth's turn came, she showed no more filial respect than her sister. Records show that she did consider continuing with the project but rejected several designs, hampered no doubt by the reluctance to spend too much money on it. After all, her own considerable monument, taking many years to complete and requiring a fortune in white marble, was of more immediate importance.

Through the Commonwealth and the Restoration periods the half-finished monument and the chapel that housed it fell into further disrepair, its ruinous condition being recorded as late as 1749. In 1804 when the architect, James Wyatt, began work on a huge royal catacomb on the site of the chapel, Henry's tomb was put into storage. As his memory faded into the past, plans for Henry VIII's memorial faded with it. The tomb was never completed, and the huge black sarcophagus intended for Henry is now in St. Paul's housing instead the bones of England's hero of Trafalgar, Lord Nelson—who has so many monuments.

And so Henry and Jane stayed where they were beneath the floor of St. George's Chapel at Windsor, but they were not left in peace. In 1649 the tomb was opened up to make way for Charles I. One wonders, after executing so many lesser men, what Henry makes of sharing his tomb with a defeated and executed King. You can almost hear his indignant roar, "It wouldn't have happened in my day."

At the end of the seventeenth century the tomb was opened again for the burial of a stillborn child of Princess George of Denmark (later to become Queen Anne) and again to allow a casket of relics appertaining to Charles I to be interred.

At that time a light was lowered into the tomb and revealed Henry's coffin to be *"in a condition of great dilapidation. The King's skull, with its very broad frontal, his thigh bones, ribs and other portions of the skeleton are exposed to view as the lead has been extensively ripped open...."*

The grave remained unmarked until 1837 when in King William IV's reign it was inscribed as follows.

IN A VAULT
BENEATH THIS MARBLE SLAB
ARE DEPOSITED THE REMAINS
OF
JANE SEYMOUR, QUEEN OF KING HENRY VIII
1537
KING HENRY VIII
1547
KING CHARLES I
1648
AND AN INFANT CHILD OF QUEEN ANNE.
THIS MEMORIAL WAS PLACED HERE
BY COMMAND OF
KING WILLIAM IV. 1837.

So, our great Tudor monarch lies in a modest tomb in mixed company while many of his contemporaries, people who bowed and scraped before him, lie in splendour elsewhere in the kingdom.

The graves of his wives are more resplendent than his, even those who died disgraced. Katherine of Aragon has a black marble grave marker with her name written above it in large gilded letters. Anne Boleyn and Catherine Howard lie beneath decorative grave markers at the Chapel of St. Peter ad Vincula at the Tower of London where flowers are left regularly by modern day sympathisers.

Anne of Cleves has a marked tomb at Westminster Abbey which, if a little difficult to find, still has substance. And at Sudeley Castle an effigy of Henry's last wife, Catherine Parr, lies upon a resplendent tomb.

Henry's son, Edward VI has a tomb fit for a monarch at Westminster Abbey, as does Elizabeth who shares her grave with her half-sister Queen Mary I. Even Henry's bastard son, Henry Fitzroy, lies in some majesty in St. Michael's church at Framlingham in Suffolk.

Many of Henry VIII's contemporaries have superior monuments to their king. Thomas Howard, Earl of Surrey, third Duke of Norfolk has a sumptuous memorial at Framlingham Church, and Henry's great rival King Francis I has a huge effigy in the Basilica of St. Denis in Paris with a separate gigantic urn to house his heart.

And Henry's last victim, Henry Howard, Earl of Surrey, who was beheaded just one day before the king died, has a resplendent effigy marking the tomb he shares with his wife Frances, at Framlingham in Suffolk.

Henry's elder brother Arthur, who was Catherine of Aragon's first husband and died before he could ascend the throne, has an ostentatious tomb in a designated chapel.

I could go on and on, but I will resist. Henry's parents, grandparents, wives, children, cousins, siblings, friends—most of the Tudors rest in splendour and, I hope, peace.

It is only Henry, who in life was the most ostentatious of them all, that lacks the majesty of a proper monument.

Tudor England's Most Infamous Villain: Richard Rich, 1st Baron Rich of Leez

By Beth von Staats

Sir Richard Rich, 1st Baron Rich of Leez, Essex—was there ever a more evil or manipulative man in sixteenth century British history? Simply stated, no. In fact, many historians would be hard pressed to find any British man who walked the earth with less redeeming qualities. With no moral center, not even the religious fanaticism common for the era, the Baron Rich of Leez lived his life flip-flopping to the whims of the monarchs he served, resourcefully allying with and then stepping on anyone in his way to advancement and wealth.

Unfortunately for many in the realm, Rich was long-lived, spreading his venom throughout the reigns of King Henry VIII, King Edward VI, and Queen Mary I, amazingly remaining unscathed. With the varying political and religious agendas of these monarchs, ranging from staunch Roman Catholicism to near Calvinist Protestantism and everything in between, just how did he pull this off? Let us count the ways through this admittedly incomplete list.

TEN DASTARDLY DEEDS OF SIR RICHARD RICH

1. Sir Richard Rich, by 1535 Attorney General of Wales and Solicitor General of England, is famously known for his persecution of those who refused to take the Oath of Supremacy during the reign of King Henry VIII, a vow that assured the King was the acknowledged Head of the Church in England. In the case of Bishop John Fisher, Rich tricked the man into admitting his loyalty to the Roman Catholic papacy, promising to tell no one. Rich then testified to Fisher's statements at trial.

In Thomas More's case, Rich flat out lied to the same. Thomas More reportedly told him at trial, *"In faith, Mr. Rich, I am sorrier for your perjury than for my own peril, and you shall understand that neither I, nor no man else to my knowledge, ever took you to be a man of such credit as in any matter of importance I or any other would at any time vouchsafe to communicate with you."*

Though the source of the quote is actually from More's son-in-law William Roper, truer words were never spoken. Both Saint John Fisher and Saint Thomas More were executed by decapitation for high treason based on Rich's dubious testimony.

2. In 1536, along with his other titles, Sir Richard Rich was appointed Chancellor of the newly created Court of Augmentations. In this role, he worked in partnership with the Vice-gerent and King's Principal Secretary Thomas Cromwell to dissolve all abbeys, monasteries, and nunneries in England and Wales, displacing thousands and completely upending a way of life going back centuries.

What did Sir Richard Rich have to gain by this? Well, he acquired wealth and territories, of course. At bargain basement prices, he procured the monastery at St. Bartholomew, the priory of Leez, the manors of Lighes Parva, Magna Lighes, Felsted and Fyfield in Essex. Not satisfied, he added to his land gains by procuring the nunnery of St. Bride at Syon, several manors in Essex once belonging to Christ Church, Canterbury and several more manors once owned by St. Osth's at Chic and the Holywell Priory, Middlesex.

Our Baron Rich of Leez was on his way.

~ೱೱ~

3. In 1540, Sir Richard Rich turned on his close ally and benefactor of his great wealth and land acquisitions, again performing commendably as a "chief witness", this time against Thomas Cromwell, who was just four months earlier elevated to Earl of Essex. Cromwell was soon executed by decapitation for sacramentary heresy and treason, the charges and testimony falsified.

Thomas Cromwell made his opinions of Rich known to King Henry VIII in a letter after his arrest. From prison he wrote, *"What master chancellor has been to me, God and he knows best; what I have been to him your Majesty knows."*

The Baron of Leez was "off the hook" for perjuring himself in court this time, though. Cromwell was condemned on attainder; thus Rich's lies were solely to Parliament, the Privy Council, and the King.

~ೱೱ~

4. Sir Richard Rich was an incredibly resourceful villain. As King Henry VIII's religious views swayed from evangelical to conservative and back again, Rich went along for the ride, playing the role of henchman brilliantly. In July 1540, on the heels of Cromwell's execution, three men were burned at the stake, declared heretics for preaching doctrines opposed to King Henry's Six Articles of Faith.

On the same day—that's right, the same day—three more men were hanged, drawn, and quartered for denying the Royal Supremacy. Think about that for a minute. Three Evangelicals and three Roman Catholics were put to death at the hands of Sir Richard Rich on the same day. Was there anyone more expert in riding the waves of King Henry VIII's ever changing religious doctrine? I think not.

~ೱೱ~

5. Well, yes, this time in 1541 the parties were actually guilty of wrong doing both from a legal and moral standpoint, so perhaps we can give Sir Richard Rich the benefit of the doubt that his extensive involvement in the fall of Queen Catherine Howard, as well as his participation in the special Commission for the trials of Thomas Culpepper and Francis Dereham, were solely done for the benefit of the King's honor and the realm's security.

If you are shaking your head disbelievingly, I don't blame you.

⁂

6. In 1546, the Baron of Leez was a busy guy. Along with Lord Chancellor Thomas Wriothesley and Bishop Stephen Gardiner, Rich engaged in a witch hunt, working to discredit and upend minor evangelicals in the hopes of snagging the major players, most notably Katherine Parr, Queen of England; Catherine Willoughby, Duchess of Suffolk; and Thomas Cranmer, Archbishop of Canterbury.

One such "minor evangelical" was martyred preacher Anne Askew. Unwilling to testify with whom she associated, Sir Richard Rich and his cohort Wriothesley tortured the woman, racking her by turning the wheeled levers themselves. To punctuate the evilness of the act, the Constable of the Tower of London refused to participate and rushed to court to inform the king. Before he could gain an audience, the damage was done. Anne Askew became the only known women to ever be tortured at the Tower of London in its over thousand year history.

With arms, legs, elbows, and knees dislocated from the rack, Anne Askew was burned at the stake on July 16, 1546.

⁂

7. Upon the death of King Henry VIII and ascension of King Edward VI in 1547, Sir Richard Rich once again did what he did best, turn on one of his closest allies to seek his own advancement. To reach his goal, Rich successfully worked with his other "allies of the moment" and secured the fall of his "interrogation and torture partner" Lord Chancellor Thomas Wriothesley.

Things did not work out quite as planned. William Paulet was appointed in Wriothesley's place. No problem—Baron Rich of Leez quickly convinced Lord Protector Edward Seymour and the Privy Council of Paulet's "incompetence", securing the Lord Chancellorship for himself.

⁂

8. Throughout the reign of King Edward VI, Lord Chancellor Rich was a "staunch Protestant". Thus, along with Archbishop Thomas Cranmer, he ensured the destruction of all "images and idols" in the realm's churches. Throughout the realm great roods and stained

glass were destroyed. All church and abbey walls were whitewashed, priceless works of art covered and replaced with the Ten Commandments—in English, of course.

Just how "staunch" was Rich's Protestantism? Baron Rich of Leez was heavily involved in proceedings leading to the arrests and imprisonments of conservative and later avowed Roman Catholics, Bishop Edmund Bonner and Bishop Stephen Gardiner. Taking things a step further, in his role as Lord Chancellor, Rich worked tirelessly to ensure the Eucharist mass was not celebrated, arresting those performing mass for the ever defiant Lady Mary Tudor.

Sir Richard Rich dutifully delivered a letter to the King's Roman Catholic sister from Edward VI himself, commanding her to cease and desist. The Lady Mary's response? She commanded that Rich keep his lecturing short. Her celebration of the Eucharist continued.

❧❧❧

9. What goes around comes around, even for the brilliantly manipulative Sir Richard Rich. In December 1551, he was compelled to resign his long sought powerful position as Lord Chancellor of England and Wales, feigning illness. The poor man took to his bed at his estate at St. Bartholomew's.

Why? Like those in modern times who carelessly hit the "send button" before ensuring they are emailing or private messaging the correct person, a befriending letter of manipulative warning intended to be sent to the imprisoned Edward Seymour, Duke of Somerset was delivered instead to the also imprisoned Thomas Howard, Duke of Norfolk.

I suppose addressing the wax sealed parchment "The Duke" was not quite specific enough for a missive sent to the Tower of London. After all, throughout Tudor history, there always seemed to be a few dukes, earls, or barons in the pokey.

What a great opportunity for Norfolk to gain potential release! Though ultimately unsuccessful (for now), the Duke sent the missive along to John Dudley, Duke of Northumberland. Rich's days as Lord Chancellor were over.

Phew! Finally we are done with him. Or are we?

❧❧❧

10. Upon the death of King Edward VI in 1553, both Mary Tudor and Elizabeth Tudor were usurped in favor of the King's cousin, Jane Dudley. Sir Richard Rich was solicited for support of the new Queen. Knowing this was his chance to regain power within the realm, the Baron of Leez did what he is now infamous for. Rich flipped his support to the one whom he gauged would ultimately reign and proclaimed his loyalty to the woman he had previously persecuted, Mary Tudor.

The Baron of Leez always the ultimate host, Queen Mary Tudor spent a few days visiting with Rich and his family at his home in Wanstead before heading to London to take her rightful crown.

What was Sir Richard Rich's most noteworthy service to the realm in Queen Mary's reign? This should come as no surprise. Baron Rich, loyal subject that he was, became one of Queen Mary's most active persecutors, orchestrating the arrest and execution by burning of all convicted Protestant "heretics" in his home county of Essex.

Perhaps to make amends for his previous work as Chancellor of the Court of Augmentations, the Baron of Leez worked towards the large and unfinished task of restoring the monasteries. He granted the Queen what remained of the monastery at St. Bartholomew, where she established Black Friars.

⚜

After five years supporting the Roman Catholic agenda of Queen Mary Tudor, Sir Richard Rich rode into London with Queen Elizabeth Tudor when she ascended the throne. In one of his only acts showing disagreement with a reigning monarch, Rich refused to support Queen Elizabeth's Act of Uniformity, voting against it in Parliament's House of Lords in 1559 with the Roman Catholic minority.

Sir Richard Rich mellowed in his last years, perhaps in penance and preparation for meeting his God. The Baron of Leez founded a grammar school in Felsted, which in time educated two sons of Oliver Cromwell. He also founded almshouses to care for the poor and built the tower of Rochford Church.

The father of at least fifteen children, eleven legitimate from his longsuffering wife and at least four known bastards, Sir Richard Rich, 1st Baron Rich of Leez, died on June 12, 1567. He rests under his magnificent, albeit disconcerting tomb and statue at Felsted Church, Essex.

SOURCES

"Chapter X: Sir Richard Rich." In *The Records of St. Bartholomew's Priory and St. Bartholomew the Great, West Smithfield*, Volume 1. (Originally published by Oxford University Press, Oxford, 1921.) *British History Online.* http://www.british-history.ac.uk/st-barts-records/vol1/pp289-297

"Richard Rich, 1st Baron Rich." (Excerpted from Pollard, A. F. "Richard Rich, first Baron Rich," *Dictionary of National Biography*, Vol. XVI, Sidney Lee, ed., New York: The Macmillan Company, 1909, pp. 1009-1012.) *Luminarium Encyclopedia Project: England under the Tudors.* http://www.luminarium.org/encyclopedia/richardrich.htm

MYSTERY OF THE CHEQUERS RING

By SANDRA BYRD

SHE HELD THE REALM'S FINANCES IN HER GRASP AND THE CROWN JEWELS ROUND HER neck or on her head, but there were only two pieces of jewelry that Queen Elizabeth I was reliably said to have never removed: her coronation ring, which she considered to be her "wedding" ring, and her ruby and pearl locket ring. This latter ring, shrouded in mystery, tells us as much about the queen's heart as does the former.

The ring is generally referred to as the Chequers ring because its permanent home is now at the British Prime Minister's country home, Chequers, and under the authority of its trustees.

In 2008, Prime Minister Gordon Brown lent out several pieces of art from Chequers to the museum at country house Compton Verney. Kathleen Soriano, head of exhibitions at Compton Verney, said of the ring, *"It's a very moving piece because it's so delicate and small and really evokes the sense of the story. It's a very powerful object."*

Just what is that story evoked?

Most sources place the first appearance of the locket ring at 1575. Although some assert that the Queen had it commissioned, there is no trail or definitive provenance for that claim. Traditionally, lockets are gifts. Inside might be a portrait of a lover or a child, or perhaps a lock of hair from someone who had passed on. The idea is to keep close to heart someone who is likely far removed by death or convention, politics, or sea. The idea, too, is to be able to shield or shroud the identity of the loved one by clasping and keeping the locket closed.

English locket jewelers Lily & Will tell us that, *"When Elizabeth I wore a locket ring... it marked a new beginning for the locket. It started to rise in popularity as Elizabeth I gave gifts of jewel encrusted lockets to many of her favourite loyal subjects—Sir Francis Drake being one of them."* The Scottish National Museum holds among its collection a locket with portraits of Mary, Queen of Scots, and her son James, given to a trusted servant on the eve of her execution.

Then who is to be found inside of the ring so cherished by Queen Elizabeth? Another royal, executed mother, and her beloved only child. When opened, the Chequers ring reveals two portraits which face one another. One is clearly Queen Elizabeth, seemingly in her early forties, neatly fitting with the year 1575. The second portrait is widely understood to be her mother, Queen Anne Boleyn.

Because there is no direct provenance, there has been speculation that the portrait could be of the young Queen Elizabeth herself, or even of Queen Kateryn Parr,

Elizabeth's stepmother. It's unlikely that the Queen would have worn two portraits of herself throughout her life and in any case, there would have been no need for those portraits to be kept hidden.

Although Elizabeth bore tender affection for Parr, the portrait within does not clearly resemble Parr, nor does the French hood worn by the subject fit in with the French hoods known to have been worn by Parr. It does, however, perfectly match the French hoods Anne Boleyn was well known for.

The British Museum says of Anne Boleyn:

> Of the mid-sixteenth century representations of her, the most reliable must be the tiny miniature set into a ring of about 1575 which belonged to her daughter, Queen Elizabeth I (The Chequers Trust; see "Elizabeth" exhibition catalogue edited by Susan Doran, London, The National Maritime Museum, 2003, no.7). This likeness comes from the same source as the painting in the National Portrait Gallery.

There is another miniature of Anne which Charles I had copied by John Hoskins the elder in the seventeenth century, which is endorsed, "from an ancient original." What might this ancient original have been?

Anne's principle biographer, historian Eric Ives, states that it is *more likely that Hoskins had access to an earlier image of the kind from which the NPG image originated.* Ives continues, *"A full-length portrait of Anne was owned by Lord Lumley in 1590 and existed as late as 1773. Could it even be that Hoskins' source was or was derived from a Holbein painting now lost?"* Perhaps there was one early portrait or sketch that Hoskins, the painter of the NPG portrait, and maybe even the painter of the locket miniature based their work upon.

Although Elizabeth likely could not remember what her mother looked like, there were those at her court old enough who would remember, and there were also those who still held quiet affections for and perhaps an illustration of Queen Anne. And just like that, the generosity of fiction allowed me to consider who might have loved and understood Elizabeth enough to risk giving her a ring with a portrait of her beloved, but taboo, mother inside.

An Enduring Tudor Mystery: What Happened to Lady Mary Seymour?

By SANDRA BYRD

Lady Mary Seymour was the only child of Queen Kateryn Parr and her fourth husband, Thomas Seymour. Parr died of childbed fever shortly after giving birth to Mary, and the baby's father, Thomas Seymour, was executed for treason just a few short years thereafter. But what happened to their child, who seems to have vanished without trace into history? This is an enduring mystery and one which has intrigued Tudor readers for years.

The last known facts about the child include that her father, Thomas Seymour, asked as a dying wish that Mary be entrusted to Katherine Willoughby, Duchess of Suffolk, and that desire was granted. Willoughby, although a great friend of Mary Seymour's mother, Queen Kateryn Parr, viewed this wardship as a burden as evidenced by her own letters which pleaded for relief.

According to Parr's biographer Linda Porter,

> In January 1550, less than a year after her father's death, application was made in the House of Commons for the restitution of Lady Mary Seymour. ...she had been made eligible by this act to inherit any remaining property that had not been returned to the Crown at the time of her father's attainder. But in truth, Mary's prospects were less optimistic than this might suggest. Much of her parents' lands and goods had already passed onto the hands of others.

The £500 required for Mary's household would amount to approximately £100,000 British pounds, or $150,000 U.S. today, so you can see that Willoughby had reason to shrink from such a duty. And yet the daughter of a Queen must be kept in commensurate style. There were many people who had greatly benefited from Parr's generosity throughout the short years of her marriage to Henry. None of them stepped forward to assist Baby Mary.

Biographer Elizabeth Norton says that, "The council granted money to Mary for household wages, servants' uniforms, and food on 13 March, 1550. This is the last evidence of Mary's continued survival." Susan James says Mary is, "probably buried somewhere in the parish church at Edenham."

Most of Parr's biographers assume that Mary died young of a childhood disease. But this, by necessity, is speculative because there is no record of Mary's death anywhere: no gravestone, no bill of death, no mention of it in anyone's extant personal or official correspondence. Parr's biographer during the Victorian ages, Agnes Strickland, claimed that Mary lived on to marry Edward Bushel and become a member of the household of Queen Anne, King James I of England's wife. It's possible. There are other possibilities.

Various family biographers claimed descent from Mary, including those who came down from the Irish shipping family of Hart. This family also claimed to have had Thomas Seymour's ring, which was inscribed *"What I Have, I Hold,"* until early in the twentieth century. I have no idea if that is true or not, but it's a good detail and certainly possible.

According to an article in *History Today* by biographer Linda Porter, Kateryn Parr's chaplain, John Parkhurst, published a book in 1573 entitled *Ludica sive Epigrammata juvenilia.* Within it is a poem that speaks of someone with a "queenly mother" who died in childbirth, the child of whom now lies beneath marble after a brief life. But there is no mention of the child's name, and 1573 is twenty-five years after Mary's birth. It hints at Mary, but does not insist.

Fiction is a rather more generous mistress than biography, and I was therefore free to wonder. Why would the daughter of a Queen and the cousin of the King not have warranted even a tiny remark upon her death? In an era when family descent meant everything, it seemed unlikely that Mary's death would be nowhere definitively noted. Far less important people, even young children, had their deaths documented during these years; my research turned up dozens of them, most of whom were lower born than Mary.

Edward Seymour requested a state funeral for his mother (which was refused) as she was grandmother to the King. Would then the death of the cousin of a King, and the only child of the most recent Queen, not even be mentioned? The differences seem irreconcilable. Then, too, it would have been to Willoughby's advantage to show that she was no longer responsible for the child if Mary was dead.

The turmoil of the time, in which Mary's uncle the Lord Protector was about to fall, the fact that her grandmother Lady Seymour died in 1550, and the lack of motivation any would have had to seek the child out lest they then be required to pay for her upkeep, all added up to a potentially different ending for me. The lack of solid facts allowed me to give Mary a happy ending in my novel, *The Secret Keeper: A Novel of Kateryn Parr,* an ending I feel is entirely possible given Mary's cold trail and one which I feel both Queen Kateryn and her little Mary deserve.

Thomas Cranmer's Everlasting Legacy: Poetic Prose

By BETH VON STAATS

BLESSED Lord, who hast caused all holy Scriptures to be written for our learning; Grant that we may in such wise hear them, read, mark, learn, and inwardly digest them, that by patience and comfort of thy holy Word, we may embrace, and ever hold fast, the blessed hope of everlasting life, which thou hast given us in our Saviour Jesus Christ. Amen.
— Thomas Cranmer, Archbishop of Canterbury

THOMAS CRANMER IS REMEMBERED AS A GREAT PROTESTANT MARTYR, A TORTURED soul who found his courage just in time to die with the knowledge that his salvation was only guaranteed by his faith and his faith alone.

Most history lovers think of Thomas Cranmer as the man plucked up from obscurity to become Archbishop of Canterbury for the specific role of settling King Henry VIII's "Great Matter" once and for all, a task he dutifully committed by finding the King's marriage to Catalina de Aragon invalid. Others think of Cranmer as the ever cautious reformer, who, hiding behind the front man and principal driver Thomas Cromwell, helped pave the way to the Henrican Reformation and introduction of an English language Bible. Then there are those who also look to him as the lead and principle change agent for the sweeping Protestant reforms that ravaged through England during the reign of King Edward VI.

As memorable as these historical events were, and as dramatic and heroic his ultimate martyrdom was, Archbishop Thomas Cranmer's greatest gift to the world is something most people never think about, his brilliance in composing a liturgical vernacular written specifically to be read aloud, the literary genre we now know as poetic prose.

The Book of Common Prayer, Thomas Cranmer's lasting liturgy for the Church of England, now extended worldwide to the Anglican Communion, is a literary masterpiece—his words contained profoundly embedded into the very cultural soul of the British people, the lyrical vernacular deeply imprinted into every English speaking person worldwide. As Cranmer openly admitted, *The Book of Common Prayer* was not his entire original creation. Through his scholarship of theology, Cranmer dove head first into the Latin of the English Catholic Church, most notably a book known as the *Sarum Missal,* the liturgy of choice of the priests and monks of Salisbury Cathedral. Cranmer also borrowed from the liturgy of the Reformed Church of Cologne and prayers from the Byzantine rite.

Though today some may call this literary plagiarism, these compositions were written in Latin for the clergy. Thomas Cranmer's intent instead was to create an English language liturgy that was universally gospelled throughout all parishes of the Church of England, one whose beauty lay in its simplicity and scriptural truth. Cranmer's steadfast and primary goal in his religious reformation was to ensure every person, whether educated or illiterate, could understand God's word. Thus, he didn't trifle with originality, but instead celebrated the richness of English religious traditions then only understandable to Latin scholars and translated them with his gifted hand of literary genius.

This acknowledged, it is critical to note that many of the most eloquently written and profoundly beautiful collects and prayers of *The Book of Common Prayer,* notable for their grace, simplistic grandeur, idioms, imagery, repetitions, contrasting reversals, general rhythms and lyric poetic cadence were of Thomas Cranmer's original composition.

Even Cranmer's writings in general through his scholarly articles and personal letters hold beauty and depth of feeling. Thus there is no Tudorphile alive who cannot quote Cranmer's professed love for Queen Anne Boleyn, *"Now I think that your Grace best knoweth, that, next unto your Grace, I was most bound unto her of all creatures living...."*

Since the inception of *The Book of Common Prayer,* countless novelists, screenplay writers and poets show plainly in their writing styles and plots strong influence from the poetic prose of Thomas Cranmer. The first notable author to look to Cranmer for inspiration was none other than William Shakespeare. In fact, literary historian and Professor Daniel Swift argues that *The Book of Common Prayer* was absolutely essential to the playwright.

> *"See a prayer book in his hand,*
> *True ornaments to know a holy man."*
> —*Richard III,* William Shakespeare

Although some historians believe Shakespeare was Roman Catholic, Swift convincingly demonstrates the playwright's use of Cranmer's liturgy in his early comedies, while the marriage rite is used in other plays. Also pronounced is Shakespeare's focus on church ceremonies for the departed in the connected rites of Communion and burial. *Macbeth* is the play Swift notes as most influenced by Thomas Cranmer's liturgy, demonstrating without question that Shakespeare clearly utilized *The Book of Common Prayer* as source material for his writing, taking what he wished and leaving the rest.

So engraved is Thomas Cranmer's literary style in English vernacular, many writers and composers, knowing and often unknowing "borrow" from it, enhancing the quality, rhythms and poetic cadences of their work. Most commonly this takes the form of the use of triplet repetitions, which is often seen in the writing of Charlotte Bronte and Jane Austen. It's no surprise to learn then that both women were daughters of Anglican clergymen. Examples of Cranmer's use of commonly known "triplets" include:

...Earth to earth, ashes to ashes, dust to dust; in sure and certain hope of the Resurrection....

What the heart loves, the will chooses and the mind justifies.

O God, from whom all holy desires, all good counsels, and all just works do proceed; Give unto thy servants that peace which the world cannot give....

Thomas Cranmer's poetic and rhythmic liturgical vernacular is as pronounced in our modern times as it was to Shakespeare, Bronte, and Austen. Regardless of religion, many of us when marrying vow, *"...to have and to hold from this day forward, for better for worse, for richer for poorer, in sickness and in health...."*

Thomas Cranmer's prayer for the dead lives on eternal, as well. David Bowie and Faith No More fans sing aloud in the shower to tunes entitled "Ashes to Ashes", a theme continued in the novel titled *Ashes to Ashes*, by Tami Hoag and a play titled the same by Harold Pinter. Perhaps most notably, in Great Britain viewers tune in faithfully to BBC One's popular science fiction and television police drama *Ashes to Ashes*.

Another famous Cranmer line is: *"Give peace in our time, O Lord."* World War II history buffs will harken to Neville Chamberlain's policies of appeasement, declaring the most cherished "peace in our time", a theme continued in a politically charged song by Elvis Costello. Even President Barack Obama controversially invoked Thomas Cranmer in his second inaugural address, again striving for "peace in our time". Conservatives slammed Obama in the social media incorrectly citing Chamberlain as the source.

Thomas Cranmer, Archbishop of Canterbury was a literary genius, who if novels had been envisioned in his lifetime, would surely have crafted masterpieces rivaling the greatest fiction writers in history. Cranmer's brilliance lay in his sonorities and structure of the English sentence and his knack of being as astute a listener as he was an author. Thus, on this anniversary of Thomas Cranmer's martyrdom, rather than remembering the circumstances of his tragic death, celebrate instead the man with the depth and quality of composition that leads literary historians to place him alongside William Tyndale and William Shakespeare as the founding influences of the English language as we know it now to be.

Many people today will remember the right hand of Thomas Cranmer. After all, it signed the recantations that Cranmer told those listening to his last speech *"troubleth my conscience"*, so much so that he announced and then did thrust it first into the fire that consumed him.

Instead, today I prefer to cherish the words that flowed from the quills it held, and the man who wrote with *"...an outward and visible sign of an inward and spiritual grace."*

SOURCES

Aitkin, Jonathan. "Common Prayer, Uncommon Beauty." *The American Spectator.*

Swift, Daniel. *Shakespeare's Common Prayers: The Book of Common Prayer and the Elizabethan Age.* Oxford University Press, 2012.

Woods, James. "God Talk: The Book of Common Prayer at Three Hundred Fifty." *New Yorker Magazine* (October 22, 2012). http://www.newyorker.com/magazine/2012/10/22/god-talk

The Birth of a Queen: Marie Stuart, December 8, 1542

By Linda Root

At the time of the birth of Mary Tudor to Queen Catherine of Aragon and later, that of her half-sister Elizabeth to Queen Anne Boleyn, neither were considered likely to become sovereigns. Both of their mothers had childbearing years ahead of them, and Henry Tudor would have been the first to declare himself the most virile man in England. Surely there would be sons!

Four centuries later, the same could be said of Princess Elizabeth of Windsor when her grandfather King George V died in 1936 and her personable uncle David became Edward VIII. And then came the famous words of abdication: *"But you must believe me when I tell you that I have found it impossible…to discharge my duties as King as I would wish to do without the help and support of the woman I love."* Sixteen years later his gentle-spirited niece succeeded his brother George VI to become Elizabeth II of England and Elizabeth I of Scotland, titular head of the British Commonwealth.

But it was an entirely different story when Princess Marie Stuart was born. When her mother entered her birthing chamber, a Scottish army far superior in numbers to the English defenders had suffered an embarrassing and unnecessary rout at Solway Moss, and despondent King James V had retreated to his luxurious hunting lodge at Falkland and taken to his bed. The cream of the Scottish nobility had been herded to London as hostages to be seduced to Henry VIII's cause, and the common soldiers had deserted in great numbers even before the battle had been joined, principally due to their distrust of the military hierarchy led by the King's ineffectual favorite Oliver Sinclair and the deference given to the Frenchmen in the chain of command.

To weather such a crisis, both King and country were in need of a healthy heir apparent who was male. But two weeks after the defeat at Solway Moss, Princess Marie Stuart was born under the cloud of the Scottish defeat and the unfortunate nature of her sex. This was not an occasion when Scottish skies were alight with bonfires.

The full impact of the birth of a female heir apparent did not strike until six days later, when her father James V turned his face to the wall of his bedchamber and died. And thus, the disappointing Princess Marie became the even more disappointing Queen of Scots, leaving the nation ripe for exploitation from those without and factionalism from those within.

Decades later, the mighty but personally insecure Elizabeth Tudor called her cousin Marie Stuart, Queen of Scots, "the daughter of debate," a statement that borders on the prophetic. After hundreds of years, historians are divided as to whether Marie was a martyr or a murderess, an incredibly forgiving wife or an adulteress, a competent sovereign facing insurmountable odds or an utter failure who orchestrated her own ruin.

Thus it should be no surprise that not even her date of birth is settled. Most historians accept December 8, 1542 on the Julian calendar, although some historians advance the argument that it actually occurred on December 7 and had been altered later to make it fall upon the Feast of the Holy Virgin. At least there is a consensus as to the place—Linlithgow Palace in Lothian.

Linlithgow Palace was a favored residence of a chain of Scottish consorts due to its picturesque setting and clean air. When Marie of Guise first saw it, she was delighted to find its setting equal in beauty to the chateaux along the Loire.

She joined with her husband James in a major effort to make it as lavishly decorated inside as it was magnificent on the outside. Together they selected furnishings, art, and tapestries and imported items from France that created an environment as comfortable as the Queen's late husband's ducal palace in Orléans or at Grande Jardin in Joinville, the most elegant of the many residences of the House of Guise. Linlithgow was indeed the show place of Stuart Scotland, and Queen Marie de Guise chose it for the birthplace of the third child of her marriage to the Scottish king.

John Guy in his excellent 2004 history of the Queen of Scots, *My Heart is My Own*, published in the United States under the title *The True Life of Mary Stuart, Queen of Scots*, adds his talent for using words to creating vibrant visual imagery of Scotland in the grips of an unprecedented cold spell at the time of Marie Stuart's birth. Even the mighty Clyde had frozen over in late November of 1542.

It was an odd time for the King to decide to launch a major military excursion into England via the Debatable Lands. Some historians including Antonia Fraser attribute the unwise decision as a response to his uncle Henry Tudor's saber-rattling when James refused to travel to England for a meeting at Christmas. Henry VIII has been insisting that his nephew, son of his older sister Margaret, meet with him on English soil or English armies would avenge the slight by marching into Scotland.

For whatever reason, James sent a huge raiding party into England, and it resulted in a rout. James did not personally participate in the battle, and when he heard the news, his first concern was not for the hundreds of Scots who had been slaughtered or who had drowned or the thousands captured, but for his unpopular favorite Oliver Sinclair.

After leaving the borders, James stopped by Linlithgow to exchange courtesies with his wife who was about to begin her confinement and traveled on to his favorite hunting lodge at Falkland. According to Guy, he was suffering from deep depression after the defeat at Solway Moss which he blamed on the high rate of desertions within the Scottish ranks, not the incompetence of their leaders.

Whether he died of despair is debatable. There is a possibility that he had contracted cholera or had caught whatever fever had recently claimed the life of his friend and confidant the Earl of Athol. The salient fact is that six days after her birth, Marie Stuart's father was dead and she was Queen of Scots.

Early twentieth-century historian Thomas Finlayson-Henderson speculates that James more than likely did not love his second wife Queen Marie de Guise, citing the fact that he sired at least nine bastards to numerous mistresses. However, those of the King's illegitimate children with known birth records were conceived long before his marriages to either of his French consorts, first to the frail Princess Madeleine, who died childless within months of her arrival in Scotland and whom James apparently adored, or his second marriage to the Dowager Duchess of Orleans, Marie of Guise in 1538.

The Guises were a powerful family from the Duchy of Lorraine, and after Lorraine's annexation to France they were considered French princes. Marie was the oldest daughter. She was an established beauty of keen intellect, and at least during her youth, a woman of robust health.

Lady Antonia Fraser remarks in her seminal biography first published in 1969, *Mary Queen of Scots*, that the physical characteristics we associate with Marie Stuart are consistent with the tall and handsome members of the House of Guise, not the less impressive Stewarts. Her temperament, elusive illnesses, and her tendency to impetuousness, however, are attributed to her father's line. In any case, there is no doubt that Marie of Guise was a much sought after marital partner; Henry VIII, who was between marriages when the Duke of Longueville died, had been his nephew's rival.

Finlayson-Henderson's speculation is probably based on the established truth that James V would have preferred to marry the already married Margaret Erskine, Lady Douglas of Loch Leven, the mother of his favorite child Lord James Stewart. The lady was the acknowledged love of his life, rather than either of his French brides.

James V, however, was not the consummate romantic that his remote descendant Edward VIII became in 1936. While he did not like it much, he was indeed able to stumble on without the help and support of the woman he loved, who went back to her husband Sir Robert Douglas of Loch Leven and is best known for her role in later life when she became Marie Stuart's jailer at Loch Leven Castle in 1567.

A good deal of the problems that befell Marie Stuart as an adult stemmed from the fact that Lady Margaret indoctrinated her son Lord James Stewart, Earl of Moray, with the idea that she and the King had engaged in a hand-fasting and thus he, not his half-sister Marie, was the rightful sovereign of Scotland.

Marie de Guise, the Dowager Duchess of Longueville, came to the bed of the Scottish King with an established record for bearing sons. She had already given birth to two, one of whom survived and was left in Joinville in the care of his maternal grandmother Antoinette de Bourbon, Duchess of Guise.

King James also had established himself as a worthy sire of sons, albeit illegitimate. Of his many bastards of record, only one was a daughter, Princess Jean Stewart, Countess of Argyll. The two childless years of the royal marriage were causing alarm to both the Scottish nobility and the Guises when the first of two sons was born in 1540 and became Prince James, Duke of Rothesay, his birth celebrated with all of the requisite bonfires and bells. In April of the following year a second prince was born, named either Robert or Arthur, who lived for just two days.

By the end of April 1541, both of the Scottish infant princes were dead, apparently of natural causes. Scots preparing for the coronation of the elder soon found themselves mourning both. Scots critical of the King blamed it on a vengeful God rendering punishment for his libido and moral laxity, but infant mortality in the sixteenth century was hardly rare. Both families assured the couple that they were young, and there would be more sons coming. And thus, in the bleak winter of 1542, the fate of Scotland and the mental health of its King rested on a hope and promise that did not come to be.

The circumstances related to the birth of Marie Stuart were shrouded in mystery and misinformation.

Thomas Finlayson-Henderson in his 1905 biography *Mary Queen of Scots* reports that several days before her birth, news reached Edinburgh of a premature delivery. In some versions the child was male and in others, female, and in some versions, it died. Henry VIII certainly received such a report. But Linlithgow was only a few miles distant from Edinburgh, and soon those rumors were dispelled, and the nation returned to a period of watchful waiting.

When the Queen of Scots was born in early December, the weather in Scotland was so foul that it took six days for the messengers heading to London with the news to reach Northumberland south of Berwick-on-Tweed. More disastrous news had arrived a few days earlier. The King of Scots was dead.

Finlayson-Henderson writes that the child's father, King James V, had been at Falkland Palace where he had taken to his bed in despair over the defeat at Solway Moss and the uncertain fate of his favorite Oliver Sinclair when a courier arrived with news that the Queen had delivered a daughter. This was not the news that James wanted to hear. Following the death of his two infant sons he had pinned his hopes on a new male heir. Those hopes too were dashed.

Within a week of Marie Stuart's birth, the disparaged King died, apparently of natural causes, possibly from cholera. Two weeks later reports circulated in London that both mother and child, by now established to be female, were seriously ill and unlikely to survive.

One explanation for the dissemination of such dire but unsubstantiated news was the unusual reclusiveness of the Dowager. An effort was made by Marie of Guise to insulate her daughter from the intrigues of the factions vying for control of her daughter during what was certain to be a protracted period of regency. A second factor had to do with the death of the King and the resulting funeraries which curtailed the usual celebrations surrounding the birth of a monarch.

The Queen of Scots was quietly christened at the nearby parish church of St. Michael without any of the usual pomp and splendor or exposure to the deadly cold that she would have faced had she traveled to either of the chapels royal at Holyrood or Stirling. Her coronation was delayed until the following September.

Marie Stuart's most formidable modern critic Retha Warnicke, in her 2006 tightly written biography *Mary Queen of Scots*, gives us a glimpse of what followed in her remarks on the political atmosphere surrounding the Queen's birth. Although there was no opposition to her ascension and no legally justifiable argument to raise against it after the parliamentary entail ended in 1536 with the death of the Duke of Albany, succession of a female was by no means popular with the Scots. Long before John Knox's *The First Blast of the Trumpet Against the Monstrous Regiment of Women*, David Lindsey, the Lion Herald, spoke out against it in verse.

The one positive result of the Queen's ascension was that for the first year of her life at least, Henry VIII called off the dogs of war and pursued a marriage game instead. His son Edward, Prince of Wales, was five years old, and Henry saw a way of establishing the long asserted English suzerainty over Scotland without bloodshed by means of a dynastic marriage—provided, of course, that the infant Queen of Scots survived. When the English diplomat Ralph Sadler was shown the unswaddled little queen in March, he reported to Henry VIII that she was *"as goodly a child as I have seen of her age and as like to live, by Grace of God."*

By the time of her coronation in September of 1543, she was a healthy, bright, and pretty child, and the battle for control of her future began.

A large contingent of the Scottish nobility were Anglophiles and many of them Calvinists. The Dowager Queen of Scotland, however, was French, a daughter of the ultra-Catholic House of Guise, and strongly allied with the standard bearer of the Scottish Catholics, Cardinal David Beaton, Archbishop of Saint Andrews, who sought control of the little Queen. His rival was the Scottish heir-apparent James Hamilton, Earl of Arran, whom Marie of Guise accurately called *"the most inconstant man in the world".*

Marie de Guise had another nominee, Matthew Stuart, Earl of Lennox, who at the time was a bachelor with claims to both the Scottish and the English crowns and a sworn enemy of the Hamiltons. The new widow exercised her feminine wiles and enticed Lennox to become her champion. Thus, the major issues during the first year of Marie Stuart's life were: 1) who would be her regent? and 2) whom would she marry?

Soon Henry Tudor released the contingent of Scottish hostages known as "Assured Scots" whom the English King had wooed and won, and the incompetent but pro-English Earl of Arran was ratified as Regent. Initially, there was a compromise that placed Beaton as Chancellor, but that did not last long. Soon Lennox was ousted, and Beaton was arrested. A treaty was negotiated between the regent and the English which, among other things, promised Marie Stuart as the future bride of little Edward Tudor. The Dowager Marie de Guise had another candidate in mind.

Roderick Graham in his 2009 biography, *An Accidental Tragedy—The Life of Mary, Queen of Scots*, presents an excellent analysis of why the English betrothal did not happen. In essence, while the diplomats were dispensing bribes and Henry Tudor was flexing his muscles, Marie de Guise, one of the most competent women of her time, realized that the key to her daughter's safety was to keep her close.

While the others bartered and threatened and bribed and cajoled, Marie de Guise tightened the circle around her daughter and herself, agreed to conditions she never intended to honor, and until she saw her daughter safely off to France in 1548 under the protection of the French King Henri II, she held on firmly and did not let go. She was very likely the one person in Marie Stuart's life who consistently acted in what she believed to be in her daughter's best interest, often at the expense of her own health, happiness, and peace of mind.

In 1548, just short of Queen Marie Stuart's sixth birthday, her mother sent her to France to be raised in the French royal nursery in anticipation of her betrothal to the Dauphin Francois. The Dowager traveled to France for a visit three years later. She returned to Scotland a year later to protect her daughter's interests and never saw the little Queen again.

She died in 1560 after years of confrontation with the Protestant Lairds of the Congregation and was buried in the chapel at Saint Pierre les Dames in Rheims after the Scots refused to allow her interment in the Chapel Royale at Holyrood alongside her husband James V and her infant sons. Twenty-seven years after the death of Marie de Guise, the captive Marie Stuart, Queen of Scots, made a similar request of her cousin Elizabeth Tudor that her body be sent to Rheims after her execution to be interred beside her mother at Saint Pierre les Dames. That request, too, was denied.

More lines have been written about Marie Stuart, Queen of Scots, than practically any other regnant queen. There have been nursery rhymes and cut-out dolls and songs and plays and movies, and now the blatantly sexy and inaccurate but colorful mini-series *Reign*. But there is little trace of her at the site of her birth.

Her remains are in London at Westminster Abbey across the aisle from those of her cousin Elizabeth Tudor, the person who either inadvertently or purposefully signed her death warrant. Her tomb is the far more elegant of the two, probably due to guilty feelings on the part of her son James VI and I who had turned his back on her while she lived. And thus Marie Stuart, Queen of Scots, reigns over legions of the royal dead and other dignitaries buried within a magnificent abbey in the capital she never visited, in a country she never ruled.

Thus, her exile remains, a fact that perhaps lends bittersweet importance to the recent unveiling of a statue on the grounds at her birthplace at Linlithgow. It portrays her as elegant, tall, athletic, and dignified.

The seven-foot-tall statue was designed by the late Aberdonian sculptor Anne Davidson and has been scaled up and cast by well-known sculptor David Annan. The costs came from private donations, and was a major fundraising project of the Marie Stuart Society. The physical site is at Linlithgow Peel on the palace grounds and will be maintained by Historic Scotland. Linlithgow is one of the only sites associated with Marie Stuart accessible to the public year round. Thus, at least symbolically, the Queen of Scots has come home.

Mary, Queen of Scots: A Kingdom Lost

By BARBARA KYLE

THIS IS THE STORY OF HOW MARY QUEEN OF SCOTS LOST HER KINGDOM. TWICE.

Mary Stuart was crowned Queen of Scotland when she was five days old. At the age of six she was sent to France to join the French royal family in preparation for marrying the king's heir, François. The two teenagers were wed, and a year later, in 1560, François became king. Mary, at seventeen, was queen of France.

At this time the young English queen, Elizabeth Tudor, was in the first year of her reign. She feared a French invasion through Scotland, and to prevent it she sent an army to back Scottish rebels who had risen up against their mighty overlords, the French. A leader of the Scottish rebels was Mary's Protestant half-brother, James, and with Elizabeth's help he and his fighters beat the French army, ending French domination in Scotland and putting a Protestant government in power.

Elizabeth's victory over the French in Scotland was a turning point in her fledgling reign. By gambling on intervention she had defied France, elevating her status at home and in the eyes of all Europe, whose leaders had to acknowledge her as a formidable ruler. She did this at the age of twenty-six.

Elizabeth could not have realized that her problems with Mary Stuart had just begun. The two were cousins: Henry VII, the first Tudor monarch, was Elizabeth's grandfather and Mary's great-grandfather. With undisputed Tudor blood Mary publicly maintained her claim to the throne of England.

In 1561 Mary's husband, the young French king, died. A widow at eighteen, she came back to Scotland to take up her birthright as its Queen.

She found a country that had undergone the Protestant Reformation in her absence. Her return upset the balance of power among the Scottish nobility, setting off a sporadic civil war between her supporters, who were mostly Catholic, and those of her Protestant half-brother, James, now the Earl of Moray, the *de facto* head of the government. For six years this unrest smoldered.

Mary fell in love with a young Englishman, Lord Darnley, and against the advice of her council she married him. She gave birth to a son, James, but the marriage quickly turned sour. Everyone at court knew that Mary and Darnley were fighting.

Mary began to rely on a tough, soldierly man on her council, the Earl of Bothwell. Many whispered that the relationship was adulterous.

In the winter of 1567 the rivalry between the power-seeking factions came to a head when Darnley was killed in an explosion; the house he was staying in was blown up with gunpowder. Three months later Mary wed Bothwell. Suspicion for Darnley's death fell on them both. Moray acted quickly to take power. He indicted Mary for masterminding her husband's murder, took charge of her baby son, and imprisoned her. Bothwell fled to Denmark.

Mary Queen of Scots, at age twenty-four, had lost her kingdom.

Mary's prison tower rose from an isolated fortress, a castle on an island in Loch Leven. She had been a captive for ten months when one of her young supporters helped her slip out of the castle dressed as a country woman. He rowed her the mile across the lake. Waiting on the other side were her loyal nobles.

All of Europe gasped at the news of Mary's escape. She was notorious for the scandals that had swirled around her: Was she a murdering adulteress who had deserved to be deposed, or an innocent victim horribly wronged? Everyone had an opinion—and waited to see what would happen next. It held enormous significance for every leader. The kings of Spain and France, fiercely Catholic, were eager to see Moray's Protestant government destroyed. If Mary ventured to reclaim her throne, it could start an international war. Elizabeth, once again, feared invasion.

Mary quickly gathered an army. So did Moray. They faced each other on the Glasgow moor near the village of Langside. As Mary looked on from a hilltop her commander, Lord Herries, led a cavalry charge that forced Moray's men to retreat. But when another of the Queen's commanders led his infantry through the village's narrow street they met close fire from hackbutters (arquebusiers) that Moray had placed behind cottages and hedges. Hundreds of the Queen's men fell under the gunfire. Moray's main force, moments ago in retreat from Herries' cavalry charge, turned and attacked. Mary's demoralized men began to flee, deserting. Moray's men chased them. The Battle of Langside was over in less than an hour.

Mary had lost her kingdom for a second time.

She panicked. She galloped down the slope, terrified of being captured again. Several lords loyal to her rode after her, begging her to take flight for France, but Mary galloped south. In her terror she wanted to put Scotland behind her as quickly as she could. She rode for England.

It was the worst decision of her life. She would never see Scotland again.

DID THE QUEEN KILL HER HUSBAND? THE FIRST TRIAL OF MARY, QUEEN OF SCOTS

BY BARBARA KYLE

THE NEWS THAT REACHED LONDON ASTONISHED QUEEN ELIZABETH AND ALL HER court. Her cousin Mary, Queen of Scots, had been defeated on the battlefield near Glasgow and in terror had fled to England. She had arrived in a fishing boat on the coast of Cumbria with nothing but the clothes she stood up in. It was May 1568.

Mary instantly wrote to her "dear cousin" Elizabeth asking for her protection and her support. Eager for revenge, Mary wanted to rage back to Scotland at the head of an army and vanquish her enemies. Those enemies were led by her own half-brother, the Earl of Moray.

Arriving in England as a royal refugee, Mary fully expected the support of her cousin Elizabeth. Mary was often blind to reality when she had a passionate stake in a situation, and never was she more blind than when she asked Elizabeth for help.

That's because Mary's arrival in England created a terrible quandary for Elizabeth. England was Protestant, but a large, disgruntled portion of its people were Catholics who believed that Mary, a pious Catholic, should be on the throne, since they regarded Elizabeth as illegitimate and a heretic. Both queens had Tudor blood.

Elizabeth, unmarried at thirty-five, had no children, and Mary had the best claim to succeed her. Elizabeth feared that Mary would be a lightning rod for disaffected English Catholics to rise up to depose her. If they tried, Mary could expect the backing of the mightiest power in Europe, Catholic Spain.

Elizabeth's councillors were appalled at the thought of Mary moving freely around England to draw Catholics to her cause, and they advised her to imprison Mary. Elizabeth recoiled at that, for she took her cousin's royal status very seriously. However, she knew that Mary was a dangerous threat to her throne. So, crafty ruler that she was, she found a way forward.

Her solution was Machiavellian—and pure Elizabeth. She let it be known that, much as she sympathized with her fellow queen, she could not support her if Mary was, indeed, an adulteress and a murderer. To discover the truth, she proclaimed, she would hold an inquiry into the charges against Mary.

In soothing letters to her cousin she assured her that if the charges proved unfounded, as Mary vehemently insisted, Elizabeth would wholeheartedly back her in restoring her to her Scottish throne. Elizabeth's tactic was one that modern-day crafters of smear campaigns would appreciate. Dirt, once it is hurled, tends to stick. If it did, Elizabeth would be free to abandon Mary and uphold the alliance she wanted with Moray's Protestant government in Scotland.

It was not called a trial, since English courts had no jurisdiction over foreign rulers, but for all intents and purposes, a trial is what it was. Elizabeth set the venue; the proceedings would take place at York, then move to Westminster. She invited the Earl of Moray to come and argue his case before her commissioners. He eagerly agreed and set out from Edinburgh with a rookery of lawyers.

Mary was furious. She said there was only one way she would appear to answer charges made by her subjects: if they were brought before her in chains. She refused to attend the inquiry. It was one of the many impetuous decisions she made that doomed her, for by all accounts she had extraordinary charm, and had she attended she might have won the commissioners' sympathy. Instead, she appointed commissioners to act in her name, Lord Herries and the Bishop of Ross. These men were staunchly loyal to her, but they did not have her "star" power.

Elizabeth appointed the Duke of Norfolk, the premier peer of her realm, to preside. But Norfolk, like just about everyone involved in this intricate piece of political theater, including Elizabeth, had a hidden agenda. Mary, ever seeking to enhance her power base in England, had made Norfolk an offer he could not resist: marriage. Secretly, in letters, the two formed a marriage plan. For Norfolk, it was the brass ring. Mary had the best claim to be Elizabeth's heir, and if she came to the throne, then he, as her husband, would be king. Norfolk, therefore, was secretly predisposed to find Mary innocent.

But something happened that changed the course of the proceedings and of history. Moray presented evidence to the English commissioners: eight letters written by Mary to the Earl of Bothwell while she was married to Darnley. These have become known as the "casket letters," so named because, Moray said, they were found in a small silver casket in Bothwell's house after he had fled the country. Found under a bed.

How convenient, Mary raged. She had good reason to rage, for she only heard of this development from leaks. Moray had presented the letters to Elizabeth's commissioners alone, in secret. Mary was not allowed to see the evidence that was to damn her.

And damning it was. The letters were the intimate words of a woman to her lover. She called herself *"the most faithful lover that ever you had or shall have,"* and wrote, *"I end, after kissing your hands...your humble and faithful lover who hopeth shortly to be another thing unto you for my pains...Love me always, as I shall love you."* In another letter, she wrote, *"I remit myself wholly unto your will."* Worse, they indicated that Mary and Bothwell had indeed been plotting to kill Darnley. *"Burn this letter, for it is too dangerous."*

News of the letters, carefully leaked, shocked all of Europe. Mary swore to her dying day that the letters were forged. And the fact that she was allowed no rebuttal at the inquiry was such a miscarriage of justice that her furious commissioners withdrew in protest.

Elizabeth gave Mary one last chance to come before the inquiry and defend herself. Mary refused, sure that such a desperate move would be a virtual confession of guilt. But the damage had already been done. Mary's reputation was in tatters. Even many of her

Catholic followers turned away from her. Elizabeth was satisfied. She wrapped up the inquiry without even proclaiming a verdict. She didn't need to.

Did Mary plot with Bothwell to murder her husband? We may never know. The casket letters no longer exist. Moray took them back to Scotland where they eventually ended up in the possession of Mary's son, James. He became king, and the letters were never seen again.

Mary never regained her freedom. Elizabeth kept her under house arrest for the next nineteen years. Hers was a comfortable captivity, spent in a series of old castles with a small retinue to serve her, but it was captivity nonetheless. During those nineteen years she plotted ceaselessly to take Elizabeth's crown.

Eventually, she was part of a plot in which her own writings—irrefutable this time—proved her guilt. Elizabeth had had enough. Charged with conspiring to murder Elizabeth, Mary came to trial in October 1586. This time, it was not her reputation that was in jeopardy, it was her life.

The trial was a mere formality, its outcome never in question. Three months later Mary was executed, beheaded at Fotheringhay Castle.

The famous rivalry between these two queens has enthralled the world for over four hundred years. It enthrals us still.

Unveiling Marie Stuart: The Poetry of the Queen of Scots

By LINDA ROOT

IT IS SMALL WONDER THAT ONE OF SCOTLAND'S TWO CONTRIBUTORS TO THE LIST OF technically accomplished royal poets of the sixteenth century wrote her verse in French.

It is more puzzling to explain how easily the creative aspect of her character is trivialized. The poet of whom I speak is Marie Stuart, a woman we know as the French Queen Consort and anointed Queen of Scots, but often forget that she was a student and life-long confidante of Pierre Ronsard, the leader of the Pléiade, frequently called the Prince of Poets, and that both Ronsard and the scholar-historian Brantome acknowledged her expertise. Nevertheless, at least one competent Marian historian opines that if Marie Stuart lived today she would be a runway model jet setter, and that is the image that sticks.

While many members of the historical fiction writer's audience consider England and Scotland as united by more than politics and geography but also by a common heritage, during much of what is called the Renaissance, Scotland was linked not to England but to France. The relationship has a name, "the auld alliance", and it is generally considered to have come into being before the end of the thirteenth century.

There were periods in the fifteenth and sixteenth centuries when dual citizenship was afforded to citizens of the respective kingdoms, and villages existed in Northern France where there were as many Scots as French. When the French monarchy needed a rescue during the fifteenth century, its own aristocracy turned away, leaving Stuarts, Melvilles, Douglases and Carmichaels fighting with Joan d'Arc at the Siege of Orleans.

There was another player in the dynamic of "the auld alliance," and that was the auld enemy England. Dating to the days of Edward Longshanks, the pattern was established—the English invaded and the French defended. The thought that Marie de Guise somehow ceded all that was Scottish to the House of Valois when she sent her toddler daughter to France in 1548 is a misconception. The Dowager of Scotland sent her daughter away to escape Hertford's army which sought to establish its suzerainty over Scotland by kidnapping its five-year-old Queen as a future bride for Henry VIII's son Edward VI.

Again, the auld enemy was in assault mode, and the auld ally came to the rescue and spirited her to France. As a result, the adolescent widow who entered Leith harbor in 1561 to assume personal rule of Scotland was a French girl.

THE FRENCH CHILD

Marie Stuart was not without her flaws. Nevertheless, she was skilled in the areas where a French queen consort was expected to excel—poetry, music, dance, and needlework.

When she was a child at Saint Germain, her Scottish friends were expelled to a nearby convent to insulate Marie from their Scottish speech and mannerisms. In the ordinary course of life, never again should she have set foot on Scottish soil.

Her training was not meant to create a regnant queen. The Salic law precluded a female from assuming the French throne. But while the objective of Marie Stuart's education was not meant to create a sovereign, it was hardly lightweight. While still a child, she delivered a scholarly recitation to the court of King Henri II—not in French, but in Latin. While the words were probably scripted by her uncle Charles de Guise, Archbishop of Rheims and Cardinal of Lorraine, her presentation was flawless.

While her poetry is not as sophisticated as her English rival Elizabeth's, her works are far more introspective. It is not the work of the shallow-minded sycophant she is often portrayed as being. It is full of wordplay and puns, and like her embroidery, it is replete with symbolism.

Unfortunately, as demonstrated below, those features are hard to appreciate when translated from their original French into modern English. Perhaps we tend to make light of her achievements not because of what Marie Stuart was, but because of what she definitely was not—for she was not an astute politician. And while her poetry is technically competent, she was not always circumspect in determining what themes to express and which thoughts to keep to herself.

In the end, it was what she put to paper that sent her to the scaffold. I offer some samples of her work to perhaps give a glimpse of the woman who was Marie Stuart, Queen of Scots, a woman who is in some respects as enigmatic her cousin Elisabeth.

While students at the royal nursery at Saint Germain en Laye were expected to do daily exercises in penmanship and verbal expression, usually in the form of letters which were rarely sent, we see early works of both Marie Stuart and Elizabeth Tudor written in prayer books, Psalters, and the like.

When she was seventeen and Queen of France, Marie wrote the following quatrain in her aunt's prayer book. In translation it does not show the artful play on words prominent in the original idiomatic French or her use of the words *ordonne* and *l'ordonnance* in a manner that reveals how she perceived herself. Robin Bell translates it thus:

> *If I am ordered to write in this space*
> *Because you desire a souvenir,*
> *I ask you to always save my place*
> *And ne'er withdraw the order I have here.*

Another translation of the same work appears in the excellent book, *Royal Poetrie: Monarchic Verse and the Political Imaginary of Early Modern England* by Peter Herman, discussed below, and while the translations are similar, there is a shift of emphasis that exposes the difficulty in translating poetry, especially that written in a language as idiomatic as French.

Herman says, *"Furthermore, the use of 'ordonne/ ordonnance"* not only anticipates the use of wordplay in her later works, notably one of the Bothwell sonnets, but *"gives the poem a distinctly legislative air".* Whether or not he is correct is a matter of conjecture.

Compare Marie's quatrain to the verse young Elizabeth Tudor wrote in a French Psalter at some point before she ascended the throne at age twenty-five, after she had spent years subjected to scorn, distrust, and imprisonment.

> *No crooked leg, no bleared eye,*
> *No part deformed out of kind,*
> *No yet so ugly half can be*
> *As is the inward suspicious mind.*

While Elizabeth's work is usually described as having been written in her French Psalter, an item on display in the Royal Library, Windsor Castle and published in Paris ca. 1520, Elizabeth did not keep the book. She wrote her inscription when she presented it to a servant or lady-in-waiting as a memento.

Elizabeth signs her little quatrain as *"Your loving Mistress, Elizabeth"* making the inscription very personal. By comparison, Marie writes her quatrain in a Mass Book belonging to her aunt, Anne of Lorraine, Duchess of Aerschot and signs it *"Reine de France Marie."* This coincides with Peter J. Herman's observation that Marie's simple verse reveals the importance she placed on status. Note that she identified herself first by her position as queen (Reine) and only then by name.

In Herman's interpretation, the Queen of Scots asserts the power of her position by phrasing her inscription as an order and signing it as Queen while Elizabeth is comfortable relying on the thought expressed in her revealing anecdote. Her sentiment, not her signature, is the message she wishes to leave in the book. Perhaps this is a clue that Elizabeth Tudor was self-reliant but Marie Stuart was not. It is also indicative of someone who had been Queen since six days old as opposed to a girl who had been a princess only to become the bastardized Lady Elizabeth at age three.

The Queen of Scots wrote two of her most widely read poems in 1560-1561 when she was Dowager Queen of France, mourning the death of her adolescent husband Francois II. They tend to be long and doleful. Here is an excerpt from one of two odes written on his death.

> *I shall cease my song now*
> *My sad lament shall end*
> *Whose burden aye shall show*
> *True love cannot pretend*
> *And, though we are apart*
> *Grows no less in my heart.*

Marie and Francois had been informally betrothed when she was five and he was four. He was an object of ridicule and pity. He had a sallow complexion, distorted posture and a constantly runny nose. He was small for his age and dominated by his mother, the redoubtable Catherine de' Medici.

Marie, on the other hand was very tall and, by the time of their wedding, was nearly six feet in height. Her ivory complexion and striking coloring were legendary. She was a notable beauty long before she was a bride. They were a physical mismatch, but in spite of it, they were soulmates.

Because of her position as an anointed queen, Marie took precedence over the Valois princesses Elisabeth and Claud and later, Margot, and on state occasions, she sometimes took precedence over Francois, since she was an anointed regnant queen, and he remained the heir apparent until his father was mortally wounded in a tournament in 1559.

Comparing the poetry written by Marie upon the death of Francois with the poetry written by an albeit much more mature Elizabeth lamenting the departure of her last serious suitor, the Duke of Alençon, whom she called Monsieur, (c.1582) highlights the difference in the personalities of the rival queens.

Elizabeth couches her lament of Alençon's departure in terms of what it means for her future. At the time she was fully aware it was the last card to be played in the marriage game. Note that Elizabeth uses the personal pronoun "I" eight times in six lines of verse compared to Marie's once.

> I grieve and dare not show my discontent,
> I love and yet am forced to seem to hate,
> I do, yet dare not say I ever meant,
> I seem stark mute but inwardly to prate.
> I am and not, I freeze and yet am burned.
> Since from myself another self I turned.

Even in the mournful poems following the death of Francois, Peter Herman points out Marie's recognition of her change in status. In the first stanza of the above poem, his translation, again differing slightly from that of Robin Bell, Herman has Marie recognizing that her best years (i.e., as Queen of France) are behind her.

ROBIN BELL'S TRANSLATION

> In my sad quiet song,
> A melancholy air
> I shall look deep and long
> At loss beyond compare,
> And with bitter tears
> I'll pass my best years.

By way of contrast, Herman's version is different in tone, especially in the tense used on the last line. In Herman's version, the best years are fading with the last views of the French coastline and the loss is suffered in the present. It is a subtle but poignant difference.

PETER J. HERMAN'S TRANSLATION

> *In my sweet and sad song*
> *of most lamenting tone*
> *I look deeply at my incomparable loss*
> *and in bitter sighs*
> *I pass my best years.*

This is the vision I endeavored to portray in my sketch from *The First Marie and the Queen of Scots,* illustrating the scene in which Marie Stuart is said to have looked wistfully back at the coast of France, calling out, *"Adieu, Dear France, Adieu. I fear that I shall never look upon you again."* And of course, she never did.

THE POET AS THE REGNANT QUEEN OF SCOTS

Unfortunately, one of Marie Stuart's early pieces written shortly after her decision to assume personal rule of Scotland has been lost. It survives in the form of two differing translations.

The poem is addressed to Elizabeth. It is what we would call a gift enclosure card, and the gift, like the subject of the poem, is a diamond ring. In it, the diamond is speaking. Its giver of the gift is not subservient to the recipient, although obviously courting favor. It is commonly entitled "The Diamond Speaks."

Bell admits that his translation is largely interpretative and based on divergent French translations of the missing original, tempered by his own analysis of Marie Stuart's poetic style. Here is an interesting excerpt from "The Diamond Speaks." Note how artfully Marie places sentiments that might be presumptuous if attributed to her as coming from the diamond!

> *May it please, from these omens I shall gather strength*
> *And thus from Queen to equal Queen I'll pass at length*
> *Or would I could join them with an iron band alone*
> *(Though all prefer gold) and unite their hearts as one*
> *That neither envy, greed nor gossip's evil play*
> *Nor mistrust nor ravaging time could wear away*
> *Then they'd say that among treasures I was most renowned*
> *For I'd have two great jewels in one setting bound....*

The poem, according to Bell, was forwarded along with a heart-shaped diamond that symbolized Marie's desire to live as a "good sister" to Elizabeth. *"I know of nothing that can resemble my good will to my sister better than that,"* she told her friend, the English ambassador Nicholas Throckmorton.

The good will, if there ever was any, did not last long. Elizabeth, in spite of her indictment of the "suspicious mind" as penned in her lady's Psalter, had grown one of her own, and not without cause. She had distrusted her cousin ever since Marie Stuart's father-in-law, Henri II, induced her to quarter the English coat of arms along with those of France and Scotland and style herself as Queen of England after the death of Mary Tudor in 1558.

Not all English Catholics honored Elizabeth's claim because they did not recognize Henry VIII's divorce from Catherine of Aragon and subsequent marriage to Anne Boleyn. Elizabeth did not take Marie's action lightly and never forgot it, but during the early years of her reign, and later during the Northern Rebellion of 1569, the threat was genuine.

Most of the communications between the Queens after Marie Stuart arrived in Scotland as a widow were couched in diplomatic prose or in messages passed from the lips of envoys who often came bearing gifts. Both Queens toyed with the image of an enduring sisterhood, but eventually Elizabeth struck back.

After Marie fled to England in 1568, what had been a nagging annoyance became a materialized threat. In 1569, Elizabeth's Catholic subjects in the northern counties rebelled. Marie became the reluctant champion of their cause and never fully rehabilitated herself in Elizabeth's eyes. Elizabeth responds in her poem, "On Future Foes" (written between 1568 and 1571), in which she pins Marie Stuart with a tag that sticks by calling her "the daughter of debate." The last eight lines are indicative of Elizabeth's sentiments toward her cousin, but the entire piece is worthy of inclusion.

> The dread of future foes exiles my present joy,
> And wit me warns to shun such snares as threaten mine annoy.
> For falsehood now doth flow, and subject's faith doth ebb;
> Which would not be if Reason ruled, or Wisdom weaved the Web.
> But clouds of toys untried do cloak aspiring minds,
> Which turn to rain of late repent by course of changed winds.
> The top of hope supposed the root of ruth will be,
> And fruitless all their graffed guiles, as shortly ye shall see.
> Those dazzled eyes with pride, which great ambition blinds,
> Shall be unsealed by worthy wights whose foresight falsehood finds.
> The Daughter of Debate, that eke discord doth sow,
> Shall reap no gain where former rule hath taught still peace to grow.
> No foreign banished wight shall anchor in this port;
> Our realm it brooks no stranger's force, let them elsewhere resort.
> Our rusty sword with rest shall first his edge employ,
> To poll their tops that seeks such change and gape for joy.

The poem has been criticized by some as the work of a novice because of its contradicting imagery—some of it agricultural and some of it, maritime—until a deeper analysis shows how appropriately they are interwoven. Most critics now believe that it was deliberate. The meter is iambic throughout which is the emergent favorite form for much English poetry of the period.

Again the work is not particularly introspective. Elizabeth is not whining about her troubles. She is casting the gauntlet at the feet of her adversaries.

Reading it as a companion to her Tutbury speech tells us much of what we need to know about Elizabeth. The Cecils may have orchestrated her policy but they did not dictate her poetry. The Queen of Scots was foolhardy to cast Elizabeth in the role of benevolent sister. Expecting Elizabeth to help her regain her throne and crossing the Solway into England was the last of a parade of disasters that began with her second marriage to Henry Stuart, Lord Darnley. But before analyzing the dynamic of Marie's nineteen years of captivity it seems appropriate to take a look at the earlier pieces which help explain exactly how she got there.

THE MYSTERY OF THE TWELVE SONNETS FROM THE CASKET

The next major examples of Marie's poetry are of controversial provenance. They are the twelve sonnets included in the items which the Earl of Morton produced at the hearings held in York in 1568, the collection that history knows as The Casket Letters. Historians disagree as to their authenticity. They were recovered among letters said to have been written to Bothwell while Marie's second husband, King Henry Stuart, known to history as Darnley, was still alive—specifically, during the period of her trip to Glasgow to fetch her estranged husband King Henry (Darnley) home.

The entire body of evidence produced from the casket by her enemies is suspect, although more attention has been given to the letters than the poetry. Some of the letters seem to refer to events that had not yet happened and to references that make little sense. They are not dated, and there is a strong inference that if not total forgeries, they are alterations of authentic letters written at a different time—what we would call a "cut and paste job".

The sonnets raise different issues. The first concerns their form. Prior to these sonnets having been attributed to her, Marie usually expressed herself in couplets. The discipline of the sonnet form was something new. This does not, however, resolve their authenticity.

The form was becoming popular, as evidenced by the works of Philip Sydney (and later, by William Shakespeare). It was obviously within her capabilities, since much of her later poetry was in the sonnet format. Other scholars claim that their authorship is suspect because the poet is very unlike the dignified Queen of Scots. These are written by a venomously jealous woman who sometimes seems close to hysterics, not the young woman whose usual poetic expressions were introspective and at times, almost sublime.

On the other hand, it can be suggested that such critics have never found themselves hopelessly in love with the wrong partner, which seems to have been one of Marie Stuart's consistent states. Her second marriage was such a disaster as to cause a rift and a rebellion of her lairds. Her third marriage was to a man who had been divorced for just a week and who was the prime suspect in the murder of her second husband.

At about this same time, Sir William Kirkcaldy of Grange, who had known Marie Stuart since they both were at the Valois court of Henri II, told Thomas Randolph (who passed it onto Cecil) that the Queen had declared to him that she would gladly follow Bothwell to the edge of the world in nothing but a white petticoat. This is the same Marie Stuart who surrendered at Carberry to her enemies on the condition that they allow her bridegroom Bothwell to leave the field unmolested. Might that same woman have said (as in the first sonnet), *"I would renounce the world were it his whim. I'd gladly die if it should profit him"*?

In the second sonnet, the writer gets "down and dirty" when it comes to the matter of her rival, her lover's lawful wife, presumably Bothwell's wife, Lady Jean Gordon. In the second piece, the rival woman is described as having made her husband's acquaintance through her kin. This fits. Jean Gordon's brother George, Earl of Huntly, was one of Bothwell's closest friends and had brokered the marriage between his sister and the flamboyant Earl.

In the next sonnet, the writer speaks of her rival as having through marriage restored her honor and estate and thus gained more than her kin could hope for. The reference again points directly at Jean Gordon, Bothwell's reluctant countess. Jean's father, the previous Earl of Huntly had died in his saddle at the Battle of Corrichie Burn, and on Marie's orders his body was salted and thereafter tried, convicted, drawn and quartered.

Jean's favorite brother John was similarly dispatched without having the good fortune to have died beforehand. The Earl of Huntly had been the most powerful Catholic in Scotland, called the Cock o' the North, and he had sent agents to France the year before to pledge the loyalty of the Catholics in the North to the new widow and to encourage her to make her landing in Glasgow from whence they would purge Scotland of its Protestants. There is a good argument that Marie launched her campaign against him to prove to Elizabeth Tudor that she did not intend to restore Catholicism to Scotland.

After Marie's army defeated Huntly at Corrichie, the honor and estates of the mighty Gordons had been forfeited. Thus, the words of the sonnet themselves point to Lady Jean, whose marriage to Hepburn was brokered by her family in hopes of regaining the Queen's favor. And it did confer the honor of a title of countess upon the bride.

Without belaboring the point, there is a little bit of back-story well worth retelling. Before Jean Gordon married Bothwell, she had been deeply in love with Alexander Ogilvy of Boyne. But conspiring with Jean's brother, the Queen snagged Ogilvy away from Jean to marry one of her Four Maries, Marie Beaton, who was suffering a tarnished reputation due to indiscretions with the English envoy, Tom Randolph.

At the time, Boyne was considered a rather lackluster catch for one of the Queen's famous Four Maries. Apparently Jean was entirely blindsided. Then the Queen and Jean's brother stage-managed her marriage to Bothwell, who needed Jean's huge reinstated dowry to pay his debts. Is it a guilty conscience that in sonnet three causes the author to describe her rival as having come out well in her marriage to the jealous author's lover at small cost to herself?

Said the poet, *"She had to give up nothing, save the embrace of a tiresome dolt she once loved dear".*

The dolt sounds suspiciously like the easily manipulated Alexander Ogilvy. But the jealous poet is not finished with Lady Jean. Next she takes a swipe at her rival's clothes taste in what is perhaps the pettiest of the barbs in the sonnets.

> *...In her dress she showed without a doubt*
> *She never feared taste might blot her out*
> *From the affection of your loyal heart....*

At Jean's wedding to Bothwell and during their brief marriage, the Countess of Bothwell's taste in clothes was very much an issue. In spite of the fact that the Queen gave the bride eleven ells of expensive fabrics for a wedding gown, Lady Jean took to wearing mourning for her lost love. She was widely criticized for her unorthodox wardrobe choice, and Bothwell expressed his disapproval of it.

But the poet's criticism of her rival did not stop with her clothes. In the same sonnet (#8), the author also paints her rival as a frigid bed partner.

> *While you made love, she lay with cold disdain.*
> *If you were suffering the heat of passion*
> *That comes from loving with too much emotion*
> *Her hand would make her heart's revulsion plain.*

Finally, the poet accuses her rival, who had apparently been writing conciliatory letters to her husband, of having to employ a ghost-writer, since she did not have the intelligence to write them herself:

> *...with writings tricked out in a learned tone*
> *that could not be the product of her brain.*

Having twice deprived Lady Jean Gordon of a husband does not enhance the portrait of a Marie Stuart who was kind and charitable to her ladies-in-waiting, which is how she is depicted even by biographers who are otherwise critical. Perhaps it is that perception of the Queen that prompts critics to question the authenticity of the twelve pieces by offering the alternative explanation that they were written by another of Bothwell's jealous lovers, of which there had been several.

The usual suspects include an unknown French courtesan and the wealthy Norwegian woman Anna Throndsen who was the mother of Bothwell's only child. Anna and Bothwell had hand-fasted before Bothwell fleeced and jilted her in favor of the anonymous French lady.

However, there is no known poetry attributed to either.

Anna, who was considered the Earl's wife under the laws of Denmark where the marriage was contracted and consummated, definitely bore a grudge. However, the pen was not her weapon of choice. Anna was more litigious than literary. She followed Bothwell to Scotland and filed a lawsuit; but by then he had spent her money and was judgment-proof, and Anna returned to Denmark. She did get more than mere poetic justice the year after Carberry when Bothwell fell into the clutches of the Danes.

She was a well-connected heiress who put enough pressure on the Danes to keep Bothwell locked away in Dragholm castle where he eventually went insane and died chained to a post.

Some claim that the love sonnets are too far beneath the level of Marie Stuart's expertise to possibly be hers. But that is fodder for the counter-argument that from the time of her second husband Darnley's assassination and her surrender at Carberry, the sometimes suicidal Queen was far too distraught to worry much about her cursive or the form and meter of her verse.

The final piece in the set of twelve is incomplete, perhaps the work of a lover with a desperate need to express herself but who had given up the will to vent.

Marie Stuart had good reason to be discombobulated. If Robin Bell's dates of authorship are correct, the Queen of Scots was pregnant, and her future was uncertain. Bothwell was still a married man who kept visiting Jean Gordon on the side. That habit continued even after the Queen and Bothwell's marriage late in May 1567, one week after his divorce from Jean.

The love sonnets recovered from the silver casket bear similarities to the Queen's earlier works in their use of meter, cadence, and occasional play on words. But they also show a less regal and seriously flawed Marie Stuart if she is indeed their author. The writer of the sonnets displays a growing lack of confidence in the depth of her lover's commitment, the classic lament of the other woman in a triangle. Yet the factual references in the sonnets suggest that Robin Bell is correct and that Marie Stuart was the desperately jealous poetess.

Shortly after the date Robin Bell gives the sonnets, the pregnant Queen and Bothwell led their army to Carberry Hill near Musselburgh. It was unusually hot, and the loyalist troops were facing into the sun and drinking wine. The ragtag rebel force had the sun at its back and was drinking water, and the citizens of the villages along the way were sporting the makeshift white banner of the little prince.

"Judge and Avenge my cause, O Lord," said the cartoon character of the boy kneeling by his father's corpse (adapted by the rebels from William Drury's crime scene sketch sent to Cecil). By the end of the day, much of the Queen's force had deserted. On a promise of safe conduct for her husband and a show of respect for herself, the Queen surrendered to Kirkcaldy of Grange, whilst Bothwell rode off to oblivion.

Although Marie Stuart did not know it yet, her marriage to the Earl of Bothwell was over, and so was the love affair between the common Scots and their auburn-haired Boadicea. The promises made to the Queen assuring her safety were broken by the time she was escorted to Edinburgh. After midnight on the second day of her captivity she was taken to Loch Leven Castle.

THE CAPTIVE OF SCOTS

In early spring of the following year, the Queen escaped her prison on Loch Leven island and mustered a sizable army, but she remained free for less than two weeks. She fled to England following an indecisive battle at the village of Langside near Glasgow.

Just as at Carberry Hill the year before, she refused to wait for reinforcements which might have altered the outcome, and she crossed into England against the advice of every member of her support group. She remained there in various levels of detention until 1587, a period of nineteen years. During her captivity, the Queen honed the skills she learned as a child at Saint Germain en Laye. Unfortunately, she did not limit her endeavors to her verse and her embroidery. Finally Elizabeth's minister Cecil and her spymaster Walsingham had garnered the goods to kill her, and Elizabeth had run out of reasons to save her.

Thereafter, the Queen of Scots prepared to assume the role of a martyr. She had been growing into it since the sonnet below was written early in her captivity. The work known as "Sonnet" written during the Queen's Imprisonment was published in 1574 as part of the papers of the Bishop of Ross. It is the inspiration and theme of my book *1603: The Midwife's Revenge*, in which Marie Stuart's son ascends to the English throne.

In the poem the Queen expresses a wish to be free to live out what remains of her life in a chaste, devout, and humble body with a mind that dwells in constant prayer. From the content of her sonnet, it is easy to believe reports that she repeatedly asked Elizabeth to let her leave England and retire to Saint Pierre les Dames in Rheims where her aunt, Renee de Guise, was abbess. This poem was written at the time that Edinburgh Castle fell, ending the Marian military presence in Scotland.

Four hundred and twenty-six years after her death, her words still inspire and puzzle those who write about the Queen of Scots.

> *The wrath of God is not appeased by blood*
> *Of goats and oxen on the altar laid;*
> *No incense or any sacrifice made*
> *Brings satisfaction to the Lord our God.*
> *Those who seek to please you must maintain,*
> *O Lord, their faith in immortality*
> *And to mankind bear hope and charity*
> *And do good works, nor take thy laws in vain.*
> *The only offering that pleases you*
> *Is a mind that dwells in constant prayer*
> *In a living, chaste body, devout and humble there*
> *Almighty God, grant that it be my due*
> *To bear these gifts in my heart all my days*
> *And offer them to your eternal praise.*
> *Marie Stuart, 1573*

In her last years, despair and physical impairment made writing poetry difficult. Yet she continued to write. One of her last efforts was a poem she intended as a thank you note to the Prince of Poets, Pierre Ronsard, who had recently dedicated a book of his poetry to her. Like many of her last pieces, it was full of strikeovers, so she left it unfinished and sent him two thousand pounds and a silver vase instead. This is one of her last couplets, and while she was not sufficiently pleased with it to send it to her mentor, it might well have served her as a model for her own epitaph.

> *Alas! Tell not of the heights to which he rose.*
> *But that he'd fain be succoured in his woes.*

Below is one of her last pieces, written at Fotheringhay shortly before her execution. The last stanza shows the depth of her despair and her reconciliation with her pending death.

> *Alas what am I? What use has my life?*
> *I am but a body whose heart's torn away,*
> *A vain shadow, an object of misery*
> *Who has nothing left but death-in-life.*
> *O my enemies, set your envy all aside;*
> *I've no more eagerness for high domain;*
> *I've borne too long the burden of my pain*
> *To see your anger swiftly satisfied.*
> *And you, my friends who have loved me so true,*
> *Remember, lacking health and heart and peace,*
> *There is nothing worthwhile that I can do;*
> *Ask only that my misery should cease*
> *And that, being punished in a world like this,*
> *I have my portion of eternal bliss.*
> *Marie Stuart, Queen of Scots (1542-1587)*

SOURCES

Bell, Robin. *Bittersweet within My Heart: The Love Poems of Mary, Queen of Scots*. San Francisco: Chronicle Books, 1992.

Fraser, Antonia. *Mary Queen of Scots*. London: Weidenfeld and Nicolson, 1994.

Guy, John. *'My Heart is my Own': The Life of Mary Queen of Scots*. London: Fourth Estate, 2004.

Herman, Peter J. *Royal Poetrie: Monarchic Verse and the Political Imaginary of Early Modern England*. Cornell University Press, 2010.

Wilson, Katharina M. *Women Writers of the Renaissance and Reformation*. Athens, GA: University of Georgia Press, 1987.

Lost from Her Majesty's Back: Tudor Gowns and Finery

By VICTORIA LAMB

In Tudor films, you often see the women slipping easily out of their gowns at bedtime. But in reality, their clothing was a fiendish affair which would have left modern women ready to scream. Poor women and lesser gentry might be able to get away with a smock-like one piece gown, pulled simply over the head. But wealthy Tudor woman had to contend with layers of clothing, some of which had to be fastened together as they were put on.

The kirtle or foreskirt went over any undergarments—rarely worn—and often had a highly decorative front panel. Sometimes the kirtle was already attached to a bodice, but might also be laced into place at the time. Over this would be hung an overskirt with a wide V-style opening to reveal the decorative kirtle. In the later Elizabethan era, a hoop or farthingale might be worn below the kirtle to swell it out like a bell. A "bum-roll" was also used to help support this structure and to provide contrast between the narrow waist and chest—helped along by a stiffened or bone-strengthened bodice holding a lady's assets down—and the swaying skirts.

Sleeves were normally separate from the rest of the gown and could be worn in a mix and match way so that women might have "favourite" sleeves which they used with different gowns. These would be tied on with laces or ribbons. For some of Queen Elizabeth I's more elaborate outfits, however, it was not unusual for the sleeves to be so heavy with fur trimmings or jewels they would need to be sewn on at the time of dressing. The stitches would then be patiently unpicked by her small army of ladies-in-waiting at the end of the day.

Only imagine the boredom of such a lengthy disrobing ritual which for Queen Elizabeth could take as long as four hours! Perhaps the literary cliche of lusty gentlemen ripping high-born ladies' bodices off in sheer frustration may not be so far from the truth.

All these expensive clothes would have been stored in chests that accompanied the Queen everywhere, including on visits away from her royal palaces, and were guarded zealously by the Keeper of the Royal Wardrobe. Any jewels which snagged and fell off unnoticed while Elizabeth was out walking would be marked down in a Day Book now charmingly known as *"Lost From Her Majesties Back"*, which was kept religiously by her ladies. Every tiny pearl that disappeared from a sleeve or hem was noted down in this book, presumably allowing replacements to be ordered.

Given how many lost jewels appear in this book, it must have been quite a worthwhile pursuit to follow the Queen about on state occasions hoping to grab any lost jewels as they fell from her gowns, some of which were fairly bristling with expensive jewels—a point made by Janet Arnold in her fascinating book, *Lost from Her Majesty's Back* (The Costume Society, 1980), which may be available from some university libraries if you are looking to pursue this topic further.

A Masque, a Mask, and a Mystery

By Sandra Byrd

ALTHOUGH SHE BORE NO CHILD, QUEEN ELIZABETH I MID-WIVED A NUMBER OF bright achievements during her reign which persist to this day, among them a settled religious faith, a healthy national commerce, and a nursing of the fine arts, specifically, the development of theater. London still has one of the finest, if not the premier, theater districts in the world. But in truth, the English love of drama began much earlier than the sixteenth century.

Theater: A Crash Course by Rob Graham states:

> *During the 12th century, nonliturgical vernacular plays based on biblical stories were performed at festivals, such as Christmas. These were called the Mystery Cycles (the "mystery" was redemption...). Local lads from the crafts guilds and companies performed those "passions" on rough wagons in procession through the streets or on fixed circular stages.*

These plays, staged locally, were mostly enjoyed by the lower classes. The upper class enjoyed theater, too, especially when they put it on themselves. To plays based solely upon Scripture, courtiers added topics such as Greek and Roman gods, comedy, tragedy, and life as they (and their countrymen) knew it.

Henry VIII was well known as a person who loved to sponsor and act in masques and disguisings. He preferred, of course, to play the valiant knight, or sometimes (what else?) the sun itself!

Later in the sixteenth century, plays, playwrights, and performers came into their own, and the love of theater spread. *The Age of Shakespeare* by Frank Kermode shares that poets and playwrights depended on aristocratic patrons for support. Many of the most highly titled men in Elizabeth's court sponsored their own troupe, known by the sponsor's name. For example, The Earl of Leicester's Men were sponsored by the Queen's favorite, and later, The Queen's Men were sponsored by Her Majesty herself.

When the Queen finally sponsored her own troupe, the cloudy reputation of players and playwrights finally lifted. The Lord Chamberlain's Men were sponsored by Baron Hunsdon, Queen Elizabeth's cousin by Mary Boleyn. William Shakespeare wrote many of his plays for the troupe sponsored by The Lord Chamberlain, including *Hamlet, Othello,* and *Macbeth.* Others were writing and performing too. Kermode tells us that, *"between 1558 and 1642 there were about three thousand* [plays], *of which six hundred and fifty have survived."*

Shakespeare was not only a playwright—he sometimes acted in secondary roles, and later, when partnerships began to sponsor performances for financial gains, he was an investor. He was among those who received a grant of arms and a great deal of money for his talents. Some of his better known colleagues and competition weren't so lucky. Christopher Marlowe was stabbed to death at age 29; Ben Jonson was often in jail and ended up with a branded thumb. Plays were also used for political purposes, even against the Queen who allowed them to flourish.

Historian Simon Schama tells us that the traitorous Earl of Essex sponsored a special production of *"Richard II—which deals with the murder of an incompetent king...to gee up his supporters against Elizabeth...."*

Elizabeth herself approved a play written by Sir Henry Lee, *The Hermit's Tale,* which celebrated a woman who chose her father's dukedom and duty over her own love. She used the tale, masterfully, to signal to her courtiers and her people that she would always put her true husband, England, first.

Then, and now, drama allows us to explore our lives, our problems, our hopes and dreams, and our loves and losses. In fact, we, too, are players, for as William Shakespeare wrote,

> *All the world's a stage*
> *and all the men and women merely players:*
> *they have their exits and their entrances*
> *and one man in his time plays many parts,*
> *his acts being seven ages.*

BOY ACTORS TO THE GREAT QUEEN ELIZABETH

By STEPHANIE COWELL

The world of the theater of Shakespeare's day was completely masculine. Young boys were trained to play the women's roles. The first Juliet and the first Ophelia were boys whose voices were not yet broken. It was a very new profession and did not even have a Guild. Professional actors had grown from the medieval theater. When they gathered together to play in the sixteenth century, it was first in inn yards. The first real theater was not built until 1576. Within ten years, theater had begun to soar, particularly because the Queen and her court patronized it.

Women did not appear on the Elizabethan stage (though they played in court masques); it was considered indecent for a woman to appear in a play. On the contrary, the Puritans felt it was indecent for boys to play women; they were fairly horrified at this cross-dressing and believed it encouraged homosexual lust. So everyone regarded something as indecent on this subject! This tug of war continued to the fall of the King when *all* theater was forbidden by 1640. Until then, the boys played on in wigs and rouge and petticoats.

But in 1593, theater was blossoming in London. A new rising playwright from Stratford called Shakespeare was filling the seats of the open-air hexagonal roofless Theater in Shoreditch, and picking up extra money playing for the Court especially on holidays: tender love stories, invigorating histories, riotous comedies. Boys between perhaps ten and sixteen were needed to play the women.

Boys needed a great deal of training very quickly before their voices broke or they grew to bearded men six feet tall. Many of the principal adult actors took a few boys into their households where they were trained in fencing, acting, singing, dancing, playing instruments. To portray credible women, the boys wore wigs and breast padding and makeup. For the first Cleopatra, a role of tremendous difficulty, I imagine they used a boy in his mid-teens whose voice was light in texture.

The names of some of the boys have come down to us. Alexander Cooke was apprenticed to John Heminges, an actor and Shakespeare's dear friend. Robert Goffe created the role of Juliet in *Romeo and Juliet*. And then there was the amazingly handsome Nathan Field. His father was a Puritan preacher who preached against the sins of playgiving, and yet (likely to his father's horror) he was impressed, much as soldiers were then, into appearing with the Queen's choir and, as a side occupation, with a troupe of all boy players called The Children of the Chapel Royal. What could his outraged father do? The Queen needed the boy's beautiful face and charm and likely sweet singing voice, and what the Queen needed, she was given. (Field grew up to be a true lady's man and gorgeous.)

The difficulty and delight of their profession! And what fun it must have been and yet what a responsibility to speak great lines, to have an audience weep over you and idealize you, and to perform before the Queen. For noble and royal patronage protected the new acting troupes. Queen Bess loved theater and many times a year, especially around Christmastide, the acting troupes were summoned to play before her.

The boy players were serious and dedicated on stage. I imagine them to have been a little like the young actor I saw a few years ago as Billy Elliot, receiving his applause breathless, amazed. Did one of the boy actors who played at Court ever sit by his fire years later and tell his grandchildren this? "Aye, I remember acting in a play with Will Shakespeare on a cold night in Greenwich Palace before the great Queen Bess...and after we bowed before her and danced, and then we gathered up our costumes and props and took a boat home on the Thames. Those were the great days of theater, my loves! They shall not come again."

THE EXECUTION OF THOMAS DOUGHTY BY FRANCIS DRAKE

BY DAVID WESLEY HILL

I LEARNED OF THE TRIAL AND EXECUTION OF THOMAS DOUGHTY FROM *THE WORLD Encompassed by Sir Francis Drake,* a history of the second circumnavigation of the globe. Despite its title, this book was not written by Drake himself but by a nephew thirty years after Drake's death.

According to *The World Encompassed,* Doughty and Drake were good friends and companions, but even so, Doughty apparently had been plotting against Drake since *"before the voyage began, in England"* and sought not only to murder *"our general, and such others as were most firm and faithful to him, but also* [sought] *the final overthrow of the whole action."*

Eventually Doughty's transgressions became so egregious that Drake was forced to take action. He ordered Doughty into custody and convened a formal trial. Forty men were chosen as jurors. *"Proofs were required and alleged, so many and so evident, that the gentleman himself* [Doughty], *stricken with remorse of his inconsiderate and unkind dealing, acknowledged himself to have deserved death...."*

Thomas Doughty was convicted of treason by unanimous vote. After the verdict was returned, Drake offered the guilty man three options. *"Whether you would take,"* he asked Doughty, *"to be executed in this island? Or to be set a land on the main? Or to return into England, there to answer for your deeds before the lords of her majesty's council?"*

Doughty, however, refused this leniency, replying:

> *Albeit I have yielded in my heart to entertain so great a sin as whereof now I am condemned, I have a care to die a Christian man.... If I should be set a land among infidels, how should I be able to maintain this assurance? ...And if I should return into England, I must first have a ship, and men to conduct it...and who would accompany me, in so bad a message? ...I profess with all my heart that I do embrace the first branch of your offer, desiring only this favor, that you and I might receive the holy communion again together before my death, and that I might not die, other than a gentleman's death.*

Drake granted Doughty's request. The next day they celebrated communion with Francis Fletcher, pastor of the fleet, and afterward Drake and Doughty dined together, *"each cheering up the other, and taking their leave, by drinking each to other, as if some journey only had been in hand."* Then *"without any dallying or delaying"* Doughty knelt down, preparing his neck for the blade. His final words were instructions to the executioner to *"do his office, not to fear nor spare."*

My immediate reaction to this story was that it simply was not credible. I could not believe any man would choose death when given the alternative choice of a sea voyage home.

The Queen's displeasure was a distant threat, after all, while the executioner's sword was a very near danger. I also doubted that Doughty would value his immortal soul over his mortal life and turn down Drake's offer of exile in Peru. Whoever this man was, it was unlikely that he was a saint.

I suspected that *The World Encompassed* was a fabrication either in whole or in part. In fact, the book has known to be unreliable since the mid-nineteenth century.

Although claiming to be *"carefully collected out of the notes of Master Francis Fletcher, Preacher in this employment, and divers others his followers in the same",* the parson's notes were expurgated. This only became clear in 1854, however, when the Hakluyt Society released *The World Encompassed* in an edition that included Fletcher's original notes as well as an account of the voyage by John Cooke, who sailed with the adventure.

To Cooke, Francis Drake was not a charismatic leader but a villain who *"in tyranny excelled all men."* His appraisal of Drake was so damning that the editor apologized for printing it.

Some historians, such as Sir Julian S. Corbett in *Drake and the Tudor Navy*—the biography of Drake against which others are measured—admitted that Cooke's narrative, although *"the one most unfavorable to Drake",* was *"probably the most correct, if allowance be made for the adverse construction the author puts on all Drake's actions."*

Henry B. Wagner, in *Sir Francis Drake's Voyage Around the World,* the authoritative study of the circumnavigation, printed the complete Cooke manuscript—except for the parts about Drake and Doughty.

Zelia Nuttall, whose *New Light on Drake* is a masterpiece of historical detection, claimed without proof that Cooke's narrative *"plainly shows that it consists of a report of the Doughty affair which was subsequently tampered with for the malicious purpose of injuring Drake's reputation."*

Despite this Victorian hand-wringing, contemporary scholars have reconciled themselves to the general accuracy of Cooke's account. The story he tells is too internally consistent for it to be made up, and many of its details are verified by other sources.

The World Encompassed glosses over Doughty's exact position in the adventure, but Cooke states explicitly that he and Drake were *"equal companions and friendly gentlemen."* It is likely that Drake was in charge of the ships and the sailors while Doughty had charge of the soldiers accompanying the fleet, particularly considering that in the Cape Verde Islands Doughty led the expeditionary force dispatched to explore inland and engage the Portuguese.

Although they were apparently friends at the start of the voyage, their relationship deteriorated during the Atlantic crossing. Whenever there was foul weather, Drake would say *"Thomas Doughty was the occasion thereof,"* and call him *"a conjurer and witch"* and a *"seditious fellow and a very bad and lewd fellow."*

Doughty himself told anyone who would listen that *"the worst word that came out of his [Drake's] mouth was to be believed as soon as his oath."* At one point Drake attempted to gather testimony against Doughty from other crew members, an effort which back-fired in the case of Thomas Cuttle, master of the *Pelican*. After talking with Drake, Cuttle departed in fury, jumped overboard, and threatened to maroon himself rather than bear false witness against Doughty.

Cooke's version of the trial also differs significantly from that in *The World Encompassed*. Doughty neither admitted to any crime nor showed any remorse. He vigorously rebutted the charges against him and was assisted with his defense by Lenard Vicary, a lawyer, whom Drake dismissed as "crafty".

At the start of the trial, in order to secure a conviction, Drake gave the jury his word that the death penalty was off the table, but after the verdict he reneged on this promise. Nor did Drake offer Doughty leniency only to have Doughty choose death instead. In fact it was Doughty himself who requested exile, saying, *"Seeing that you would have me made away, I pray you carry me with you to Peru and there set me ashore."*

Drake refused. *"No, truly,"* he replied, *"I can not answer it to her Majesty if I should so do. But how say you, Thomas Doughty, if any man will warrant me to be safe from your hands, and will undertake to keep you sure, you shall see what I will say unto you."*

John Winter, captain of the Elizabeth, volunteered to keep Doughty in custody. After a pause, however, Drake said, *"Lo, then, my masters, we must thus do: We must nail him close under the hatches and return home again without making any voyage."*

This, as Drake very well understood, would mean financial ruin for both the adventure's investors, who stood to lose their capital if the ships returned to England with empty holds, and for the ordinary men, whose wages would be reduced or not paid at all. It was unsurprising that the assembly—or, as Cooke termed them, *"a company of desperate bankrupts"*—cried, *"God forbid, good General."* Thomas Doughty's fate was sealed.

Here the Cooke account agrees with *The World Encompassed*. Doughty met his end bravely.

"Now, truly, I may say," he joked with the headsman, *"as did Sir Thomas More, that he that cuts off my head shall have little honesty, my neck is so short."*

From Cooke it is clear that Francis Drake and Thomas Doughty were at loggerheads for most of the voyage but it is less obvious what caused the antagonism between them. Was it Doughty's ambition, as claimed in *The World Encompassed*, that caused Drake to execute the man who had once been his friend—or did Drake have a more personal motive?

Both Cooke and Fletcher wrote that their enmity began when Doughty accused Drake's brother, Tom, of pilfering from the *Santa Maria*, the Portuguese merchant vessel captured in the Cape Verde islands.

In England, however, rumor suggested that:

Thomas Doughty lived intimately with the wife of Francis Drake, and being drunk he blabbed out the matter to the husband himself. When later he realized his error and feared vengeance, he contrived in every way the ruin of the other, but he himself fell into the pit.

A more likely supposition than this adulterous speculation is that the relationship between the two commanders fractured over an issue so important that it could only be resolved by the death of one of them. Unfortunately, there is no way of knowing what was at stake because to this day no one is sure of the true goals of the adventure.

Some historians believe that the voyage was a peaceful merchant expedition while others contend that its intentions were piratical from the start. Were their investors' instructions to sail east around the Cape of Good Hope or west through Magellan's passage? To seek out the mythical northwest passage, the Straits of Anian? To establish factories in the New World and found the colony of New Albion? No one can say.

The only surviving plan of the expedition was damaged by fire. The words that remain tease the reader by almost, but not quite, making sense.

Few questions were asked either when the *Pelican*—renamed the *Golden Hind*—returned to Plymouth harbor because she had aboard one of the greatest pirate treasures of all history. In her hold was more money than the English government received in taxes during an entire year.

The Queen alone was given £100,000 plus a diamond cross and a crown in which were five emeralds, three of them as long as a finger and two round ones worth 20,000 crowns. The backers of the expedition realized a return of 4,700 percent on their investments, while Drake himself became a millionaire.

Given the amount of money involved it is unsurprising no one wanted to look too deeply into the execution of Thomas Doughty. Only Doughty's brother, John, pursued the matter, filing suit against Drake for murder. However, since the execution had taken place outside of the country, the suit could only be filed in a special court—which Elizabeth refused to appoint.

Eventually John Doughty became such a nuisance that he was jailed in Marshalsea prison. A year later he petitioned that he be either *"charged and called to answer"* or be set at liberty. This manuscript has survived. On it someone wrote: *"Not to be released."* We know nothing more of John Doughty.

Perhaps the best assessment of the situation came from Don Bernardino de Mendoza, Spanish ambassador to Elizabeth's court, spymaster, and propagandist, who surreptitiously printed an account of Drake's doings in the Pacific.

M. Drake and his company returned from this very hot and hardy service... and brought all his treasure into England. Where he has so well welcome, and so liberal in the division of shares to some courtiers, that notwithstanding the gallows claimed his interest, it near got so great a bravado, for in very sight of Wapping [the Admiralty dock where pirates were hanged], *he was at Deptford rewarded with the honor of knighthood, and in the same ship, wherewith he had been abroad aroving. And although some poor pirate or other has been cast away upon Wapping shore, yet was there seldom or never restitution. Only the ones who stole too little suffer....*

SOURCES

Corbett, Sir Julian S. *Drake and the Tudor Navy*. London: 1898.

"John Winter's Report, June 2nd 1579", in E. G. R. Taylor, "More Light on Drake," *Mariner's Mirror*, XVI (1930).

Nuttall, Zelia, ed. and trans. *New Light on Drake*. Kraus Reprint Limited, 1967.

Penzer, N. M., ed. *The World Encompassed and Analogous Contemporary Documents concerning Sir Francis Drake's Circumnavigation of the World*. New York: Cooper Square Publishers, Inc., 1969.

Wagner, Henry R. *Sir Francis Drake's Voyage Around the World, Its Aims and Achievements*. San Francisco: 1926.

The World Encompassed by Sir Francis Drake, being his next Voyage to that to Nombre de Dios collated with an unpublished manuscript of Francis Fletcher, chaplain to the expedition, ed. W. S. W. Vaux. Hakluyt Society, 1854.

FOOD STANDARDS AGENCY SIXTEENTH CENTURY STYLE, OR WHAT'S IN THAT MEAT PIE?

BY MARGARET SKEA

READERS IN THE U.K. MAY OR MAY NOT BE CONCERNED ABOUT THE RECENT "HORSE-meat labelled as beef" scandal.* For those of you in the U.S. or elsewhere who might not have heard, there was recently a Europe-wide crisis with horsemeat DNA having been found in many supposedly beef ready-meals, burgers, etc., with Food Standards Agencies running rings round themselves, testing everything in sight to discover the scale of the fraud.

For the record, I'm not worried, though I would prefer to know what I'm eating. And if I'm not currently enjoying any burgers, I am at least enjoying the host of jokes that the crisis has spawned—my (suitably historic) favourite: "After finding Richard III in a Leicester Car Park, scientists have found his horse in a Tesco burger."

Is the mis-labelling and adulteration of food a new problem?

Definitely not.

I imagine it's been an issue for millennia, though I personally haven't delved further back than the fifteenth and sixteenth centuries. It was certainly a problem then, however, and to protect the customer and avoid disorder there were strict market regulations governing what could be sold, where, and in what form.

In Scotland, some regulations came from the burghs themselves, some by statute, and the penalties for breaching them were suitably harsh.

Take bread, for example. Scotland, in common with most of Europe suffered from "bread riots", with one notable difference—the rioters in Scotland were not the poor, desperate for reasonably priced food, but the bakers or "baxters" themselves, protesting about price restrictions imposed by the burgh authorities in response to regular Acts of Parliament.

Most bread was made from wheat, though the poorest households probably made their own from flat and fairly indigestible barley bannocks. The price and weight of bread was set but fluctuated according to the price of wheat. Burgh records describe the bailies taking flour ground from a *firlot* (roughly equivalent to an imperial bushel) of wheat to a baker and watching as the bread was baked.

The resulting loaf was the standard against which all other loaves were measured. Any baker selling underweight bread risked, at best, a fine and confiscation of his stock, and at worst, his oven being broken.

Often the sale of bread, as of other foodstuffs, was restricted to freemen or women—those with burgess status. "Outlanders", coming into the burgh from outside, were sometimes allowed to trade, but only if they paid the burgh for the privilege. Quality was also controlled, different grades of bread being classified as "white" or "gray"—not the most appealing of names—but all was to be "good" and "dry", which probably meant well-fired and well-risen—nothing worse than a damp and soggy loaf!

Ale was also strictly regulated—the price dependent both on the price of malt and the quality of the ale. Tasters, or "conners" were appointed on annual contracts, and having graded the ales they chalked the set prices on the shutters or door of the brewsters so that they could be clearly seen. Anyone found to be over-charging could have the bottom knocked out of his brewing vessels. (Interesting that sixteenth century burgh authorities were concerned with imposing a maximum price for alcohol, while the current debate relates to minimum pricing.)

As now, horse was not a normal part of the sixteenth century Scottish diet—they were in any case much too valuable to eat. There is however plenty of evidence of the consumption of beef, mutton, pork, and goat in the burghs, along with salmon and seawater fish in coastal areas. Meat regulation was primarily concerned with quality and, as in the current horsemeat scandal, with ensuring that customers knew exactly what they were buying.

There has been much discussion on the length of our food chain, with meat being shipped all round Europe before it lands on a British table. Back then the food chain was extremely short: animals were to be slaughtered outside, in public view, and importantly, at the point of sale—one way to ensure that a customer knows what animal they're about to eat.

There were other issues too—the sale of meat from "longsoucht" (lung-diseased) animals was banned, as was the sale of damaged or poorly butchered meat.

Efforts were made to outlaw dishonest practices designed to improve the appearance of meat, for example blowing air into an entire carcass, which plumped it up—to much the same effect, I imagine, as the modern practice of the addition of water, or the bleeding of animals before slaughter, which masked last minute feeding.

Not everyone was so well protected though—a rather shocking regulation stated that putrid pork or fish should be removed from sale and given to lepers.

But to come back to the meat pie of the title.

One of the most interesting restrictions of all on the activities of butchers or "fleshers" is found in the *Ancient Laws and Customs of the Burghs of Scotland*—prohibiting them from trading as pastry cooks—an attempt to stop them putting poor quality meat into pies? Perhaps, which begs the sobering thought—three hundred years on and nothing much seems to have changed....

FURTHER READING

March, M. S. "The trade regulations of Edinburgh during the 15th and 16th centuries." *Scot Geogr Mag* 30 (1914): 483-88.

* This article was written in 2013 following the Europe-wide horsemeat scandal.

THE OTHER COUSINS: WILD FRANK AND HIS COUSIN JAMES OF SCOTLAND

By LINDA ROOT

COUSINS

WHEN WE THINK OF FAMOUS AND INFAMOUS COUSINS FROM THE PAGES OF HISTORY, few readers and writers of historical novels would overlook Elizabeth Tudor and Marie Stuart. The English Queen and Marie Stuart's father James V of Scotland were first cousins, making the famous Queens first cousins once removed.

There was friction between them beginning with Elizabeth's coronation. Shortly thereafter Marie, who at the time was Dauphine of France as well as the anointed Queen of Scots, began quartering the arms of England on her standard and having her heralds announce her as Queen of Ireland and England as well as Scotland and the Isles.

The adolescent Queen of Scots was probably not behind the controversial move, which is usually attributed to her powerful uncles of the House of Guise and her father-in-law Henri II, King of France. Nevertheless, she did nothing to prohibit it, and Elizabeth never forgave her for it. In essence, Marie thought her claim was justified. Catholic Marie considered Protestant Elizabeth a bastard and thus barred from inheriting the Throne of Saint George. In her mind, England was hers by Divine Right.

The French King Henri II petitioned the Pope to excommunicate Elizabeth which would have absolved her subjects from obedience, and that early in her reign, such a move might have altered history. However, the Pope was not ready to go quite that far. Nevertheless, at the time Elizabeth was well aware of the tenuous nature of her hold on the English crown and appreciated the French claim as a realistic threat. Thus, from the time when Elizabeth was twenty-five and Marie was sixteen, the cousins had reason to be wary of one another.

The hostilities did not lessen with time and culminated when Marie was forty-four years old and had been Elizabeth's prisoner for almost two decades. A frustrated and ailing Queen of Scots was not as cautious as she should have been, and when she dropped her guard, Elizabeth's henchmen were ready to strike her dead. Whether or not Elizabeth meant to sign the death warrant, she surely had endorsed her cousin's death. She merely had her own idea of how it should be orchestrated.

She wanted the Queen's jailer to poison his charge, but he refused. After the deed was done, the English Queen gave her cousin a lavish funeral and had her interred at Peterborough Cathedral alongside Catherine of Aragon. Then she tried to recover a portion of the costs from Marie's son, King James VI of Scotland.

But the Queens were not the only royal cousins on Britannia who came close to resolving their religious differences and rivalry with bloodshed. James VI had a troublesome cousin of his own. However, while the ladies expressed their exasperation and sometimes their affections in letters, the gents got up close and personal. Marie's son, James VI, was once accosted by his cousin Francis while seated on the royal privy hole, an invasion every bit as audacious as the acts of his notorious uncle James Hepburn when he kidnapped the Queen of Scots, carried her off to Dunbar, and ravished her. If it happened as Melville reported it (and he was there), we would call it rape.

Most historical novelists and history buffs are well aware of the misdeeds of the 4th Earl of Bothwell, many of which had to do with his treatment of the women in his life, but fewer are acquainted with the bizarre antics of his nephew, Francis Stewart, the 5th Earl, who was every bit as dangerous, and regarded by many as a witch and perhaps the personification of the Devil.

WHO WAS WILD FRANK STEWART?

The tensions between James and Francis began when they both were children. Frank's father was the only child of Marie's favorite brother, Lord John Stewart, Commendator of Coldingham, and his mother was the Queen's notorious third husband Bothwell's flamboyant sister, Jean Hepburn. Those familiar with the Queen of Scots may recall that not long after she returned to Scotland to assume personal rule of her kingdom, there was a scandal concerning the conduct of her brother John and her uncle Rene de Guise, Marquis of Elbeuf, who had allowed themselves to be drawn into a lurid caper instigated by James Hepburn, the 4th Earl of Bothwell, famous for his womanizing and his audacity.

The episode involved the sexual assault of a girl named Alison Craik, a relative of Hepburn's and the lady friend or mistress of mad James Hamilton, 3rd Earl of Arran, whom Hepburn made a sport of harassing. The incident took on a life of its own once the Queen was involved, and when it was smoothed over public criticism settled on the Queen.

She then placed her brother John on what teens today would call "restriction" until his forthcoming wedding and confined his step-cousin Rene de Guise to house arrest at Holyrood Palace. The instigator was detained briefly and then sent to his castle to plan his sister's wedding. Lord John's bride was none other than Bothwell's sister Jean whose own reputation had been sullied in letters that British ambassador Tom Randolph sent home to Cecil and Elizabeth.

Like many of Randolph's reports, it was full of innuendo and scant on detail. Jean was also rumored to dabble in the occult. There were flaws in the characters of both Lord John Stewart and Bothwell's sister Jean sufficient to give notice that offspring of the marriage might be hard to handle.

It is unfortunate that only one authentic portrait exists of the 4th Earl—the wedding miniature that commemorates his marriage to the heiress Lady Jean Gordon—and none at all are found of the 5th. Considering the vanity of both, one concludes that there was a dearth of portraitists in Scotland.

During this same period, no portraits were painted of the Queen of Scots, a fact that complicated the recent facial reconstruction currently on display in Edinburgh. The most trustworthy likenesses of the Queen were painted in France. The ones painted while she was a captive in England are suspiciously stylized and differ greatly from one another. During the forty-odd years of Sir Francis Stewart's life, not a single likeness appears, although there is one caricature that resembles Pre-Columbian art more than a sixteenth-century portrait.

The Hepburn earls of Bothwell of the sixteenth century were of medium height, considerable intelligence, and capable of displaying great charm. A survey of the biographies of Francis Stewart discloses little about his youth. At some point he came under the guardianship of the Regent James Douglas, Earl of Morton. This may have been prompted by reports of his mother and her friend Janet Beaton's interest in the occult. Jean was likewise prohibited from exerting influence over her nephew, William Hepburn, James Hepburn's son who was regarded as illegitimate under Scottish law.

Francis was given his uncle's forfeited title to the Bothwell earldom by his cousin James VI at Stirling in late November 1577 in the presence of his guardian Morton four days before his marriage to Margaret Douglas, one of Morton's relatives and the daughter of the Earl of Angus. She was the older of the two, and they were not permitted to cohabit, ostensibly because of Stewart's youth. Morton had been deprived of a continental education and remedied it with his ward, who in spite of his marriage was shipped first to the Sorbonne and Rouen, and later, to Italy where he studied art in Florence.

He was summoned back to Scotland by the adolescent King in time to align himself with another cousin of the young James VI, Esme Stuart. Esme was a flamboyant French aristocrat who had been awarded the Lennox title after sharing a controversial intimate correspondence with the adolescent King that some say bordered on the erotic. His expatriate father, John Stuart, was a famous member of the French King's *Garde Écossaise* and the brother of the Scottish King's paternal grandfather Matthew Stuart, Earl of Lennox, who was killed in a raid on Stirling by a band of Marians in 1572.

During the period from Esme's arrival in Scotland in 1579 until he fell from grace when the Ruthven faction took the King captive and forced Esme's ouster and exile, Esme Stuart and his cohort Captain James Stuart, who was named the Earl of Arran, ruled Scotland as a team. But in 1582, Esme and James turned their backs just long enough to let the Ruthven Earl of Gowrie and his Ruthven Raiders kidnap the King, providing the following explanation for their acts:

> We have suffered now about the space of two years such false accusations, calumnies, oppressions and persecutions, by the means of the Duke of Lennox and him who is called the Earl of Arran, that the like of their insolencies and enormities were never heretofore born with in Scotland.

But in 1582, the Ruthven faction repeated the mistakes of Esme and Arran and permitted James Stuart (Arran) to exercise a degree of power in the government in hopes that he could rein in some of Ruthven's dissenters. That strategy proved to be a huge mistake. Soon Arran was again in control, and the Ruthvens were in England living off Elizabeth's meager dole. By 1583, the 5th Earl of Bothwell was firmly in the Ruthven camp and out of favor with his cousin James. At some point Francis Stewart joined the exiles in England, but his itinerary was sufficiently flexible for him to sire eight children to Lady Margaret Douglas.

Things seesawed back and forth for Francis Stewart for the next years depending upon who was controlling the King until 1585 when the faction opposing Arran returned again from English exile, but in a rare show of largesse on Elizabeth's part, this time they came with an army.

The Earl of Arran recognized the inevitable and retired with his head intact, and although the King was growing concerned with Cousin Frank's wild ways, like his famous uncle, Francis managed to charm his way back into the royal favor. But that only lasted until the execution of the King's mother Marie Stuart, Queen of Scots.

FRANCIS STEWART ADOPTS A CAUSE

After a brief bit of saber rattling, the King adopted a conciliatory stance concerning what Bothwell and his followers considered an outrage. King James wanted an apology, but Wild Frank Stewart wanted war. When the court at Holyrood was told to don mourning attire in honor of the woman referred to as "The King's Mother", Bothwell came to court in full armor and told the king to his face that his ameliorating attitude ought to get him hanged. If James VI had been anything like his great-grand-uncle Henry VIII, Cousin Francis would not have lived to repeat such insolence.

Francis Stewart's defiance was consistent with his heritage. His grandfather the 3rd Earl of Bothwell, Patrick Hepburn, had remained loyal to Marie Stuart's mother, Marie of Guise, from the time she first arrived in Scotland to the period when she was regent for her daughter who was living in France. Later, Frank's uncle James Hepburn, the notorious 4th Earl of Bothwell, stood among Marie of Guise's champions when she was warring with the Lords of the Congregation. That loyalty transferred to the Queen of Scots when she assumed personal rule of Scotland. James Hepburn may not have been faithful to his wives and lovers, but he was faithful to his queen.

Likewise, his nephew Francis was outraged that there was such a weak response to Marie Stuart's execution. He tried to raise a military force of his own when the King refused to do so, but his efforts failed. Like his uncle before him, he had the power and charisma needed to muster a band of Border Reivers, but he lacked the wherewithal to raise an army. There was little left for him to do but lay low. King James shared his mother's tendency to forgive the transgressions of errant relatives, and on July 8, 1587, Lord Francis Stewart was sworn as a full member of the Privy Council, and King James assumed that Cousin Frank would behave himself. James should have known better.

THE AUDACITY OF THE 5TH EARL OF BOTHWELL

The man dubbed "Wild Frank Stewart" was not of a complacent nature. There were brawls and duels here and there, and a growing interest in the Black Arts, probably inspired and tutored by his mother Jean. And thus it is in the role of a witch and as the devil's disciple that Francis Stewart leaves a historical record approaching that of his famous uncle. Whether the next acts resulted from Bothwell's instability or a belief that he was next in line to the throne should James die childless, he focused his energies on thwarting the King's marriage to Princess Anna of Denmark.

The accounts are based on credible reports of Bothwell's raids on Holyrood. He had also planned one at Stirling that did not materialize. When the King went on the offensive, he almost caught his culprit cousin, but his horse lost its footing and sent the King cascading into the mud. For the remainder of Frank's life he was obsessed with capturing the King and either bending him to his will or killing him. After the prince was born, he included capturing the heir apparent in the game plan.

According to some accounts of the raids on Holyrood, the target had been the Chancellor and not Bothwell's royal cousin. But the raids continued long after Chancellor Thirlestane fell from grace. While there were but two penetrations of the King's chambers at Holyrood, there were many other incidents, and the King was becoming less eager to forgive him. Even the Earl's wife was becoming weary of his antics and was imploring him to make peace with his cousin King James.

FRANCIS STEWART'S CONVERSION

But Francis, who had grown into his given moniker "Wild Frank", was not finished yet. When his fellow ardent Protestants among the peers began distancing themselves from Bothwell, he merely changed allegiances and became a Catholic. After all, Henri IV of France had traded Paris for a Mass—why should he not trade Scotland for a similar conversion designed to capture Catholic support? And he did not stop at the altar. He sold his services to the King of Spain.

Up until that abrupt change, many Scots believed that Frank was motivated not by blind ambition but by his Protestant zeal. His espousal of the Spanish cause changed all that. As his support group dwindled to the few ardent Catholic lairds in the north, Stewart was not dissuaded. He found sanctuary in England until Elizabeth saw the degree to which his politics and religion had shifted, and then she cut him off. He fled to the Spanish Netherlands where he brokered an invasion to Philip II, an attack which he planned in conjunction with Philip's generals in the Netherlands and which was dependent upon a Catholic uprising in Scotland that did not play out. He next became a pensioner of the King of Spain and moved to Madrid.

Finally Philip, who was dying, grew tired of having Stewart on the dole while all he did was laze about the Spanish court. He increased his new minion's stipend and sent him to Flanders to plan an invasion that never happened. Philip had the will, but he did not have the money.

CHANGES

When Philip II died, he left Spain fiscally depressed and facing bankruptcy for the fourth time during his reign. Upon his death, the Hapsburg Empire underwent alterations with Philip III retaining sovereignty over Spain and Portugal and Spain's overseas possessions while his sister the Infanta and her husband the Archduke Albert of Austria ruled the Spanish Netherlands as an independent state. That made a coordinated invasion of the island kingdoms of ancient Britannia by means of a landing in either Scotland or England less likely.

Stewart hatched invasion plan after invasion plan, some of which were seriously considered by Philip III, but the great Spanish maritime power had become over-extended from dealing not just with the marauding English, but with the new European menace to Spanish interests presented by the Dutch Republic and its formidable fleet.

By the late 1590s Elizabeth had her own problematic hot-head to subdue in the Earl of Essex. Chancellor Robert Cecil was as canny as his famous father Burghley had been and had no desire to antagonize the Scots by providing an alternative haven for the Earl of Bothwell, what with Elizabeth's health declining and the queen reluctant to stare death in the face by naming an heir. It was as if the re-forming political climate of Europe had left Francis Stewart behind. In spite of his wife's pleas that he come back to Scotland and make peace with his cousin, Francis Stewart lived his remaining days in Italy where he was said to dabble in the occult.

CONCLUSION

When James ascended the English throne in 1603, there were no more madcap schemes coming from Wild Frank. It was too late for military intervention, and Bothwell had run out of charm. He died in Naples in November of 1612, some say of grief over the death of his young kinsman Henry, Prince of Wales, who had died earlier that month. Bothwell had expected the boy to intercede with his father the King on his behalf when he petitioned for reinstatement of his property and titles.

But it was far too late for that. The new English King James I had left Scotland behind and Bothwell with it.

It was reported that Frances Stewart supplemented what stipend he was able to eke out of the Hapsburgs by telling fortunes other than his own. Yet, no matter how bizarre his antics, he came incredibly close to putting an end to the Stuart dynasty.

FURTHER READING

For additional information on the topic, the author recommends *Bothwell and the Witches* by Geoffrey Watson (1975). For an excellent blog that focuses on Francis Stewart and the occult, see "Francis Stewart, Fifth Earl of Bothwell: A Devil in Disguise?" at blog site *Strange* Company—a walk on the weird side of history.

THE REIVERS AND THE RESCUE OF KINMONT WILLIE: THE STORY BEHIND THE SMAILHOLM PANEL

By MARGARET SKEA

LAST SUMMER I AGREED (RATHER FOOLISHLY AS I AM NOT AN EMBROIDERER) TO TAKE part in a huge project called "The Great Tapestry of Scotland".

It is to be the longest tapestry in the world at over 130 metres, the panels being stitched by volunteer community groups all over Scotland, and will tell the story of the history of Scotland from pre-historic times to the present day.

As Smailholm village lies in the centre of the Borders, my group, excitingly for us, was given the panel depicting "The Border Reivers and the Rescue of Kinmont Willie". Our panel is now partially stitched, and our target is to be finished by the end of April.

But who were the "reivers"? And why are they significant in the history of Scotland? Alistair Moffat says in *The Reivers* that they were:

> a people who lived beyond the laws of England and Scotland, who ignored the persistent efforts of central government to impose order, who took their social form and norms from the ancient conventions of tribalism, who invented evermore sophisticated variants on theft, cattle-rustling, murder, and extortion.... And they spoke and sang beautiful, sad poetry and told a string of stirring, unforgettable stories.

Many of the notable "reiver" surnames including Armstrong, Elliot, Graham, Scott, Johnstone, Kerr, and Maxwell are still common in the Scottish Borders today.

Central to the reivers' activities was an area termed the "Debatable Land". It straddled the border between Scotland and England, and for over three hundred years its inhabitants effectively answered to neither government.

Beyond the Debatable Land a wide stretch of territory on both sides of the notional "border" was divided into "marches" and officials, called "wardens", were appointed by both governments. Thus, for example, there was a warden of the English middle march and a corresponding warden of the Scottish middle march. Equally disregarded by the reiving families, the wardens sometimes co-operated across the border in seeking to maintain order.

Customary law forbade the building of any permanent dwelling in the Debatable Land. But one of the methods used to enforce this was interesting, to say the least. In 1551 the Crown officers of England and Wales made the declaration:

*All Englishmen and Scottishmen, after this proclamation made, are and shall
be free to rob, burn, spoil, slay, murder and destroy all and every such persons,
their bodies, buildings, goods and cattle as do remain or shall inhabit upon any
part of the said Debatable Land without any redress to be made of the same.*

More likely to add to rather than reduce the lawlessness, it didn't clear the area of inhabitants: one notable family, the Grahams, who were present in large numbers on both sides of the border, are known to have had five tower houses there, and they were not the only ones.

The sandstone tower on our panel (the part that I embroidered) depicts one of the Armstrong fortified houses—Gilnockie—belonging to Johnnie Armstrong, hanged on the order of James V along with thirty or forty (depending on which account you believe) of his followers at Carlanrig, near Hawick. The circumstances of what seems summary justice (all the records state that they were hanged on growing trees rather than gallows, and it was likely therefore to have been an impulsive and possibly dishonourable act) are unclear. A grey tower on the opposite side represents Hermitage, an isolated but imposing castle, home to James Hepburn, Lord Bothwell, who later became Mary, Queen of Scots' third husband.

In 1552, a compromise solution to the vexed issue of jurisdiction was proposed—to draw a straight line from east to west where Armstrong and Graham land met. The result was the building of "The Scots Dyke": a four-mile long earthwork approximately nine feet wide and eight feet high. It would have been hard to miss, but whether it had any positive effect is another matter. Especially as it wouldn't take very long on horseback to ride around either end!

Far from the wardens being in control of the borderland, it was the heads of local clans who were the authority, their power in proportion to their numerical strength. Which in some cases was considerable—George Macdonald Fraser, in his book, *The Steel Bonnets*, suggests that the Armstrongs alone could muster 3000 men. Not a force to be lightly challenged.

The number of reivers involved in an individual raid would of course be much smaller, but still considerable, typically anything from thirty to around a hundred men. In the centre of our panel are two reivers wearing their normal garb of steel bonnets (hence Fraser's book title) and padded jerkins, the sheep and cattle imprisoned in their gauntleted fists, symbolising their core activities of cattle-rustling and sheep-stealing.

Seeing an hundred or more of them thundering across the moor towards your door, one hand on the reins, the other holding the long spears that flank the panel, must have been a terrifying sight.

Interestingly the three-year-old grandchild of one of the ladies involved in sewing the panel stared at them for a moment, then said, before running away, "I don't like those men." An instinctive reaction that may be an echo of hundreds of children before her.

The "Day of Truce" mentioned in one of the scrolls at the top of the panel was a day when the Scots and English came together to witness the trials of criminals from both sides of the border. The jury comprised six Scots—chosen by the English—and six English—chosen by the Scots.

There were agreed penalties for perjury by witnesses, an attempt at ensuring honest testimony; interestingly the most important and effective penalty wasn't a fine or imprisonment but a formal statement that no future testimony would be accepted or believed. Honour among thieves was part of the reiver code. All witnesses and those who came to the Truce were to be given safe conduct through others' territory and were honour-bound to refrain from confrontation and not to offend by "word, deed or countenance" as long as the Truce lasted.

When large numbers of sworn enemies attended, it isn't surprising that tempers often frayed, the wardens struggling to maintain order. What is surprising is that most, though not all, Truce Days appear to have passed without major incident.

Although the main design of each panel has been done by a wonderful artist called Andrew Crummy, the stitchers are allowed some input. In our case, it is the mane and raindrop infill on the horses and most of the wording.

The curse which links the two reivers: *I curse thair heid and all the haris of thair heid"* comes from the "Great Monition of Cursing against the Border Reivers" by Gavin Dunbar, Archbishop of Glasgow 1525—a lengthy and comprehensive "cursing", which should have put the fear of God into all who heard it.

The quotation at the foot of the panel: *"My hands are tied but my tongue is free and who will dare this deed avow"* comes from "The Ballad of Kinmont Willie."

At sixty-six Willie had, by the time of his capture, been reiving successfully for some fifty years and led a notorious gang called "Kinmont's Bairns".

While his imprisonment in Carlisle Castle was undoubtedly deserved, given a lifetime of crime, his seizure was illegal—captured on his way home from a Truce Day in March 1596. One month later a carefully planned and perfectly executed plan to rescue him was carried out by Scott of Buccleugh, himself a law officer on the Scottish side.

Buccleugh had first protested the illegality of the capture and requested Willie's release, but when this was denied, he acted. A clear indication of the flexible attitude to reiving among border folk, even those appointed to uphold the law.

He rode on Carlisle Castle and with a small party of men entered the castle by a locked postern door, having levered out the stone in which the bolt was shot. Without discovery or a shot being fired they spirited Willie away—a daring rescue that was to be one of the last significant border raids.

Sir Walter Scott's *The Minstrelsy of the Scottish Border* brought together many of the ballads, including that of Kinmont Willie, along with the tunes to which they were sung. Although the tales are often romanticised, they do provide a flavour of the reiving lifestyle and the superstitions and beliefs of the time.

But the writing was on the wall for the reivers. James I's accession to the English throne in 1603 abolished the border between Scotland and England. Re-naming the area the "Middle Shires", James set in train a dismantling of the reiver way of life and a bringing of law and order to this most unruly part of Great Britain.

The reivers have left their mark on the border landscape in various ways: in the form of innumerable and mostly ruined tower houses; in literature and music through the Border Ballads; and on tradition, in the annual festivals in all the major and some of the smaller border towns which commemorate the riding of the marches.

They have left their mark too on the English language: the words "blackmail" and "bereave" derive from their activities. A sombre legacy indeed.

TO REIVE IS TO THIEVE

BY TOM MOSS

THE BORDER REIVERS DOMINATED THE COUNTRY ON EACH SIDE OF THE SCOTTISH English Border, from the Solway Firth in the west to Berwick and the North Sea in the east, from the thirteenth to the beginning of the seventeenth century. Born out of adversity, suffering from the inroads of both Scottish and English armies in a bitter war in which Scotland sought independence from England and lasting on and off for two hundred and fifty years, they resorted to the theft of cattle and sheep as a last resort to starvation as their lands were devastated. It became a way of life that neither monarchy nor authority could subdue and resulted in murder, blackmail, and deadly feud.

The Border Reiver clans of southern Scotland and the surnames (families) of northern England were often at war with each other. These quarrels were not just a product of a natural animosity between the Scots and English resulting in many a cross-Border dispute. They were the result of incessant theft, often maiming, and murder.

Loyalty on each side of the Border began and ended with the clan of family. Nationality meant nothing to the Border people. Reivers stole from their own countrymen. They had been abused for centuries by their own monarchies and governments and found, through bitter experience, that loyalty began and ended with their own folk.

In the Scottish southwest in the sixteenth century two families vied for predominance. These were the Johnstones and the Maxwells. They were the warlords, the predominant families of Dumfriesshire, refined families with illustrious ancestry. The feud between them had festered for almost a century when the events of 1593 were to bring it to a head. It would conclude with one of the biggest and bloodiest family battles in British history.

At the time the Johnstone chief was Sir James Johnstone of Dunskellie whilst the Maxwell clan were ruled by John, Lord Maxwell. He was the Scottish West March Warden and thus nominally in charge of the whole of the Scottish West. It was a post that had often changed hands between the two clans at the whim and dictate of the monarch, James VI, forever nervous of the power of his Border lords. The change from one to the other was the root cause of the animosity and resentment that dominated the relationships of the two West March lords.

Early in 1593 Willie Johnstone, known as the Galliard, stole a black horse, amongst other beasts from the stables of Lord Crichton. Crichton's men pursued the thief and rode him down. On the orders of the Lord, being caught at the "red hand" or "in the deede doinge", he was hanged not far from where he was apprehended. "Redhanded" is a word we have inherited from the Border Reivers.

In revenge the Johnstones of Wamphrey came out, led by Willie Johnstone of Kirkhill, and attacked the Lord Crichton's people. Border Reivers of some renown, they burned and stole as they made their way through the steadings and villages. In the process they killed fifteen of Crichton's men.

Crichton, incensed to the point of irrationality, sought out James Johnstone and demanded that he hand over the Wamphrey raiding party. Johnstone was loth to do this saying that he would deal with his own men, in his own way, in his own time. He had the power to do this as he had his own court of justice under licence from the King. And anyway nobody knew where Willie Johnstone and the band of Wamphrey men were. They had gone into hiding since the devastating raid on Crichton land.

Lord Crichton was appalled by such an approach. He made for Edinburgh to petition the King, James VI, for a firmer kind of justice. Following a brief meeting with the King who promised an answer after discussing the affair with his Privy Council, Crichton paraded fifteen women up the Canongate. They walked whilst displaying a set of bloodied sarks (shirts). They were the fifteen wives and mothers of the men who had lost their lives in the devastating raid carried out by the Johnstones of Wamphrey; the sarks taken from the bodies of their loved ones. Hundreds of the Edinburgh citizens followed the women, and by the time they had returned to Holyrood Palace to await the King's response to Crichton's plea there was such a clamour from the horde gathered outside the gates that the palace guard came out to investigate.

James VI, famous for indecision and vacillation, responded with unaccustomed alacrity on this occasion and gave his permission that John, Lord Maxwell should pursue James Johnstone of Dunskellie, apprehend him and convey him to Edinburgh to await the King's pleasure.

Lord Crichton was more than satisfied with the outcome.

James Johnstone refused to hand himself over to Maxwell.

There were other Lords in the Scottish south-west who would welcome the demise of James Johnstone of Dunskellie and the whole of his clan. The Lords of Closeburn, Lag, and Drumlanrig, after much discussion, signed a band of Manrent with John, Lord Maxwell. They meant to add their military support to Maxwell. A band of Manrent was a bond wherein a person of lesser standing sought the security provided by a more powerful lord in return for his aid in times of conflict or strife.

By now it was obvious that some form of military contest would ensue, and both clans mustered their fighting men. The Johnstones could only gather three hundred men. With some support from the Scotts, Elliots, Irvines, and Grahams, they could count on no more than four hundred.

The Maxwells, on the other hand, had numbers including some Armstrongs and Douglas fighters, in all about two thousand men at their call. They mustered in the grounds of Lincluden Collegiate church; the Johnstones at Lockerbie.

The two armies met at Dryffe Sands, near Lockerbie, on a grey day in December 1593. (The cemetery that houses a memorial to the unfortunate victims of the 1988 Lockerbie air outrage is nearby.) Maxwell, confidence rising at the meagre number of Johnstones encountered on the other side of the Annan water, deliberated his next move. Sure, he and his army had to cross the river, but that was but a slight impediment.

He was not prepared for what happened next.

The small party of Johnstones on the opposite side of the river hurled insults at the great Border chief. His wife and mother were not spared lewd insinuations. At the same time the Johnstones goaded the Maxwells to cross the water and pursue the outcome.

All of a sudden Maxwell, incensed beyond any rational thought, ordered a charge. The first phase of his army splashed in and headed across the water. The small contingent of Johnstones, now feigning terror, turned and made a mad rush for some low hills to their rear. The Maxwells, confident that they could ride down with ease the seemingly feckless rabble that preceded them, followed them at pace and ran into an ambush as the main body of Johnstones left their place of concealment behind the hills. The Maxwells were hemmed between the Johnstones and the second phase of their own men and suffered appalling consequences.

The main body of the Maxwells was still detached, still trying to cross the river. Many turned back panicked by the death throes of their friends before them.

Maxwell was struck from his horse, and though he tried to surrender, he was despatched on the spot. The hand of the arm he stretched out in a call for mercy was struck off and nailed to the door of Lochwood Tower, a major Johnstone stronghold, the vestiges of which still remain today. What was left of him was buried at Lincluden.

One of the Johnstone army is particularly remembered to this day. Robert Johnstone of Raecleuch was eleven years old when he joined the Johnstones on that fateful day. He survived.

It is significant to note, and typical of the approach that resulted in constant animosity and confrontation throughout the Border Country, that two years after Dryffe Sands, Johnstone, a Border lord who had defied his King, was invested in the post of Scottish West March Warden. James VI did little to bring peace and harmony with such an appointment.

It is often said that the origins of the deadly feud that beset these two powerful Scottish Border families has been lost in time. The Battle of Dryffe Sands in 1593 is seen as the near culmination of a century of strife, resentment, and confrontation between these two great Dumfriesshire clans. What is known is that the animosity which reigned between the Maxwells and Johnstones can be traced back at least half a century before 1593.

In or about 1546 the Laird of Johnstone violated the terms of the bond of Manrent in which he had bound himself to assist Lord Maxwell at times that he might need aid against his enemies.

Lord Wharton, an English West March Warden, renowned for his victory over the Scots at the Battle of Solway Moss (Longtown, Cumbria) in 1543, had endeavoured to create discord between the two great warlords and had even offered Johnstone money to entice Maxwell into his power. Such was the hold of the Maxwells over the fortified strongholds that littered the Scottish West March that Henry VIII of England, seeking to hold sway over and control Scotland, was prepared to go to any length to weaken Maxwell resistance to his aims and desire to create a united kingdom under the rule of the English Tudors.

The creation of enmity between Maxwell and Johnstone was one way in which the stranglehold of the Border Lords of south-west Scotland might be broken.

Although Johnstone ostensibly entered into the plot with gusto, he, according to Wharton, was not to be trusted; Johnstone and his allies *were all so false, that he knew not what to say*. Again the loyalty to the clan took precedence.

Inconsistency, treachery, and double-dealing were the result of the English intrigues. Resentment, hatred, and bitter feud and conflict were the inevitable outcome between the houses of Maxwell and Johnstone.

Even should the feud have lasted only the half a century between the 1540s and the 1590s, and not the century that is so often quoted, it is still evidence that feud in the Scottish-English Borders was truly the "canker" that so troubled the mind and actions of James VI of Scotland. Moreover it is proof positive that monarchs, in this case Henry VIII of England, actively encouraged conflict between the clans of southern Scotland and the families of northern England in times of unrest when the threat of war between the two countries was on the horizon. The same monarchs and authority came down with a heavy hand on these same people when diplomatic relations between the two countries followed a less troubled course.

It is little wonder then that the clans and surnames (families) of the Border country, both English and Scottish, turned inwards and looked to their own for aid and support in the times of the Border Reivers.

Early in 1592 efforts were made to end the deadly feud that existed between the Maxwells and the Johnstones. An agreement was reached between the two chiefs by which they *"freely remitted and forgave all rancour of mind, grudge, malice and feuds that had passed, or fallen forth, betwixt them or any of their forebears in any time bygone"* and promised that *"they themselves, their kin, friends, should in all time coming live together in sure peace and amity".*

Events of the following year, 1593 and beyond, even down to 1608, would prove different.

In order to understand the feud that bedevilled the houses of Maxwell and Johnstone in the sixteenth century, it is necessary to have a broad look at the history of the two clans both before and after the irrational violence that took hold in 1593 at the Battle of Dryffe Sands.

In 1578 John Johnstone was not only knighted but also made Warden of the Scottish West March, a position of great significance in the Scottish Borders. Now he was responsible for the actions of all the clans who inhabited his March including the Maxwells, a clan equally or even more powerful than the Johnstones. James VI of Scotland did little to encourage cordial relations with this decision. Yet he had a mindset that saw no farther than the Johnstones and Maxwells for such a pivotal position.

The Maxwells resented Johnstone's appointment and were up in arms when he put himself forward as a candidate for the position of Provost of Dumfries, a post more often than not held by the Maxwells or their associates. Johnstone's temerity in applying for

Provost was to rub salt in the wounds of the Maxwells who were already smarting at his selection as Scottish West March Warden.

The situation only added fuel to the feud which had been simmering for decades.

Maxwell quarrelled with the favourite of James VI, Lord Arran, and was put "to the horn" (i.e. declared an outlaw). Johnstone was ordered to arrest Maxwell, and two bands of soldiers were sent to assist him achieve this goal.

They were confronted and defeated at Crawfordmuir by Maxwell's half-brother, Robert. Lochwood Tower, seat of the Johnstones, was burned.

It is said, that Robert Maxwell, on burning Lochwood, observed that the flames would at least aid Lady Johnstone in setting her hood.

Johnstone retaliated by attacking his rival Maxwell, but his audacity failed and he was taken prisoner. Released within a year when James VI sought to reconcile the two factions, their stand-off, and feud, he died soon afterwards.

It is often said that he died of a broken heart, in despair at the shame that followed his defeat and imprisonment. The year was 1586.

As we have already seen Maxwell fell at the Battle of Dryffe Sands. His hand was severed and nailed to the door of Lochwood Tower. Some versions state that not only his hand was to adorn the massive oak door of the Johnstone stronghold. It is said his head followed suit.

John, Lord Maxwell, son of the Maxwell who fell in the savage encounter that was Dryffe, nursed a hatred that all but consumed him, and vowed revenge, not only for the death of his father but the callous, insensitive manner in which he was dispatched. He waited for the day when he would exact his revenge.

He made no secret of his intense hatred of Johnstone and held no regard for the threats of the King, James VI, who endeavoured to bring peace to the two families. Even entreaty and cajolement from a monarch who was not renowned for patience and sub-tlety fell on deaf ears. So much for the control of the Scottish monarch. So much for the contempt in which he was held by the Maxwells at this time.

When Johnstone was granted the ministry of the Scottish Middle Marches, Maxwell, following some disturbances in which he was instrumental, was imprisoned in Edinburgh castle. He escaped and sought a meeting with Johnstone as a prelude to resolving their differences, forgetting and forgiving times past, looking forward to a new beginning.

They met in April 1608.

Each had one attendant at his side. Very soon a quarrel arose between them. When a pistol was fired, Sir James Johnstone endeavoured to intervene and separate the two combatants. As he turned his back on his great rival, Maxwell shot him twice. Johnstone died on the spot.

Maxwell escaped to France and remained there for a few years, but eventually, the inevitable pull of his homeland was to lead to his undoing. Venturing back to Scotland in 1612, he was apprehended in Caithness, caught at the home of his relative, Earl George

Sinclair, and brought to trial in Edinburgh. Sinclair, in order to ingratiate himself with the government, basely betrayed him.

Maxwell was indicted for the murder of Sir James Johnstone, but a second charge, that of fire-raising, a treasonable offence, was also levelled against him. The latter crime, under ancient Scottish law, meant that his lands were forfeit.

Thus James VI, true to his penchant for enriching favourites and toadies, bestowed Maxwell's lands on others, including Sir Gideon Murray.

Lord Maxwell, refusing any religious instruction as he claimed to be not of the religion of the ministers gathered to offer him some consolation, but a Catholic, was beheaded at the Cross of Edinburgh on 21 May 1613.

Thus ended one of the longest and deadliest of feuds in British history.

Stuart Period
(1603–1714)

Henry Hudson's Search for the East Indies from the North, 1610

By KATHERINE PYM

IN THE FIRST DECADE OF THE SEVENTEENTH CENTURY, HENRY HUDSON WORKED FOR several merchantmen companies both in England and Holland. His goal was to find the northern route to the Spicerie Islands in the South Pacific.

He worked for the Muscovy Company, England's East India Company, and the Dutch East India Company. These companies pooled their resources, made their captains sign extensive contracts, gave them long lists of rules and regulations, then sent them on their way to find the easiest, fastest passage to Spicerie ports of call.

The route south through the Cape of Good Hope was fraught with danger, i.e., weeks of calm or killer storms, scurvy, the bloody flux, pirates. Once into the Cape, there were added dangers of rogue waves that came out of nowhere, swamping and sinking a ship to the depths of the sea.

If it weren't for the ice that filled the northern regions, that route would have been far easier to navigate. When they went north toward Greenland or west to Newfoundland, these intrepid explorers found a vast ocean crowded with so many fish that they leaped into their boats rather than be netted. They brought home stories of ling cod, and whale meat/lard. Fishermen sent their ships to these waters, and the English dinner table began to find new foods that delighted the palate. Oil lamps and candles began to smell of whale lard.

When Hudson worked for the Muscovy Company, he did not find a Northwest Passage but alerted his employers of a place where one could catch many whales. The Dutch East India Company (V.O.C.) had so many failures that when they heard of Hudson they enlisted his services.

Hudson promised better things. He was certain the passage could be found. All their previous captains could not find the passage, and the directors wanted to know how he would go about it.

Henry replied that he followed Petrus Plancius' theory. Plancius was one of the founders and cartographers of the V.O.C., so the directors nodded their approval. When Hudson offered this theory, Plancius was still alive. He could be consulted for confirmation.

The theory was of a temperate, open sea in the North Pole not covered with ice. What Hudson professed was a mild climate above *"74 degrees latitude—the point at which the Dutch ships had always found their path blocked by ice".* Hudson not only affirmed to have seen this, he raised the stakes higher by adding that the depth of the sea was so great at this point, the swells could never freeze. In this temperate area, Hudson declared to have seen a new land with many animals and sweet grasses wherein the animals grazed. It was a veritable paradise.

Hudson further added if he could go above 83 degrees latitude, he would sail west to the Pacific then south into the warmer seas of the East Indies. V.O.C. demanded more proof, so Hudson sent for Petrus Plancius. The gentleman, also an astronomer and clergyman, nodded his concurrence at Hudson's every point. He added the sun's long days and white nights during the summer kept the waters warm enough so that ice could not form. As a result, Henry was given the opportunity to seek a northern route to the South Seas.

Once aboard ship, Hudson disregarded all instructions by the V.O.C. He used his own maps and went northwest through bad weather. Finding the way too difficult, Hudson tootled south. He expected to find a waterway along the American coast where he could travel to the Pacific. He did not find it, but he did find a land rich in fisheries and game with trees so big they would make excellent ships.

Hudson had found Manhattan Island. The V.O.C. was not impressed, but other merchants were which started the colonization of that area.

In 1610, this time financed by English merchants, Hudson tried again. He found his way into what is now the Hudson Bay. The seas were filled with ice. His crew turned surly and one night mutinied. They grabbed hold of Henry Hudson and a few faithful crewmen, put them in a small boat without food, water, or warm clothing, and set them adrift. Henry Hudson disappeared into the night, never to be seen again.

SOURCE

Milton, Giles. *Nathaniel's Nutmeg: Or the True and Incredible Adventures of the Spice Trader Who Changed the Course of History*. Penguin Books, 2000.

THE GOLDEN WEED: TOBACCO IN VIRGINIA, 1610

By ANNA BELFRAGE

WHEN THE FIRST ENGLISH COLONY WAS ESTABLISHED IN VIRGINIA (AND I DON'T count the Roanoke debacle—which anyway was in present day Northern Carolina) in 1609, the eager participants came with dreams and hopes of easy riches, something akin to what the Spanish had discovered down in South America.

Sadly, Virginia had no mountains of almost pure silver like Potosí, nor was gold abundant in any way. Rather the reverse, actually. And those stories of rivers full of sturgeon, of woodlands crammed with mulberry trees (and the accompanying silk worms) proved as false as the myth of El Dorado, leaving the colonists in the rather unfamiliar situation of having to work—and work hard—to survive.

One would assume anyone intrepid enough to set off for an unknown continent would be expecting to have to labour hard to achieve some sort of foothold. Unfortunately, more than half of the first 105 settlers were gentlemen—or their servants—and as such most reluctant to set their hands to farming. No, they wanted to explore and look for gold, all of them hoping to return home extremely wealthy men. Most of them died during the first year.

During the first few decades of its existence, the Colony of Virginia was something of a death machine with mortality rates so high it became difficult to attract new settlers. Food was constantly scarce, and to stop people from stealing from the communal warehouses, theft was punished by death. One poor man was caught stealing oatmeal and was therefore chained to a tree and left to starve to death....

Things changed fast when tobacco was introduced to the colony. This addictive golden weed thrived in Virginia's fertile soil, and with a huge and growing demand for tobacco in Europe, the colonists had at last struck gold.

In actual fact, tobacco was already growing in Virginia when the first English settlers landed, but this was a rougher, less tasty variant than the one the Spanish were importing to Europe. The Spanish cultivated the tobacco on huge plantations in the Caribbean, and it wasn't until someone decided to fetch (steal?) some seeds from these islands that the tobacco industry in Virginia was born.

It is impossible to talk about tobacco in Virginia without mentioning John Rolfe—the man who procured those Caribbean seeds. John set off for Virginia in 1609, was shipwrecked on Bermuda, lost his new-born daughter and wife along the way, and landed in Virginia in May 1610.

In 1614 he married Pocahontas, daughter of the Powhatan chief, and from what can be gleaned from the few historical documents left to us, it seems he was in love with this new wife of his, despite her heathen background. One hopes Pocahontas—or Rebecca as she was called after her christening—was in love with him. (No, Pocahontas was never, as far as we know, in love with dashing John Smith.) Pocahontas gave birth to a son, accompanied her husband to England, and sickened and died, whereupon John left his son in the care of relatives and returned to Virginia.

It seems John dedicated the rest of his life to improving the quality and quantity of the Virginia Tobacco. He must have reaped quite some success, as twenty thousand pounds of exported tobacco in 1617 had become half a million pounds in 1630.

By then John Rolfe was long dead. He died in 1622, a year in which a third of the colonists in Virginia were massacred by the Native Americans. In a desperate attempt to rid themselves of the intruders, the Powhatan attacked the colonists in one well-planned nightly raid, destroying most of the settlements outside of Jamestown. Whether John was one of their victims is uncertain.

Tobacco is a labour-intensive crop. With ever more acreage being put under cultivation, the colony of Virginia screamed for people to work the expanding fields, and so the age-old system of indentured servants was transplanted from England to the colony—in a somewhat reworked form.

The indenture system set in place in Virginia meant that the planters carried the cost for transporting over the servants, who paid nothing for their passage and were placed under contract for four to seven years to work off the debt of transportation. The life that awaited the newly arrived labourers was harsh: acres to be cleared, planted, and harvested, day after gruelling day in a hot and unfamiliar climate, and all to produce hogshead after hogshead of fragrant tobacco leaf, thereby enriching the plantation owners further. Conditions were so severe that forty per cent of the indentures died before the contract ended.

Most indentured servants came over voluntarily. Quite a few indentured servants went anything but willingly, being deported by the powers that were for various reasons. Some were criminals, others were outspoken defenders of their faith, yet others simply protested against the system in general. As early as 1620, King James VI decided that shipping out these unwanted elements to the colonies was a smart way of reducing their presence in his kingdom while furnishing much needed labour to the plantations. Over the coming decades, both Oliver Cromwell and the latter Stuarts would continue doing so.

Tobacco built a lot of wealth in colonial Virginia. A man cultivating a few fields of tobacco by himself would on average earn five to seven times more than a skilled craftsman in England. Add some more land, five or six field hands, and the annual income would be close to that of a wealthy gentleman. Without the tobacco, it is questionable whether Virginia would ever have achieved the importance it came to have at the birth of the American nation. Actually, without tobacco Virginia might have become yet one more failed colonial attempt.

But for the people who were forced to participate in the production of the golden weed, the tobacco was nothing but a cruel and demanding taskmaster—a taker of life, rather than a giver of gold.

SNUFF AND "DRINKING TOBACCO"

BY DEBORAH SWIFT

CHRISTOPHER COLUMBUS WAS RESPONSIBLE FOR BRINGING SNUFF, OR GROUND TOBACCO, back to Europe in 1496 after one of his party noticed the native people of Haiti using it. It quickly became fashionable among the French and Spanish, and the Frenchman Nicot (from whom we get the term "nicotine") imported larger quantities to France during his travels abroad in the mid-sixteenth century. Initially unpopular with the French monarchy, its fortunes were revived when Catherine de Medici was given snuff by Nicot as a treatment for migraine. The resulting "cure" popularized snuff amongst the French aristocracy.

Snuff was expensive as it had to be imported and the grinding process was laborious. Originally the tobacco plug was dried in an oven and then ground by hand in a hand mill by your servant to your requirements. This meant it was mostly available only to the rich. A whole culture grew up around the habit in the following centuries with the manufacture of snuff boxes and bottles and elaborate "mouchoirs" or handkerchiefs. In England, snuff was made even more fashionable in the seventeenth century when Charles II returned to England from his exile in France and brought with him his snuff habit.

Many different snuff mills grew up next to watercourses in London, Sheffield, and Manchester to supply the habit. Retailers soon set up shops solely dealing in snuff and snuff accoutrements. Tiny, decorative boxes were popular, because prolonged exposure to air causes snuff to dry out and lose its scent. Snuff boxes were so small because they were designed to hold only one day's worth of snuff.

Snuff was brought over to America when the colonies were formed and was an essential part of early American life. America produced its own unique snuff that had a smokier aroma than its European counterparts and a sweeter taste. Snuff is usually scented or flavoured in unique blends, and typical blends would be floral, mentholated, or spicy. Ingredients used to scent the snuff would include things such as cinnamon, nutmeg, sandalwood, or camphor. Nowadays you can even get Cola-scented or cherry-scented snuff!

The use of snuff was at its height in the eighteenth and nineteenth centuries, and it was recommended by doctors as a general cure-all, ironically as a treatment for coughs, colds, or headaches.

Professor A. Phillips Griffiths has been a regular snuff user since the 1940s. He says the habit is catching on with a new generation since the ban on smoking here in the U.K. But if you are writing about a period any time between the sixteenth and the twentieth century, chances are at least one of your characters would be familiar with the stuff.

In the coffee houses of the seventeenth century, people took tobacco in three forms—as snuff inhaled into the nose, as chewing tobacco, and by smoking it through a pipe. Nobody in my books "drinks" tobacco, which is a pity because that is actually the word that was used for smoking in the seventeenth century. So I used the word "smoke" even though it is technically incorrect. Cigarettes did not exist of course, so all smoking was through a pipe, and the smoke was drunk, sipped, or swallowed. Smoking was a word only applied to the tobacco itself when it was alight!

Tobacco was very expensive, so pipe bowls were small, allowing less than an ounce of tobacco. The stem of the pipe was long and slender, and the hole through which you drank, tiny. You would have had to suck quite hard to get your hit of tobacco.

Clay pipes were very decorative, especially those made for women, and I have an example at home which has flowers around the bowl. The pipes were cast from a mould after the original shape was carved from wood or fashioned from clay. For more examples you can't do better than to visit the website of Heather Coleman, an amateur archaeologist and expert on clay pipes. Beth Maxwell Boyle has a collection of pipes and smoking related memorabilia on her website.

Pipes were also used by children in the age-old fashion even in the seventeenth century as Michaelina Woutiers' "Boys Blowing Bubbles" from the 1640s shows us. This painting is in the Seattle Art Museum and is a wonderful resource for costume detail. There is a shell used for holding the bubble-blowing liquid. Let's hope the boys did not "drink" the contents!

SOURCES

Ayto, Eric G. *Clay Tobacco Pipes*. Shire Books, 2008.

Boyle, Beth Maxwell. "Women and Pipes." *Rams Horn Studio*. http://www.ramshorn-studio.com/pipe_smoking.htm

Coleman, Heather. "Dutch Clay Tobacco Pipes." *Dawnmist*. http://www.dawnmist.org/dutchpipes.htm

Griffiths, Phillips. *Snuffs and Snufftaking*. http://www.snuffbox.org.uk/

Seattle Art Museum. http://www.seattleartmuseum.org/

THE STRUCTURED COURT OF CHARLES I

BY P.L. FARRAR

CHARLES II, KNOWN BY SO MANY AS THE "MERRY MONARCH", HAD A BRILLIANT COURT where life was one non-stop party, correct? He opened the theatres and pubs and allowed dancing once again. But before the interregnum there had been another king, and he had a court too. Except his was nothing like his son's....

Charles I's inspiration for his court came from Spain, where he had attempted (unsuccessfully) to woo the Spanish Infanta in 1623. He was impressed by the way the court was designed: a perfect example of order and structure. This was to be the template upon which he based his own court.

At a time of personal and absolute monarchy, the court reflected the personality of the ruler. In direct contrast to the bawdy and vulgar court antics of his father, James VI and I, it was Charles' composed and sophisticated nature that came through in his court most prominently. Charles was at the top of this stately hierarchical pyramid, and everyone beneath him knew their place in the social order.

A common event at court was the masque. Charles I and his wife Henrietta Maria appeared as the principal characters. The plots of these masques were basic in that there was always some trouble that led to chaos throughout the land. These problems disappeared the moment the wise and just King appeared with his loving and beautiful Queen.

Charles, like Louis XIV after him, exercised strict control over the movements of his courtiers. The majority of his courtiers were of the higher nobility. The gentry, on the other hand, were made to remain in their local parishes to enforce law and order, and there were, in fact, cases of nobles being fined for not seeking the King's permission to be at court or in London.

Many members of the court were also Catholics. Charles' French Queen, Henrietta Maria, had many French ladies-in-waiting who were not sent back to France.

The great number of Catholics with whom Charles surrounded himself, the highly structured ceremony, and the Church-like opulence gave rise to the perception that the court was exclusively for Catholics, and that Charles himself was Catholic.

Charles was in fact a devotee of Arminianism, or early Laudianism. Thus he did not believe that a select group of people were predestined to go to heaven, and equally, he wanted to focus on "the beauty of worship" (including an emphasis on sacred music), not merely on the sermons. There were elements of Catholicism such as having an altar and a railing instead of a Communion table, but he was essentially a Protestant. However, the issue of his alleged Catholicism was of major concern for everyone as they feared the absolutism and tyranny which they believed was connected to Catholicism. They also feared a return to Papal rule.

Charles I's court was one of great beauty. He loved to collect art, and of all subsequent rulers, his was the most significant contribution to the Royal Collection. He continually lured the great European painters over to the English court, just as he had observed the Spanish doing. Charles commissioned Rubens to paint the ceiling of the banqueting hall at Whitehall Palace, and he made Rubens a knight as well as offering him a house and pension if he remained as the court painter.

Charles commissioned Van Dyck, the premier Dutch portrait painter, to capture the essence of his "kingship" in a series of portraits. This talented painter was ordered to compensate for the king's shortcomings. This resulted in a number of equestrian portraits which depicted the king as a conquering hero on a great steed—very kingly and regal. (Charles I was a very short man but in these portraits his height ceased to be an issue.)

And Van Dyck used his artistic license to make Charles look five years older which was intended to add an element of wisdom and gravitas.

Together with his Queen, Henrietta Maria, Charles intended for his court to set the tone of the age as one of grace, splendour, and majesty. And although the Republic, led by Cromwell, sought to destroy or sell off anything that might belong to or evoke the Carolingian splendour, his son—that Merry Monarch to be—did his best to restore his father's regal and artistic legacy.

Of Stubborn Scots, an Obdurate King, and a Little Book of Prayer

By ANNA BELFRAGE

In a simplified version of history, the Scottish Covenanter movement sprang from a smouldering fire to a huge bonfire through the actions of one Jenny Geddes. A devout member of the Scottish Kirk, Jenny was in St. Giles the day the dean chose to read from the new *Book of Common Prayer*, and so incensed was she by these proposed changes to her familiar liturgy that she stood up and spontaneously hurled her stool at the poor dean.

Whether spontaneous or not—and a lot of things point to this being a well-planned protest—it is a fact that when the new *Book of Common Prayer* was introduced, the majority of the Scots were already convinced this was a fiendish attempt at weaning them away from the true religion as advocated by the Scottish Kirk, luring them into the dangerous mires of popery.

Had Charles I understood just what havoc his insistence on implementing this new Prayer Book was to have, he would probably have desisted. However, being anything but prophetic, Charles I took a mulish approach to the loud protests from Scotland, and in so doing fanned the flames of religious fervour into a devastating inferno that was to consume his three kingdoms and ultimately cost him his life.

Charles I was neither unintelligent nor uneducated—rather the reverse, in fact—but he does seem to have had a tendency to compensate his short stature with an authoritarian approach to most things in life. As anointed King, he firmly believed it was his responsibility and duty to care for his subjects, leading them up the right path in all matters, including faith. Minor obstacles such as the said subjects' reluctance to follow him down the chosen path, mainly because they did not agree with their King's opinion in matters of faith, were generally ignored by Charles, who to further undermine his religious credibility in his kingdoms committed the *faux pas* of marrying a Catholic princess—not a popular move in a time and age when the whole of Europe was a battlefield between the Protestants of the north and the Catholics of the south.

So what was the argument about? What were those principles of faith that had the majority of the English—and Scottish—citizens of the seventeenth century walking about with their knickers in a twist? (Not that all that many of them had any knickers to twist in the first place....) Well, to answer that we must leapfrog backwards a century to the heady age of the Reformation.

In England, Henry VIII proclaimed himself the Head of the Anglican Church, disbanded the clerical orders, and severed his ties with Rome. But the rituals remained virtually unchanged, the Anglican Church building on the medieval (and therefore Catholic) rites that were already well-established within the kingdom.

In Scotland, the Reformation was led by John Knox, a disciple of Calvin himself, but was ultimately a bid for Scottish independence from the French interests as represented by Marie de Guise, mother of Mary, Queen of Scots. The hundred or so Scottish nobles that headed this coup probably found it convenient to set a religious label on their actions—it had a better ring to it than to admit they were only doing this to protect their own interests. However, in difference to England, the Reformed Scottish Kirk very quickly divested itself of "popish" ritual and practise, emphasising instead the importance of the Word (Scripture) and faith.

By the seventeenth century, the Scottish Kirk was a robust and thriving organisation in which the local parishes played a strong role. It was also an organisation dominated by leaders who shuddered at the thought of having their cleansed and purified Kirk besmirched by the papist trappings that still lingered in the Anglican Church. So when Charles I decided to harmonize the religious practices in his three kingdoms by advocating a *Book of Common Prayer* he was throwing a lit fuse into a munitions store, and eventually the whole thing exploded in his face.

A *Book of Common Prayer* valid in all three kingdoms was not a new idea. Already James I (VI) had tried to go down that way, but having far better political instincts than his unfortunate son, he backed off in light of the Scottish protests. Unlike Charles, James understood his Scottish subjects, having spent his first 37 years as King of Scotland only. Charles, on the other hand, was born in Scotland but was raised and educated in England, and his first visit to Scotland as an adult was for his coronation in 1633. As stated above, Charles was also somewhat jealous of his royal prerogative, and where his father would have been open to discussions about the incendiary book, Charles refused to budge. He was the King and knew best what his subjects needed to fortify their spiritual life.

The Scottish Kirk wasn't about to keel over without a fight. Upon hearing that Charles was planning a new *Book of Common Prayer*, the Kirk began its countermoves which involved all the parishes but also a massive PR effort with a number of printed documents (pamphlets, tracts) defending its principal tenets of faith. Well before the *Book of Common Prayer* had been published, "everyone" in Scotland knew that it was full of potentially popish garbage, and matrons in Edinburgh were heard protesting about this terrible little book well in advance of Jenny's stunt with her stool.

On Sunday, 23 July 1637, a number of loyalist ministers and bishops set out to their respective churches to use the new *Book of Common Prayer* for the first time. By the time the sun set, all of them had realised that implementing the new liturgy was a bad idea. Too bad they never got Charles to understand this. Over the coming months the protests did not abate—rather the reverse—and when Charles finally grasped just how serious the situation was, it had already snowballed into an unstoppable avalanche.

The protest culminated in the document known as the National Covenant. Drafted by Alexander Henderson, the Covenant was an elegant piece of work that professed the Kirk's loyalty to God and the King—in that order—thereby attempting to avoid being labelled as treasonous. The Covenant listed several acts of parliament against superstitious and papist rites, imposed an oath to uphold the true reformed religion, plus included an oblique reference to the King's obligation to uphold the Kirk. More importantly, there were a lot of things *not said* in the covenant, but implicit in the entire document was a clear threat: "Back off our Kirk, Mr. King, or beware of the consequences."

Charles I recognised the Covenant for what it was: a thrown gauntlet telling him quite clearly that should he not hold to his coronation oaths, well then.... Unfortunately for him—and the thousands upon thousands of civilians that were to lose their lives, homes, and families in the coming conflict—Charles severely underestimated his adversary, calmly convinced that his forces would prevail against whatever army the Covenanters might put together. They didn't, and even worse, the Covenanters inspired people of similar beliefs in England to also take up arms. The rest, as they say, is history, ending for Charles I on a cold January day in 1649 when his head was severed from his body.

THE PRICE OF CONVICTIONS

BY ANNA BELFRAGE

W HEN I WAS A LITTLE GIRL, I DEVOURED ALL KINDS OF HISTORICAL FICTION, AND
when the novels didn't tell me enough I went to the history section, checking out
heavy, dusty tomes to further dig into what details there were. During one rather long
period, I was stuck in the English Civil War with my heart firmly in the Royalist camp.

Today, I am still stuck in the Civil War—or rather its aftermath, as I have a particular
fondness for the latter half of the seventeenth century—but these days I root for the
Parliamentarians. Always. A somewhat fruitless position one could argue, given that ultimately Charles II was reinstated, but there you are.

As we all know, the Restoration as such was a bloodless event. The returning King
was wise enough not to demand redress for years of exile and penury, nor did he actively
persecute former Parliamentarians—well, with one exception, the regicides.

Fifty-nine commissioners signed Charles I's death sentence, and of these, twenty
were already dead when Charles II ascended the throne, nineteen were imprisoned for
life, three were disinterred and executed "after the fact", so to say, and nine were hanged,
drawn, and quartered.

The story surrounding the arrest of three of the regicides reads like a seventeenth
century James Bond. It starred George Downing of His Majesty's Secret Service. (In actual
fact he was the English ambassador to the Netherlands, but I prefer imagining him as a
sinister guy in immaculate black velvet, rapier in hand as he trawls through the seedier
parts of Delft in search of the wanted men.)

George Downing spent his childhood in England but accompanied his family to Massachusetts when he was fifteen. He was in the first class ever to graduate from Harvard,
spent some time in the West Indies, and subsequently ended up as a chaplain in a regiment commanded by one John Okey.

The coming years had George seeing very much fighting first-hand, and through
a series of advantageous career moves plus, one must assume, considerable skills, he
advanced steadily from spymaster all the way to one of Cromwell's most trusted diplomats.

So far, George had been a steadfast supporter of the Commonwealth cause. His whole
career had been built on his staunch Puritan convictions and his loyalty to the Protector.
Unfortunately for George, Oliver Cromwell went and died in 1658.

Fortunately for George, at the time he was the English ambassador to the Netherlands and managed to cling on to this post throughout the eighteen months of turmoil
that followed Cromwell's death. And while he was at it, dear George took the opportunity
to mend his fences with Charles Stuart—also in the Netherlands—expressing that his life

so far was a lie built on the erroneous principles that had been inculcated in him during his years in the radical Colonies.

I'm not sure Charles bought this "volte-face". I do, however, believe that Charles Stuart had learnt the hard way how important it was to surround himself with capable men, and George Downing was nothing if not impressively capable. A tenuous relationship was established resulting in George still being the ambassador to the Netherlands when Charles set off to claim his throne.

There were a number of people in Charles' inner circle that were anything but thrilled by this development, and somehow George needed to quench all doubts as to where his loyalty lay. (A sarcastic person would conclude he was mostly loyal to his own interests rather than to his professed convictions....) A golden opportunity to do so arose in early spring of 1662.

After several years as a spymaster and an ambassador, George had a number of spies in his service, one of whom lived in Delft and was called Abraham Kick. How unfortunate for the three regicides, Barkstead, Corby, and Okey—yup, George's former commanding officer—that they used Kick as their contact when fleeing the long arm of royal justice. But George, well, he must have rubbed his hands together in glee at this most happy turn of events.

The Dutch were ambivalent to the new English king and were on the whole very sympathetic to Puritans fleeing England. George couldn't risk such sensitivities getting in the way of his plan, and once he had a warrant for their arrest, he set off to do the actual arresting on his own with people he could trust.

Night was closing in when George and his men burst into Kick's house. I wonder what he said to Okey, if he could look these former comrades of his in the eyes when by his actions he was effectively condemning them to gruesome death. Whatever the case, he had the three regicides dragged off to Delft's town jail and set about organising the logistics of transporting them back to England and the waiting gallows.

The people of Delft were not pleased by George's night-time raid. The magistrates demanded that the three unfortunates should have their case tried, and public opinion was loud in their support. For a while, it seemed this most juicy plum was about to be plucked from George's hand, but resourceful as ever he secured a handover document at lightning speed from the powers that were.

Imagine a cold March dawn in seventeenth century Delft. Mists hung like sheer veils over the network of narrow canals, and this early there were no lights, no sounds but the occasional bark of a dog. A soft splash, a muted curse, and a small boat appeared through the fog, rowing up the canal that led to the back entrance of the jail. In the prow sat George with his precious document, and minutes later three bound men were bundled into the boat, muted screams leaking through their gags. Well before sunrise the boat had left Delft far behind, and some days later Downing's precious cargo was deposited on English soil.

In April 1662, Barkstead, Okey, and Corby were hanged, drawn, and quartered.

In July of 1663, Downing was made a baronet, dying a couple of decades later as a very wealthy man. But now and then I suspect it came back to haunt him, that day when he arrested those three men. Did he twist in bed as he recalled Okey's frenzied pleading that he please not do this? He could have let them run. He chose not to. Did he sometimes shiver awake in the predawn, convinced that it was Okey's hand that clutched at his neck? I somehow hope he did.

BRILLIANA HARLEY AND THE
SIEGE OF BRAMPTON BRYAN

By ALISON STUART

IN A QUIET CORNER OF HEREFORDSHIRE ARE THE REMAINS OF BRAMPTON BRYAN Castle. There is little to be seen except the great gatehouse and part of a wall. Having withstood the ravages of time, the castle was not to outlast the English Civil War.

Although mentioned in the Domesday Book, the present structure was probably constructed in the late thirteenth or early fourteenth century by Robert Harley who had inherited the castle through marriage to the daughter of Bryan de Brampton. The Harleys held Brampton Bryan in an unbroken line through to the seventeenth century.

As England lurched towards Civil War, Herefordshire showed itself solidly and staunchly Royalist in sympathy. The Harleys, Puritans and supporters of Parliament, rapidly found themselves the butt of unpleasant taunts and rumours long before the first shot had been fired. When the war finally broke out, Sir Robert Harley, a Member of Parliament, remained in London, leaving his wife Brilliana to hold the castle.

Brilliana was the third wife of Sir Robert Harley, and it can be seen from the letters (some of which were written in a clever secret code) that passed between Brilliana and her husband that it was a strong and affectionate partnership. They had three sons and four daughters, all of whom survived into adulthood.

With her husband and sons away, Brilliana and her daughters found themselves living as an island of Parliamentary sympathy in a sea of Royalists. Being a practical woman, Brilliana turned her mind to what she would need in the event of hostilities and added powder, match, and flintlocks to her housewifely shopping list.

The early months of the war did not go well for the Parliamentarians, but it was not until July 1643 that Brampton Bryan found itself the centre of Royalist attention. Brilliana's former neighbours, friends, and relatives suddenly found themselves ordered to "reduce" Brampton Bryan. An awkward correspondence between besieger and besieged ensued, but Brilliana politely but firmly refused to surrender Brampton saying *"...my dear husband hath entrusted me with his house but according to his pleasure, therefore I cannot dispose of his house but according to his pleasure...."*

Hostilities commenced; the village of Brampton Bryan was razed and artillery brought to bear on the castle. Despite heavy bombardment, casualties within the castle were surprisingly light. A personal offer of terms from the King did not move the lady, who played for time in the knowledge that the Earl of Essex was going to the relief of the siege of Gloucester, which would divert the Royalist forces.

After seven weeks the siege was lifted, and Lady Harley set about replenishing stores within the castle. Encouraged by the news that the siege of Gloucester had been lifted, she went on the offensive, sending out foraging parties and an attack force to the town of Knighton. By early October the Royalists were again poised to renew the siege.

Brilliana wrote to her son Ned on 9 October 1643:

> *...I have taken a very great cold, which has made me very ill these 2 or 3 days, but I hope that the Lord will be merciful to me, in giving me health, for it is an ill time to be sick in. My dear Ned, I pray God bless you and give me the comfort of seeing you again....*

Sadly, Brilliana was never to see her husband or sons again as she died of pneumonia on 31 October, leaving *"the saddest garrison in the three kingdoms"*.

In the spring of 1644, Brampton Bryan Castle was besieged a second time and finally fell to the Royalists. The castle was "reduced" (a term meaning destroyed so as not to be capable of defence again), but the lives of the defenders were spared and the fame of Brilliana Harley spread, earning her the *"admiration and applause even of her enemies"*.

Despite this apparent victory, the Royalist cause was lost. Sir Robert Harley was compensated for his loyal support of the Parliamentary cause and was paid the sum of 13,000 pounds (worth now well over 1,000,000 pounds) for the loss of his home.

THE ENGLISH CAVALIER AND HIS STOMACH

By DEBORAH SWIFT

IT HAS LONG BEEN RECOGNISED THAT AN ARMY MARCHES ON ITS STOMACH—THAT THE importance of food to morale is vital. Apart from just the sustenance, the regularity of meals provides a routine in what can often be chaos during a war or campaign. Eating together has always bonded people and created friendships and loyalties which extend onto the battlefield. Particularly in cold, wet weather (and England is often cold and wet!) the cheer of a good hot meal cannot be underestimated.

In the English Civil War, a period I am researching right now, the official ration for a Cavalier was two pounds of bread, one pound of meat, and two bottles of beer.

Meat was considered essential by both armies in the conflict, and between January and June 1645 (a six month period) the two hundred Roundheads stationed at Chalfield House, Wiltshire ate:

40,000 lbs beef
1600 lbs bacon
580 lbs pork
1900 lbs mutton
64 lbs veal

As well as this heavy diet of meat, they also ate:

15,000 pints of wheat
27,000 pints of oats
20,000 pints of malt
5000 pints of beans
5000 pints of peas

All this was supplemented with small amounts of cheese and dairy produce (statistics from Charles Carlton, *Going to the Wars*).

The fact that vegetables are not mentioned does not necessarily mean that people ate no vegetables; it is perhaps that their cost does not appear in records in the same way as other foods. Pulses were widely grown in England and formed an essential part of most people's diet. Who remembers this old rhyme?

Pease Pudding hot, Pease Pudding cold,
Pease Pudding in the pot, five days old.

So how did the troops keep up this diet whilst on the move? When the Earl of Essex came to the aid of Gloucester, the thousand sheep and sixty cows that they drove along with them for food slowed them down. The meat had to be killed, skinned, and butchered as they went, often in unsanitary conditions. The carcasses were left behind to rot, but were taken by local people who used the bones for glue.

Once farther from a garrison town, food became scarcer, and scrounging or plundering food was a common occupation. Many citizens during the English Civil War found themselves with unwelcome guests from the foraging armies. After their victory in Taunton in 1644, the Roundheads were so hungry that they stopped chasing the King's Army and went in search of food. The Royalists counter-attacked, killing many with the bread still "in their mouths".

Plundering was a way to show high spirits, but also a way for defeated troops to vent their anger and shame. After the battle of Edgehill, one Royalist platoon got out of hand and brutally plundered their own hometowns of Droitwich and Bromsgrove. And in a blind rage after being beaten at Marston Moor, Prince Rupert's men seized cattle, sheep, and chickens, killing all who tried to stop them.

Because the troops sometimes could not carry all their plunder, special market days were arranged where they would sell off what they had pillaged. Records show for example that Joyce Hammon managed to buy back gold plate and also some beaver hats that troops had stolen from her house in Hereford.

Feeding the soldiers on the march was compulsory—in the sense that refusal led to threats and violence. Householders were expected to billet soldiers at a set rate in exchange for an IOU that was often never paid. They were expected to provide food and ale and to feed their horses. The soldiers (on both sides) fresh from blood and battle were often the worst kind of house guests—violent, greedy, and out of control.

The cost to England of free quarter and plunder was enormous. In Cheshire £120,000 of free quarter was said never to have been reimbursed, not to mention the claims of villages in the same county which lost as much as £190,000 worth of goods and livestock in plunder. Often a lifetime's hard work could be laid waste in one night.

Women alone in their houses whilst the men were at war feared the arrival of troops from both sides, even from the side they supported. In her memoirs Lucy Hutchinson condemned plunderers as "the scum of mankind", and Milton wrote in his "Poem to The Lord General Fairfax",

> In vain doth valour bleed,
> Where avarice and rapine share the land.

SOURCES

Ashley, Maurice. *The English Civil War*. Palgrave MacMillan, 1997.

Carlton, Charles. *Going to the Wars: The Experience of the British Civil Wars 1638-1651*. Routledge, 1994.

Fraser, Antonia. *The Weaker Vessel: Women's Lot in Seventeenth-Century England*. Vintage, 2014.

Hunt, Tristram. *The English Civil War at First Hand*. Penguin, 2011.

THEY SEEK HIM HERE, THEY SEEK HIM THERE: THE LIFE OF A RELIGIOUS REBEL

By ANNA BELFRAGE

RECENTLY—WELL, FOR THE LAST THREE YEARS OR SO—MUCH OF MY TIME HAS BEEN spent with a slight man with sparse hair, beautiful grey eyes, and a voice that can reduce a congregation to tears—or have his followers on their feet, roaring like lions. Not that I have any idea if Alexander Peden matches the above description, but that is how I see this charismatic seventeenth century minister—a man who became a legend during his lifetime.

"Legend?" you might ask, scratching your head in an attempt to bring forth some sort of information about this Alexander person. Yes, legend—but not far beyond the borders of his native Ayrshire, which might explain why the majority of us have never heard of Prophet Peden. You may, however, have seen his mask, a little thing on display at the National Museum of Scotland. In this disguise, Alexander Peden flitted over the Scottish moors like some sort of religious Zorro, even if he never showed any inclination to mark his victims or foes with a flamboyant Z.

Alexander Peden was a stubborn, brave man of God as per the Scottish Kirk, not as per the Anglican Church. Peden couldn't care less what the Anglican worthies might have thought of him. Had not Charles II been restored, Alexander Peden would probably have lived out his life as a capable minister in his small living in New Luce, Galloway. As it was, with the Restoration came a number of changes that would drive Alexander—or Sandy, as those of us close to him prefer to call him—into rebellion.

Some background: Charles II seems to have been a reasonable man in matters of faith—I suppose he learnt the hard way that religious contention could lead to nasty repercussions and death. I'd hazard he lived in constant awareness of the fact that his father—an anointed king—had been executed, and while Charles I's faith was never cited as a reason for his execution, it must have struck his son that had only Charles I handled the religious conflicts that sparked the Civil War better, things might have ended very differently.

Whatever the case, Charles II was prepared to be conciliatory in most matters—but he held no great love for the powerful Scottish Kirk. Besides, Charles II's closest advisors were Anglicans, and after years of penurious exile they saw an opportunity to get their own back.

In 1662 a set of laws commonly known as the Clarendon Code were passed through Parliament. As per these laws, it became illegal to hold religious meetings outside the Anglican Church, it was mandatory to recognise the King as the head of the Church, and all able-bodied men were called to take the Oath of Abjuration, whereby they were required to disavow themselves from any previous oaths in conflict with the new laws. With this legislation in place, the time was ripe to grind the Scottish Kirk into submission.

Someone seems to have forgotten about the Scots and their independent—and stubborn—streak. The Scottish Kirk was not an institution to be brushed aside as inconsequential, and so the recently restored King had a new religious conflict on his hands—this time mercifully contained to parts of his northern kingdom, but still....

The ministers of the Scottish Kirk who refused to recognise the King as the head of their church were evicted from their livings in 1663. This more or less meant all ministers, Alexander Peden being one of them. Their congregations were urged to attend the Anglican services instead, but rather than flocking to hear the word of God from the King's chosen representatives, the people of Ayrshire—and elsewhere—chose to follow their ministers out into the wilderness, breaking the law by attending unlawful Conventicle meetings, further breaking the law by having the evicted ministers christen their babies and bless their marriages.

Sandy Peden already had a reputation as a gifted preacher. In the present circumstances, his fame grew exponentially and wherever he preached, Sandy told his flock to never turn their back on the true Kirk, to never kowtow to the Anglican Church, papist whore that it was.

For doing this, and for further heinous acts such as baptising children (many children—on one occasion he baptised close to thirty babies) and wedding young couples, Sandy was formally outlawed in 1667, with a hefty price set on his head. Over the coming years, an intricate manhunt played out over the Ayrshire moors and beyond. The English soldiers chased. Sandy ran, aided and abetted by his countrymen and women.

I imagine Sandy Peden dashing off over the moor, his threadbare cloak standing like a billowing sail around him. In my head, the moor is an orgy of flowering heather, here and there dotted with stands of bright yellow gorse, the air permeated by its nutty scent. In reality, poor Sandy squelched through mud and freezing water, ducked down to hide behind a stand of stunted trees, his forearm pressed to his mouth to muffle his constant cough—a consequence of far too many nights sleeping under the bare skies.

For over a decade, Alexander Peden led the English soldiers a merry dance over the rugged landscapes of his native Ayrshire. In his wake sprung stories of divine intervention, describing how God would help his favourite minister by creating timely fogs into which he could disappear. (Given that this is Scotland, it would seem God was doing a lot of fogging well before Sandy and long after him as well.)

And then there were all of Sandy's prophecies, the most well-known of these being when he officiated at the wedding of John Brown to Isabel Weir in 1682. According to legend, Sandy took the bride aside after the ceremony and told her she should keep linen by her side to make her new husband a winding sheet, as John was to die shortly. I'm not quite sure this shows much sense for timing, but Sandy was sadly proved right; in 1685, James Brown was shot dead at his home by John Graham of Claverhouse (Bluidy Clavers as he was known in Ayrshire), this for refusing to take the Oath of Abjuration—and for having a number of illegal weapons in his house.

In 1673 Alexander Peden was arrested—betrayed, some say—and after several years on Bass Rock he was set aboard a ship in 1678 to be deported to the colonies. When the boatload of deportees landed in London, there to be transferred to another vessel, Sandy Peden succeeded in convincing the captain of this new ship that to deport him and his companions would not please God, and so they were left behind on the docks. Sandy and his Merry Ministers walked all the way back to Scotland, receiving a lot of help along the way.

The remaining years of his life, Sandy spent in Scotland and in Ireland, always running, always hiding. And he continued to baptise children and officiate at weddings (as demonstrated above when he wed John Brown and Isabel). In 1686 he was staying on his brother's farm when he died—in bed, as he had prophesied.

Upon hearing Alexander Peden was dead, English troops chose to disinter him, having the intention of hanging the dead man from the Cumnock gallows. The local powers interceded, worried that this might cause an uproar among the people of Ayrshire. Instead, Sandy Peden was reburied by the gallows—in itself an insult.

Many years later, a monument was erected over Sandy's final resting place. Personally, I think he wouldn't be all that impressed. Sandy never wanted a monument—all he wanted was the freedom to praise God according to his beliefs.

SEVENTEENTH CENTURY TRADE

By KATHERINE PYM

THE EAST INDIA COMPANY ALMOST DIED UNDER THE REIGN OF CROMWELL. THE DOUR religion disallowed many things. Gold and silver did not help the "saints" into heaven.

Calicoes from India were not allowed during the Commonwealth. Only dark and homespun woollens prevailed. Spices brought about the fall of man, so little sold in England. The East India Company was forced to trade spices for other goods in the foreign markets. Pepper traded for coral in Italy sold in India at a 90% profit.

It brought the Dutchman Company, called V.O.C. or United East Indian Company, into power. They took advantage of England's weakened Navy and merchant ships to increase holdings in the Far East. In Persian waters, Dutch merchant ships outnumbered the English four to one. The Dutch gained control of one port after the other. After the English Civil Wars, Cromwell went to war with the Dutch. In the South Seas a battle completely destroyed Pulo Run Island's nutmeg industry.

English merchant ships were virtual warships that carried cannon and shot. If the crew survived periods of calm in the seas, scurvy, or the treacherous waters off the Cape of Good Hope, they invariably fought the Dutch and other sundries as pirates to gain ports of call where they could trade. This continued until after Charles II regained the throne.

Enter the Portuguese Infanta, Catherine of Braganza in 1662. Portugal had been in the South Seas trade industry for well over one hundred years. Her dowry brought a wealth of cash, artisans, new designs in furniture, and ports of call in India. They included stations in the Far East, warehouses called factories, counting houses, and residences.

Her dowry ship to England used sugar for ballast.

My resources indicate tea was introduced in England about 1660 by Thomas Garway. He felt it preserved one's health until old age, but it was expensive—ten shillings per pound with the East India Company (the one belonging to England) having the sole right to import it. Called China tea, it was transported in square wooden boxes lined with lead. The new Queen, Catherine of Braganza gave tea popularity. She felt the quality of water in England terrible. Her first drink when she arrived was a horn of ale. She shook her head, and asked for "tee".

Along with the new ports of call came a plethora of new items from the South Seas. Porcelain had made its original entry to Europe through the Crusaders. Queen Elizabeth I was given by Lord Burghley a *"poringer of white porselyn, and a cup of greene porselyn"*. She also wore *"an armlet of pearls and enclosed thereof a clock"*. But few others enjoyed such riches.

When Catherine of Braganza came to England, food was eaten out of bowls and trenchers, liquid slurped from horn cups, tankards, two-handled cups, or posset pots (generally called dishes). These were made of earthenware, wood, or tough leather. Porcelain for the general public did not really hit England's shores until after King James II went into exile.

King William and Queen Mary brought porcelain with them when they came to England to rule. Europe, who had been the recipient of Dutch trading for years received a further taste for tea, sipped from porcelain and served from lacquer-ware.

As time marched toward the end of the seventeenth century, shiploads of 250,000 porcelain pieces at a time were brought to England. No longer were the habits of good Englishmen as they had been during the Restoration. Breakfasts were then a dish of new beer, bread, Cheshire cheese, or gruel served with a heavy meat. In the early eighteenth century the Tatler stated a breakfast of *"tea and bread and butter...have prevailed of late years."*

Even though Catherine never gave Charles II an heir, she brought to England a new way of living with the finer things of life. England's taste became more dignified and refined.

SOURCE

Thomas, Gertrude Z. *Richer than Spices*. New York: Alfred A. Knopf, 1965.

THE PARADOX OF MOTHERHOOD IN SEVENTEENTH CENTURY ENGLAND

BY SUSANNA CALKINS

IN EARLY MODERN ENGLAND, THE IDEA PREVAILED THAT A DISCIPLINED FAMILY WAS AT the heart of the social order. This notion forms much of the backdrop of my debut novel, *A Murder at Rosamund's Gate*, a historical mystery set in seventeenth century London.

In the most simplistic sense, wives were expected to obey their husbands, servants their masters, and children their parents. In return for this obedience and fidelity, the head of the household, more a benevolent patriarch than a tyrant, was expected to perform his duties as husband, father, or master properly and to maintain the family livelihood.

Women, idealized as "chaste, silent, and obedient," were expected to maintain their homes in a godly manner and to oversee the spiritual and physical nourishment of their husbands and children. Such ideas were derived from scripture, disseminated in household manuals, and affirmed in children's catechisms. Children were viewed as the reward of God, and husbands and wives were expected to follow the biblical injunction to go forth and multiply.

Within this context, there was a highly prescriptive understanding of what it meant to be a "good" mother, found in sermons, advice manuals, and other similar directives. Even before giving birth, the good mother was expected to *"take tender care of herself,"* which included among other things, praying, consulting with almanacs (to assure an auspicious birth), and avoiding vigorous activities like dancing. After birth, mothers were expected to breastfeed their infants and otherwise stay close to them.

As William Gouge heartily admonished: *"Be not so unnatural as to thrust away your own children"* (Gouge, 1622, pp. 18-19)—which may well have been a warning to upper class women who sent their babies off with wet nurses.

Nor did injunctions for "good" motherhood seem to change for mothers of older children. Richard Baxter, a non-conformist, admonished parents to raise their children on a *"temperate and healthful diet,"* and to keep them busy in order to avoid idleness of mind and body (Baxter, 1624, p. 5). Mothers were to be diligent, keeping their children from pursuing vices (*"gaming for money, from cards, dice and stage plays, play books and love books and foolish wanton tales and ballads"*) or untoward familiarity with tempting persons of another sex (Baxter, 1624, p. 5).

While, of course, women may not have achieved this ideal (or even wanted to, for that matter), the expectations for good motherhood were at least generally clear. What's interesting, however, is that there was a newly emerging understanding of motherhood arising in the writings of Quaker women during the 1650s-1680s, indicating a renegotiation of the ideal mother.

On the one hand, Quaker mothers, like all mothers, were expected to teach their children the proper ideas about God, the right way to behave, the right way to carry themselves with each other and in society. William Penn advised parents to love their children wisely, to explain *"the folly of their faults,"* and to use the rod sparingly and judiciously. The virtues extolled in this literature implicitly assumed that a good mother was physically present, corrective, and watchful of her child.

However, on the other hand, Quaker women as a group did not adhere to this ideal in practice.

First, Quaker mothers were not purified ritualistically after childbirth, nor did they have their babies baptized, two expectations of good motherhood held by the Anglican Church. Second, Quaker mothers often ignored the expectations for good motherhood established by the medical community. After all, there are examples of Quaker women— either pregnant or new mothers—withstanding long bouts in prisons, traveling long distances by foot or horseback, and even crossing the Atlantic.

Third, many wives and husbands stayed apart from one another in a deliberate attempt to minimize pregnancy as the presence of young children impeded women's abilities to carry out their mission for God (Trevett, 2000).

Moreover, Quaker women who left their children to follow the will of God were clearly uneasy or anxious over their actions. For example, in 1670, Elizabeth Stirredge was allegedly stunned when God called her to leave her children:

> *"...I did not think that the Lord would make of such a contemptible Instrument as I, to leave my habitation, and tender children...to go to King Charles which was an Hundred miles from my habitation, and with such a plain testimony as the Lord did require of me, which made me go bowed down many months...."* (Stirredge, 1810, p. 37)

Quaker mothers seem to have navigated this tension by ultimately creating a new ideal of motherhood. Although they were separated from their children, many sought to become spiritual mothers of the community. Such "Mothers in Israel" offered solace, comfort, religious training, and physical and spiritual nourishment to fellow Friends.

In such ways, the Quaker women offered a fascinating reinvention of what it meant to be a "good" mother; transcending expectations imposed on women, while still pursuing what mattered most to them.

SOURCES

Baxter, R. *The Poor Man's Family Book.* London, 1624.

Gouge, W. *Of Domesticall Duties.* London, 1622.

Penn, W. *Advice to Children.* In J. Fothergill (Ed.), *Select Works of William Penn.* London, 1771.

Stirredge, E. *Strength in Weakness Manifest: In the Life, Various Trials, an Christian Testimony of that Faithful and Servant of the Lord.* Second Edition. London, 1810.

Trevett, C. *Quaker Women Prophets in England and Wales 1650-1700.* Lampeter, Wales: Edwin Mellen Press, 2000.

ALCOHOL AND SAMUEL PEPYS: DRUNK AND DISORDERLY?

BY GRACE ELLIOT

Thence Jenings [sic] and I into London (it being through heat of the sun a great thaw and dirty) to show our bills of return, and coming back drank a pint of wine at the Star, Cheapside.

–Samuel Pepys' Diary

WHEN PEPYS CASUALLY MENTIONS DRINKING A PINT OF WINE IN THE SAME SENTENCE as the thaw and the pub, it makes me smile. Apparently, Pepys didn't think imbibing such a quantity of alcohol was anything out of the ordinary, which arguably it wasn't.

In this excerpt we learn that Pepys drank at The Star in Cheapside. Amongst the general population literacy rates were low, and people liked places that were easily identifiable with a picture. Hence pubs such as The Star, Bull, or Bell, denoted with a painting on their sign were popular.

In the modern age the majority of people reading this essay will have access to clean, sanitised drinking water, but this wasn't the case in the seventeenth century world. Although germ theory (i.e., disease is caused by micro-organisms) wasn't discovered until the late nineteenth century, instinct must have warned people that drinking dirty water led to awful stomach upsets. As such, alcohol was consumed widely by everyone from children and servants to labourers and royalty, and perceived as being safer to drink than water.

Even though people didn't understand why, they perhaps recognised the result that the brewing process made water safer to drink. Of course we now know that boiling water, fermenting, and alcohol have disinfectant properties on some water-borne bugs.

Was the population permanently drunk? Possibly!

However, seventeenth century alcohol wasn't as strong as the modern-day equivalent. One reason for this was that the yeasts weren't as hardy as our modern varieties, and they were less tolerant of the alcohol produced during fermentation. This meant that the brews were naturally limited in strength, because once they reached a certain level of alcohol, the yeast died and the process stopped. Incidentally, these yeasts made for a cloudy drink rather than the clear ales and wines of today, but the cloudiness was disguised by metal tankards or frosted glass.

As an aside, the small beer or wine produced was much sweeter than modern brews. Again, this was because the yeast died before all the sugar was converted to alcohol. Also, it is interesting to reflect that grain stores were vulnerable to spoilage by rodents—so the safest way to protect your harvest was to convert it to beer, which preserved the sugar and calorie content! (Don't forget, sugar was a hideously expensive commodity.)

So was the population permanently drunk? Quite probably. And finally, one unfortunate effect for the inimitable Pepys was that the quantity of alcohol he consumed contributed to the formation of his bladder stones, so drinking wasn't all pleasure even without the hangovers.

A PROPER EDUCATION:
STUART SCHOOLS

BY DEBORAH SWIFT

IN THE STUART ERA IT WAS NOT UNUSUAL FOR A GIRL TO BE MARRIED AT TWELVE OR thirteen and for a boy to finish school and go to university by the age of sixteen. Girls were seldom educated unless they were of wealthy families, and even then the subjects taught were usually French, dancing, music, needlework, and household management. Only a few were taught mathematics or sciences as these skills were thought inessential in a wife.

Boys of course were educated. The leading schools were Eton, St. Paul's, Winchester, Westminster, and The Merchant Taylors Schools, which were founded by men from the Guild. The Merchant Taylors used to be armourers. The Linen Armourers, an allied craft to the Tailors, originally made the padded tunics or *gambesons* worn under suits of armour and by the seventeenth century had grown to be one of the most influential guilds in London. The London School was founded in 1562 but burnt down in the Great Fire of 1666 and had to be rebuilt.

The Merchant Taylors Company also founded schools such as the one in Mill Street, Ashwell, Hertfordshire. It was built in 1681 by the Merchant Taylors Company as a result of a bequest for this purpose made by Henry Colbron, a London scrivener.

For the unfortunate pupils school days began at 6 a.m. and went on until late afternoon when the light was best. Study would be undertaken by means of slates to write on and horn books which the teacher used as text books.

The boys would be severely disciplined for laziness or stupidity in a way we would find unacceptable today. The birch rod was a symbol of a master's authority as servants were frequently beaten, and it was exactly the same in school. Whether you were an apprentice or at school, you were likely to be on the receiving end of corporal punishment. Flogging was frequent and severe, as it was thought to drive devils from the body. It was thus used for every moral lapse or failing, and the boy would typically have his bottom beaten until blood flowed. Another common punishment was to use a *ferula*, a flat ruler with a rounded end into which a hole had been cut. This was used to strike the hand or mouth, and the hole brought up a terrible blister.

Some noble boys were educated at home, but by the seventeenth century the private tutor was much less popular as numbers of schools increased. Grammar Schools took day pupils, and Colleges were residential and took boarders. But occasionally boys were placed in the homes of a suitable tutor. They would go to Oxford or Cambridge Universities usually at fourteen to sixteen years old. Childhood was certainly short in those days.

Young gentry were often sent on a Grand Tour which was a rite of passage that introduced them to the cultural riches of Europe and gave them an insight into foreign affairs and diplomatic relations. A typical tour would include Paris, Geneva, Turin, Florence, Venice, and Rome. All through his schooling life the boy would have leisure time with his friends which more often than not involved blood sports such as falconry, shooting, stag hunting, and badger baiting. At University there was *"swearing, drinking, rioting and hatred of all piety"* (Simonds d'Ewes, Cambridge 1620).

There were one or two attempts to introduce the idea of French Academies: for example, in 1635 the Museum Minervae was established under royal patronage by Sir Francis Kynaston in Bedford Square, and its course included the arts, antiquities, and military studies as well as mathematics and languages. Charles I himself donated books, antiques, and other apparatus. Unfortunately, the fortunes of the Museum Minervae Academy declined when its patron was executed!

Once schooling was over the boy would often be sent abroad—wherever there was a War—to gain military experience. During the Thirty Years' War many young men from England went to fight on the continent. No doubt their experiences were useful when they returned and needed to fight during the English Civil Wars.

SOURCES

"Birth and Education: English Civil War Notes and Queries." *The Sealed Knot*. http://www.thesealedknot.org.uk/

Merchant Taylors' Company. http://www.merchant-taylors.co.uk/

"Proposals for an English Academy." *Wikipedia*. https://en.wikipedia.org/wiki/Proposals_for_an_English_Academy

GRINLING GIBBONS: THE MICHELANGELO OF WOOD

By GRACE ELLIOT

*There is no instance of a man before Gibbons who gave wood the loose and
airy lightness of flowers, and chained together the various productions of the
elements with free disorder natural to each species.*

–Horace Walpole

IN EARLY AUGUST I WAS FORTUNATE ENOUGH TO BE INVITED TO PREVIEW THE NEW
"Line of Kings" exhibition at the Tower of London. Amongst the exhibits are a number
of wonderful wooden horses. These were carved in the late seventeenth century as props
on which to display the armor of kings. At the preview, two historians debated in excited
tones which of the carved horses had been created by Grinling Gibbons. Their reverential
voices and the way their faces came alive made me curious to discover just who Grinling
Gibbons was.

Described as "the Michelangelo of wood," Grinling Gibbons (1648-1720/1) was the son of
English parents living in Holland; as a young man he trained as a stonemason in Amsterdam.

Attracted by the promise of work rebuilding London after the Great Fire, Gibbons
sailed for England in 1667. He worked successfully for several years, but his big break came
in 1671 when John Evelyn found him carving a copy in wood of Tintoretto's *"Crucifixion"*:

*I saw the young man at his carving, by the light of a candle. I saw him to be
engaged on a carved representation of Tintoretto's 'Crucifixion', which he had
in a frame of his own making.*

Evelyn was so impressed by what he saw that he told a colleague, the architect Sir
Christopher Wren. In turn, Evelyn and Wren arranged for their new prodigy to be introduced at the court of Charles II. The quality of his work delighted and amazed. Gibbons'
skill was to bring lightness and grace to the cherubs, flowers, and fruit he carved in lime
wood. Such was his ability that he created a lace-cravat out of lime wood— the detail of
which is absolutely stunning.

Over his career Grinling Gibbons was commissioned to work on royal residences such
as Windsor Castle, Hampton Court Palace, and Kensington Palace. His carved panels
of cherubs and ripe fruit were symbolic of the wealth and prosperity that the monarch
brought to the country. (He had a trademark peapod which he incorporated into panels
of fruit and flowers; if the peapod was open, it meant he had been paid for his work; if

closed, he hadn't!) Indeed, his carvings in the royal apartments impressed King William III so much that in 1693 he appointed Gibbons as master carver to the Crown.

Gibbons also worked widely for Wren on projects such as the choir stalls and organ case at St. Paul's Cathedral. The cultural significance of his carving was such that during World War II it was removed from St. Paul's and stored in a place of safety. Sadly, more harm than good was done when the pieces were replaced in the 1950s. Clumsy restoration with iron nails led to the panels splitting when the nails rusted—thankfully, recent restoration techniques have undone a lot of this damage.

And now I begin to understand the excitement of those historians at the Tower of London. A carved horse would have been something of a departure for Grinling Gibbons...and a fine example of the flexibility of his amazing talent. Not only that, but to stand so close to an object that Gibbons would have smoothed and chiselled with his own hand makes the great man seem so much closer....

Early Georgian Era (1715-1800)

A Hound? No Sir, You Have It Wrong!

By Anna Belfrage

AT TIMES, ONE STUMBLES UPON THINGS BY ACCIDENT: *"...AND THAT CONCLUDES today's programme on typefaces. I hope you enjoyed learning more about Baskerville."*

I have no interest in typefaces. I do, however, react to names I recognise, and Baskerville was such a name, conjuring up the hideous image of a slavering, murderous giant of a hound. It intrigued me that this fictional horror should have given his name to a typeface. He hadn't, as it turned out. Instead, it seems the hound takes his name from the designer of the typeface.

John Baskerville was born in Worcestershire in 1706 but would spend most of his life in Birmingham. While his family was financially comfortable, it was not comfortable enough to have young John loitering about as a gentleman, and so at the early age of seventeen, John was already hard at work engraving and designing tombstones. (Given John's future adventures as a corpse, this early trade is quite ironic, but more about that later.)

Apparently, John took to this trade with aplomb, stone chips flying as he pummelled each perfect, individual letter into being on whatever stone the deceased was to lie under.

As a side-line, John taught writing and book-keeping, and when his father died in 1738, this talented young man invested his inheritance in the lacquering (or "japanning") industry. Bright, curious, and innovative, John Baskerville went on to revolutionise the industry, becoming something of a household name with his "japanned" goods. Trays, bread baskets, useful little boxes—he inundated the market with these pretty trifles at (relatively) affordable prices, thereby recouping exponentially on his original investment.

Now very, very rich, John Baskerville enjoyed flaunting his wealth. His carriage was a rolling advertisement for his business, every single square inch covered by exquisite— and expensive—lacquer work. His clothes were always ostentatious, going to the extreme of being adorned with gold lace on important occasions, and he made a comfortable home for himself in the mansion Easy Hill just outside of Birmingham.

At this point in time John was the man about town, no doubt with quite the line-up of potential wives presented to him. John wasn't interested. He had met the woman of his life some years earlier, and he scandalised all of Birmingham by having his beloved Mrs. Eaves move in with him. Mr. Eaves was not in a position to protest; a forger, he had fled the country to avoid arrest.

Far worse than his disreputable liaison with Sarah Eaves, was the fact that John was an outspoken atheist. This made him something of an outcast in polite society—not that it seems to have bothered him unduly. No, John had other matters on his mind, first and foremost how to improve the art of printing.

With his background as an engraver, John was not all that impressed by the quality of much of the printed work at the time, and at the age of 44 he focused his considerable intellect on re-engineering the entire printing business. Due to a combination of paper, ink, and types, most volumes printed in the early eighteenth century had lettering that was somewhat indistinct around the edges, and this John Baskerville did not like. He wanted his typeface bold and clean-cut; he wanted the text to bounce off the page with consistent colour and sharpness.

John started by designing a typeface. He went on to experiment with woven paper, a relatively new product at the time. He used new types of ink, and to all this novelty he added the final touch of introducing heat in the printing process, using heated copper cylinders to set the type on. ("Why heat?" one might ask. Heat dries the ink faster, thereby minimising risk of smudging.)

As a financial professional, I regard all this innovation with a certain level of suspicion, having learnt the hard way that not all innovations pay their way. After all, if people were willing to accept uneven colour in the ink, somewhat smudged letters, and a deficient paper quality, who would be willing to pay for Baskerville's books? John himself couldn't care less. He didn't need the money—he was doing this for Science, for Art. (He was a member of the Royal Society of Arts, through which he came into contact with another famous printer, Benjamin Franklin.)

John wanted to print beautiful books, and beautiful books did he print, his most noteworthy contribution being a splendid folio Bible—even today considered one of the most beautiful Bibles ever made—which can be perceived as somewhat hypocritical given his beliefs, but there you are.

I envision John as being a rather content man in his last two decades. A woman he loved by his side, a successful business to fund his interest in his beloved printing, a life of ease and comfort, and the respect of his contemporaries—well, not all of them, but those who didn't approve of him were those John didn't much approve of either.

Despite the lavish effort he had expended on his printed version of the Bible, John remained to his death an atheist, leaving firm instructions that he was to be buried in un-consecrated ground. When John died in 1775, a bereaved Sarah ensured his last wishes were respected, burying him on the grounds of their home. Some sources say John insisted on being buried standing up, but I find that difficult to believe, so let's just assume he had a regular burial with someone uttering commemorative words while leaving any mention of God, the hereafter, or "dust to dust" out of it.

That could have been the end of Mr. Baskerville, but his house was wrecked in the Priestley Riots of the 1790s, the land was sold, and in the first decades of the nineteenth century a canal was dug through his former property, bringing his lead coffin to light in 1821. The coffin was opened, and there, lo and behold, was Mr. Baskerville, in surprisingly good condition despite almost five decades underground.

People didn't know what to do with him—the man was a confirmed atheist, so placing him in a church or a graveyard was out of the question, and apparently reburying him in a park somewhere was not considered an alternative. His coffin became a commodity with one intrepid soul earning quite a lot of money by displaying his body to whoever might want to see it. Many did. All this exposure to fresh air was not doing our dead friend any good, and as a consequence a cloying odour clung to the remains. So the coffin was nailed shut, shoved into a warehouse, and left there for several years.

At some point the warehouse was sold—including the coffin—and the new tenant, a plumber, used the coffin as a workbench for a number of years, now and then enhancing his income by allowing people a peek at the by now rather decomposed remains. Mr. Baskerville was becoming something of a deadweight (!) round the poor plumber's neck. He didn't want an unburied body in his workshop—who would?—but the available burial grounds were closed to this particular coffin, and so the plumber was more than relieved when he was approached by a certain Mr. Nott, a bookseller who was very disturbed by the whole spectacle of Mr. Baskerville's rotting corpse.

Mr. Nott devised a cunning plan. As not one single church was prepared to allow Mr. Baskerville to rest in their precincts, he decided to smuggle the coffin into his own private family vault, located in Christ Church. Picture the scene before you. It is dark—it has to be—the lead coffin weighs a ton—it must—the bribed warden is standing by the door hissing that they must hurry—easy to say when you're not doing the carrying—and on top of that it was probably raining—it always rains in England when you least need it. Whatever the case, the mission succeeded, the coffin was safely stowed in the vault, and while Mr. Baskerville might be rotating in disgust at being on consecrated ground, no one was around to hear his protests. Everyone could relax—until the church was razed to the ground several years later.

As per today, Mr. Baskerville's coffin—or what is left of it— therefore resides in the Warstone Lane Catacombs. Being an atheist, Mr. Baskerville did not aspire to life after death, and so we must assume (hope) he is blissfully unaware of the adventures his remains have lived through.

So where does the hound come into all this? Well, apparently Conan Doyle spent quite some time in Birmingham and must have heard about the flamboyant Mr. Baskerville. Why he chose to name his fictitious beast after him is unclear, but I guess this rather reflects a liking for the name than any attempt to pin the qualities of a hound on John Baskerville. After all, that would have been very unfair; a man with so much passion for the printed word must have been a decent sort, no matter that he lived in sin, died in sin, and cared not one whit what others might think about him.

Next time I catch the tail end of a radio programme, I might decide not to listen. But on the other hand, had I not done so, I would never have come upon the intriguing, energetic Mr. John Baskerville. That would have been a loss—at least for me.

Colour My Tableware Bristol Blue

By MIKE RENDELL

THE CITY OF BRISTOL, LYING A HUNDRED MILES TO THE WEST OF LONDON, HAS BEEN famous for many things over the centuries. In the Middle Ages it was a significant port, and the city was second in size and importance only to London. It was from Bristol that the explorer John Cabot sailed off on board *The Matthew*, returning later with the news that he had discovered "new found land" (Newfoundland, now part of Canada). Later, in the Victorian era it became irretrievably linked with the import of tobacco (the huge bonded warehouses still remain) and with the activities of Isambard Kingdom Brunel (Clifton Suspension Bridge, the Great Western Railway and the *SS Great Britain*). But in the eighteenth century the city was famous for something totally different: the manufacture of glass. Indeed the city gave its name to a particular type of glass—Bristol Blue—although much of the blue glassware was actually made elsewhere, and Bristol itself produced vast quantities of clear glass (used in bottles, windows etc.) as well as the brilliantly coloured rich blue glass used in decorative tableware.

How did this come about? There are records to show that small quantities of blue glass medicine bottles were being manufactured in Bristol in the middle of the seventeenth century. The underlying glass-making skills flourished due to a huge local demand: the fine new houses in the city and in nearby Bath all needed large quantities of glazing. Indeed it has been estimated that over fifty per cent of all glass used in England in the eighteenth century was produced in Bristol (to say nothing of the glass exported to the colonies). Added to this was the demand for bottles to cope with the burgeoning wine trade. Harveys and Averys were both wine shippers based in Bristol with their roots in the 1790s.

At some stage the manufacturing process received a huge boost with the (English) invention of the conical chimney, enabling noxious gases from the furnaces to be drawn upwards and out into the atmosphere. Coal needed to fire the furnaces was readily available—it was mined in many areas around the city. The choking and often dangerous conditions in which the men worked started to improve and the cone-shaped kilns started appearing all over the city—at one stage there may have been as many as sixty, and a commentator at the time remarked that in Bristol there were as many glass chimneys as church spires. Only one chimney remains (or at least in part) as The Kiln Restaurant in what used to be the Ladbroke Dragonara hotel near St. Mary Redcliffe. I believe it is now known as The Ramada Bristol City, but for all I know it will soon be re-designated as the Hilton Sheraton Hyatt Holiday Inn....

Churning out window glass and bottle glass established the skill and manufacturing base, and it was from this base that the next phase took off: the manufacture of lead crystal (then known as Flint Glass). The process had been invented by the chemist George Ravenscroft in the 1670s. He discovered that adding lead gave the glass a harder, more brilliant, finish—one which could be engraved to give a sharp image. Lead was available from the nearby Mendip hills, where it had been extracted since Roman times. For a time factories had to choose between making either window glass or Flint Glass—they were prohibited from combining the two because up until 1845 Flint Glass was taxed at a much higher rate. Excise Men toured the factories to make sure that no Flint Glass was produced unless the tax was paid. One effect of this was to make it more logical for the Flint Glass to move "up-market" with smaller factories producing high class products. This in turn meant links were established between the glass manufacturers and the skilled craftsmen needed to engrave and decorate the glassware.

It is at this juncture that two men appeared on the scene to transform the City's glass-making reputation. The first was the Bristol merchant and potter named Richard Champion. He used the glass-making technology to develop a recipe for making porcelain. This he patented and then approached the chemist William Cookworthy—he wanted a way of emulating the blue-on-white porcelain of the Far East. Cookworthy knew of the cobalt oxide, known as smalt, which was being mined at the Royal Saxon Cobalt Works in Saxony. When production ceased in around 1753, Cookworthy bought the exclusive rights to all remaining smalt stocks, and over the next twenty years they were brought into England by ship into just one port—Bristol.

And so it was that the Flint Glass makers of Bristol suddenly found themselves with easy access to the mineral which they could mix with the lead glass to make a beautiful soft-blue material. Other glass makers in other cities had to buy the cobalt from Cookworthy in Bristol, and this helped give rise to its name—Bristol Blue.

Into this scene entered a man who had no previous background in glass making, one Lazarus Jacob. He was from a Jewish family and had come to England from Frankfurt in Germany around the middle of the century; he was a wheeler-dealer, selling linen and bankruptcy stock. It looks as though he married outside the faith (and quite possibly into a local glass-making family) and by the 1760s had established glassworks in Temple Street Bristol. The first reference to him in the Bristol Journal is in February 1771 when Lazarus is described as a *"glass cutter opposite Temple Church"*. Lazarus died in 1791, but the business was taken over by his son Isaac Jacob who in 1805 advertised his newly completed *"Non Such Flint Glass manufactory"*. Trade boomed phenomenally as demand for this luxury tableware soared—George III was one of his patrons. With the Royal Warrant came fame and, for a while, fortune. And what made the Jacobs family famous—and uniquely popular with collectors today—is that they introduced the idea of signing each piece individually. This had never been done before.

For perhaps thirty years decorating your table with Bristol blue glass was *de rigeur*—blue decanters for cognac, rum, and gin, blue cruet sets, blue coolers (holding iced water, with drinking glasses suspended round the edge so that the bowl of each glass was kept chilled), blue finger-rising bowls beautifully decorated with gold Greek key motifs, and blue wine glasses.

In time, Isaac over-expanded the business. It is not clear whether the import of smalt ceased because of the Napoleonic Wars or because supplies became exhausted. But cease it did. Added to this, Isaac had made some disastrous business loans—friends defaulted and left him with huge liabilities. At the same time, he had started work on building a huge house at great expense at nearby Weston Super Mare. Up until then Weston was little more than a fishing village on the mud banks of the River Severn, but it had started to become a popular resort, and Isaac was determined that his house, Belvedere, would impress. In practice he was forced to sell it as soon as it was finished, but his creditors were circling, and he was declared bankrupt shortly afterwards. He died a broken man in 1835.

Nowadays Bristol blue is eminently collectable. Replica glassware is still being made in Bristol, and there is a small exhibition of items made by Lazarus and Isaac Jacob in the Bristol Museum.

WHY THE ENGLISH TOOK TO TEA

By DEBORAH SWIFT

I WOULD CERTAINLY NOT HAVE BEEN ABLE TO FINISH ANY OF MY BOOKS WITHOUT MY regular top-up of that quintessentially English drink, tea. I have inherited a number of teapots from my mother, and tea drinking has always been a big part of my family life.

Of course tea is not really English at all; it came first from China and later was introduced to India by the British as a way of supplying the British Empire with a cheaper product.

At the end of the seventeenth century almost nobody in England drank tea, but by the end of the next century nearly everyone from King to commoner did. In 1699 six tons were imported, but by the turn of the eighteenth century eleven thousand tons were imported annually!

The sudden enthusiasm for tea can be attributed to a number of factors—the first of which was the King's marriage to Catherine of Braganza. Her enormous dowry, suited to her position as daughter of King John IV of Portugal, included the trading posts of Tangier and Bombay, a fortune in gold bullion, and—a large chest of tea.

Catherine loved her tea and drank it from delicate thimble-sized cups. This tea-drinking caught on like wild-fire amongst the aristocracy leading to many ladies also demanding this new elegant drink.

Because women were excluded from coffee shops, drinking tea also became sociable, particularly amongst women, and in 1717, Thomas Twining of Devereux Court, who already owned a coffee shop, opened up a tea shop to furnish women with this fashionable and popular commodity.

Tea was still so expensive that ladies could not trust their servants to buy the tea for them as it would mean entrusting them with large sums of cash. So now the ladies could take a sedan to the shop carrying their tea caddies which were equipped with locks to prevent pilfering. They were able to buy directly from the shop or stay a while there to meet their friends and enjoy tea freshly prepared and served in porcelain dishes.

A whole ritual then evolved as a means of demonstrating how sophisticated and cultured you were. Books and articles were written on the etiquette of serving tea, and small snacks were introduced to cleanse the palate between tastings. Great effort was made to ensure the dishes and plates were as dainty and genteel as possible and the food as refined. Bread and butter was the usual accompaniment, cut up very small. This later became a whole afternoon meal, our Afternoon Tea.

Tea Gardens then opened up, a place where women could meet and also a respectable place to meet members of the opposite sex. The first to open was in Vauxhall Gardens in 1732. An article about Vauxhall Pleasure Gardens can be found on the Museum of London Blog.

Of course none of this would have been possible without the British East India

Company which during King Charles' reign grew to become a manifestation of British power in the East Indies. The first tea imports were from Bantam (now in Indonesia) in 1669, and it was part of a cargo of pepper, silk, and other textiles. As the company grew it managed to establish trading posts in China and, despite warring with the Dutch, was able to retain control over the importation of tea.

For the poor, tea became an essential once people realised that it improved health and productivity. It was healthy because of its natural anti-bacterial effects (of course this was not understood then) and the fact that it was made with boiled water. It was also more suited to a labouring workforce as it was a stimulant and, unlike ale, would not send you to sleep!

SOURCES

Hoh, Erling. The True History of Tea. Thames and Hudson, 2009.

Standage, Tom. A History of the World in Six Glasses. Walker Publishing Company, 2006.

Rose, Sarah. For All the Tea in China. Arrow, 2010.

TAKING TO THE SKY

By LAURIE ALICE EAKES

FROM AT LEAST AS FAR BACK AS THE ORIGINS OF THE GREEK MYTHS, FLIGHT HAS FASCInated man (and woman). Many tried and pretty much all failed—until the hot air balloon.

No one is quite sure who invented the idea of filling a bag with hot air and attaching a "car" (a.k.a. the basket) for flight. As with many inventions, speculation and half-formed theories abound from the Chinese to the people of the Nazca culture in Peru. Europeans, however, made ballooning a reality to the early modern world.

In 1783, two Frenchmen, Jean-François Pilâtre de Rozier and the Marquis François d'Arlandes, took to the sky in the first untethered flight. Before this, many men had sailed aloft while the balloon remained attached to the earth by ropes; therefore, the highest flight was only 80 feet and not precisely flying.

Flying is rather a misnomer with ballooning. In truth, all one can do in a balloon is drift. With favorable wind currents, you may even get where you want to go. Balloons, however, are not steerable. Many have tried to find a way to do so using paddles and sails, but none proved effective. Balloonists achieved some sense of ordered direction by raising and lowering the level of the balloon in order to find the most favorable wind currents.

In the early years, before propane tanks provided the gases, going far, even with favorable currents, was not particularly feasible for the simple fact that the balloons needed to carry fuel, and a great deal of it. The air did not stay in the balloon due to the lack of airtight fabric. At the high elevations at which people flew, the air cooled off rather quickly, and the balloon began to sink.

Some chemical compounds helped with the air seepage. These included rather combustible chemicals such as bird lime, which was an oily substance used by hunters to make birds stick to tree branches. When mixed and added to linseed oil, aeronauts cooked it to the right consistency as a sealant. It worked fairly well, but if it got near fire...poof!

Balloonists also double-stitched the silk of the balloon fabric which helped the seals, but all that was still not good enough. The hot air needed constant replenishment.

Those men and women who took to the skies went up in a wooden basket with live fire, straw, iron shavings, and acid.

A brazier held the fire, which the aeronaut fed regularly with straw to keep it going. If that fire extinguished, the air would cool, the balloon would sink, and the passengers would likely die in a crash. If the brazier spilled...well, fire was a very real and too often deadly possibility.

Above the fire, the balloonist suspended a beaker filled with iron shavings and acid. When heated, this toxic combination formed hydrogen. That hydrogen rose from the beaker to the balloon through a wax-coated canvas tube.

Ballooning is still not precisely a safe form of flight. Using a propane tank at ten thousand feet above the earth holds its risks, and balloons are still subject to capricious wind currents. But propane seems positively foolproof compared to going aloft with live fire and acid—just the idea of going aloft with live fire and creating hydrogen, a highly flammable element, makes me queasy. Yet the men and, yes, women who pioneered balloon flight considered the risk worth the experience and potential for navigation.

Sadly, especially for those who died in the trying, ballooning never became a viable form of transportation. With the need to carry live fire and fuel and being subject to the direction of the wind, no one could, for example, sail over enemy territory during a war. Balloons just did not have that kind of range. But the aeronauts let mankind know that flying was not in the realm of dreams, but a real possibility.

"A Very Fine Cat, a Very Fine Cat Indeed..."

By GRACE ELLIOT

LEXICOGRAPHER AND WRITER, DR. JOHNSON, WAS A CAT LOVER. IT WAS WHILST HE WAS in residence at 17 Gough Square, London that he owned his most well-known cat, Hodge. To this day a statue of Hodge, appropriately seated on a dictionary, forms part of a memorial to the great man at the far end of the square where he once lived.

Indeed, such was Johnson's love of cats that the diarist and biographer, James Boswell, thought to record it. "*Nor would it be just...to omit the fondness which he* [Johnson] *shewed for animals which he had taken under his protection.*"

This kindness extended to visiting the fish market in person, in order to select the best oysters for his cat since Johnson didn't want to put the servants out and cause resentment against Hodge.

> *I never shall forget the indulgence with which he treated Hodge, his cat: for whom he himself used to go out and buy oysters, lest the servants having that trouble should take a dislike to the poor creature.*

Boswell must indeed have been a firm friend and admirer of Johnson, since he himself disliked cats and was most probably allergic to them.

> *I am, unluckily one of those who have an antipathy to a cat, so that I am uneasy when in the room with one; and I own, frequently suffered a good deal from the presence of this same Hodge.*

Johnson, however was unstinting in his affection for his feline companions, as Boswell goes on to record.

> *I recollect him* [Hodge] *one day scrambling up Dr Johnson's breast, apparently with much satisfaction, while my friend smiling and half-whistling, rubbed down his back and pulled him by the tail.*

Poor Boswell seems to have at least made an effort to fit in with his cat-loving friend as this excerpt recounts.

> *When I observed he was a fine cat...* [Johnson] *saying 'Why yes, Sir, but I have had cats better than this.' And then as if perceiving Hodge to be out of countenance, adding, 'but he is a very fine cat, a very fine cat indeed.'*

And the final words go to Percival Stockdale in this excerpt from his elegy on the death of Johnson's favourite cat:

Shall not his [Hodge's] worth a poem fill,
Who never thought, nor uttered ill;
Who, by his master when caressed
Warmly his gratitude expressed;
And never failed his thanks to purr,
Whene'er he stroked his sable fur?
The general conduct if we trace
Of our articulating race,
Hodge's example we shall find
A keen reproof of human kind.
He lived in town, yet ne'er got drunk,
Nor spent one farthing on a punk;
He never filched a single groat,
Nor bilked a tailor of a coat;
His garb when first he drew his breath
His dress through life, his shroud in death.

A Painful Transition for Some, a Benefit for Others: The Enclosure Acts

By J.A. BEARD

Not so large, I dare say, as many people suppose. I do not mean to complain, however; it is undoubtedly a comfortable one, and I hope, will in time be better. The inclosure of Norland Common, now carrying on, is a most serious drain. And then I have made a little purchase within this half year— East Kingham Farm, you must remember the place, where old Gibson used to live. The land was so very desirable for me in every respect, so immediately adjoining my own property, that I felt it my duty to buy it. I could not have answered it to my conscience to let it fall into any other hands. A man must pay for his convenience, and it has cost me a vast deal of money.
— John Dashwood, in Jane Austen's *Sense and Sensibility*, Chapter 33

MR. DASHWOOD'S COMMENTS DON'T INITIALLY SEEM TO BE ALL THAT IMPORTANT IN the grander discussion of the nature of socio-economic disparity and economic realignment in Georgian and Regency England. His off-hand mention of *"the inclosure of Norland Common"*, however, touches upon a rather significant series of land reforms that had major impact on the rural lower classes in England.

Enclosure/inclosure was the process by which land was consolidated, separated from neighboring properties, and deeded to private owners. The name comes from the way these lands were marked off from others: enclosure with a wall, hedge, fence, or other obvious marker of division. Much of this process involved consolidation of irregular areas into more contiguous lands, but there were also cases of just simple conversion from common use to private use. The combination of consolidation, demarcation of borders, and simple ownership assignment eliminated any ambiguity about who owned what and effectively eliminated most common-use land in England.

For a good chunk of English history, an open system was in place in many (but certainly not all) areas where peasants could make use of common-use land for grazing, small-scale planting, small-scale forestry, and similar subsistence activities. Although various minor cases of enclosure occurred throughout the centuries, the process really picked up speed during the Georgian era with a huge number of Enclosure Acts being passed by Parliament between the mid-eighteenth century and the mid-nineteenth century. While these were acts passed by the legislature, it should be noted that the process of acquiring enclosed land during most of the Georgian era involved a private citizen petitioning Parliament (until the mid-nineteenth century at least), and so many of these Parliamentary acts were the culmination, in a sense, of private concerns and petitions rather than autonomous, top-down decisions by the government. Even excluding the major Enclosure Acts, many smaller-scale private acts were passed by Parliament at the direct petition request of individuals.

It should be noted that in some cases enclosure was done to basically cut down on illegal use of private property. A man might own a swath of land, but a lack of clear borders allowed people to come in certain areas, pick berries, graze their livestock, et cetera. That being said, in other cases there were centuries-old common areas that were destroyed by enclosure.

The act of enclosure, given that it removed many economic/food-related rights from peasants in local villages and nearby areas, had widespread secondary effects. Once land was controlled by an owner, usage, if allowed, would require rent, which poorer families may have not been able to afford. Whereas previously they could potentially get by making limited use of common land, many now had to seek out employment. Arguably, without the Enclosure Acts, the huge number of cheap laborers necessary to help fuel the Industrial Revolution in England would not have been available.

Even if one is not particularly politically inclined, it's easy to see how these acts might be viewed with suspicion by some. A person (and many have) could make the argument that formerly self-sufficient people were forced to go seek out work, sometimes far from home (thus disrupting village life), whereas only a small percentage of individuals found themselves in a stronger economic position.

The often unpleasant labor conditions of the early Industrial Revolution or the low-security life that accompanied service were arguably tolerated because of the flood of workers desperate for new means to sustain themselves. Was enclosure nothing more than people of superior means consolidating resources and land at the expense of people of lesser means? Some argue that rather strenuously.

On the other hand, the ostensible logic behind enclosure was in some cases simple protection of property rights and in other cases about improving efficiency of the land. Some historians suggest that by pushing people out of low-level subsistence farming, enclosure may have ultimately contributed to greater social mobility potential in the long run. General improved economic efficiency combined with the slowly eroding social resistance to things like trade and investment among gentry arguably led to a consolidation, enrichment, and investment cycle that benefited the nation as a whole. Under this argument, the workers flooding into the factories of the Industrial Revolution, in turn, expanded the economy and helped shift the poorer English away from having effectively zero chance at social mobility.

It's also undeniable that in many areas over-use and agricultural inefficiency were the legitimate motivation for enclosure. This is the so-called tragedy of the commons. In such a situation, as no one involved in the use of land/resource has true ownership, they will not take special measures to conserve it because others using the resources may not. This cycle of use and self-interest leads to the depletion of the resource. The various people who supported enclosure often based their argument on economic reasons (fencing associated with enclosure allowed high-value pasturage), agricultural efficiency, and land restoration.

Did this mean that every enclosed area was actually some horribly depleted over-farmed and over-logged deadland that needed the help of the gentry to rescue it? Doubtful. While there were areas where this was the case, it's not as if during the process of enclosure the government first did some sort of complicated land-use analysis. Mostly they were responding to petitions filed by people with enough wealth to hire lawyers to file petitions.

Many enclosed areas had been successfully maintained for centuries. Though, as noted above, in some cases enclosure was about making property borders more concrete rather than a more active attempt to expand land holdings. The nature and appropriateness (depending on one's point of view) of enclosure likely varied by case.

Regardless if you feel enclosure was some sort of land-grab by the elite or if it was a painful but necessary part of an economically maturing England that benefited everyone, it most definitely played a role in changing the nature of the English countryside and working classes.

DEATH IN THE
EIGHTEENTH CENTURY

By MIKE RENDELL

I RECENTLY CAME ACROSS THE BILL SUBMITTED TO MY ANCESTOR RICHARD HALL BY THE Funeral Director on the occasion of the death of his first wife Eleanor in 1780. The undertakers (that is to say, the company which undertook the arrangements...) were John Cooper & Co. It gives some idea of what was involved in a funeral in the Georgian era in the latter part of the eighteenth century.

Eleanor Hall had died in her 47th year—she got up and had breakfast as normal on 11 January 1780 at her home at One London Bridge, had a splitting headache at midday, and was dead by six in the evening. In all probability she suffered a brain haemorrhage. It must have been a terrible shock for Richard, who had married Eleanor nearly 27 years earlier, and for their three grown-up children, who all lived at the property.

Richard records her death in his diary:

> Oh the affliction of this Day. My Dear and Affectionate Wife was suddenly seiz'd with a pain in her head after Twelve at Noon, which issued in a Fit; no Prescription of Physician Avail'd.

Richard was devastated and made a beautiful cut-out in paper as a memorial. The memento is only just over one inch across and is extraordinarily delicate.

He would have employed the firm of John Cooper & Co. to make all the arrangements for the funeral, which was to take place at Bunhill Burial Grounds (where many Dissenters were buried). Richard and Eleanor were both Baptists, and as an additional incentive to choose Bunhill, it was where both her parents had been buried back in 1754. The expenses even included opening up the family vault and constructing a tent over it so as to keep prying eyes at bay.

The invoice starts by showing the actual funeral as taking place on January 18, exactly one week after Eleanor's death.

To start with, the actual coffin and furniture:

- *Inside Elm Coffin lined and ruffled with fine Crape and a mattress (£1/11/6)*
- *A Superfine Sheet, Shroud and Pillow (£1/15/00)*
- *An outside lead coffin with plate of Inscription (£4/10/00)*
- *An Elm case covered with fine Black Cloth, finish'd in the best Manner with black nails and drape, Lead Plate Cherubim handles, lead plate and wrought Gripes [that is to say, grips] (£5/10/00)*

Then there were the extras:

- *4 Men going in with Lead Coffin and Case (10/-)*
- *7 Tickets and Delivering—7 shillings* [these would have been official invitations to attend the funeral service, sent out to close friends]
- *Hanging the Shop and Stair-case in Mourning* [in other words, draping black cloth over the entire ground floor and stairs of One London Bridge, from where the funeral procession started its sad and solemn journey]
- *Use of 16 double silver'd sconces and Wax Lights for ditto*
- *2 Porters with Gowns and Staves with Silk cover & hats & gloves*
- *The best Pall* [i.e. the cloth spread over the coffin]

There then follow a few items which are hard to decipher. What looks like:

- *A coffin lid of black feathers and man in hatband and gloves*
- *Crape hatbands*
- *Silk ditto*
- *Rich three quarter Armageen* [a type of material] *scarves for a Minister*
- *12 Pairs of Men's laced kid gloves*
- *2 Pairs of Women's ditto*
- *6 Pairs of Men's and Women's plain and one pair Mitts*
- *Use of 11 Gent Cloaks*
- *A Hearse and 4 coaches with Setts of horses*
- *Velvet Coverings and black feathers for hearse and six*
- *10 Hearse pages with truncheons , 6 of ye bearers*
- *10 Pairs of gloves and favours for ditto*
- *Eight coach pages with Hatbands and gloves*
- *Use of 5 Coachmans cloaks*
- *10 pairs of gloves for ditto and Postillion*
- *Paid at Bunhill for opening the Vault and for Tent*
- *Fetch and carrying Company*
- *Turnpike and drink for the Men*

The total came to £51 8s. 6d. You would need to multiply by perhaps seventy to give a modern day equivalent (i.e £3500 or $5250). On the other hand, a farm worker might have had to scrape by on half that amount for a whole year, so it is fair to assume that the funeral was something of a statement: the Hall family have arrived, and we can afford to put on a good show.

It must have made a sombre and imposing sight as the funeral cortege wended its way north of the Hall household on its one mile journey to the graveside. As Richard noted in his diary that night, it had been *"a very damp day, some part Foggy, not very Cold."* You can almost see the black horses with their black plumes, attended by page boys dressed from tip to toe in black, the heavy coats of the pall bearers, the coffin lined with black velvet....

AULD LANG SYNE

By LAUREN GILBERT

NEW YEAR'S EVE—THE DAY WHEN MOST OF US LOOK BACK AT THE OLD YEAR PASSING away, celebrating the good things that happened, mourning our losses, and generally taking stock. We also look forward to the New Year approaching, preparing to shake off the dust and move forward. Parties and celebrations are the order of the day, a happy way to speed the old year out and the New Year in. Many traditions are involved in the New Year's celebration, and one of these is the singing of "Auld Lang Syne."

The lyrics of "Auld Lang Syne" are attributed to Scottish poet Robert Burns (1759-1796). However, this is a much older song than we really know. Variations of "Auld Lang Syne" abound. Over the years, as is the way with many traditional songs, the lyrics and melodies have varied to suit the time and those singing it. Although not published, a written record of lyrics for this song (then a lament about a faithless lover) was found in the Commonplace Book of James Crichton, 2nd Viscount Frendraught, for 1662. James Watson included a version in his *Choice Collection of Comic and Serious Scots Poems*, published in 1711. Allan Ramsay also included "Auld Lang Syne" in *A Collection of Songs* published in 1724.

In September of 1793, Robert Burns wrote a letter to George Thomson, an editor working on an anthology of songs. Burns commented on songs that Thompson had proposed for the anthology and suggested that Thompson include one more, which was "Auld Lang Syne." Burns indicated that he wrote down the words while listening to an old man sing them. Burns' lyrics appeared in Volume 5 of James Johnson's *Scots Musical Museum*, published in 1796, and are indicated as *"old verses with corrections or additions."* The music published with it then was different, and Burns apparently did not care for it. When Thomson's anthology *Select Collection Of Original Scottish Airs* was published in 1799 (after Burns' death), he changed the music to that which we know now. The Morgan Library and Museum website has a wonderful online exhibition where you can look at and listen to a reading and the musical variations of this song.

"Auld Lang Syne" was associated with the Scottish celebration of Hogmanay (a traditional New Year's event). Whether it was because it was a traditional song or because of its theme of remembrance, it gradually became associated with the New Year's events in the United Kingdom, and it spread to the colonies. However, it was not a "popular" song in the modern sense until 1929 when Guy Lombardo adopted "Auld Lang Syne" for his annual New Year's Eve broadcasts on radio and then television.

Depending on the version of choice, the number of verses varies, and the meaning of the song can be obscure because of the dialect. Commonly, the first verse and refrain is what we sing as the ball drops at midnight. I thought it would be nice to include the first verse and refrain with some clarification:

Should auld acquaintance be forgot,
And never brought to mind?
Should auld acquaintance be forgot,
And days of auld lang syne?
Chorus:
For auld lang syne, my dear,
For auld lang syne.
We'll tak a cup of kindness yet,
For auld lang syne.

"Auld"—old. "Auld lang syne"—literally old long since, by-gone days, old times. "Tak"—take.

SOURCES

"Auld Lang Syne—The Story of a Song." *The Morgan Library & Museum Online Exhibitions.* http://www.themorgan.org/exhibitions/online/AuldLangSyne/default.asp

Barger, Michael. "History Behind Auld Lang Syne: The New Year's Eve Song." *Yahoo! Voices,* 12/8/2008. http://voices.yahoo.com/history-behind-auld-lang-syne-years-eve-song-2278848.html

Koster, Kristen. "A Regency Primer on Christmastide & New Year's." *Kristen Koster blog,* 12/27/2011. http://www.kristenkoster.com/2011/12/a-regency-primer-on-christmastide-new-years

Prentice, Claire. "'Auld Lang Syne': New Year's song has a convoluted history." *Washington Post Style Section* online, 12/30/2011. http://articles.washingtonpost.com/2011-12-30/lifestyle/35287090_1_auld-lang-syne-auld-lang-syne-burns

"Scottish Hogmanay Customs and Traditions at New Year." *AboutAberdeen.com.* http://www.aboutaberdeen.com/hogmanaycustoms.php

Strawberry Hill House: A Neo-Gothic Castle Which Heralded an Architectural Revolution 1747-80s

By MIKE RENDELL

In 2010 a remarkable house, situated southwest of London, emerged from its chrysalis of scaffolding and protective cladding and was revealed in all its original glory: Strawberry Hill House. It has been likened to a wedding cake on account of its beautiful white exterior finish called "harling" (a lime and pebble stucco render). It may be decorated like icing, but to me it is altogether lighter—more like a confection made of whipped cream! It really is a masterpiece, and its resurrection is all the more remarkable because by the end of the twentieth century the place was in a terribly dilapidated state. Three cheers for English Heritage and the Lottery Fund, who between them raised the majority of the nine million pounds needed to restore the building which kicked off the neo-Gothic movement!

I cannot claim that I am enamoured with what Victorian Gothic became (think of the heavy, over-ornate architecture of the Houses of Parliament) but I have to say that its Georgian precursor of Strawberry Hill Gothic (as the style became known) is astonishingly delicate, vibrant—and fun!

The style is down to the vision and verve of Horace Walpole, who bought what was an eighty-year-old villa near the banks of the River Thames at Twickenham in 1747. The previous owner was a well-known shopkeeper who sold toys and trinkets by the name of Mrs. Chevenix, and Horace Walpole described his purchase as *"a little plaything that I got out of Mrs. Chevenix's shop and is the prettiest bauble you ever saw."* Over the next fifty years he transformed it into a Gothic fantasy—into what he whimsically described as *"the castle I am building of my ancestors".*

Walpole used it as his summer residence. In those days it was half a day's ride from the centre of London, eleven miles away. It was not in a particularly fashionable area, but Walpole created a wondrous confection to impress and amuse his friends—and to house his astonishing collection of books, paintings, furniture, coins, and historical artifacts.

He could hardly have come from a better-connected family: his father Robert was the first British Prime Minister, and Robert had built his rather solid ancestral home in Palladian style at Houghton Hall in Norfolk. Horace was the youngest son, and he did what was expected of him: he went to Eton, went up to Cambridge, failed to take his final examinations, and then set off on the Grand Tour for a couple of years. He returned in 1741 and immediately entered Parliament, but his main interest seems to have been the acquisition of paintings and artworks. Strawberry Hill was his chance to showcase the collection; he had some 4000 items including drawings by Holbein, paintings by Sir Joshua Reynolds, Renaissance armour, and *objets d'art*. The architectural symmetry so favoured by contemporary architects disappeared out the window to be replaced by crenellations, gothic window frames, Tudor turrets, Jacobean chimneys, and details from his imagination.

Horace Walpole never intended it to be built to last—he himself doubted if it would remain more than ten years after his lifetime. Why? Because it was jerry-built, a piece of froth, a sham. Where others used plasterwork Walpole used papier mache, but to what effect! The interiors were stunning, and it is thanks to a brilliant restoration programme that they have been put back to their former glory. In all there are twenty-five show rooms which have been meticulously restored on the ground and first floors. Most significantly, all the cement render has been hacked off and the exterior put back to its white stucco finery.

Horace Walpole was a remarkable man—an effete, an aesthete, a dilettante, a collector, and an innovator. He died in 1797 at the age of eighty.

Of course it is a shame that none of the contents remain. In an act of cultural desecration the contents were sold off separately in 1843, although the Victoria and Albert Museum was able to track down nearly three hundred of these items in a major exhibition in 2010.

Outside, Walpole's pride and joy was his lime tree grove, and this is now being replanted. As Walpole wrote in 1753: *"it is an open grove through which you see a field which is bounded by a serpentine wood of all kind of trees and flowering shrubs and flowers"*. Nothing much can be done about the fact that the fields have been replaced with modern housing, but hopefully the gardens will soon prove to be a magnificent setting for this extraordinary creation, one which triggered off the architectural movement which dominated the ensuing century.

Strawberry Hill House is at 268 Waldegrave Road, Twickenham, TW1 4ST and is administered by the Strawberry Hill Trust.

THE BOARD OF LONGITUDE: WHAT DOES SPACEFLIGHT HAVE TO DO WITH A WATCHMAKER, JAMES BOND, AND A DEADLY SHIPWRECK?

By J.A. BEARD

IN 2004, SPACE TRAVEL ENTHUSIASTS CHEERED THE AWARDING OF THE ANSARI X PRIZE for sub-orbital flight. For those unfamiliar, the prize was awarded for a demonstration by a private entity of launching a reusable manned spacecraft into near-outer space twice within two weeks (100 kilometers). The prize itself was worth ten million dollars, but the winners of the prize, and for that matter most of the people attempting to earn the prize, ended up putting considerably more money into earning the prize for various reasons (seeking glory, seeking the attention winning the product would grant for business ventures).

The X Prize Foundation itself, which has several prizes dedicated toward impressive achievements, is simply interested in stirring innovation in particular areas that might aid humanity in general.

This is of course not a new idea. Even the Ansari X Prize itself had the goal of helping promote efforts in space by entities other than government agencies. The idea being that such efforts would lead to an expansion of private efforts into the last frontier, something that is needed given the stagnation of government programs.

That particular prize was inspired by certain aviation prizes in the twentieth century, but the idea of offering a prize to encourage people to develop technologies that would aid in travel also made an appearance in Georgian England, though in this case, it was driven by a government prize.

Now, of course, back in Georgian England, space travel and even aerial travel weren't areas that people were particularly worried about trying to crack. They had a more fundamental problem they were attempting to solve for sea-going vessels: knowing your longitude.

Of course, today, we have satellite GPS systems to deliver latitude and longitude with extreme precision. In the eighteenth century, even with centuries of maritime tradition, navigation was a far trickier affair.

Latitude, at that point, wasn't a major issue for experienced sailors as both charts and tools were available that could give fairly decent latitude readings. Without going into detail, the ability to see either the Sun at noon during the day or Polaris (the North Star) at night in general allows a determination of latitude at sea.

Determining longitude can theoretically make use of similar tools as used for latitude (which are various devices, really, just to determine the angle between the horizon and Sun or stars), however, due to the geographical (and for that matter geometric) nature of longitude, accurate determination of longitude also requires another piece of information: time.

Time has a strong relationship to longitude because the Earth rotates at fifteen longitude degrees per hour. Accordingly, if a sailor knew the time at a fixed reference location and then knew the local time, they could, through the wonders of math (or at least the wonders of a chart) figure out their longitude.

Finding out the local time wasn't typically a major problem at the time, but the fly in the ointment in the aforementioned system is knowing the time, accurately, at the used fixed reference location. Note this isn't just a matter of having a chronometer, but one that's extremely accurate, as a single degree of longitude could be a fairly decent distance in terms of kilometers (the actual distance varied relative to the distance to the poles).

Prior attempts to solve the longitude problem involved some very bright minds, including Galileo and Edmond Halley, examining the issue with a particular focus on celestial bodies. Improved sextants and the development of a method using the moon, the so-called lunar distance method had some utility in the mid-eighteenth century, but at the beginning of the eighteenth century, the longitude problem remained a critical issue, and even the later lunar distance method still had some accuracy issues.

One of the main practical methods of longitude calculation actually used at the time was dead reckoning, which involved making estimates based off course and speed in relation to a known starting point. This method is subject to severe cumulative error, and that is assuming that the navigators are keeping good records.

In addition, a lack of accurate knowledge of longitude could cause navigators to lean more on their knowledge of latitude. For example, they might establish travel until they were at the known latitude of their destination and then just sail directly toward it by maintaining latitude. This might, in many circumstances, mean they were not traveling the most direct route.

Now, one might ask, "What's the big deal? So they didn't have the most accurate navigation in the world. They got around, right? Heck, they got across the ocean to the New World."

First of all, for those not traveling the most direct route, this meant more time on the ship. If they were in the middle of the ocean, this meant issues with supplies.

Second, incorrect navigation away from the coast could be downright dangerous. This was spectacularly demonstrated in 1707 when a fleet commanded by Sir Cloudesley Shovell attempted to return from a failed naval campaign in Gibraltar.

From September to October, the fleet traveled without serious incident. Bad weather had slowly put them off course. This all came to head on October 22. The fleet, at the time, thought they were much farther west than they actually were, and, as a consequence, were not aware they were sailing right into the Isles of Scilly off the Cornish Peninsula.

By the time they realized their mistake, it was too late. The fleet struck ground. Four ships were lost and at least 1400 sailors died.

While this was not the only such disaster, it was a particularly high-profile one. Something had to be done to save the lives of English sailors. In 1714, the Longitude Act was passed, and the Board of Longitude was established. The Board offered prizes for men who could solve the longitude problem.

There were three main longitude prizes: 10,000 pounds for a method that could accurately determine longitude within sixty nautical miles, 15,000 pounds for a method for within forty nautical miles, and 20,000 pounds for a determination within thirty nautical miles.

Although it is difficult to completely accurately determine the relative inflation between 1714 and now, that still puts the rough value of the prizes in the neighborhood of tens of millions of modern pounds. So, in other words, the Board of Longitude was throwing around just as much money, in equivalent terms, as the Ansari X Prize.

Although many brilliant men tackled the problem, an autodidact carpenter and clockmaker is the man who ultimately solved the issue in a lasting and accurate way. He spent decades of his life attempting to construct accurate clocks that would allow for accurate time-keeping on the ship and keep track of the time from the reference point. Ultimately, he designed a series of large watch maritime chronometers for the purpose.

Despite the accuracy of Harrison's later devices, the Board of Longitude claimed, basically, that he'd gotten lucky. Now, there are many possible reasons for that, but two major reasons commonly cited by historians include the presence of a professional rival on the Board of Longitude at the time of certain critical tests and an academic preference for non-chronometer-based methods, as certain alternate methods, such as the lunar distance method, were viewed by the scientific establishment as being more reflective of science. There's also some suggestion that the Board may have been biased against Harrison because of his relatively humble background.

Eventually, nearing the end of his life and finding the Board intransigent, Harrison managed to appeal to King George III, who tested Harrison's most advanced watch himself in 1772 (though at the palace, not on a ship). With the king vouching for the accuracy of his devices, Parliament begrudgingly was forced to award some money to Harrison, though he was never officially awarded the Longitude Prize, even though he obtained about the same amount of money overall through various payments from Parliament. He didn't have long to enjoy it, as he died in 1776, though his family at least benefited.

As they never officially granted the prize, the Board of Longitude had no reason to close up shop, but they would officially be disbanded by Parliament in 1828.

I should briefly note that other countries also established similar sorts of longitude prizes and navigation awards. This was one of the foremost scientific and maritime issues of the seventeenth and eighteenth centuries.

As mentioned above, the lunar distance method had gained some popularity in the middle of the eighteenth century and traction over marine chronometers because it was cheaper, but ultimately Harrison's chronometers (and later marine chronometers) were more accurate, and so in the nineteenth century, chronometers came to dominate.

Even modern GPS is, ultimately, a time-based technology, as demonstrated, interestingly enough, in the James Bond movie *Tomorrow Never Dies*, where a disruption in a satellite chronometer is used by a villain to disastrous navigational effect against a Royal Navy frigate. So, Harrison definitely got the last laugh in the long run as no supervillains have yet made use of the lunar distance method for their plots.

No Lead in Your Pencil?
That's Because It's Graphite

By MIKE RENDELL

HERE IS A STORY (QUITE PROBABLY APOCRYPHAL!):

> The year—1564;
>
> The place—Grey Knotts, Seathwaite Fell in Borrowdale, near Keswick, England;
>
> The action—a tree fell down;
>
> The result—locals discovered the world's only known deposit of solid graphite in the form of black lumps of "stone" caught on the tree roots. They found that the substance was useful for marking sheep (always good to count them before you go to sleep...). Local workers were able to saw the "black lead" or plumbago as they called it into sheets and then into thin rods.

Graphite is in fact a form of carbon and has nothing to do with lead. To start with, the material was wrapped in string or sheep wool to facilitate holding it, but then in the 1700s an Italian carpenter decided to sandwich the graphite between two bits of juniper wood, and the modern pencil was born. It never has contained lead (although possibly it gets its reputation from the lead stylus used by the Romans to etch marks on wax tablets).

For many years there was no other source of graphite apart from in the Lake District—and even today it has never been found as a solid block. The mining area was requisitioned by The Crown because it was found that the material was useful in lining moulds used to manufacture cannonballs and the substance was considered too valuable to "waste" on mere pencils. So the locals started smuggling it out....

I still have a pencil belonging to my ancestor Richard Hall, from the 1780s, linked to a small "aide memoire"—thin sheets of ivory held together by a clasp and holding a tiny pencil within a leather loop. It is strange to think that 250 years later it is possible to pin-point exactly where the pencil came from! There is still a pencil making tradition in Cumbria (Derwent started in 1832), and a Museum of Pencils exists at Southey Works in Keswick.

In the eighteenth century the lack of available solid graphite caused a problem, not least to the French who were peeved when the wars with England towards the end of the century meant that supplies were cut off. A chemist called Nicolas Jacques Conté (who later went on to be an officer in Napoleon's army) wanted to do something about it—and he succeeded. Conté experimented with mixing ground graphite (which was found in France) with differing quantities of fine clays before baking it in a kiln. He discovered that this enabled the hardness of the pencil to be controlled—a fact for which artists have been eternally grateful. His patent was taken out in 1795 and the process is essentially the same as is used today.

Conté can claim to be the father of the modern pencil, but he is not the only one. The title is also claimed by a German cabinet maker, one Kaspar Faber, who in 1761 in a village called Stein, just outside Nuremberg, started to insert strips of graphite between pieces of wood. He sold his pencils in the local market and 250 years later the business of Faber-Castell is still going strong.

And the eraser, the pencil's faithful companion? Charles Marie de la Condamine, a French scientist and explorer, was the first European to bring back the natural substance called "India" rubber. He brought a sample to the Institute de France in Paris in 1736.

In 1780 the scientist Joseph Priestley noted that rubber erased pencil marks from paper. Previously, bread crumbs would have been used for that purpose. The same year (1770) saw the first commercial sale of rubber erasers when an English engineer, Edward Naime, started selling them. Naime claims he accidentally picked up a piece of rubber instead of his lump of bread and discovered the possibilities.

However, rubber was not an easy substance to work with because it went bad very easily—just like food, rubber would rot. It was not until 1839 that Charles Goodyear discovered a way of "curing" rubber, thereby creating a lasting and useable material. He called his process vulcanization, after Vulcan, the Roman god of fire. The process was patented by Goodyear in 1844.

A dozen years later an American came up with the idea of "marrying" the eraser on to the pencil and patented the idea, only to have it challenged by A. W. Faber (the company founded by the son of the original Faber mentioned earlier). It was held that merely combining two items already in existence did not in itself constitute something "new", and the patent failed.

And why is it traditional (at least in America) for pencils to be yellow? After all, it is estimated that about three quarters of the 2.8 billion American pencils produced each year are this colour. Why? Initially, it was because the early pencil manufacturers in that country found an alternative source for graphite—in China. Yellow was a Chinese colour symbolising nobility and rarity, and the yellow caught on as a way of showing the origin and superior quality of the "lead" in those pencils. Now, it is more a case of being as common as muck!

Propelling pencils (in America they are called mechanical pencils) differ in that the graphite is not attached to the holder, but is pushed out often with a spring or click mechanism. The earliest known example was found on the wreck of the ship HMS *Pandora* which went down in 1791. It sank with the loss of 31 crew—as well as four of the mutineers from the *Bounty* who had been recaptured by the ship's crew and kept on board the vessel in a cage or box ("Pandora's Box"). Quite who the propelling pencil belonged to is not known. It was not until 1822 that a patent was granted (to Sampson Morden and John Isaac Hawkins) for a refillable pencil with a lead propelling mechanism.

And the sharpener? At first penknives were used to sharpen pencils (literally, a knife which was used to sharpen quill feathers to make pens). In 1828, Bernard Lassimone, a French mathematician applied for a patent on an invention to sharpen pencils. However, it was not until 1847 that Therry des Estwaux first invented the manual pencil sharpener as we know it.

I rather like the development of the sharpener called the "Love Sharpener." John Lee Love came up with the simple, portable pencil sharpener that many artists use. The pencil is put into the opening of the sharpener and rotated by hand, and the shavings stay inside the sharpener. He patented his idea in 1897. So we move on from having no lead in your pencil, to the introduction of the Love Sharpener....

THE LEARNED PIG

BY GRACE ELLIOT

DURING THE EIGHTEENTH CENTURY THERE WAS A CRAZE FOR PERFORMING ANIMALS: dancing dogs, musical cats, counting horses, acting canaries, and retrieving tortoise—but most popular of all was The Learned Pig.

A shoemaker turned animal trainer, Samuel Bisset owned the pig that started a craze for porcine performers. By all accounts Bisset was an interesting character with acts such as a cat orchestra and a tortoise that could fetch things like a dog (albeit very slowly!). Always on the lookout for "the next big thing", at a market in Belfast Bisset paid three shillings for a black piglet and trained him over the next two years.

A poet, Robert Southey, with an interest in learned pigs (how niche is that!) interviewed a man who lived near Bisset's yard about the animal's treatment.

> He told me he never saw the keeper beat him; but that, if he did not perform
> his lessons well, he used to threaten to take off his red waistcoat - for the pig
> was proud of his dress.

The Learned Pig first made his debut in 1783 in Dublin. He knelt and bowed, used cardboard letters to spell out names, and could point to the married people in the audience. The act succeeded Bisset's wildest dreams, and it seemed the couple were destined to be welcomed in novelty seeking London.

But all did not end well for Bisset, who was attacked in Dublin and although he made it to England, he died en route to London—according to his biographer as a result of his beating.

So convincing was the pig's performance that some religious people claimed he was possessed and *"corresponding with the devil".* Others saw it as proof that the soul could migrate, suspecting that: *"The spirit of the grunting Philosopher might once have animated a man."*

Whilst the secret of the Learned Pig's training died with Bisset, it seemed likely that he used a system of hand signals and rewarded the pig with sliced apple for responding correctly.

A Mr. Nicholson, about whom little is known, took the pig on and continued to London. Nicholson was a canny publicist and placed several compelling advertisements.

> *...solves questions in the four rules of arithmetic, tells by looking at a...watch,
> what is the hour and minute and is the admiration of all who have seen him.*

> *...the tongue of the most florid orator...can not sufficiently describe the wonderful performance of that sagacious animal.*

The act amazed and astonished the audience as the pig spelt out names using cardboard letters. Crowds flocked to see him, and with four shows a day, it was rumoured Nicholson took the huge amount of 70 pounds a week in ticket sales.

After a long London run, the pig joined a circus performing at Sadler's Wells Theatre. A group of acrobats, incensed at being asked to share billing with a performing pig, threatened to resign and were sacked on the spot. By 1786, in the world of entertainment the Learned Pig ruled. Robert Southey touted the pig as: *"a far greater object of admiration to the English nation than ever was Sir Isaac Newton."*

During the Learned Pig's career newspapers reported that he earnt more money *"than any actor or actress within the same compass of time."* But in November 1788, several papers carried the story that their favourite, the Learned Pig, had died, and his master had been confined to a madhouse in Edinburgh! Such a sad end to an illustrious career.

FORK HANDLES? NO, FOUR CANDLES!

By MIKE RENDELL

M Y ANCESTOR RICHARD HALL, LIVING IN THE SECOND PART OF THE EIGHTEENTH century, had access to four different forms of candle—beeswax, tallow, sperma-ceti, and rush-light. At a time when the world was either dark or it was light, choosing the correct candle would have been very important. Candles formed a significant part of Richard's budget since his accounts show that in 1797 he was spending £4.8.04 p.a. on candles (roughly equivalent to £250 today) as against more than double that amount for coal (£10.17.00).

By far the best and most expensive candles were made from beeswax—they would burn with an even, sweet-smelling light, but they were a luxury. As an aside, the pres-tigious store of Fortnum & Mason has its origins in the sale of beeswax candles. The Royal Family insisted on new candles being used every night, which meant that there was a constant supply of half-used candles which were left to the footman (one William Fortnum) to dispose of. William's landlord was Hugh Mason. Together they decided to go into partnership selling on these part-used candles along with general groceries. 300 years later the firm is still going strong!

Back in the Georgian era tallow candles were made from suet (animal fat from beef or mutton usually) and these had the disadvantage of spitting and spluttering as well as smelling pretty foul. They had the added drawback of being soft, particularly in the heat of the summer, meaning that the stems would bend and become useless.

Spermaceti was certainly used by Richard in the 1790s because he specifically men-tions it in his shopping order of 21 January 1791 where he bought two ounces of the stuff.

The purchase reflects the huge increase in whaling in the latter part of the eighteenth century. Whales meant far more than just meat and blubber, and in the case of the sperm-whale it was found that it contained an odourless, waxy substance which could be used to make candles. The spermaceti was extracted from the whale's head (in a large whale there could be several tons of it). It could then be poured into a mould and allowed to crystallise. Spermaceti candles had the added advantage of being more or less odourless, and being a much harder substance, they withstood the heat of summer. They also burned more brightly than tallow candles, and at a far more constant rate, and their light became a measure of brightness for scientists—one *candela* being the amount generated by a "standard candle".

For Richard there was also a fourth alternative—rush-light candles. These would have been home-made and were probably used as lighting for dark corners rather than for reading. The inventory of Richard's house in Bourton, made after his death, showed that there were various rush-light holders in use. Sometimes these were like pliers (with a spring-loaded clip which fastened around the rush-light) and a spike at the other end so it could be nailed into the wall.

Other holders were more like a conventional table-mounted candle holder. Either way, they would burn for perhaps 40 minutes before needing to be replaced. They would have given off a dim and often fluctuating light.

I still have Richard's pen knife, and it is easy to imagine Richard going down to the River Windrush at Bourton, pulling out the knife, cutting down several dozen rushes, and taking them back across the meadows to his home. Here he would split each rush in four, peeling back the green outer layer to reveal a white pithy substance inside. These white strips would be placed in the sun to dry.

Whenever any spare fat was available, e.g. from cooking, the strips would be dipped in the fat and left to cool. They could then be clipped into the holder and lit—no good at all for reading or sewing but acceptable for residual background light.

FANNY BURNEY, SURVIVOR

BY LAUREN GILBERT

FANNY BURNEY (1752-1840) WAS A FAMOUS AUTHOR, A RELUCTANT CELEBRITY IN HER time, and an inspiration to other authors, including Jane Austen, who subscribed to *Camilla*. She is known for her four novels, but she also wrote plays (only one of which was performed in her lifetime). However, we are not going to discuss her novels or writings specifically. Before anything else, Fanny Burney was a survivor. She had an amazing life, which she chronicled in her journals and letters.

While her fame as a novelist opened many doors for her, I suspect that Fanny Burney would have had an eventful life even if she had never published at all. Her journals and letters reveal intelligence, a talent for observation, and a gift for expression. In her novels, her heroines made mistakes and suffered consequences; her skilled observation of her time and society gave her characters and their dialogues a liveliness and reality that paved the way for later authors. She used her writing skill to illuminate perceived wrongs. However, it is in Fanny Burney's journals and letters that we find her spirit and her indomitable passion for writing which sustained her through the remarkable ups, downs, and turns that her life took.

Fanny Burney's father was Dr. Charles Burney, a prominent musician and writer. He performed with theatre orchestras and in other venues, and was also employed by the composer George Frederick Handel. His music was his introduction to the highest level of society. Her mother was Esther Sleepe, who was of French extraction and a Roman Catholic and considered kind, gentle, and intelligent by those who knew her. She was the daughter of a musician and a talented musician herself.

Charles and Esther were both well-read, musical, fond of poetry, interested in philosophy, and were extremely happy together by all accounts. The date of their marriage was apparently deliberately muddled, as it seems their eldest child, Esther (known as Hetty), was born before their marriage was solemnized. Esther and Charles produced six living children of whom Fanny was the fourth.

Born June 13, 1752, Fanny was small (about 5'2" as an adult), very shy and sensitive, with poor eyesight. Fanny was very quiet and considered backward as she did not know her letters or how to read until after she was eight years old. Her limitations fostered her sharp memory and her talents for listening and observation.

By contrast with Hetty, who was outgoing and something of a musical prodigy, performing before audiences by age ten, Fanny had a more serious nature and disliked being in the limelight. She was very close to her mother, possibly because of her shyness and other difficulties. This made it extremely difficult for Fanny when her mother died on September 27, 1762, after becoming ill following childbirth (her ninth pregnancy). The violence of Fanny's grief was a concern to her family, as she would not be comforted. Fanny started writing not long after her mother's death. This was the first big tragedy of Fanny's life.

In October of 1767, her father eloped with Elizabeth Allen, a beautiful, intelligent, and educated widow with three children of her own. Her sister had been a friend of Esther's and was loved by Dr. Burney's children. Unfortunately, Fanny and her brothers and sisters did not like Elizabeth (she doesn't seem to have been particularly popular with her own children). She seems to have been intrusive, managing, and short-tempered.

During these years, Fanny did her writing in secret. At age fifteen, she destroyed her journals and other writings, supposedly in an effort to keep her stepmother from seeing them, and vowed to stop writing for fear of committing an impropriety. In March 1768, however, about nine months after destroying her earlier work, she started another journal to record her thoughts and observations, which she continued one way or another for over 70 years, still in secret.

Fanny was aware that she was expected to marry. She was ambivalent. On one hand, she was very romantic and had her share of "crushes". On the other hand, as she matured she recognized the danger to women in their dependence on men, saw problems women experienced with faithless men, and, of course, had experienced her mother's death as the result of childbirth. She resented the restrictions imposed by etiquette on women, in particular the waste of time in paying calls and worrying about dress. Interestingly, neither her father nor her stepmother showed significant concern with Fanny or their other daughters' welfare in society as marriageable young ladies. In fact, Dr. Burney seemed in no hurry to have his daughters marry.

In addition to her journal, Fanny also wrote a novel, *Evalina*. It was published anonymously and in secret when she was twenty-five years old with the assistance of her brother. It was immediately successful and acclaimed. Even her father read and admired it. When her identity was made known, celebrity followed. She also earned some money.

Her father's society connections had already resulted in her acquaintance with influential people. These connections and her sudden fame resulted in her acquaintance and friendship with Dr. Samuel Johnson, Hester Thrale, and the Bluestockings, including Mary Delaney. She was very uncomfortable with her fame. Once her father and his friend Samuel Crisp realized she was the author of a successful novel, they were more than willing to offer advice. (Her father was also very concerned to keep Fanny at hand to assist him with his own projects; she acted as his secretary on his massive work on the history of music.)

Starting in 1778 or 1779, Fanny wrote a play, *The Witlings*, which was a comic satire on Society. Despite her confidence and pride in it, and interest shown in it, both Dr. Burney and Mr. Crisp put pressure on Fanny not to pursue it as they were concerned that influential people such as Mrs. Thrale would recognize themselves and be offended.

It appears that Dr. Burney was as much concerned about possible fall-out for himself as problems for Fanny. At any rate, reluctantly, Fanny gave in to their pressure and did not pursue publication or performance of this play, abandoning it in 1780. They then began pressing her for another novel. The result was her second novel *Cecilia* which was published in 1782. Available data indicates that Fanny was not as happy with *Cecilia* as she had been with *Evalina*, that she felt rushed and pushed. *Cecilia* was not as well received as *Evalina*, but did reasonably well.

Mrs. Thrale took Fanny up and made an effort to help her in society, although her own letters seem to indicate a certain level of exasperation with Fanny's apparent lack of interest and gratitude. Fanny did build a friendship with Mary Delaney, one of the Blue-stockings and a friend of Queen Charlotte and King George III. This friendship resulted in Fanny's presentation at court and ultimately an invitation to serve as second mistress of the robes for the Queen in 1786. Fanny did not want to do this. However, her father and Mr. Crisp were both eager for her to go, seeing the prospect of multiple advantages.

She was extremely bored, as much of her time was spent waiting for the Queen. The long hours and restrictions affected her health, and personality issues with another of the Queen's ladies, Elizabeth Schwellenberg, combined to make her very unhappy with the position. She served in this position for five years before she convinced her father that it was necessary for her to resign. The Queen awarded her a pension of 100 pounds a year (half of her salary).

During a visit to Surrey, Fanny became acquainted with French émigrés living there, one of whom was General Alexandre D'Arblay who had served with Lafayette. She married him July 28, 1793 in spite of his penniless state and her father's disapproval. (Dr. Burney refused to attend the ceremony, even though he ultimately became very fond of Alexandre.) They had one child, a son named Alexandre, born on December 18, 1794. Their finances were very strained; the publication of *Camilla* in 1796 saved the day and allowed them to build a cottage.

In spite of their financial struggles, they seemed to have been very happy together. Fanny's pension and her earnings from her books provided their support. Alexandre dreamed of recovering his estate and status in France. Fanny continued writing, completing three comic plays between 1797 and 1801.

In 1800, Fanny lost her younger sister Susanna (known as Susan in the family). Susanna's death hit Fanny extremely hard; they had shared everything and were considered as close as twins. In many ways, Susanna's death was as difficult and painful for Fanny as was her mother's death. She was unable to speak her sister's name after her death.

In 1801, General D'Arblay was offered a position in Napoleon's France. Seeing this as a way to start the process to recover his estate and status, Alexandre accepted. Fanny and their son joined him in France in 1802. This period coincided with the Peace of Amiens, which ended in May of 1803.

Fanny lived in France for ten years, much of the time as an English woman in enemy territory. Although she wrote to her family when she could, she discouraged letters from them to discourage any accusations of spying for England. This must have been an incredibly lonely and trying time. On top of everything else, her pension from the Queen stopped because she was no longer in England.

In 1810, she was diagnosed with a cancer of the breast, which led to a mastectomy by

Napoleon's chief surgeon, Dr. Dominique Jean Larrey, in September of 1811. This was performed without anaesthesia, and she wrote a detailed account of the surgery in a journal letter to her sister, Hetty. After ordering the preparation of bandages, lint for packing, and other necessities for her surgery, she had to expose her body to the knife not knowing until that moment that the whole breast was to be removed. Her graphic description of this ordeal is incredibly powerful. The wonder is that she survived and made a full recovery. During her years in France, she worked on her fourth novel, *The Wanderer*.

In 1812, Fanny brought her son Alexandre to England with her. She was terrified that he would be conscripted into Napoleon's Army and was desperate to see her father. She and her son went aboard with passports stamped for Newfoundland or some coast of America and were almost halted by the French customs and subsequently almost becalmed.

Fanny brought the manuscript of *The Wanderer* with her and by the time she landed was so relieved to be ashore she picked up a pebble to commemorate her landfall. Her brother Charles did not recognize her, as age and her experiences had altered her appearance. Her father was aged and had lost much of his hearing, becoming something of a recluse. She caught up with her family's news, and in 1814, just before her father's death, *The Wanderer* was published. This was the least successful and most criticized of her four books, garnering some very harsh reviews.

In November of 1814, in spite of her reluctance, Fanny returned to France in a small open boat in stormy weather. She had to be carried off the boat due to dehydration upon landing. In the process of her arrival, her husband Alexandre was injured when he was struck by a horse and cart—it took him several days to recover enough to go on to Paris. Both were ill during the winter.

When Napoleon escaped from Elba in March 1815, neither Fanny nor her husband expected him to return to Paris. Their only preparations were to make sure Fanny had a properly stamped passport and Alexandre was armed. When Napoleon was outside of Paris, General D'Arblay mounted his horse and rode off shouting "Vive le Roi!" Apparently, it had not occurred to Fanny until then that he might actually join the fighting.

She received a letter from him telling her to leave Paris, and she left for Belgium in the middle of the night, arriving in Tournai on March 23, 1815. She and her husband were briefly reunited in April when he found her in Brussels. He went on to Treves. They knew battle was coming, just not when. When the Battle of Waterloo finally began, Fanny did not know where General D'Arblay was or what was happening. She was especially anxious, as her husband had signed an oath of loyalty to King Louis XVIII; if Napoleon won, this would be fatal. Rumours had Napoleon, then Wellington, then Napoleon winning. After hours of anxiety, hearing firsthand accounts of the carnage, she finally learned of the British victory.

In the meantime, General D'Arblay was stuck in Treves awaiting orders which never came. Fanny sent him Wellington's Proclamation issued June 22. He was injured when kicked in the leg by a horse, and the wound became infected. As a result of inept treatment without anaesthesia, he slipped into a coma. Finally hearing of his situation, Fanny decided to go to him but had a series of misadventures (missed diligence, passport issues in Prussian-controlled territory, getting lost, and suffering major anxiety) before finally being united with him on July 24, 1815.

It took an additional month of convalescence before he was able to make the journey to Paris. He was extremely depressed, not only because of his injury, but because of his country's humiliation, and his realization that he was never going to recoup his family's fortune and estates in France. They finally returned to England, landing on October 17, 1815, reuniting with their son and settling in Bath.

By April of 1816, Alexandre was planning to return to France in hopes of settling his business matters. Their son was attending Cambridge, and his success was a source of anxiety as his and his parents' futures depended upon it. He was on scholarship but not happy with the course of study required; at the same time, he was caught up in his social life.

General D'Arblay further strained the situation by trying to arrange a marriage for their son with a French girl in spite of Fanny's objections. He had returned to Paris in the hope of salvaging something and met a family he and Fanny had known in 1802 whose daughter seemed a likely match for Alexandre. The difficulties of their separation during this time were exacerbated by this disagreement and other misunderstandings. The general returned to England a few weeks later, having had to abandon his dream of recovering his estates and of settling his son's future in France.

In 1817, in spite of his own ill health and issues with his son (who did pass his examination), General D'Arblay returned to France. Depressed, he had a portrait of himself done so that his son would not forget him and worried about his son and the lack of an inheritance for him. His health further deteriorated. Later in the fall, he returned to England with nothing accomplished. Fanny and their son noticed the deterioration in his health. Finally, in early 1818, in great pain, he was diagnosed with rectal cancer and was told it was too late for surgery. Alexandre did succeed in getting his degree, but the General's health continued to deteriorate. He finally passed away May 3, 1818.

After her husband's death, Fanny would not go out for some months except to go to church on Sundays. Fanny left Bath and settled in London with her maid and her dog. (Her son returned to Cambridge.) She spent time with family and started working on her father's papers. She planned to sort and edit them to publish a memoir with correspondence. Dr. Burney had left twelve notebooks of memoir material.

Unfortunately, after three years, Fanny had little to show for it; her father's notebooks were of little help, and she felt that much of the material would actually tarnish his memory. She ended up writing her own account of his life, leaving out anything that was controversial, embarrassing, or otherwise less than flattering. The resultant work was published in November of 1832. She was criticized for her ruthless editing of his materials.

Concerns for her son proceeded to dominate her life at this time. Alexandre had travelled but achieved little; he had been ordained in 1818, but was uninterested in teaching or being a cleric. He would disappear for weeks or months at a time. He was undisciplined and apparently unable to focus on a specific goal. He accepted a living but disappeared periodically, leaving no one to handle the services. He was a serious worry to Fanny, who was concerned for his health and his future.

In May of 1835, Alex became engaged to Mary Ann Smith whom Fanny liked very much. However, lack of money prevented their marriage. He could not figure out how to resolve the issue and was unable to make a decision or take any action. They remained engaged but never married. In 1836, he moved from place to place, never sticking to anything. He caught a chill which developed into influenza and died at Fanny's home on January 19, 1837.

At this point, Fanny was 85 years old and had only one close family member still living—her sister Charlotte. She was plagued with money problems. Fanny was very deaf and almost blind (she had cataracts). Alex's fiancée Mary Ann continued to watch out for Fanny. Her sister died on September 12, 1838, leaving Fanny alone. She had communion brought to her every week and had regular visitors. She divided up her papers, giving her personal papers to her sister Charlotte's daughter, Charlotte Barrett, and her father's papers to her brother Charles' son, Charles Parr Burney. She signed her final will on March 6, 1839. Her health was so poor that she spent much time in bed. She finally died January 6, 1840, and was buried beside her husband and son.

Fanny Burney D'Arblay lived a long life, surviving a serious of losses and blows, any combination of which could have brought her to a stand-still. She survived a major surgery without anaesthetic and recovered fully, not suffering an infection or a recurrence of the cancer. She lived in France during the Napoleonic wars. She travelled between England and France in spite of weather and political turmoil. She outlived her nearest and dearest, including her husband and only child. A shy person, Fanny learned to cope with her celebrity status; a sensitive person, she learned to accept some searing criticism of her work. There is no doubt that she had great courage, strength, and determination. Her journals and letters show that, in spite of everything, she never lost her interest in people and events around her.

SOURCES

Chisholm, Kate. *Fanny Burney: Her Life*. Random House, 2011.

Burney, Fanny. "Breast Cancer in 1811: Fanny Burney's Account of Her Mastectomy." Introduction by Michael Kaplan. *New Jacksonian Blog*, 12/2/10. http://newjacksonianblog. blogspot.com/2010/12/breast-cancer-in-1811-fanny-burneys.html

D'Ezio, Marianna. "Transcending National Identity: Paris and London in Fanny Burney's Novels." 2010. http://ressources-cla.univ-fcomte.fr/gerflint/RU-Irlande3/Ezio.pdf

"Fanny Burney 1752-1840." *Norfolk Women in History*. http://norfolkwomeninhistory. com/1751-1799/fanny-burney

"Frances (Fanny) Burney (married name D'Arblay)." *The Burney Centre at McGill University*. http://burneycentre.mcgill.ca/bio_frances.html

A TAX ON DOGS

BY GRACE ELLIOT

IN 1796 A SEEMINGLY INNOCUOUS PIECE OF TAX LEGISLATION CAUSED UPROAR IN England. The new law provoked a debate about the very nature of the human spirit and whether owning a dog was a right or a luxury.

At the end of the eighteenth century the English government was desperate for money to finance the ongoing war with France. One way of raising the necessary cash was taxation. Tax was raised on everything from soap, to tea, tobacco, windows, and lace—and indeed it didn't stop there. Servants were a taxable asset under the auspices of the Male Servants' Tax bill 1777-1852 and the Female Servants' Tax bill 1795-1852, but fortunately (or unfortunately?) wives and children were not taxable assets! There was a Horse Tax (on carriages and saddle horses) and a Farm Horse Tax (on horses and mules used in trade) but none of these taxes created quite the same stir as the imposition of the Dog Tax in 1796.

The crux of the disquiet lay in the very English relationship between man and dog. It raised a serious debate about whether having a dog was a luxury or a natural part of being human. The tax tapped into questions about the emotional bond between the two. By putting a tax on dogs it implied a shift in relationship from one of nurturing and caring to servility and subordination—and dog owners were enraged. To many this was tantamount to taxing spouses and children, and people weren't happy. This wasn't about the financial aspect of the tax but the moral implication.

Those that supported the bill pointed out that pet dogs were a luxury and consumed food that could have been better used to feed the poor. Opponents argued back that to need things beyond the essential—such as a dog—was a distinctly human trait. These people considered pets to be their friends, and putting a tax on them turned the language of friendship to that of slavery and service.

Interestingly, the idea behind the dog tax may have originated in France (the very country the English needed to raise funds to fight!). In 1770, a French census suggested a population of four million dogs; an extrapolation of the amount of food they consumed was equivalent to feeding a sixth of the population. The French dog tax was proposed to discourage dog ownership as a means of disease control and to increase food availability.

French authorities also insisted dogs belonging to the poor spread disease, especially rabies. This was considered a disease of dirty and hungry dogs, so poor labourers who "can scarcely feed themselves" should be discouraged from owning dogs by means of a tax. The difference between France and England was that in the former the tax remained as a proposition, whereas in the latter it was acted upon.

Whatever the moral argument, the English government won in the end—the Dog Tax was imposed and stayed in place until 1882.

LET THE CAT OUT OF THE BAG...

BY JONATHAN HOPKINS

FLOGGING—THE VERY WORD CONJURES IMAGES OF BACKS SCARRED FOR LIFE BY THE instrument of this largely military form of torture—the cat o' nine tails.

The British army and navy of the eighteenth and nineteenth centuries comprised huge numbers of "volunteers". Whether these men took "the King's shilling", were made offers they could not refuse by magistrates, or were legally "impressed" to serve by navy shore-parties, many proved unsuited to military life and its harsh discipline. Theft and insubordination, even violence and desertion, were commonplace.

To maintain order a simple way to administer punishment was needed, the severity of which could be varied to fit the crime. Not only that but it had to be enough of a deterrent to plant fear in the hearts of potential offenders. Flogging was such a punishment. And the preferred instrument of martial law was the cat o' nine tails.

Widely used by the end of the seventeenth century, the cat was a whip made from heavy cable (rope). A four-foot length was split into its three component strands to produce a two-and-a-half foot tail, each strand being separated again into three to produce the requisite nine "tails". These were knotted at the free ends to prevent fraying and the handle part then back-spliced both to provide a good handgrip and stop it unravelling, though in later examples the nine lashes were bound to wooden handles. Once made, the cat was stored in a canvas or baize bag ready for use, from whence the title of this essay comes.

Methods of punishment were roughly similar in army and navy. The guilty man would be tied hand and foot to some suitable structure: in the navy a ship's grating (hold cover) tied upright, in the army a triangle made of three sergeant's halberds lashed together. Apparently cavalry regiments, which had no halberds, habitually used a vertical ladder. The ship's crew or soldier's regiment were formed up and made to watch, presumably to remind them of the consequences of rule-breaking.

A drum-major, cavalry farrier-major, or boatswain administered the punishment, the number of strokes having been previously agreed upon at the victim's trial. Men chosen for this task needed to practice: the whip had to be applied only across shoulders and upper back, avoiding the more vulnerable neck and kidney areas. Twenty-five lashes was considered a minimum number of strokes in the army, with 1200 the maximum allowed. The latter was almost a death sentence, to be administered only to the most serious offenders. And to ensure the prisoner was fit to take his punishment, a surgeon had to be present. He could step in at any time to stop the flogging if the condemned man lost consciousness, or too much blood, but if the punishment was curtailed for medical reasons that might not be the end of it. The man was allowed to recover, for days or weeks, before whatever remained of his sentence was carried out.

In the navy a seaman might be flogged "around the fleet" as an example to others, his sentence in number of lashes being divided between ships. After having the requisite number on his own vessel he would be cut down and taken by tender to the next where he was re-tied and "catted" again.

A navy rope cat was usually replaced after a single use unless a number of men were being flogged when it would be scrubbed in a bucket of seawater between prisoners. Unbeknown to those involved, this made navy floggings less likely to result in infected wounds, added to the fact navy punishments were often for fewer lashes. Seamen were less easily replaced than landsmen, and one who could not do his job while flogging wounds healed not only meant his shipmates had to cover his work as well as their own but his absence from duty might compromise the ship's performance in action. Notwithstanding this, it is reckoned more than 50 men were flogged for various offences aboard *Victory* in the weeks before the Battle of Trafalgar. And on the already horrendous retreat to Corunna in 1809, General Edward Paget had drawn his regiments of the rearguard into a square ready to flog three men for looting when he was told the enemy were only several hundred yards behind them!

Despite the Duke of Wellington's insistence that his "scum of the earth" could not be controlled without the lash, George III was never fond of flogging, and as the nineteenth century drew on, the number of lashes permissible was reduced. Perhaps the increasing use of whipcord and leather-thonged cats caused more severe injury in fewer strokes than the original rope whips. With the rise of more effective communications, increased awareness of the effects of flogging caused disquiet among the general population, and several high profile cases where men died after being whipped hastened the end of the cat. Its use was abolished on mainland Britain in 1871. It could still be used abroad, however.

The navy kept the cat, but use declined until in 1879 it too was banned by the Admiralty. The writing was on the wall, and following the senior service's lead, the following year the army got rid of the lash. The last British soldier was flogged in July 1880, in Afghanistan, for sleeping on sentry duty. The ban was confirmed by Act of Parliament the following year.

The reminders were a few horribly scarred backs, and soon they too were lost to time until only a phrase remained....

The Glorious(ish) First of June

By JONATHAN HOPKINS

When France's revolutionary government declared war on Britain in 1793, the country breathed a collective sigh of despair. Since being drummed out of America in 1776 things had not gone well for the British militarily.

They were forced from their toehold on the French mainland at Toulon thanks largely to the clever tactics of a young artillery captain called Napoleon Buonaparte. And the Duke of York's campaign in Flanders was becoming bogged down after minor early successes.

Britain needed a victory. Something to shout about: to help restore collective morale and take people's minds off growing social unrest at home. So when in the spring of 1794 the Admiralty got wind of a large enemy grain convoy returning to France from America, the English Channel fleet under Admiral Lord Howe was ordered to intercept it.

Sixty-nine years old at that time, Richard Howe had joined the navy at thirteen, and having been successfully involved in many previous naval actions he was highly regarded, both by his peers and the ordinary seamen serving under him, as a master tactician and humanitarian. Which two didn't often go together.

Howe's fleet of twenty-six ships of the line (battleships) and twelve support vessels sighted the enemy on 27 May, in heavy seas, four hundred miles out into the Atlantic from the French coast. By next afternoon his leading ships were close enough to trade shots with the rearmost warships of the French escort squadron before rain and fog closed in, effectively putting an end to the action.

The following day the wind had dropped from gale force. With the French fleet still ahead and in more favourable winds Howe ordered his ships to tack. Angling upwind gave the British a speed advantage, and they soon caught up with the enemy. But they were still too far away to engage in the most usual form of sea battle, a broadside-to-broadside cannon duel with their opponents.

So Howe determined on a tactic later to be made famous by Nelson at both the battles of the Nile and Trafalgar. With the enemy fleet sailing stretched out line-astern (nose to tail), he ordered his leading ships to turn almost at right-angles to break through their line.

Howe knew only too well this was a risky plan. Approaching the enemy bows-on meant though the British ships made smaller targets they could bring few guns to bear, while the French could fire all cannon, on one side, at them. The attackers must wait, enduring French gunfire, for it was only as a British ship broke through the enemy line that it could fire back. Then it could use cannon on both sides and so engage the bow of one ship and the stern of another without much in the way of retaliation possible from either.

When that happened, carnage was the usual result. A ship's gundeck was one long, clear space allowing crews as much room as possible in which to work. Any cannonball smashing through bow or stern could in theory travel the whole length of the deck, mangling anything in its path. A French sailor at Trafalgar reported a single shot killing and maiming ten men as it passed through his ship.

The weather then intervened again. A sea mist came down in the evening, prompting Howe to sensibly disengage, avoiding the risk of accidental collision and "friendly fire". Several ships on both sides had been badly damaged and during the night jury-rig sails were hurriedly prepared to keep them on the move. By morning the French fleet had moved off, and when the fog cleared in the afternoon Howe realised they were now too distant to attack that day.

The first of June dawned cloudy and with a heavy swell. Despite the French having pulled further ahead during the night, with the best of the wind Howe soon caught them and by 9:30 a.m. was once again ordering his fleet to turn, in line-abreast this time, to engage the enemy.

The battle lasted four hours. Many ships having fought themselves to a standstill, Howe then signalled a halt. A dozen French warships had been disabled, and though the enemy managed to take five under tow, the British captured six. The French 84 gun *Vengeur* sank, and despite rescue boats launched from a British frigate to pick up survivors many of her sailors drowned.

The loss of any ship this way was classed a major disaster. Oak warships could take a huge amount of punishment and still remain afloat unless fire took hold, exploding the powder magazine. Sinking an opponent in battle was not the idea, rather disablement and capture whence hull and contents could be sailed or towed to a friendly port and sold, providing prize money for the victorious captain and his crew. And since a huge number of sailors were unable to swim, casualties from sinkings were always high.

Talking of which, the British suffered 287 killed and 811 wounded in the whole engagement, the French approximately 1500 killed, 2000 wounded, and 3500 made prisoner.

So how "glorious" was the first of June?

Despite Howe's prizes (and some captains complained he should have let the action continue until more enemy ships were boarded to be taken in tow), the enemy merchant fleet escaped, prompting the French to count the battle their victory and to honour seamen who died when the *Vengeur* sank as martyrs to the revolutionary cause.

In Howe's defence he had engaged and half-destroyed a French battle fleet of more heavily armed ships than those he commanded, he was by now 600 miles out to sea, and many of his own vessels needed repairs before they could make for home.

And be fair—at his age, after four days continuous alert and action he was entitled to a rest!

In any event, the battle prompted wild celebration on both sides of the English Channel. Howe was hailed a hero and once again enhanced his reputation as a commander; presented with a jewelled sword by George III, he ordered it sent around every ship in the fleet together with a letter of praise from the King which was read out to ordinary sailors, the men who had borne the brunt of the fighting. Knew how to boost men's morale, did Howe. Apparently one of Nelson's most treasured possessions was a note of congratulation he received from Howe after the Battle of the Nile.

Anyway, after the Glorious First of June, Britain never lost a major sea battle during the whole Revolutionary and Napoleonic wars. That was pretty glorious, really.

Boy Sailors during the Age of Nelson and Napoleon

By M.M. Bennetts

Anyone who has thrilled to the dramas of naval derring-do such as *Horatio Hornblower* or *Master and Commander* will have observed that on the British ships of the late eighteenth and early nineteenth centuries, there were a great many boys—often as young as twelve—serving aboard His Majesty's ships.

Indeed, it had been a twelve-year-old boy who had saved the day and the general (in this case, Sir Francis Drake) back in 1578 after a fracas with natives near the Island of Mocha. So boys, working their way up the ladder, as it were, proved a common feature of the English navy from its beginnings. And they were called "Younkers".

The eighteenth century saw a great rise in charitable institutions which were often founded to enable the poorest of London poor to climb out of the gutter and provide for themselves in a legitimate trade. In 1756, The Marine Society was just one of these ventures—others included the Foundling Hospital and the Royal Hospital School. At the first meeting of the founders, held at the King's Arms Tavern in Cornhill, they met to approve *"A Plan of the Society for contributing towards a supply of Two or Three thousand Mariners for the Navy."*

They began an *Entry Book for Boys* on 5 August 1756. In this document, they recorded all the pertinent information they received about the boys: their age (if known), whether they had parents or were fatherless, their place of abode. They also used the term "friend-less", which was in their eyes a worse condition than being an orphan.

The next meeting of this Society stated their aims:

> *John Fielding having procured 24 boys for sea service, they were all clothed by the Society...Order'd that 10 of said boys be sent to Admiral Broderick and 14 to Capt. Barber of the Princess Royal at the Nore and that each boy shall have a Testament, Common Prayer Book, Clasp Knife and a printed list of their Cloths.*

In 1756, of course, Britain was on the brink of entering the Seven Years' War. During that period of time, the Royal Navy's manpower requirements rose swiftly—from 10,000 men to 80,000. Moreover, there was an endless need for servants aboard ship, for cabin boys, loblolly boys, carpenters' mates....

Indeed, the Society launched a massive newspaper campaign to recruit:

> *All stout Lads and Boys who incline to go on board His Majesty's Ships, as servants, with a view to learn the duty of a seaman, and are upon examination,*

approved by the Marine Society, shall be handsomely clothed and provided
with bedding and their charges borne down to the ports where His Majesty's
Ships lye, with all proper encouragement.

By 1772, the Regulations of the Marine Society were including a great deal more information about the boys they received. There were columns in which to note if a boy was "good" or not so good; some are recorded as having *"little or no guard against temptation"*, while others are said to be *"abominably corrupted* [by the] *most wicked company, in the most wicked parts of these kingdoms"* or *"hardened in iniquity"*.

Still, the Marine Society was offering these boys, described by the magistrate John Fielding as: *"numberless miserable, deserted, ragged, and iniquitous pilfering Boys that at this Time shamefully infested the Streets of London"* a new life, one which included an education of sorts leading to a lifelong trade, steady rations, safe housing, and a kitbag which included a felt hat, a kersey pea jacket, two worsted caps, waistcoat, shirts, trousers, three pairs of drawers, and a pair of shoes. It seemed a good deal for many.

And over time, as the Society grew along with the need for more boys to feed the ever-expanding British naval workforce, magistrates, beadles, parish officers, aldermen, and bishops all came to use the Society's provision as one option for criminal youth—a positive choice as opposed to the Gallows—which boys were then referred to, unsurprisingly, as "Scape Gallowses".

But what of young teenage officers? The midshipmen? For the call of the sea wasn't just heard by those on the streets, but also by the middle-class sons of merchants, doctors, lawyers, yeoman farmers, all up and down the land for whom the navy promised adventure, dashing careers, promotion, and enrichment through limitless prize money.

Many, such as the small twelve-year-old boy, a son of a Norfolk clergyman, who would become Admiral Lord Nelson in time, would go to sea courtesy of a relation or patron, a serving captain perhaps—someone who had position and influence in the navy and who would take them under their wing, providing them with a classroom at sea where they would learn all the necessary skills and tools to—one hoped—eventually pass their examinations and rise above the post of Mid-Shipman.

For others of the gentry classes, there was the necessity of a good naval education at one of many institutions such as the Portsmouth Naval Academy, founded in 1729, which was open to *"the Sons of Noblemen and Gentlemen, who shall not be under thirteen years of age nor above sixteen at the time of their admission."*

And it was here, at these Naval Academies, that one can see the breadth of the education required for a young man who hoped to succeed in the navy of Nelson's time. It was an immensely broad plan of education, requiring no less than two years' study:

It being intended that the Master of the Academy shall instruct Scholars in
writing, arithmetic, drawing, Navigation, Gunnery, Fortification and other

noteful parts of Mathematics, and also in the French Language, Dancing, Fencing and the exercise of the Firelock.

But that wasn't all, for the Academy also required that boys engage in a whole range of technical training which they would need as potential naval officers, including: *"The Description and Use of the Terrestrial Globe, Geography, Chronology, Spherics, Astronomy, Latitude, Longitude, Day's Work, and Marine Surveying."*

Two of Jane Austen's brothers attended the Portsmouth Academy. Francis Austen enrolled there in 1786 at the age of eleven, and he was a model student, going to sea two years later. His brother, Charles, who was sent to the Academy in 1791, was not so assiduous in his studies, and he did not leave the Academy until he had served the full term of his work there, in 1794, when he was sent aboard HMS *Daedelus*. Both of Austen's brothers would in due time become admirals.

Interestingly, however, the Portsmouth Academy also had its detractors, many of whom considered it, *"a sink of vice and abomination, [which] should be abolished...."* And it finally closed its doors in 1806, although many other such institutions—such as the Naval Academy at Chelsea—carried on, providing unequalled training for a future within the wooden walls.

PRINT SHOPS: PAST AND PRESENT

BY GRACE ELLIOT

IN GEORGIAN TIMES, THEN AS NOW, PEOPLE WERE FASCINATED BY VISUAL IMAGES; OF course, in those days there was no television or cinema, and so art was the draw. However, only those with spare income could afford the entry fee into art exhibitions, and indeed, the free, annual Royal Academy exhibition was so popular that it was mobbed by unruly crowds, and eventually an entry fee was levied to keep the poorest out. But in the eighteenth century with the rise of the print shop, their window displays became the new galleries, drawing crowds to gaze on the latest works of art.

Prior to 1740, most prints were imported from France, and in 1744 when Hogarth made engravings for "Marriage a la Mode" he called up two Frenchmen. Indeed, during the first half of the eighteenth century print sellers sold mainly French wares, the British equivalent being cheap copies and poor quality.

It took printer John Boydell to give a leg up to English engravers when he spotted a potential market amongst middle income earners for artwork to put on their walls. He commissioned prints of familiar London scenes, and his business instinct was amply rewarded as he made a small fortune. The public taste for prints was kept fresh by rapid developments in technique: mezzotint 1760s, aquatint 1770s, and stipple in 1780s. Indeed such was their popularity that one observer, Sophie La Roche, described the wide pavement outside a print shop in Cheapside: "[to] *enable crowds of people to stop and inspect the new exhibits.*"

Boydell's art was mainly classical, and with the French Revolutionary wars his export trade floundered, but around the same time a new vogue arose—that of the caricature.

Perhaps Hogarth stimulated this new trend with scenes depicting moral corruption; indeed, James Gillray (a heavyweight in the golden age of caricature) cites Hogarth as one of his greatest inspirations. Gillray was a political satirist of genius, and his work still gives the modern social historian a priceless insight into the Georgian world.

In the late eighteenth century, 6d (plain) to 1s (coloured) would purchase a print to brighten the walls of a tavern, lodging house, or workplace. Caricatures tickled the English sense of humour and quickly became all the rage with a commensurate increase in the number of shops selling them.

James Gillray (1756-1815) was one of the greatest artists of this type, regularly making fun of the Regent's pretensions to knowledge and the King's miserly tendencies. Gillray became so influential on public perception that the King tried to suppress one of his prints ("*L'Assemblie Nationale*") and paid a huge amount of money to buy the original plate.

Gillray's publisher was a Miss Hannah Humphrey, and his name was linked with hers romantically. He lived above her print shop in St. James' until his death in 1815, and his print "Very Slippery Weather" shows crowds gathered around the window.

One of Gillray's competitors, Cruikshank, records how the artist worked with prodigious speed:

> Sometimes he would at once etch a subject on the prepared copper plate... unable even to submit to the process of drawing it upon paper.... [H]e worked furiously, without stopping to remove the burr thrown up by the [burring]; consequently his fingers often bled from being cut by it.

The period 1789-1815 is widely acknowledged as the height of print influence and popularity, and it was with interest that I passed a print shop the other day on modern day St. James' Street. It didn't have crowds round the window, but people were stopping to look at the prints, reminding me of a bygone time.

Ann Radcliffe: The Mighty Enchantress

By J.A. BEARD

READING, THAT OH-SO-WONDERFUL PLEASURE, WAS OF COURSE APPRECIATED BY MANY in Georgian England. The expansion of literacy among women during the period also helped to provide new popularity for many types of fiction.

In the later decades of Georgian England, the rise of the Gothic novel particularly stands out. Crumbling castles, brooding noblemen, virtuous women terrorized by supernatural wickedness in the darkness. These are all part of the early tradition of Gothic fiction. Fixated on atmosphere, the Gothic tradition was a mix of horror, melodrama, and romantic elements. Whenever Gothic fiction is considered, there's one woman who helped to shape and popularize the genre: Ann Radcliffe.

An excerpt:

> While Emily gazed with awe upon the scene, footsteps were heard within the gates, and the undrawing of bolts; after which an ancient servant of the castle appeared, forcing back the huge folds of the portal, to admit his lord. As the carriage-wheels rolled heavily under the portcullis, Emily's heart sunk, and she seemed, as if she was going into her prison; the gloomy court, into which she passed, served to confirm the idea, and her imagination, ever awake to circumstance, suggested even more terrors, than her reason could justify.
>
> Another gate delivered them into the second court, grass-grown, and more wild than the first, where, as she surveyed through the twilight its desolation—its lofty walls, overtopt with briony, moss and nightshade, and the embattled towers that rose above—long-suffering and murder came to her thoughts. One of those instantaneous and unaccountable convictions, which sometimes conquer even strong minds, impressed her with its horror. The sentiment was not diminished, when she entered an extensive gothic hall, obscured by the gloom of evening, which a light, glimmering at a distance through a long perspective of arches, only rendered more striking. As a servant brought the lamp nearer partial gleams fell upon the pillars and the pointed arches, forming a strong contrast with their shadows, that stretched along the pavement and the walls.
>
> — The Mysteries of Udolpho, 1794

While not the first author to write what we would now consider a Gothic novel,

Radcliffe helped to popularize and bring Gothic novels into the literary mainstream. For this reason, she's often considered the true definer of the genre.

Although she was wildly successful during her lifetime, she wrote only a book of poetry and six novels: *The Castles of Athlin and Dunbayne* (1789), *A Sicilian Romance* (1790), *The Romance of the Forest* (1791), *The Mysteries of Udolpho* (1794), *The Italian* (1797), and *Gaston de Blondeville* (1826). If you're wondering about the large number of years between her fifth and sixth novels, the last was actually posthumously published by her husband.

Her works tended to focus on virtuous and imperiled heroines of breeding dealing with the aforementioned brooding noblemen, mysterious exotic castles, and supernatural elements. Radcliffe, however, in contrast to many other Gothic writers was rather explicit in showing that the supernatural elements in her stories all actually had rational, non-supernatural explanations (with one exception, *Gaston de Blondville*, though as noted above, it would only be published after her death).

One of the continuing elements in her works is a heroine desperately resisting an onslaught of emotion and instead, eventually, applying reason to the situation. For the time, especially given many people's sentiments about women in general, this was actually somewhat feminist, though a type of feminism considered mostly acceptable by late Georgian society.

Indeed, her combination of sensible heroines, lack of true supernatural elements, and virtue allowed her brand of Gothic novels to be acceptable for the literary mainstream. Critics at the time hailed her as the "mighty enchantress."

Surprisingly, at the height of her popularity at the age of 32, she stopped writing. As she kept a rather low personal profile, it's not certain her exact reasons for quitting, but many literary historians attribute it to her personal disgust with the direction Gothic fiction was taken, particularly in terms of then-prurient disreputable supernatural content. For example, *The Monk*, published in 1796, gained some popularity. The novel features and references, among other things, demon pacts, rape, and incest.

Radcliffe's works remained popular and influential throughout the nineteenth century both in England and the United States. She would influence many other authors who would go on to influence their own literary descendants. So, even if she isn't a household name anymore, her influence lingers.

Her nineteenth century popularity is easily attested to by the direct references to her works in period works and later fiction. One of the more famous and familiar to modern readers would be the several references to her work, particularly *The Mysteries of Udolpho*, in Jane Austen's *Northanger Abbey* (1817), a parody of many elements popular in Gothic fiction and Radcliffe's books. I should note that Ms. Austen was far from the only one parodying Gothic excess at the time.

So, whenever you read a book or watch a movie where some young woman is running down a spooky mansion/castle corridor, take a moment to think of Ann Radcliffe.

Late Georgian and Regency Era (1800–1837)

MISTRESS OF THE MANOR: WHAT DID SHE DO ALL DAY?

By MARIA GRACE

PERIOD DRAMAS HAVE LEFT MANY OF US WITH THE NOTION THAT LADIES OF THE landed gentry in the Regency era had little to do but dress in lovely gowns, embroider, and gossip. Reality could not be farther from this image. In general, both masters and mistresses of the house did a great deal of work around the estate, often working alongside the servants in the efforts to get everything done.

Labors tended to be divided along gender lines, so much so that single men sought female relatives to manage their households. Bachelors looked to sisters or nieces while widowers often called upon daughters or the dead wife's kin. So, even if a woman did not marry, there was a very strong possibility she might take on the responsibilities of a household sometime in her lifetime. Gentlemen tended to respect the household mistress' authority; her contributions to the home had worth equal to his.

RESPONSIBILITIES OF THE MISTRESS

The role of an estate's mistress was, depending on the size of the estate, the equivalent of managing a small hotel all the way up to being the CEO of a major corporation. She oversaw the finances, food service, hiring and training of the staff, procurement, charitable contributions of the "company," as well as the interior design of the "corporate headquarters." Depending on her intelligence, she might also assist her husband with overall estate business. While accomplishing all this, she was also expected to raise her children and care for sick family members. Talk about a working mother....

CHILDREN

The mistress' responsibilities to her children are perhaps the most obvious. She was expected to provide them, in the first place. Once they were born, it was on her shoulders to hire the nursery maids and governess, if the estate could afford them. If not, she would care for them herself. She was responsible for their education, whether she conducted it herself or hired others to teach them.

As her daughters grew older, it was her role to ensure they acquired the necessary accomplishments that would be expected of them, including, interestingly enough, sufficient understanding of mathematics to manage household ledgers. She would also tutor them in the skills necessary to manage a household of their own.

FINANCES

Managing the household budget and accounts made up a large part of the mistress' efforts.

Numerous domestic manuals, including Mrs. Rundell's *A New System of Domestic Cookery,* were available to assist women in the process. Mrs. Rundell warned *"the welfare and good management of the house"* depended on their careful surveillance. Accounts should be regularly kept and *"not the smallest article"* omitted. That included weighing meat, sugar, and similar commodities when they came from the retailer and comparing them with the charge. So, the mistress also served as the CFO of her domestic organization.

She might earn some additional money from managing the dairy and poultry, which was almost exclusively a female domain. Selling eggs, milk, and surplus fowl could bring a tidy sum into the household, if carefully managed. Of course, doing so also meant more that required her attention.

SUPPLYING THE MANOR

All manner of supplies for the home were handled by the mistress. What could not be made in house was purchased. What could be made was. Planning for and managing the creation of necessary products could be a huge year-round endeavor.

All manner of foodstuffs and herbs were raised and preserved using recipes and instructions passed down from mothers and grandmothers. To neglect this process was to risk the family going without during the winter when it was often difficult to purchase supplies.

Beyond this, the mistress of an estate oversaw the making, mending, and cleaning of the family's clothes. Clothing for the servants might also be included in her purview. Making soap for laundry and household use required animal fat and wood ashes to be saved and stored until needed. Water from boiling rice and potatoes was saved for starching clothes. Animal and even human urine (yikes!) was also saved for wash day.

SERVANTS

Although men were legally responsible for hiring and firing servants, the mistress oversaw the engaging, instructing, and supervising of domestic servants. Close control and supervision could be necessary. Many records of the era note inefficient and dishonest servants were commonplace. Not only did the mistress manage the servants, she was also in a position to care for their needs. She typically kept herself informed about their families, illnesses, and needs, and provided for their care.

COMMUNITY

The responsibilities of a landowner's wife extend beyond the home into the community at large, both to those who were her social equals and to those below her in social rank.

To those on her level, she would be expected to host dinners and social gatherings. Regular calls would be normal among her social circle.

To her social inferiors, she owed another kind of duty. In rural areas where no doctor was available, she might be called upon for her advice in treating the sick and injured. The village children needed to be educated—she was the one to organize the dame school to teach them to read and write. At Christmas time, she would provide gifts of baby clothes, blankets, shawls, coats, stockings, and flannel petticoats to the villagers.

The mistress of the estate also was expected to care for the poor. She might meet with the local clergyman to find out their needs and determine how to meet them. It was her role to visit them, deliver food, give advice, and listen to their complaints. Since the indigent had no other support system, the gracious provision of the estate's mistress provided a needed safety net.

So much for covering screens and eating biscuits. The Regency estate's mistress was no lady of leisure; she was a full time working mother, business partner to her husband, and ideally, a leader in her community.

SOURCES

Davidoff, Leonore & Catherine Hall. *Family Fortunes: Men and Women of the English Middle Class 1780-1850*. Routledge, 2002.

Horn, Pamela. *Flunkeys and Scullions, Life Below Stairs in Georgian England*. Sutton Publishing, 2004.

Le Faye, Deirdre. *Jane Austen: The World of Her Novels*. Harry N. Abrams, 2002.

Sullivan, Margaret C. *The Jane Austen Handbook*. Quirk Books, 2007.

Vickery, Amanda. *The Gentleman's Daughter*. Yale University Press, 1998.

Morning Calls and Formal Visits: Socializing in the Regency Era

By Maria Grace

IN THE 1800S, THE MONEYED MINORITY IN ANY LOCALE WAS EXPECTED TO MIX SOCIALLY with one another, whether or not they were personally agreeable to one another. In general, people only mixed socially within their own social class, so the company could become confined and unvarying quickly. Hence, new families of the right social standing would quickly be paid an obligatory visit by their neighbors in order to initiate an acquaintance and effectively broaden the social circle.

Until a formal acquaintance was recognized, members of the families could not socialize with one another. Established members of the neighborhood would take it upon themselves to call upon the newcomers. Only men called upon men; women did not initiate the relationship themselves. Once the man of the house performed introductions for the women in his household, they could interact socially and even introduce the newcomers to others.

Commonly the social inferior was introduced to the superior, and men to women, rather than the reverse. Unlike in town, where one had to wait for the call of a superior, in the country it was acceptable for a man to make a call or leave a card with someone of higher social standing if that person was new to the neighborhood. Acceptance by those above one's social status was a key to social mobility in Regency society, so such acquaintances were highly sought after.

Social connections were usually formed through a series of meetings, usually beginning with morning calls to the homes of those in fashionable society.

CALLING CARDS

Morning calls or visiting upon a household had an established protocol. Those who failed to follow it risked being shunned. First a calling card was presented to the household's servant.

Calling cards became popular at the end of the eighteenth century and bore the visitor's name, title, and residence. Their purpose was to prevent errors by forgetful servants. After all, one could not trust one's social future to a mere servant's memory.

One would generally leave not a single card, but three: one from the lady for the house's mistress, one from the gentleman for the house's mistress, and another for the house's master. Calling cards were displayed on special trays often set up on the front hallways, visible to all who came into the house. Cards from high ranking individuals and titled folks gave additional status to the household displaying their cards.

If one came without a card, he or she might be snubbed. When a servant received the cards, they would be conveyed to the mistress who would then decide whether to admit or reject the caller. If the servant informed the caller that the mistress was "not at home", this was code for not wishing to make the acquaintance. On the other hand, if a reciprocal card was formally presented to the visitor, this indicated there was a chance for the relationship to develop.

If one was uncertain as to the reception one might receive, the safest course would be to leave his or her card without asking if the mistress was at home. This would oblige her to reciprocate the call the next day, if only by leaving her own card. Failure to do so was a rebuff, but certainly a less painful one than being rejected at the door.

FORMAL CALLS

There were several other types of "visits in form", calls considered a duty rather than a pleasure. Duty visits were hard to evade as a decent level of social exchange was expected and individuals could be rebuked for their inattentiveness. These duty visits included calls to acknowledge hospitality, the newly-married, childbirth, bereavement, and those in straitened circumstances.

Calls for condolence and congratulations were typically made about a week after the event. Ceremonial visits to acknowledge parties, balls, and other invitations were paid sooner, a day after a ball, within two days of a dinner party, and within a week of a small party. These calls would be paid later in the day than "morning calls", typically between three and four in the afternoon.

Wedding visits were rigorously observed, extending a month or two after the marriage. The neighbors of gentry status would call on the couple in their own home. Then the visits would be returned and possibly one or more parties held in the couple's honor.

Calls to the bereaved and suffering were part of the duties of an estate's mistress. It was up to her to look after her less fortunate neighbors with a personal visit every week or two. On such visits she might deliver food and medicinal preparations made in her own kitchen and still room, give advice, and lend an ear to their complaints. These visits were often the only support system for the indigent in the neighborhood.

MORNING VISITS

Less formal visits, morning calls were actually paid between the time of rising and that of eating dinner, effectively between eleven in the morning and three in the afternoon. Earlier calls might interfere with breakfast or a lady's morning household duties. Later visits might suggest indecorous attempts at securing an invitation for dinner. The earlier in the day, the less close the acquaintance; the later, the greater degree of intimacy between the parties.

Morning visits were expected to last for at least fifteen minutes, but certainly not more than half an hour. Callers were received by men in their business room or library. Women took calls in the morning room or in their drawing-room. Pets and children, both regarded as potentially destructive and annoying, were not welcome on morning calls.

WHAT TO DO DURING A VISIT?

The heart of polite sociability was conversation. The whole purpose of conversation was to please other people and to be deemed pleasing. In general, conversation was tightly controlled by rules of etiquette as well.

During the quarter of an hour a call usually lasted, conversation was expected. Politeness demanded a visitor inquire after the health of absent members of the household. Beyond that though, polite individuals did not ask direct personal questions of recent acquaintances. To question or even compliment anyone else on the details of their dress might also be regarded as impertinent. Discussion of current events (non-controversial, of course) such as literature, music, and travel would always be welcome.

In order to take advantage of afternoon light, women would continue their needlework during a call. Sometimes visitors brought their own work or the hostess would offer her visitors pieces to work on. It was considered more genteel to continue with one's "fancywork" rather than "plain" shirt-making or mending.

SOURCES

A Lady of Distinction. *The Mirror of Graces* (1811). R.L. Shep Publications, 1997.

Banfield, Edwin. *Visiting Cards and Cases*. Wiltshire: Baros Books, 1989.

Black, Maggie and Deirdre Le Faye. *The Jane Austen Cookbook*. Chicago Review Press, 1995.

Byrne, Paula. In *Jane Austen in Context*. Cambridge University Press, 2005.

Day, Malcolm. *Voices from the World of Jane Austen*. David & Charles, 2006.

Downing, Sarah Jane. *Fashion in the Time of Jane Austen*. Shire Publications, 2010.

Hughes, Kristine. *The Writer's Guide to Everyday Life in Regency and Victorian England, from 1811-1901*. Cincinatti: Writer's Digest Books, 1998.

Jones, Hazel. *Jane Austen & Marriage*. Continuum Books, 2009.

Lane, Maggie. *Jane Austen's World*. Carlton Books, 2005.

Lane, Maggie. *Jane Austen and Food*. Hambledon, 1995.

Laudermilk, Sharon & Teresa L. Hamlin. *The Regency Companion*. Garland Publishing, 1989.

Le Faye, Deirdre. *Jane Austen: The World of Her Novels*. Harry N. Abrams, 2002.

Pool, Daniel. *What Jane Austen Ate and Charles Dickens Knew*. New York: Simon & Schuster, 1993.

Randall, Rona. *The Model Wife Nineteenth-Century Style*. London: The Herbert Press, 1989.

Ray, Joan Klingel. *Jane Austen for Dummies*. Wiley Publishing, Inc., 2006.

Ross, Josephine. *Jane Austen's Guide to Good Manners*. U.S.A.: Bloomsbury, 2006.

Selwyn, David. *Jane Austen & Leisure*. The Hambledon Press, 1999.

Trusler, John. *The Honours of the Table or Rules for Behavior during Meals*. Literary-Press, 1791.

Vickery, Amanda. *The Gentleman's Daughter*. Yale University Press, 1998.

A PRIVATE REGENCY BALL

By MARIA GRACE

The characteristic of an English country dance is that of gay simplicity. The steps should be few and easy, and the corresponding motion of the arms and body unaffected, modest, and graceful.

–The Mirror of Graces, 1811

IN A SOCIETY GOVERNED BY STRICT RULES REGULATING THE INTERACTION OF THE SEXES, the dance floor provided one of the only places marriage partners could meet and courtships might blossom. The ballroom guaranteed respectability and proper conduct for all parties since they were carefully regulated and chaperoned. Even so, under cover of the music and in the guise of the dance, young people could talk and even touch in ways not permitted elsewhere.

As far as the opportunity to meet people went, private balls had the very great advantage over public ones in that the hosts controlled who attended. One could be assured of the quality of guests at a grand house, so chaperons could rest a little easier that their charge was not interacting with someone below her station.

Hosting a ball was no small matter. Musicians had to be hired and supper for all the guests provided. Cards or invitations were sent out no less than two to three weeks prior to the event and a reply was imperative within a day or two. After the ball, thank you notes were expected of all the guests in appreciation for the hospitality.

Balls were, of course, formal occasions which allowed one to show off their finery. But even here there were degrees of formality. The dress ball which usually began with minuets was the most formal, a cotillion ball somewhat less so. "Undress" or "fancy" balls invited the guests to appear in all manner of historical or fanciful costumes. Whatever the form of dress, gloves were essential lest the dancers touch one another directly.

OPENING THE BALL

Early in the Regency era, balls were opened with a minuet. By the early 1800s the practice fell from favor as it took far too long for all the couples to have a turn to display in the slow, elegant dance.

Later in the period, the ball would be opened by the hostess, the lady of highest rank or the person in whose honor the ball was given (like a debutante or new bride) who took the top position of the first dance. The top lady would "call the dance", determining the figures, steps, and music to be danced. Polite young ladies were cautioned that if they should lead a dance they should not make the figures too difficult for the other dancers, especially if there were younger dancers present.

DANCE PARTNERS

Every dance required a partner. At a private ball, unlike a public assembly, everyone was considered introduced, so any young man could ask any young woman to dance. A young lady signaled she was interested in dancing by pinning up the train of her gown. If asked to dance, she could not refuse unless she did not intend to dance for the rest of the night.

Gentlemen, unless they retired to the card room, were expected to engage a variety of partners throughout the evening. Failing to do so was an affront to all the guests. A gentleman might request a dance in advance, but saving more than two dances for a particular partner was detrimental to a young lady's reputation.

Even two dances signaled to observers that the gentleman in question had a particular interest in her. The day after a ball, a gentleman would typically call upon his principle partner, so a young lady who danced two sets with same gentleman might rightfully expect continued acquaintance with him.

Oftentimes women outnumbered men at these affairs. As a result, it was not uncommon for women to dance with other women rather than sit out the entire evening.

FOOD

Halfway through the evening, dancers would pause to refresh themselves with a meal. Depending on the hostess, the ladies might proceed to the dining room together, parading in rank order, or might be escorted in on the arm of a gentleman whose rank matched their own.

One's dance partner for the "supper dance" usually would be one's dining partner for the meal as well.

Each gentleman would serve himself and his neighbors from the dishes within his reach. He also poured wine for the ladies near him. Soup (especially white soup made from veal or chicken stock, egg yolks, ground almonds and cream) served with negus (sugar mixed with water and wine, served hot) were staples. If a dish was required from another part of the table, a manservant would be sent to fetch it. It was not good form to ask a neighbor to pass a dish. It was equally bad manners for the ladies to help themselves or to ask for wine.

During dinner, a gentleman would be expected to entertain the ladies nearest him with engaging conversation. Many topics were unacceptable. A polite individual did not ask direct personal questions of someone they had just met.

DANCES

Supper was quite necessary as most of the ball dances were lively and bouncy. Country dances, the scotch reel, cotillion, quadrille made up most of the dancing.

One dance not likely to be found in balls held in the first decade of the nineteenth century was the waltz. When it was first introduced, the waltz was regarded as shocking because of the physical contact involved. However by 1812, it was a regular feature of private London balls, according to Lady Caroline Lamb—although Lord Byron was scandalized by the prospect of people "embracing" on the dance floor. It was unlikely to have been seen often in public assemblies until the latter part of the Regency era, and even then, not often.

SOURCES

The Complete System of English Country Dancing. 1815.

Day, Malcolm. *Voices from the World of Jane Austen.* David & Charles, 2006.

The Gentleman & Lady's Companion: Containing the Newest Cotillions and Country Dances; to which is added Instances of Ill Manners to be carefully avoided by Youth of Both Sexes. 1798.

A Lady of Distinction. *Regency Etiquette, the Mirror of Graces (1811).* R.L. Shep Publications, 1997.

Lane, Maggie. *Jane Austen's World.* Carlton Books, 2005.

Laudermilk, Sharon and Teresa L. Hamlin. *The Regency Companion.* Garland Publishing, 1989.

"Regency Dances." *Britain Express.* http://www.britainexpress.com/History/regency-dances.htm

Ross, Josephine. *Jane Austen's Guide to Good Manners.* U.S.A.: Bloomsbury, 2006.

Selwyn, David. *Jane Austen & Leisure.* The Hambledon Press, 1999.

Sullivan, Margaret C. *The Jane Austen Handbook.* Quirk Books, 2007.

DANCING THE NIGHT AWAY

BY MIKE RENDELL

A S ALL JANEITES WILL KNOW, JANUARY 27, 2012 MARKED THE 200TH ANNIVERSARY OF the publication of *Pride and Prejudice*. And as every film or TV adaptation of every Jane Austen novel has a dance or ball as its centrepiece I thought it would be useful to look at the role of the dance in eighteenth century—and in particular, Regency—etiquette.

Quite simply, a formal dance was one of the few places where a young person could hope to meet a prospective spouse from outside the immediate family or the circle of the parents' friends. Maybe that is why my own family tree is littered with marriages between cousins— perhaps they weren't especially adept at dancing and therefore at making new friendships!

Suppose your family came to Bath for the Season: you could expect the Master of Ceremonies to come round to your lodgings and assess the eligibility of the young gentleman or lady. An invitation to attend the Assembly Rooms at a specified time would then be given. (It would be chaos if all the carriages bringing the guests arrived at the same time.)

The Master of Ceremonies would carry out suitable introductions, and the couple would then be able to dance—never all evening, but perhaps for two sets. Each set would consist of two dances, each perhaps lasting twenty minutes. There would be no question of a gentleman hogging the company of one girl all evening, or of a man walking up to a girl who caught his eye and suggesting a twirl around the floor! This explains one of Jane Austen's letters, sent in 1796, when she says:

> There was one gentleman, an officer of the Cheshire, a very good-looking young man, who, I was told, wanted very much to be introduced to me, but as he did not want it quite enough to take much trouble in effecting it, we never could bring it about.

Remember too that this was a time when young girls were chaperoned and where anything more affectionate than holding hands in public would be frowned upon, so the art of dance—how to move fluently and to behave appropriately, how to impress and how to engineer a repeat dance—was a social skill which was well worth learning.

Charging down the row the wrong way, or moving awkwardly into the path of another couple, was hardly likely to endear you to your partner—or to the anxious parent watching from the sidelines. I am not convinced that the dances shown in some of the re-enactments are correct—they seem to be throw-backs to the stately dances of the Elizabethan era rather than showing the lively, energetic dances of the Regency period.

Of course, the waltz was not yet socially acceptable—indeed it was considered outrageous. It was the very first dance in which the couple danced in a modified Closed

Position—with the man's hand around the lady's waist. Full of movement and menacing passion is Gillray's 1810 take on the waltz, entitled *"La Walse—Le Bon Genre"*. Why, it positively reeks of indecency!

No, far more respectable was the cotillion (eight dancers in a square performing the dance routine with ten changes); the minuet (beginning to go out of fashion by the Regency period); and the boulangers, or circular dances performed mostly at the end of the evening when participants were getting exhausted and in need of something less strenuous! And then of course there was the country dance which could rumble on for a whole hour.

Learning to dance was something you started while at school—my ancestor's diaries show that he was happy to fork out a guinea a term for lessons for both Anna and Benjamin, the children by his second wife. But dance steps were constantly changing—additional arm movements, or clapping, or a hop-and-a-step might be introduced. One of the favourite arm and hand movements was termed the Allemande (from the French, meaning "German"). These changes in what was currently in vogue on the dance floor meant that adults would take lessons to stay up to date.

One of my favourite sets of dancing pictures was by the caricaturist William Bunbury. In 1787 he published what was in effect the first ever strip cartoon entitled "A Long Minuet as Danced at Bath". Other caricaturists and satirists had endless fun lampooning people learning to dance—especially overweight middle-aged gentlemen desperate to master the latest dance craze.

Of Refinement and Good Manners

By MARIA GRACE

ETIQUETTE IS AN INTEGRAL PART OF EVERY CULTURE. ALTHOUGH THE DETAILS DIFFER among regions and historical periods, the concept of correct and incorrect ways to behave remains constant. Rules of polite behavior are essential elements of communication within a society, a social code that enables individuals to understand motives and subtle messages that are otherwise cumbersome to display through words alone.

These social rules are adopted and adapted over time. Some may be written into elaborate manuals, though many are unwritten, caught rather than taught among the population at large.

In general these rules reflect the values of a society. Following these rules demonstrates respect for the common morality and for other people. Obedience to the guidelines of good manners also reflects on the character of the individual and suggests one is well bred and refined.

In periods of great social transition, like the Regency, published manuals are especially abundant. Many pages in Regency era manuals were filled with comments on general deportment and the behavior to be exhibited by individuals of good breeding. When trying to rise into higher levels of society, a family's social standing could be made or broken by the ability to conform to all the conventions associated with polite behavior.

Although these patterns of etiquette might appear awkward and restrictive, especially for women, they did act as a safeguard against misunderstanding and embarrassment for both parties. This was particularly true as well-bred women were thought to have a "natural" sense of delicacy. Taste and poise should come naturally to a lady, and it was an indictment against her breeding to be worried about looking correct.

MARKS OF GOOD BREEDING

In line with the emphasis on elegance and formality, people were encouraged to maintain an erect posture when sitting or standing. Slouching or leaning back was regarded as slothful unless the individual was infirm in some way. Similarly, a well-bred person walked upright and moved with grace and ease. Moreover, such a person maintained an elegance of manners and deportment and could respond to any social situation with calm assurance and no awkwardness.

Etiquette demanded a person behaved with courteous dignity to acquaintance and stranger alike at all times. Well-bred individuals and those seeking to be seen as such were instructed to keep at arm's length any who presumed too great a familiarity. Icy politeness was the best weapon in putting so-called "vulgar mushrooms" in their place.

To be considered well-mannered, individuals had to control their features, their physical bodies, and their speech when in company. Extremes of emotion and public outbursts were unacceptable, as was anything pretentious or flamboyant. A woman, though, could have the vapors, faint, or suffer from hysteria if confronted by vulgarity or an unpleasant scene.

All forms of vulgarity were unacceptable and to be continually guarded against. Laughter, too, was moderated in polite company, particularly among women. Men might engage in unrestrained mirth in the company of other men or among women of low repute for whom the rules of etiquette were more or less irrelevant.

SHOWING RESPECT

These marks of good breeding were one means by which respect for others was demonstrated. Rituals of bowing and curtsying accomplished similar ends.

A bow or curtsy would be performed according to the status and relationship of the person encountered and with respect to the particular circumstance. For example, a bow or curtsy would be made on entering or leaving a room, though good friends and family were not always bowing to one another.

Bows and curtsies were expected at the beginning and end of a dance, and on encountering any person one wished to acknowledge. Children generally bowed or curtsied on meeting their parents for the first time each day.

When encountering people in public, etiquette suggested it was the woman's duty to acknowledge an acquaintance first by a slight bow with the head and shoulders. If she did not make such an acknowledgement, a gentleman should not acknowledge her.

Such recognition could only occur if the two individuals had been previously introduced.

INTRODUCTIONS

It was unacceptable to speak to anyone of good breeding without a formal introduction by a third party. The higher ranking individual (or the woman in the case of two equally ranking individuals) would indicate whether he or she wished to permit the introduction of an inferior. In the case he or she desired an introduction, a third party would be asked to make one. At a public ball, the Master of Ceremonies would conduct this service to enable gentlemen and ladies to dance. However, if the higher ranking person did not desire an introduction, one could not be forced upon him.

In some circumstances, the higher ranking person could introduce himself or herself to the lower one. When introduced, the people of lower rank bowed or curtsied. Gentlemen and ladies of equal rank bowed and curtsied when formally introduced to each other and again when parting.

Touching and tipping one's hat was a standard salutation; not returning it would be very rude. After being introduced, individuals always acknowledged each other in public, at minimum with a tip or touch to the hat or a slight bow of the shoulders. Failure to acknowledge an acquaintance was a breach in conduct and considered a cut. Manuals warned that a lady should never "cut" someone unless "absolutely necessary", and only ladies were truly justified in delivering a "cut".

SERVANTS

Servants and social inferiors were, of course, the exception to this rule. They were always kept at a proper distance but without arrogance, pride, or aloofness. The well-bred individual spoke to servants with an appropriate degree of civility and avoided the casual informality with which a person might address an equal. Private business was not discussed in the presence of servants, and they were generally ignored at mealtimes. Mocking or belittling servants or their families was deemed undignified and a sign of bad manners.

CONVERSATION

The heart of polite sociability was conversation. The whole purpose of conversation was to please other people and to be deemed pleasing. In general, conversation was tightly controlled by rules of etiquette as well. The list of unacceptable topics far outnumbered the acceptable ones.

Personal remarks, however flattering, were not considered good manners. Etiquette manuals counseled such comments should be exchanged only with close family and intimate friends.

Similarly, scandal and gossip should be omitted from public conversation. Any references to pregnancy, childbirth, or other natural bodily functions were considered coarse and carefully sidestepped. A man could sometimes discuss his hunters or driving horses in the presence of ladies though it was generally discouraged. Greater latitudes of conversation were allowed when the genders were segregated, particularly for the men.

TOUCH

Not surprisingly, good manners required all forms of touching between members of the opposite sex were to be kept to a minimum. Putting a lady's shawl about her shoulders, or assisting her to mount a horse, enter a carriage, and for a gentleman to take a lady's arm through his to support her while out walking were considered acceptable forms of courtesy.

Shaking hands, however, was not. In the Regency era, shaking hands was considered a mark of unusual affability or intimacy. Only gentlemen of about the same social class who knew each other well shook hands. Moreover, the intimacy of shaking hands was a mark of condescension if offered by one of a higher rank.

Shaking hands with a person of the opposite sex was less frequent and less proper. A pressure of the hands was the only external sign a woman could give of harboring a particular regard for certain gentleman, and it was not to be thrown away lightly. According to some contemporary conduct guides, a woman should avoid even touching the hand of a man who was not a family member.

Between sisters or ladies of equal age or rank, a kiss on the cheek was acceptable. A gentleman might kiss a lady's hand, but kissing it "passionately" was a gesture of excessive intimacy.

Though these rules might seem excessive, adherence to them was crucial, especially for ladies whose reputations were especially brittle. For those seeking admission to higher society, any breach in etiquette could be fatal to one's social standing.

SOURCES

Black, Maggie & Deirdre Le Faye. *The Jane Austen Cookbook*. Chicago Review Press, 1995

Byrne, Paula. In *Jane Austen in Context*. Cambridge University Press, 2005.

Day, Malcolm, *Voices from the World of Jane Austen*. David & Charles, 2006.

Downing, Sarah Jane. *Fashion in the Time of Jane Austen*. Shire Publications, 2010.

Jones, Hazel. *Jane Austen & Marriage*. Continuum Books, 2009.

A Lady of Distinction. *Regency Etiquette, the Mirror of Graces (1811)*. R.L. Shep Publications, 1997.

Lane, Maggie. *Jane Austen's World*. Carlton Books, 2005.

Lane, Maggie. *Jane Austen and Food*. Hambledon, 1995.

Laudermilk, Sharon & Teresa L. Hamlin. *The Regency Companion*. Garland Publishing, 1989.

Le Faye, Deirdre. *Jane Austen: The World of Her Novels*. Harry N. Abrams, 2002.

Ray, Joan Klingel. *Jane Austen for Dummies*. Wiley Publishing, Inc., 2006.

Ross, Josephine. *Jane Austen's Guide to Good Manners*. Bloomsbury U.S.A., 2006.

Selwyn, David. *Jane Austen & Leisure*. The Hambledon Press, 1999.

Trusler, John. *The Honours of the Table or Rules for Behavior during Meals*. Literary-Press, 1791.

Vickery, Amanda. *The Gentleman's Daughter*. Yale University Press, 1998.

TAMBOUR WORK

BY LAUREN GILBERT

REGENCY NOVELS FREQUENTLY REFER TO "TAMBOUR FRAMES" AND "TAMBOUR WORK". One novel contained an amusing story where a lady used a tambour frame as a weapon. I assumed it was a form of embroidery. I knew nothing about it, but I enjoy needlework and thought it would be interesting to see what it was.

Tambour embroidery was a very popular and fashionable craft. Thought to have originated in China, it was supposedly introduced to France in the mid-eighteenth century and subsequently spread to England and Western Europe. Ladies occupied their time with tambour work as well as other needlecrafts, while professionals used this technique on a larger scale until machines were able to produce similar effects. The stitcher uses a needle with a hook, similar to a modern latch hook, and makes a chain stitch on fabric stretched in a round frame.

The frame is a two-part object with an inner frame over which the fabric is stretched with the exterior frame holding it in place. It is called a tambour or tambour frame because it resembles a drum ("tambour" is French for drum). It is similar to modern embroidery hoops, but much heavier. (I can now see how it could actually do some damage if used to strike someone!) The thread is held underneath with one hand, while the other hand pushes the hooked needle through the fabric to catch the thread and pull it through.

Bringing the thread back up through the same hole forms a loop, and the pattern evolves as each new stitch is formed near the previous stitch, catching the loop from that stitch. The stitches form a continuous chain. The hooks used were small, sometimes not much more than a wire bent at the tip, and produced a lacy design. It was commonly used to produce white on white design such as the flower and vine designs popular on white muslin. Tambour work was used to embroider gowns, shawls, reticules, and other wearable items. Using the finest hooks and threads, the chain stitch would also lend itself to monogramming handkerchiefs. Obviously, fabrics with a more open weave such as muslin, gauze, and net lend themselves beautifully to tambour work.

Tambour embroidery is now also referred to as tambour crochet. Crochet work as we know it seems to have evolved from tambour embroidery at least in part, being worked as a continuous chain using a hook and thread or yarn without the background fabric. Tambour embroidery is still done today. There are numerous resources on the internet for supplies, hooks, frames, and videos of instruction.

SOURCES

De Dillmont, Thérèse. *The Complete Encyclopedia of Needlework.* Third edition. Philadelphia, PA: Running Press, 1996.

Hopper, John. "Tambour Embroidery Work." *The Textile Blog*, 7/22/2010. http://thetextileblog.blogspot.com/2010/07/tambour-embroidery-work.html

McConnell, Megan. "Tambour Work." Embroidery Site. *BellaOnline: The Voice of Women*, 2010. http://www.bellaonline.com/articles/art67103.asp

CHOCOLATE THE REGENCY WAY

BY MARIA GRACE

O F THE THREE LUXURY BEVERAGES OF THE REGENCY ERA, TEA DOMINATES THE CON-
versation, but coffee and chocolate were regularly enjoyed by many in the higher
classes. Chocolate was typically served at breakfast, although specialty coffee and chocolate houses served it at all times during the day.

While some chocolate candy did exist in the Regency era, dipped chocolates and
sweet chocolate bars would not appear until much later. French cookbooks dating from
1750 contained recipes for chocolate disks sprinkled with nonpareils, chocolate truffles,
and fudge-like chocolate conserve. Recipes for ices, ice creams, custards, and various pastries and tarts abounded in English cookery books. Even so, chocolate in the Regency era
generally referred to drinking chocolate.

Preparing drinking chocolate was a time consuming, labor intensive process, beyond
the means of many, particularly if started from dried cacao nibs.

Hannah Glasse offered two recipes for preparing the nibs for use.

How to make Chocolate.

*TAKE six pounds of cocoa-nuts, one pound of anise-seeds, four ounces of
long-pepper, one of cinnamon, a quarter of a pound of almonds, one pound
of pistachios, as much achiote as will make it the colour of brick, three grains
of musk, and as much amber-grease, six pounds of loaf-sugar, one ounce
of nutmegs, dry and beat them, and scarce them through a fine fire; your
almonds must be beat to a paste, and mixed with the other ingredients; then
dip your sugar in orange-flower or rose-water, and put it in a skillet, on a very
gentle charcoal fire; then put in the spice, and stew it well together, then the
musk and amber-grease, then put in the cocoa-nuts last of all then achiote,
wetting it with the water the sugar was dipped in; stew all these very well
together over a hotter fire than before; then take it up, and put it into boxes,
or what form you like and set it to dry in a warm place. The pistachios and
almonds must be a little beat in a mortar, then ground upon a stone.*

Another Way to make Chocolate.

*TAKE six pounds of the best Spanish nuts, when parched, and cleaned, from
the hulls, take three pounds of sugar, two ounces of the best cinnamon,
beaten and sifted very fine; to every two pound of nuts put in three good
vanelas, or more or less as you please; to every pound of nuts half a drachm
of cardamom-seeds, very finely beaten and searced.*

These recipes, which might also include cardamom, aniseed, cloves, or bergamot, produced a hard, gritty chocolate tablet. A few people ate them straight as a type of candy, but most believed they would cause indigestion if eaten in that form. These tablets were the basis of Regency drinking chocolate.

Even with premade chocolate tablets, it took thirty minutes or more of strenuous effort and several specialized kitchen items to prepare a cup of drinking chocolate.

First, a specialty chocolate grater would be used to shave the necessary amount of chocolate from the solid tablet. The powdered chocolate would be added to a large pan containing water, milk, or possibly a mixture of water and wine or water and brandy and placed over heat.

The chocolate/liquid mixture would be brought to a boil with constant stirring to prevent scorching. After it came to a boil, the cook removed it from the heat and used a special tool, known in England as a chocolate mill (in France a *molinet*, in Spain a *molinilla*) to agitate the mixture. At this point eggs, flour, corn starch, or even bread might be added to the mixture to thicken it. The cook would spin the chocolate mill between her hands for several minutes to incorporate the thickeners into the drinking chocolate.

After beating, the pot was returned to the heat and brought to a boil again while stirring constantly. At this stage, cream might be added. The chocolate mill would be employed once more to fully blend the mixture and raise a head of froth, without which drinking chocolate was not considered fit to be served.

The finished drinking chocolate would be transferred to a special chocolate pot for service. A chocolate pot was taller and straighter than a tea pot, with a shorter spout than a coffee pot, placed high on the pot. It also sported a hinged finial on the lid to allow a chocolate mill to be used while the lid was down to prevent splashing.

Chocolate cups were taller and narrower than coffee or tea cups. Their unique shape made them more likely to spill, so special saucers known as chocolate stands developed to steady the unstable cups.

Those who could not afford all the specialty items made do with what they had, cooking their chocolate in skillets and drinking it out of whatever vessels they had.

If they could not afford chocolate at all, Hannah Glasse offered this recipe.

Sham Chocolate

TAKE a pint of milk, boil it over a slow fire, with some whole cinnamon, and sweeten it with Lisbon sugar; beat up the yolks of three eggs, throw all together into a chocolate-pot, and mill it one way, or it will turn. Serve it up in chocolate-cups. [Gingerbread might also be added to this beverage as a thickener.]

This modern recipe captures many of the flavors of Regency drinking chocolate:

Spiced Hot Chocolate
- *2 cups water*
- *¼ cup sugar*

- *1 strip lemon peel 1" by 2"*
- *1 3" cinnamon stick*
- *pinch of ground cloves*
- *¼ cup cocoa powder*
- *1 tsp vanilla*
- *½ cup heavy cream*

Heat the first 5 ingredients to boiling, reduce heat, simmer 3 min. Remove from heat, whisk in cocoa and vanilla until foamy. Strain into warmed cups. Top with whipped cream.

SOURCES

Boyle, Laura. "A Passion for Hot Chocolate." *Jane Austen.co.uk*, January 9, 2011. http://www.janeausten.co.uk/a-passion-for-hot-chocolate/

Glasse, Hannah. *The Art of Cookery Made Plain and Easy.* W Strahan, 1784.

Rundell, Maria. *A New System of Domestic Cookery.* J Geave, 1839.

SOME LIKED IT HOT! COOKING CURRY IN JANE AUSTEN'S TIME

By LAUREN GILBERT

O N MY FIRST TRIP TO ENGLAND, ONE OF THE FIRST THINGS I WANTED TO TRY WAS Indian food, particularly curry. I used to think that trying spicy food from other places was a modern taste, and it was not a concept that I associated with typical English cuisine of Jane Austen's time. However, history proves me wrong. Cookbooks and recipes from the eighteenth and nineteenth centuries show that flavorful food was important, and herbs and seasonings were as important to cooks then as they are today. Trade and colonies yielded new seasonings and tastes. Travellers and immigrants had brought different seasonings and dishes into England, as did returning soldiers, sailors, and traders. Spices, especially pepper, at different times were an exchange item, valued as money. Clearly, strong, distinct, spicy flavors had been incorporated into the culinary landscape, and hot seasoning was a part of that. I had intended to present a broad overview of the use of herbs and spices in cooking during Jane Austen's day. However, I was distracted by Martha Lloyd's curry recipes, so today our focus will be curry in Jane Austen's time.

There is a perception that the popularity of spices in earlier times was based at least in part on their value as preservatives, which is actually not correct. It was driven by flavor and medicinal values. Lack of refrigeration resulted in the "high" (tainted) flavor of meat, fish, and poultries, so seasonings were used to disguise the taste. (Spices were not effective as preservatives and were too expensive to use in a quantity required for preserving the way salt is used). Cubeb and cayenne are both hot and spicy and are listed in Culpeper (which indicates they could be grown in England). Uses of sauces and strong tastes, such as nutmeg, cloves, cinnamon, etc. produced complex, sophisticated flavors that appealed to the wealthy. When combined with the supposed medicinal values (hot spicy seasoning balanced cool moist humours of meat and fish), we can see how the desire for spices grew.

Before the thirteenth century, the taste for spice came back with the crusaders. Originally, the spice trade was controlled by the Arabs in the Middle East, but the Dutch and Portuguese became competitors, with the Dutch ultimately assuming control. In order to participate in (and to try to ultimately control) the spice trade, the British East India Company was formed in 1600 to compete with the Dutch. In 1608, the British East India Company established its first base in India and, for the first time, Britain had access to spices that were not controlled by the Dutch. Spice trade was driven by the craving for varied and exotic tastes as well as the medicinal values of various spices. (Spice was the first globally-traded commodity, one of the first pushes to globalization.) It is interesting to note that hot peppers (capsicum-cayenne peppers) were introduced into Asia by European traders after they were found in the New World (the name "Indian peppers" relates to the New World, not India).

English traders began to settle in India in the early 1600s. Indian seasonings gained increasing popularity in England as their flavors were brought with returnees from India who desired to recreate flavors they had come to enjoy and shared them. The cost of spices remained high in spite of English control of spice trade—almost constant warfare disrupted trade and consequently affected cost and availability.

There is disagreement on the origin of the word "curry", but it was applied to Indian dishes with spiced sauces by the English in the seventeenth century. The Hindostanee Coffee House was opened by Dean Mahomed in London in 1809 advertising Indian dishes better than any curries made in England before. (Hookah pipes could also be smoked there.) Although Mr. Mahomed went bankrupt in three years (people did not dine out then as commonly as now), this restaurant remained open for some years under various owners. Popularity spread to middle classes in spite of cost. (Note that the cachet of spices lessened somewhat as their perceived medicinal value declined due to improved modern medical knowledge, a loss of status which may have resulted in a slightly reduced monetary value that may have allowed them to be a bit more easily purchased by other than the wealthy classes. However, the cost did not reflect any significant decline during the Georgian era, thanks to war, blockades, and piracy.)

Curry was an established element of English cooking in the Georgian era. In the first edition of Hannah Glasse's *The Art Of Cookery Made Plain And Easy*, she included a recipe for "Fowle Rabbit Currey" in which rabbit is stewed with rice flour (thickener), coriander seeds, and black peppercorns, which would have been very mild (in the fourth edition, ginger and turmeric are included). Hannah Glasse's original recipe may have been one of the earliest examples of changing a recipe to suit a different population's taste. The 1774 new edition contains a recipe for "To make a currey the Indian way" (chicken with turmeric, ginger, salt, and pepper) and for "A Pellew the Indian Way" (rice pilau with pepper, mace, and cloves) on page 101.

John Mollard's *The Art Of Cookery Made Easy and Refined,* second edition, had a recipe for "currie" (curried chicken) on page 81, referring to two tablespoons of "currie powder" and cayenne pepper to taste, which seems to indicate an increasing fondness for the Indian spices and for heat. There is also a "Currie of lobster" on page 83 and "A Peloe of rice" (pilau of rice) on page 95, while on page 254 there is a recipe for "Currie (Pepper Water)" which is apparently a version of what became known as Mulligatawny Soup. Available information indicates that curry powders were widely known and subject to individual tastes; recipes for curry powder were highly variable.

Curry is mentioned in Martha Lloyd's household book: curry powder, curry soup, curried chicken. Martha was Jane Austen's friend, and lived with Jane, her mother, and sister, before she finally married Jane's brother Francis. It is safe to assume Jane Austen would have had curry dishes. Note that Martha mentions use of cayenne and black pepper "to your taste..." so it seems evident that the heat level was a personal matter even then.

Martha's recipe for curry powder contains turmeric, galangal (a ginger relative), cayenne pepper, and rice flour. (The use of few spices could be a matter of taste, a matter of cost, or elements of both.) I made it up and used it in a dish similar to "A Receipt to Curry after the Indian Manner" from *The Jane Austen Cookbook*. It is very mild and has a nice flavor, perfect for someone who has never tried curry or for someone who doesn't care for a strong or pungent curry. The flavor could be deepened by increasing the turmeric and/or galangal, or by adding other Indian spices, such as cumin or coriander. One source indicated the rice powder would be a thickener of the sauce, but I noticed very little thickening effect.

Curry maintained its popularity through the nineteenth century, coming to a peak in Victoria's reign. It declined in the early twentieth century but has become a staple of British cuisine again. While the flavors may be somewhat different than those with which Jane Austen and her family may have been familiar, the concept and the spices combined to make curry would not be foreign to her.

SOURCES

Black, Maggie and Deirdre Le Faye. *The Jane Austen Cookbook*. Toronto: McClelland & Stewart Ltd., 1995.

"East India Company Timeline." *The East India Company website*. http://www.theeastindiacompany.com/24/timeline

Freedman, Paul. "Spices: How the Search for Flavors Influenced Our World." YaleGlobal Online. (3/11/2003) http://yaleglobal.yale.edu/print/396

Glasse, Hannah. *The Art Of Cookery Made Plain And Easy*. 1784. https://play.google.com/books/reader?id=xJdAAAAAIAAJ&printsec=frontcover&output=reader&authuser=0&hl=en

Hickman, Peggy. *A Jane Austen Household Book with Martha Lloyd's recipes*. North Pomfret, Vermont: David & Charles Inc., 1977.

Jahangir, Rumeana. "How Britain got the hots for curry." *BBC News Magazine*. (11/26/2009) http://news.bbc.co.uk/2/hi/8370054.stm

Mollard, John. *The Art Of Cookery Made Easy and Refined*. 2nd edition. 1802. https://play.google.com/books/reader?id=3nEEAAAAYAAJ&printsec=frontcover&output=reader&authuser=0&hl=en

O'Rourke, Kevin H. "The Worldwide economic impact of the Revolutionary and Napoleonic Wars." *National Bureau of Economic Research website*. May 2005. http://www.nber.org/papers/w11344

Smith, David W. "A History of Curry." *The Curry House Online*. 2012. http://www.curry-house.co.uk

Tannahill, Reay. *Food in History*. New York: Three Rivers Press, 1988.

A Profitable Vice: Gambling in Regency England

By J.A. Beard

Games of chance have been with mankind from our most ancient days. Even in cultures and times where currency and property were unknown ideas, staring down fate and wagering something of importance was known. In many ancient cultures, gambling was even linked to mystical, religious, and ritualistic practices. The pervasive allure of gambling also affected the English of the Regency period.

While the Regency English did not elevate gambling to a mystical experience, the pastime was tremendously popular during the period. It's important to note this fondness for games of chance and profit/loss cut across all levels of society. It was arguably most pronounced among the top tiers of proper society as the elite could enjoy the special thrill that came with extremely high stakes.

Both men and women were drawn in by Lady Luck's tests of chance, though there were differences in regards to their typical approaches to gambling. Men, in general, bet on a wider range of activities including cards, dice, and sporting events (e.g., boxing and races). Really, though, the true gamblers, would bet on almost anything. Women, however, particularly women of higher social standing, tended to keep their gambling more focused on cards and also tended to keep their stakes lower. Whist, faro, piquet, and loo were all popular card game choices for men and women who wanted to toss a bit of coin around and challenge fortune.

This is not to say that women never played for larger stakes, and there even was the occasional titled woman who decided that there was good money to be made in facilitating gambling and taking a cut. After all, the house always wins, right? Men also had their gambling facilitated by its more prominent presence at their clubs and their greater social freedom to frequent "gaming hells."

Although there were some who looked askance at gambling as a moral failing, there was no general social condemnation against the activity in polite society. Excessive gambling, as with other excessive behaviors, was frowned upon, but people of great social respectability could freely gamble without a lasting taint on their reputation, even with the occasional playing at one of the seedier gaming dens. Though larger bets meant great reward, they obviously also carried greater risks, and it wasn't unknown for people to even bet and lose property, a rather serious matter in a society that so tied land to status.

Indeed, arguably, the main social condemnation related to gambling at the time (other than cheating) applied only to those who acquired gambling debts and then did not pay them off. As with all things during the Regency, social class differences heavily colored the view of a gambling debt. A titled gentleman would feel pressured to promptly pay back his debts to another titled aristocrat of similar rank. A titled aristocrat might feel he could take his time, though, if he owed debts to a common merchant. Although the general tendency of social classes to mix with those of their own kind kept the overall amount of extreme class differences between debt holders and their debtors relatively low, there were more than a few gentlemen of means who found themselves owing a large sum to their alleged social inferiors. They would get their money...eventually. Despite the "advantage" that came with being able to leisurely repay one's social inferiors, it was somewhat offset with the reality that owing money to a social inferior was very damaging to one's reputation.

Gambling could also reinforce social classes in a different way. In *Pride and Prejudice*, Lizzie Bennet finds herself a bit put off, not by the presence of gambling but by what she assumed were too-high stakes:

> On entering the drawing room she [Elizabeth] *found the whole party at loo, and was immediately invited to join them; but suspecting them to be playing high she declined it, and making her sister the excuse, said she would amuse herself for the short time she could stay below with a book.*
> —*Pride and Prejudice*, Chapter 8

I'm guessing that once she became Mrs. Darcy, she was a bit less nervous about high stakes.

FUN AND GAMES ON REGENCY EVENINGS

By MARIA GRACE

THESE DAYS, MOST OF OUR EVENING ENTERTAINMENT CENTERS AROUND ELECTRICITY: television, video games, internet. Even our lighting is almost entirely electric. If the power goes out, we grow agitated, wondering what we are supposed to do to keep ourselves entertained until the power comes back on.

In the days before electricity, evenings, particularly winter evenings which kept families indoors with poor lighting, proved challenging for entertainment. Consequently, young ladies were often accomplished musicians and called upon to entertain their fellows in song. Cards were also popular but often could only accommodate a small group at a time. To include larger groups at once, house parties turned to parlor games to while away the long evening hours.

Rachel Revel, spinster, published a book in 1825, *Winter Evening Pastimes or The Merry Maker's Companion,* that offers guidelines for various amusements suitable for genteel company in the drawing room. Many of the games are somewhat familiar, though we often consider them children's games rather than adult pastimes. Even more interesting is the way that normal strict social conventions might have been bent or even ignored for the sake of the play.

Some games allowed for the potential of physical touch that would earn censure in other contexts.

> *Buffy Gruffy is recommended as a fit substitute for Blindman's Buff for those good folks whose nerves could ill support the racket of the legitimate Blindman's Buff, or were afraid of having their toes trod on, or their furniture bruised and battered. One player, with a blindfold over the eyes, stands in the middle of the room. The others arrange their chairs in a circle and silently trade places. Someone claps to start the game. The blindfolded person passes around the chairs and stops in front of one. The player may use his knees to determine if someone is sitting in that chair, physical contact generally not permitted in polite social contexts, especially between gentlemen and ladies.*
>
> *The blindfolded player begins questioning the seated player who answers while disguising their voice as much as possible. Here is an excellent opportunity for an individual to mock someone they do not like all under the guise of polite hilarity. After three answers, the blindfolded player must guess who they*

have questioned. If they are correct, the seated player takes the blindfold and play begins anew. Else, the blindfolded player moves on to question another.

Other games opened the possibility for people to say things most shocking. I can easily imagine a group of young ladies or young men conspiring together to cause their friends to say very surprising things in the course of this game.

Cross Questions and Crooked Answers: Players are seated in a circle. The starting player asks his right-hand neighbor a question, as for example, "What is the use of a cat?" The person interrogated might answer, "To kill the rat, that ate the malt, that lay in the house that Jack built," or some other similar and somewhat ridiculous response. The player who has answered then turns to their neighbor and asks their own question, perhaps "What is the use of a looking-glass?" to which the answer might be "To reflect our perfect likeness."

The play continues around the circle with each player recalling the question they have asked and the answer they have given for at the end each player will recite the question asked of me was_____ and the answer is of course_____. In this case, they would say "The question asked of me was what is the use of a cat, and the answer is of course to reflect our perfect likeness." If any player cannot recite their question and answer correctly, they must pay a forfeit.

Other word games offered the opportunity to ask questions of someone of the opposite sex that might not be otherwise asked. It is not difficult to imagine humor used as front for something more serious.

Short Answers: The players are seated in a circle, with a lady and gentleman alternately. A lady commences the game by asking her right-hand neighbor a question, to which he replies with single syllable words. Longer words will exact a penalty, one for each additional syllable. He then turns to the next lady with a question to be answered with a single syllable. The questions may be mundane as in: Pray, Sir, permit me to ask if you love dancing? Or unique as in: Pray, Madam, what wood do you think the best for making thumb-screws? The challenge comes in that neither question NOR answer may be repeated. Any player who repeats a question or answer incurs a forfeit.

Musical magic provided, with the assistance of one's friends, the perfect opportunity to flirt openly under the cover of being a good sport.

Musical Magic: One of the party is made to quit the room until the rest determined what task he will be required to perform. The task can be as simple as snuffing a candle, for a novice player, or as complex as kneeling before another player, removing their ring and placing it on the finger of the other player, for an experienced player. The player is guided in divining his task by the playing of music from soft or loud. When the player is close to the object or action he must do next, the music becomes louder until it stops when he has gotten it right. The further away the player the softer the music. If the player in despair, gives up a forfeit must be paid and another player takes his place.

The Aviary provides even greater latitude, allowing the players to confide a secret to another, openly and in public.

The Aviary: The person who leads this game (the birdman) should have a very good memory to avoid blunders or a piece of paper and pencil to keep track of all the birds in the aviary. All of the players select a bird to be in the aviary and whispers their choice to the birdman. The birdman then instructs: Ladies and gentlemen, my aviary is complete, and I will thank you now to inform me to which of these you give the preference, or which are objects of your dislike. The birdman then asks each player three questions: To which of my birds you will give your heart? To which you will confide your secret? From which will you pluck a feather?

The player will answer for example: I give my heart to the goldfinch; my secret to the parrot; and pluck a feather from the crow. The birdman notes down these answers. Should the player select a bird not on the list, he must pay a forfeit and select another until the answers are complete.

Once all the players have responded the birdman reveals the identity of each bird. Then each player kneels to the bird to whom he has given his heart; discloses something in confidence to the bird chosen for the secret; and the person from whom a feather was plucked pays a forfeit.

I must admit, after reading these, and many others of the games included in this book, I was quite surprised at how close to the line of impropriety many of these games might be. It is not difficult to imagine young people conspiring together to make these games work to their advantage in serious endeavors of flirtation and matchmaking. I wonder how many hearts were won and lost in the mists of these popular winter pastimes.

WOMEN'S PERIODICALS DURING THE REGENCY: *ACKERMANN'S*

By LAUREN GILBERT

W HEN THE NAME ACKERMANN'S COMES TO MIND, THE FIRST THING ONE THINKS OF is the fashion plate, the beautifully drawn illustration of the current mode. However, there was so much more than that....

Rudolph Ackermann published the *Repository of Arts, Literature, Commerce, Manufactures, Fashions and Politics* (also known as *Ackermann's Repository*) in London beginning in 1809 as a monthly periodical.

Originally, this periodical was much more than a fashion magazine. As its title indicates, each month the reader was treated to a selection of articles about a wide variety of subjects, ranging from art and architecture to domestic issues (including needlework patterns and home furnishings), biographical sketches of historical or current figures, and reviews of books and art exhibitions. Even political matters were explored. Fashion was only one of many subjects addressed in these early magazines.

Women's buying power was also acknowledged, in that there were product advertisements, not only for cosmetics (like Gowland's Lotion) but for larger purchases such as furniture (like the patent pianoforte advertised in 1812).

I took the opportunity to browse through the *Repository of Arts, Literature, Fashions, Manufactures, &c.* Vol. II, No. VII (July 1, 1816).

Articles included information about architecture (a Gothic Conservatory and the new Customs House were the focus in this edition), saloon draperies, a needle-work pattern (a design for muslin), instructions on how to dye various fabrics certain colors from *The Domestic Commonplace Book*, poetry, and short stories. Under "Miscellanies", there was a fascinating article titled "Some Particulars Illustrative of the Character of Prince Leopold of Saxe-Coburg." The fashion items appeared later in the periodical discussing English and French fashion issues.

The periodical ceased operations in 1829. By that year, it was known as *Ackermann's Repository of Fashion* and was dedicated primarily to fashion and needlework.

A quick review of *Ackermann's Repository of Fashions*, No. I January, 1829 (Price 2s.) shows the beautiful fashion plates, with detailed descriptions and a needlework pattern. The February 1829 edition includes masquerade costumes and "General Observations on Parisian Fashions" as well as a needlework pattern.

Considering that by this time there was already a shift towards the mores and values we associate with the Victorian period—including the idea that a woman's place was in the home and that she should not take an interest in matters such as politics—the change in content is significant.

FURTHER READING

Blum, Stella, ed. *Ackermann's Costume Plates: Women's Fashions in England, 1818-1828.* New York: Dover Publications, Inc., 1978.

R. Ackermann's Repository of Fashions [4th ser. of the Repository of arts, literature, fashions, manufactures]. https://books.google.com/books?id=d1AEAAAAQAAJ

The Repository of Arts, Literature, Fashions, Manufactures, &c. The Second Series. Vol. II, No. VII (July 1, 1816). https://books.google.com/books?id=TEIFAAAAQAAJ

THE LADY'S MONTHLY MUSEUM

BY M.M. BENNETTS

URING THE LAST YEARS OF THE EIGHTEENTH CENTURY AND WELL INTO THE EARLY nineteenth century, as female literacy and affluence increased, there was a growing body of publications designed to meet the burgeoning demand for feminine entertainment.

This is an age when great poetry not only sells, it sells well—Byron's *Childe Harold* doesn't just sell well, it's a runaway best-seller along the lines of *The Da Vinci Code*. Austen's *Sense & Sensibility* causes such a sensation, Lady Caroline Lamb's mother is writing about it, saying that everyone in the Spencer household is wholly taken up with it and talks of nothing else.

It is—make no doubt—a literate society, and whilst the salons of English ladies may not reach the intellectual and political heights achieved by Frenchwomen of the period, that doesn't make them literary slouches.

The Lady's Monthly Museum or Polite Repository of Amusement and Instruction: Being an Assemblage of whatever can tend to please the Fancy, interest the Mind or exalt the Character of The British Fair, written "By a Society of Ladies", was one of the immensely popular periodicals published during this period. (I did not make up that title, I can assure you. I merely copied what is in the frontispiece of the volume at hand.)

It was published by Vernor and Hood in London, from 1798 until 1832, and provides a rather different window into the world of the early nineteenth century lady than one might imagine based on novels and histories about the age.

Volume five (being the one I possess) is a good example. The contents include an article about one Miss Linwood (who apparently is a painter of some note), and the following articles, titled: "Impostors", "The Generous Host", "Habit", a series of invented letters called "The Old Woman", three chapters of a serialised romance by the title of *The Castle De Warrenne*, the Editor's "Reply to Mrs. Saveall's Letter—with some useful hints upon the government of the Temper", "On Celibacy and Marriage", "A Character", "The Poor Sailor Boy", "On a Passage in Sterne"...and last, but not least, *Jane of Flanders; Or, the Siege of Hennebonne, Scene III of a Drama in Two Acts*, which is continued from Volume IV (perfect for home dramatics).

(Later issues contain a great deal of poetry, a "Pattern for a Carpet in Needlework", articles on the "Manners of Parisian Ladies" and under School of Arts, "To destroy Bugs". And curiously enough, my copy does not have—with the exception of the needlework pattern—fashion plates or pictures of any kind.)

Equally, it's vital to bear in mind that each of these volumes had an enormous reach. Though initially received by one household, once read, the volume would have been lent about the neighbourhood, and each of the articles probably read or heard by well over 50 women.

My favourite offering from this particular volume is the Romance—*The Castle De Warrenne*—possibly because it's so silly, but just as much because it provides an insight into what they were reading, what books and ideas were popular, how they spoke and wrote, and how early nineteenth century females perceived themselves, how they perceived heroism and romance.

This is the opening:

> *Slowly and heavily the bell of the great clock in the turret tolled out three: the gloomy mists of night were gradually dispersing, while a faint yellow, tinging the eastern atmosphere, already indicated the approach of day.*
>
> *Matilda started from her couch yet wet with tears, and which had that night afforded her but broken and imperfect slumbers. Fearing that she had exceeded the appointed time, she hastily arrayed herself in her simple habit, and, bending mournfully over the bed of the yet sleeping Raymond, bestowed innumerable kisses on his dimpled mouth.*
>
> *"Sweet babe!" cried she in an agony of tears: "perhaps I for the last time view thy lovely countenance!—no longer shall I receive pleasure from thy innocent endearments! Oh! Why does Virtue demand this painful sacrifice!—My dear Lady, too,—all—all lost!!"*
>
> *Again she pressed her lips to those of the child, who opened his eyes, and, fixing them on Matilda, smiled sweetly. The smile undid all her resolution; and, seating herself by his side, she soothed him with her accustomed tenderness, heedless of the passing time. The clock again reminded her of her tardiness, and with reluctance, she replaced the child; and, casting a mournful look round her little apartment, departed.*
>
> *With trembling steps and perturbed heart she descended the great staircase. All was yet profoundly still. At the appointed spot she met Jaques, who waited (faithful to the trust reposed in him) to open the gate for her.*

(I shall skip ahead to the description of our heroine now, because you won't want to miss this.)

> *Matilda, at this period, had just completed her fourteenth year. Her figure was elegantly formed, and though it had not yet attained its perfect stature, was nevertheless far from contemptible. Her complexion, exquisitely fair, was admirably contrasted with a profusion of chestnut-coloured hair, which fell in careless ringlets over her forehead and bosom. Her eyes were bright and piercing, and the contraction of the eyes at the temples gave an expression of archness highly fascinating.*
>
> *Her dress consisted of a gray camlet jacket and petticoat, neatly bound with black ribbon, which served to exhibit to advantage her fine shape. A net fillet*

confined the superfluous hair, over which was tied a little black chip hat; and
a pair of blue silk mittens completed her dress, at once simple and becoming.

It's great stuff! She runs away to her parents' house, where she finds her father dying... plenty of opportunity to get lachrymose there...and on it goes.

And whilst we may laugh at the naivety of the writing and the overwrought sensibilities, this is exactly the sort of thing that Marianne Dashwood would have found appealing (and Willoughby too, no doubt) and which was being read (devoured) up and down the country by ladies of all ages.

No wonder *Sense & Sensibility* was such a hit!

STRIKE A LIGHT!

By MIKE RENDELL

Does your Regency hero pose nonchalantly by the window, pull out a cheroot, and light it with a match struck against the rough stone surface of the mullion window through which he gazes at his beloved? If so, you may have to re-think the scene, because striking a match was not known until a British invention in the year 1827.

Up until then your hero would have taken a taper from a lit fire, or, if no fire burned in the grate, would have had to resort to using a tinderbox. And that meant several minutes of messing around getting very frustrated and probably grazing his gorgeous knuckles....

My family still have a couple of tinderboxes belonging to my Georgian ancestors. One of my forebears was called Richard Fairfax; his box is dated 1812 and I suspect was one of many thousands of steel, hinged tinderboxes churned out by metal workers in Birmingham in the reign of George III. They are usually around five inches long and just under an inch deep.

It made me think: how were the tinderboxes used, and when did congreves/vestas/lucifers/matches come into vogue?

The tinderbox usually contained at least three items—a flint, a firesteel, and a piece of tinder (typically charcloth). It might also contain "matchsticks," made of wood dipped in brimstone, which would be lit from the charcloth, and a damper (to extinguish the charcloth after it had been used).

The charcloth was made by scorching a piece of material so that it was easy to ignite. An old piece of linen would be held by tongs close to the flames until it blackened. It would then be allowed to burn for a fraction of time before being extinguished, and popped into the box for future use. If charred cloth was not available then straw might be used or even, or if you were French, a thin slice of a mushroom known as *amadou* dipped in saltpetre. In England it was known as "horse's hoof fungus" because of its shape.

The firesteel was held rather like a knuckle-duster. Repeated downward strikes of the firesteel against the flint would send a shower of sparks down onto the charcloth. After two or three minutes, with many attempts and often with knuckles knocked red-raw from being caught on the flint, the cloth would smoulder and be blown gently into life; the flame would be transferred to the matchstick (known as a "punk" or sometimes a "spunk") which would then flare into life; from there the flame could be transferred either to a candle or to the hearth to light the kindling wood. *Voilà!*

The tinderbox had been in use for hundreds of years with very few modifications. When my ancestor bought his in 1812, he would have little thought that it would become obsolete within a matter of only a few years.

In 1827 a Stockton on Tees chemist called John Walker began experimenting with chemicals which would burst into flames. According to Wikipedia he came up with the idea of *"wooden splints or sticks of cardboard coated with sulphur and tipped with a mixture of sulphide of antimony, chlorate of potash and gum, the sulphur serving to communicate the flame to the wood."* At first Walker simply called them "friction lights". He declined to apply for a patent, and his involvement in the development of the friction match only really became apparent after his death in 1859.

His price for a box of 50 matches was a shilling, and each box came with a piece of sandpaper, folded double, through which the match had to be drawn to ignite it. Walker named the matches Congreves in honour of the inventor and rocket pioneer Sir William Congreve.

Despite Walker selling his first Congreves in April 1827, credit for the invention was claimed by Samuel Jones, a Londoner who copied Walker's ideas to the letter and who launched his own Lucifers in 1829. Others came up with their own ingredients for "safety" friction matches, and suddenly fire was portable, instant, and safe. All those tinderboxes became museum objects almost overnight.

THE DUEL THAT SHOCKED
THE NATION

BY M.M. BENNETTS

O N THE TWENTY-FIRST OF SEPTEMBER 1809, JUST AFTER THE DAWN OF A SUNNY AND clear morning, Viscount Castlereagh made his way with his cousin, Lord Yarmouth, toward Yarmouth's cottage, discussing as he went the fashionable soprano, Angelica Catalani, and even humming the tunes of her arias. Awaiting them at the cottage were George Canning and Charles Ellis, Canning's second.

After Ellis made one final attempt at reconciliation between the two principals, at shortly after six, Lord Castlereagh and Mr. Canning took the ten required paces, turned and took aim, both missing their first shot. After which, Castlereagh declared himself unsatisfied and the pair resumed their positions.

This second time Castlereagh's aim proved more accurate and Canning collapsed on the grass with a bullet in his thigh. Castlereagh, honour now satisfied, rushed to his fallen adversary's side, and taking him by the arm, carried him to a neighbouring cottage to receive medical attention.

However, within weeks, *The Battle of the Blocks*, a satire mocking the profligacy and arrogance of the duellists, was published to the delight of the jeering classes. And it was only the first of many such poems and satires.

But what can have occurred to have brought a man like Castlereagh, about whom one of his fellow diplomats would later write, *"the suavity and dignity of his manners, his habitual patience and self-command, his considerate tolerance of difference of opinion in others...his firmness, when he knew he was right, in no degree detracted from the influence of his conciliatory demeanour..."* to be involved in such a scandalous activity as a duel?

Look no further than his opponent and rival, George Canning.

Under the aegis of the aging and somewhat sickly Duke of Portland as Prime Minister, a government had been formed in March 1807 with Spencer Perceval as the Chancellor of the Exchequer and leader of the House, Canning at the Foreign Office, and Castlereagh at the War Office.

Castlereagh, with customary diligence, threw himself into his work reorganising the Volunteers and the militia to bolster Britain's expeditionary forces, as well as commissioning a series of reports from intelligence agents across Europe in an attempt to find the weak points in Napoleon's empire.

In the Lower House, he was also frequently called upon to stand firm against the attacks from the Opposition on the conduct of the war, in particular defending the actions and honour of Sir Arthur Wellesley, first in regard to his action in Denmark and latterly over events in the Peninsula which had culminated in the disastrous Treaty of Cintra.

(In a nutshell: Wellesley had trounced the French at the Battle of Vimeiro on 21 August 1808. All well and good. Within a day however, Wellesley was superseded by two older armchair generals, Sir Harry Burrard and Sir Hew Darymple, who negotiated a completely ruinous treaty with the French General Junot, in which Britain was required to transport all the defeated French troops back to France carrying with them their "personal" items, which happened to be all they'd looted from the Portuguese. When news of the treaty got out in London, there was a huge outcry—and Wellesley was blamed, though he had not been a signatory to the Treaty.)

By late September, as the news of the Battle of Vimeiro was published and the details of the dishonourable treaty leaked out, Canning, in private, grew strident in blaming both Castlereagh and Wellesley for the debacle.

Though a new Commander-in-Chief, Sir John Moore, was given command of the Peninsular Campaign, by the end of January 1809 he was dead, and the surviving British troops had been evacuated following the Retreat to Corunna. (No, things weren't looking great on the war front....) Nevertheless, by April, heartily supported and endorsed in Parliament by Castlereagh, Wellesley was on his way back to the Peninsula as Commander-in-Chief to aid the beleaguered Portuguese and Spanish in ridding themselves of the Napoleonic yoke.

At the same time, Castlereagh proposed within the Cabinet attempting to open up another front in the war against Napoleon, this time in northern Germany near Flushing— later this would be known as the Walcheren Campaign.

And it is at this time, around Easter 1809, that Canning's campaign to discredit and undermine Castlereagh got going. Thus, as the months of meetings with his fellow Cabinet-members moved forward, as Castlereagh relied on their support and expertise and trust for his pursuit of the country's war aims, Canning was pursuing a secret campaign to have him removed from office even as in public he made a show of friendship and support. A letter here, a comment there, it was a perpetual drip-feed of undermining criticism, and although the Prime Minister was unwilling to act on Canning's advice and remove Castlereagh, Canning's duplicitous backstabbing and insidious whispering campaign continued unabated.

And no one, not even his uncle, said a word, leaving Castlereagh completely and utterly in the dark.

In early September, as the sick troops began to return home from the disastrous Walcheren Expedition and Castlereagh felt that the weight of responsibility for the debacle lay upon his shoulders, he also learned of Canning's efforts to unseat him and his fellow Cabinet members' silence on the subject. Shocked and demoralised, on 8 September he resigned from the Government.

Over the next few weeks, as more and more details emerged of Canning's ambitious plotting, including his letter to George III suggesting himself as a new Prime Minister (an unprecedented act) and the deal he had struck with Portland to replace Castlereagh or he himself would resign, Castlereagh felt more and more keenly the humiliation of his position. Thus on 19 September, he wrote to Canning that he had acted:

> *in breach of every Principle of good Faith, both public and private.... It was therefore your act, and your conduct, which deceived me, and it is impossible for me to acquiesce in being placed in a situation by you which no man of honour could knowingly submit to, nor patiently suffer himself to be betrayed into without forfeiting that character.*

Castlereagh's letter left Canning—who had never fired a shot in his life—with little alternative but to agree to the duel which had previously been suggested. (Castlereagh was known to be a crack shot....)

Following the duel and the news of it leaking to the press and every scandal-monger in Britain, both Castlereagh and Canning remained on the backbenches of the House of Commons and outside the Cabinet for some time.

Castlereagh's reputation recovered first and he was soon offered the position of Foreign Secretary by Spencer Perceval, now the Prime Minister, a position which he held from February 1812 until his death in 1822, becoming over the course of those ten years one of the most renowned diplomats of the nineteenth century and possibly the greatest of Foreign Secretaries for his work at the Congress of Vienna in 1814.

It wasn't until after Castlereagh's death that George Canning held office again—a high price for his ambitious machinations against a fellow Cabinet member. (And he limped.)

A Shilling a Day

By Jonathan Hopkins

IN THE EIGHTEENTH AND NINETEENTH CENTURIES BRITAIN'S STANDING ARMY WAS MADE up entirely of "volunteers". They weren't forced into joining the military or obliged to serve by statute as in many European countries. While officers mostly purchased their commissions from the Crown, the rank and file were recruited from local militia groups, Yeomanry, and fencibles, from amongst prisoners, and from within the general population.

Joining the army of the time was not seen as the good career move it often is today. In peacetime soldiery was considered by the public as rabble—gangs of uncouth, unprofessional troublemakers, regularly used by government to police instances of public disorder with unnecessary violence. Women who married soldiers were pitied as fools, not surprising since those whose husbands were sent to serve abroad would often be left destitute unless they had another source of income.

It is difficult to see what, bar a sense of adventure, encouraged young men to enlist. Perhaps they believed, after the hardships of farm or factory, the army could not be worse.

And there was the bounty, of course: that purse beloved of recruiting sergeants; the *"forty shillings on the drum"* of the song. That actually refers to "attestation" money, the amount a recruit received on first signing up, which amounted to two pounds two shillings (forty-two shillings, or two guineas).

- Bounty paid to an infantry recruit: £16 16s 0d
- Bounty paid to a cavalry recruit: £13 8s 0d

This was probably more money than most men had ever seen in their lives! But, of course, it was a pike to catch a minnow: in reality a fresh recruit rarely saw any of it. What wasn't drunk away in the short-lived euphoria of a new life was retained by the army to pay for the soldier's board and lodging until he was fully signed up and approved, which also meant paying for a doctor to examine him to confirm he was "fit to serve", and for a magistrate to co-sign his papers.

And his necessaries: those items of kit Army Regulations deemed the man should supply himself, things the Commander-in-Chief at Horseguards, and thus the government, refused to provide from the public purse. Initial cost of these worked out at £2 14s 0d for an infantryman and a whopping £3 15s 0d for a new dragoon—he had to buy equipment for his horse, too!

NECESSARIES

- Infantryman - shirt (4), shoes (2 pairs), stockings (2 pairs), gaiters/leggings, stock and clasp, pack, greatcoat strap set, brushes and blackball, combs (2), sundries.

- Cavalryman - Breeches and slings (braces), stable jacket, stable trousers, forage cap, shirt (3), shoes (2 pairs), night cap, stockings (3 pairs), gaiters, stock and clasp, shoe clasp, shoe brush (3), comb (2), razor and soap, clothes brush. *Plus* nose bag, watering bridle and log, worm & picker, mane comb, sponge, hoof pick, scissors, emery oil, pipeclay, blacking, powder bag and powder, carbine-lock case, saddlebag/valise.

Army pay was certainly not particularly attractive in itself. Private infantrymen received 1 shilling (£0 1s 0d) a day, which doesn't sound too bad until you consider a skilled loom operator could earn three times that for a week's work. Though to be fair, a farm labourer probably earned less than £10 a year. A light dragoon earned (gasp!) 1s 3d (one-and-thruppence) a day, one reason the cavalry had less trouble attracting recruits than regiments of foot.

The problem was that the soldier suffered deductions from this amount to pay for food, accommodation, and any items of equipment which needed replacing before their due date. Everything had a standard lifetime in the army, except the men. And because a dragoon's necessaries covered his horse's essentials as well as his own, his deductions were proportionally higher. So cavalrymen were probably worse off in the long run.

EXAMPLE OF EQUIPMENT LIFETIMES
- *Hat - 1 year*
- *Gloves - 1 year*
- *Coat - 2 years*
- *Boots (Infantry) - 2 years*
- *Boots (Cavalry) - 6 years*
- *Bridle - 12 years*
- *Saddle - 16 years*
- *Ammunition pouch - 20 years*

In fact a dragoon might be much worse off. If you were stationed in some foreign country and your horse galloped off, together with all the equipment strapped to it, unless you could persuade your commanding officer the animal was lost *"through the actions of the enemy"* you might be forced to cover its cost. With a replacement animal alone costing £35 (two years pay, before deductions), woe betide the man who was bucked off if he could not catch his mount.

There was one bright spot in all this financial gloom, though—inflation was non-existent. The cost of horses, for example, remained the same from Wellington's day until the beginning of the First World War. In an 1810 despatch (*The Dispatches of Field Marshal the Duke of Wellington* by Gurwood, Vol 6 p 578) he suggests the army pay 35 guineas for horses "suitable for immediate service" either purchased in Britain or imported from the US, and in 1914 the army were still paying £30-£40 for cavalry mounts and light draught horses.

So it may come as little surprise that in 1914 an infantry private was still being paid...a shilling a day. Though the army did supply his boots!

Figures quoted in this article come from *The British Army against Napoleon* by Robert Burnham and Ron McGuigan, originally sourced from Thomas Reide's *A Treatise on Military Finance* (1805).

An Officer and a Mendicant

By JONATHAN HOPKINS

O NE FEATURE OF THE BRITISH ARMY IN THE NINETEENTH CENTURY WHICH SEEMS almost incomprehensible to us today is its system of appointing officers. Commissions and promotions were purchased and thus involved the prospective candidate or his family in considerable expense.

The thinking behind this practice was twofold: any man with a financial interest in his career was not only more likely to take it seriously but was also unlikely to risk losing his investment by rebelling against the Crown, who held his money. In times of great political change, where army-backed republicanism was a real fear, potential insolvency, if a commission were to be forfeit, was considered a significant deterrent.

What the purchase system meant in real terms was that officers tended to come from the moneyed middle classes and higher up the social scale. It was the norm for regiments to be officered by "gentlemen" to the extent that the occasional ranker promoted to command through some singular act of bravery might find himself shunned by former comrades as too low-caste to be a real officer. Bigotry worked both ways, as it does today.

Most of the time all a young gentleman required to enlist, apart from the money, was a letter of recommendation, usually from a serving officer. This might be a family member, friend, acquaintance, even a "friend of a friend", and knowing royalty, however minor, meant almost certain acceptance. Potential soldiering ability was hardly ever considered. Patronage, dear fellow, was all important.

COST OF COMMISSIONS (SOURCE 1)

Price varied depending on the status of the regiment, those with connections to the monarchy (Lifeguards, Royal Horse Guards, and Foot Guards) being both costlier and more difficult to get into. For ease of comparison I have stuck to Line Infantry and Cavalry regiments, since these provided the vast majority of commissions on offer.

	Dragoons/Light Dragoons	Foot Regiments
Lieutenant Colonel	£4982 10s	£3500 0s
Major	£3882 10s	£2600 0s
Captain	£2782 10s	£1500 0s
Lieutenant	£997 10s	£550 0s
Cornet (cavalry)	£735 0s	-
Ensign (foot)	-	£400 0s

Once a commission was approved by the regimental colonel it then had to be accepted by the King before details were published in the London Gazette (hence the term "gazetted").

Any step up in rank would only require payment of the difference (e.g. Ensign to Lieutenant would cost the purchaser £150, since that officer's lower rank would be sold on at its original cost). And from the figures it can be seen that the jump from Lieutenant to Captain was the most difficult in financial terms.

At one time it was common for the second sons of the wealthy (since these unfortunates were unlikely to inherit family estates) to have a commission purchased for them at birth, particularly in a "family" regiment. And because promotion was sometimes by seniority alone, this meant in theory it would have been possible for a child with sixteen years "seniority" to become a Lieutenant Colonel without ever having seen a barracks. So in 1795 the Commander-in-Chief (Frederick, Duke of York at that time) introduced a set of rules governing how long an officer must have actual service in each rank before he could be promoted to the next step.

Again, wartime often meant such rules were flouted, when a junior officer might be given a field or "brevet" promotion through necessity rather than because he could afford it or had the requisite years of service. However, unless such higher rank was subsequently approved in the usual way he would still be viewed as having his regimental (lower) rank once he returned home.

HIDDEN COSTS

Unfortunately for a new officer, buying his first commission was not the end of it. He had also to provide his own uniform and weapons, neither of which was exactly cheap.

(i) Uniform and Equipment. For an infantry Ensign, a basic uniform would comprise a bicorn or shako, sword and sword knot, silk sash, gorget, sword belt, coat, waistcoat and breeches, which might be got for a total of £9 13s. (Source 2)

It was also expected, though in practice not essential, that he had a horse and associated saddlery. It is difficult to establish with any accuracy how much a mount might have set him back, but for an infantry officer it's probably nearer the price of a cavalry troop horse (£30-£40) than the *"no more than £100"* which procurers of the 15th Light Dragoons were ordered to spend on horses *"suitable for officers' chargers".* Of course, in the latter case the colonel would hope to sell such animals on to horseless officers at a profit!

Because to set oneself up as a cavalry officer was far more expensive. In 1806, a 15th Light Dragoons enquiry (Source 3) concluded that the *"expense attending the equipment of a subaltern officer"* (Cornet or Lieutenant) including two horses (though the army would provide forage for these plus one other on campaign), uniforms, arms (dress and fighting swords plus pistols) and appointments, to be no less than £485. By the time a servant and living allowance over and above board and lodging to support himself *"in that situation as an officer and a gentleman"* his overall costs were *"likely to be in the region of £1000, and he would need a further £500 per annum to maintain his lifestyle".*

Some cavalry subalterns were too poor to afford a horse. Cornet Arthur Mayer of the 7th Hussars (later killed at Waterloo), embarking for the Corunna campaign in October 1808, was forced to rely on his commanding officer, Lieutenant Colonel Sir Richard Hussey Vivian, to provide him a mount. (Source 8)

(ii) Signing Fee. The new officer also had to pay a fee to the King for signing his commission papers. The Sovereign's fee (Source 3) for a Cornet was £6 0s 6d, and for an Ensign £4 11s 10d.

Even very senior officers were not exempt from this. Promotion from regimental commander, for example, to the command of a brigade attracted "Staff Commission." Sir Arthur Wellesley, when selected as Commander of the Forces for the expedition to Portugal in 1809, had to pay £29 19s 6d for the privilege!

PAY

Officers received more than the private soldier's "shilling a day". One reason the cavalry was more popular than the infantry was that a Cornet received 8s 0d a day compared to an Ensign's 5s 3d. But this was not all it seemed—even in the 1800s deductions were taken before the officer saw a penny of his pay, based on:

(i) **Poundage.** This was a commission to the regimental agent, who would have dealt with the officer's original purchase and continued to act on his behalf, in financial and contractual matters, throughout his career. It was only paid by captains and higher ranks and varied, but was usually 5% of pay.

(ii) **Income tax.** Introduced in 1799 to pay for the war with Napoleon, this was levied at 10% for those making £150 per year or more and 5% for those making less.

(iii) **Agency fee.** 5%.

(iv) **Chelsea Hospital.** Every soldier was deducted 1 day's pay per year to finance this institution.

(v) **Rations and accommodation.**

The list below shows how much an Ensign's pay would come to once these deductions were made (Source 1):

- Yearly pay £95 16s 3d
- Regimental Agent £4 1s 9½d
- Agency fee £2 5s 0d
- Income tax £4 1s 9d
- Chelsea Hospital £0 5s 3d
- Rations, etc. £77 11s 3d (4s 3d per day)
- Total Deductions £88 5s 1d

- Net Yearly pay £7 11s 2d

- Net Daily pay £0 0s 5d

That's right—fivepence! Out of this pittance he then had to find any out-of-pocket expenses, so it's easy to see why new officers needed a private income or sponsor.

EQUIPMENT REPLACEMENTS

The problem with clothing and equipment is that it wears out, and more quickly on campaign, despite which officers received no extra allowance to pay for replacement. (They could, however, claim for anything lost *"due to the actions of the enemy."*)

Captain Edward Charles Cocks (16th Light Dragoons) wrote to his brother Thomas on 22 December 1810 requesting:

> ...*Second, would you order me a new hussar saddle with accoutrements complete from Whippy* [horsey readers of a certain age will recognise that name!].... *Third, would you order me a new helmet from Hawkes* [and maybe that one too!].... *Fourth, a new sabre and belt from Prossee.... Fifth, four pairs of new hussar boots, not open, from Gilbert, three pairs of laced half boots with spurs to them all....* (Source 5)

All this came out of his own pocket.

On campaign, clothing and equipment could sometimes be bought cheaply second-hand. The effects of officers killed in battle were often auctioned and the proceeds sent home to his family. Bullet holes could be patched and bloodstains washed out. After the battle of Talavera in July 1809, commissary August Schaumann says at the auction of the belongings of deceased Colonel Gordon he bought *"...for a mere song, his extremely fine dark blue overalls with two rows of buttons. And I wore them a very long time."* (Source 6)

And Captain James Naylor (1st Kings Dragoon Guards) records that in May 1815 in Flanders he was able to buy a packhorse "for 15 Napoleons"—roughly £9—which would have cost him double in Britain.

But that might not be the end of it because colonels, even the Commander-in-Chief, regularly made changes to regulation regimental clothing and accoutrements which an officer was expected to comply with at his expense, from simple accessories such as feather plumes to expensive gold and silver-braided cavalry dolmans and pelisses (overjackets). For example, the uniform of the 20th Light Dragoons, not even one of the more fashionable regiments, had major alterations in 1796, 1802, 1808 and in 1811, when all Light Dragoon regiments suffered general (and much criticised) amendments to their uniforms at the instigation of the Prince Regent. (Source 4)

NON-PURCHASED COMMISSIONS

It was, however, possible to be commissioned, and in particular promoted, without purchase. Royal Artillery and Engineer officers were promoted strictly by seniority, and in just one random example, from the London Gazette of 31 July 1804, Thomas Munro was commissioned as an Ensign, without purchase, in the 42nd Foot.

Historian Michael Glover studied the promotion of junior officers listed in the London Gazette between September 1810 and August 1811, and between March 1812 and February 1813 (Source 1). He found that in regiments of foot only 12.3% and in cavalry regiments 42.7% were purchased. This again shows demand for cavalry appointments was higher than for the infantry, but also that perhaps the greater risks inherent in commanding regiments of foot in wartime reduced their attraction as investments. It seems more infantry colonels were content to fill vacancies created by promotion through recommendation, rather than struggling to find purchasers, even though this might create a problem for a promoted officer trying to sell his earlier rank.

Taking the whole of the Napoleonic Wars, Glover reckoned only 20% of promotions were purchased, the remainder being by seniority (70%) and patronage of the Commander-in-Chief (10%).

One problem with promotion other than by purchase was that the officer could not sell his higher rank, if promoted again, unless he had at least ten years' service: even then he had to apply to the Commander-in-Chief for permission. Can't have a fellow making money from a freebie, now can we?

Purchase of commissions declined gradually as older men retired but was eventually abolished only in 1881, mainly because to repay the cost of every serving officer's investment in one fell swoop would have cost the government a *lot* of money.

Perhaps they had this in mind when the notorious Earl Cardigan, of "Charge of the Light Brigade" fame, was allowed to purchase command of the 11th Hussars in 1835. Despite being relieved of his colonelcy of the 15th Hussars two years earlier, when he was court-martialled and "cashiered" (i.e. he lost his investment) for abusing a fellow officer, his family paid the War Office £40,000 to obtain his new position (Source 7), more than £1.6 million in today's money!

They must have been desperate to get him out of the house!

Mendicant—one who relies for his subsistence on the generosity or charity of others.

SOURCES

Burnham, Robert and Ron McGuigan. *The British Army against Napoleon*. Frontline Books, 2010.

James, Charles. *The Regimental Companion*. 1811.

Glover, Gareth. *From Corunna to Waterloo: The Letters and Journals of Two Napoleonic Hussars, 1801-1816*. Greenhill Books, 2007.

Franklin, C E. *British Napoleonic Uniforms*. The History Press, 2008.

Page, Julia. *Intelligence Officer in the Peninsula: Letters & Diaries of Major the Hon. Edward Charles Cocks, 178 -1812*. Spellmount, Limited Publishers, 1986.

Schaumann, August. *On the Road with Wellington*. 1924 translation.

Royle, Trevor. *Crimea: The Great Crimean War, 1854-1856*. 1999.

Vivian, Hon. Claud. *Richard Hussey Vivian: A Memoir*. 1897.

REGENCY MILITIA: A DIFFERENT BREED OF OFFICER

By MARIA GRACE

IN MANY REGENCY ERA BOOKS, COMPANIES OF SOLDIERS ARE ENCOUNTERED STATIONED in England. These men are members of the militia, not the regular army. While at first blush there may seem little difference between the regulars and the militia, the differences are striking and significant.

WHAT WAS THE MILITIA?

The militia served as a peacekeeping force on home soil, embodied only in wartime to free the regulars for combat abroad. In theory, they suppressed riots, broke up seditious gatherings, and if needed, repelled invading enemy forces. Unfortunately, the militia was a dubious peacekeeper. It was not uncommon for its members to sympathize with their rioting neighbors they were sent to subdue. For this reason, militia units served outside their own counties.

Militia men were required to have weapons and to be skilled in their use. However, their lack of training made them amateurish compared to the regulars since only small numbers were selected for more serious training, the so-called trained bands.

JOINING THE MILITIA

The nation did not maintain a standing militia. The militia was embodied in wartime or in times of national emergency to guard against invasion or rebellion and to take over various policing duties normally performed by the regular army. Popular opinion painted the citizen-soldier as a fierce defender of home and country. History had taught that a regular army could be a great threat to civil liberties, so the virtues of the militia were sometimes overstated.

Parliament controlled the size of the militia. Though the militia was considered a volunteer force, all Protestant males were required to make themselves available for service. The King required the Lord-Lieutenant, usually a local nobleman, of each county to gather a force of able-bodied men between eighteen and forty-five years of age to fill the quota for his area. Militia service required a five to seven year commitment to service on home soil with no chance of being sent overseas. Only clergymen were exempt from service.

If a man did not wish to serve he could pay a substitute to serve in his stead. The going rate started at £25 and could go as high as £60. (For comparison, £50 a year would be a rough equivalent of today's minimum wage.)

Most militia officers were drawn from the local gentry and were led by a colonel who was a county landowner. Officers' commissions were not purchased as they were in the regular army. Officers' ranks were directly related to the amount and value of property they or their family held. For example, to qualify for the rank of captain, a man needed to either own land worth £200 per year, be heir to land worth £400 per year, or be the son of a father with land worth £600 per year. A lieutenant needed land worth £50 a year.

Officers drew an allowance, but this was not expected to do more than cover expenses since their primary income would be from their property. Poor families of militiamen were eligible for support from the parish whereas those of the regulars were not.

In practice it was difficult to find officers, particularly lower grade officers, for militia service. So the property qualifications for lieutenants were often ignored. While this leniency allowed many to join the ranks of officer who would not otherwise have such an opportunity, it did bring down the perceived status of the militia officer. Possibly to combat this issue, many regiments selected their recruits for their handsome appearance which would improve the look of their regiment and thus its prestige.

LIFE IN THE MILITIA

Service in the militia carried little threat of front line duty. Officers had a great deal of leave and often enjoyed a busy social schedule provided by the local gentry. Since all officers were supposed to be property holders of some measure, they were all considered gentlemen and afforded the according status.

In summer the militia's regiments went into tented camps in the open countryside to engage in training exercises. Camps were located throughout the southern and eastern coasts, the largest at Brighton.

Military reviews, held on open hillside or common land, made excellent entertainment for the local residents. Reviews included displays of all sorts of military actions: marching, drilling, firing at targets, and even mock skirmishes often for the benefit of a visiting general.

Prior to 1796 when barracks were provided, the militia quartered for the winter wherever accommodation could be found for them in the nearby towns and villages. These were supposed to be paid for by the soldiers themselves, but since they would only remain a short time in any one place, it was not uncommon for them to run up bills and leave town without paying them.

PUBLIC ATTITUDE TOWARD THE MILITIA

All in all, the militia was not popular. Inhabitants resented assessments of equipment and money to cover the needs of the militia. Men resented being drafted to serve and were apt to do everything they could to avoid their military training. Tradesmen and innkeepers resented them leaving town without paying for services and wares.

As a peacekeeping force, the militia had little to do but drill. With so much free time on their hands they developed a reputation for a wild lifestyle of parties and frivolity. Not surprisingly, parents often saw militia officers as a threat to their marriageable daughters since their families were unknown, and they might disappear from the neighborhood very quickly.

SOURCES

Collins, Irene. *Jane Austen, The Parson's Daughter*. Hambledon Press, 1998.

Day, Malcolm. *Voices from the World of Jane*. Austen David & Charles, 2006.

Downing, Sarah Jane. *Fashion in the Time of Jane Austen*. Shire Publications, 2010.

Holmes, Richard. *Redcoat, the British Soldier in the Age of Horse and Musket* W. W. Norton & Company, 2001.

Le Faye, Deirdre. *Jane Austen: The World of Her Novels*. Harry N. Abrams, 2002.

Southam, Brian. *Jane Austen in Context*. Edited by Janet M. Todd. Cambridge University Press, 2005.

Tomalin, Claire. *Jane Austen, a Life*. Random House, 1999.

Watkins, Susan. *Jane Austen's Town and Country Style*. Rizzoli, 1990.

"Spy? Why, Sir—I Am No Spy!" A Quick Guide to Information Technology During the Peninsular War

By JONATHAN HOPKINS

MILITARY INTELLIGENCE IS A CONTRADICTION IN TERMS, OR SO THE OLD JOKE RUNS. Of course that was based on generals' continued fallback option in later wars: throwing masses of lightly armed and unprotected men against emplaced infantry, machine guns, and artillery in the forlorn hope they commanded higher numbers than the opposition and the basic tactic of eighteenth century warfare still worked.

It's far different nowadays, in an age of satellite imaging and unmanned drones. But even though the Duke of Marlborough had famously written that *"no war can be conducted successfully without early and good intelligence"* it wasn't until 1803 that a Department of Military Intelligence was proposed in Britain by Robert Brownrigg who had accompanied Frederick, Duke of York as his military secretary on the abortive expedition to Holland in 1799 and who realised the system of using local knowledge, in widespread operation at that time, was rubbish, basically.

But Brownrigg found recruiting operatives to the D.M.I. was a major headache. Though governments employed spies, the army was above such ungentlemanly shenanigans. Intelligent young officers, attracted originally by a home posting, soon found sifting through mounds of often conflicting information far less attractive than they had first imagined, apart from the fact that many were ostracised by friends once their occupation became known.

A spy? Harrumph! Not the done thing, old boy.

Most transferred out of the fledgling department pretty sharpish once they realised this, so by the time Wellington landed on the Portuguese coast in August 1808, he was no better off than Marlborough had been on his march across Europe to the Danube a hundred years earlier.

The first problem the British had was a dearth of maps. Wellington originally relied on those of cartographer Tomas Lopez ("tolerably accurate" according to the University of Southampton). Their main failing was they showed few contour details, critical information when it came to moving large numbers of troops and quantities of equipment by road. Or dirt track, which is what Iberian thoroughfares usually were.

It was exactly this which prompted Sir John Moore, in the autumn of 1808, to gamble on splitting his force in three when he crossed Portugal into Spain. Locals convinced him that because of the state of the roads, the only way he could get his horse drawn artillery safely to Salamanca was on a circuitous journey through Estremadura, to the south of his preferred line of march. As it turned out, the guns could have managed Moore's central route without too many problems, so since he did not know exactly where the French were he had risked any one of his under-strength divisions meeting the enemy unexpectedly through a lack of good intelligence.

Once Wellington returned to Iberia the following year, he set about solving these problems. He saw immediately how useful intimate local knowledge was when Colonel John Waters, who had remained in Portugal after the British left, found boats which enabled Wellington's troops to cross the Douro at Oporto un-noticed by Marshal Soult's army and create a strongpoint from which they were able to run the French out of the city and thence from Portugal, at least for a time.

The Duke had no specialist cartographers, but he did have a few engineers who possessed similar skills. When not required on other projects, these men were sent out, often with a cavalry escort, initially to map areas ahead of the British line of advance but later to survey vast tracts of Portugal and Spain. As they moved about the country and became familiar to the local populace, they would often receive information from the natives about French positions which they passed on to headquarters, and thus the more generally known role of "Exploring Officer" (they were called "Observing Officers" in many period dispatches) was born.

Edward Charles Cocks was one such officer, though he was a captain in the 16th Light Dragoons rather than an engineer. As well as mapping the countryside, Cocks watched for troop and supply movements which might indicate where the enemy were likely to strike next. His cavalry escort meant he was usually able to pass messages back quickly without needing to either return to headquarters personally or risk Portuguese or Spanish couriers of unknown reliability.

As the war progressed, however, the network of known partisans grew. Messages could travel shorter distances between couriers so they went faster. In addition, Wellington had made it known he paid cash for captured French dispatches, and it seems he did not much care how they were obtained. There are anecdotal tales of them being received still smeared with their original carrier's blood. For their part the French pursued a policy of extermination against any individual or group they believed had helped the British, fueling the growth of Iberian guerrilla movements and ensuring even more information reached Wellington's ears.

Exploring Officers wore full uniform for the simple reason that if they were captured they could claim they were combatants (which, technically, they were) and should be afforded all privileges their rank demanded. Spies caught in civilian clothes would likely be shot, though that did not stop many Exploring Officers going about in disguise. Captain Dashwood, an officer on Moore's staff, dressed himself in a Spanish shepherd's cloak and hat before walking brazenly into the occupied village of Rueda to check on the numbers of French troops in residence before strolling casually back out again.

The most important piece of Exploring Officer's equipment was usually a good horse. John Waters was captured at one point but bided his time until his escort was distracted. Then he galloped off, outrunning pursuers thanks to his mount's superior fitness and stamina.

Being able to live by your wits helped, too. When Colquhoun Grant was captured in 1812 he somehow got sight of a letter from Marshal Marmont accusing him of spying and suggesting he be refused exchange for a captured French officer, normal practice at the time. Grant considered this allowed him to break his parole—his promise not to try to escape. Passing himself off as American, he made his way to Paris and mailed a number of intelligence reports to Wellington from the capital before escaping back to Britain by boat.

Eventually, semaphore stations were constructed in Portugal, helping messages travel even faster, though these were restricted to coastal areas. They never made it into the Spanish interior, and it seems likely that was due to the terrain. But given the number of times the British advanced into and retreated from Spain between 1809 and 1813 it's unclear how much use they would actually have been.

And I suppose the final piece of our IT jigsaw was George Scovell's success in finally cracking the Grand Chiffre, France's method of coding messages.

So there you have it. The Peninsular War was really won using wits, pen and ink, fast horses, and friendly Spaniards. They would've loved Google Earth and SatNav.

Well, maybe not SatNav....

SIR FRANCIS BEAUFORT: THE MAN WHO CAUGHT THE WIND

BY ARTHUR RUSSELL

THE BEAUFORT SCALE FOR MEASURING THE STRENGTH OF WIND WAS DEVELOPED BY Sir Francis Beaufort who was born in Navan, Co. Meath, Ireland on 27 May 1774. He was the son of Daniel Augustus Beaufort, a Protestant clergyman, cartographer, and member of the Royal Irish Academy who had himself created a new map of Ireland in 1792.

The Beaufort household into which Francis was born was located on Flower Hill in the provincial town of Navan, which is located where the River Blackwater meets the River Boyne. The old house where he was born and reared survived until very recently but eventually succumbed to the "development mania" that plagued Celtic Tiger Ireland in the last decades of the twentieth century. A modern apartment complex now occupies part of the site where the rambling Beaufort house once stood. All that now shows where the scientist was born is a simple plaque which has been erected under a large tree in front of a school which has also been erected on the site.

The Beauforts of Navan were descended from French Huguenot refugees who had come to Ireland in the aftermath of the Massacre of St. Bartholomew's Day during the sixteenth century religious wars in France.

As a young man, Francis showed early interest in the sea and joined the British Navy. By the time he had reached his sixteenth birthday, he had already experienced shipwreck. The fact that this was caused by faulty charts fuelled his interest in hydrography and the creation of accurate nautical charts.

He saw his share of action in the Napoleonic Wars and was seriously wounded on HMS *Phaeton* in the course of the capture of the 14-gun *Calpe* near Malaga in 1800. During his convalescence, he spent two years helping his brother-in-law, Richard Lovell Edgeworth (father of Maria Edgeworth, authoress of *Castle Rackrent*), in the construction of a semaphore line between Dublin and Galway which was capable of transmitting messages across the breadth of Ireland in eight minutes. He refused to be paid for this work, preferring to subsist on his meagre naval pension.

When he recovered his health, he returned to active naval duty and was quickly made ship's captain. During his time at sea, he immersed himself in taking readings at sea, updating and creating new charts, and educating himself to the point where he became recognized as a leading expert in sea charts and nautical maps. It was during these years that Beaufort developed his earliest version of a wind force scale and weather notation coding which he continued to use and perfect during his long scientific career.

Where his colleagues sought leisurely pursuits, Beaufort spent his leisure time taking soundings and bearings, making astronomical observations to determine latitude and longitude, and measuring shorelines, which he assiduously applied to new, improved charts. Beaufort's first ship command, HMS *Woolwich*, afforded him a unique opportunity to conduct a detailed hydrographic survey of the Rio de la Plata estuary in South America.

Experts in the British Admiralty were very impressed by the completed survey that Beaufort brought back to them. Most notably, Alexander Dalrymple, the first hydrographer of the British Admiralty, remarked in a note to the Admiralty in March 1808:

> *Captain Beaufort did more in the month he was in the Plate to acquire a correct knowledge of its dangers, than was done by everyone together before. We have few officers (indeed I do not know one) in our Service who have half his professional knowledge and ability, and in zeal and perseverance he cannot be excelled.*

What was most remarkable about all this was the fact that Beaufort was largely self-educated yet demonstrated masterful knowledge and had established himself as a pioneer in his chosen field. As such he was destined to rub shoulders with some of the greatest scientists and mathematicians of his time. Among these were John Herschel, George Airy, and Charles Babbage.

THE BEAUFORT WIND SCALE

Perhaps his most enduring and well-known legacy is the Beaufort Wind Scale which is a methodology for measuring the strength of the wind as it impacted sailing ships and later steam ships which replaced them during the nineteenth century. Measuring wind was not a new idea in nautical circles. Beaufort's achievement was the fact that he was able to have his system universally accepted, where no standardised system existed before.

The first proposed scale presented in 1806 ranged from calm (level 0) up to storm force (level 13) in which wind strength was correlated with the amount of sail a full-rigged ship would carry appropriate to the wind conditions. It was first used officially by Robert Fitzroy in 1831 and thereafter adopted by the British Admiralty in 1838. As sail gave way to steam, the scale was modified by defining levels in terms of the state of the sea or wind speed.

A LONG AND DISTINGUISHED CAREER

In 1811-1812, shortly after being promoted to Captain, Beaufort charted and explored southern Anatolia in Turkey and succeeded in locating many classical ruins there. An attack on the crew of his boat by Turks at Ayas, near Adana, in which he sustained a serious bullet wound in the hip, interrupted his work. He returned to England and drew up the charts based on records and readings taken during his time there. He also published his book, *Karamania*, in 1817, which is a brief description of the South Coast of Asia Minor and of the remains of Antiquity he had explored.

In 1829, at the relatively late age of 55 years, when most seamen would be expected to retire from active service, Beaufort was appointed British Admiralty Hydrographer of the Navy, a post he held for a further twenty-five years. During this period of his long and distinguished career, Beaufort converted what had been a minor chart repository into the finest surveying and charting institution in the world. Some of the excellent charts the Office produced during Beaufort's time are still in use.

One of the practices he introduced to the office he led for so long and which is still meticulously followed is that no chart or other document may ever be published by the Hydrographic Office without first undergoing the Chief Hydrographer's personal scrutiny. He also took over the administration of the great astronomical observatories at Greenwich, London and at the Cape of Good Hope in Africa and directed some of the major maritime explorations and experiments of the time. Among these, he directed the Arctic Council during its search for the explorer, Sir John Franklin, who was tragically lost in his last polar voyage in search of the North-west Passage between the North Atlantic and the Pacific Oceans.

BEAUFORT'S LINK WITH THE VOYAGE OF HMS *BEAGLE* AND OTHER PROJECTS

Beaufort trained Robert Fitzroy, who was put in temporary command of the survey ship HMS *Beagle* after the ship's previous captain had committed suicide. When FitzRoy was reappointed as Commander for the famous second voyage of the *Beagle* he requested Beaufort *"that a well-educated and scientific gentleman be sought"* to accompany the voyage. Beaufort's enquiries led to an invitation to Charles Darwin, who subsequently drew on observations made during the voyage to formulate his theory of evolution which he presented in his book, *The Origin of Species.*

As a council member of the Royal Society, the Royal Observatory, and the Royal Geographic Society, of which he was a founding member, Beaufort used his administrative position to interact with the most prominent scientists of his time. Beaufort recommended the geographers, astronomers, oceanographers, geodesists, and meteorologists to the Hydrographic Office and gave significant support to many research projects.

Overcoming many objections, Beaufort obtained government support for the Antarctic voyage of 1839-1843 by James Clark Ross, which investigated the Earth's magnetic forces.

He also promoted the development of reliable tide tables for Great Britain and Ireland which motivated similar research elsewhere in Europe and North America. He supported his friend William Whewell and attracted the support of the Prime Minister, the Duke of Wellington, in expanding record-keeping at 200 British Coast Guard stations. Beaufort gave enthusiastic support to his friend, the Astronomer Royal and noted mathematician Sir George Airy, in achieving a historic period of measurements by the Greenwich and Good Hope observatories.

BEAUFORT'S LEGACY

It is a measure of the regard in which Beaufort was held that he finally retired from the

Royal Navy with the rank of Rear Admiral on 1 October 1846, at the relatively advanced age of 72 years. Two years later, in April 1848 he was appointed Knight Commander of the Bath (KCB) and was henceforth known as Sir Francis Beaufort.

Beaufort's private life had its share of scandal, which did not become public until after his death when portions of his private memoirs, written in a cipher developed by himself, were finally deciphered. It appears from these that from 1835 until he married Honora Edgeworth in November 1839, he had an incestuous relationship with his younger sister Harriet. The entries also show he was tortured by guilt over the relationship.

This son of Navan, Co. Meath, Ireland, who contributed so much to the world of nautical science, as well as to our understanding of the oceans and seas which occupies 71% of the surface of the planet on which we live, died on December 17 1857, and is buried in St. John's Church Gardens in London.

THE SUMMER THE ALLIED MONARCHS CAME TO TOWN

By M.M. BENNETTS

I T MAY SEEM ALMOST IMPOSSIBLE TO IMAGINE, NOW, 200 YEARS ON...BUT IN THE EARLY years of the nineteenth century, Napoleon Bonaparte—the French Emperor—was the most hated and feared man on the planet.

When he wrote the opening of *War and Peace*, which begins with a discussion in which Napoleon is referred to as the great Antichrist, the literary giant, Tolstoy, wasn't indulging in a fit of hyperbole:

> *Well, Prince, so Genoa and Lucca are now just family estates of the Buona-*
> *partes. But I warn you, if you don't tell me this means war, if you still try to*
> *defend the infamies and horrors perpetrated by that Antichrist—I really do*
> *believe he is Antichrist—I will have nothing more to do with you and you are*
> *no longer my friend....*

He was telling the truth. Yet by the summer of 1814, all that seemed to be in the past.

For from his calamitous invasion of Russia beginning in the summer of 1812, Napoleon had suffered one ruinous disaster after another, one blistering defeat after another, losses France could no longer afford.

Thus in the spring of 1814, with France invaded in the east by the Allied armies of the Russians, Austrians, Prussians, and Swedes and in the west by Wellington and his British troops, Paris fell, the Generals capitulated, and Napoleon abdicated power and was on his way to exile on the island of Elba.

All of Europe rejoiced—many of them in the cafes and gambling clubs of Paris.

And as they cobbled together the Peace of Paris, the Allied Sovereigns considered their next move. Obviously a European lap of honour was required, and where better to start than in Great Britain, the country which had funded the decades-long fight against Bonaparte and his *Grande Armée*?

Equally, (with the exception of Peter the Great's visit in 1698) this would be the first time in over two centuries, since the days of Henry VIII and Elizabeth, that foreign crowned heads were paying a visit to Britain—a not insignificant event, then.

From the British point of view, there were a few minor problems, though. With the exception of the rather run-down and lived-in-by-his-ailing-parents Windsor Castle, the Prince Regent didn't have a superlative setting for statecraft—there were no Hermitages or Palais du Louvre or Versailles here. (Which may go some way to explaining his later mania for building and improving the royal residences....)

Instead, the royal Dukes were chucked out of their apartments in Cumberland House and their rooms rapidly refurbished: the Duke of Cambridge's rooms assigned to the Emperor of Russia and his royal aides, the Duke of Cumberland gave up his rooms for the Emperor of Austria, and Clarence's rooms were to be used by King Frederick William III of Prussia.

In early May, it was announced that Princess Charlotte would marry—in the presence of all those Crowned Heads—William, the Prince of Orange, who had already arrived in Harwich and was travelling under the name of "Captain H. George". This royal wedding was to be the highlight of the royal visitation.

It was all to be a Peace Celebration such as the world had never seen, and the Brits were ready to party! Or were they?

May went by without any royal visitors arriving. By the end of the month, it was said that the Austrian Emperor would not be visiting at all, and that the Tsar's visit was also delayed.

Then, at last, on 3 June, the Foreign Secretary, Lord Castlereagh, arrived back in Dover (following his six months abroad representing Britain in the Allied sovereigns' control tent) with the details of the Treaty of Paris which had ended France's hegemony in Europe, and the announcement that the sovereigns would be arriving on the following Monday.

The Dover Road was besieged by those wishing to get a glimpse of the Royal Liberators. Carriages and foot-traffic alike battled for position along the road. Union Jacks were flying, as were the flags of the Allied nations—Prussia, Russia and Austria. But they were to be disappointed.

The sovereigns didn't land until late that night. Word also spread that other illustrious visitors had slipped ashore late Sunday evening—a company of Don Cossacks, the Austrian foreign minister, Prince Metternich, the Russian commander, Count Barclay de Tolly....

London waited too as the east wind grew colder.

The veteran Prussian field marshal, Gebhard von Blucher, hero of Leipzig and Paris, was the first to arrive—in an open carriage—to the rapture of the crowds. And he delighted the huzzah-ing press—women were waving handkerchiefs and begging for even one of his white hairs—with his courteous bowing and his broken thank-yous: *"Me ferry tankvoll! ferry, ferry tankvoll...."*

Two military bands played, competing, all afternoon on the forecourt of Cumberland House. The crowds waited, drooping, then went home. Eventually, the tall (he was over six feet), blond, athletic figure of Alexander I, his Imperial Highness, Emperor of all Russia, (accompanied by his poodle) was seen on the balcony of the Pulteney Hotel in Piccadilly, where already a new crowd had gathered, cheering wildly (for the Tsar and/or his attendants had judged the offered rooms in Cumberland House not up to snuff and had gone elsewhere....)

What followed was a month of delight and intrigue.

Tsar Alexander had brought his favourite sister and confidante with him, the widowed Duchess Oldenburg Holstein, the Grand Duchess Catherine of Russia—and she was determined to break off the engagement between Princess Charlotte and William of Orange.

At the first of many grand and multi-course meals given by the Prince Regent at

Carleton House, the Grand Duchess wore black and insisted she was still in mourning and then, as the Italian musicians sought to fill the evening air with music to dine to, Catherine announced, "Music makes me sick!"

It was either the commencement or the confirmation of a mutual violent hatred between the Grand Duchess and the Prince Regent. Which, curiously, played well in London where the Prince was not loved, but badly in the rest of the country, where they liked him fine, and hence was a serious diplomatic and political error on the Duchess' part.

Alexander, on the other hand, could not have been more popular. By the second day of his visit, already a protocol was established. The great crowds of people would gather beneath his balcony, give a huzzah, and the Emperor and Grand Duchess would come out onto the balcony as the cheers grew ever louder. Alexander would bow repeatedly for three minutes, then disappear inside...this was a royal who had rapport with the crowds.

There was a grand military review in Hyde Park. And nightly, there were the most amazing Illuminations, sponsored by various individuals, by commercial businesses, by enterprise.

The most spectacular Illuminations were at the Bank of England, where 50,000 lamps were arranged in columns and rows to border the pediments and columns, while in the midst was a vast transparency meant to represent the "genius of France reviving".

Oxford Street, where the preparations had gone on for weeks, was now formed of two parallel lines of light. Carleton House was lit up with yellow and green flares which glowed between huge palm trees in painted tubs. Many houses were lit up with transparencies of "Peace". There were firework displays in Hyde Park. And even Lord Castlereagh's home at 18 St. James' Square was illuminated with the transparency of a Dove with an olive branch in its beak.

Every night saw many grand dinners, private balls and soirees, all of which were thrown to honour the visiting conquerors of Napoleon.

So much so, that the seventy-one-year-old Field Marshal Blucher eventually wrote:

> The French could not succeed in killing me, but the Regent and the English are in a fair way to doing it...I am inhumanly exhausted...It will be a miracle if I don't go crazy...I have to watch myself that I don't make a fool of myself.

But he would also say just before departing,

> I have come out of England alive, but worn and weary. Words fail to express how they treated me; no one could have had shown to him more kindness or goodwill....

Among other honours, Oxford University had conferred upon Blucher the degree of Doctor of Law, while Cambridge University had entertained him at a grand dinner at Trinity College and had awarded him the degree of Doctor of Civil Law.

(Also, in recognition of the sacrifices endured by their allies, at this time, the British public contributed £100,000 for those living in the villages around Leipzig, while

Parliament voted to add another £100,000 to this fund—which is among the earliest examples of a foreign nation recognising the need for and sending monetary aid to a war-ravaged area and its inhabitants. Which I think is quite cool....)

However, by the time the monarchs departed at the end of June, relations between them and their hosts had soured. There was the expense, of course, which Parliament hadn't much liked. Princess Charlotte, egged on by Catherine, had broken off her engagement to the bewildered Prince of Orange.

And Tsar Alexander had confounded everyone by his unflagging ability to party all day and night—for example, he attended the evening ceremonies at Oxford on the fourteenth, then drove through a thunderstorm that night to reach London, where he changed his clothes, then danced from two until six in the morning at Lady Jersey's ball; and was at ten announcing his plans for that day—which would include a dinner at Lord Castlereagh's home, followed by a performance at Drury Lane Theatre, after which he turned up at a ball at the Marchioness of Hertford's home.

On the twenty-second, the Prince Regent accompanied the Allied sovereigns to Petworth House in Sussex, where Lord Egremont offered them an early dinner in the Marble Hall, there. From thence, the monarchs travelled through Sussex and Kent—the roads of which were decorated with arches and trophies of laurel and oak leaves and flags—to Dover. On Monday, 27 June, the Prussian King boarded HMS *Nymphen* and sailed away. That evening, Catherine and her brother, the Tsar, boarded the *Royal Charlotte*....

The Prince Regent returned home. The first party was over...but after twenty years of continuous war, the party here in Britain was just beginning. And would continue all summer.

THE JILTING PRINCESS

By M.M. BENNETTS

YES, SHE WAS A PRINCESS. AND YES, SHE HAD TO MARRY FOR REASONS OF STATE RATHER than reasons solely based on her personal fancy, but Princess Charlotte (1796-1817), daughter of the Prince Regent and Caroline of Brunswick was no pawn—kind of more the opposite....

Bear in mind that at the time when ministers of state, and latterly her parents, were scanning the horizon for suitable royal consorts for her, the Napoleonic wars were heading towards, they hoped, a close. At the same time, the remaining heads of state—those which had survived—were wondering how best to restore order to Europe and reinstate legitimate government (read monarchies) to those countries which Napoleon had annexed to France. So the task of choosing a royal mate was a little more complex than usual.

Nevertheless, in 1812, the government hit upon a plan. Wouldn't it be perfect if Princess Charlotte were to marry William of Orange? He was of an age with Charlotte, neither too old nor too young, he'd seen active service in the Peninsula, so he was a dashing military hero, and he was a Protestant (a necessity). What could be better?

William of Orange had been raised in exile in England (so he spoke English!), he'd spent two years at Oxford, and from 1811, he'd served in the Peninsula under Wellington, by whom he was known as "Slender Billy".

Perhaps he wasn't great-looking, but he was known to be amiable, and there had been another hugely successful marriage between a Prince of Orange and an English princess.... And, bliss of blisses, someday he would rule the Netherlands—so through him and any children they might have, Britain would regain a toehold on the Continent, moreover a toehold that was right across the North Sea, thus securing the sea lanes to the Baltic. It was ideal!

There was only one problem: Princess Charlotte.

Because you see, in the autumn of 1812, she had conceived a rather violent passion for a Captain Charles Hesse of the 18th Hussars, and whilst at Windsor had gone out riding with him every day.

And after that, she'd been meeting with him secretly at her mother's home in Kensington, where her mother, helpfully, would:

> ...let him into her own apartment by a door that opens onto Kensington Gardens...[then] leave them together in her own bedroom, [with the words] "a present, je vous laisse, amusez-vous." [For the moment I'm leaving you, amuse yourselves....]

As you may appreciate, when the Prince Regent discovered this, he was incandescent with rage. And Charlotte was pretty much locked away with a new governess and with very little company. As the Prince said with some feeling (and almost in echo of Austen's Mr. Bennet):

> *I know all that passed in Windsor Park; and if it were not for my clemency I would have shut you up for life. Depend upon it, as long as I live you shall never have an establishment, unless you marry.*

Hence, when the proposed match with William was put to Princess Charlotte in February 1813, she was not keen. As she said of him, *"I think him so ugly, that I am sometimes obliged to turn my head away in disgust when he is speaking to me."* (Ouch!) But the idea did eventually take hold—marriage would allow her her own establishment and financial independence. And the princess was already in debt to the tune of £22,000 (over a million pounds in today's money).

The Prince Regent was delighted and held a dinner at his home at Carlton House so that the two might meet on 11 December, and Charlotte was enjoined to give her father her *"fair and undisguised opinion"*. After the usual fits and starts, by the end of the evening, Charlotte told her father, *"I like his manner very well, as much as I ever have seen of it."* The Prince Regent was rapturous. Charlotte would later speak of the whole thing as *"a dream"*.

Then, in early April, having been fought to a standstill in France, Napoleon abdicated. Then followed another remarkable bit of news: for the first time in centuries, European royalty were to visit England! Caught up in the euphoria of the moment, in early May, the government announced the intended marriage between Charlotte and William, the Hereditary Prince of Orange (who suddenly had a throne again!).

William himself had already arrived in Britain, ahead of the other European princes—Tsar Alexander and Kaiser Wilhelm and their entourages. But then, a spoke appeared in the marital-diplomatic wheel—the Grand Duchess Catherine, the Tsar's confidante and sister, who allegedly had designs on William herself—or rather, Russia also wanted a toehold in western Europe.

The visit of the crowned heads that June offered an opportunity for endless rounds of parties, balls, dinners, and diplomacy, but Princess Charlotte was not invited. Instead, she remained cooped up in her residence at Warwick House, next door to Carlton House, sequestered away from the fun, even as Grand Duchess Catherine worked on her, visiting, taking tea, souring whatever remained of Charlotte's affection for Slender Billy—especially by recounting just what her fiancé was getting up to.

While Charlotte was locked away, William was repeatedly getting drunk, attending all the social events, having a whale of a time—when he'd gone to the Ascot Races, he'd returned to London hanging off the outside of a stage coach.

And there was one other looming problem. Where would the young couple live? Charlotte feared that if she left the country and her father obtained a divorce as he wished to do, her father might remarry and produce a new heir. And where would that leave

Charlotte? So the demand made in the proposed marriage settlement that she should spend some time with her husband in the Netherlands, as she put it, *"living in Holland amongst the fogs and dykes"*, each year proved the final straw.

(Though it's also said that she'd been secretly seeing the Prussian king's nephew, Prince Frederick, who was said to be very handsome and she was much enamoured....)

Charlotte therefore requested that William pay her a visit on 16 June. Their consultation together ended with Charlotte's *"positive declaration that she will not leave England now"*. And later that evening, Charlotte wrote to William informing him that she was jilting him, that their engagement was *"to be totally and for ever at an end"*.

It was a public humiliation for William...and initially, it didn't work out so well for Charlotte either...though later, she did marry the rather spiffing Prince Leopold of Saxe-Coburg, and he was her choice.

Fact or Holmesian Fantasy?
The London Fog

By M.M. BENNETTS

There was no dawn, just a slow thinning of night into the obscuring mist which lay sagging and inert over the city like a slattern in her bed. Jesuadon gazed out of one clouded window to the dockside and drank down his tankard of flip. Fistfuls of fog swirled and eddied before fading about the forest of masts—all he could see of the multitude of boats, skiffs and barges, all confined to port, becalmed beneath the stagnant sky, the bustle and rush of St. Katharine's Docks brought to a muffled, deadening halt.

IT LOOKS SO GOOD IN ALL THOSE COSTUME DRAMAS, DOESN'T IT? THE SWIRLS OF FOG rising, the mist clotting the air through which the gorgeously or raggedly costumed actors emerge from alleys onto Baker Street...I mean, it's an atmospheric masterstroke, isn't it, into which baddies and goodies can disappear at will—just on the street—no special effects required.

But....

But the truth is...the truth is, the London fog was fact—a very big, very present, very smelly fact.

It wasn't just a delicious figment of Sir Arthur Conan Doyle's or Charles Dickens' pen. And it had been around for years and years, centuries even, before those two ever caught the writing bug....

In Shakespeare's day, visitors approaching the city or leaving it were known to remark that one could smell the place from fifty miles away. (And in 1600, fifty miles was a fair distance—a couple of days' journey probably.)

By the early nineteenth century, London was a sprawling metropolis of some one million inhabitants, the largest city in Europe (Naples was second), and it had the vapours and stench to prove it. The whiff of the city's smoke *"could always distinguish a London letter...on putting it to the nose."*

A visitor to the city, Louis Simond, wrote:

> *London does not strike with admiration; it is regular, clean, convenient (I am speaking of the best part) but the site is flat; the plan monotonous; the predominant colour of objects dingy and poor. It is altogether without great faults and without great beauties.*

Speaking of the fog, he continued:

> [In winter] *smoke increases the general dingy hue, and terminates the length of every street with a fixed and grey mist, receding as you advance.*

And he wasn't joking. And he was speaking of every day.

Early 1814 saw the worst fogs since November 1755—during the few weeks of the Great Frost Fair—which caused chaos and great consternation. Carriages were regularly over-turned as the drivers couldn't see more than a few paces in front of them. The mails (which began in London) were held up and neither dispatched nor received.

Only a few of the capital's hackney carriages were willing to venture forth—and those only at walking pace with an assistant leading the horses. And on any street, all one saw were lanterns bobbing and moving in all directions, joined by muffled cries of "Mind! Where are you? Have a care!" And that was during the day.

But even in summer it was disgustingly bad (and bad for your health). For even then, there were those people who were astonished if they could look out of their window and see up to the end of their street.

And those who lived in the posh newly-built squares of the West End were delighted if they could see the houses across the square. They certainly didn't look out and see the sunlight glinting off the dome of St. Paul's...or off any other dome for that matter. The fog would have obscured all such clarity of vision.

The painter J.P. Malcolm wrote of his surprise on a particularly fine August morning:

> *Then lengthened perspective, and enabled the eye to penetrate depths unfath-omable at eight o'clock, and shewed retiring houses at distances I had never seen them before. The fanciful decorations of shop windows, doors, and the fresh-painted fronts, had each their relief; and the brazen appearance of the gilt names* [that] *had vanished with the smoke now darted with due lustre....*

(It kind of ruins the idea of a spinster seeing everything by standing behind her lace curtain though, doesn't it? I mean, she could twitch all she liked, but what actually would she have been able to see? Not very much.)

So what caused this notorious, pestiferous, stinking, mottled blanket of dingy obscu-rity which lay over the city? A combination of factors—the location of the city on the tidal estuary of the Thames, England being an island and a fairly soggy one at that, but most of all, the use of coal to heat the homes and fire the furnaces of the factories that were beginning to line the Thames and fill the poorer parishes of the city.

If you haven't smelled coal smoke, it is surprisingly acrid and there's a sharpness about it. A bite. It is entirely unlike wood smoke or the relatively smokeless heat produced by charcoal (which is how houses were heated in Paris and Vienna). Coal also produces soot on an unprecedented scale.

Yes, it does heat to a hotter, higher degree than wood—hence its desirability in industry (iron work, foundries, horse-shoeing). But it coats absolutely everything with a black film, and as a city, not just the buildings of London would be blackened with coal soot, but the air itself would be laden with small flecks of soot....

(Which is why, during the Regency for example, those gentlemen who could afford it had their shirts laundered far enough away from the city so that when the clean laundry was hung out to dry, they wouldn't be soiled by the very air. Oh, and they would have smelled a great deal more pleasant.)

Also, by the early nineteenth century (though it had been growing and growing for years) small industry was firmly established in the nation's capital. It was a city of slaughterhouses (around Whitechapel), knackerers, shipbuilding, tanneries (the main ingredient for tanning leather being urine), small foundries, the brick makers, and all sorts... and all of these cottage industries spewed their toxic by-products into the Thames and through their tall chimney stacks into the atmosphere.

So, the London fog? Yes, absolutely! And if it wasn't foggy, it was probably raining....

The Worker Revolt Against Progress or Just Standing Up for the Little Guy? The Luddites, 1811

By J.A. BEARD

The Industrial Revolution, a product of the concerted application of "natural philosophy" and engineering, did not please everyone in England. Indeed, in the early years, some productivity gains associated with this economic shift led to such instability that thousands of troops were fielded to suppress discontent. Such was the case with the Luddites.

In early 1811, stocking factories in Nottingham started receiving letters from *"General Ned Ludd and his Army of Redressers."* Among other wage grievances, these letters outlined threats against employers over the use of stocking frames—an early type of semi-automated knitting machine. The advance of the Industrial Revolution had spread various types of textile processing machines throughout northern and mid-England. While these machines allowed the cheaper production of textiles, they also hurt the livelihood of traditional handloom weavers. Even when the automation process didn't completely eliminate jobs, they still resulted in a severe downward pressure on wages and longer hours. Other economic issues contributed to the climate of discontent. Thus, the Luddites quickly gained a great deal of popular support among the working classes.

The Luddites started breaking into factories and destroying stocking frames. The discontent and destruction spread. Soon, the newly established Prince Regent was offering reward money for information on these so-called "frame-breakers" and "frame-smashers."

So, who was General Ned Ludd? The historical evidence suggests there likely was no such man. Instead, the name was likely inspired by a 1782 incident involving an angry farm laborer who smashed some frames. Whether there was a real General Ludd didn't seem to matter much. The Luddites weren't a tightly organized movement as much as various different groups of agitated workers arising in different locations. Many of their clashes with authorities were more riots than anything else. This was one of the reasons they would initially prove hard to suppress. There was no head of the dragon to cut off. The factors leading to their discontent weren't things that the government and authorities could do much to directly address in an efficient manner.

The Luddite cause spread throughout the industrial areas of England, including Yorkshire, Derbyshire, Lancashire, and Leicestershire. Although it had started with the weavers, other textile workers vented their wrath on various machines threatening their jobs and their general frustration over increasing concerns about economic inequity.

The chaos would continue to spread. Seemingly constant frame breaking and attacks on mills escalated into occasional attacks on mill guards, mill owners, and others opposing the Luddite cause. Though there were some arrests for murder and executions, the responses of local authorities did little to quell the decentralized movement. A combination of several factors, including the on-going Napoleonic Wars on the Continent, contributed to exploding wheat prices in 1812. This poor economic climate combined with concern over food led to even greater militarization of many workers. Despite the passionate opposition of a small minority of Luddite-sympathizing politicians, such as the controversial Lord Bryon, Parliament passed the Frame-Breaking Act, which made frame-breaking in and of itself a capital crime. In addition, troops were sent into the areas suffering from Luddite trouble.

By 1813, the show of force succeeded in bringing the Luddites to heel. Mass trials were followed by executions and transportation to Australia for many. Though Luddite-related riots, frame-breaking, and violence would sputter back into life over the next few years, by 1817 the Luddites were finished as a movement, even if their name would live on as a slur directed at anti-technology people.

A Surprising Greek Hero: The Very English Lord Byron

By J.A. Beard

George Gordon Byron, the 6th Baron Byron, was one of the more colorful characters of the late Georgian period. Many remember him to this day for his poetry and his many, many scandalous love affairs. After all, this man at one point was declared (albeit by an ex-lover) as *"mad, bad, and dangerous to know."*

There was another side to this man, though. His practical and political side would lead this English poet to have a small role in the history of labor and the history of another nation: Greece.

For Lord Byron, one aspect of his birthright was a seat on the House of Lords—a fortunate convenience for a man very critical of the status quo. Byron's poetry was often full of scathing critique and satire of both domestic and international political issues, and he made many impassioned speeches in Parliament to champion the causes he felt just. His first period in Parliament (March-June 1809) was brought to an end by a trip to Europe. He would later return to Parliament in 1812, though his permanent departure from England in 1816, forced both by rumors about his behavior and heavy debt, would end his domestic political career.

During his time in Parliament, Lord Byron championed many reformist causes, or by some people's reckoning, revolutionary causes. For example, he supported Irish independence both in poetry and political speeches:

> *Thus has Great Britain swallowed up the Parliament—the constitution—the independence of Ireland, and refuses to disgorge even a single privilege, although for the relief of her swollen and distempered body politic.*

He later would even pen poetry suggesting some support for the independence of India. These were not exactly popular positions at the time.

He also supported the Luddites. They were an anti-industrialization movement centered around textile workers whose jobs were being eliminated by new technologies. Protests turned to a campaign against mills in the north of England. The destruction of mills combined with attacks on magistrates led to the deployment of thousands of troops against the Luddites.

As one can surmise, the Luddites were not some genteel opposition movement. They were a near revolutionary force that conservative aristocrats viewed with disgust and trepidation. In contrast, Lord Byron viewed the Luddite cause as arising from social justice concerns by people being harmed and destroyed by dubious automation that benefited others more than the workers. He supported the movement both in Parliament and in his poetry. Whether one thinks him a fool or praises him for that, it definitely was a very radical position.

Even after leaving England, Byron would continue to contribute to political newspapers and discussions, generally supporting causes that placed him firmly in opposition to many landed, aristocratic interests. A lot of this was heavily influenced by his Romantic worldview.

Byron later became involved with the Greek independence movement. At the time, the Greeks were under the heel of the Ottoman Empire. He'd spoken and written of his belief in Greek independence for some time, but the start of open insurgency in 1821 further crystallized his support. While some of this support was just part of his natural tendency to support most independence movements, Greece also held a special place in the hearts of many Western intellectuals of the period due to its ancient contributions to Western thought.

Generous financial and literary support by Byron gave way to more direct military aid in 1823, including his formation, using his own money, of the Byron Brigade (including refitting warships). Besides helping with equipment, he also ended up in command of Greek rebel soldiers.

Despite his literary talents, he had no military experience at all, but it seems the Greeks weren't going to risk offending a man who was giving them a considerable amount of money and for whom they had a great deal of respect. He was to take part in a major assault on a Turkish fortress, Lepanto, but before the force could depart toward the objective, he fell ill. Over the next few months he fought disease, incompetent doctors, and infection until he finally succumbed to his aliments at Missolonghi, Greece on April 19, 1824 at the not-so-ripe age of 36.

Despite Byron's very minimal involvement in the actual fighting, years of financial, political, and literary support garnered him a large amount of Greek respect. In Greece, many still consider him, despite his non-Greek background, a hero of the Greek War of Independence. There was even a three day period of mourning following his death there and a city northeast of Athens still named after him, Vyronas (Βύρωνας). His death in Greece helped focus even more international attention on the conflict and arguably helped to contribute to the entry of other Western powers on the Greek side.

Pretty good for a man who was *"mad, bad, and dangerous to know."*

Newfoundlands: Lord Byron's Bear and Other Stories

By Jonathan Hopkins

Byron had a tame bear. I knew that, but what I didn't know was that he also kept a pair of Newfoundland dogs called Thunder and Boatswain.

A couple of years ago when I wrote the outline for my current work in progress, I decided the young naval lieutenant in the story should own a dog. And since the action took place on board ship that dog should be a Newfoundland. It just made logical sense that in an age when few sailors could swim a "water-dog" offered fresh plotting opportunities.

My first mistake was making the dog black. Apparently, this colour was very uncommon in Britain before 1840. Most Newfoundlands of the day were pied—white and black, or white and brown. Today this colour is known as "Landseer" after Sir Edwin Landseer who painted a number of these dogs' portraits

But I got the name right. My Newfoundland was called "Cuthbert" after Admiral Collingwood. Apparently Frederica, Duchess of York, owned a Newfoundland called "Nelson" at that time, so I'm in good company!

Newfoundlands had been imported to Britain from...well, Newfoundland, since the mid-sixteenth century. Their origin is obscure, but they are believed to have been developed from crosses between husky types, retrievers, collies, and even mastiffs. Some think their ancestry may even date back to Viking bear dogs.

Early examples often exhibit a decidedly collie-like muzzle, quite different to today's breed, which brings us back to Lord Byron. So fond was he of Boatswain that he had his portrait painted. Though it must have been a good likeness (or he would likely not have paid the artist) at the beginning of the twentieth century its provenance was disputed on the grounds it was too unlike a Newfoundland, so if it was really Boatswain was he actually a cross-breed?

With imported Newfoundlands costing twenty guineas in Byron's day, it's doubtful even he would have spent good money on a dog of dubious parentage. And there's another noticeable difference between then and now because Boatswain and Thunder were used as guard dogs, suggesting a more aggressive temperament, bred out through subsequent generations to produce today's far more equable, some would say soppier, individuals. In fact Boatswain was well known for fighting with just about every other dog he encountered, his owner being an early example of irresponsible dog ownership. Byron's darker side took advantage of this trait—he used his two Newfoundlands to bait his bear, and Boatswain's tooth-edged metal collar, which still survives, shows stark evidence of such fighting in its scrapes and gouges.

When the dog died in 1808 of hydrophobia (rabies) caught from another dog he fought, Byron had an ornate memorial built in the grounds of his home, Newstead Abbey. (Out of interest, this property was later owned by Colonel Thomas Wildman of the 7th Hussars, ADC to Lord Uxbridge at Waterloo—my sole mention of anything cavalry-related in this essay!)

One specific point of conformation encouraged by selective breeding is the Newfoundland's webbed feet. There are huge numbers of incidents recorded of dogs saving the lives of drowning people and other animals. Their size and strength, together with a double-layered pelt, gives them both endurance and buoyancy. Many dogs happily dive into deep water, sometimes from a height, and have been known to retrieve objects below the surface, this despite having open ears and nostrils which, unlike those of a seal, are not designed to close underwater.

A report in the *Portsmouth Telegraph* of 23 June 1800 about a Newfoundland which refused to let any stranger approach its master who suffered a fit in the street says the dog previously saved him from drowning when he fell overboard in the harbour.

This is by no means unusual—there are hundreds of such stories of dogs saving lives, both when deliberately encouraged to enter the water and simply of their own accord. They have retrieved the unfortunate victims of drowning, swum out with ropes to stricken vessels, towed drifting small boats to shore, even retrieved smaller dogs which had swum out of their depth.

Such was the Newfoundland's reputation that river police on the Seine kept a team as rescue dogs in the early twentieth century, though despite some successes they were eventually disbanded, apparently through lack of use. There was even a story that a Newfoundland's barks attracted the attention of *Carpathia* to an errant lifeboat when *Titanic* was sunk, but this was later found to be a hoax. Shame, really.

Obviously intelligent, several Newfoundlands became famous "animal actors" before there were such things. They were used to haul small loads and small children in carts. They collected for charities, particularly those connected with seafaring. Nowadays many are still trained and used as lifesaving "water dogs".

It continues to amaze me what you discover when researching for historical fiction.

SOURCES

Bondeson, Jan. *Those Amazing Newfoundland Dogs*. CFZ Press, 2012.

My grateful thanks to Jackie Bagnall of Newfinch Newfoundlands for her help with this article.

VOLCANOES, VAMPIRES, AND MAD SCIENCE: THE BIRTH OF SEDUCTIVE VAMPIRES AND SCIENTISTS PLAYING GOD

BY J.A. BEARD

IN 1815, A SERIES OF LESSER VOLCANIC ERUPTIONS WAS FOLLOWED BY THE ERUPTION OF Mount Tambora (one of the largest eruptions in over 1000 years). This occurred in combination with cyclical lows in solar activity. While modern scientists aren't completely sure, they believe this particular convergence is responsible for the phenomena that occurred in 1816 that we now know as the "Year without a Summer."

Overall temperatures around the globe, particularly in the Northern Hemisphere, were temporarily reduced. This, in turn, caused summer frosts, increased rain, and various other climate effects that resulted in the summer season resembling more an extended autumn. These climate impacts had numerous negative effects, including reduced crop yields from early frosts and excessive rainfall (leading to flooding) in many areas. This led to subsequent downstream economic effects. All in all, the experience wasn't pleasant for much of the world.

During the normal "summer" months of that year, a small group of intellectuals were staying near Lake Geneva for a summer holiday. The unrelenting rain forced them inside for most of the summer. Absent the modern conveniences of the internet, television, radio, or even not-so-modern conveniences such as a large, expansive library, these sad vacationers, being of the literary bent, decided to have a contest of sorts to see who could create the most frightening tale. The dark, grim summer along with various other ghost stories served as inspiration (perhaps with the aid of a little alcohol or laudanum for some as well, according to a few sources).

Now, these weren't just any random collection of people. The primary host of this vacation gone awry was none other than Lord Bryon, the often morally questionable bad boy Romantic poet. In addition to Lord Bryon, the poet and radical Percy Shelley was also in attendance along with his new young wife, Mary. They only added to the scandal factor of the gathering. The main reason the Shelleys were abroad had to do with the fact that Percy left his first wife, who was pregnant at the time, and child to run off with the then sixteen-year old Mary in 1814. Percy and Mary didn't marry until Percy's first wife committed suicide in 1816. Many people in their social circles were suitably scandalized, so they fled England to tour Europe. Rounding out the party was Mary's stepsister, Claire Clairmont, and John William Polidori, a writer and physician.

Of the stories produced during the contest, two were later expanded and have had a lasting impact on literature.

Mary Shelley penned a story she later expanded into none other than *Frankenstein: The Modern Prometheus,* which she published in 1818. Though Hollywood has often rendered Frankenstein's Monster into a pathetic, easily spoofed parody, the original story relates the creation of an intelligent and philosophical artificial being.

Whatever one thinks of the literary merits of the book (it was not well received upon release), it is rather notable that the creation of the monster was specifically inspired by what was then cutting-edge science rather than some type of supernatural cause. This, arguably, makes it an early example of science fiction, in addition to horror. Various stories about a scientist going "too far" with experiments and receiving a suitable, if predictable, karmic reward for trying to "play God" arguably have some descent from *Frankenstein*.

Notably, there had been some discussion shortly before Mary wrote the initial version of the story of the experiments of the Italian scientist, Giovanni Aldini. Giovanni was intensely interested in experimenting with stimulating muscles with electricity. He performed a particularly high profile experiment in 1803 where he applied electrical current to a dead condemned criminal. Some witnesses, upon the seeing limb movements and facial expression changes due to the artificial stimulation, thought Giovanni was actually bringing the man back to life.

These experiments, along with some similar experiments performed by other scientists on animals, were well-known among the intellectual set, including Mary Shelley. It's easy to see how such experiments at a time where even the educated had only a mild handle on biochemistry and physics could lead an intelligent young author to pen a story where forbidden science is used to animate an artificial human.

The other major story to come out of that summer in 1816 was *The Vampyre* by John William Polidori. Like Shelley, Polidori would rework and expand his story over a few years. He published the final novella in 1819.

In the story, an Englishman, Aubrey, meets and travels with a mysterious aristocrat, Ruthven. After an incident in which Ruthven is apparently killed and an earlier incident where a vampire kills a mutual acquaintance, Aubrey is surprised to see the man quite alive. Ruthven then begins to seduce Aubrey's sister. Aubrey is powerless, because of an earlier oath, to tell his sister that he saw the man already die. Eventually, on her wedding night she is found dead, drained of blood.

This tale was wildly successful both because of the existing interest in Gothic horror at the time and the fact that for many years people attributed the story to Lord Byron rather than Mr. Polidori. It would go on to inspire countless vampire tales during the Regency and Victorian era. Eventually, it would inspire the now more famous *Dracula* by Bram Stoker. The transformation of the vampire from some pseudo-ghoul corpse walker symbol of plague that was far more prevalent in folklore to a manipulative, aristocratic creature of canny planning and frightening patience was Mr. Polidori's innovation. The influence of Mr. Polidori's story still reverberates to this day.

That's something to keep in mind. Whenever one complains about vampires being seductive creatures rather than just ghoulish monsters, they should remember the seductive-vampire motif goes all the way back to 1819 and Mr. Polidori.

CHAWTON TODAY: A WALK IN JANE AUSTEN'S VILLAGE

BY M.M. BENNETTS

ALTHOUGH SHE DIDN'T SETTLE IN THE VILLAGE OF CHAWTON IN HAMPSHIRE UNTIL 7 July 1809, it's now one of the places we most associate with Jane Austen.

It's there that the cottage she lived in with her mother and sister Cassandra is found, and can be visited...and it's there that she wrote and rewrote during the most productive years of her short life.

As probably everyone knows, the Austen family had been living mostly in Bath and roundabout for a number of years, since 1800—though Jane, rather like her heroine Anne Eliot of *Persuasion*, did not like it there. Thus, when her brother Edward offered the family the use of the small seventeenth century cottage in Chawton that was his as owner of the "big house" in the village, Chawton House, it was a welcome change.

Between moving to the cottage in Chawton in 1809 and her death in July 1817, Austen wrote or revised the novels which would change the face of fiction forever.

Though Austen's niece described the family's life there thusly: *"It was a very quiet life, according to our ideas, but they were great readers, and besides the housekeeping our aunts occupied themselves in working with the poor and in teaching some girl or boy to read or write...",* I think it's fair to say that while Austen's life may have appeared quiet, her imagination and her pen were busier than ever.

Starting with the publication of *Sense and Sensibility* in October 1811, she went on to publish *Pride and Prejudice* in January 1813, which was followed by *Mansfield Park* in May 1814, and *Emma* in December 1815. (*Northanger Abbey* and *Persuasion* were published posthumously in December 1817.)

It's been 200 years since Austen published *Pride and Prejudice* from that most modest address and to celebrate, the village of Chawton opened their gardens to visitors, and Chawton House, besides opening their gardens, also brought a company of Regency dancers to perform in the grounds as well as to teach some of the dances to visitors.

Over the past few years, a great deal of work has been done on the Chawton property to open more of it to the public and to provide an education centre as well. Among other things, the garden has been carefully planted with flowers and shrubs that were available at the time of Austen's living there, rather than with modern cultivars, and the effect is wondrous.

Walking the still-quiet lanes, peering into the beautifully kept gardens, observing the dancing at the big house—all of this is part of the life that Austen would have known when she resided there. So many of the cottages might easily have belonged to Miss Bates or housed the school where Miss Smith had grown up, don't you think?

So please, take a moment to walk with her and see what she might have seen, to hear the distant bleating of lambs, and smell the scents of roses, pinks, and rich earth as she did in those heady weeks after the publication of her most famous novel, when she had no idea how famous she would become, nor how many of us would make the pilgrimage to this tiny village in northeast Hampshire.

What Were the Royals Doing? And What Was in the Theatre? August 16-18, 1819

By DEBRA BROWN

I AM ENTHRALLED WITH THE WORDING AND THE POINTS BROUGHT OUT IN AGES-OLD newspapers. I make sure my table is spotless and my hands are clean before I bring out my treasures—in this case, an 1819 London *Times*. "Papers" were made, back then, of fabric, often rags, and they have a different feel. Paper made from trees was yet a few decades away. I also get out a magnifying glass as the print is miniaturized, apparently meant to be read by a grasshopper.

Just as publications today report on the schedule of the Queen (and the Royal Family) and inform us of what she had with her tea, there were details for royal watchers in the old newspapers:

> Cowes, August 16.—The Duke of York will certainly be here to-day, and, with his Royal Highness the Prince-Regent, will honour the Earl of Cavan, at Eaglehurst, with their company at dinner. To-morrow, Lord Henry Seymour is to have the honour of entertaining his Royal Highness at his splendid mansion at East Cowes. His Lordship is universally beloved in the island, and his liberal and hospitable spirit has induced him to open his lawn and grounds to the public, who are to be treated with refreshments at his Lordship's entire expense. The Prince-Regent has directed Sir B. Bloomfield to look out for land whereupon he can build; and already the moorings for the Royal Yacht are fixed in our roadstead. He says he shall pay us an annual visit for a month together. The Prince at present intends to remain here a fortnight longer.

> Windsor, Aug. 17.—Lord St. Helen's, as a Member of the Council, is in waiting here on the King. Saturday, the Duchess of Glocester, accompanied by the Princess Augusta, rode to Bagshot, to view the alterations, improvements, and repairs, which have been proceeding there for some months past. Their Royal Highnesses returned to the palace for dinner.

> THE DUCHESS OF KENT'S BIRTH-DAY.—Yesterday being the Duchess of Kent's birth-day, the Duke made arrangements for

rejoicing on the occasion. In the morning, at half-past six o'clock, the Princess Feodor, attended by her music-master and the whole of the domestics, was in the room adjoining the Duke and Duchess's, to serenade her Royal mother with God Save the King. In the course of the day several distinguished characters called at the Palace, to leave their names and dutiful respects on the happy return of the day. Their Royal Highnesses had a dinner party in honour of the day. Among the company were, the Duke of Sussex, the Princess Augusta, the Duchess of Glocester, the Duchess of York, and the Princess Sophia Matilda. After dinner the company adjourned to the apartments of the Duke of Sussex, in the Palace, where his Royal Highness entertained them with tea, coffee &c. and a select concert, under the direction of Sir George Smart, who presided at the grand pianoforte.

That was it. Not enough? I could share with you some of the Theatre information.

For the BENEFIT of Mr. WARDE.
THEATRE-ROYAL, HAYMARKET
THIS EVENING, THE FOUNDLING OF THE FOREST.
Count de Valmont, Mr. Warde.
After which, BLUE DEVILS.
To conclude with THE PRISONER AT LARGE.

⁓⭒⭒⭒⁓

THEATRE-ROYAL, ENGLISH OPERA-HOUSE.
THIS EVENING, THE PADLOCK.
After which, (11th time), an entirely new Operetta called
BELLES WITHOUT BEAUS!
or, The Ladies among themselves.
To which will be added, a new Entertainment, in one act, called
ONE, TWO, THREE, FOUR, FIVE, BY ADVERTISEMENT.
To conclude with WALK FOR A WAGER.

⁓⭒⭒⭒⁓

SADLER'S WELLS.
From the great approbation bestowed on the new
Aquatic Melodrama
It will be repeated every evening till further notice.
THIS and three following EVENINGS
the entertainments will commence with a romantic melo-dramatic
burletta, called

THE BOLD BUCANIERS; Robinson Crusoe, Mr. Campbell; Friday, Mr. Grimaldi,
Iglou, Mr. Bologna; Paraboo, Mr. Hartland.
After which a new musical interlude,
called the CALIPH AND THE CADI;
or Rambles in Bagdad:
characters by Messrs. Campbell, Mears. Barnes, O'Rourke,
G. Crisp, and Miss Neville;
principal dancers, Mr. W. Kirby, and Mrs. Best.
To conclude with a new Aquatic Melodrama,
called THE IDIOT HEIR.
The whole of the last scene exhibited on real water, representing the overthrow of the usurper, and total destruction of the castle by fire.
Doors open at half-past 5; begin at half-past 6.

VAUXHALL.
Under the Patronage of His Royal Highness the Prince Regent.
THIS EVENING, Aug. 18th, a GRAND GALA; when Monsieur, Mademoiselle, and Madame Saqui, will go through their surprising evolutions. At the end of the concert, Madame Saqui will make an astonishing ascent on the Tight Rope, amidst a brilliant display of Fire-works by Signora Hengler.
Admission 3s. 6d. Doors open at 7; the concert to begin at 8 o'clock.

There you have it. A brief summary of what was going on in mid-August, 1819 and how it was written up in the newspapers.

THE HANDSOME MASTER OF ACIDS: SIR HUMPHRY DAVY

BY J.A. BEARD

OFTEN WHEN THINKING ABOUT THE LATE GEORGIAN ERA AND THE REGENCY PERIOD, it's easy to fixate on the many cultural and political changes that occurred. Controversial and charismatic men like Lord Byron challenged social mores, and decades of war in the form of the Napoleonic Wars presented an additional stress to a country that was already undergoing rapid change due to industrialization.

Sometimes lost in discussions of aspects of the period such as industrialization is that the late Georgian era was also a time of impressive scientific progress. It is easy, in the light of modern genetic engineering, nanotechnology, and control of nuclear power to be dismissive of the achievements of these "natural philosophers" who set the stage for the massive advances in science and technology that define the modern human condition. Today, I will spotlight one of these pioneers: Sir Humphry Davy.

Sir Humphry was born into a respectable, though untitled and not particularly wealthy family in 1778 in Penzance. As a young child, both at home and school, he quickly demonstrated above-average intelligence, concentration, dedication, and attention to detail, all traits that would serve him well. He also had the fortune, while a student, to have as an early mentor Robert Dunkin. Though Mr. Dunkin's background was more business than anything, he had a keen interest in many areas of burgeoning interest in natural philosophy, and he inculcated in young Sir Humphry the principles of the experimental method and exposed to him devices such as the Leyden Jar (a sort of primitive capacitor that can store static electricity) and other apparatuses that would kindle an interest in electricity and exploring the principles behind electrochemistry. He would remain friends with and discuss scientific principles with Mr. Dunkin even after leaving his tutelage.

After the death of Sir Humphry's father in 1794 (Sir Humphry was fifteen at the time), the boy was apprenticed to a surgeon. This proved fortuitous for his growing interest in chemistry as it gave him a ready supply of reagents with which to experiment, not, if some of the anecdotes and statements of the time are accurate, with the greatest attention to personal safety.

A chance encounter with Davies Giddy, a member of the Royal Society, led to Sir Humphry's introduction to a number of men of science and engineering. He was given the chance to experiment in more dedicated and well-equipped laboratories and received exposure to certain electrochemistry phenomena that were being actively explored at the time, such as the galvanic corrosion (due to the copper and iron construction) of floodgates in the city of Hayle. Though there was initially some resistance by his surgical master (who wanted Davy to stay as a surgeon in Penzance), Davy would eventually leave Penzance with Dr. Thomas Beddoes, a physician and writer.

In 1798, Sir Humphry joined the Pneumatic Institute, a research center founded by Dr. Beddoes to study the medical applications of newly discover gases (particularly oxygen and hydrogen). While at the Institute, Sir Humphry spent time studying nitrous oxide (a.k.a laughing gas), but, unfortunately, the potential as anesthesia seems to have escaped him (as it would many others) for several decades. Again, while at the Institute, he continued to not always practice what we would consider modern safe experimental practice and nearly killed himself more than once in the pursuit of knowledge. Indeed, in later years, he damaged his vision due to an accident with a laboratory acid experiment.

He also published several scientific studies and continued his intense work with electrical conductors and galvanic electrochemical reactions. In addition, he had the time to establish connections with a variety of men of influence, both scientific and otherwise, including James Watt (the Scottish master of the steam engine whose work was pivotal to the Industrial Revolution) and poet and philosopher, Samuel Taylor Coleridge.

With the establishing of the Royal Institution, a major multi-disciplinary research organization in London, Sir Humphry made the move to London and, as it were, "the big time." His youth, handsome looks, and dramatic speaking style which included flashy chemical demonstrations quickly turned his public lectures into popular events. He also was not one to downplay the perceived importance of his own work, as can be seen from this excerpt from an 1801 lecture on galvanism:

> The relations of galvanism to the different branches of physical science, are too numerous and too extensive to be connected with the preceding details; and, although in their infancy, they will probably long constitute favourite subjects of investigation amongst philosophers, and become the sources of useful discoveries....
>
> The connexion of galvanism with philosophical medicine is evident. The electrical influence in its common form, as excited by machines, has been employed with advantage in the cures of diseases; in a new state of existence it may possibly be possessed of greater and of different powers.

For several years, Sir Humphry explored electrochemistry and gas chemistry. Among other things, he was the first to isolate magnesium, potassium, boron, and barium. Although he did not discover chlorine (that honor belongs to the Swedish chemist, Carl Scheele), he gave the substance its current name and also proved several important facts about chlorine, such as the fact that pure chlorine contains no oxygen.

In 1812, his various contributions to science earned him a knighthood (thus, he finally actually became Sir Humphry). He married and along with his wife traveled to the Continent in 1813. He was also accompanied by his assistant, a man who would go on to be another pivotal figure in science, Michael Faraday. Unfortunately, in later years, Sir

Humphry's ambition and suspicion would cause him to have a falling out with Faraday (whom he accused, among other things, of plagiarism).

During the next couple of years in Europe, Sir Humphry received a medal from Napoleon (yes, that Napoleon) for his scientific work, demonstrated iodine was an element, and proved diamond was pure carbon.

When he returned to England in 1815, he worked on a number of projects, including improved coal mining lamps with wire gauze that would not leak gas into the environment. This, unfortunately, may have inadvertently led to increased mine-related deaths by encouraging workers to probe more deeply into areas of mines they would have previously avoided due to safety concerns.

He also expanded on his acid-base theories to classify acids as substances with metal-replaceable hydrogen groups and bases as substances that formed water and a salt when combined with an acid. These definitions are not as specific as the more modern Lewis and Bronsted-Lowry Acid-Base definitions but were useful enough to help facilitate a considerable amount of brilliant electrochemistry and acid-base chemistry in the decades after Davy's death.

For those of you unfamiliar with chemistry, please note that the number of realms that electrochemistry and acid-base chemistry touch is vast. Indeed, proper understanding of acid-base chemistry is critical for everything from understandings of drugs and biochemistry to industrial manufacturing. Obviously, Sir Humphry did not fully develop our understanding of this area, but he made very important contributions to the areas for others to build on.

In 1819, his continued contributions to science were recognized by the awarding of a baronetcy (an inheritable non-peerage title, unlike knighthoods which are non-inheritable non-peerage titles). It should be noted this put him higher in honors for science work than even the master of physics, Sir Isaac Newton.

Sir Humphry died in 1829 from a heart issue. Although his name is less recognizable to many than someone like Michael Faraday, his work was important and influential and echoes even today in the twenty-first century in a wide variety of applications ranging from hybrid cars to sensor design.

THE ROYAL NAVY'S
FINEST SAILOR?

By M.M. BENNETTS

ASK ANYONE FAMILIAR WITH THE NAPOLEONIC WARS THAT QUESTION AND THEY will probably answer, "Horatio, Lord Nelson, of course! Hero of the Nile, of Copenhagen, and of Trafalgar!" And they'd be right. To a certain extent.

But the problem with that answer is that Lord Nelson died at Trafalgar in October 1805. And the war(s) with Napoleon lasted for another decade, during which time Britain was called upon not just to rule the waves and blockade the Continental ports belonging to Napoleon's vast European Empire, but, for a brief period, to wage war upon a Napoleonic ally—the fledgling United States.

(We sometimes believe we invented economic warfare and sanctions and all that. We didn't. Nor did the U.N. The European powers of the early nineteenth century were pros in the art....)

In June 1812, when war was declared by the U.S. Congress upon Great Britain, Britain was already engaged in an existential struggle for survival with Napoleonic France, as the U.S. well knew. Hence, there was little in the way of a military presence that could be sent across the world to Canada—our troops were tied up and winning in Spain. So the Admiralty, with the War Office's full support, decided on a war of economic attrition—and this was something Britain was good at. Very good at. (Wars are very costly....) And, realistically, it was all Britain could afford.

Philip Bowes Vere Broke was born on 9 September 1776, the eldest son of a prosperous Suffolk country gentleman and heir to a fine estate. He was not meant to be a sailor; he was intended to be a gentleman or at the very least an army officer.

But after years of determined nagging, his father consented to send him to the Portsmouth Naval Academy to learn the trade of seamanship. By 1792, he was at sea as a midshipman. And he first took command in 1805. Then, in September 1806, he was given command of HMS *Shannon*—a standard British fifth rate frigate—a new 38-gun 18-pounder frigate—and this is where the magic begins.

Because Broke was fired with enthusiasm, devotion to country, to honour, and duty, he was determined that his ship should be the very best. And to that end, he invested heavily in it, with his time, with his intellect, with his seamanship, and out of his own pocket. Gun carriages and guns alike were adjusted carefully to achieve straight horizontal fire when required. He had the decks marked so that every gun on the broadside could be directed to a single target, which would produce devastating destruction.

Furthermore, he insisted that the crews drilled to fight in silence so that all commands could be heard above the cacophony of battle. And over the next five years, he would keep up a relentless pursuit of battle perfection, with daily drills, daily firing practice, daily training in small arms combat.

In the summer of 1811, in response to a fracas between the large USS *President* and the tiny British schooner, *Little Belt,* the Admiralty ordered Broke to join the North Atlantic Squadron, headquartered in Halifax, Nova Scotia, and from thence to patrol the Atlantic coast for privateers and slave ships, but not to provoke the Americans. He reached Halifax on the twenty-second of September and from thence sailed to Bermuda. Early in 1812, he sailed back north....

Even after the declaration of war by the belligerent Congress, however, Broke's orders were to avoid conflict and maintain a blockade. The British government and its diplomats were convinced that things might be peacefully and diplomatically resolved, firmly believing that the American people did not want war.

(For example, in early 1812, a million bushels of American wheat were shipped from Baltimore to feed Wellington's soldiers in the Peninsula—what the British believed the Americans wanted was trade, not war!)

The tiny American navy had other ideas though. And led by the increasingly myopic (that's not a joke—he was terribly short-sighted) Commodore Rodgers, the few captains aboard the few American warships were keen for their slice of glory against the overbearing British. The iconic USS *Constitution* defeated the much smaller HMS *Guerriere* on the nineteenth of August.

By early September, the entire sail-power of the American navy were blockaded in Boston: *President, Constitution, United States, Congress,* and *Chesapeake,* together with a pair of sloops...all waiting for an opportunity to slip back to sea.

Maintaining a blockade may be an effective form of economic warfare, but it's hardly exciting, as Broke's letters back home to his wife, Louisa, tell us. He hated it. The tedium of endless months at sea, doing little but drill and appear threatening. And above all, there's little opportunity for glory!

Nor did the war fizzle into nothing as the British diplomats had hoped...and orders were now received by the North Atlantic Squadron *"to make them* [the Americans] *feel all war...."*

At last, fed up with the months of cruising, few battles, and only minor prizes, and anticipating needing to return his worn-out ship to port for rebuilding and re-victualling, Broke sent a written challenge to the Captain Lawrence of the *Chesapeake.*

> As the Chesapeake *now appears ready for sea, I request that you will do me the favor to meet the Shannon with her, ship to ship, to try the fortune of our respective flags.... You must, Sir, be aware that my proposals are highly advantageous to you.... I entreat you, Sir, not to imagine that I am urged by mere personal vanity to wish of meeting the* Chesapeake.... *You will feel it a compliment if I say, that the result of our meeting may be the most grateful Service I can render my country.... Favor me with a speedy reply. We are short*

of provisions and water, and cannot stay long here.... Choose your terms, but
let us meet.

Though Captain Lawrence never received Broke's letter, he was ready for the challenge anyway, and on 1 June 1813, he would put to sea. The pair would meet off Cape Ann, just north of Boston, and the events of that day would be seen by many who'd come out to watch in small fishing boats, certain of an American success to match Lawrence's naive braggadocio.

Broke, a professional in all situations and all conditions, kept his ship to its regular routine: breakfast, cleaning the ship and drying it, and at 10:00 a.m. mustering the crew for their daily gunnery practice.

By noon, *Chesapeake* had fired a single gun reply to *Shannon*, and a flag emblazoned with the words *"free trade and sailors rights"* (the slogan of America's challenge) was hoisted. Broke ordered his ship for Cape Ann (far from where any American gunboats might join the fray) and had lunch served on the quarterdeck for himself and his officers, using the ship's finest silver and glassware. Once the meal was cleared away, the surgeon went below decks to prepare his instruments and the men were given their grog ration.

At 5:10 p.m., Broke mustered the crew onto the main and quarter decks—the men had cotton ready to stuff into their ears, they were stripped to fight, and the officers were dressed in their oldest or second-best uniforms, armed with swords and pistols.

Addressing them all, Broke urged them to remember:

> *...that there are Englishmen in the frigate who still know how to fight.... Don't dismast her. Fire into her quarters: main deck to main deck: quarter deck into quarter deck. Kill the men and the ship is yours. Don't hit them on the head, for they have steel caps on, but give it to them through the body. Don't cheer. Go quietly to your quarters. I feel sure you will all do your duty; and remember you have the blood of hundreds of your countrymen to avenge.*

Broke had commanded *Shannon* for seven years and now, at last, he was going to have his fight. He was wearing full uniform so that all his men would recognise him amidst the heat and smoke of battle. He presented to them the same commander they had always known: confident and calm, waiting patiently for the enemy to close, for he wished for that enemy to be nearly upon them before he opened fire. It was a test of nerves in the eerie silence of that spring afternoon.

Captain Lawrence also addressed his men: *"Peacock her my lads! Peacock her!"* he yelled, referring to an earlier engagement where they'd de-masted and crippled the British ship. He had ordered his gun crews to load canister and bar shot onto the round shot and grape shot.

(Bar shot is an anti-rigging projectile which cripples the rigging or destroys it, leaving the ship unsailable, after which, broadsides can finish it. Bar shot is often made up of 12" long iron bars which are connected by chain links, then folded up to be fired from 18 and

32 pounder cannon. The bars open out into four sections which are joined by a central ring and are used to rip away the shrouds and bring down masts.)

In the straining tense silence, amidst the slap of the waves on the hull, Broke held his nerve while Lawrence manoeuvred, until the two ships were a mere 40 or 50 yards apart, broadside to broadside, near enough to give *Shannon's* well-trained gunners a perfect platform for accurate horizontal fire. As *Chesapeake* ranged closer, Broke himself chose a grenade, trimmed its fuse short and lit it. It was 5:50 p.m.

Two balls smashed through the American ship, a tin case of musket balls ripped through the port and destroyed the gun crew. As each of *Chesapeake's* gun ports came into view, *Shannon's* starboard battery fired in succession. In just over two minutes many of the American ship's forward gun crews were dead or seriously wounded and many guns disabled. At the same time, the Royal Marines poured volley after volley of musket fire at the quarter deck, mowing down those in command....

The American ship, contrariwise, had come up too fast, overshooting the mark, and exposing the ship's wheel to the eager and accurately directed British fire.

Equally, though the American gunners returned fire gamely, their ship wasn't steady and many of their broadsides smacked against *Shannon* at the waterline, causing little or no damage, while the anti-rigging barshot, which they were so keen on, was simply wasted.

The captain, Lawrence, had been hit, William White had been decapitated, the midshipmen were also dead and the First Lieutenant had been taken below, wounded, but not fatally. The American command was finished, and only Lawrence, wounded in the groin, remained on deck, described by one observer as a "slaughter pen". It was 5:58 p.m.

Then, a cartridge box on *Chesapeake's* quarterdeck exploded, adding to the destruction. As he stumbled down the gangway, Captain Lawrence called out for more boarders, saying, *"Tell the men to fire faster! Don't give up the ship!"* Though it has gone down in American naval lore as the ultimate in heroism, it was the order of a desperate man, one unacquainted with the full damage his ship and crew had suffered.

And there remained only one young officer to take the order—an acting lieutenant named Cox. And as he lay on the surgeon's table, Lawrence would have felt his ship crash into the *Shannon's* starboard bow. Only ten minutes had passed since the first shot had been fired.

Broke took the opportunity to order the two ships lashed together and called for a pre-chosen boarding party. Ten minutes previously, the deck had held forty-four American marines... now all but one officer and one NCO were dead or wounded, leaving about a dozen men to buckle before the adrenaline-charged rush of British sailors. Within moments, the Americans were overwhelmed.

Though two Americans tried to rally and regain control of the ship, their efforts were vain. Several Americans surrendered, a few sailors in the mizzenmast continued to fire upon the British boarding party, but even so, in two minutes, the British boarders had taken the ship.

From below, Lawrence bellowed "Blow the ship up!" It was too late.

Broke moved to regain control over his enthusiastic tars, but at this point, three of those who had surrendered snatched up their weapons again and attacked Broke, splitting open his skull, only to be hacked down by others in the British party.

There was, at the time, no doubt that those who had attacked Broke after surrendering were known deserters from the Royal Navy—had they been taken alive, for having fought for an enemy power in time of war, they would have been returned to Britain in chains to face trial for treason.

The British boarding party demanded that the Americans surrender, stating that they had 300 men still on board and that they would shoot them all if the Americans did not lay down their arms. Broke had collapsed from shock and loss of blood. The battle was over—in not even twelve minutes.

The Marines secured the prize. Broke was taken to the surgeon who cleaned the wound and wrapped his head in gauze. The boatloads of American spectators scrambled for shore, stunned by the speed and efficiency of the British win, by the shocking loss of life—they had not believed that war could be this savage, this devastating and deadly. The pre-arranged celebratory public dinner in Boston was cancelled, unsurprisingly.

The two ships were sailed slowly back to Halifax. Captain Lawrence died on the journey of an infection to his wound. Broke, shockingly, survived, though his health would always remain frail.

A comparison made of the two ships' hits found that the British had scored twice as many as the Americans, with the *Shannon* taking thirteen 32-pounder hits to the *Chesapeake's* twenty-five; twelve 18-pounder hits to the *Chesapeake's* twenty-nine; and 119 hits of grape shot to the *Chesapeake's* 306. The Americans had been outmanoeuvred, outfought, and outgunned by possibly the greatest fighting crew that ever set sail.

And although the Admiralty wished their hero to remain in command, by August, they realised that they were asking too much of Broke and ordered *Shannon* home. Britain rejoiced at the news. Broke was the first officer to be honoured with a naval gold medal for a frigate action. When he reached Britain on 2 November, he discovered that he had been made a Baronet.

Within a year, Broke's tactics had been adapted throughout the Royal Navy. A fall from a horse in 1820 further immobilised him, though he remained an artillery expert for the Royal Navy. In 1830, he was made Rear-Admiral. He died in 1841.

No other naval commander has ever delivered such a decisive victory in so short a time.

LONELY LIVES AND DEATHS: FRENCH NAPOLEONIC PRISONERS OF WAR IN BRITAIN

By ANTOINE VANNER

THOUGH THE FOCUS OF MY OWN WRITING IS ON THE LATE-VICTORIAN PERIOD, I retain a lively interest in the Napoleonic era. I have always found the plight of prisoners of war of this time particularly poignant.

Over 100,000 of them were brought to Britain during the wars with France that raged from 1793 to 1815 with only a one year break in 1802/3. Enlisted soldiers and seamen had the worst of it, with many being confined in horrific conditions on moored hulks. The luckier ones were housed in the specially built prison on Dartmoor, to which many American prisoners were also sent from 1812 to 1815.

Officers were, however, given the opportunity to give their parole—their word of honour, in writing, not to escape—and to live relatively normal lives in lodgings in a few specified British towns. The French established a similar regime for British officer-prisoners at Verdun in Eastern France.

Unlike in earlier wars between Britain and France, only limited exchanges of prisoners took place in the Napoleonic period, and those unfortunate enough to be captured early in the wars faced long periods in detention. In the case of seamen, removal of skilled men from active service was of particular benefit to the captor. This reflected the fact that, given the technology of the time, an effective soldier could be trained in a matter of weeks whereas mastery of nautical skills demanded years of experience.

For French and British officer-prisoners—and for the large number of wealthy British civilian tourists whom the French somewhat unsportingly interned in 1803—life was as close to normal as was possible in the circumstances. Social relations seem to have been relaxed, and even warm, as discussed later in this article.

Once the initial fervour of Revolution had died down and social stability had been restored by Napoleon, ideological differences as we understand them today were almost non-existent. The concept of "a gentleman" transcended national boundaries, and apart from the painful necessity of fighting each other occasionally, personal animosity seems to have been remarkably low between the British and the French at all levels of society. This may have been due to the facts that Britain's civilian population was never exposed to French foraging and that when Britain did invade France, in 1814, Wellington ensured that French civilians were spared the sort of rapine that had disgraced British victories in Spain at Badajoz and San Sebastian.

The most notable French prisoner in Britain was Napoleon's brother, Lucien, who had fallen out with the Emperor in 1809 and who attempted to flee from Italy to the United States. He was captured by the Royal Navy and brought to Britain, where on landing he was apparently cheered by a crowd that approved his part in the family quarrel. Placed under liberally-interpreted "house arrest", Lucien was permitted by the British Government to purchase a large country house at Thorngrove in Worcestershire and to establish himself as a member of local society. His son, also Lucien and later a distinguished philologist, was born there, and two of his daughters would later marry into the British aristocracy.

Large numbers of less highly connected officers also spent long periods in Britain. On arrival in Britain an officer-prisoner was the responsibility of the Admiralty's Transport Board. Once he had signed a parole document he was provided with a copy of its terms in French and English. It also carried a physical description of him, so that it served as an identity card which he was thereafter required to carry.

Formalities complete, the prisoner was assigned to a "parole town". One such was the Alresford, one of no less than eleven such towns in Hampshire and one which still contains sad memorials to these men. The Transport Board had an agent in each town—in Alresford's case a solicitor called John Dunn—who arranged for billeting the prisoner on a suitable local family.

Each prisoner was required to report to the agent twice a week, an obligation made less onerous by being also the occasion for drawing one shilling and sixpence a day for subsistence. The agent heard and resolved complaints, supervised conduct, and submitted reports and accounts to the Transport Board, which hoped to recover costs from the French Government at the end of hostilities. Should a prisoner die then the agent arranged the funeral, sold his possessions, and as far as circumstances allowed transmitted the proceeds to his family. Some prisoners had their wives living with them, possibly captured at sea and choosing to stay with their spouses in captivity.

In Alresford prisoners were free to walk up to one mile along the turnpike road—now the A31 highway—which led eastwards towards Guildford, thirty miles away, and westwards to Winchester, eight miles distant. The prisoners were not permitted to leave the highway or cross fields and it is not clear if they were allowed to walk on lesser roads leading from the town. Any such prohibition would have been very painful since Alresford is set in one of the most beautiful rural landscapes in Britain and strolling in it would have been some solace to the prisoner.

The village of Chawton, home of Jane Austen, lies a mere nine miles to the east and she would have used the turnpike on her visits to Winchester. As she passed through Alresford, Jane would almost certainly have seen French prisoners. She would perhaps have felt a chill at the realisation that her two brothers in the Royal Navy might someday endure a similar fate in France. Though she makes a naval officer the hero of *Persuasion*, and as her cousin Eliza's French husband had been guillotined during the Terror, it is perhaps regrettable that she did not work in a French prisoner as a character.

The Transport Board's daily allowance seems to have been on the meagre side and many of the prisoners supplemented their incomes by giving lessons in French, fencing, or drawing. Others seem to have made for sale tobacco boxes, sets of dominoes, and bobbins used in making lace. Some may have built model ships of the type made from bone and rigged with human hair which are associated with French prisoners—one occasionally appears at auction houses. Whether to supplement their diet or to satisfy French gastronomic taste, prisoners were frequently seen gathering snails, much to the amazement of the locals.

The most notable reminder of the prisoners in modern Alresford is to be found in the graveyard of the ancient church of St. John the Baptist. Here one can find headstones which commemorate four prisoners, and the wife of another, who lie buried here. A small plaque alludes to deaths brought on by tropical diseases carried back from the West Indies. Though brief, the inscription on each stone tells a tale of tragedy:

- **Pierre Garnier**—Sub-Lieutenant of the French 66th Regiment of Foot, died on July 31, 1811 at the age of 36. I have been unable to locate a book written about him by Audrey Deacon entitled *The Prisoner from Perrecy* (1988), but his details appear to be that he had served since 1796 and sailed to Guadeloupe in 1810, being captured that year in the British attack that eliminated this last French base in the Caribbean. Garnier arrived in Alresford in June 1811 but already appeared to be ill, possibly due to a fever brought from West Indies. Before dying he prepared a claim for arrears of half-pay to which he was entitled as a prisoner, but the claim was not settled (on behalf of his heirs) until six years after the end of the war.

- **Jean de Lhuille**—Lieutenant of Artillery died August 6, 1812 at the age of 51. He was the oldest commemorated with a headstone and considering his junior rank one wonders what his story might have been. Was he a promoted ranker? Was he perhaps a civilian but enrolled in some part-time militia on Guadeloupe and captured at the same time as Pierre Garnier?

- **Joseph Hypolite Riqueffe**—Naval Ensign, died December 12, 1810, aged 28. It is interesting that his affiliation is given as the "Imperial and Royal" French Navy and not the "Imperial" alone. He was *"regretted by his comrades and all who knew him"* and one suspects that the latter category was not confined to Frenchmen.

- **Mr. C. Lavau**—Merchant Navy officer, died December 23, 1811 at the age of 29. Given that much of Britain's naval war against Napoleon was a war against commerce and conducted with higher standards of humanity than the U-Boat wars of the twentieth century, there is a good chance that he might have been captured at sea.

- **Madame Marie Louise Fournier**—wife of Captain F. Berlet of the French Artillery, died April 11, 1812, aged 44. This is the saddest of the gravestones and one wonders how she had come to be in Alresford. Had she perhaps been captured with her husband, perhaps in Guadeloupe, and had she volunteered to stay with him? Had he perhaps been wounded and needing nursing? Or had she offered to come to Britain to stay with him after he had been captured somewhere else?

Yet in parallel with these tragedies life went on as pleasantly as it could, and relations between British hosts and reluctant French guests seem to have been generally cordial. French prisoners seem to have participated in social gatherings, and one such was to be at The Swan Inn (still in business and proud of having hosted Oliver Cromwell) in 1810 when the agent, John Dunn, and other Alresford notables were invited to attend an Anglo-French assembly to celebrate Napoleon's marriage to Marie-Louise of Austria. Somebody must have tipped off the Admiralty's Transport Board which then prohibited the celebration as being unpatriotic.

It is also notable that the tradition of prisoner of war theatricals, which was so much a feature of WW2 camps, especially British ones, seems to have been well established in Alresford. On one occasion some spoilsport at the Transport Board got wind of the fact that French officers had formed a theatre and warned John Dunn that if it continued the prisoners would be moved elsewhere. One hopes that this warning was treated with the contempt it deserved!

Other than Conan Doyle's Brigadier Gerard's brief captivity in Britain, I know of only one notable work of fiction which builds on social relations between the British and their French prisoners. This is a tragic short story by Rudyard Kipling in his *Rewards and Fairies,* and it centres on a girl who, unknown to herself, is dying of consumption. Her father has become friendly with a French prisoner, a doctor, René Laennec, who is in the process of inventing the stethoscope. Another friend is Arthur Wellesley, later Duke of Wellington, who is just back from India. The climax of the story is an unbearably poignant account of a dinner at which all three men realise that the girl is dying, but she does not know it herself. Wellesley, who himself was partly educated in France, would have had no hesitation to be on friendly terms with a cultivated Frenchman, prisoner or not. I'd like to think that social interactions of this type were not uncommon—and there's scope here for many a convincing fictional plot!

SOURCE

In preparing the above article I have been heavily indebted to the *About Alresford* website and to an article on it by Peter Hoggarth, dating from 1991, on the French prisoners.

A VIENNESE CHRISTMAS

BY M.M. BENNETTS

IMAGINE IT! FOR OVER TWENTY YEARS, GREAT BRITAIN HAD BEEN CUT OFF FROM CONtinental travel and culture. And when I say cut off, I mean, cut off.

War is always bad for international trade and social and cultural intercourse. And since 1793, the Continent had been embroiled in a series of wars, first with the newly formed French Republic and subsequently with Napoleonic France.

Then, with the imposition of the Berlin Decrees in November 1806 and the Milan Decrees in 1807, the French Emperor had effectively severed all commercial ties between the Continent and Great Britain. If things hadn't been difficult enough, now it was impossible (unless you were a smuggler, and in that case, business began to boom...).

Hence British merchants, travellers, scientists, and diplomats (and their wives) had had to find other markets, other places to do business, other cities to visit and enjoy, other more exotic lands to investigate. Books, music, and ideas had perhaps continued to be exchanged between the Continent and Britain—a bit—but only because these could easily be sent or smuggled without damage.

And then, finally, in 1814, came peace. The holiday-abroad-starved Brits (who had become quite insular over the past two decades) flocked to the Continent and especially to Vienna in the autumn of 1814, where the great European Congress, the first ever international peace conference, was being held.

Great Britain's Foreign Secretary, Viscount Castlereagh, arrived with his wife and brother in tow and a diplomatic mission of some 80 others. There were fourteen assistants, including Lord Cathcart and Lord Clancarty, Edward Cooke, the Under-Secretary of State, and Joseph Planta, Castlereagh's private secretary.

The parties and balls that autumn were extravagant and endless as European heads of state, diplomats and their entourages, and those representing special interests such as printers and publishers, the Papal representative, or the Jewish delegation, engaged in a ceaseless round of business-mingling and flirtation that accomplished little. Meanwhile, the Viennese shopkeepers, wine-sellers, brothel-owners, hoteliers, gambling dens, restauranteurs, and secret service made money hand over fist.

Then, as December came to Vienna, snow began to fall occasionally, the days were shorter and colder, and the city began to celebrate Advent and prepare for Christmas. It would be the first Christmas without war in twenty years....

From the thirteenth century, Viennese traders had held a special December Market, the *Thomasmarkt*, from before Christmas through New Year, which sold wonderful gingerbread and pastries. In the Am Hof market though, the sale of this special gingerbread (a study of contemporary invoices tells us) had expanded to include Christmas goods too for the first time—angels, silver-plated nuts, ribbons, lametta (thin strips of metallic decorative work formed into stars, snowflakes, icicles, etc.), and candles—alongside the standard market fare.

Then, just before Christmas, there was a great party at the Arnstein mansion held by Fanny von Arnstein, a prominent Viennese hostess, where guests found in the salon a great, tall fir tree, decorated all over with gifts, lametta, and candles. It was the first Christmas tree ever seen in Vienna, and it's referred to in the diaries of diplomats and the reports of the many spies of the Congress, as "the Berlin custom".

The many guests were enchanted.

The French embassy were among the first to adopt the custom as their own. There, the French ambassador's hostess, Dorothee, Duchesse du Perigord, convinced the ambassador to decorate the mansion Berlin-style. Nor was she content with just one tree. In the great hallway, guests were greeted with a huge fir tree, adorned with *"colourful garlands and lit candles"* while another even larger tree stood near the mansion's famous staircase, and everywhere too, there were platters of German-style marzipan delicacies formed into fruits and small animals, gingerbread, and butter biscuits.

And that year, when Dorothee hosted a party on Christmas Eve, gifts were exchanged that night, again, German-style—not as they did in Catholic countries like Austria and France, on New Year's Eve.

It was the start of a whole new way of celebrating Christmas. Imagine that....

Victorian Era and Twentieth Century (1837-1950)

Victoria's Early Years: Kensington Palace

By GRACE ELLIOT

Recently I visited Kensington Palace to see the King's Grand Staircase, commissioned by George I in the early 1700s. Kensington Palace is still home to royalty (when in London, Prince William and his wife, Catherine, stay there) and since the seventeenth century has been entwined with royalty: from William III to Princess Diana, from George II to Princess Victoria. It is the link to Victoria that struck me as particularly interesting.

Kensington Palace's connection to Victoria is obvious as you approach the building; an imposing statue of the young Queen stands outside the east façade. The composition of Victoria in her coronation robes was designed by her daughter, Princess Louise, and unveiled in 1893. The statue is a fitting reminder that three key events in Victoria's life took place at Kensington Palace.

PRINCESS VICTORIA IS BORN

At Kensington Palace on 24 May 1819 a princess, Victoria, was born to the Duchess of Kent. The infant Victoria grew up at Kensington and had a somewhat lonely childhood. Her father died before she was a year old, and Victoria was kept isolated, away from the excitement of court life and without friends of her own age to keep her company.

Her mother, the Duchess of Kent, along with an equerry, Sir John Conroy, oversaw her education. They devised "The Kensington System"—which ostensibly was to equip Victoria for her future role as queen—whilst some people muttered it was also a means of keeping the young princess firmly under their control.

VICTORIA'S ACCESSION TO THE THRONE

At 6 a.m. on 20 June 1837, Victoria was woken by her mother. The news was so urgent that the eighteen-year-old Victoria donned her dressing gown to receive the Archbishop of Canterbury and Lord Conyngham. It was their grave duty to announce that the King was dead, and Princess Victoria was now Queen.

> Lord Conyngham then acquainted me that my poor Uncle, the King, was no more, and had expired at 12 minutes past 2 this morning, and consequently that I am Queen.

That morning, the new Queen held her first council meeting in the Red Saloon at Kensington Palace. This young woman was surrounded by much older men, including the Duke of Wellington and the Dukes of Sussex and Cumberland. The Prime Minister,

Lord Melbourne, had written a short speech for her and despite the circumstances it was noted that Victoria handled everything *"with perfect calmness and self-possession."*

MEETING ALBERT, PRINCE OF SAXE-COBURG AND GOTHA

There are few people who haven't heard of Victoria's love for her husband, Albert. But did you know that the couple first met at Kensington Palace?

On 18 May 1836, Victoria caught sight of her cousin Albert, and his brother Ernest, as she loitered on the stairs at Kensington Palace. Albert made a good impression, as recorded in her diary:

> *Albert, who is just as tall as Ernest but stouter, is extremely handsome; his hair is about the same as mine, his eyes large and blue, and he has a beautiful nose and a very sweet mouth with fine teeth.*

The visit went well, and Victoria was delighted by the gift of a tame parrot. To encourage the romance, the Duchess of Kent threw a ball at Kensington at which Victoria and Albert danced until three in the morning. But time flew by all too quickly and when on Friday, 10 June, Albert departed Victoria wrote in her journal: *"I embraced both my dearest cousins most warmly, as also my dear Uncle. I cried bitterly, very bitterly...."*

The rest of their courtship and marriage is, as they say, history.

Victoria was born, acceded to the throne, and then found love at Kensington Palace—quite a legacy for a building still home to royals today.

THE HEALTH OF MR. GLADSTONE...AND PRIVACY ISSUES

By DEBRA BROWN

M̲R. WILLIAM GLADSTONE, OF SCOTTISH BLOOD AND BORN IN LIVERPOOL, SERVED four times as Prime Minister of England and was the leading statesman of the century—though he was disliked by Queen Victoria. She once complained about Gladstone, *"He always addresses me as if I were a public meeting."*

He entered politics as a Tory but became the leader of the Liberal party. He focused on reforms which were to reduce the power of privilege and opened certain institutions such as the military and civil service up to the common man. He doggedly pursued the vote for working class men and added about six million to the ranks of Parliamentary voters.

As a young man in 1832 he was recruited by the Duke of Newcastle and voted into Parliament as a Conservative. At the time he opposed the abolition of slavery and factory legislation. In 1833 he entered Lincoln's Inn to become a barrister, though he continued also in Parliament. He gave up the career direction of barrister in 1839.

Gladstone married Catherine Glynne that same year. His marriage was happy, and he and Catherine had eight children. Catherine was not interested in entertaining as a politician's wife was expected to do, and at age thirty-three his daughter Mary, for the most part, took over the role of hostess. Mary was politically minded, and some saw her as a way to reach her father.

Gladstone walked the streets of London beginning in 1840 and even decades later as Prime Minister trying to talk prostitutes into giving up their careers. He offered them shelter and a way to make another life. As a result, some questioned his sanity or, because he would enter their houses, even his motives.

During his first term as Prime Minister, Gladstone became very interested in "the Irish question", and he worked toward improving conditions for the Irish peasantry. Though it was considered to be quite radical, he worked toward Irish "home rule" on into the later part of the century.

His nemesis was Benjamin Disraeli who was the other leading politician of the time, and who was in Victoria's favor. They intensely disliked each other and fought each other's policies—Gladstone being effective in his efforts. When Disraeli died, Gladstone refused to attend his funeral. Despite such controversial ways, he remained popular with the voters and continued to be returned to power.

He resigned as Prime Minister for the last time in March 1894 and left Parliament in 1895. There is much more to be said about those 60 years in public service, but for now...I thought I might pry into personal matters of his health as did journalists of the nineteenth century.

Gladstone lost a finger in an accident with a gun in 1842.

He was obsessed with physical fitness and to that end would fell trees with an axe.

In 1892 William Stead wrote that:

> Mr. Gladstone...must somewhere have discovered the elixir of life or have been bathed by some beneficent fairy in the well of perpetual youth. Gladly would many a man of fifty exchange physique with this hale and hearty octogenarian. Only in one respect does he show any trace of advancing years. His hearing is not quite so good as it was, but still it is far better than that of Cardinal Manning, who became very deaf in the closing years. Otherwise Mr. Gladstone is hale and hearty. His eye is not dim, neither is his natural force abated....

On Friday, December 11, 1896, the *Daily Graphic* printed an article: "The Health of Mr. Gladstone."

> Some uneasiness has been felt owing to the reported indisposition of Mr. Gladstone during the week, but the authentic facts are of a reassuring character. On the early morning of Thursday, December 3rd, after a rather longer walk than usual on the previous damp and chilly afternoon, Mr. Gladstone felt some oppression of the chest and difficulty in drawing a deep breath, which disturbed his usually tranquil sleep. These symptoms, however, passed off the next day under very slight treatment, and on the afternoons of Friday and Saturday he felt well. On the Sunday evening, which was very wet, he drove to church in a close carriage. During the night he had a return of the uneasiness with some disturbance of sleep, but to a lesser degree. A careful examination of the chest disclosed nothing wrong beyond a few dry crepitations. The heart sounds were free from bruit and under simple remedies he has practically been restored to good health. There has been no angina, and the symptoms appear to have been due to chill of the intercostal muscles. Mr. Gladstone is strongly advised by Dr. Dobie to go to Cannes after Christmas.
> —British Medical Journal

Apparently, privacy issues were not what they are today, and quite intimate details could be shared. It sounds like the reporter was given a copy of the patient's chart! Gladstone went on to live till 19 May 1898, nearly a year and a half longer, when finally his heart gave out. Or, as a different source states, he died of cancer.

After his death, his son opened a letter Gladstone had written that stated:

> *With reference to rumours which I believe were at one time afloat, though I know not with what degree of currency: and also with reference to the times when I shall not be here to answer for myself, I desire to record my solemn declaration and assurance, as in the sight of God and before His Judgment Seat, that at no period of my life have I been guilty of the act which is known as that of infidelity to the marriage bed.*

This was no doubt written for those who questioned his morals in the matter of the prostitutes.

VICTORIAN VIOLENCE: REPELLING RUFFIANS, PART ONE

By TERRY KROENUNG

The housebreaker freed one arm, and grasped his pistol. The certainty of immediate detection if he fired, flashed across his mind even in the midst of his fury; and he beat it twice with all the force he could summon, upon the upturned face that almost touched his own.

She staggered and fell: nearly blinded with the blood that rained down from a deep gash in her forehead; but raising herself, with difficulty, on her knees, drew from her bosom a white handkerchief—Rose Maylie's own— and holding it up, in her folded hands, as high towards Heaven as her feeble strength would allow, breathed one prayer for mercy to her Maker.

It was a ghastly figure to look upon. The murderer staggering backward to the wall, and shutting out the sight with his hand, seized a heavy club and struck her down.

—*Oliver Twist*, Charles Dickens

To JUDGE BY THIS DISTURBING SCENE (OR, INDEED, ANY EPISODE OF *RIPPER STREET*) it was as much as a man's life was worth to walk the streets of Victorian London. Robbery and murder were commonplace; pickpockets were as ubiquitous as fleas on a mongrel, and as for an unaccompanied woman, well....

But was that true? Or were the news reports of that era just as slanted toward the sensational as are our own? "If it bleeds, it leads" is the motto of modern media and certainly British journalism of the nineteenth century could hardly claim to be more scrupulous. The truth is that we do not know with any degree of certainty.

Then as now circumstances and geography dictated risk. Jack the Ripper's outrages were committed in sordid Whitechapel, after all, and not in genteel Kensington. A critical mass of the poor and desperate has always led to increased criminality.

Wise ladies and gentlemen preferred to avoid dirty, ill-lit areas with foul reputations. Forewarned is forearmed and all that. Yet an assault could happen at any time and place. It was no respecter of persons, either. In 1862 a Member of Parliament was garroted and robbed in broad daylight in Pall Mall.

Earlier centuries may well have been worse. The gin-soaked gutters of Hogarth's time, with none of Robert Peel's bluebottles or even the Bow Street Runners to keep the peace, were likely a horror-show. A noticeable decrease in wretchedness did occur with the advent of the Metropolitan Police, though it took until the 1880s for that force to gain widespread respect. Ennui was not a risk faced by the Peelers.

In a typical Dickensian year (1856) the force arrested over 73,000 people. And we would do well to remember that an enormous percentage of crimes went unreported or unrecorded. The citizenry did not trust its own officers, often with good reason. Particularly in the early days, the policeman was often just as likely as the most hardened East Ender to be guilty of an offense.

Even if the bobby was honest, many residents felt it a waste of time to make a complaint, since so many crimes were not solved. Let us give savagery the benefit of the doubt and presume that it was enough of a concern that measures had to be taken.

To this end most men of the middle and upper classes considered training in pugilism and singlestick to be an essential part of their education. When faced with a determined defender, many a hooligan would likely seek easier prey. Quite apart from such practical considerations, the manly arts also served to toughen the mind and spirit, preparing a fellow for the rugged vicissitudes of life. Instructional manuals abounded, all stressing this point:

> *Physical education is indispensable to every well-bred man and woman. A gentleman should not only know how to fence, to box, to ride, to shoot and to swim, but he should also know how to carry himself gracefully, and how to dance, if he would enjoy life to the uttermost. A graceful carriage can best be attained by the aid of a drilling master, as dancing and boxing are taught. A man should be able to defend himself from ruffians, if attacked, and also to defend women from their insults.*
>
> —Our Deportment, 1879

Naturally certain of these skills were better-suited to the country house than the alleys of the metropolis. Be that as it may, expertise with stick and fist doubtless preserved many a life when faced with a resolute robber in a fetid corner of the Empire's capital. At a minimum it would have enabled the victim to keep a cool head and react with grace under pressure.

VICTORIAN VIOLENCE: REPELLING RUFFIANS, PART TWO

By TERRY KROENUNG

GENTEEL SELF DEFENSES

I can almost hear people say, "Oh, this is all rubbish; I'm not going to be attacked; life would not be worth living if one had to be always 'on guard' in this way." Well, considering that this world, from the time we are born to the time we die, is made up of uncertainties, and that we are never really secure from attack at any moment of our lives, it does seem worthwhile to devote a little attention to the pursuit of a science, which is not only healthful and most fascinating, but which may, in a second of time, enable you to turn a defeat into a victory, and save yourself from being mauled and possibly killed in a fight which was none of your own making.

Added to all this, science gives a consciousness of power and ability to assist the weak and defenceless, which ought to be most welcome to the mind of any man. Though always anxious to avoid anything like "a row," there are times when it may be necessary to interfere for the sake of humanity, and how much more easy is it to make that interference dignified and effective if you take your stand with a certainty that you can, if pushed to extreme measures, make matters very warm indeed for the aggressor?

The consciousness of power gives you your real authority, and with it you are far more likely to be calm and to gain your point than you would be without the knowledge. Backed up by science, you can both talk and act in a way which is likely to lead to a peaceful solution of a difficulty, whereas, if the science is absent, you dare not, from very uncertainty, use those very words which you know ought to be used on the occasion.

—Rowland George Allanson-Winn, 5th Baron of Headley, 1890

Professional pugilism has died out, as much choked by the malpractices of its followers as strangled by public opinion.... The noble art of self-defence is not, however, altogether neglected, but finds its place among the athletic sports, and the clubs by which it is encouraged may be congratulated on keeping alive one of the oldest institutions, in the way of manly exercise, on record.

—Charles Dickens, Jr., 1879

PUGILISM

As we are concerned with the employment of self-defense techniques in the protection of one's person and loved ones on the streets of Victorian London,

476 | *Castles, Customs, and Kings*

it is not our purpose here to elaborate upon prize fights. Yet it is indisputably true that the one informed the other. Effective methods of pugilism were developed in the ring and then adopted by gentlemen on the boulevards. British boxing arose from the Age of Enlightenment's love of all things classical. The ancient Greek sport of pankration, renowned for its brutality, and subsequent Roman variants, were revived in much more genteel versions in the mid-eighteenth century.

It was the upper-classes who led the way in this, as simple brawling with fists had never died out among the working folk. Naturally, gambling was the impetus for injecting rules and order into what had been a mere vulgar scrap. A way had to be found to settle disputes when great sums were being wagered on gentlemen's champions.

Thus the first regulations were set in place by former fighter John Broughton. His interest in fair play—gloves, set rounds, no attacking a downed man, etc.—was somewhat selfish: he ran a school to teach pugilism to men of refinement, and they did not wish to take broken jaws and black eyes home to their ladies.

Here we see the beginnings of the later Victorian attitude that boxing was a quintessentially English activity to be practiced by the "quality." To be sure, those less-mannered had always been beating one another to a bloody pulp in the alleys of London, but by the 1780s pugilism began to evolve into an art that eventually replaced fencing in the hearts of the British middle and upper classes.

The decades-long struggle with France accelerated this urge toward the good manly virtue of boxing. Fisticuffs were seen as an antidote to the effeminate ways of the Continent. Less lethal than dueling (a strong selling point with every man needed to carry a musket against Bonaparte) and purely egalitarian (man vs. man with no underhanded doctoring of weapons), boxing became a national craze.

But it was a fad that suffered from early Victorian attitudes. That age's philosophy stressed morality, faith, and family rather than the violence that Napoleon's threat had necessitated. So the vogue waned for some time, as fighting was considered beneath the dignity of a proper man. But when it returned it did so with a vengeance. The Queensberry Rules of 1867 were adopted with alacrity and became so widespread that the very nature of boxing changed.

With padded gloves an absolute requirement, tactics and footwork had to shift. First off, there actually could be tactics, rather than mere flailing away until someone collapsed. In bare-knuckle boxing the defense, such as it was, was with the forearms rather than the hands. To protect one's face the stance was upright, leaning the head back to keep it away from the opponent's fists. Now the heavy gloves served as a shield to crouch behind.

In order to defeat this barrier, the now-familiar bobbing and weaving came into play, along with active footwork. Counter-intuitively, this all made the sport rather more dangerous. With bare knuckles a fighter had to pull a punch somewhat or risk a shattered hand. Now blows were delivered with much more fury and with greater rapidity. As a result men were struck harder and more often, since fights resulted in less bout-ending blood and broken teeth than before.

The cumulative effect of many punches caused more damage and actual knockouts than a few nasty but less forceful knuckle strikes. Brain injuries became common.

In a sense the popularity and widespread adoption of the Queensberry Rules might have been the downfall of many a well-trained but rule-bound gentleman when it came to actual no-holds-barred self-defense in the street. When accosted by an alley ruffian intent on relieving him of his wallet or watch, the club-trained man of means may have found himself at a disadvantage when kicked, grappled, or struck with a club. One can imagine him being overwhelmed mentally, as well, as the thug did not conform to the rules. Fair play did not enter into the equation.

But one can also imagine the contrary. Assailed by an unskilled, desperate, possibly intoxicated street thief, the training in pugilism might have made for a brief encounter. For the value in boxing does not lie only in simple techniques, but in the intangible qualities of confidence, cool-headedness, and quick judgement of the opponent's strengths and weaknesses. Indeed, simply knowing how to take a punch, and how to mitigate the impact of it, would be of immeasurable value in itself. Attacked by an over-confident, swaggering hooligan who launched a clumsy haymaker, the gentleman's schooling at his club could very well have resulted in the automatic response of step into the attack/block it/simultaneously punch with other fist.

Here we would be well-advised to recall the words of Allanson-Winn at the beginning of this essay, that pugilism is *"a science, which is not only healthful and most fascinating, but which may, in a second of time, enable you to turn a defeat into a victory, and save yourself from being mauled and possibly killed in a fight which was none of your own making."*

Victorian Violence: Repelling Ruffians, Part Three

By Terry Kroenung

I was not surprised when Holmes suggested that I should take my revolver with me. He had himself picked up the loaded hunting-crop, which was his favourite weapon.
—"The Adventure of the Six Napoleons"

The light flashed upon the barrel of a revolver, but Holmes's hunting crop came down on the man's wrist, and the pistol clinked upon the stone floor.
—"The Adventure of the Red-Headed League"

"I'm a bit of a single-stick expert, as you know. I took most of them on my guard. It was the second man that was too much for me."
—"The Adventure of the Illustrious Client"

WEAPONS

When a lady or gentleman of the Victorian upper or middle class ventured into a less-than-savory district, a variety of defensive aids was available, from the lethal pistol and knife to the simple cudgel, walking stick, and umbrella. In this essay we shall eschew firearms and confine ourselves largely to the items most likely to be either carried by someone of refinement or by those rogues who preyed upon them.

Violence upon propertied people was probably not as widespread as novels and press reports of the time, both depending on sensationalism for sales, would have us believe. That being said, incidents of self-defense against the criminal element did occur with enough frequency that a brisk trade in protective means existed.

CUDGEL

A mere club, the cudgel was more likely to be employed against our unfortunate gentleman than by him. It could be as crude as a limb wrenched from a handy tree or as refined as a gaily-painted policeman's truncheon. Shorter and more rudimentary than the walking stick (generally less than an arm's length), its affordability and ease of concealment made it popular, particularly with the lower sort.

Indeed, the late Victorian police truncheon was only fifteen inches in length and lived in a specially-built pocket of the officer's trousers. For even though the servant of the law could claim authority to employ his cudgel, it was not considered proper to wantonly display the threat, since moral suasion was the first line of a Peeler's defense. Particularly in the first half of Victoria's reign these sticks would be ornately decorated, as they were the officer's mark of authority as well as his weapon.

Cudgel tactics were unsophisticated compared to the exotic joint-locking techniques taught today. Chiefly it was a case of "brain him" with a stunning blow to the offender's cranium. As can be imagined, this often resulted in a dead suspect and rather less labor for the magistrate.

LIFE-PRESERVER

A variant of the club was the so-called life-preserver, which a respectable man might carry, though not as often as he might a proper cane. Easily hidden at about a foot in length, it had a flexible shaft of whalebone or some such supple core, leather-wrapped, with a weighted knob at one end. Their construction ran the gamut from crude to almost artistic. Principal targets were the head and wrist.

The knobstick was closely related, but its weighted end was a lead ball wrapped in string, rather than leather. It cushioned the blow somewhat, though it remains a point of conjecture as to whether the recipient often appreciated the consideration.

LOADED HUNTING CROP

As seen in the Arthur Conan Doyle excerpts above, Sherlock Holmes favored a variation of the life-preserver. The loaded hunting crop contained a steel or lead core wrapped in leather. Less legally problematic than a pistol, and not as likely to permanently ruin a man whose testimony might be required to solve a case, they would be employed much as a life-preserver or cudgel.

KNUCKLEDUSTER

Rather on the more brutal end of the spectrum lay the knuckleduster, a remnant of the sword hilt which had always been used when a duel got to close quarters and blades could no longer be effectively brought to bear. This had the advantage of being readier to hand than a pocketed cudgel, since in seamier districts it could remain on the fist. One version, marketed as the "Highway Protector," sported a spike on the little-finger side for striking behind.

Even easier to conceal was the Apache ring, essentially a knuckleduster for one finger but operating in the same manner. Named for the vicious French street gangs of the Belle Époque who favored them, they often had fearsome projections that would leave ghastly wounds on the faces of their victims to serve as warnings against future trespass.

WALKING STICK

Naturally the gentleman's weapon most associated with the Victorian era in the popular imagination would be the cane or walking stick. Appearing in a bewildering variety of shapes, sizes, materials, and gadgetry, the stick was essential equipment for a man or woman of means. A substitute for the sword as an article of refined dress, its phallic symbolism is best left for another essay. The actual employment of canes and umbrellas in defense will be discussed in part four of this series.

The nineteenth century saw the height of the aristocratic stick's popularity, both as ornament and as weapon. (Victorian London boasted some 60 walking stick shops.) It sprang from Louis XIV's adoption of an embellished stick as a symbol of his majesty, a form of scepter. He even banned commoners from sporting them. Overnight, as with so much else in the Sun King's orbit, fancy sticks became essential at court.

The eighteenth century had seen both smallsword and stick carried together. After the Napoleonic era the former gave way to the less lethal (and arguably cheaper, for the masses) stick. Functional jewelry, sticks could be decorated to the level of the bearer's wealth as a symbol in a very status-conscious age. Almost incidentally, a stick also kept a gentleman upright in dodgy ground and in dodgy company.

Canes could be utilitarian, of course, like a good Irish blackthorn. A certain type of confident gentleman would favor one of these, proclaiming to the world that he had no time to waste concerning himself with mere foppery. There was the added benefit that such a stick made a more than serviceable weapon and its owner was less likely to wail if it shattered upon the thick pate of a luckless thug.

For self-defense two types stood out. A crook-handled stick had much to recommend it inasmuch as it could snare the limbs and even necks of assailants. As it lacked a solid punch, however, a gentleman might eschew it for a heavy knobbed affair that could cave in the skull of a determined adversary. The ultimate example of this sort of formidable stick would be the knobkerrie, originally a native weapon from South Africa that could even be thrown like a missile.

SYSTEM STICK

Naturally some gentlemen preferred to employ less brute force and more surgical precision in a crisis. For them the discerning designers of the Industrial Age could provide system sticks, so called because they contained any number of clever devices, from brandy flasks to complete medical kits. Simplest was the classic swordstick, a steel blade inside the hollow shaft.

A few opted for spring-loaded stiletto points that could pop out of the end. One wicked French version had razors that would snap out along the whole stick, to the great inconvenience of anyone foolish enough to seize it. And the added advantage of a swordstick was that once it was drawn the user had a pair of weapons, for the hollow body made a splendid cudgel/parrying stick in its own right.

It goes without saying that any arms race will always increase in lethality. Once the criminal element in a particular region embraced firearms, then a segment of the gentry would follow suit. Quite a few canes became vessels for powder and ball. Yet turning one's stick into a shotgun could be considered a step backward for the genteel man.

UMBRELLA AND PARASOL

As ubiquitous as the walking stick, and seemingly an unofficial passport declaring one's *bone fides* as an English citizen, the brolly may have been used in defense more often by women than men. Indeed, a significant body of literature exists outlining tactics to be employed by ladies with umbrellas. While specialized uses similar to stick-play were the norm, this did not exclude the manufacture of umbrellas with daggers, swords, etc.

HATPIN

While ladies' fashions varied widely in the period, from enormous hoop skirts to bustles to leg-of-mutton sleeves, hatpins were a constant for much of the age. Particularly when bonnets tied under the chin gave way to hats perched atop the head, and even more so with the advent of wide-brimmed affairs easily caught by the wind, hatpins became utterly essential items for all women. So large was the demand that one Gloucestershire factory employed over 1,500 workers.

CONCLUSION

Thus we have examined a number of common street weapons of the Victorian age. While no means an exhaustive account (the entire range of firearms and knives being reserved for another day, along with such exquisite rarities as belt buckle pistols and garrotes), the reader or author of nineteenth century literature may now be confident of a basic grounding in the more likely devices to be encountered or employed.

Victorian Violence: Repelling Ruffians, Part Four, or Elegant Brutality for Ladies and Gentlemen of Discernment: A Bartitsu Primer for Authors

By **TERRY KROENUNG**

The usual homeless lads had returned to the Oxford Street alley. Paragon noted their drunken snores and detoured around them. Within four paces of exiting the dark, narrow passage what little light had been visible at its opening vanished. A wide-shouldered figure in an immense topper blocked his way. While his brain absorbed that, the supposedly-sleeping pair he had just passed scrambled to hobnailed feet. One glance over his shoulder revealed stout cudgels and handkerchiefs across their faces.

These were no beast-men. Merely hired London bully-boys. Still, Paragon did not quite manage to evade the blow aimed at his right ear. He pivoted left, but still caught it on the shoulder. His Malacca stick clattered to the ground as his arm went numb. On his left the other man swung his cudgel at his exposed temple.

Paragon stepped inside the arc of the arm and used his would-be slayer's own impetus to fling him into his partner. With no feeling in his right arm yet, and his stick out of reach in any event, he had to rely on some particularly unsavoury Parisian street fighting.

Whenever traveling in dangerous areas Paragon liked to slip on his Apache ring. A complex steel Medusa's head with a small grip that rested against his palm, he had removed it from a deceased French gangster in Montmartre who had endeavoured to garrote him. Before the attackers could recover from his counter-stroke, he snapped a coup de pied bas into the knee of one with his aluminum foot. The vicious low kick brought the wincing man's face down to the perfect height for a powerful left cross to his jaw. Paragon's dreadful ring left Medusa's bloody portrait on the bloke's face as it put him down and out.

His opposite number tried to sneak in a killing blow to the crown of the actor's head, since the boater offered little protection. Sliding left, Paragon let the fellow's cruel cudgel spend itself on empty air. With the rowdy's balance upset the fellow could not evade a powerful aluminium side kick to his ribs. The hapless villain's body smote the unforgiving wall with a wet smack. As the fellow bounced from it Paragon elbowed his throat and turned to engage the giant who blocked his escape.

Except that the third man had gone.

THIS EXCERPT FROM MY PENDING STEAMPUNK NOVEL, *PARAGON OF THE ECCENTRIC*, illustrates a few principles of the first true mixed martial art in the West since ancient Greek Pankration, the first to blend Asian and European techniques. Though the name Bartitsu can promote snickers and occasional calls of *"Gesundheit!"* it is a deadly-serious means of self-defense and can claim a rich legacy in the annals of combat and literature. (Arthur Conan Doyle had Sherlock Holmes employ it to defeat Professor Moriarty.) Appearing, albeit in somewhat altered and anachronistic form, in such works as Will Thomas' Barker/Llewelyn novels and the recent Sherlock Holmes films, Bartitsu is a wonderful means of spicing up your Steampunk or Victorian writing.

Bartitsu is a portmanteau word derived from a blending of the surname of its inventor, Edward Barton-Wright, and the Japanese discipline of ju-jitsu. Barton-Wright studied the latter when he was in the East working as an engineer in the 1890s. He returned home to find the London papers full of outrage about a wave of street crime. Proper gentlemen and ladies were being regularly assaulted and robbed. To address this thuggish violence he developed a system of personal defense which he claimed could *"meet every kind of attack, armed or otherwise."*

His system blended techniques found in boxing, wrestling, French savate, la canne (walking stick), and ju-jitsu. Of these, the last named features most prominently in Barton-Wright's description of Bartitsu's guiding principles:

1) to disturb the equilibrium of your assailant,

2) to surprise him before he has time to regain his balance and use his strength,

3) if necessary to subject the joints of any part of his body whether neck, shoulder, elbow, wrist, back, knee, ankle, etc. to strain which they are anatomically and mechanically unable to resist.

Any modern student of aikido (my martial art of choice, also a child of ju-jitsu) will recognize these principles. The opponent's own momentum and strength are redirected and used against him. This was no sport for effete British dilettantes. Indeed, there is no competitive form of Bartitsu at all. From the first it was intended to be a means of defense against ruthless alleyway assailants. Fast, violent, and effective, Barton-Wright's system aimed to put an attacker down as soon as possible and render him incapable of further outrage (though he took pains to advise that it not be taken to extremes or be used to hurt a man who has been made helpless).

This system embraces every possible eventuality and your defence and counter-attack must be based entirely on the actions of your opponent. Even though Barton-Wright's original Pearson's articles mentioned some 300 reactions to common situations, he insisted that the essence of Bartitsu was the fluidity of mind and body to respond to the circumstances of the encounter.

It was expected that the middle-class patrons trained at his Soho Bartitsu Club would never initiate an attack, but only take action when threatened. To this end there are few purely offensive techniques described, though an unscrupulous practitioner could always adapt Barton-Wright's principles to the wrong ends.

Bartitsu tends to be fast and fluid, offering the writer a great variety of exciting moves when used in an action scene. There is little toe-to-toe pounding involved. If a tactic fails or is blocked, the Bartitsu fighter immediately abandons it in favor of another.

Besides the five primary disciplines already mentioned, great store is set on the employment of clothing and found weapons. Barton-Wright mentioned bowlers, coats, umbrellas, hatpins, and even bicycles as equalizers in a fight. In my books I have included all of these and more. They make for dandy spectacles of mayhem. What follows are a few very basic descriptions of the basic disciplines.

STICK

Barton-Wright naturally presumed that anyone in his audience would likely be in possession of a walking stick or umbrella when in the street. To that end Bartitsu relies quite a bit on stick play inherited from saber tactics and prior stick-fighting systems. Much of this came from his stick instructor at the Bartitsu Club (located in the appropriately-named Shaftesbury Avenue in Soho), French/Swiss military man and combat expert Pierre Vigny.

The stick is held like a club, thumb wrapped around the fist, rather than like a sword with the thumb along the shaft. Preference is given to remaining out of distance of the opponent and striking his arm or head. Often this involves inviting a particular attack and then sliding or pivoting out of danger while simultaneously swinging the stick at a vulnerable spot.

Also favored is defending and attacking in a single move, such as blocking a club aimed at one's head and continuing on to assail the foe's own body. Closing the distance to get inside the arc of a punch or stick-swing is recommended. While wrapping and disabling the attacking arm, the handle of one's stick may then be used against vulnerable areas. Alternatively, the shaft can leverage joints.

What is not advised is engaging in a pure fencing match with another stick or club. Of great utility is holding the stick in two hands like a rifle with bayonet, relying on thrusts with the point. Concentrating the force in such a tiny area is very effective. One should keep in mind that the stick, like the other disciplines, is not used alone, but in combination with kicks, punches, and throws.

SAVATE

French kick-boxing, derived from the tough waterfronts of Marseilles, gives Bartitsu a handful of useful tactics. Barton-Wright did not go into detail in print about the kicks used in Bartitsu, so some speculation is involved; however, he does specify three savate kicks. A coup de pied bas mentioned in the opening selection, is a low front kick to the knee or shin. This would most likely be used as a spoiling move against an advancing opponent, or as a setup/distraction in combination with a stick strike or punch.

The chassé bas lateral, a low side kick, requires a bending of the rear leg and straightening the front one while turning the outside edge of its foot up. It is then thrust at the thigh, knee, or shin, the blow landing with the heel or outer part of the foot. From personal experience while sparring I can attest that it will absolutely stop an onrushing attacker in his tracks when used against his kneecap.

Finally, the chassé croise median aims for the foe's solar plexus or stomach. Skipping the rear foot behind and past the front, the latter is then pistoned out at the enemy's midline.

Another use for the foot, though not borrowed from savate, is to maneuver behind one's attacker and collapse his knee joint by simply stepping on it. Very little force is required and gentle pressure on collar or shoulder will drop the largest man.

BOXING

> In order to ensure as far as it was possible immunity against injury in cowardly attacks or quarrels, they must understand boxing in order to thoroughly appreciate the danger and rapidity of a well-directed blow, and the particular parts of the body which were scientifically attacked.

Barton-Wright also seemed to believe that every Englishman of any breeding would already know the basics of pugilism, because he said precious little about it other than to note that street fighting and Marquis of Queensberry boxing were very different and the latter had to be adapted to ensure success in a battle for survival against the expected unscrupulous opponent. In point of fact, much of what he said about it seemed to be aimed at knowing how to defeat the expected moves of a trained boxer.

Viewing film of boxing matches from 1894 (indeed, some of the oldest movies in existence), one sees that the style of Barton-Wright's time called for a very upright stance with the arms extended. The thumb would be on top of the fist instead of wrapping it around for safety as we would now do it.

Whereas today we would keep the hands close to the face, hunkering behind them in a close guard, the realities of bare-knuckle boxing called for a different approach. The opponent was to be kept literally at arm's-length, since his hands weren't padded and could do significant damage.

The milling of one's fists is no movie parody but was an actual technique of the age. It confused the foe and kept the hands primed for use, much like a volleyball player "dances" the feet to be more ready for a quick reaction to the spike. Punches often tended to be almost lunges, the lead foot and fist moving together, though there was also plenty of swinging from the rear foot in the old films. Blocking with the arms more resembles defense in an Asian striking discipline than in modern boxing. The movements tend to be more exaggerated, not tiny and controlled.

WRESTLING

As with pugilism, the references to standard freestyle wrestling are not extensive, possibly for the same reason, that Barton-Wright expected all young men to have practiced the basics. But he also borrowed from Swiss schwingen, a grappling style inherited from medieval times that chiefly involved grasping the opponent at the hips and throwing him. Many of its techniques are nearly indistinguishable from judo moves, which themselves evolved from ju-jitsu in the nineteenth century. Since Bartitsu's founder relied primarily on ju-jitsu for close-quarters work and ground fighting, he likely taught standard wrestling as much for knowing how to counter it as for using it in a fight.

JU-JITSU

Much enamored of this Japanese discipline, since he had studied it in its native land and was convinced of its efficacy, Barton-Wright wrote and spoke more about it than any of the other principle techniques. He clearly prized it, since he incorporated its final syllables into the name of his art. In fact, he went so far as to import three ju-jitsu masters when he returned home. Some of the attention he paid to it might be put down to its sheer novelty in Britain, as it required much more explanation. It was also what made Bartitsu so very different from other combative systems in the West.

It is the essence of ju-jitsu which informs Bartitsu's core principles. It can be translated as "the art of yielding." This is appropriate, since it teaches practitioners to use the enemy's own momentum and strength against him. Developed by samurai to fall back upon when disarmed and fighting an armored foe, it replaced futile hand strikes with joint locks. As previously stated, it depends upon disturbing an assailant's equilibrium, inviting hostile motion so as to make use of the foe's own energy, and taking pre-emptive action with offensive defense.

This is the aspect of Bartitsu that gives it a grace and elegance while at the same time enabling its violent character when joined with the other disciplines. Stepping into an assault, blending with its direction and carving circles in space while rendering the opponent helpless looks almost dance-like when performed well. When employed along with punches, kicks, and stick-play, it makes for an exciting and unique fight scene readers will enjoy.

CLOTHING AND FOUND WEAPONS

Apart from walking stick display, this is the area of Bartitsu where the Steampunk author can add Victorian flair and color to her writing. Hats, overcoats, parasols, and pins are all mentioned by Barton-Wright as adjuncts to the Bartitsu practitioner's standard arsenal. He recommended flinging a bowler into the opponent's face as a distraction while closing to engage, or tossing a coat over his head. A sturdy hat could even serve as a buckler in the off-hand while striking with a stick. This is all absolutely efficacious, as I discovered in a full-speed Bartitsu free-play exercise. My student charged me with a stick with no choreography. Unarmed, I flung my hat into his eyes, pivoted, wrapped his stick arm with my left, and disarmed him with my right. Despite his knowing Bartitsu, he still lost to this move.

Barton-Wright was not remiss in advocating that ladies practice Bartitsu. Umbrellas, particularly those with crook handles, made fine weapons. Offending arms and legs could be hooked and the brolly's tip into the throat would deter any ruffian.

A fourteen-inch hatpin to the eye would certainly end a fight in the lady's favor. It is known that suffragettes such as Edith Garrud defended themselves against the police with ju-jitsu, though whether they actually trained at the Bartitsu Club itself is conjectural. Also an established fact is that the sister of Boy Scouts founder Lord Baden-Powell was an expert at defending herself with both parasol and walking stick.

GROUP FIGHTING

Since it was well-established that the criminal element rarely offered a fair fight and commonly attacked in groups to ensure success, Bartitsu included tactics for engaging several assailants at once. Naturally Barton-Wright preached that one should not stand on ceremony or honor in such situations but rather flee with all haste. If one were to be trapped, however, he offered means to clear a path to safety. These depended on having a stick and employing it in wide sweeps and vigorous back-and-forth motions to prevent surprise from the rear. Once room had been made, then the single man could proceed as the situation dictated.

We will end with a final fight scene from *Paragon of the Eccentric:*

> *She grasped a straight stick in her gloved hands and returned to the centre of the mat. Queue assumed the attitude of some ill-paid thug with minimal training as a fighter. Her stick sliced straight down at his skull while she bulled her way toward him.*
>
> *Paragon pivoted on his front foot. Her impetus as the blow missed took her a step past him. Almost casually he stepped on her knee joint from the rear, causing her to fall onto that knee. A painless rap to the back of her shoulder with the light stick neck ended the first exchange.*
>
> *Again they faced off. This time she swung her stick with both hands, as a frustrated rowdy might do. Like a batsman trying for six she chose a more horizontal path. Not so easy to avoid as a vertical attack.*
>
> *Knowing this, Paragon did not attempt evasion. Instead he slid directly into her, body against body. Now the stick body was past him, unable to inflict harm. Adding his own force to hers, left arm across her stick arm, they spun like a top. He simply bent his knees as they went around, causing her*

to fall forward out of the spin. She landed on her back with a boom, his stick point against her throat.

After assisting her to rise, they met for a third time. Now she feinted another descending sabre cut, but as he raised his stick with both hands wide apart to parry it she shifted to a spiking bayonet-style strike at his chest. Leaving his stick up high, Paragon pivoted out of her stick's path with a simultaneous left cross to her jaw. Despite her armour, the impact of the fist sent her sprawling.

Cursing under his breath, Paragon cast his stick aside and rushed to the immobile woman. He pulled off her bulky helmet to give her air. Queue's eyes remained closed, her breathing shallow. "We need some help in here!" he bellowed, half-turned toward the door. "Halloo!"

The room swiveled as if on ball bearings. Before he could comprehend his predicament he lay flat on his back, staring into the painful glare of the electric ceiling lamps. A leg made of cast iron clamped onto each side of his arm, which was stretched high over his head. One heel bored into his throat. His air and voice were cut off. Jolts of pain shot along his arm as Queue hauled back on it, bending his elbow across her thigh. For good measure she ruthlessly twisted his wrist in a direction it had definitely not been designed to go.

I'll be damned if I'll tap out for her satisfaction.

Another three seconds showed him how much in error that last belief had been. Queue yanked on the arm as if trying to pull a locomotive down the track. At the same time her heel pressed in another two inches, until he positively gurgled and drooled.

Hopefully these few precepts concerning the Victorian/Edwardian fighting art will embolden you to craft exciting scenes of Steampunk or Victorian mayhem. While the normal tropes of the genre (those gears, clocks, and airships) are growing stale, Bartitsu is still fresh and unspoiled. Despite its century-old pedigree, book lovers are unfamiliar with it. Nothing thrills a reader quite so much as seeing a cool, well-dressed hero or heroine dispatching ill-mannered blokes. So let the sticks, feet, and erudite quips fly. Grace under pressure has always been the hallmark of good breeding and Bartitsu is certainly a means to that end.

LONDON: HOME TO HENRY JAMES AND JOHN SINGER SARGENT

BY MARY F. BURNS

I GREW UP IN LOVE WITH ENGLAND. EVEN BEFORE THE BEATLES SHOWED UP ON THE scene, I'd been reading about King Arthur and the Knights of the Round Table, and I longed to visit Camelot and Stonehenge and the Tower of London. Mary Stewart's deep and imaginative rendering of the Arthurian legend through the eyes of Merlin—from young boy to ancient spirit of the woods—was a constant inspiration and delight.

In college, I read Jane Austen for the first time, and I also fell deeply in love with Henry James—probably the most prominent American to love England so much he ultimately became a citizen of that country. He did so on 26 July 1915, about six months before he died, as a declaration of loyalty to his adopted country and in protest against America's refusal to enter the war. James lived in London for many years, was a member of the Reform Club (which I visited in 1993—they were finally allowing ladies in for luncheon), and settled in Rye, at Lamb House, which is a National Trust property.

In 1999, I came across the paintings of John Singer Sargent at a huge exhibition in Washington, D.C. and found that he was another American who lived most of his life in Europe, and especially in England, after 1884 until his death in 1925. I was overwhelmed by his stunning, enormous portraits and vowed I would write a novel about him. While conducting research about Sargent, I discovered that he not only knew Henry James but also that James was an active patron of the young painter and was very influential in persuading him to leave Paris and come to live in London.

I had no trouble imagining why these men preferred England (or Europe) to America. James' novels are the quintessential exploration of the differences between the Old and the New Worlds, usually as seen through the eyes of a fresh, young, innocent American who comes upon the landscape of the tired, cynical, and sinful Europeans who both misunderstand and underestimate the newcomer. But it's clear that James nonetheless admires those very cynics, those inveterate, experienced sinners, and is convinced there is much to learn from them, knowledge to be gained that one simply cannot get in the United States (just read *The Ambassadors*). Sargent, on the other hand, was actually born in Florence, Italy—his mother was an expatriate who vastly preferred Europe to America, and they rarely went back home to Boston despite her husband's longing to do so.

Sargent spoke five languages; he was a talented musician and obviously a brilliant artist. He settled in Paris after his art training, when he was in his early twenties, and he intended to stay there—but scandalous circumstances in 1884 made it impossible for him to earn a living in Paris, so he fled to London and was assisted by Henry James and other friends in making himself known to potential clients. He eventually rented a studio on Tite Street in Chelsea, just north of the River Thames. In the late nineteenth century, Tite Street was a favored and fashionable location for people of an artistic and literary disposition. Sargent's residence was at No. 31 and his studio at No. 33, formerly the studio of James McNeill Whistler. Other famous people who lived at Tite Street at the time were Oscar Wilde and Edwin Austin Abbey.

In a way similar to the experience of the Impressionists in Paris, whose paintings were rejected so thoroughly by the academic Salon held every year that they started their own gallery (helped by wealthy friends) to exhibit their *"plein air"* paintings, the upstart artists in London were enormously assisted by the opening of the Grosvenor Gallery in 1877 by Sir Coutts Lindsay and his wife Blanche (née Rothschild). Initially, the Grosvenor was a showcase for the works of the Pre-Raphaelite painters—such as Edward Burne-Jones, William Holman Hunt, John Everett Millais, Dante Gabriel Rossetti, and Walter Crane— whose paintings were not approved by the Royal Academy of Art for its annual exhibition. Unlike the Royal Academy and especially the French Salon, the Grosvenor approached art exhibitions in a completely new way, placing several works by an artist in the same room, arranged with ample space and natural lighting to help the viewer appreciate the works as part of a whole style or way of painting.

In 1877, a famous incident occurred there when the art critic John Ruskin visited the gallery, where an exhibition of paintings by Whistler was on display. Ruskin's savage review of Whistler's work led to a long-drawn-out libel case between the two men. Sadly, although Whistler won the case, the judge awarded him a mere farthing in damages, leaving the American artist bankrupt and bitter. But the case made the gallery famous as the home of the Aesthetic movement, which was satirized in Gilbert and Sullivan's musical *Patience*, a play about the folly of chasing fads, which includes the lines, *"A pallid and thin young man, A haggard and lank young man, A greenery-yallery, Grosvenor Gallery, Foot-in-the-grave young man!"*

Henry James wrote essays on art criticism for both London and New York magazines, and frequently attended the Grosvenor Gallery, where in 1882, Sargent exhibited three Venetian studies, of which James spoke highly. A large and brilliant portrait by Sargent titled *Dr. Pozzi at Home* was exhibited the same year at the Royal Academy—James referred to it as "splendid" and, comparing it to two portraits of Cardinals (*Manning* by Watts, and *Newman* by Millais), wrote that *"Sargent's flamboyant physician out-Richelieus the English Cardinals, and is simply magnificent."* An English friend of Sargent's, Violet Paget (whose pen name was Vernon Lee), wrote to a friend about this portrait:

> I went to the Academy, poor stuff for the most part, but John's red picture,
> tho' less fine than his Paris portrait, magnificent, of an insolent kind of magnificence, more or less kicking other peoples pictures to bits.

As in Paris, Sargent was able to straddle the accepted and the new worlds of art in

London, too. He became so in demand by the London aristocracy and wealthy merchant class that his popularity was depicted in a cartoon by the famous Max Beerbohm showing wealthy female clients lined up at his door and Sargent peering warily out the window at them. By the early 1900s, Sargent was thoroughly tired of portraiture, and as he'd earned vast amounts of money in the previous decades, he spent more time painting landscapes or more "impressionistic" figures in landscapes. A great way to take a look at hundreds of Sargent paintings is to visit the online site http://www.jssgallery.org.

John Singer Sargent died on April 14, 1925, and is buried in Brookwood Cemetery, Surrey. Henry James died on February 28, 1916, and is buried in Cambridge Cemetery, Cambridge, Massachusetts.

FEMALE PIONEERS OF AVIATION

By DIANA JACKSON

EVERYONE HAS HEARD OF AMY JOHNSON AND AMELIA EARHART, PIONEERS IN AVIA-tion in the 1930s, but during my research I have discovered many women whose endeavours matched the male counterparts of their era as far back as 1910. Their daring to venture into what was seen as a man's world accomplished much more than their achievements in flying alone, although these were certainly remarkable.

They also designed clothes, opened factories, began flying schools and fought prejudice at many levels. They were not, as I had imagined, all rich young ladies with plenty of time on their hands, but women who dared to be different.

HARRIET QUIMBY, 1875-1912: "THE GREEN EYED BEAUTY"

Harriet Quimby came from a poor American family, but by working up from journalism and theatrical writing she became a competent and successful screenwriter for the silent movies of her time. It was after attending the Belmont Park Air Tournament on Long Island that she decided she must learn to fly.

In 1911 she gained her pilot's licence and became the first female American to gain an Aero Club of America Certificate. Like many pilots of her day, Harriet gained experience and a way to fund her ambitions by participating in several air shows, but her main achievement was in April 1912 when she was the first woman pilot to fly across the English Channel.

Unfortunately she met her early death as a passenger in a two-seater Bleriot only three months later in July 1912.

Harriet was noted for her beauty and her dignified manner, but her other notable legacy was that she designed a suitable style of dress for women pilots of her day. She was known for her purple satin one piece flight suit which converted into pants (trousers) when flying but to a skirt when out of the aeroplane so that she did not offend the dress expectations of her era.

KATHERINE STINSON, 1891-1997: "THE FLYING SCHOOLGIRL"

Katherine Stinson originally took up flying to save up to travel to Europe to study music, but she was a naturally gifted flier and soon became quite famous for her daring feats. She gained her pilot's licence in 1912 and a year later participated at exhibition flights.

It is claimed by some that Katherine was the first woman to perform a loop and to fly solo at night, but she was certainly the first woman to be authorised to carry mail and to do pre-flight inspections on her aeroplane.

Her other claim to fame was that she invented night skywriting, amazing her audiences worldwide. Not being allowed to participate as a pilot in WW1, Katherine, like many of her counterparts, raised money for the Red Cross through exhibiting her daring feats.

Unlike many of her fellow female fliers Katherine defied early death and lived to an amazing age of 106!

RUTH BANCROFT LAW, 1887-1970: "RUTH LAW'S FLYING CIRCUS"

A student at a private academy in New Haven CT, Ruth Law saw her first plane in the sky and fell in love with the idea of flying.

She gained her pilot's licence in 1912 and set the non-stop cross country record from Chicago to New York. It is also claimed that *she* was the first woman to do a loop the loop and to fly at night.

During WW1 she formed "Ruth Law's Flying Circus" to raise money for the Red Cross where cars raced aeroplanes, and she flew through fireworks.

Due to her determination to contribute in a more substantial way to the war effort, she was dismayed at the army's rejection of her application to fly for them, but finally they allowed her to wear an NCO uniform whilst raising money for their cause, the first lady ever to do so.

The New York Governor chose Law to illuminate the Statue of Liberty which she circled three times with flares on the tips of her wings and a banner with the word "Liberty" on the fuselage.

It was her husband who decided enough was enough and put a stop to Law's flying antics by writing her notice of retirement in the newspaper in 1922!

Ruth Law died at the good age of 83 years.

HILDA BEATRICE HEWLETT, 1864-1943

Born into a large and wealthy family, she was educated at Kensington Art School in wood carving, metalwork, and sewing, all skills she used later in life. Hilda married Maurice Hewlett, a successful novelist and poet, and through him she became interested in motorcars, becoming a passenger and mechanic to a female racing driver, Miss Hind.

In 1909 she became a friend of an engineer Gustave Blondeau through whom she gained an interest in aviation and began to save up to buy an aeroplane. She travelled to France where she worked alongside the men building her aeroplane, where she called herself Mrs. Grace Bird.

They returned with the aeroplane, called *The Blue Bird*, and set up a flying school at Brooklands where Hilda learned to fly. At 47 years old Hilda was the first English woman to gain a pilot's licence in 1911. Alongside their flying school, where incidentally Tommy Sopwith also learnt to fly, they began making aeroplanes.

In 1912 Hilda moved to Leagrave in Bedfordshire where she set up her own aeroplane factory where women were trained to build planes for The Great War. By 1918 they employed 300 men and 300 women. (Even her sewing skills came into use here in sewing the fabric on the wings of the planes.) Later, she was the first woman passenger to make the eleven day through flight from England to New Zealand, and she was also involved in an airline.

Hilda Hewlett died at 79 years of age.

BESSIE COLEMAN 1892-1926: "QUEEN BESS"

One of thirteen children of a sharecropper, Bessie had to walk four miles to school each day, where she excelled in mathematics. In 1915 she worked at a barber's shop as a manicurist which is where she heard stories of pilots arriving home from WW1.

She dreamed of learning to fly, but even black U.S. airmen wouldn't train her so, undeterred, she learnt French and headed to Paris. In 1921 she became the first African American to obtain her international aviation licence. Still unable to make a living flying in the U.S.A. or to find anyone willing to train her as a stunt pilot, she returned to France, gaining instruction there and in Germany too by a pilot at the Fokker Corporation.

On returning to the U.S. she appeared in air displays and became known as "The world's greatest woman flier."

Bessie was noted as saying, *"I decided blacks should not have to experience the difficulties I had faced, so I decided to open a flying school and teach other black women to fly."*

Unfortunately she did not live long enough to fulfil this dream because in 1926 a plane she flew in with William Will crashed, and both died.

It was after her death that she made the impact she'd hoped for in life, when "Bessie Coleman Aero Clubs" sprang up throughout America.

London Landmarks
in Wartime

By GRACE ELLIOT

As a writer of historical fiction, I aim to bring the past to life. To help imagine the sights, smells, and sounds of the past, it's become a bit of a hobby of mine to visit historic sites in London. This can be a bittersweet experience, because some important houses are now surrounded by the most monstrous architecture—a result of the rapid rebuilding of areas destroyed during the Blitz in World War II.

One of the great survivors of WWII was St. Paul's Cathedral. Of course the original cathedral was destroyed in the Great Fire of London in 1666. The original building was in a poor state of repair in the 1660s. Wooden scaffolding erected to effect repairs on the damaged roof was in part responsible for kindling the flames that ultimately destroyed the building.

The replacement cathedral was designed by Christopher Wren and took nine years of planning. Construction started in 1675, and it took 35 years to complete the build. The greatest challenge to the survival of this iconic building came during the Blitz when the German Luftwaffe bombed the capital for 67 consecutive nights.

That St. Paul's survived was down to the courage of the fire-fighters assigned to protect the iconic landmark. 29 bombs fell in or around the environs of St. Paul's. One device landed on the dome, smashing through to lodge in wooden supporting timbers. The fire-fighters had to climb up through the rafters to get to the bomb and accidentally dislodged it, whereupon it fell to the ground and was disarmed.

Fire-fighters were an important part of keeping London safe. Impromptu fire stations were set up throughout the city to keep a watch for incendiary bombs. Houses such as that of the famous lexicographer, Dr. Johnson, were enrolled as fire stations.

Dr. Johnson's house survived intact, but not all places of historical significance escaped. A parachute bomb landed on the Chiswick home of the eighteenth century artist, William Hogarth, and gutted it. Fortunately, in later years the house was restored and is now a wonderful evocation of how it was in Hogarth's day.

Historical Tidbits across the Ages

A Book Lover's Paradise

By ANNE O'BRIEN

ANY TOURIST VISITING THE LOVELY HISTORIC CITY OF HEREFORD IN THE WELSH Marches will have on the "to see" list the *Mappa Mundi* which gives us the magnificent representation of the medieval view of the world. Housed in Hereford Cathedral—worth a visit in its own right for its solid Norman atmosphere—the map maker's masterpiece is displayed in the anteroom to another treasure which must attract any travelling book-lover.

This is the famous chained library. It is a breathtaking remnant of the past.

The chained library at Hereford Cathedral is a unique treasure in England's rich heritage. The earliest and most important book kept there is the eighth century Hereford Gospels, but it is only one of the 229 medieval manuscripts which occupy two bays of the chained library. And there are many more historic books, covering a wealth of subjects from theology to law to horticulture.

Chaining books was the most effective security system in European libraries from the middle ages to the eighteenth century, and Hereford's seventeenth century chained library is the largest to survive with all its chains, rods, and locks intact.

A chain is attached at one end to the front cover of each book; the other end is slotted on to the rod running along the bottom of each shelf. This system allows a book to be taken from the shelf and read at the desk below, but not to be removed from the bookcase.

The books are shelved with their fore-edges, rather than their spines, facing the reader—the wrong way round to us—because this allows the book to be lifted down and opened without needing to be turned around. This avoids tangling the chain.

The specially designed chamber at the Cathedral means that the whole library can be seen in its original arrangement as it was from 1611 to 1841.

To our good fortune, the library survived the seventeenth century Civil War pretty much unscathed. During the Second World War the medieval manuscripts and *Mappa Mundi* were removed to safety and returned in 1946.

To visit this library is like stepping back into history; it is a special moment to stand in this room, surrounded by such a collection of past knowledge and erudition. Even breathing in the air seems to be a privilege. Although for the casual tourist it is definitely a case of look but don't touch, it is an awe-inspiring place and not to be missed. Long may it remain safe and secure for those who come after us. Do visit it if you ever get the chance.

LEEDS CASTLE: A CASTLE
FIT FOR A QUEEN...

BY ANNE O'BRIEN

...or even six of them.

NOT ONLY IS LEEDS CASTLE A ROMANTIC RUIN IN A SUPERB SETTING—SOMETIMES described as the loveliest castle in the world—and so a "must-visit" spot on any tourist or historical itinerary, it has a particular attraction for me as a writer of medieval historical fiction. During its time as a medieval royal residence, Leeds Castle has been home to at least six queens of England.

Why? Because Leeds Castle became part of the Queen of England's dower, granted to her on her marriage to give her future security in the case of her husband the King predeceasing her.

Situated in Kent, near Maidstone, the original castle was probably a simple motte and bailey construction of wood and earth, but a more formidable stronghold was built in 1119 by Robert de Crevecoeur.

Its importance in history began when it fell into royal hands in 1278 when King Edward I took over. It soon became, not surprisingly, one of his favourite residences, and he made much investment there, creating the beautiful setting that it enjoys today. It is thought that Edward was the man who created the lake which surrounds the castle, linking the three islands in the River Len with a causeway. For the pleasure of his beloved wife Eleanor of Castile, he built a *gloirette*—a D shaped tower with residential apartments—on the smallest of the three islands, giving magnificent views of the surrounding countryside. I am sure they enjoyed living there during the summer months although I imagine it would be incredibly damp in winter.

So who were the Queens who spent time there?

- **Eleanor of Castile**, wife of Edward I, for whom most of the early improvements were made. She is the Eleanor of the crosses, marking her final journey in death from Lincoln to her burial in Westminster Abbey.

- **Margaret of France**, Edward I's second wife. She was only twenty when she married him, and he was sixty, but when she was widowed eight years later she never remarried, saying *"when Edward died, all men died for me."*

- **Isabella of France**, wife to Edward II. After his death in 1327 and her fall from grace when her son Edward III took control of England, she lived primarily at Leeds castle.

- **Anne of Bohemia**, the fifteen-year-old bride of Richard II, spent the winter of 1381 at the castle on her way to be married to the youthful king.

- Henry VIII transformed the castle with much new building in 1519 for his first wife **Catherine of Aragon**. They stayed at Leeds together, with the entire English Court, on their way to the Field of the Cloth of Gold to sign the treaty with Francis I of France. The wood and plaster work in the courtyard looks to be a Tudor addition, but the stonework is old enough for the castle's medieval beginnings.

And my own particular interest in Leeds Castle? It was the home of two of my favourite ladies, both of whom appear in my novel for 2013, *The Forbidden Queen:*

- **Joanna of Navarre**, second wife to Henry IV and stepmother to Henry V. Joanna was imprisoned at Leeds for witchcraft—a spurious accusation for which there was no evidence but which enabled Henry to get his hands on her dower to pay for the increasingly expensive war in France. This was not Henry at his best! Joanna was released just before Henry's death. I doubt that she enjoyed her enforced stay at Leeds.

- **Katherine de Valois**, wife to Henry V and Owen Tudor. Katherine was not always free to visit Leeds, condemned as she was to live in the household of her son, the boy King Henry VI, after her unwise association with Edmund Beaufort. But after her demand for independence and her subsequent marriage to Owen Tudor, I imagine they spent much time together there in so idyllic a setting.

What a rich sense of history this castle has. Is it possible that the spirit of any of these royal inhabitants still lingers in this lovely place? Not that anyone has noticed. But it is said that a large black dog haunts the ruins, a monstrous creature associated with Eleanor Cobham, Duchess of Gloucester, (married to the brother of Henry V) who was tried and convicted of necromancy, witchcraft, heresy, and treason. She was held prisoner at Leeds for a short time before her trial. Perhaps her unsettling presence caused the black dog to roam the ruins.

Black dogs notwithstanding, I like to think that the shades of Katherine and Owen still walk the ruins together on a summer evening, hand in hand.

HOLYROOD ABBEY AND THE PALACE OF HOLYROODHOUSE

BY LAUREN GILBERT

THE PALACE OF HOLYROOD HOUSE IS ONE OF THE MOST HAUNTING PLACES I HAVE ever visited. It is inextricably linked to Mary Stuart, Queen of Scotland, who lived there during much of her reign. However, its history extended back centuries and continued after her. It was built next to Holyrood Abbey where its history actually began.

The Abbey of Holyrood was founded in Edinburgh, Scotland for the Canons Regular of St. Augustine by King David I in 1128. There is a legend that the foundation was laid as an act of thanksgiving by the King for a miraculous escape from a hunting accident on Holy Cross Day. A hart was deflected from goring the King by the reflection of sunlight on a crucifix, according to the legend. An alternate version has a crucifix appearing between the antlers, while the King was trying to save himself by grabbing the antlers. Either way, the Abbey was founded and named Holyrood ("rood" meaning cross) in honor of the King's escape on Holy Cross Day. A fragment of the True Cross was housed in the Abbey church. It had been brought to Scotland by King David's mother, Margaret (canonized as St. Margaret of Scotland), from Waltham Abbey, and became known as the Black Rood of Scotland. The Abbey survived and continued through the next few centuries.

The Abbey suffered invasion by the English twice, once when it was burned by Richard II in 1305, after which it was restored, and again in 1322 when it was sacked by Edward II's army. In 1346, at the Battle of Neville's Cross, the Black Rood of Scotland was captured by the English and carried off to Durham Cathedral, from where it subsequently disappeared during the Reformation.

Edinburgh became the capital of Scotland in the fifteenth century, and the guest house of the Abbey of Holyrood was used more and more frequently by the royal family, apparently in preference to the fortress of Edinburgh Castle. James I of Scotland's twin sons were born within the Abbey in 1430, and his Queen Mary of Gueldres was crowned there in 1449. The younger of the twins became James II and he was crowned in the abbey, married there, and was finally buried there. In July of 1469, James III married Margaret of Denmark (who was only thirteen years old) at least in part to resolve the feud between Scotland and Denmark over the Hebrides.

During the period from about 1500-1504, James IV built a palace for himself and his bride Margaret Tudor (Henry VIII's sister) next to the Abbey, of which little remains. His son James V extensively rebuilt the palace, possibly for his bride Madeleine (daughter of Francis I of France). His second wife, Mary of Guise, was crowned in the Abbey of Holyrood. The north tower, a large tower with round corner turrets built to be royal lodging between 1528 and 1532, still stands at the front of the palace. In 1535-36, further rebuilding was done on the other wings. During this time, Edinburgh Castle was used more as a place to confine political prisoners. James V died of fever December 15, 1542, after the Scots were defeated by the English at the Battle of Solway Moss, leaving his only legitimate child, the infant Mary, to become Queen. During the "rough wooing", the Abbey was burned and looted by the English in 1544; finally, in 1547, the English destroyed the choir, lady chapel, transepts, and monastic buildings of the Abbey. Although some repairs were made, it was never fully restored.

In 1548, Mary left Scotland for France, and the French troops ended the English occupation. Her mother, Mary of Guise, governed on her behalf until her death in 1560. During this period, the Reformation gained momentum, and Scotland became increasingly Protestant. After the death of her husband, Francis II of France, also in 1560, Mary returned to Scotland and made the Palace of Holyrood House her residence. This remained her primary residence through her tumultuous years as Queen. Ironically, what may be the only building in Scotland directly attributed to her still remains: the bath house near what was the north side of the palace in her time.

In July of 1566, Mary married Henry Stuart, Lord Darnley (her cousin) in 1566 in the Abbey church. The next year, Mary's secretary, David Rizzio, was murdered in her private apartments at the Palace, setting in train a series of events that led to the murder of Darnley, her marriage to James Hepburn, Earl of Bothwell, and ultimately the end of her reign. Religious differences accelerated and exacerbated the tumult; also in 1567, the interior of the church was pillaged by the followers of John Knox. The bloodstains left by David Rizzio's murder are still visible on the floor in the palace.

Between the Reformation and the Restoration, the palace and abbey were largely neglected. However, in 1633, some renovations were carried out to mark the coronation of Mary's grandson, Charles I. Unfortunately, during the Civil War, Oliver Cromwell's troops were quartered in the palace, which resulted in much more damage caused by fire.

Charles II was crowned in Scotland in 1651 (before the restoration in 1660). In the 1670s he ordered a massive rebuilding under Sir William Bruce, Scottish architect, at which time the Abbey Church was made into the Chapel Royal. When James, Duke of York, succeeded him as King James VII of Scotland/II of England, he restored the Catholic services at Holyrood and used it as the chapel for the ceremonies of the Order of the Thistle. Unfortunately the Abbey was plundered again in 1688 by the Edinburgh mob to show their outrage at King James' Catholic leanings.

Again there was a long period of neglect. At one point, "grace and favour" housing was provided there to poor and distressed aristocrats. For a brief period, things improved when Bonnie Prince Charlie used Holyrood as his headquarters in 1745 during his unsuccessful attempt to reclaim the throne. After that brief moment of glory, the palace sank into neglect again. The Abbey Church roof collapsed in 1768.

The site was left as it was until the early nineteenth century. Money was voted to improve Holyrood because of George IV's state visit to Scotland in August of 1822. George

IV decreed that Mary's apartments in Holyrood should be preserved. Subsequently, after Queen Victoria fell in love with Scotland and purchased Balmoral, she reintroduced the custom of the Royal Family staying at Holyrood, which inspired the Scots to renovate the palace extensively. Renovations were continued by King George V and Queen Mary, installing electricity, bathrooms, and other twentieth century conveniences. Today, the palace is still in use by the Royal Family when in Scotland. When they are not in residence, the palace is open for tourists. Mary Stuart's apartments, complete with David Rizzio's bloodstains can be seen, just as George IV would have wanted.

SOURCES

"History of Palace of Holyroodhouse." *Castles and Palaces of the World.* http://www.everycastle.com/Palace-of-Holyroodhouse.html

"Holyrood Abbey." *Catholic Encyclopedia.* http://www.newadvent.org/cathen/07423a.htm

"Holyrood Abbey – Edinburgh, Scotland." *SacredDestinations.com.* http://www.sacred-destinations.com/scotland/edinburgh-holyrood-abbey-and-palace

"The Palace of Holyroodhouse & Holyrood Abbey." *Mary Queen of Scots.com.* http://www.marie-stuart.co.uk/Castles/Holyroodhouse.htm

"The Palace of Holyroodhouse." *Website of the British Monarchy: The Royal Residences.* http://www.royal.gov.uk/TheRoyalResidences/ThePalaceofHolyroodhouse/History.aspx

Phillips, Charles. *The Illustrated Encyclopedia of Royal Britain.* New York: Petro Books, 2009.

Steel, David and Judy. *Mary Stuart's Scotland: The Landscapes, Life and Legends of Mary Queen of Scots.* New York: Crescent Books, 1987.

FLEET PRISON, LONDON

BY KATHERINE PYM

THE FLEET PRISON WAS AROUND SINCE THE TIME OF WILLIAM THE CONQUEROR. THE term Fleet comes from Saxon times and loosely means "a large enough stream to navigate". Records show it could handle a dozen ships loaded with merchandise and barges of considerable size and weight. The tide flowed as high as Holborn Bridge. Even at low tide, the water was still at least five feet deep.

Through the years, the River Fleet became fouled with all manner of excrement and garbage. In 1606, the Lord Mayor and Aldermen demanded it be cleaned. Eventually, it disappeared with an open thoroughfare over it called Farringdon Street.

From the Doomsday survey, the Fleet Prison was held in conjunction with the See of Canterbury and the English Crown. Between the kings and archbishops, the wardenship of the prison passed down from one knight to another beginning with the family of Leveland in County of Kent. For over one hundred years, this family held custody of the king's palace in Westminster and Fleet Prison and any monies these garnered.

Custody of the Fleet could be bought for high prices. In 1594, it was held by Sir Robert Tyrrel, Knight, who sold it to Sir Henry Lello for the considerable amount of £11,000.

From the fifteenth through mid-seventeenth centuries, the Fleet was the prison of the Star Chamber or Court of the Privy Council wherein the inhabitants were of the upper crust—political and religious dissidents. After being judged by those of the Star Chamber they were thrust in the Fleet. Sir Walter Raleigh, charged with treason, resided there for a time. The Star Chamber had supreme jurisdiction of the Crown. It stood by itself. No other courts could challenge the Star Chamber. The Privy Counselors sent the higher people of the land to the Fleet without appeal. There were no juries and no witnesses. They could inflict heavier punishments than any other court.

This was abolished by an act of Parliament in July 1641. After this, the Fleet became a debtors' prison. It was also a paying prison. There were no freebies there. The prisoner paid for everything. He'd pay for his food and lodgings, pay for the guard to turn the key to his cell. He'd pay for putting on and removal of his shackles. The warden and his officers received monies for all things in Fleet Prison. A debtor could leave the prison for a day or so only if the family paid the guard a day's wages to compensate for loss of monies garnered through fees.

The warden received 20d per day from every man in the prison. Some wardens abused their power. During the reign of Charles II, a warden named Mr. John Huggins allowed several persons to escape from the Fleet. One fellow who owed more than £10,000 was allowed to travel to France to conduct his affairs. The warden extorted money from folk as they fled the prison. His superiors declared him guilty of "notorious breaches of trust".

The amount of monies depended on who the prisoner was. For instance, during the reign of Elizabeth I while still the prisoner of the Star Chamber, an Archbishop, Duke, or Duchess was to pay £21 10s for a week's worth of food. They also paid for anything beyond normal, such as wine: £3 6s 8d. A yeoman paid for his weekly fare £1 14s 4d. If he wanted wine, it was another 5s. A poor man had no food. If he could pay for weekly fare, it would cost him 7s 4d.

The poor devil who couldn't pay was allowed a moment at a grilled door that looked out on the street. There he begged for a coin or two. This beggar would not be allowed in the upper floors with the more well-to-do but in the cellar or "Bartholomew Fair". These people generally died quickly from "Gaol Fever".

Mid-seventeenth and into the eighteenth century the Fleet became notorious for its Fleet marriages. Fifty to sixty couples were married per week in the Fleet Chapel by ministers in prison for debt. The marriage shop in Fleet became big business, and for a fee, with no questions asked, couples were married. These weren't children marrying, either. The average ages for men and women marrying during the seventeenth century were in the mid to late twenties.

Marriage paperwork was almost nonexistent. Clergy in prison for debt hid behind the walls to keep from being fined for these marriages. If caught, they would be fined £100. If not caught, these clergy could amass piles of money in this business.

Around 1710-1753, these marriages expanded to a sanctuary area outside the prison where clergy imprisoned for debt could make a living. This gave the clergy freedom to marry customers day or night. The certificates issued looked official, mostly stamped paper. For a fee, false entries of marriages were entered in registers. If the bride was pregnant, the entries could be backdated. Witnesses afterward were not easy to find.

This all ended with the Marriage Act of 1753.

SOURCES

Ackroyd, Peter. *London: The Biography*. Vintage, 2001.

Browne, W. A. F. *The Fleet, A Brief Account of The Ancient Prison Called "The Fleet", in the City of London, Abolished by Act of Parliament, 1842*. Henry Wix, 1843.

Stone, Lawrence. *Uncertain Unions: Marriage in England 1660-1753*. Oxford University Press, 1992.

A Delicious Sense of History at the Lord Leycester Hospital

By Anne O'Brien

ANYONE OF AN HISTORICAL TURN OF MIND VISITING WARWICK WILL AUTOMATICALLY make Warwick Castle their first port of call. It is without doubt a marvelous site. But for me, the Lord Leycester Hospital should take priority as a unique historical and architectural gem.

The name hospital is used in its ancient sense of *"a charitable institution for the housing and maintenance of the needy, infirm or aged."* It was established by Robert Dudley, Earl of Leicester in 1571, as a retirement home for old soldiers disabled in the service of Elizabeth I. It takes the name Leycester from the original spelling of Leicester's name in his will.

However, the building has a continuous, well-documented history from a much earlier date. The original chapel of St. James the Great was built in 1123 over the West gate into Warwick, but most of what we see today is from the fifteenth century when the United Guilds of Warwick moved to the site and the whole was rebuilt under the patronage of the Earls of Warwick. After Leicester's death without a direct heir, it became the property of Sir Philip Sidney, the celebrated poet and soldier. His descendants have been patrons of the Hospital until the present day.

The true miracle is that this building has survived at all. When the Great Fire of Warwick swept through the town in 1694, it wrought havoc with the medieval timber framed buildings. Today it is easy to follow its route. The buildings approaching the Hospital along High Street are constructed in stone and brick, showing the path of destruction of the fire driven by a strong southwesterly wind. Miraculously the fire stopped just before it reached the Hospital.

Today the Lord Leycester's Hospital is open to visitors and is a delight, a visual feast, but there are some aspects that particularly draw the eye and the imagination. There is no electric lighting in the beautiful chapel. Every weekday morning (except Mondays) the Brethren who still live in the Hospital gather there for prayers in exactly the same wording as laid down by Robert Dudley in 1571. Such a breath of history! Because there was some renovation in the nineteenth century, there is also a lovely window by the pre-Raphaelite artist, William Morris, who also designed the altar hangings.

The Great Hall is superb, dating from 1383. Particularly fine is the beamed roof. What an impressive place to hold a wedding reception, a concert, or a dance. Any opportunity to spend time in this room with such a sense of history would be perfect....

The Guildhall was for me the star of the show, built in 1450 by Richard Neville, the "King-maker" Earl of Warwick, as a private chamber for the Guilds to meet and carry out business. There are mementos here of the visit of James I to the room, but it is the Warwick connection that is so strong. The structure of the room is magnificent, and so is the original table around which the Guild members sat. And you can actually sit at it and touch it....

Entering the Courtyard is striking. The gallery that faces the doorway is decorated with shields depicting the devices of families associated with the Hospital over the past 450 years, including of course the bear and ragged staff. It is an opportunity simply to stand and stare.

And then if sustenance is needed, a visit to the Brethren's Kitchen is a must. This is where the Brethren ate together until 1966 when the Hospital was provided with self-contained flats. Now it caters for the exhausted visitor. The oak cupboard from Kenilworth is said to have once belonged to Elizabeth I, and there is a framed piece of embroidery by Amy Robsart, the first ill-fated wife of Robert Dudley, to admire as you drink a cup of tea.

What a splendid place it is. What a sad loss it would have been if the 1694 Fire had continued to sweep through Warwick. Whatever you do in Warwick, make time for the Lord Leycester's Hospital. I defy you to be disappointed!

BEDS AND BUGS THROUGH THE CENTURIES

BY DEBRA BROWN

I RECENTLY RAN ACROSS A STATEMENT ABOUT MINT PLACED IN STRAW BEDDING. How pleasant, I thought! It reminded me of having lain in a pile of fresh-smelling straw in a friend's barn in childhood, listening to the rain hitting the metal roof.

In this day of plush mattresses—though I must say mine is quite welcoming—we have got away from the sounds and smells of nature. And that means we've got away from the negative ions that rolling in the hay kicked up. I've read that there was less insomnia in a time when a person was "grounded" electrically by sleeping on natural bedding—even on animal skins on the hard ground—and wearing cotton nightclothes rather than polyester. The things we've done to ourselves!

The earliest beds were piles of straw, leaves, or simply skins. These things were plentiful and easy to obtain. They could be replaced as needed. In time, large bags (ticks) of fabric (ticking) were made to encase straw, leaves, pea shucks, moss, cotton, wool, or feathers. These were used at home, but travellers might bring along a rolled up tick and stuff it full of straw wherever they needed to lay down their heads.

Some early houses had built-in frames, like boxes or tubs, where straw could be piled up and contained. Eventually, frames were built of wood or stone to elevate the bed materials in order to keep the damp and pests away. (You don't mind vermin, do you?)

Noble Anglo-Saxon families evidently had better beds. Bed burials, usually of young women with rich grave goods dating back to the seventh century, have been found in the southern counties of Cambridgeshire, Suffolk, and Wiltshire, but a few have also been found in Derbyshire and North Yorkshire. These beds were wooden frames with iron fittings. The quality of the jewelry found in some graves indicates that the deceased may have been princesses. Some of the young women buried on their beds in the Ixworth, Roundway Down, Swallowcliffe Down, and Trumpington areas have pectoral crosses or other emblems buried with them which suggests that they may have been abbesses, who in the early Anglo-Saxon period were recruited from noble families.

Box beds, or beds enclosed in an alcove built into the wall, were common (for the living) in the Scottish Highlands.

Early medieval lords and their families slept in the manor's great hall, but in time they began to want more privacy. The first step in this direction came with the hung beds perhaps built into alcoves with drapes hanging from the ceiling or walls around them. They would have a fabric celure at the head of the bed, the fabric matching the curtains and coverings. During the day the draped fabrics might be pulled back or folded to permit the bed to be used for seating. Such beds became a symbol of wealth or prestige from the thirteenth to fifteenth century.

By the thirteenth century, wooden frames began to be decorated by carvings. By the fourteenth century the carving was less important in some countries. The wood was being covered by drapings of Italian silk, velvet, or even cloth of gold, sometimes lined with fur and richly embroidered. By the sixteenth century, the bedstead might have posters and rods called testers above which held the curtains. At first there were two posts at the foot of the bed along with the celure at the head, but in time, four posters and a wooden headboard became common. This was called a sealed bed or wainscot bed in Elizabethan times and was still used only by the wealthy, but shortly thereafter yeoman farmers began to use them, too.

In the fourteenth century wealthier people could own feather beds or what we would now call feather mattresses. When the middle classes began to prosper they wanted the soft beds as well. Downy breast feathers from the guest of honor at a duck or goose dinner were saved up over the years, as were their other feathers, though those would need some trimming to be comfortable in a bed. Servant girls might be allowed to save the feathers they'd removed from poultry over time for their future marriage beds. These beds were placed over something firmer, perhaps a straw bed. Feather beds were something to be passed on in a will, as were poster beds.

Every third year or so the feathers would have to be pulled out of a mattress to clean them. So, I wondered, where would they put them? Out in the sun or on the floor to air, while the women washed and waxed the ticking cover—wax or even soap would be rubbed onto the fabric to keep the feathers from poking through. The beds (mattresses) could be sent out for steam cleaning in later years. Shaking and plumping was a regular housekeeping process with feather beds.

Down comforters, duvets, or continental quilts as they are called in England, were common on the continent long before they were used in England, where they are a fairly recent addition.

By the sixteenth century bedsteads became lighter in weight though beautifully made. Why? Royals and lords would take them along when they went on progress. Can you imagine the chore traveling became? It is no wonder a large household required many servants.

England had simpler beds than some other countries, though often with four posts. Cast iron beds appeared in the eighteenth century, sold as beds that would not harbor some of the critters and vermin which were commonly found in wood.

In France the bed was a place where a woman would visit with intimate friends surrounding special occasions such as marriage, childbirth, and even mourning, and the bed was richly designed and decorated. Starting with Louis XI, ceremonial beds were placed for honoring guests such as ambassadors or great lords. Louis XIV loved staying in bed and often held court in his bedroom. He had 413 beds.

Less expensive beds in Victorian times were stuffed with wool flocking, which became lumpy. The wool might also become fodder for moths. Therefore the mattresses would have to be disassembled and the wool washed, boiled, and teased. After that was finished the mistress would hire someone to come in and stitch the mattress back together.

No matter their station in life one might be visited by the bed bug, and it was no picnic to get him to move along. One could probably blame it on the maids, but it did not give them a better night's sleep to do so. A woman in the nineteenth century wrote about tossing twenty pails full of water on the kitchen floor trying to drown the bugs. All the parts of her bed were then immersed in water, after which they were laid out in the sun for two days. The bed's joints were painted with mercury ointment (they were unaware of the mercury vapor's toxicity), and the curtains were taken down and washed. These were often thick, heavy fabric to help keep the cold out, and just getting them into the boiling pot would have taken a bit of energy. Bed bugs can live within the walls of a house, so depending on whether you lived in a stone hut or a stuccoed Belgrave Square mansion, you might have had to learn what could be done to evict them from between the stones or plaster.

The first coil-spring mattress was patented in 1865—what luxury! I'm sure you appreciate the advances in beds as I do.

SOURCE

"The Historic Design Influence on the Design History of the Classic Poster Beds." *Classic Beds.* http://www.classicbeds.us/history/index.htm

Let's Hear It for the Smith

By DEBORAH SWIFT

WITHOUT THE SMITH MOST OF LIFE IN PREVIOUS CENTURIES WOULD BE UNTHINKable, yet he often does not appear in historical novels. Nearly all of life was supported by the smith. Forged tools were used by all other craftspeople such as shear hooks for thatchers or chisels for carpenters. All farmers and agricultural workers relied on him for scythes, ploughs, rakes, and so forth. Women used iron cooking pots, metal spoons, and knives, all hand-made by the smith.

There were several different types of smith—the traditional blacksmith who shod horses and was an expert in veterinary practice, but also the brightsmith or whitesmith who polished his work to a higher degree of finish. Cutlers and weaponry makers would come under this category. Some smiths made bells and included the business of bell-hanging in their trade; some were locksmiths manufacturing only locks and keys. Often they worked closely with wheelwrights and wainwrights to make the parts of wagons and coaches—a trade as complex as manufacturing a car today. In the period I enjoy writing about, the seventeenth century, all transport was by horse, or horse and trap or carriage.

As well as making large items, the blacksmith would often have apprentices making nails, hooks, hinges, and other small items for everyday use. Nails were used to hold everything together—furniture, shoes, and musical instruments all required hand-made nails.

As the demand for nails was so great, some parts of the country specialized in nail-making. The improvement of slitting the iron into bars came from the France early in the seventeenth century, and this helped create an English nail trade. Godfrey Box built the first slitting mill in England at Dartford, Kent in 1590. It used water power to slit the iron.

Many forges were close to water because of the need to "quench" the iron between heatings and because the wheelwright often required water to soak and bend the wood for wheels. Because their trade involved keeping a fire going all day, villages often built the bake-house with its bread-oven near the smith's. So a symbiotic relationship between all the trades developed with each using the advantages of the other. I'm sure many smiths enjoyed the benefit of a hot pie at the end of their day's work!

Some blacksmiths specialized in making cutlery and so came to be known as "cutlers". They had a great knowledge of the properties of iron and how to control the heating and cooling processes to achieve a particular result. These men made knives, scissors, razors, and swords.

SOURCES

Drury, Elizabeth and Eric Drury. *A Book of English Trades*. English Heritage, 2005.

Grant-Jones, Simon. "History of the Blacksmith." http://www.simongrant-jones.com/history_of_the_blacksmith.html

Willetts, Arthur. *The Black Country Nail Trade.* Dudley Leisure Services, 1987.

SWORDS: PARTS AND PIECES
OF A MASTERPIECE

BY SCOTT HOWARD

Swords populate the world of English history and the books we love. Whether your favorite character(s) went on Crusade, haunted the tourney circuit, lived through the Anarchy, or strolled the courts of intrigue under the shadow of a Tudor, a sword was an everyday staple. Some were ornate and ceremonial and rarely saw the heat of battle, while others were the difference between life and death or glory and shame.

This weapon was much more than simply a piece of steel. There were many parts and pieces that made a sword both a formidable weapon and a work of art. Balance, weight, its edge, the grooves along the blade, the handle (grip), the scabbard, the crossguard, and the pommel all played a small, but vital part in a sword's construction and long-term use. When these disparate chunks of leather and steel were crafted together as a whole, a masterpiece was the result; they could even become an extension of your character.

THE POMMEL

Designs varied and range from functional to beautiful. Rampant lions, sunbursts, crosses, or jewels would be etched or embedded into round, octagonal, ring, swallowtail, or fishtail pommels. Additionally, coats of arms, Latin inscriptions, or filigree patterns could adorn that hunk of steel and, for some, price was not a constraint nor were the artistic touches.

When it comes to function, the pommel of a sword acted as a counterweight to the rest of the sword, resulting in a balanced whole. A long blade provoked the need for something that could equalize and distribute the weight. A knight or some other stripe of gallant, while the epitome of fitness, could still become weary swinging a sword at a practice dummy on some fine and mist-shrouded English morning.

Pommels could knock an opponent senseless when in close quarters. A fight or skirmish in a tight room or a winding stone staircase left little room for maneuverability. When thrusts, jabs, swings, and parries fail and an attacker's odorous breath becomes overwhelming, the flares and mass of a swallowtail can quickly end a fight with a downward thrust to the head or the back of the neck.

Additionally, the pommel served as a means of securing the full tang of the blade; the tang being the thin, unsharpened part of the blade that passes through the grip and through the ring below. The round retainer at the end could be screwed or otherwise made fast to the tang. Swords of lower quality had the tang ending in the grip, while those of a higher caliber passed entirely through. This method of construction could help prevent defeat and embarrassing situations—imagine a penniless knight fighting for honor, prestige, and a lady's favor at a tourney, only to have his cheap and blunted blade sail through early morning sunshine (reflecting the day's warmth and brightness, of course) and knock his love-interest squarely on the forehead with the flat of the blade.

THE CROSSGUARD

The crossguard was the transition piece between the blade and the sword grip. The typical medieval sword fell under the "cruciform" style, owing to its cross shape when the tip is pointing down. Religious symbolism and certain types of imagery were important to Crusaders and knights during the Middle Ages, and many agree that this design's purpose was to remind a soldier of his faith. However, it seems that many a knight missed this subtle message.

Similar to the pommel, crossguards had a myriad of designs. The most common design was a flat piece of steel extending three to four inches perpendicular to the blade; the blade actually passed through a notch in the guard and was held secure against the handle. Those of great wealth could have jewels, crosses, filigrees, or various inscriptions adorning this part of the sword. In addition to the flat crossguard style, designs could vary—lions' heads, fishtails, flared ends reminiscent of a cross pattée, or unique designs that reflected the wealth and status of the user.

Defense was paramount when a green and untried English knight faced a veteran on some unnamed thirteenth century meadow. When thrusts and parries failed, the crossguard could stop an attacker from removing one's hand, arm, or perhaps worse, depending on the angle of the strike. A downward swing could be stopped by a quick twist of the grip where the guard absorbs the force of the blow.

Additionally, the crossguard was an offensive part of the sword. In a melee or close-quarter fighting the crossguard could be jabbed at an angle into an opponent's exposed face or other un-armored parts of the body. Moreover, the end could be thrust downward onto the head or a mail-clad shoulder causing short-term pain and perhaps an opportunity.

Those most skilled at swordplay would find that the guard could be used to disarm an opponent. With swords locked at the crossguards in some smoke-filled great hall, a deft twisting of the wrist could change the fortunes of your favorite protagonist based on just a slight concavity to the guard. This curve could act as a type of lever to wrangle an opponent defenseless by pivoting the attacker's wrist toward his body and combining that with a thrust to the sword hand from a mailed fist.

Imagine how the game could change for one's character and the possibilities that could arise if Sir Knight, weary and winded, had a burst of sudden clarity and used this part of the sword to end an otherwise even fight—to breathlessly utter, "Yield!"

THE GRIP OR HANDLE

To state the obvious, the handle is the part of the sword that enables the user to properly wield the sword. Wood was a typical cover over the blade's tang, which then could be wrapped in leather, or even wire, to prevent slippage. The most common grips were one-handed, two-handed, and the hand-an-half—also called the bastard sword.

Two-handed swords allowed an armored knight to wield his sword with both hands for those devastating strikes. However, atop a destrier, perhaps with a shield on the left arm, two handed operation would be difficult at best. Two hands gripping this type of sword was more suited when dismounted—manning a wall or within a press of knights making a last ditch effort during a siege.

But is a two-handed sword even usable for a mounted knight? It depends! If your arms are well-muscled and your stamina strong then ride on to glory. Or, and here is where the "sword magic" is on display—the pommel can balance the sword in such a way that its feel becomes light. A lever and a fulcrum come to mind.

One-handed swords generally have a shorter blade, which allows the user to wield it with relative ease. Since it is shorter in length, Sir Knight can swing and parry the way he was chivalrously trained—on top of his warhorse.

However, even a sword of this type could be used with two hands. One could rest his hand on the pommel or take up a double grip. While this is not ideal, there are advantages in terms of speed and strength of strike.

The hand-an-a-half sword, or bastard sword, was generally shorter than a two-handed sword, and its design combined the better qualities of the two preceding types. It was a versatile weapon, which allowed a mounted knight ease of use, while allowing the same knight to make that last stand against William Marshall as he scales the wall and draws you into a fight on the wall walk (a chivalrous nod of the helm to Elizabeth Chadwick and her favorite).

This type of sword allows the user to comfortably grip the base of the pommel, thus giving it a two-handed feel without the weight. When one-handed use is warranted, its relatively light weight resembles that of a one-handed sword—great news when your protagonist is mounted or defending a spiraling stairwell.

This article merely scratches the surface of sword construction. To those that read, write, and otherwise love those epic days of yesteryear it is my hope that this snippet has given you added color for the characters you read about and those you create from your dreams. Historical fiction allows us to live vicariously, perform the greatest of feats, and press onward, heedless of our limits, through the lives of our heroines and heroes.

THE REMOVAL, REASSEMBLY, AND RECONSTRUCTION OF ST. TEILO'S CHURCH

BY JUDITH ARNOPP

ALL OVER WALES YOU WILL FIND ANCIENT MEDIEVAL CHURCHES, MANY OF THEM IN out of the way places, the sole reminder of a once thriving rural community. St. Teilo's church in Llandeilo Talybont was just such a building.

Saint Teilo was from Penalun in Pembrokeshire, a British Christian monk, bishop, and founder of monasteries and churches. "Llandeilo Talybont" translates as *"the church of St. Teilo at the head of the bridge"* and refers to the first crossing point of the river near the Roman fort of Leucarum. The site of the church, on a tidal marsh, gives it the local name of *"the Church of St. Teilo on the Marsh"*.

Although worship at the site dates back to the sixth century, the only remaining parts date to the thirteenth century. Additions were made in the late fourteenth century and further alterations added to the south of the nave in the fifteenth. Mercifully, it was left untouched by the Victorians.

The church was cared for, cherished, the hub of village life and in constant use until 1852 when a new, larger parish church was built in the expanding town of Pontarddulais. Services continued to be held at Talybont three times a year until 1971. Built on marsh land, St. Teilo's was always vulnerable, and when in the autumn of 1984 thieves made off with the roof slates, rain and periodic flooding quickly undermined the fabric of the walls leaving the church in ruin.

Local societies and groups fought to save the building, but poor access made repairing it on site very difficult and in the end, when the Welsh Folk Museum became involved, it was decided to dismantle the church, stone by stone, and relocate it to the museum at St. Fagans.

I was sceptical about this at first. Although the motives of the museum were noble, I feared the restoration might result in a horrific Disneyfication of our medieval past. I have now come to review that idea and confess that the positives far outnumber the negatives.

The earliest painting (circa 1400) depicts St. Catherine, while scenes from the Passion and a large painting of St. Christopher were added around 1500 and painted over during the Reformation. They were photographed and recorded by the Royal Commission on Ancient Monuments in Wales, and then a team of archaeologists from Cardiff University began work to conserve them. Once the paintings were recorded and preserved the church was carefully measured and slowly dismantled, each stone numbered. It must have been a nervous moment for the mason who removed the first stone for, at the time, St. Teilo's was the only church to have been reassembled on another site.

The project, which took twenty years, brought together Wales' greatest craftsmen, and during reconstruction only medieval techniques were used (where health and safety permitted). This involved pit sawing, splitting, and adzing of timbers, carving the arch-braced collar beams, mixing the lime, and finally reapplying the wall paint.

The church now provides an excellent resource for students, writers, historians. It is refurbished to an approximation of its appearance around the year 1530, complete with all the elements associated with a late medieval church, including a rood screen and loft, altars, carvings, and brightly coloured interior.

St. Fagan's, now known as The Museum of Welsh Life, is a fascinating place with over forty buildings making it possible for visitors to travel through time, passing through furnished homes and businesses from different historical periods. For me, of course, the church of St. Teilo has to be a favourite.

Nuns, Monks, Priests, and Believers: Writing about Spiritual Matters in English Historical Fiction

By Stephanie Cowell

I ONCE TOLD A FRIEND THAT IT WAS IMPOSSIBLE FOR ME TO WRITE A NOVEL WITHOUT A nun or a priest in it. In my household this has become a bit of a joke; my husband likes to say, "Oh, you wouldn't like this book or movie! No one's searching for God!" Well, sometimes it is true.

I am myself a church mouse; I can hardly pass an old church or chapel in England without slipping inside. Oh the history! Sometimes a thousand years or more in one church. Women were praying for their families seven hundred years ago in the very spot where you stand.

Roughly I can put the nuns, priests, and devout characters in novels in three categories: sleuth, spiritual seekers, and secondary characters who slip in and out of pages baptizing and burying (in the many periods of historical fiction, religion was a major part of one's life). And of course the first two categories intermingle.

There are so many such novels or series that I can mention only a few. The sleuth nuns in both *The Crown* by Nancy Bilyeau and the Margaret Frazer *Dame Frevisse* series; the monk in Ellis Peter's *Brother Cadfael* mysteries—all are wonderful portraits of sleuths who are devout as a matter of course as they try to bring a little justice and grace into the world and find the inevitable murderer. On the other hand, Margaret of Ashbury in Judith Merkle Riley's *A Vision of Light* is not a sleuth. She does not need to pursue spiritual light; it overcomes her, and she has no idea why. On page 121 in a poor parish church, Margaret sees *"something very strange, like a veil of light...I was seized with inexpressible ecstasy."* I was reading this fascinating book and came across these pages. I had found one of the truest descriptions of spiritual ecstasy not in my shelf of books of theology and sermons, but in a historical novel. I was spellbound and cheered.

I would like to depart the shores of England for a moment and mention that, though this novel is set in Germany (her previous was set in England), I felt a deep spiritual sense in Mary Sharratt's writing even before she decided to tackle the medieval nun Hildegard of Bingen. I read *Illuminations* with great fascination. To write a historical novel with no central love story, indeed where the love story is for a true realization of God, is a very brave thing, and she succeeds beautifully.

It is difficult to write about spiritual matters. They are the most intimate of our feelings and more difficult to express in words than physics, which is most deeply expressed in mathematics. And words are all we have as novelists. Yet a good historical novel can transplant a reader to spiritual places and feelings which a theological book can seldom do. Novels can be a gate to "things that are unseen."

I'll end with an absolute favorite, now out of print but so much loved by me! A novel of John Donne, *Take Heed of Loving Me,* by Elizabeth Gray Vining. Pure poetry! Donne is the author of the words *"No man is an island",* and James I made him Dean of St. Paul's in 1621. You can find his statue there in his shroud, one of the few things which survived the 1666 fiery destruction of the earlier St. Paul's.

OF HANDS, HEADS, AND OTHER BITS AND PIECES

By ANNA BELFRAGE

I T IS SAID THAT WHEN FRANCISCO FRANCO LAY DYING IN 1975, HE HAD THE DESICCATED hand of St. Teresa right beside him on his pillow. No doubt the dying dictator was hoping Spain's patron saint would guide him all the way to heaven—personally, I have serious doubts as to whether he qualifies.

Franco was by his own reckoning a most devout person, motivated not only by power but also by a desire to defend the Catholic Church when he took up arms against the Spanish Republic. As an aside, the Republic did go overboard on several occasions vis-à-vis the religious organisations, but that is totally unrelated to this essay—as is Franco, apart from him clutching St. Teresa's hand when he died.

This essay, you see, is about the hands, the finger joints, the bits and pieces of various saints and martyrs that have travelled the world, carried from one dusty monastery to the other in the hope of bringing with them some part of the saintliness that imbued their original owner.

In the case of St. Teresa, this remarkable woman was an anomaly. First of all, she was of Jewish descent. Her father was a *converso* and had been forced to wear the *sambenito* robes at every church in Toledo for seven consecutive Fridays while being pelted with refuse and verbally abused for being a doubtful Christian—and there are *a lot* of churches in Toledo. Secondly, she was a woman at a time when the religious authorities were very negatively inclined to women who attempted to study and interpret scripture or, even worse, claim to have spiritual visitations from Christ. Thirdly, while Teresa was a nun, she was also a very attractive nun, a woman who didn't think twice about utilising her feminine wiles to get what she wanted.

And still, despite these obvious drawbacks—I mean, a woman saying she was talking to God? Come on! After all, Spain had San Juan de la Cruz doing the chatting with Jesus, and the country didn't need one more direct line to God, did it?—Teresa was recognised already in her own lifetime as being something very, very special. She levitated, she was overcome by visions, and she wrote inspired books about all these her experiences, books that were viewed with much suspicion by the Inquisition—so much, in fact, that Teresa herself was hauled before the Inquisition two years before her death.

Whatever the case, Teresa was obviously destined for great things after death, and no sooner had the poor woman expired than people began squabbling over her remains. The nunnery where she died hastily buried the body, hoping to keep it. Down came Teresa's confessor, ordered the grave opened, marvelled at her un-decayed flesh and...sliced off her left hand (the one adorning Franco's pillow, four centuries or so later).

The body was taken to Ávila; it was disinterred several times more as various parties squabbled over her final resting place, and at every such disinterment poor Teresa lost a part of her fantastically preserved remains. An arm ended up at the convent where she died, her jawbone and her right foot reside in Rome, part of her cheek is in Madrid, and her heart is carefully preserved in a reliquary in Alba. There is a finger with a ring on it in Ávila, and other bodily parts now live in Brussels, México, and Paris. Poor woman: come Resurrection, she will have a hard time collecting all her bits and pieces.

This is where it all becomes quite interesting. As per the Christian faith, the dead will rise again upon the Day of Resurrection; they will stand up intact from their graves and be returned to some sort of life. (Nowadays, Christian faiths don't worry overmuch about an intact body—cremation is an accepted practise—but they definitely did back then!) I assume this only goes for the good ones, the ones deserving to live forever in Paradise, and reasonably this should include all the saints. Unfortunately, all the saints will have problems similar to St. Teresa's, namely that they won't be able to locate all their parts— or even worse, they will locate too many parts.

Take Swithin of Winchester, for example. Now, this is a somewhat odd saint, as nothing really noteworthy was written about him until a century or so after his death, when he was chosen as patron saint of the new cathedral in Winchester. This brought about quite the Swithin revival, and suddenly this rather insignificant man was credited with miracles, with wisdom—and with saintliness. His bones were moved out of his original tomb to the new basilica, and people came from afar to pray at his tomb.

So far, Swithin's bodily remains were still rattling around in the same coffin, but this state of affairs was not to last. His head was sent off to Canterbury, an arm went to Peterborough, and bit by bit the poor man's bones went on a reluctant walkabout.

Any church worth its name wanted a relic, something to entice the faithful to come and visit. In some cases, people went to great lengths to acquire such relics, like St. Hugh of Lincoln, who reputedly bit off a piece of St. Mary of Magdalene's arm while visiting a convent in France. Sounds a bit too gruesome to be true, but undoubtedly this fascination with relics led to a brisk trade in them—and most of the finger bones, embalmed hearts, fragments of the True Cross, were forgeries.

In some cases, potential saints had their bodily parts separated from the rest of their bodies prior to death—or upon being executed. (After all, by severing someone's head and hanging it on a spike for some years before dropping it to sink in the Thames, the authorities were symbolically ensuring that person would never make it through the Resurrection—denying the unfortunate the possibility of eternal life.)

Such a saint is St. Oliver Plunkett, the last person to die as a Catholic martyr in England. Oliver Plunkett was the Archbishop of Armagh, an Irish Catholic who had the misfortune of being a contemporary with the extremely anti-Catholic fanatics that dominated English political life in the 1670s.

England was unhappy with its Catholic Queen and with its royal Catholic heir, James, Duke of York. Charles II's brother had probably converted to Catholicism as early as 1669, but this change of faith only became public when the Test Act was introduced in 1673, whereupon any person wishing to hold office had to condemn certain practices within the Catholic Church as superstitious and idolatry. James refused, thereby making it known to all and sundry that he was no longer of the "right" faith.

To further add fuel to this infected fire, along came Titus Oates, a slimy character gifted with a very vivid imagination and a glib tongue. He "revealed" the infamous Popish plot whereby even the Queen was accused of intending to murder her husband. It was all lies, but the lies were craftily constructed, and the people—Parliament especially—wanted to believe the Catholics were up to no good, and as a consequence more than twenty people lost their lives before Oates was revealed as being a perjurer.

As part of this Popish plot, Plunkett was accused of conspiring with the French, aiming to invade England. There was not a shred of evidence supporting this, but Plunkett was brought to England, placed on trial and convicted of treason—despite "everyone" knowing that he was innocent of anything but being Catholic.

He was hanged, drawn, and quartered at Tyburn in 1681, originally buried in two (?) tin boxes, but his remains were exhumed in 1683, and his head was sent off to Rome, most of his body was buried in England while bits and pieces ended up in France, the Americas, Germany, and Australia. The head has since then been returned to Ireland and is now displayed in St. Peter's Church, Drogheda. Just like St. Teresa, poor Oliver will have to do quite some globetrotting to find himself....

Nowadays, the Vatican takes a negative stance on relics—and especially on the trade in relics. For those wannabe saints that are presently living out their lives amongst us, all those who work so hard at being good, at being charitable and doing good deeds, this means that they need not worry about being chopped up after death. I hope this comes as a relief to all those that consider themselves included.

No, modern day saints will be buried whole, they will remain in the ground whole, and whatever shrines are built in their names will instead include real time footage of miracles and speeches, available for download if you have the right app. Sadly, I think the biggest problem in this world of ours is that there are too few of us who aspire to saintliness. After all, being good to others is so "last year" in a society that more and more embraces the simplified cult of "me".

THE CORPSE ROAD

By DEBORAH SWIFT

Now it is the time of night
That the graves all gaping wide,
Every one lets forth his sprite
In the church-way paths to glide
　　　　　　　—Puck, in Shakespeare's *A Midsummer Night's Dream*

WHEN I WAS OUT WALKING LAST WEEK I WAS TRAVELLING WHAT IS KNOWN AS A "coffin route" or "corpse road." So what exactly is a "corpse road"?

In the Middle Ages there were only a few mother churches in England that held burial rights. This meant that when someone died, the corpse had to be transported long distances, sometimes through difficult terrain. Because of the landscape, often a corpse had to be carried miles by the bearers unless the deceased was rich and had left instructions for a horse-drawn bier.

One well-known funeral way is the one that runs from Rydal to the church in Ambleside in the Lake District where you can still see a coffin stone on which the coffin was placed while the parishioners rested.

Many of the corpse roads are now long gone, but there are clues in the names of footpaths and fields. Fields crossed by church-way paths often had names like "Church-way" or "Kirk-way Field".

Where I was walking the coffin had to be carried up the side of a limestone rock face known locally as "the Fairy Steps" because there was no burial ground in Arnside. The coffin had to be carried over the marshes to nearby Beetham church, a beautiful historic building dating back to Saxon times, with lovely medieval-style carvings above the door. The coffins were hoisted over the limestone cliffs using metal rings embedded in the rock. In 1866, the church at Arnside was consecrated, and the long coffin walk between Arnside and Beetham was no longer necessary.

The church was also besieged by Parliamentarians in the Civil War in 1647, where local landowners' tombs were desecrated by having the heads removed from the statues.

But to return to corpse roads—there was much superstition associated with the coffin route. For example, the feet of the corpse had to be kept pointing away from the family home on its journey to the cemetery, to prevent the deceased wanting to walk back home.

To prevent the dead returning, the route often went over bridges or stepping stones across running water which it was believed spirits would not be able to cross. Sometimes it led over stiles or through various other hazardous locations, such as the Fairy

Steps. This was supposed to deter the ghosts from wandering. Ghosts and spirits were an accepted part of everyday life right up until the twentieth century.

The corpse light, representing the soul of the dead, was supposed to linger on these roads, and there were many accounts of people seeing them.

SOURCES

"Coffin Path, Rydal." *Cumbria Heritage Trails*. http://treasuresofcumbria.org.uk/images/uploads/audio/CoffinPath.pdf

Neighbors, Joy. "The Legend and History of the Corpse Road." *A Grave Interest* (March 30, 2012). http://agraveinterest.blogspot.co.uk/2012/03/legend-history-of-corpse-road.html

OF WITCHES, MIDWIVES,
AND CHILDBIRTH

By SAM THOMAS

FOR MANY YEARS, HISTORIANS THOUGHT ONE OF TWO THINGS ABOUT MIDWIVES IN pre-modern Europe. If you asked medical historians, they were decrepit old crones with no medical training. They were untrained, lived on the margins of society, and probably dabbled in witchcraft.

If you asked (some) women's historians, they would agree that midwives practiced witchcraft, but in this account, they were the distant heirs to a pre-Christian religion, practitioners in an early modern Earth-Mother cult. These rebellious figures rejected the Church's authority and for their trouble were often burned at the stake.

Both of these accounts are complete bunk.

The connection between midwives and witchcraft dates back to the notorious *Malleus Maleficarum* (Latin for *Hammer of Witches*), written in 1486 by two Dominican inquisitors, Jacob Spernger and Heinrich Kramer. In *Malleus*, Sprenger and Kramer offer lurid accusations that midwives murdered newborn children and sacrificed them to the Devil.

While *Malleus* has influenced generations of historians, it is less clear that it had much influence on its readers. Kramer's behavior at a witch trial in 1485 so outraged his fellow-inquisitors and a local bishop that they came to the defense of the accused witch, and even the Spanish Inquisition warned its inquisitors not to take it too seriously. More significantly, when historians have studied witch trials, they find midwives not among the women accused, but testifying for the prosecution. While thousands of women were tried for witchcraft, only the tiniest handful were in any way connected to midwifery.

If midwives weren't witches, who were they? Just because the medical historians were wrong about the witchcraft, were they right that midwives were poor old women who lived on the margins of society?

Wrong again.

It turns out they were not much different than women in England. Many midwives were quite well-off, often referred to with the honorific "Mrs.", and we know that the wife of the Lord Mayor of Chester practiced midwifery. Letters written on behalf of Martha Baker describe her as *"a Gentlewoman of great Judgement & skill,"* and the will of Bridget Hodgson of York includes large cash gifts and refers to her family's coat of arms. It is not uncommon to find midwives married to Anglican ministers, which is hardly the mark of poverty and disdain.

That said, poor midwives did exist. Court documents describe Anne Doughty as *"very poore & hath very small employment,"* and say that Johanna Thompson *"is very low and*

526 | *Castles, Customs, and Kings*

poore in the world." In some cases, there is evidence that women receiving poor-relief were encouraged to take up midwifery in order to reduce their reliance on public funds.

It thus seems that midwives were young and old, rich and poor, married, widowed, and even spinsters.

Once we have figured out who midwives were, the question then becomes: *What did midwives do?* Sure they delivered children, but in a world before anesthetics and instruments, how did they do this? What was it that made midwives different from the other women who helped mothers when they were in labor?

It is first important to note that in the pre-modern world midwifery was not a science in the modern sense of the world. Rather, practitioners described their work as an "art" and, significantly, a "mystery." The 1689 testimonial for the wife of James Phillips noted that she was *"a Civill & discreet Matron & one well skilled & knowing in the Art & Mistery of Midwifery."* A few years later, Elizabeth Arrandell was described as *"well skild in the Mystery of Midwifery...."*

In keeping with its status as an art, there was much room for variation in the delivery room, but a midwife would check the cervix to see how far along the labor was and prepare the mother for delivery by lubricating the birth canal, usually with oil or animal fat. She might give the mother an enema, rub liniment on her belly, and give the mother "caudle," a hot drink somewhere between gruel and spiced wine.

In the day of modern anesthetics, such work might seem (to some) to be of questionable value, but in the early modern period a good midwife made labor less painful, moved it along more quickly, and could be the difference between life and death. In the midst of her labor, Susanna Watkin cried out, *"Godsake either fetch Ellin Jackson* [being a midwife] *or else knock me on the head."* Another woman—complaining when her desired midwife was late—claimed that she *"might have been delivered two houres sooner if she had had... helpe when they desired it."*

Once the child was born, the midwife had the honor of cutting the umbilical cord, and it was she who washed and swaddled the child before returning it to the mother. She then made the decision whether to deliver the placenta manually or to let nature take its course.

While it would be a mistake not to acknowledge the importance of this work, as one historian noted, the *"majority of births...were uneventful whether attended by a physician, a midwife or a stork."* So what made one midwife better than another? I would argue that a midwife's skill lay less on the medical side of the equation and more on the social side. A good midwife could effectively manage the mother and the delivery room.

Naturally enough, a midwife's social work focused on the mother. She ruled the delivery room, assigning tasks to the other women present and managing any conflicts between the mother and her birth attendants or among the gossips themselves. The midwife also encouraged the mother in the last stages of labor, as in 1739 when a midwife assured her patient that *"in less than Two Minutes the Child would be in the World."*

The midwife also would have reassured anxious fathers during labor and consoled them in the event that the birth ended in the death of mother or child. In performing these tasks, from calming a panicky mother to controlling quarrelling gossips, a midwife would have had to project a great deal of authority—this was not a profession for a shrinking violet!

A good midwife thus had to have the ability to take control of difficult and dangerous situations and convince her friends and neighbors to do as they were told. She was as authoritative a woman as you'd find. But a midwife's role in the neighborhood went well beyond labor and delivery and could take her into the world of law enforcement as she investigated and helped to prosecute a variety of crimes.

FURTHER READING

Cressy, David. *Birth, Marriage, and Death: Ritual, Religion, and the Life-Cycle in Tudor and Stuart England.* Oxford, 1997. (An excellent book full of great stories!)

Gowing, Laura. *Common Bodies: Women, Touch and Power in Seventeenth-Century England* New Haven, 2003.

Harley, David. "Historians as Demonologists: The Myth of the Midwife-witch." *Social History of Medicine* 3, no. 1 (1990): 1-26.

Lindemann, Mary. *Medicine and Society in Early Modern Europe* Cambridge, 1999.

Marland, Hilary, ed. *The Art of Midwifery: Early Modern Midwives in Europe.* London: 1994.

LET'S GO A-BARBERING

By KATHERINE PYM

FIRST, A LITTLE TECHNICAL HISTORY. BACK IN THE DAY, MONKS WERE BARBER-SURGEONS. They took care of all men's needs, from spiritual to physical. They groomed men and performed surgery on them. It was a monopoly.

But in 1163 at the Council of Tours, Pope Alexander III declared clergy getting their hands bloody was contrary to healing souls, and they were therefore banned from the practice. Enter the lay person where the profession of Barbery combined the services of grooming and doctoring.

Barbers let passers-by know they'd leech or perform surgery by putting a bowl of blood in their windows, but in 1307 an Ordinance forbade that little advertisement. Accumulated blood must be privately taken to the River Thames and dumped into its waters. If not, barbers were fined two shillings by the sheriff. Not to be outdone, barbers continued to advertise with red rags in the window.

The next year in 1308, the barber guild was formed. The first master of Barber's Company was Richard le Barber. In 1462, the guild received a royal charter by King Edward IV.

In 1540, the guild's title was changed to Barber-Surgeon, and disputes erupted. Finally, King Henry VIII enacted: *"No person using any shaving or barbery in London shall occupy any surgery, letting of blood, or other matter, except of drawing teeth."*

This law was not followed or enforced. Barbers often performed surgical procedures. They would barber in one part of their shop, and on the other do surgery, and surgeons—to make extra coin—practiced barbery.

The barber had long hours. King Henry VI issued an edict:

> *No barber* [shall] *open his shop to shave any man after 10 o'clock at night from Easter to Michaelmas, or 9 o'clock from Michaelmas to Easter, except it be any stranger or any worthy man of the town that hath need: whoever doeth to the contrary to pay one thousand tiles to the Guildhall.*

Well, to cut that edict to a nubbin, it meant anyone with a coin could be barbered whenever he wanted, which included Sundays and holy days. Barbers traipsed around town all days, from sunup to sundown and beyond. Pepys was often barbered on Sunday mornings before he went to church or late at night before he went to bed.

From *Visible World* published in 1658 and considered the first illustrated schoolbook, the barber in his shop *"cutteth off the hair and the beard with a pair of sizzars or shaveth with a razor which he taketh out of his case. And he washeth one over a bason with suds running out of a laver and also with sope and wipeth him."*

The barber's shop was a world unto itself. Gallants met there to be barbered—or sewn together after suffering sword wounds. Carbuncles would be lanced and drained and medicines dispersed. Those waiting played musical instruments and gossiped. The barbershop was where men went to learn current events or the latest scandals.

Once in the chair, their beards were starched and their hair trimmed.

In *Quip for an Upstart Courtier* published in 1592, we read that:

> [T]he courtier sat down in the throne of a chair, and the barber, after saluting him: "Sir, will you have your worship's hair cut after the Italian manner, short and round, and then frounst with the curling irons to make it look like a half-moon in a mist; or like a Spaniard, long at the ears and curled like to the two ends of an old cast periwig; or will you be Frenchified with a love-lock down to your shoulders...."

After the barber finished with the hair, he'd attack the beard. There were several ways to fashion the facial hair. Beards and mustaches could be formed into the Roman "T," a stiletto-beard, soldier or spade beard, bishops' beard, or the well-known Vandyke. You could have the "court cut" or "country cut." You could look fierce to your enemy or friendly to the ladies.

Some barbershops created a veritable spa environment. Nose and ear hairs were snipped. They'd foam and wash the patron's beard, dab it with fragrant waters, and anoint his closed eyes, then pull a rotten tooth.

Or should the barber have pulled the tooth, first?

SOURCE

Andrews, William. *At the Sign of the Barber's Pole, Studies in Hirsute History*. Cottingham, Yorkshire: J.R. Tutin, 1904.

A BRIEF HISTORY OF MENTAL ILLNESS AND ITS "CURES"

BY DEBRA BROWN

MENTAL AND EMOTIONAL ILLNESSES HAVE BEEN EXPLAINED BY MANY "CAUSES" OVER the millennia, from demon-possession to sainthood or witchcraft.

Treatment, of course, was determined by the cause. Skulls from the Stone Age have been found drilled with holes, probably to release demons which were believed to be causing the person's illness.

Plato (428-348 B.C.) believed that there were three possible causes of mental disturbance—disease of the body, or imbalance of base emotions, or intervention by the gods. He wrote about conditions that are recognized today—melancholia or depression, in which a person loses interest in life, and manic states, in which a person becomes euphoric or agitated. He argued that these be treated, not by chanting priests with snakes, but by convincing the person to act rationally, threatening him with confinement, or rewarding him for good behavior. There was hope even then!

Hippocrates (c. 460-377 B.C.) proposed treating melancholia by inducing vomiting with herbs to rid the body of humors, specifically black bile. Then the body was to be built up with good food and exercise. He taught that pleasures, sorrows, sleeplessness, anxieties, and absent-mindedness came from the brain when it is not healthy, but becomes *"abnormally hot, cold, moist, or dry...Madness comes from its moistness".*

The Greek physician Claudius Galen (A.D. 129-216) accepted the theory of humors, but he dissected cadavers to study the body, and he believed that a network of nerves carried messages and sensations to and from every part of the body to the center of the nervous system, the brain.

While sophisticated progress was being made in many places on the earth during the Dark Ages and Medieval period, Europeans equated madness with demonic possession or witchcraft. Fear of madmen showed up as taunting and abuse. Ships' captains were paid to remove mad persons to distant towns. They were driven out of the city walls at night along with lepers and beggars. Poor Tom in Shakespeare's *King Lear* was forced to fend for himself in the woods and fields:

> *Poor Tom; that eats the swimming frog, the toad,*
> *The tadpole, the wall-newt and the water;*
> *That in the fury of his heart, when the foul fiend rages,*
> *Eats cow-dung for sallets; swallows the old rat and the ditch-dog;*
> *Drinks the green mantle of the standing pool;*

Who is whipped from tithing to tithing,
And stock-punished, and imprisoned;
Who hath had three suits to his back, six shirts to his body,
Horse to ride, and weapon to wear;
But mice and rats, and such small fare,
Have been Tom's food for seven long year.

Some fared better. If a disturbed person came from a loving aristocratic family, they might be sheltered in a castle's turret. Treatment might be sought from a priest; a relic, an item reputed to have been touched by Jesus or a saint, might be applied, or an exorcism performed. They might even seek help from a physician who had studied the writings of Hippocrates or Galen. Poor folk sought cures from women who blended superstition and a knowledge of herbs. One such was recorded in *The Leech Book of Bald*, compiled in England in the eleventh century:

> *When a devil possess a man or controls him from within with disease, [give]*
> *a spew drink [to cause vomiting] of lupine, bishopwort, and henbane. Pound*
> *these together. Add ale for a liquid. Let it stand for a night. Add cathartic*
> *grains and holy water, to be drunk out of a church bell.*

If the illness manifested as obsessive praying, fasting to the point of starvation, or claiming to see visions, the person might be thought to be in special communication with the Holy Spirit. Others were not so fortunate.

Freedom of speech and religion had no place in medieval Europe. The Church maintained its power by instilling fear of punishment in this world and terror of damnation in the next. Any opposition meant heresy, and heresy was punished by death. Thousands of Jews were executed for religious heresy.

"Witches", who did the devil's work on earth, were heretics of the highest degree. In 1484 Pope Innocent VIII issued a Bull calling upon the church to seek out and eradicate witches throughout Christendom. How were they to be identified? Two German monks, Heinrich Kramer and James Sprenger, published a book called *Malleus Maleficarum* or *The Hammer of Witches* explaining how they could be recognized and prescribing methods for making them confess. Anyone who tried to oppose the witch hunt would himself be suspect!

> *All wickedness is but little to the wickedness of a woman. Wherefore St. John*
> *Chrysostom says: 'It is not good to marry, What else is woman but a foe to*
> *friendship, an inescapable punishment, a necessary evil, a natural tempta-*
> *tion, a delectable detriment, an evil of nature, painted with fair colors!'*

Any woman who talked wildly, wandered aimlessly, and insisted that she heard strange voices or saw visions was likely to be a witch. Inquisitors would be sent to extract a confession. She would generally confess under torture. For two hundred years, clerics referred to the pages of *Malleus Maleficarum*, arresting tens of thousands of supposed witches, many of whom were likely mentally or emotionally ill women, and sent them to their deaths.

By the early seventeenth century, the hunt for heretics had lost its driving force. The mad were seen, more and more, to suffer from a form of illness. They needed protection—and society needed protection from them.

I love the title of the fourth chapter of my resource, "Out of Mind, Out of Sight." Here I quote from the book, which is titled *Snake Pits, Talking Cures, & Magic Bullets: A History of Mental Illness* by Deborah Kent.

> *When St. Mary of Bethlehem Priory, in London, opened its doors to the sick and destitute in 1329, its nuns acted within the longstanding tradition of Christian charity. At first they took in only a few unfortunates at a time— perhaps a dying leper, or a frail old woman in need of shelter. In 1375 the priory was seized by the Crown, and in 1403 a royal edict turned it into a 'madhouse,' or shelter for the insane. Records show that the madhouse held six insane men during its first year of operation. The city of London took over the hospital in 1547, and it served as a city hospital for the mentally ill until 1948. By Shakespeare's time the name Bethlehem was shortened to 'Bedlam,' a word that endures in the English language to this day, connoting unbridled noise and disorder. The word carries an echo of the cacophony that must have reigned in that London institution some five hundred years ago.*

Perhaps a reason for that cacophony, besides the mental illness itself, is brought out by Urbane Metcalf in *The Interior of Bethlehem Hospital, 1817*:

> *It is to be observed that the basement is appropriated for those patients who are not cleanly in their person, and who on that account have no beds, but lie on straw with blankets and a rug; but I am sorry to say it is too often made a place of punishment to gratify the unbounded cruelties of the keepers.*

By the middle of the seventeenth century, hospitals sprang up all over Europe. These early hospitals were not so much designed to heal the sick as they were to protect society from them. The sick and poor might be brought by officials, and some persons, desperate with poverty, pleaded for admission. The hospital provided food and lodging, but it exacted a heavy price in suffering and humiliation.

Inmates were often kept in damp, or even wet, conditions, cold in the winter, and many were bitten by rats. Some were kept in cages and fed like livestock. To the hospital directors, the workers, and the general public, the inmates were not fully human. The rational mind was the essence of humanity.

Kent writes that:

In 1815, testimony before the British House of Commons revealed that curious visitors were admitted to view the lunatics at Bedlam for a penny each Sunday. In one year Bedlam collected four hundred pounds in pennies from some 96,000 visitors.

While public hospitals made little attempt to provide treatment, families wanted help for their disturbed relatives. Late in the seventeenth century, individuals—not always doctors—converted manors into small hospitals. For a goodly fee, they offered treatments, and some made extravagant claims.

In Clerkendale Close...there is one who, by the blessing of God, cures all lunatic, distracted, or mad people. He seldom exceeds more than three months in the cure of the maddest person that comes in his house. Several have been cured in a fortnight, and some in less time. He has cured several from Bedlam and other madhouses in and about the city.

This ad in a London newspaper concludes with "No cure, no money".

Physicians continued to try to understand and cure madness in all its forms. Some of the efforts and changes in succeeding centuries will be discussed in my next essay.

FROM MADHOUSE TO ASYLUM: THE EVOLUTION OF THE TREATMENT OF MENTAL ILLNESS

BY DEBRA BROWN

M Y PREVIOUS POST DISCUSSED HOW WHILE IN SOME PARTS OF THE EARTH ADVANCES were made in the understanding and treatment of mental illnesses, in Europe superstition and religious edicts and misinformation combined to increase the suffering of the sick and the fears of the rest of the population. The mentally ill were thought to be demon-possessed, witches, or at least subhuman.

As time went on, more attention began to be paid to the possibility of mad behavior being caused by poor health of the mind.

In the mid-seventeenth century Richard Morton treated an eighteen-year-old girl who refused to eat until she looked like *"a skeleton clad with skin"*. Morton applied plasters to her stomach to draw out the bad humors. He forced her to inhale ammonia fumes to subdue her violent passions and tried to build up her strength with medicines containing iron. She died within a few months, and likely would have without this treatment, but at least he was trying to help.

As European doctors learned more about the brain, they gave up the concept of the four humors and ascribed emotional disturbances to problems of the nervous system. Women were considered prone to "nervous complaints"—at least wealthy women, while poor women in the same condition were "mad".

The cause of the illness? Some doctors returned to an ancient Greek notion that the womb wandered throughout the body in search of children, causing hysteria (thus the hysterectomy connection). Privileged women were warned to avoid study or hard work which might overtax their delicate nervous systems. Their menfolk tried to prevent excitement which might bring on an attack of "the vapors".

In 1728 Daniel Defoe, the author of *Robinson Crusoe*, protested the horrors of the madhouse system. He wrote an outraged exposé about husbands:

> ...sending their wives to madhouses at every whim and dislike, that they may be more secure and undisturbed in their debaucheries.... This is the height of barbarity and injustice in a Christian country. ...If they are not mad when they go into these cursed houses, they are soon made so by the barbarous usage they there suffer.... Is it not enough to make anyone mad, to be suddenly clapped up, stripped, whipped, ill-fed, and worse use? To have no reason assigned for such treatment, no crime alleged or accusers to confront, and what is worse, no soul

to appeal to but merciless creatures who answer but in laughter, surliness, con-
tradictions, and, too often, stripes [lashes with the whip]?

After a series of similar protests, the British Parliament investigated private mad-houses in London and found that sane persons were indeed incarcerated against their wills. In 1774 Parliament passed a law requiring a medical certificate before any non-pauper [!] could be locked away as insane. Medical certificates, however, were all too easy to obtain, even to incarcerate persons of means.

Somehow, this well-intentioned effort of Parliament did not do much good for even the beloved King George III, who apparently had a physical disorder, porphyria, which caused severe psychiatric symptoms. Agitated, irritable, and incoherent, he received the full horrors of eighteenth century treatment. The Countess Harcourt said:

> *The unhappy patient...was no longer treated as a human being. His body was immediately encased in a machine which left it no liberty of motion. He was sometimes chained to a stake. He was frequently beaten and starved, and at best he was kept in subjection by menacing and violent language.*

He was purged, bled, and given emetic drugs. His madness, however, helped to stir Parliament's interest in the treatment of the mentally ill.

In 1793, in the Age of Enlightenment, Philippe Pinel was appointed director of a noto-rious Paris madhouse, Bicetre. The bloody French Revolution promised equality, liberty, and brotherhood. Yet Pinel found many of the patients locked in filthy cells or chained to the walls. He hoped to treat these patients humanely and bring forth their inborn humanity as he had seen accomplished in Spain and other places. He was deeply impressed by the wife of a hospital official, Madame Poussin, who treated the patients with kindness and used her imagination successfully to reach into the private realm of the sick.

Pinel determined to unchain the madmen of Bicetre. Many Parisians were alarmed. As he predicted, however, the patients were grateful for their freedom and did not attack him or other members of the staff. Evidence of humanity!

Also in the 1790s, William Tuke led an investigation of English madhouses. At York Hospital he discovered a tiny room, eight feet square (six square meters), where thirteen women slept on filthy straw. Like Pinel, he was convinced that mad persons should be treated with kindness rather than cruelty. He determined to create *"a place in which the unhappy might obtain refuge—a quiet haven in which the shattered bark may find a means of reparation or safety."* His York Retreat opened in 1796. It heralded in a new era in the treatment of the mentally ill, the age of the asylum.

William A. F. Browne, superintendent of the Montrose Asylum in Edinburgh, Scot-land wrote:

> *The inmates...all are busy, and delighted by being so.... You meet the gar-*
> *dener, the common agriculturalist, the mower, the weeder.... The bakehouse,*

the laundry, the kitchen, are all well supplied with indefatigable workers....
There is in this community no compulsion, no chains, no corporal chastise-
ment, simply because these are proved to be less effectual means of carrying
any point than persuasion, emulation, and the desire of obtaining gratifica-
tion.... You will pass those who are fond of reading, drawing, music, scattered
through handsome suites of rooms, furnished chastely but beautifully.... In
short, all are so busy as to overlook, or are all so contented as to forget, their
misery. Such is a faithful picture of what may be seen in many institutions,
and of what might be seen in all, were asylums conducted as they ought to be.

Was this the end of the terrible treatment of the mentally ill? Could they now begin to heal in peace and plenty? Surely some were greatly benefitted in the improved conditions, and their gratitude would have moved them to cooperate as best they could.

SOURCE

Kent, Deborah. *Snake Pits, Talking Cures, & Magic Bullets: A History of Mental Illness.* Twenty-First Century Books, 2003.

MENTAL HEALTH TREATMENT: FURTHER ATTEMPTS

BY DEBRA BROWN

M Y LAST ESSAY DISCUSSED THE BEGINNINGS OF CIVIL TREATMENT OF THE MENTALLY ill. Indeed, advances were made, beginning in the eighteenth century, of kind, considerate treatment instead of chaining, caging, and tormenting the poor victims.

Even the government began to take mental conditions into account.

> In 1843 a Glasgow carpenter named Daniel McNaughton attempted to assassinate British Home Secretary Sir Robert Peel, and accidentally killed Peel's assistant instead. In the celebrated court case that followed, McNaughton's lawyers proved that he had delusions of persecution. For months he had been tormented by the idea that public officials were pursuing him. McNaughton was acquitted of murder on the grounds that he was insane and could not distinguish between right and wrong. The McNaughton case is the foundation of the "insanity plea" that is sometimes invoked in courtrooms to this day.

Dorothea Dix (1802-1887) visited England during a low point in her life. She was depressed and alone, and she did not know how she could go on living. Fortunately, she carried a letter of introduction to William Rathbone III. The Rathbones took her into their home and brought her through her melancholy with their heartfelt kindness. At their home she met Samuel Tuke, the grandson of the founder of the York Retreat. She saw and felt the value of what he called "moral treatment".

Dorothea returned to America where she visited state legislatures and convinced many of the need for reform in the treatment of the insane. She had great success, and the dream of places of asylum for them began to be met. The view was that the patients were in need of respite from the pressures of life and family and that kindly medical care would be a help to them. And it was. Hospitals were small, and each patient was under the care of a doctor trained in this new method of treatment. Rates of cure were considered to be high.

In time, however, populations grew, and it began to be seen that many more people needed this respite from troubles to regain their mental stability. State legislatures balked at rising costs. In 1851, a superintendent said to Dorothea Dix, *The tendency now is not to make hospitals as fit as possible, but as cheap as possible.*

Hospitals became much larger and more impersonal, and they were staffed more and more with poorly trained attendants who spent their time struggling to keep the patients under control—this, while thousands of mentally ill persons were still being held in almshouses and prisons. By the late nineteenth century, asylum life bore a disheartening resemblance to that in Bedlam two centuries before. Restraints were used well into the twentieth century.

Deborah Kent writes:

> White Americans sometimes argued that immigrants and African Americans had a special tendency toward mental illness. In the years before the Civil War, several 'scientific studies' supposedly proved that free blacks had a higher rate of physical and mental illness than did slaves. Thus blacks must be unfit to cope with freedom, and were better off under slavery.

A Dr. Samuel Cartwright detailed two "mental diseases" that were unique to blacks. One "illness", *Drapetomania*, was caused, he said, by owners that treated their slaves as equals, causing them to have a tendency to run away. *Dysaesthesia Aethiopis*, the second, resulted in a desire to avoid work and cause mischief. I have my doubts that any of those symptoms related to disease!

In the late 1700s Franz Anton Mesmer enjoyed studying the new science of electricity. A practicing physician in Vienna, Mesmer conceived a startling new theory to explain human illnesses. An invisible fluid, which he called "animal magnetism," fell from the stars to the earth. This fluid, with its positive and negative charges, existed in all living things, and it flowed from one to another. If they became unbalanced, the charges caused disease.

To bring the charges into balance, Mesmer sat facing his patient. He held the patient's thumbs and stared into her eyes. He ran his hands up and down her arms and legs. Patients burst into fits of laughter, tears, or shaking. After this, what Mesmer called a "hysterical crisis", the patient's symptoms disappeared.

In 1778 the authorities accused Mesmer of touching his female patients inappropriately, and they drove him out of the city. He settled in Paris, where he came to have eager patients among the French aristocracy. Eventually Louis XVI ordered an investigation into the scientific validity of Mesmer's claims. Benjamin Franklin was in France at the time, and along with other investigators, he considered the magnetic fluid to be an unsound theory:

> The violent effects observed...are to be attributed to the touching, to the aroused imagination, and to that mechanical imitation which leads us, in spite of ourselves, to repeat that which strikes our senses....

A hundred years later, Jean-Martin Charcot became interested in the practice of Mesmerism, which had persisted and been refined. Charcot was in charge of insane patients in Salpetrière, a Paris hospital. Many of his patients had symptoms with no known physical cause. He decided to use a form of Mesmerism which he called hypnosis on some of these hysterical patients. Often a patient would awake from his trance free of his or her previous symptoms.

The young doctor Sigmund Freud believed all mental illness had biological roots, but he studied under Charcot in 1885 or 1886, and he began to wonder how hypnosis touched the psyche of the patients and helped them.

Back in his home town of Vienna, Freud and an older doctor, Josef Breuer discussed an interesting case, that of a woman they called "Anna O" in their later book *Studies in Hysteria*. Breuer had treated a woman for strange symptoms—she lost her appetite, forgot her native German language for a time, and even thought her braids were snakes trying to choke her. She had radical personality changes and believed the people around her were wax figures.

Breuer began to question her about her life during the time the illness set in. She talked freely about the stresses she had been under while caring for her dying father. She came to call these discussions her "talking cure". Indeed, she felt they were the reasons her symptoms disappeared.

Freud began to feel that talking, even without the use of hypnosis, would have therapeutic results. He had his patients lay on a couch and talk about whatever came to their minds. Freud called this "free association", the beginning of psychoanalysis. We see in this a start of accepting trauma as a cause of emotional illness and talk as a healing therapy.

Though some of Freud's followers turned away from him as his theories developed, the idea began to grow that if talking about trauma relieved emotional distress, why not prevent the distress to begin with? Child guidance clinics throughout the United States began training parents in compassionate child-rearing and providing treatment for troubled children as well as wholesome sporting and recreational programs. But a good thing could not be left alone.

Along came the thought from some psychoanalysts that mental illness in children had to be the mother's fault. Deborah Kent writes, *"Mother emphatically did not know best. She was either overprotective or rejecting, demanding or neglectful. No matter what she did, she was seen as a destructive force in her child's life."* Cold "refrigerator mothers" were the cause of autism. Many women bore the distress of seeing their children suffer mental conditions while guilt compounded their sorrow. In later decades of the twentieth century, severe mental illness was finally seen to have biological origins.

Dr. Henry Cotton in early twentieth century New Jersey was convinced that tooth decay was a leading cause of mental illness—possibly because the mentally ill had no presence of mind to care for their teeth, and they were in poor condition. Without scientific evidence backing his theory, he extracted their teeth for some thirty years. A hospital visitor wrote in 1930 that she saw hundreds of people without teeth. They suffered with indigestion, she said, because they could not chew their food.

Patients were submerged in ice water for up to three hours, perhaps every day for two or three weeks.

Insulin shock therapy was used beginning in 1934, resulting in the deaths of one percent of the patients. Nevertheless, this treatment continued until the 1960s.

An Italian psychiatrist, Ugo Cerletti, examined a group of epileptic patients and came to the conclusion that epilepsy and schizophrenia did not mix—that an epileptic patient could not have the second condition. He felt that if he produced convulsions in schizophrenic patients, their illness would disappear. This led to the use of electrical current therapies. Though he was wrong in his understanding about epilepsy and schizophrenia, the use of electrical currents seemed to be a major breakthrough for easing the minds of schizophrenic patients and lifting depression.

A Portuguese doctor, Egas Moniz, developed a grim treatment that he said calmed highly disturbed patients, and this came to be used frequently for a time. Nerves in the front portion of the brain were severed in a process called lobotomy. Some surgeons entered the brain by drilling holes in the skull, much like the ancients did apparently to allow the escape of demons. (Does it seem we went full circle?) Other surgeons went through the eye. Crucial areas of the brain were destroyed, and many had terrible effects. Dr. Moniz was awarded the Nobel Prize for Medicine in 1949.

The sister of the American President John F. Kennedy underwent a prefrontal lobotomy. Massive brain damage resulted, leaving Rosemary unable to communicate or care for her basic needs. She was placed in a nursing home. The public did not learn the truth about this until 1996.

For the most part, the treatments that had been tried in more modern times, even those that resulted in tragedy, had the best of intentions. Not all, however, could make that claim.

We can be thankful for the vast improvement in understanding and development of treatments made by researchers and professionals of recent decades. Though we may long for the past, my history-loving friends and I prefer today's medical care!

I recommend to you my resource, the book *Snake Pits, Talking Cures, & Magic Bullets: A History of Mental Illness* by Deborah Kent, a Young Adult book full of fascinating information.

MALLENDERS AND SALLENDERS...AND A FEW OTHER NASTY COMPLAINTS.

BY JONATHAN HOPKINS

VETERINARY SURGEONS—DON'T YOU JUST LOVE 'EM?
 My gripe with horse vets is that when you call them out they always ask what the problem is. So you tell them, they look at the horse, agree with you, and when the bill arrives they've charged you for their diagnosis!

But—in the small hours of a wet and windy winter morning when you have a colicky horse you can't do anything for? That's when you really appreciate them; when you're eternally grateful most still abide by Siegfried Farnon's famous assertion to James Herriot in that author's semi-autobiographical series of books: "You must attend."

Where would we be without our vets, eh? Probably still reliant on farriers, or reaching further back the village healers, "wise women" herbalists. But they treated man and animal alike, whereas a farrier really only treated horses. Frankly, horses were that important.

In fact the term "farrier" has obscure origins in this context (it's generally believed to derive from the Latin for "ironworker") because, up until fairly recently, a smith shod horses while a farrier was a horse doctor. "Farrier" didn't become synonymous with shoeing until the eighteenth century. Work that one out.

As in most trades, farriers served an apprenticeship, but with few standard medicinal or surgical treatments for any specific disease there must have been a wide variety of skill levels. The problems this could cause were recognised as early as the twelfth century, when the mayor and aldermen of London approved the formation of the Marshals of the City of London, with powers to inspect the work of farriers operating in and around the capital. (Did you know "Marshall" comes from the original Frankish for "horse-servant"? Nor me.)

Unfortunately the Great Fire disrupted many livery companies to such an extent that in 1674 a new charter was granted by Charles II to the Brotherhood of Farryers within our Cities of London and Westminster, an organisation which eventually became today's Worshipful Company of Farriers, the U.K. training and licensing body (together with the Farriers Registration Council) for Registered Shoeing Smiths.

A lot was known about horse anatomy by the eighteenth century, yet despite George Stubbs' sensational series of etchings based on his dissections and published originally in 1766, there was still no real scientific approach to the treatment of their ailments, at least in the U.K.

The very first veterinary college had been founded in Lyon, France in 1761 and one of its graduates, Charles Vial de St. Bel, hit upon the idea of opening a similar institution in Britain. On a visit to England he was fortunate to meet up with Granville Penn, great-grandson of Admiral Sir William Penn (and thus related to the founder of Pennsylvania) who had the same idea and managed to raise funding where St. Bel had failed. As a result the Veterinary College, London eventually opened its doors to students in 1792, with St. Bel at its head.

A veterinary school was particularly good news for the army which was desperate to reduce losses of expensive horseflesh on campaign. So in 1796 cavalry and artillery colonels were ordered to employ a graduate in each regiment as "Veterinary Surgeon" (to differentiate him from the Regimental Surgeon), the first time such a designation was used.

How existing army farriers felt about this usurpation of their responsibility isn't known—perhaps that's when they began to take an interest in horseshoes, or maybe such duty was foisted upon them. They'd have certainly felt aggrieved that as a Warrant Officer, in 1806 the Veterinary Surgeon was paid eight shillings a day (rising to ten shillings after three years' service) compared to a Farrier and Smith's rate of three shillings and four-pence, three-farthings. But employing qualified vets helped to begin standardising treatments for certain animal ailments, and, as had been found with surgeons, dealing with battlefield and campaign casualties helped push the boundaries of veterinary knowledge.

One of the biggest problems farriers and vets faced was the increase in incidence of infectious disease. As urban populations grew, so did the number and size of livery and haulage yards to service them. A burgeoning equine population, together with the generally insanitary conditions of the time produced ideal breeding grounds for bacterial and viral infections when these ailments were not understood as such.

Probably the nastiest of these, and the one appearing most frequently in novels, is glanders which, according to Clater (Source 1) has *"baffled the farrier more than any other to which this useful animal is liable."* In fact this bacterial infection producing lesions and ulcers in the respiratory tract was known to pass from animal to animal (though the mechanism of transmission was not understood), so suspected cases were usually destroyed as swiftly as possible. Despite this, Clater proposed treatments to an isolated horse, by balling, drenching, injection or anointing, including such gems as a "Nitrous Acid Drink"—

> *Let one ounce of nitrous acid be mixed in three pints of water and sweetened with four ounces of treacle – To be given to the horse (as a drench) once a day or...as may be thought proper...*

Yes, we might laugh today, but at least he was trying—Lowson's advice (Source 3) on the subject was an unequivocal "shoot it". And it might surprise you to know that even though, through our use of antibiotics, glanders has been eradicated from most western nations, it's still endemic in parts of Africa, Asia, the Middle East, and South America.

Another novelist's favourite, the farcy, is a disease I'd never heard of before reading old farriery books. Lawson (Source 2) says, *"Clater, and other ignorant farriers, erroneously suppose that this disease is seated in the veins!"* Nice, huh? He also says *"This disease may be brought on by the same causes which produce the Mange",* so he wasn't as clever as he obviously thought!

They were both wrong. It's actually the same disease as glanders, but appears in different parts of the body. Clater also says, *"The farcy and the glanders appear to originate from the same source"* so he was on the right track. As a direct comparison, Strangles is still fairly common in the U.K. today, a highly contagious bacterial disease causing lesions in the lymph glands around the lower jaw and throat. This can also appear elsewhere in the body, but since we know it's the same organism the variation is called Bastard Strangles to differentiate.

These diseases were serious, and for farriers or vets of the time just about incurable. But plenty of others were treatable—wounds, strains, and sprains, surfeits (you'll have to look that one up!), most colics, foot abscesses, fistulous withers, colds, worms, spavins, and ringbones, to name but a few.

So what about Mallenders and Sallenders?

Mallenders was scurfing to the skin of the foreleg, at the back of the knee and down the tendon; Sallenders was scurfing to the skin of the hindleg at the front of the hock and down the shin. Nasty, itchy complaints. Difficult and expensive to treat, according to period farriers and vets.

In fact the pathology of both these "diseases" proved to be perfectly normal or completely benign: they weren't real ailments at all!

That's horses for you. And vets.

SOURCES

Clater, Francis. *Everyman His Own Farrier.* Original 1783. This edition revised 1861 by D McTaggart MRCVS.

Lawson, A. *The Modern Farrier.* 1820

Lowson, George. *The Complete Modern Farrier.* 1848.

WITCH HAZEL: A GIFT FROM AMERICA

By LAUREN GILBERT

THE SHRUB SPECIES *HAMAMELIS VIRGINIANA*, COMMONLY KNOWN AS WITCH HAZEL, IS native to America. It is a common deciduous shrub or small tree found on the American east coast from Quebec to Minnesota to Florida (there are other American varieties and a couple of Asian varieties as well, which will not be addressed here). It is an understory plant, found wild in forests. It is slow-growing, commonly reaching five to fifteen feet tall (although taller specimens are known, one reaching 30 feet).

It has a smooth brownish-grey bark, long slender branches growing in Y formations, and decorative leaves. The leaves are oval with scalloped edges and inverted-V veining that can reach up to six inches in length. Their color runs from a deep green during the summer to gold in the fall. It likes partial sun to light shade. It blooms in the fall (late September-October) and can bloom into December (in the south, as late as March). The blooms are yellow, and consist of four twisted ribbon-like petals. The flowers have a light fragrance. The plant is not self-pollinating, so must attract pollinators such as insects.

The flower is interesting as, when temperatures dip, the petals twist tighter to protect itself; when the temperatures are warmer, the petals relax to allow available pollinators access. In spring, it produces fruit of a fuzzy light brown capsule shape, which has one to two shiny black seeds. The fruit ripens in the summer time, and then in fall, when ready, the seed pod explodes, shooting the seed over twenty feet away. The seeds take two years to germinate (assuming they aren't eaten by birds). These seeds are white and oily on the inside and are edible, supposedly tasting somewhat like pistachios. This plant is unusual as it can have leaves, flower, and fruit on the limb all at one time.

It is unclear how the name "Witch hazel" was derived; a popular theory is that it is derived from the word *wych* which is Old English referring to pliant or bendable branches (root word of *wicker*) and hazel because the early colonists thought it was related to the species *Corylus* (hazel) due to similarities of bark & leaves. It is also known as Hazel Nut, Snapping Hazel, Winterbloom, and Spotted or Striped Alder.

American Indians were familiar with this plant and used it medicinally. The Menominee tribe (who were located in what is now modern Wisconsin) boiled it in water, creating a decoction that was rubbed on the legs to keep them flexible and on the back to relieve back pain. The Osage (modern Midwest) used it for tumors, skin ulcers and sores. The Iroquois (modern New York and Canada) brewed a strong tea that was used to combat dysentery, colds, and coughs, as a blood purifier, and as an astringent. The Mohegans (modern Connecticut) made a decoction used to treat bruises, cuts, and bites. Bark, leaves, and twigs were used fresh and dried. I could not find a reference to names by which the various tribes may have known this plant, but it was obviously widely known and used.

English colonists saw the witch hazel and noted its similarity to plants/trees at home, such as the hazel tree (species Corylus) whose flexible branches were used in wattle, fencing, and baskets. In 1588 Thomas Hariot indicated that Indians were using "wich-hazle" to make bows.

Dowsing was an ancient practice where Y shaped branches were used to seek water. Indians did this, and the practice was known in England and Europe. Supposedly, the Mohegans introduced colonists in their range to dowsing with witch hazel branches. The branches of the Witch Hazel with their slender Y-shaped configuration were similar to elm branches used for this purpose in England. One theory links the "witch" part of the name to dowsing, which was considered a form of witchcraft.

Early colonists would have had the chance to observe the Indians making and using their remedies. This knowledge was accumulated and applied. Over time, the medical uses evolved. Witch hazel was known for its astringent qualities. Bark or leaves were made into a bitter tea that would supposedly stop internal bleeding or dysentery. The tea was also applied as a poultice to ease burns, scalds, insect bites, tumors, and inflammation. Balm was made with an extract of the bark which was soothing to sores and minor burns. It was also used in a liniment. The tea was also used as a treatment for hemorrhoids via an enema or compress.

How did it get to England? Witch hazel was one of the first plants adapted to ornamental use in European gardens. It was known in private botanical collections in London, possibly as early as the mid-seventeenth century. The Oxford English Dictionary shows the name "witch hazel" in use in the mid-sixteenth century. It is not known exactly when or by whom the plant was first brought to England. However, in the eighteenth century, it was one of many American plants that became known and popular in English garden circles. "Hazel nut" (one of the common names for witch hazel) is listed in 1826 edition of *Culpeper's Complete Herbal* (additions to Culpeper's work occurred in editions subsequent to the initial publishing date of 1653). It was recommended for cough and the drying of mucus from the head; it is also recommended for stopping menstruation and diarrhea. This corresponds with the known uses for witch hazel. (It is worth noting that I found no similar medical uses for the English hazel and hazel nuts or filberts.)

Peter Collinson (1694-1768) was a Quaker born in London. A woolen draper by trade, his passion was the study of plants and botany. Largely self-taught, his trade links allowed him to obtain plant samples from all over the world, and his personal plant collections at his homes at Peckham and later at Mill Hill were remarkable. (His Mill Hill property is now the site of the Mill Hill School). His trade links with the American colonies and his connection to the Pennsylvania Quaker settlements led him to correspond with Benjamin Franklin, and he became a supporter of the American Philosophical Society which was founded in 1743 by Benjamin Franklin and John Bartram (who was a botanist and fellow Quaker). Collinson introduced German information about electricity to Franklin in 1745, which resulted in Franklin's electrical experiments, elevating the study of electricity to a science.

Under the Patronage of Sir Hans Sloane, Collinson became a Fellow of the Royal Society in 1728 and published his first paper in 1729. He had helped with Sir Hans Sloane's collection of natural curiosities by importing specimens for him from around the world—this may be considered Collinson's contribution to the British Museum which was founded in 1753 based on the Sloane collection. He was acquainted with the work of Carl Linnaeus, a Swedish naturalist, with whom he became acquainted about 1735 and with whom he corresponded. Collinson was elected to the Royal Swedish Academy of Sciences in 1747.

Collinson had a wide clientele for plant specimens, including the Royal family, Lord Bute, the Duke of Bedford, and other wealthy and influential persons. (It is not too much to say that he and the plants he introduced were known to Lancelot "Capability" Brown as many of these people were Brown's clients.) He is widely considered to have been influential in introducing the witch hazel to English garden circles.

John Fothergill (1712-1780) was a British physician, philanthropist, and naturalist; he was also a Quaker. A London physician, he published widely on medical topics, and was very interested in botany. He was acquainted with Collinson, John Bartram, and Benjamin Franklin among others, and was very interested in issues pertaining to the American colonies. He and Collinson became good friends, and Collinson introduced him to the works of Linnaeus. He became good friends with Franklin after treating him in London in 1757. Fothergill had a large botanical garden and studied plants extensively, and he is supposed to have introduced a genus of witch hazel into England. He also became a member of the Royal Society and a member of the American Philosophical Society.

In the mid-1840s, Theron Pond of Utica, NY was supposedly shown witch hazel's uses and a means of creating an extract by an Oneida medicine man. He saw the practical applications of this product and entered into an agreement with the Oneida tribe to make the extract. He developed it into a skin product called "Golden Treasure" and successfully marketed it. After he died, it became known as Pond's Extract.

About the same time (mid-nineteenth century), a steam-distilled witch hazel product was developed; alcohol was added, and the resulting product was popular for skin conditions and also for varicose veins (it acted as a constrictor and relieved the itching associated with them).

A popular ingredient in toilet water, after shave, and other similar products, witch hazel is still in use. My personal favorite product is an alcohol-free, rosewater-based toner. Witch hazel is one of a few plant substances approved by the FDA for use as an ingredient in over-the counter medication. (Many non-prescription hemorrhoid treatments contain witch hazel.)

SOURCES

Andriote, John-Manuel. "The Mysterious Past and Present of Witch Hazel." *The*

Atlantic, November 6, 2012. http://www.theatlantic.com/health/archive/2012/11/the-mysterious-past-and-present-of-witch-hazel/264553

Bremness, Lesley. *Herbs.* Eyewitness Handbooks. London: Dorling Kindersley Limited, 1994.

Culpeper's Complete Herbal & English Physician. Manchester: J. Gleave and Son, Deansgate, 1826. Reprinted by Harvey Sales, 1981.

Foster, Stephen. "Witch Hazel, Hamamelis virgiana." Stephen Foster Group. http://stevenfoster.com/education/monograph/witchhazel.html

"Hamamelis virginiana L. (Witch Hazel)." *Agriculture and Agri-Foods Canada.* http://www.agr.gc.ca/eng/science-and-innovation/science-publications-and-resources/resources/canadian-medicinal-crops/medicinal-crops/hamamelis-virginiana-l-witch-hazel/?id=1300905460520

"John Fothergill Letters: Background note." *American Philosophical Society.* http://www.amphilsoc.org/mole/view?docId=ead/Mss.B.F82-ead.xml

"Peter Collison (1694-1768)." *Quakers in Britain.* http://www.quaker.org.uk/peter-collinson-1694-1768

"The Peter Collison Heritage." *The Mill Hill Preservation Society.* http://www.mhps.org.uk/collinson-garden.asp

"The Witch Doctor...Witch Hazel." *Dooyoo website.* http://www.dooyoo.co.uk/health-products/witch-hazel/1703477

"Witch Hazel, Hamamelis virginana." *The Green Woman's Garden.* http://greenwomansgarden.com/node/36

"Witch Hazel Hamamelis virginian L." *Moonwatcher's Encyclopedia of Herbs.* http://www.nyctophilia.net/plants/witchhazel.htm

"Witch Hazel Uses and History." *Mother Earth News*, January/February 1985. http://www.motherearthnews.com/organic-gardening/witch-hazel-uses-zmaz85zsie.aspx#axzz2cHXoieko

"Witch Hazel Water." *Positive Medicine.* http://www.positivemedicine.co.uk/products/flower-waters/witch-hazel-water/prod_91.html

Dogs: Royal, Common, and Uncommon

By Katherine Ashe

"I am His Majesty's Dog at Kew. Pray, tell me Sir, whose dog are you?"

THE HANOVERIANS, LIKE MANY KINGS, WERE FOND OF THEIR DOGS AND FOND OF A jest; the poet Alexander Pope proposed this inscription for one of their royal dogs' collars.

Both King Charles I and II had a weakness for little spaniels, with two modern breeds named for them. Spaniel breeds range from two pounds to thirty pounds, with long noses or noses reduced to mere buttons shorter than the jaws and sunk between the eyes. No creature bred by mankind shows more variety of form than the dog. Goldfish are probably the closest runners-up.

Mary, Queen of Scots, found solace in her many dogs and had them about her even when she was imprisoned. Unwilling to be parted from them, she had them stuffed when they died.

The king perhaps most obsessed with dogs was Henri III of France. His passion for toy spaniels was such that his subjects took to hiding their pets lest he see them and confiscate them for his ever-growing court of canines. The breed now called Papillon, a strain of the breed now designated Phalene, was his particular obsession. These tiny spaniels were so thoroughly associated with the Court that during the French Revolution there were little guillotines for little pups and the lineage was nearly annihilated. At least in France.

One characteristic of the dog does seem to date from the time of the Revolution: the Phalene was the proper form with drooping ears heavily fringed with silky hair. After the Revolution the ears became erect, with the profuse, hanging hair forming the broad headdress that gives the strain its modern name, Papillon, as its head seems framed with butterfly wings.

The Papillon is quite small, properly two to seven pounds. He will sit silently for hours on m'lady's lap but, set down, becomes gallantly playful with a high-held head and high stepping action that mimics the gait of the noblest horse. The breed can be traced back at least to the 1500s and was as popular in Spain as in France. In appearance the modern short-haired Chihuahua seems a blend of the stocky yellow dog depicted in Central American artifacts and the much lighter bodied Papillon. The long-haired Chihuahua is practically indistinguishable from the Papillon. It would seem the darling of Europe's courtiers must have been carried by the wives of Spanish officials to the New World.

Of course, long prior to the 1500s there were tiny dogs favored by high-born ladies. Carved in stone on tombs, the portraits of medieval dead often include a small, pug-like dog curled under the deceased's feet, giving rise to questions: did the dog die of a broken heart? Was it buried with its mistress in a sort of canine suttee? Or is the image merely figurative, a sentimental reference to loyalty, as in the painting John Ruskin so praised, "The Old Shepherd's Chief Mourner," the sole mourner being a grief-stricken Collie.

But for real antiquity in tiny pups we must look to the Maltese. While she can be seen in medieval tapestries, she's far more ancient. The earliest depiction of the breed is on an amphora dating to about 500 B.C., and the little pet is described there as Melitaei. Hence she is believed to have come from the island of Malta or Miletus. Or was that simply her name, derived from the Greek word for honey? Very apt for the breed's disposition. It is Strabo, writing in the first century A.D., who opts for Malta, but that is actually a bit late in the breed's history so we may never know.

Aristocrats, certainly by the sixteenth century in Europe, bought their little pets from dog trainers who presented their offerings at m'lady's levée. It was then in the day's schedule that petitioners and salesmen were allowed into a lady's presence as she dressed and her hair was arranged, a time-consuming process well paired with other practical activity. The dogs were offered fully trained so there would be no danger to the carpets or the legs of fine furniture. Collars studded with real jewels, and tasseled satin cushions or miniature tented pavilions enabled the pup to flaunt her wealth and high position, a mirror of her mistress. Costumes too were not uncommon, with little skirts and ruffles.

While the ladies, and many gentlemen, favored tiny dogs, the hunting dog was the most numerous of canine breeds in aristocratic circles.

King Henry II of France bred a variety of hound that was all white and extraordinary for beauty as well as coursing skills.

While King Henry's dogs no doubt were derived from earlier French lines, the Talbot was quite different, although it also was a white hound used for hunting through the Middle Ages and into the Renaissance. As depicted in the dining room at Haddon Hall in the 1400s, to commemorate the marriage of Sir Henry Vernon to Ann Talbot, the dog shows a shorter snout than most hounds. There have been some efforts to recreate this extinct breed.

Most hounds that ran, coursing game as swift as deer and flying far ahead of the huntsmen's horses, were large and long of leg. The modern English hound raised for the hunt is tall and rangy, unlike the familiar Beagle used for hunting smaller game on foot. Once, when I was living in New Jersey, the Essex Hounds came streaming around our house in full cry. They were surprisingly big; one doesn't want to be in their way. Those handsome hunt prints are of tall men on tall horses with tall dogs.

Coursing hounds usually live their lives in kennels, bonding with the members of their pack and their trainer. They are not pets. But there certainly have been exceptions. George Washington kept some of his coursing hounds around him whenever he was at home, feeding his favorite bitch, Sweet Lips, from his own plate at the dinner table.

But in ages before the breeding of the sleek, spotted white hound of the hunting prints, there was the Allaunt, a large, fierce beast that could hurl himself at stag or boar. The lordly household of the thirteenth century was incomplete without its Allaunts, and

Eleanor de Montfort, Countess of Leicester, in her account roll surviving from the year 1265 makes monetary allowance for her own Allaunts and their keeper.

The rough coated medieval Allaunt looks something like a Schnauzer who has drunk Alice's enlarging potion. Its nearest surviving relatives may be the Irish Wolfhounds and Scottish Deerhounds and the Wirehaired Pointing Griffon. When I was young and living in New York and had my first dog, a Basset Hound, I used to meet another young woman walking her dog, a scruffy-looking gray fellow who had a certain raggedy charm. In a few months my friend was to be seen flying down the street behind a romping whiskery animal the size of a pony. She had no idea when she bought her puppy just how big an Irish Wolfhound would be.

There was also in medieval times the smooth-coated Allaunt, and this breed has been reconstructed as the American Allaunt, somewhat like a Great Dane with a more Mastiff-like head.

Not all aristocratic dogs were tiny or were hunters. Notably there was the dog King Louis XIV called *"the gentleman in the fur coat"*—a Great Pyrenees. This breed, brought to Gaul and the Pyrenees by Roman legions, is descended from the Italian Maremma, also a giant breed. All white, or with a slight pastel spotting of brown, the Great Pyrenees has a very thick double coat—good protection on snowy mountain tops and from wolves' claws and teeth.

For hundreds of years the Great Pyrenees has guarded sheep. It was to guard our sheep that I acquired one some years ago to protect against Eastern Coyotes. (Our local coyotes are a new wild breed of canine believed to be a blend of Western Coyote, Canadian Timber Wolf, and assorted domestic dogs. In appearance they look like ill-bred German Shepherds but they practice choruses of howling like any other coyotes.)

Our Pyrenees, Thibaut, with a bark that was *basso profundo*, kept the coyotes away solely by the impressiveness of his voice. He took his sheep guarding seriously. But when the sheep were safely in the barn for the night, he and I would dance a waltz, his forefeet gently placed on my shoulders and his head reaching seven feet high. When he rode in our station wagon for his yearned-for visits to the ice cream shop, his hind feet were on the back seat, his forefeet on the front seat and his head up against the windshield.

Aristocrats and royalty, as well as common folk like me, continue to be dog lovers. The coursing hunt has dwindled as the sport par excellence, but the comforting pet remains a mainstay. Charles de Gaulle is quoted as saying *"The better I know men the more I love dogs."* Queen Elizabeth II, when at leisure, can be seen ankle-deep in Corgis. Her Majesty has had them always, since she was a child.

Those burdened with power and position may well find relief in the companionship of dogs for, from the dog's point of view, life is simple: love and loyalty are what really count.

ENGLISH HISTORICAL CUSTOMS OF LENT

BY DEBORAH SWIFT

THE THING WE MOST OFTEN ASSOCIATE WITH LENT IS FASTING, OR THE GIVING UP OF something we enjoy. Rules of fasting for the forty days of Lent were very strict prior to the Middle Ages. One meal a day, no flesh or fish, no eggs, butter, or cheese.

In England, Lent was a season when fruit and vegetables were scarce (no supermarkets!) so the fast must have been more of a deprivation than it was in later years.

As time went by, these laws were relaxed so that by the Middle Ages fish made a return to the fast, and by the fifteenth century, milk products had been re-introduced so that effectively Lent had come to mean meals without meat, and most Lenten meals were fish and vegetables.

Fish was usually salted, dried, or cured, because fish goes off quickly without refrigeration. The onset of Lent was marked by street traders who *"beare about a herringe on a staffe, and loude doe roare, Herrings, herrings, stinckinge herrings, puddings now no more..."* (Neogeorgus), puddings of course, being like black pudding, made of meat.

After the Reformation, James I encouraged the eating of fish so that the fish and shipping trades might benefit, and Fish on a Friday became an English custom that is still favoured by schools, hospitals, and other institutions. In his diary on 10 March 1661, Pepys says he *"dined at home on a poor Lenten dinner of colewarts (cabbage) and bacon."* Not sure whether he is really sticking to the letter of the law with his bacon!

In Lent, entertainments of all kinds were curtailed; horse-racing, dancing, and even the telling of jokes were frowned upon. Rosencrantz tells Hamlet that the players will give him "Lenten entertainment" meaning poor or meagre, and the word Lenten came to mean anything grim or dismal, and "lenten-chaps" a man of dour or sober countenance.

In the seventeenth century men would leave the powder off their wigs, and even as late as 1816 it was still the custom with some old people to wear black during Lent.

But it was not all doom and gloom.

At the beginning of the season of Lent on Ash Wednesday a straw figure of Jack O'Lent would be paraded through the streets, and people would throw things at it, kick it, and eventually, when Easter came, set fire to it. The image was said to represent Judas Iscariot, but common sense tells me this is probably the remnants of an earlier more pagan rite, or more likely something borrowed from the German tradition where a figure of Carnival is sentenced to death just before Lent and burned on Ash Wednesday to mark the transition into a more reflective time of year.

Ben Jonson seems to think that instead of a straw figure, in London this role could be taken on by someone short of money:

> that when last thou wert put out of service,
> Travell'd to Hampstead Heath on an Ash Wednesday
> where thou didst stand six weeks the Jack of Lent,
> For boys to hurl three throws a penny at thee
> To make thee a purse.

This sounds like the equivalent of an "Aunt Sally" and is not a job I'd like to take on if I was short of money, I have to say!

For many poorer people in the seventeenth century Lent probably made little difference as they were not often in a position to eat meat anyway.

SOURCES

Gascoigne, Margaret. *Discovering English Customs and Traditions*. Shire Books, 2008.

Hartley, Dorothy. *Food in England: A Complete Guide to the Food That Makes Us Who We Are*. Piatkus, 2009.

Jonson, Ben. *A Tale of a Tub*.

Pepys, Samuel. *Diary of Samuel Pepys*.

APRIL FOOL!

By LAUREN GILBERT

SOMEHOW, I THOUGHT OF APRIL FOOLS' DAY AS A FAIRLY MODERN AMERICAN HOLIDAY. Something about the slapstick, whoopee-cushioned, rather raucous humor so often seen on this day just seemed so...New World-ish. It turns out that I was wrong on all counts, which is how this essay came about.

April Fools' Day has a long history. The ancient Romans celebrated "Hilaria" with masquerades and fun on March 25 in honor of the mother of the gods, Cybele, and to celebrate the end of winter (of course, it was borrowed from the Greeks). An equally ancient Hindu festival called "Holi" was celebrated in early March, also as a fun day to celebrate the defeat of evil. A similar tradition existed in Korea.

One theory of the beginning of a similar holiday in the west involves the change from the Julian calendar to the Gregorian calendar, changing the celebration of New Year's from the end of March (the spring or vernal equinox) to January first. Supposedly, when the Gregorian calendar was adopted by France in 1582, some people refused to accept this change and continued to celebrate New Year's at the end of March.

This led others to make fun of them for their stubbornness, including playing pranks on them and making jokes at their expense. This became an annual event that spread throughout Europe. The calendar theory is not universally accepted.

Be that as it may, it does seem likely that April Fools' Day is a variation or twist of traditional spring celebrations around the world. However it began, April Fools' Day as we know it is a continuation of ancient traditions.

April Fools' Day, also sometimes known as All Fools' Day, has been a popular holiday in England and Scotland since the 1700s. From there, of course, it spread to the British colonies including America (the French also carried the tradition.) Interestingly, according to the sources I've checked, in Britain one could only play jokes and pranks before noon. Once it is afternoon, April Fools' is over.

There is a fascinating history of hoaxes in England associated with April Fools' Day. The following are a couple of the most popular. People have been sent to see the "washing of the lions" at the Tower of London as long ago as 1698 (a classic example of a fruitless errand). This was especially popular in the eighteenth and nineteenth centuries, as illustrated by a ticket issued in 1857.

In 1957, a television program called "Panorama" convinced many in Britain that spaghetti grew on trees. When asked by callers how to grow their own spaghetti trees, announcers reportedly told them to put pieces of spaghetti in tomato sauce and hope for the best.

SOURCES

"April Fools Day." *Living In England*, 3/31/2006. http://resources.woodlands-junior.kent.sch.uk/customs/blog/2006/03/april-fools-day.html

"April Fools' Day – April 1." *ProjectBritain.com*. http://projectbritain.com/year/aprilfools.html

"April Fools' Day Mystery: How Did It Originate?" *NationalGeographic.com*. Daily News. http://news.nationalgeographic.com/news/2008/03/080328-april-fools

Deem, Sarah. "April Fools' Day: Origins and History." *MetroNews.co.uk*, 3/30/2012. http://metro.co.uk/2012/03/30/april-fools-day-origins-and-history-371005

Emery, David. "April Fool's Day – Origin, History." *About.Com Urban Legends*. http://urbanlegends.about.com/od/holidays/p/april_fools_day.htm

FOR THE MAY DAY IS
THE GREAT DAY...

BY LAUREN GILBERT

W HEN I WAS A CHILD, I READ OF MAY BASKETS IN LOUISA MAY ALCOTT'S WRITING (*Jack and Jill* has a whole chapter about the making and hanging of May baskets). With May Day as a spring celebration, May baskets, dancing around May poles, and other activities seemed like so much fun. In the 1970s, *Songs from the Wood* by Jethro Tull reminded me of the pre-Christian ceremonies associated with the day. (The title of this article is a quote from "Cup of Wonder" by Jethro Tull.) May Day has also acquired other connotations with the Workers' Movements. Although not as widely celebrated as it once was, it is still a bank holiday in Great Britain. May Day has significance on many levels and its traditions endure. A few of the old traditions are discussed here today.

The first of May has been celebrated as a spring festival in western countries for centuries. The ancient Gaelic festival of Beltane celebrating the return of the sun at the beginning of summer was held at the time when the sun was half-way between the spring equinox and the summer solstice. It fell roughly at the equivalent of May 7, varying from year to year. Fires were set to help the sun, and it was thought to be good luck to pass through the smoke.

Supposedly, Beltane was one of the two great celebrations of the Druids. The ancient Romans also held a spring celebration, a five-day festival called Floralia in honor of the goddess of flowers, named Flora. This fell roughly at about the same time as Beltane, and, of course, the Romans brought it with them to England. Over time, the Roman customs blended with the Gaelic traditions. These traditions celebrated the beginning of the growing season. Gathering flowers ("bringing home the May"), making garlands, giving flowers to friends and neighbors have their roots in these spring celebrations.

In time, another tradition came to be associated with May Day: the selection of a May Queen, who may also be known as the Maiden. The earliest references go back to medieval times, but the tradition could go back even further. The May Queen might have symbolized the goddess of flowers, purity, strength, and new growth. This may be derived at least in part from the Roman goddess of spring (named Maia). Once the May Queen was selected, the dancing began, sometimes around the Maiden, sometimes around a May Pole.

During medieval times, a May Day association with the Virgin Mary began, which included special altar decorations dedicated to her. Traditionally, Mary is specially venerated in May. (Being selected May Queen seems rather similar to the honor of being selected to play the Virgin Mary in Nativity pageants.)

The ancient May Pole custom is shared by England, Germany, and Sweden, and countries neighboring them. A tall pole decorated with flowers and greenery with long ribbons fastened on the top was set into the ground. Dancers, each holding a ribbon, dance around the pole, weaving the ribbons into a braid or net, depending on the pattern in which they dance. Traditionally made of hawthorn or birch, the pole evokes a pagan past, possibly connected to Germanic myths of fertility and the Norse myth of the tree that links the heavens to the underworld. May poles still make an appearance today. While in England it is linked primarily with May Day, in other areas it is also featured at mid-summer and other festivals. Morris dancing has also been a long tradition at the May Day celebration.

Yet another interesting May Day custom involves washing one's face in May dew. There was a belief that dew gathered early on the first day of May would make one's complexion beautiful, so girls and women would go out and rub their faces with dew, hoping to heal pimples and remove freckles.

As with so many fun things, May Day celebrations were squashed by Cromwell and the Puritans. After the Restoration, Charles II restored the festival with an enormous May Pole, but it never really revived completely. It was (and still is) celebrated on a local level in England with the traditions mentioned here and others but had lost some of its significance by Victorian times.

Then, late in the nineteenth century, the first of May of 1890, May Day became the international labor movement's day, a day of celebration for and of the worker. Demonstrations and strikes were held that year and in subsequent years. It also became heavily associated with Communism. Interestingly in 1955, the Catholic Church dedicated May 1 to St. Joseph the Worker. This holiday celebrating the international labor movement is still celebrated in many countries. In the United Kingdom, it is a bank holiday and protests still occur, even while the traditional May Day celebrations are still held in different areas.

Recently, interest in the ancient May Day traditions has been renewed, possibly due to increased interest in history or a revival of interest in pagan celebrations. At any rate, more spring celebrations of May Day are appearing. I think May baskets would be lovely. Shall we try it?

SOURCES

"History of May Day: History and Origin." *The Holiday Spot website.* http://www.theholidayspot.com/mayday/history.htm

"May 1st." Hillman's Hyperlinked and Searchable *Chambers' Book of Days.* http://www.thebookofdays.com/months/may/1.htm

"May Day Celebrations." *Historic U.K.,* http://www.historic-uk.com/CultureUK/May-Day-Celebrations

"Traditions and Customs of May Day." http://www.netglimse.com/holidays/may_day/traditions_and_customs_of_may_day.shtml

Wrigley, Chris. "May Days and After." *History Today.* Vol. 40, Issue 6 (1990). http://www.historytoday.com/chris-wrigley/may-days-and-after

ALL HALLOWS AND ALL SOULS

By LAUREN GILBERT

A
T THE END OF OCTOBER, AROUND THE WORLD, PEOPLE CELEBRATE IN REMEMBRANCE for the dead: specifically deceased saints and deceased loved ones. In the United States and many other western nations, Halloween has become a secular holiday, full of games, sweet treats, costumes, and fun. However, it is still celebrated as a religious tradition and has deep historical roots.

In the *Concise Oxford English Dictionary*, "Hallow" is defined as follows:

> *Verb—to make holy or consecrate;*
> *Noun—archaic word for a saint or holy person.*

In 835 A.D., Pope Gregory IV extended a holiday to the whole Catholic Church to honor all of the saints, known and unknown. It was called All Saints' Day and celebrated on November 1. This was, and is, a holy day of obligation in the Catholic Church, and attendance at mass was required. This day was also known as All Hallows' Day. As with many Christian holidays, it absorbed an earlier, non-Christian holiday, the ancient Celtic holiday, Samhain, which fell at roughly the same time.

As with other Catholic days of obligation, the evening before is the start of the celebration, or vigil. Therefore, the evening of October 31 became All Hallows' Eve, or All Hallows' Even. This is the root of Hallowe'en (now Halloween), the first known usage of which occurred about 1700. Samhain was an ancient Celtic and Gaelic holiday celebrated on the night before their New Year, which roughly coincides with October 31. On this night, the division between the living and the dead becomes blurred. Celtic customs included bonfires, sacrifices, and wearing costumes to ward off spirits.

In 1000 A.D., the feast of All Souls was established on November 2 by the Catholic Church. On this day, the office of the dead was read, and all of the faithful who had died and were in purgatory were remembered. During the service, survivors could have the names of their deceased loved ones read upon request. It was thought that the spirits of the dead returned to visit their homes, and candles were lit to guide them. Before the Reformation, poor Christians would beg for money or food, offering prayers for the dead in exchange. In England, by the nineteenth century, this morphed into a tradition called "souling" where children would sing a specific song for money or soul cakes.

The modern celebration of Halloween as a secular holiday has embraced the costumes, the bonfires and candles, and the requests for "treats" from the pagan and early Christian traditions, while losing (or ignoring) the religious solemnity.

All Saints' Day and All Souls' Day are both still celebrated today, not only by the

Catholic Church, but by other Christian denominations including the Church of England. The *Book of Common Prayer* contains this collect for All Saints Day:

> *God, who hast knit together thine elect in one communion and fellowship, in the mystical body of thy Son Christ our Lord: Grant us grace so to follow thy blessed Saints in all virtuous and godly living, that we may come to those unspeakable joys, which thou hast prepared for them that unfeignedly love thee; through Jesus Christ our Lord.*

On All Souls' Day, the Church of England celebrates the Eucharist of the Commemoration of the Faithful Departed. While it is fun to celebrate Halloween as a secular event, it is important to remember the history and roots of the celebration.

SOURCES

"All Saints' Day." *Catholic Encyclopedia Online New Advent.* http://www.newadvent.org/cathen/01315a.htm

"All Souls' Day." *Catholic Encyclopedia Online New Advent.* http://www.newadvent.org/cathen/01315b.htm

The Book of Common Prayer. Church of England website. http://www.churchofengland.org/prayer-worship/worship/book-of-common-prayer/collects-epistles-and-gospels/all-saints'-day.aspx

Chivers, Tom. "Hallowe'en: a history of All Hallows' Eve, from Samhain to trick-or-treat." *The Telegraph Online.* http://www.telegraph.co.uk/news/uknews/6468637/Halloween-a-history-of-All-Hallows-Eve-from-Samhain-to-trick-or-treat.html

Concise Oxford English Dictionary. 11th edition. Oxford, NY: Oxford University Press, 2008. Pg. 644.

"Facts about November." *Project Britain Folklore Calendar.* http://projectbritain.com/year/november.htm

"Origins of Halloween." History.com (The History Channel online). http://www.history.com/topics/halloween

Ross, Tim. "Churches attempt to take the 'dark side' out of Hallowe'en." *The Telegraph Online.* 10/31/09. http://www.telegraph.co.uk/news/uknews/8097043/Churches-attempt-to-take-the-dark-side-out-of-Halloween.html

EIGHT HUNDRED YEARS
OF PLUM PUDDING

BY MARIA GRACE

*Hallo! A great deal of steam! The pudding was out of the copper [boiler]. A
smell like washing-day! That was the cloth [in which the pudding was tied].
A smell like an eating house and a pastrycook's next door to each other, with
a laundress's next door to that! That was the pudding! In half a minute Mrs.
Cratchit entered—flushed, but smiling proudly—with the pudding, like a
speckled cannon ball, so hard and firm, blazing in half of half-a-quartern of
ignited brandy, and bedight with Christmas holly stuck into the top. Oh, a
wonderful pudding! Bob Cratchit said, and calmly too, that he regarded it as
the greatest success achieved by Mrs. Cratchit since their marriage....*

—Charles Dickens, *A Christmas Carol*

ORIGINS OF THE PLUM PUDDING

FEW FOODS CAN TRACE THEIR HISTORY BACK THROUGH MULTIPLE CENTURIES. PLUM
pudding stands out as one of those few. It began in Roman times as a pottage, a meat
and vegetable concoction prepared in a large cauldron. Dried fruits, sugar, and spices
might be added to the mix as well.

Another ancestor to the plum pudding, porridge or frumenty, appeared in the fourteenth century. A soup-like fasting dish containing meats, raisins, currants, prunes, wine,
and spices, it was eaten before the Christmas celebrations began. By the fifteenth century,
plum pottage, a soupy mix of meat, vegetables, and fruit was served to start a meal.

As the seventeenth century opened, frumenty evolved into a plum pudding. Thick-
ened with eggs, breadcrumbs, and dried fruit, the addition of beer and spirits gave it more
flavor and increased its shelf life. Variants were made with white meat, though gradually
the meat was omitted and replaced by suet. The root vegetables also disappeared. By
1650, the plum pudding had transformed from a main dish to a dessert, the customary
one served at Christmas. Not long afterward though, plum pudding was banned by Oliver
Cromwell because he believed the ritual of flaming the pudding harked back to pagan
celebrations of the winter solstice.

George I, sometimes called the Pudding King, revived the dish in 1714 when he
requested that plum pudding be served as part of his royal feast to celebrate his first
Christmas in England. Subsequently, it became entrenched as part of traditional holiday
celebrations, taking its final form of a cannon-ball of flour, fruits, suet, sugar, and spices,

all topped with holly in the 1830s. In 1858 it was first dubbed the Christmas Pudding, recorded as such in Anthony Trollope's *Doctore Thorne*.

PREPARING PLUM PUDDING

Many households have their own recipe for Christmas pudding, some handed down through families for generations. Two sample recipes from different centuries show remarkable similarity in ingredients.

A Boiled Plum Pudding (18th Century)

Take a pound of suet cut in little pieces, not too fine, a pound of currants and a pound of raisins storied, eight eggs, half the whites, half a nutmeg grated and a tea spoonful of beaten ginger, a pound of flour, a pint of milk. Beat the eggs first, then half the milk. Beat them together and by degrees stir in the flour then the suet, spice and fruit and as much milk as will mix it well together very thick. Boil it five hours.

—Hannah Glasse, *The Art of Cookery Made Plain and Easy*

Rich Plum Pudding (19th Century)

Stone carefully one pound of the best raisins, wash and pick one pound of currants, chop very small one pound of fresh beef suet, blanch and chop small or pound two ounces of sweet almonds and one ounce of bitter ones; mix the whole well together, with one pound of sifted flour, and the same weight of crumb of bread soaked in milk, then squeezed dry and stirred with a spoon until reduced to a mash before it is mixed with the flour. Cut in small pieces two ounces each of preserved citron, orange, and lemon-peel, and add a quarter of an ounce of mixed spice; quarter of a pound of moist sugar should be put into a basin, with eight eggs, and well beaten together with a three-pronged fork; stir this with the pudding, and make it of a proper consistence with milk.

Remember that it must not be made too thin, or the fruit will sink to the bottom, but be made to the consistence of good thick batter. Two wineglass-fuls of brandy should be poured over the fruit and spice, mixed together in a basin, and allowed to stand three or four hours before the pudding is made, stirring them occasionally. It must be tied in a cloth, and will take five hours of constant boiling. When done, turn it out on a dish, sift loaf-sugar over the top, and serve it with wine-sauce in a boat, and some poured round the pudding. The pudding will be of considerable size, but half the quantity of materials, used in the same proportion, will be equally good.

—*Godey's Lady's Book* (Dec. 1860)

After cooking, Christmas puddings were often dried out on hooks for weeks prior to serving in order to enhance the flavor. Once dried, they were wrapped in alcohol-soaked cheese cloth and stored in earthenware/crockery and placed somewhere cool for the duration. More alcohol may have been added during this period. The puddings might also have been sealed against air with suet or wax to aid in preservation.

PLUM PUDDING TRADITIONS

With a food so many centuries in the making, it is not surprising to find many traditions have evolved around the making and eating of plum pudding.

The last Sunday before Advent is considered the last day on which one can make Christmas puddings since they require aging before they are served. It is sometimes known as "Stir-up Sunday". This is because opening words of the main prayer in the *Book of Common Prayer* of 1549 for that day are:

> *Stir-up, we beseech thee, O Lord, the wills of thy faithful people; that they, plenteously bringing forth the fruit of good works, may of thee be plenteously rewarded; through Jesus Christ our Lord. Amen.*

Choir boys parodied the prayer.

> *Stir up, we beseech thee, the pudding in the pot. And when we do get home tonight, we'll eat it up hot.*

Christmas pudding is prepared with thirteen ingredients to represent Christ and the twelve apostles; then it is "stirred up" by all family members who must take a hand in the stirring using a special wooden spoon (in honor of Christ's crib). The stirring must be done clockwise, from east to west to honor the journey of the Magi, with eyes shut while making a secret wish.

After the family stirred the pudding, tiny charms might be added to the pudding to reveal their finders' fortune. The trinkets often included a thimble (for spinsterhood or thrift), a ring (for marriage), a coin (for wealth), a miniature horseshoe or a tiny wishbone for good luck, and an anchor for safe harbor.

When the pudding was served, a sprig of holly was placed on the top of the pudding as a reminder of Jesus' Crown of Thorns that he wore when he was killed. Flaming the pudding, as described by Dickens, was believed to represent the passion of Christ and represent Jesus' love and power. It is also a key part of the theatrical aspect of the holiday celebration.

WHY IS IT CALLED PLUM PUDDING?

And the answer to the most burning question: Why is plum pudding called that when there are no plums in it? Dried plums or prunes were popular in pies in medieval times, but in the sixteenth and seventeenth centuries they began to be replaced by raisins. In the seventeenth century, plums referred to raisins or other fruits. The dishes made with them retain the term "plum" to this day.

SOURCES

Ayton, John. *An A-Z of Food & Drink*. Oxford: Oxford University Press, 2002.

Broomfield, Andrea. *Food and Cooking in Victorian England: A History*. Westport, CT: Praeger, 2007.

Davidson, Alan. *Oxford Companion to Food*. Oxford: Oxford University Press, 2000.

Glasse, Hannah. *The Art of Cookery Made Plain and Easy*. Applewood Books, 1998.

Godey's Lady's Book, December 1860.

Griffen, Robert H. and Ann H. Shurgin, editors. *The Folklore of World Holiday*. Second Edition. Detroit: Gale, 1998.

Knightly, Charles. *The Customs and Ceremonies of Britain*. London: Thames and Hudson, 1986.

Lane, Sarah. "The Christmas Pudding: Traditions & History." http://www.classbrain. com/artholiday/publish/printer_article_256.shtml

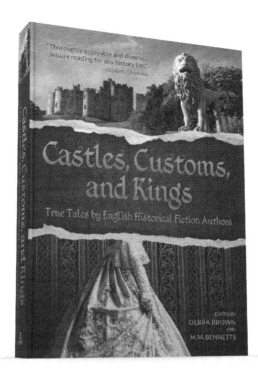

CASTLES, CUSTOMS, AND KINGS

TRUE TALES BY ENGLISH HISTORICAL FICTION AUTHORS
VOLUME 1

Edited by Debra Brown & M.M. Bennetts

ISBN: 978-0-9836719-5-4

A compilation of essays from the English Historical Fiction Authors blog, this book provides a wealth of historical information from Roman Britain to early twentieth century England. Over fifty different authors share hundreds of real life stories and tantalizing tidbits discovered while doing research for their own historical novels.

From the first English word to Tudor ladies-in-waiting, from Regency dining and dress to Victorian crime and technology, immerse yourself in the lore of Great Britain. Read the history behind the fiction and discover the true tales surrounding England's castles, customs, and kings.

20589759R00330

Printed in Great Britain
by Amazon